SAP PRESS e-books

Print or e-book, Kindle or iPad, workplace or airplane: Choose where and how to read your SAP PRESS books! You can now get all our titles as e-books, too:

- By download and online access
- For all popular devices
- And, of course, DRM-free

Convinced? Then go to www.sap-press.com and get your e-book today.

Sourcing and Procurement in SAP S/4HANA®

SAP PRESS is a joint initiative of SAP and Rheinwerk Publishing. The know-how offered by SAP specialists combined with the expertise of Rheinwerk Publishing offers the reader expert books in the field. SAP PRESS features first-hand information and expert advice, and provides useful skills for professional decision-making.

SAP PRESS offers a variety of books on technical and business-related topics for the SAP user. For further information, please visit our website: www.sap-press.com.

Bhattacharjee, Monti, Perel, Vazquez
Logistics with SAP S/4HANA: An Introduction
2018, 400 pages, hardcover and e-book
www.sap-press.com/4485

Densborn, Finkbohner, Freudenberg, Mathäß, Wagner
Migrating to SAP S/4HANA
2017, 569 pages, hardcover and e-book
www.sap-press.com/4247

Bardhan, Baumgartl, Chaadaev, Choi, Dudgeon, Lahiri, Meijerink, Worsley-Tonks
SAP S/4HANA: An Introduction (2nd Edition)
2018, 511 pages, hardcover and e-book
www.sap-press.com/4499

Michael Jolton, Yosh Eisbart
SAP S/4HANA Cloud: Use Cases, Functionality, and Extensibility
2017, 334 pages, hardcover and e-book
www.sap-press.com/4498

Justin Ashlock

Sourcing and Procurement in SAP S/4HANA®

Editor Will Jobst
Acquisitions Editor Emily Nicholls
Copyeditor Melinda Rankin
Cover Design Graham Geary
Photo Credit iStockphoto.com/519364941/© JannHuizenga
Layout Design Vera Brauner
Production Graham Geary
Typesetting III-Satz, Husby (Germany)
Printed and bound in the United States of America, on paper from sustainable sources

ISBN 978-1-4932-1641-3

© 2018 by Rheinwerk Publishing, Inc., Boston (MA)
1st edition 2018

Library of Congress Cataloging-in-Publication Data
Names: Ashlock, Justin, author.
Title: Sourcing and procurement in SAP S/4HANA / Justin Ashlock.
Description: 1st edition. | Bonn ; Boston : Rheinwerk Publishing, [2018] |
  Includes index.
Identifiers: LCCN 2017047118 (print) | LCCN 2017053630 (ebook) | ISBN
  9781493216420 (ebook) | ISBN 9781493216413 (alk. paper)
Subjects: LCSH: SAP HANA (Electronic resource) | Industrial procurement--Data
  processing. | Management information systems.
Classification: LCC HD39.5 (ebook) | LCC HD39.5 .A844 2018 (print) | DDC
  658.70285/53--dc23
LC record available at https://lccn.loc.gov/2017047118

All rights reserved. Neither this publication nor any part of it may be copied or reproduced in any form or by any means or translated into another language, without the prior consent of Rheinwerk Publishing, 2 Heritage Drive, Suite 305, Quincy, MA 02171.

Rheinwerk Publishing makes no warranties or representations with respect to the content hereof and specifically disclaims any implied warranties of merchantability or fitness for any particular purpose. Rheinwerk Publishing assumes no responsibility for any errors that may appear in this publication.

"Rheinwerk Publishing" and the Rheinwerk Publishing logo are registered trademarks of Rheinwerk Verlag GmbH, Bonn, Germany. SAP PRESS is an imprint of Rheinwerk Verlag GmbH and Rheinwerk Publishing, Inc.

All of the screenshots and graphics reproduced in this book are subject to copyright © SAP SE, Dietmar-Hopp-Allee 16, 69190 Walldorf, Germany.

SAP, the SAP logo, ABAP, Ariba, ASAP, Concur, Concur ExpenseIt, Concur TripIt, Duet, SAP Adaptive Server Enterprise, SAP Advantage Database Server, SAP Afaria, SAP ArchiveLink, SAP Ariba, SAP Business ByDesign, SAP Business Explorer, SAP BusinessObjects, SAP BusinessObjects Explorer, SAP BusinessObjects Lumira, SAP BusinessObjects Roambi, SAP BusinessObjects Web Intelligence, SAP Business One, SAP Business Workflow, SAP Crystal Reports, SAP EarlyWatch, SAP Exchange Media (SAP XM), SAP Fieldglass, SAP Fiori, SAP Global Trade Services (SAP GTS), SAP GoingLive, SAP HANA, SAP HANA Vora, SAP Hybris, SAP Jam, SAP MaxAttention, SAP MaxDB, SAP NetWeaver, SAP PartnerEdge, SAPPHIRE NOW, SAP PowerBuilder, SAP PowerDesigner, SAP R/2, SAP R/3, SAP Replication Server, SAP S/4HANA, SAP SQL Anywhere, SAP Strategic Enterprise Management (SAP SEM), SAP SuccessFactors, The Best-Run Businesses Run SAP, TwoGo are registered or unregistered trademarks of SAP SE, Walldorf, Germany.

All other products mentioned in this book are registered or unregistered trademarks of their respective companies.

Contents at a Glance

1	Introduction to Sourcing and Procurement	27
2	Implementation Options	45
3	Organizational Structure	79
4	Master Data	99
5	Operational Procurement	133
6	Automated and Direct Procurement	171
7	Inventory Management	223
8	Contracts Management	293
9	External Sourcing	339
10	Invoice and Payables Management	369
11	Supplier Management	409
12	Reporting and Analytics	435
13	Customizing the SAP Fiori UI	463
14	Conclusion	487

Dear Reader,

Your job: To collect all the right materials from all the right sources in all the right quantities. As a sourcing and procurement practitioner or an SRM consultant, you make sure everything is on hand ahead of production, and that your new ERP system is truly positioned to support each business subprocess.

Our job: To gather the right information from all the right experts in all the right chapters. As a publisher focused on SAP solutions and technologies, we know fragmented documentation abounds—so we designed this one-stop shop for procurement in the new suite. From operational procurement, inventory management, and contracts management to invoicing, supplier management and evaluation, reporting, and analytics, writers Justin Ashlock, Robert Gotschall, and Chelliah Soundar have delivered exactly that.

In your SAP S/4HANA system and on our SAP PRESS bookshelf, everything has its place. So tell us, what did you think about *Sourcing and Procurement in SAP S/4HANA*? Your comments and suggestions are the most useful tools to help us make our books the best they can be. Please feel free to contact me and share any praise or criticism you may have.

Thank you for purchasing a book from SAP PRESS!

Will Jobst
Editor, SAP PRESS

willj@rheinwerk-publishing.com
www.sap-press.com
Rheinwerk Publishing · Boston, MA

Contents

Foreword 19
Preface 21

1 Introduction to Sourcing and Procurement   27

1.1 Procurement from End to End 27
1.1.1   Ideal Procurement 28
1.1.2   Procure-to-Pay 29
1.1.3   Procurement Process Areas 29
1.1.4   Disadvantages 30
1.1.5   The Next Wave 31

1.2 Operational Procurement vs. Strategic Procurement in SAP 32
1.2.1   Operational Procurement 32
1.2.2   Strategic Procurement 34

1.3 Procurement with SAP S/4HANA 35
1.3.1   SAP Ariba 36
1.3.2   Strategic Sourcing 38
1.3.3   Procurement 38
1.3.4   Accounts Payable and Invoicing 40
1.3.5   Sourcing and Procurement Roles within SAP S/4HANA 41
1.3.6   SAP S/4HANA Sourcing and Procurement SAP Fiori Apps 42

1.4 SAP S/4HANA Enterprise Management: SAP's Digital Core 42
1.5 Summary 44

2 Implementation Options   45

2.1 Implementation Overview 45
2.1.1   Deployment Options 46
2.1.2   Cloud 47
2.1.3   On-Premise 50

2.2	On-Premise SAP S/4HANA	55
	2.2.1 Complete Functional Scope	55
	2.2.2 Installation	57
	2.2.3 Activated Appliance	58
	2.2.4 Information Technology Considerations	59
	2.2.5 Integration Options	60
	2.2.6 SAP S/4HANA System Conversion	61
2.3	SAP S/4HANA Cloud	66
	2.3.1 SAP Best Practices Scope	66
	2.3.2 IT Considerations	67
	2.3.3 Standard Integration and Customization	68
2.4	SAP Activate, SAP Best Practices, and SAP Model Companies: Quick Start Approaches and Materials for SAP S/4HANA	69
	2.4.1 Prebuilt Content and Templates: SAP Appliance, SAP Best Practices, and SAP Model Company	70
	2.4.2 SAP Best Practices	70
	2.4.3 SAP Model Company	71
	2.4.4 SAP Activate	71
	2.4.5 SAP Activate Roles	77
2.5	Summary	78

3 Organizational Structure   79

3.1	SAP S/4HANA Enterprise Management Organization Structure	79
	3.1.1 Organization Structure Terminology	80
	3.1.2 Example Organizational Structure	83
3.2	Organizational Structure Objects	83
	3.2.1 Plants	84
	3.2.2 Storage Locations	84
	3.2.3 Warehouses	84
	3.2.4 Purchasing Organizations	85

3.3 Company Code, Plant, Storage Location, Purchasing Org, and Purchasing Group Creation ... 87

- 3.3.1 Company Code Creation ... 87
- 3.3.2 Plant Creation ... 90
- 3.3.3 Storage Location and Warehouse Creation ... 91
- 3.3.4 Warehouse Creation ... 93
- 3.3.5 Purchasing Organization Creation ... 94
- 3.3.6 Purchasing Group Creation ... 97

3.4 Summary ... 97

4 Master Data ... 99

4.1 Material Masters and Material Groups ... 100
- 4.1.1 Creating a Material Master ... 101
- 4.1.2 Creating a Material Group ... 104

4.2 Batch Management and Serialization ... 105
- 4.2.1 Batch Number Configuration ... 105
- 4.2.2 Serial Number Configuration ... 106

4.3 Material Master Updates in SAP S/4HANA ... 108
- 4.3.1 SERV Product Type ... 108
- 4.3.2 Select Material Master Configuration Options ... 109
- 4.3.3 Material Master Field Character Expansion in SAP S/4HANA ... 110

4.4 Supplier Master Setup and Supplier Creation ... 111
- 4.4.1 Customer/Vendor Integration ... 111
- 4.4.2 Supplier Master Setup ... 113

4.5 Business Partner ... 114
- 4.5.1 Business Partner Objectives ... 115
- 4.5.2 SAP S/4HANA Business Partner Implementation ... 117
- 4.5.3 Customer/Vendor Integration: Conversion of SAP ERP Customers and Vendors to SAP S/4HANA Business Partners ... 118

4.6 Summary ... 130

5   Operational Procurement   133

5.1	Overview	134
5.2	Requisition-to-Pay Process	135
5.3	Procurement of Stock, Consumable, and External (Service) Items	136
5.4	**Self-Service Procurement**	**137**
	5.4.1 Creating a Requisition or Shopping Cart in SAP S/4HANA	138
	5.4.2 Confirmation and Return Delivery	140
	5.4.3 Purchase Order Collaboration	144
	5.4.4 Shopping Cart versus Requisition-to-Pay and Migrating SAP SRM Shopping Carts	145
	5.4.5 Migrating SAP SRM Shopping Carts to SAP S/4HANA	146
	5.4.6 Workflow	147
5.5	**Requirement Processing in SAP S/4HANA Sourcing and Procurement**	**148**
	5.5.1 Buyer-Driven and Automated Requirements Processing	149
	5.5.2 Navigation in SAP S/4HANA Sourcing and Procurement: Requirements Processing	151
	5.5.3 Purchase Order Processing	152
5.6	**Configuration for Self-Service Procurement**	**154**
	5.6.1 Configuration Steps: Self-Service Procurement Baseline	155
	5.6.2 Configure Catalogs (Optional)	156
	5.6.3 Cross-Catalog Search (Optional)	157
	5.6.4 Importing Catalog Data and Images	160
	5.6.5 Import JSON File	162
	5.6.6 Import Catalog via Web Service	162
5.7	**Integration with Cloud Applications**	**164**
	5.7.1 Service Purchasing and Entry with SAP S/4HANA and SAP Fieldglass	164
	5.7.2 SAP S/4HANA Cloud: Services Procurement Integration	165
	5.7.3 SAP Ariba	165
	5.7.4 SAP SuccessFactors	168
5.8	Summary	170

6 Automated and Direct Procurement 171

6.1 Automated and Direct Source-to-Pay Processes 172
6.2 Materials Requirements Planning 173
6.2.1 MRP in SAP ERP versus SAP S/4HANA 175
6.2.2 MRP SAP Fiori Apps 178
6.3 Forecasting and Planning 185
6.3.1 Forecast Planning 185
6.3.2 Reorder Point Planning 188
6.3.3 Time-Phased Planning 189
6.3.4 Forecast Collaboration 189
6.4 Contract and Source Determination 192
6.4.1 Purchasing Information Record 193
6.4.2 Source List 194
6.4.3 Quota Arrangement 195
6.4.4 Scheduling Agreement 196
6.4.5 Scheduling Agreement Release Collaboration 198
6.4.6 Blanket Purchase Order 199
6.4.7 Purchase Orders and Multitier Purchase Orders 201
6.4.8 Subcontracting 201
6.4.9 Consignment Stock 206
6.4.10 Consignment Orders 208
6.4.11 Quality Management Collaboration in SAP Ariba Supply Chain Collaboration for Buyers 209
6.4.12 SAP Supply Base Optimization 209
6.5 Configuration 211
6.5.1 Defining Master Data 212
6.5.2 Configuring Automated and Direct Procurement 212
6.6 Integration with SAP Ariba 219
6.6.1 SAP Ariba Supply Chain Collaboration 219
6.6.2 SAP Ariba Supply Chain Collaboration for Buyers and SAP S/4HANA 220
6.7 Summary 221

7 Inventory Management — 223

7.1 Inventory Management in SAP S/4HANA — 224
- 7.1.1 Inventory Management Data Model — 225
- 7.1.2 Material Master — 226
- 7.1.3 SAP S/4HANA Simplifications — 226

7.2 Stock Management in SAP S/4HANA — 227
- 7.2.1 Material — 228
- 7.2.2 Location — 228
- 7.2.3 Usability — 228
- 7.2.4 Ownership — 230
- 7.2.5 Batch Management — 230
- 7.2.6 Serialization — 231
- 7.2.7 Goods Movements — 231

7.3 Goods Receipts — 232
- 7.3.1 Posting Goods Receipts Using Inventory Management Apps — 233
- 7.3.2 Apps Used for Processing Goods Receipts via Inbound Deliveries — 239

7.4 Goods Issues — 244
- 7.4.1 Create Outbound Deliveries — 245
- 7.4.2 My Purchase Orders—Due for Delivery — 246
- 7.4.3 Manage Outbound Deliveries — 247

7.5 Stock Transfers — 248
- 7.5.1 One-Step Stock Transfers — 248
- 7.5.2 Two-Step Stock Transfers — 248
- 7.5.3 Transfer Stock—In-Plant — 249
- 7.5.4 Transfer Stock—Cross-Plant — 250
- 7.5.5 Stock Transfer Execution Using Shipping Integration — 251
- 7.5.6 Stock Transfer Reporting — 251

7.6 Transfer Postings — 253
- 7.6.1 Changes in Stock Identity — 253
- 7.6.2 Changes in Stock Usability — 253
- 7.6.3 Changes in Stock Ownership — 254
- 7.6.4 Apps Used for Transfer Postings — 254

7.7	Physical Inventory	254
	7.7.1 Creation of Physical Inventory Documents	255
	7.7.2 Entry of Physical Counts	256
	7.7.3 Posting of Physical Inventory Differences	256
	7.7.4 Physical Inventory Apps	257
	7.7.5 Physical Inventory Execution Apps	257
	7.7.6 Physical Inventory Reporting Apps	266
7.8	Reporting in Inventory Management	270
	7.8.1 Inventory Overview Pages	270
	7.8.2 Goods Movement Reporting	271
	7.8.3 Stock Balances Reporting Apps	273
	7.8.4 Apps for Monitoring Financial Inventory Values	279
	7.8.5 Inventory Management Object Pages	281
	7.8.6 Inventory Management Analytics	288
7.9	SAP Ariba Integration	290
7.10	Summary	291

8   Contracts Management   293

8.1	Contract Creation	294
	8.1.1 Types of Contracts	294
	8.1.2 Manage Purchase Contracts	295
	8.1.3 Mass Change to Purchase Contract	298
8.2	Contract Consumption	299
	8.2.1 Value Contract Consumption	299
	8.2.2 Quantity Contract Consumption	299
8.3	Contract Dashboard Reporting and Expiry Notification Setting	300
	8.3.1 Unused Contracts	301
	8.3.2 Off-Contract Spend	302
	8.3.3 Contract Leakage	303
	8.3.4 Purchase Contract Items by Account Assignment	303

		8.3.5	Monitor Purchase Contract Items	304
		8.3.6	Contract Expiry	304
8.4	**Configuration**			305
		8.4.1	Configuring Contracts	305
		8.4.2	Configuring Contract Workflow	309
8.5	**Scheduling Agreement**			309
		8.5.1	Scheduling Agreement with Release Document	310
		8.5.2	Scheduling Agreement without Release Document	310
		8.5.3	Stock Transport Scheduling Agreement	310
		8.5.4	Creating Scheduling Agreements	311
		8.5.5	Manage Scheduling Agreement	311
8.6	**Customizing Scheduling Agreements**			312
		8.6.1	Define Document Types	312
		8.6.2	Define Item Categories	313
		8.6.3	Maintain Release Creation Profile	314
8.7	**Legal Content Management**			315
		8.7.1	Legal Content Management in SAP S/4HANA	315
		8.7.2	Manage Context for Legal Content	316
		8.7.3	Categories for Legal Content	318
		8.7.4	Request Legal Content	319
		8.7.5	Manage Legal Transactions	321
8.8	**Customizing Legal Content Management**			322
		8.8.1	Define Number Ranges	322
		8.8.2	Define Reminder Types	323
		8.8.3	Define Date Types	323
		8.8.4	Define Internal Contacts	324
		8.8.5	Define Entity Types	324
		8.8.6	Define External Contacts	325
		8.8.7	Define Technical Types for Linked Object Types	326
		8.8.8	Define Linked Object Types	327
		8.8.9	Define Content Types	328
		8.8.10	Define Document Stamps	328
		8.8.11	Define Profiles	329
		8.8.12	Define Document Types	333
		8.8.13	Background Job Definitions	337
8.9	**Summary**			337

9   External Sourcing 339

9.1   Sourcing Strategies 340
9.1.1   Sourcing Process Flow 340
9.1.2   Sourcing Optimization 341

9.2   Request for Quotation 341
9.2.1   Collaborative Sourcing 341
9.2.2   Quote Automation for Procurement 342
9.2.3   Request for Price 342
9.2.4   Manage Request for Quotation 343
9.2.5   Create Request for Quotation 344
9.2.6   Monitor Request for Quotation Items 345
9.2.7   Compare Supplier Quotations 346
9.2.8   Manage Supplier Quotation 347
9.2.9   Manage Workflows for Supplier Quotation 348
9.2.10   My Inbox 350

9.3   Request for Quotation Configuration 350
9.3.1   Define Number Ranges 350
9.3.2   Define Document Types for RFQ 351
9.3.3   Define Document Types for Quote 352
9.3.4   Assign Output Channels 354
9.3.5   Assign Form Templates 355
9.3.6   Map Application and Output Type to cXML Message 355
9.3.7   Activation of Scope-Dependent Background Job Definitions 356
9.3.8   Define Document-Specific Message Customizing 357
9.3.9   Map cXML Price Modifications to SAP S/4HANA Conditions 358

9.4   Flexible Workflow 359
9.4.1   Scenario Activation 359
9.4.2   Register Event for Subsequent Workflow 360
9.4.3   Maintain Task Names and Decision Options 362
9.4.4   Visualization of SAP Business Workflow 363
9.4.5   Scenario Definition 364
9.4.6   Maintain Attribute for Workflow Task 365

9.5   Integration with SAP Ariba 367
9.6   Summary 367

10 Invoice and Payables Management   369

10.1 Invoice Processing 370
    10.1.1   Innovations in Invoice Processing in SAP S/4HANA 370
    10.1.2   Supplier Invoice Documents 371
    10.1.3   Results of Invoice Processing 373
    10.1.4   Types of Supplier Invoice Verification 373
    10.1.5   Entry of Invoice Documents 375
    10.1.6   Invoice Processing 379
    10.1.7   Other Invoice Processing Apps 381
    10.1.8   Reporting in Invoice Processing 389
    10.1.9   Object Pages 391

10.2 Accounts Payable 393
    10.2.1   Supplier Payment Processing 393
    10.2.2   Supplier Account Management 403
    10.2.3   Create Correspondence 405

10.3 Invoice Collaboration with the Ariba Network 407

10.4 Summary 408

11 Supplier Management   409

11.1 Supplier Discovery, Qualification, and Onboarding 410
    11.1.1   SAP Ariba Discovery and SAP Ariba Supplier Lifecycle
              and Performance 410
    11.1.2   SAP Supplier Lifecycle Management 411

11.2 Supplier Management 411
    11.2.1   Supplier Management with the Ariba Network 412
    11.2.2   Buyer-Side Processes in SAP S/4HANA 412
    11.2.3   Classification and Segmentation 413
    11.2.4   Supplier Segmentation and Classification Apps 414

11.3 Supplier Evaluation 421
    11.3.1   Supplier Evaluation Scorecard 423
    11.3.2   Individual Supplier Evaluation 423
    11.3.3   Supplier Evaluation by Time 424

	11.3.4	Supplier Evaluation by Price	425
	11.3.5	Supplier Evaluation by Questionnaire	425
	11.3.6	Combined Scorecard	427
	11.3.7	Operational Supplier Evaluation	427
11.4	Configuration		428
	11.4.1	Supplier and Category Management Configuration	428
	11.4.2	Supplier Evaluation Configuration	430
11.5	Integration with SAP Ariba		432
11.6	Summary		433

12 Reporting and Analytics — 435

12.1	Spend Visibility		436
	12.1.1	Multidimensional Spend Reporting in SAP S/4HANA Cloud	437
	12.1.2	Navigation and Procurement Overview Page	437
12.2	Contract Expiration		438
12.3	Sourcing		439
12.4	Supplier Performance		441
	12.4.1	Purchasing Documents Reports and Embedded Analytics	442
	12.4.2	Predictive Analytics	443
12.5	Accounts Payable Analytics and Reporting		444
	12.5.1	Aging Analysis	445
	12.5.2	Overdue Payables	446
	12.5.3	Future Payables	447
	12.5.4	Cash Discount Forecast	448
	12.5.5	Cash Discount Utilization	450
	12.5.6	Days Payable Outstanding	451
	12.5.7	Invoice Processing Analysis	452
	12.5.8	Supplier Payment Analysis (Manual and Automatic Payments)	454
	12.5.9	Supplier Payment Analysis (Open Payments)	455
12.6	Configuration		456
	12.6.1	Creating a Key Performance Indicator	456
	12.6.2	Configuring Real-Time Reporting/Queries	457

	12.6.3	Exploring Virtual Data Model and Core Data Services in SAP S/4HANA	457
	12.6.4	Integration of SAP S/4HANA with SAP Analytics Tools	458
12.7	**Integration with Cloud Applications**		460
	12.7.1	SAP Fieldglass	461
	12.7.2	SAP Ariba	461
12.8	**Summary**		462

13 Customizing the SAP Fiori UI 463

13.1	**The SAP Fiori User Interface**		463
	13.1.1	SAP Fiori Launchpad	464
	13.1.2	SAP General User Interface	467
	13.1.3	SAP Fiori Architecture	469
13.2	**User-Driven UI Tuning Options**		474
	13.2.1	SAP Fiori Edit Mode	475
	13.2.2	SAP Fiori User Settings	475
	13.2.3	SAP CoPilot	478
13.3	**SAP Fiori Configuration**		480
	13.3.1	Installing SAP Fiori	480
	13.3.2	Embedded and Central Hub Deployment for SAP Fiori	481
	13.3.3	SAP Fiori Apps Reference Library	482
13.4	**Summary**		486

14 Conclusion 487

The Author 491
Index 493

Foreword

After decades of relative stability, procurement organizations and functions are now challenged to change. Indeed, within the next five to seven years, it is expected that digital platforms and technologies will totally transform the way most procurement organizations do business.

Still, chief procurement officers continue to deliver bottom-line savings while increasing the focus on value creation for the company. They need to work with their teams to respond to key trends like hyper connectivity, big data, cloud computing, natural language processing, and superior consumer-grade user experience, disrupting the way they currently run the procurement functionality.

While most of the chief procurement officers have already achieved a high degree of spend under management, today they focus on providing more value to the business by engaging with business stakeholders on topics such as evolving from selling products to delivering solutions and services, becoming a strategic advisor by monitoring market innovations, and connecting innovative new suppliers with the engineering to leverage the latest technologies.

For more than 40 years, SAP has been working closely with chief procurement officers around the globe. This way, chief procurement officers can deliver best-practice processes and software solutions that allow procurement and finance to continuously improve their value contribution to the company and help drive bottom-line impact.

The introduction of SAP S/4HANA has established the foundation of the digital enterprise for procurement. With a state-of-the-art user interface accessible from any device, SAP HANA platform as basis for real-time analytics, and the plug-and-play SAP HANA Cloud Integration, SAP S/4HANA Sourcing and Procurement provides the necessary flexibility for every customer to digitalize every single purchasing process.

With SAP S/4HANA Sourcing and Procurement, customers can manage massive amounts of data to run live, with access to real-time digital visibility into all corners of business operations. SAP S/4HANA Sourcing and Procurement covers operational procurement processes, including purchase requisitioning, order processing, invoice processing, order confirmation, and operational contract management—all supported by real-time embedded analytics across all spend categories.

SAP provides access and outreach to partners and suppliers outside the four walls of customers' organizations by combining SAP S/4HANA Sourcing and Procurement with SAP Ariba and SAP Fieldglass solutions. Customers and their suppliers can collaborate on changed order priorities, track shipments, provide service entries, and share delivery schedules, forecasts, and inventory across the extended supply chain. These capabilities enable real-time collaboration that reduces supplier and supply chain risks.

Explore how SAP S/4HANA Sourcing and Procurement meets the key trends and how the power of SAP S/4HANA Sourcing and Procurement caters for a tangible step up in performance, speed, agility, visibility, and control.

Best Regards,
Salvatore Lombardo
Head of Development, SAP S/4HANA Procurement

Preface

SAP has been a leader in the procurement space for several decades now, having pioneered the first integrated enterprise resource planning systems to run in real-time in an integrated fashion. With the advent of the cloud, SAP has also pursued an acquisition strategy to further extend its leadership in this area, most notably with the acquisitions of SAP Ariba, SAP Fieldglass, and Concur.

With SAP S/4HANA Enterprise Management, SAP has moved the needle for speed and simplicity to a degree that also creates an array of new features and functionality on the procurement side of the ledger. No longer do users need to conduct transactions in the SAP ERP environment and then swivel their chairs to another system to conduct after-the-fact analysis. With SAP S/4HANA, the tables' overhaul and the in-memory data design mean that both transactions and analysis can be conducted directly in a single system, at exponentially faster speeds. Combine this with industry-leading cloud solutions from SAP Ariba and SAP Fieldglass, and you have SAP S/4HANA as the digital core, with SAP Ariba and SAP Fieldglass covering procurement transformation at all levels of an organization.

This book covers SAP S/4HANA Sourcing and Procurement in detail and lays out functionality, configuration, and guidelines for running successful implementations in each area. This book provides a comprehensive guide to implementing SAP S/4HANA Sourcing and Procurement, as well as key integration points in leveraging the cloud solutions from SAP Ariba.

Target Audience

This book should be of interest for anyone working with SAP S/4HANA Enterprise Management, SAP Ariba, and/or SAP Fieldglass, or those looking at rolling out procurement solutions in either an on-premise or cloud environment. Business users, procurement managers, and consultants are the primary beneficiaries of this type of book. This book assumes a familiarity with and interest in procurement solutions and terminology, as well as project management and delivery topics around these solutions. Finally, critical reasoning skills in understanding just where these solutions will provide your organization the most value individually and in concert will serve you in good stead in this journey.

Objective

This book's focus is on implementing SAP S/4HANA Sourcing and Procurement, in conjunction with key SAP cloud solutions for procurement, principally SAP Ariba and SAP Fieldglass. Together, SAP S/4HANA, SAP Ariba's solutions, and SAP Fieldglass cover a vast area of collaboration and processes between an organization and its suppliers. Although it is not possible to cover every permutation of configuration in these solutions, this book will provide an in-depth look at each of the SAP S/4HANA solution areas for procurement and will furnish system-specific guidelines, methodologies, and required roles, as well as provide guidance for integrating SAP S/4HANA with select SAP Ariba solutions.

Structure of this Book

This book is a comprehensive guide to setting up and using SAP S/4HANA Sourcing and Procurement. Starting with Chapter 5, each chapter describes the features and post-go-live use of key functionality for a given procurement topic, teaches how to configure it, and explains how to integrate it with relevant applications using system screenshots and detailed step-by-step instructions.

This book features text boxes to show readers where SAP S/4HANA functionality overlaps with SAP Ariba, or where an SAP Ariba application (e.g., the Ariba Network) can be used to optimize a particular task.

This book is organized into 14 chapters. The first four chapters cover a general SAP S/4HANA overview, implementation options, organization structure, and master data set up. The remaining chapters cover the major procurement solution areas in SAP S/4HANA, beginning with operational procurement and concluding with SAP Fiori user interface (UI) topics.

Chapter 1, "Introduction to Sourcing and Procurement," explains the software-agnostic procurement business process for today's enterprises, the boundaries between operational procurement with an SAP ERP system and strategic procurement with an SAP Cloud solution such as SAP Ariba or SAP Fieldglass, and the key simplifications introduced with SAP S/4HANA.

SAP customers can choose from on-premise or cloud versions of SAP S/4HANA implementations, which have a slightly different functional scope and IT project requirements and therefore have their own pros and cons. **Chapter 2**, "Implementation

Options," defines processes covered by each product and the relative merits of each SAP S/4HANA implementation approach. The chapter closes with a description of SAP Activate methodology and project setup for each implementation scenario.

As with previous versions of SAP ERP, defining a core organization structure foundation for SAP S/4HANA Sourcing and Procurement is a key step for a successful implementation and system adoption. **Chapter 3**, "Organizational Structure," covers organization structure design and configuration from a procurement standpoint.

Procurement requires master data to streamline transactions and facilitate the user experience and record keeping of the system. Master data setup in SAP S/4HANA is like that in previous iterations of SAP, with one significant change: the consolidation of both customer and supplier master records into a single business partner record in SAP S/4HANA. **Chapter 4**, "Master Data," covers core master data definition and setup while providing an in-depth look at the new business partner concept in SAP S/4HANA for managing both suppliers and customer records in a unified manner.

What we think of as *operational procurement* happens between the creation of a purchase order and the delivery of the invoice. **Chapter 5**, "Operational Procurement," covers the system processes involved with the purchase order, goods receipt, and invoicing.

Much of direct procurement and other reoccurring types of procurement can be automated in SAP S/4HANA, leveraging tried and true approaches such as source lists, reorder points, information records, and scheduling agreements. **Chapter 6**, "Automated and Direct Procurement," outlines the approaches and configuration steps for setting up direct procurement and automating this and other types of reoccurring procurement.

Inventory Management is fully integrated with SAP S/4HANA Sourcing and Procurement and supports many of the procurement activities and processes. **Chapter 7**, "Inventory Management," outlines the various processes in procurement that integrate with inventory management, such as reservations, stock transfer postings (STPs), and special stocks, as well as how to configure Inventory Management to support these processes in SAP S/4HANA.

Chapter 8, "Contracts Management," outlines contract functionality and usage in SAP S/4HANA Sourcing and Procurement, configuration, as well as integration with SAP Ariba Contracts. Contracts solidify pricing and volumes with suppliers, as well as terms and conditions, making contracts a must-have for orderly procurement operations. ERP systems have traditionally focused upon the operational aspects of contracts, integrating the negotiated terms into transactions. SAP S/4HANA continues this tradition while adding some nuances on the integration side with SAP Ariba.

In the source-to-pay process, sourcing can occur after forecasting and planning have been completed but prior to any transactions in the system, for a purchase requisition or order for which a source of supply has not been defined, or simply at the whim of a purchasing agent planning ahead. Sourcing in SAP S/4HANA leverages the sourcing cockpit available in previous versions of SAP ERP, along with native integration with SAP Ariba Sourcing. **Chapter 9**, "External Sourcing," outlines the various areas in a procurement process into which sourcing can be inserted, configuration of sourcing in SAP S/4HANA, and the integration activation and setup for SAP Ariba Sourcing.

Once a good or service has been requested, approved, ordered, and received, it is time for payment. **Chapter 10**, "Invoice and Payables Management," covers accounts payable invoicing in SAP S/4HANA from process, configuration, and integration standpoints, using OpenText and SAP Ariba.

The final step in the procurement process is to evaluate suppliers to determine whether it's wise to continue partnering with them. **Chapter 11**, "Supplier Management," examines supplier management and evaluation topics, providing step-by-step instructions for setup and use of key SAP S/4HANA functionality.

Chapter 12, "Reporting and Analytics," describes how to use existing SAP S/4HANA reports to analyze sourcing and procurement processes in real time. It highlights key reports for spend analysis, contract expiration, sourcing, and supplier performance, which are common to many organizations, explains how to configure those reports, and shows where they supply data to or receive the same from peripheral cloud applications.

If business users prefer to update or fine-tune the UI for organization-specific roles or user access, they can! **Chapter 13**, "Customizing the SAP Fiori UI," explains how to define roles, configure the UI, and set up the project.

Chapter 14, "Conclusion", summarizes the preceding chapters, reiterates implementation options for SAP customers, and considers how topics like big data, the Internet of Things, and artificial intelligence will impact the SAP procurement portfolio.

> **References and Resources**
>
> The following resources were used as references by the authors in the course of writing of this book and should be referred to for continued learning:

- **SAP Help**
  http://help.sap.com
- **SAP Product Documentation, Downloads, Service, and Best Practice and Integration Content**
  http://service.sap.com
- **SAP Ariba**
  http://www.ariba.com

Acknowledgments

Many colleagues and friends made significant contributions to this book. In particular, I would like to thank our Rheinwerk editors, Emily Nicholls and Will Jobst of SAP PRESS; the contributing authors, Bob Gotschall, platinum principal in the SRM Cloud Practice, and Chelliah Soundar, principal consultant and member of the SAP Regional Implementation Group (RIG) for SAP S/4HANA; our foreword author, Salvatore Lombardo, head of product development SAP S/4HANA; and Christine Hofmann, SAP S/4HANA chief product expert. I would also like to thank Alex Atzberger, president of SAP Ariba, for his support; Klaus Fischer, vice president strategic customers, procurement and business network, for contributions and edits on SAP messaging; Ulf Petzel, SAP high tech industry solution manager, supply base optimization; my mentor for all things IT and career, Professor John Leslie King, William Warner Bishop collegiate professor of information and professor of information, school of information, University of Michigan; my former manager, Bryan Bee, for introducing me to Emily Nicholls several years ago at SAP PRESS; as well as the SAP SRM Cloud practice colleagues Anil Punjala, Paul Bibb, Matthew Cauthen, John Corcoran, Lora Holst, Workman Meeks, Amar Neburi, Tuan Pham, Alan Salgado, Rachith Srinivas, Ramesh Vasudevan, Joe Wolff, Sasirekha Yuganandhan, Kannan Krishnan, Tushar Ganguly, Jaganmohan Kanala, Othon Roitman, Noel Nera, and Brendan MacBride. Special thanks and love to my wonderful wife and sons for supporting the long weekends and writing sessions.

Justin Ashlock
Chicago, Illinois
December 2017

Chapter 1
Introduction to Sourcing and Procurement

At its core, procurement is simply the purchase of a good or service by one organization or individual from another organization or individual. Companies and governments require both direct and indirect inputs of this nature to deliver the goods and services they in turn seek to deliver to the marketplace or directly to their customer base.

This chapter explains the software-agnostic procurement business process for today's enterprises, the boundaries between operational procurement with an SAP ERP system and strategic sourcing with an SAP Cloud system such as SAP Ariba or SAP Fieldglass, and the key innovations and simplifications introduced with SAP S/4HANA.

1.1 Procurement from End to End

Procurement is an essential, core process in enterprise resource planning (ERP). Without procurement, production of a good or service isn't possible, and without production no goods/services are produced. Without goods/services to provide, no spending justification can be made by a government entity, nor can sales/revenues be obtained by a firm. Following this logic to its conclusion, without input a government or enterprise can't deliver its goods and services, and without procurement you can't obtain input. Without procurement, therefore, you can't run a firm or government.

As with all core processes within an organization, procurement can be a competitive differentiator and source of strength. An organization that understands its supply base thoroughly and collaborates with its suppliers in an efficient manner can bring more innovation, lower prices, and quality to its customers than an organization that doesn't manage these processes and relationships. A company that fails to obtain effective pricing on its inputs usually begins to lose to a competitor that does. In certain scenarios in which much of the supply chain is vertically integrated into one company or entity, external procurement may not be as big a factor as other core processes in success or failure of the firm. A vertically integrated firm would not have too much to procure from outside suppliers for its direct inputs, by virtue of owning the input production upstream. Most entities today, however, are not vertically integrated as was once attempted at some automakers, where the firm owned the rubber plantations, oil fields, iron ore, components manufacturing, and so on required for making its product. Even in a vertically integrated organization, the process of procurement doesn't go away, but rather becomes an intercompany purchasing activity, an activity with its own set of intricacies and cost accounting decisions.

1.1.1 Ideal Procurement

Ideally, a procurement operation wants to understand demand down to the lowest detail level possible as far out as possible, in order to focus its procurement activities and discussions with the appropriate suppliers, discussing the appropriate quantities, pricing, and timelines. Foresight usually equals cost savings, and cost savings is one of the key value adds of procurement. Foresight can also bring the added benefit of building the appropriate level of relationship and understanding with a supplier prior to needing a product or service in a rush. The other value generator within procurement is obtaining the right product or service from the right supplier.

Too often, procurement is reduced to a tactical exercise of obtaining the lowest cost, but cost savings isn't the only goal of procurement. Lowest cost doesn't always equal optimal procurement for an organization, as the lowest cost can bring a host of trade-offs, such as lower quality and lower supplier reliability. Some commodity businesses value cost savings over many other aspects, whereas businesses competing in areas of innovation and quality value these characteristics in their supply base over cost and can be quite *cost insensitive*, so to speak.

From luxury goods to mobile phones to fast food, examples abound of companies working tightly with suppliers to ensure the best quality possible or impactful innovation or other drivers beyond cost to move the needle on their businesses. Government has countless examples as well, even in situations in which corruption or ineptitude is not the driving force behind choosing a supplier with higher prices. In fairness, it should be noted that government entities do not have a monopoly in this area. There is plenty of ineptitude in the corporate world in procurement as well, especially in industries with oligopolies or competitive moats. As with economics, our models and processes for procurement assume rational actors operating with near-perfect information, which is rarely the case.

1.1.2 Procure-to-Pay

Procure-to-pay processes in an enterprise often are extended to encompass the planning, forecasting, sourcing, and analytics steps that surround this process. This is called *source-to-pay*, but the term is somewhat misleading, as finding a source of supply may not be the first step in the procurement process every time. Sometimes the sourcing happens prior to the requisition being created and approved, but many times it happens after a requisition has been approved with no source of supply. Other times sourcing is triggered by strategic planning or even buyer hunches for upcoming demand. Regardless of how the process is organized sequentially, there are two components to procurement: a cerebral, planning- and analysis-based side; and a second, transactional component of creating and issuing agreements, whether sourcing and contracts or actual purchase orders, then receiving and paying for these purchase orders via an invoice process in accounts payable.

1.1.3 Procurement Process Areas

There is no catch-all process flow for procurement; some individual activities can move in sequence, depending on the type of procurement and the organization's and/or industry's norms for procurement processes. It's easier to break up procurement into some general areas and categories, as in Table 1.1.

Procurement Process Area	Description	Occurrence in Source-to-Pay Process	Main SAP ERP Integration Points with Other Modules
Operational Purchasing	Transactional procurement, core Purchase Order, Goods/Service Receipt, Invoice (PO-GR/SES-IV)	Before Invoice and Payables Management	Finance, Inventory Management, Production Planning
Collaborative Sourcing and Contract Management	Request for quote, purchase, information process, source selection via bidding or single source, and contract definition	Either after or before Operational Purchasing	Finance, Inventory Management, Production Planning

Table 1.1 Procurement Process Areas

Procurement Process Area	Description	Occurrence in Source-to-Pay Process	Main SAP ERP Integration Points with Other Modules
Invoice and Payables Management	Invoice submission by supplier, verification, and payment by accounts payable (AP)	After Operational Purchasing	Finance
Supplier Management	Supplier designation, master data and performance management.	Run in parallel to the other process steps and/or end of the procurement process.	SAP ERP master data
Procurement Analytics	Analysis of core, key performance indicators (KPIs), such as spend analysis, demand/forecast planning, as well as supplier performance and consolidation.	Run in parallel to other process steps and/or the end of the procurement process	Finance, Inventory Management

Table 1.1 Procurement Process Areas (Cont.)

1.1.4 Disadvantages

One of the disadvantages with ERP systems and procurement is integration with suppliers. The more tightly integrated procurement is with ERP systems, the more real-time information is available for analysis and the more that ERP modules such as finance and inventory management can support the procurement process seamlessly. However, supplier processes may differ from your internal processes, and supplier systems will differ from your internal systems. Herein lies the issue with ERP systems architecture. The supplier cannot be given access to everything in an organization's ERP system, and in many instances a firewall blocks access even to relevant information and functionality the supplier could leverage. System-to-system communication has to be negotiated on a one-to-one or one-to-network basis in ERP systems, between customer and supplier. This is costly, time-consuming to set up, and often still limits the interaction.

Areas such as request for information/proposal/quote/bid (collectively RFx) processes/bidding, contract negotiation, and supplier portals remain challenges for an

ERP-only approach to procurement, as these areas often require iterative collaboration with suppliers. SAP ERP is a transactional, command-and-control environment with high security requirements due to the sensitive data contained in many SAP ERP modules. Financial, Human Resources, and other data mandates stricter firewall requirements than needed in a collaborative environment, and if one has to preclude the other, security will almost always carry the day. This has led to earlier iterations of purchasing systems, such as SAP Supplier Relationship Management (SAP SRM), branching off from SAP ERP, but remaining integrated with the backend SAP ERP system and still installed on-premise, albeit on a separate client/server. Although this allows for focused purchasing activities, organization structures, and the support of casual users, actual supplier collaboration is limited and still requires one-to-one negotiated setup for the supplier to access the customer's portal or receive electronically transmitted purchasing documents beyond fax/email.

1.1.5 The Next Wave

The next wave of purchasing systems embraces the cloud/software as a service (SaaS) model. SAP Ariba was at the forefront of this shift, taking indirect procurement transactions into a focused, multitenant, cloud-based environment in which a much greater degree of collaboration with suppliers, improved ease of use, and richness of content are available. Most customers still need to connect to a backend SAP ERP environment, at least for financials. Many customers run a split environment, sourcing and purchasing indirect items in their SAP Ariba environments while covering their direct procurement, direct procurement meaning the purchasing of input related directly to the end products and services produced by the firm or government entity, directly out of SAP ERP.

Direct procurement and capital purchasing are particularly integrated with other modules in SAP ERP, such as Inventory Management and Warehouse Management, as well as Asset Management and Finance. For most firms, procurement is a vital aspect of their operations and their strategy, often with direct procurement deemed strategic and indirect deemed operational. This can reinforce boundaries at a system level further, as direct procurement is typically conducted out of SAP ERP and indirect out of SAP Ariba. Yet strategic sourcing for direct procurement activities often requires more supplier collaboration during the RFx process than sourcing for operational procurement.

1.2 Operational Procurement vs. Strategic Procurement in SAP

Operational procurement is transactional and conducted on a day-to-day basis to support the ongoing operations of the firm or government entity. Some direct procurement may be included in this designation, which usually is defined along the lines of cost, type, and volume. If any of these three characteristics is relatively high or classified as a direct, mission-critical input to an end product or successful execution of a service, the procurement of this good/service may be deemed strategic. By and large, strategic procurement usually centers on strategic sourcing for direct procurement activities, but an indirect product or service that has particularly high volume or cost relative to the operating costs of a company may also qualify.

1.2.1 Operational Procurement

Operational procurement keeps the lights on and the office supplies stocked for an organization. Much of this type of procurement can be driven directly at the employee level, rather than by a designated buyer aggregating demand and then placing larger orders. Depending on the industry and the process and system maturity of an organization, operational procurement is pushed all the way down to the requesting employee, centralized at a buyer level, often at the site, company division, or a centralized buying group for the entire company.

Pushing procurement down to the employee level requires system support and capabilities. Employees must be able to quickly, intuitively find what they are looking for in the system, order it and have it approved by the corresponding manager with adequate approval authority, and then have the order either routed for sourcing and processing by a buyer or, if already sourced, sent directly to the designated supplier for fulfilment.

In a buyer-brokered model, employees on a shop floor, for example, go to their point of contact for purchasing and place orders and requests. These are then routed for approval and sourced either by the designated buyer or by a buyer group once approved. Many times, this model is positioned as the only way, due to system limitations or the inability of the general staff to create coherent orders in a system. The designated shopper and/or buyer model is seen as a way to get all orders into the system cleanly and with minimal issues. However, this puts the onus on and creates a bottleneck with the designated buyers: the employees have to explain to an individual what they need purchased, and the buyer needs to translate this to an order, source it, and process the shipment or have the supplier deliver to the original requestor. Issues around transcription errors (if the supplier has questions, the buyer is caught in the middle on every order), receiving (who handles the goods receipt—the buyer or the requestor), and invoice processing (who approves payment for the order having been fulfilled) all can detract from the centralization model's strengths.

Another factor to consider is the aspect of relevance to total spend. Indirect spend usually comprises no more than 17–20 percent of total spend, which may be too small an amount to prioritize from a systems standpoint or procurement standpoint in general. Each dollar of savings is essentially profit, however. Many large companies and organizations ignore potential savings of millions in operational procurement, not realizing that they will have to sell the equivalent of hundreds of millions of dollars of additional goods and services to realize the corresponding amount they just passed up by neglecting this area of their operations.

For operational procurement, it is preferable from a systems and process standpoint to push the procurement decision-making and ordering out to the point of need—that is, the employee with job responsibilities that require this good or service. This requires enablement of the procurement process and simplification, to ensure that a casual user with a minimal amount of training can walk up, log in, and order an item in a small amount of time in an intuitive manner, providing the eventual supplier with a clear understanding of the product required, quantity with unit of measure, terms and conditions, expected delivery date, delivery address, any discounting, and a host of other information a typical casual user may not be able to provide or interested in providing. Much of the information provided in this order to the suppler needs to be automatically generated, so as to not risk burdening the casual user with unnecessary steps and requirements to complete an order.

Finally, operational procurement done correctly requires, like most iterative processes, a phase of analysis and application of lessons learned, to make the process and the procurement activities iteratively more effective at an individual and an aggregate level. The aggregate analysis, in particular, needs to be conducted by someone tasked with understanding things at this level, usually a procurement specialist.

In summary, operational procurement is best initiated at the employee level, supported by adequate system and data processes, such as intuitive UIs, approval workflows, and minimal steps, as well as clean master data, contracts, and catalog items to populate the order with all of the required information for the supplier, purchasing, and accounts payable, while minimizing manual entry on the part of the employee. Finally, each iteration needs to be examined at the process and data level to make the next time the process is conducted more efficient and cost-effective. The next section looks at this process in strategic procurement, for which the emphasis is still on cost savings and efficiencies, but with a reduced focus on the same, and with the buying group often playing with much larger stakes.

1.2.2 Strategic Procurement

Strategic procurement is the long-range procurement of goods and services that are critical for an organization to meet its objectives and obligations in the marketplace and/or for its stakeholders. An example of a direct input driving strategic procurement can be found in the airline industry. Airlines provide a service that is heavily dependent on fuel and its costs. The price of fuel can change daily, with airlines not always able to pass the costs (or, more recently, the savings) directly to their end customers. Fuel can comprise up to one-third of an airline's operating costs. At this level, fuel easily qualifies as strategic sourcing area for an airline.

Unlike one-off items ordered by employees in the office or on the shop floor, strategic procurement items have more predictable and sizeable quantity requirements and anticipated costs. If an organization fails to adequately estimate its needs in the strategic procurement area, the consequences can be severe. Securing too little fuel at an airline can mean having to buy fuel on the spot market at much higher costs, or even grounding flights. Sourcing from untested or appropriately vetted suppliers for strategic input can undermine the brand image, as products are shipped with a built-in point of failure. In severe cases, some organizations may not get a second chance to "make it right" and may be immediately cast into the dustbin of history. Quality control begins at the supplier level for any organization, especially if your products and services are the sum of your suppliers' inputs.

From a systems standpoint, strategic procurement requires three things from SAP ERP: First, you must have a robust forecasting to accurately estimate supply needs. Some companies and organizations run forecasting for the business in Excel sheets and relying on historical experience. This is a 1.0 approach and doesn't scale well for larger enterprises. Second, strategic sourcing requires an understanding of inventory and supply chain. If you have supply requirements from end customers forecasted at a certain level, what does this mean at all levels of your production? Do the suppliers have enough lead time to provide the input required? Do the areas of production have the adequate inventory and quality-management processes in place to fulfill these requirements within the timeline required? Third, do you have the right suppliers for this undertaking at the optimal price? This is perhaps the most challenging area for SAP ERP only, as it requires collaboration, a weak point for SAP ERP.

The supplier collaboration area is a weak point for SAP ERP because, by definition, SAP ERP can't connect to the outside world unencumbered by security requirements and concerns. Yet SAP ERP forms the basis for forecasting and the interconnected production planning areas in the strategic procurement equation. SAP ERP is tightly integrated with inventory management and planning modules, which can be used to drive strategic purchasing automatically for purchases, issuing POs based on stock levels and forecast models. The collaboration with suppliers is best conducted in a demilitarized zone, in which the organization doesn't have to risk its crown jewels regularly to trade simple and complex pieces of information at a system level. This is why SAP Ariba is the go-to solution for strategic sourcing execution, especially when it's time to collaborate with suppliers.

In summary, strategic procurement is central to an organization and spans many core areas, from finance to inventory and quality management to product development and production to sourcing. From a systems standpoint, both SAP ERP systems and supplier collaboration platforms/solutions are required to cover this area.

The supplier collaboration platform from an SAP solutions standpoint is SAP Ariba. To pull off all of strategic procurement, using SAP Ariba alone isn't feasible, because SAP Ariba would only be able to cover parts of the process and would need to integrate with the SAP ERP backend for others. However, handing this process entirely in SAP ERP creates its own challenges: supplier collaboration areas, from RFx scenarios to contract negotiation to network-enabled suppliers for document exchange, are not as robust as in SAP Ariba or aren't available at all in SAP ERP, as in the case of network-enabled supplier collaboration.

Now that we've covered SAP ERP processes, let's explore the innovations brought with SAP S/4HANA with regards to sourcing and procurement. The following section will introduce SAP S/4HANA and look further into these integration areas with cloud-based solutions.

1.3   Procurement with SAP S/4HANA

Rather than having to choose either on-premise or cloud for procurement activities, there is an SAP procurement strategy to fit every organization's size and needs. The core SAP procurement solution strategy today leverages SAP S/4HANA Enterprise Management as the digital core, with SAP Ariba as the go-to solution portfolio for procurement transformation, as shown in Figure 1.1. This combination of SAP S/4HANA

Enterprise Management and SAP Ariba allows you to take control in the following areas:

- **Transform procurement**
  Savings from strategic sourcing, scaling supplier management, and efficient operational procurement can be found in SAP Ariba procurement solutions.

- **Achieve digital IT transformation**
  Next-gen SAP ERP solutions for IT transformation, procurement in digital core, and simplified digital landscape can be found in SAP S/4HANA and Ariba Network.

- **Realize digital IT transformation with procurement**
  Next-gen digital landscape procurement savings and engagement at scale across the enterprise can be found in SAP S/4HANA, SAP Ariba procurement solutions, and Ariba Network.

The three main paths for procurement transformation with SAP all include Ariba Network. There is no substitute or on-premise alternative for the Ariba Network, and the power of the network for supplier collaboration at every step of the procurement process can be leveraged by small and large organizations alike.

Regardless of your choice of ERP system, you can run SAP Ariba in the cloud with the Ariba Network to transform your procurement operations. Smaller businesses with less than $1 billion in revenue annually can run their procurement operations directly in SAP S/4HANA, with supplier collaboration supported by the Ariba Network and Ariba Catalog. For larger enterprises, SAP recommends running SAP Ariba solutions and Ariba Network for all source-to-pay business processes integrated into SAP S/4HANA as the digital core.

1.3.1 SAP Ariba

SAP Ariba has cloud-based solutions for all of the major and minor areas of procurement. The most straightforward approach to understanding where SAP Ariba Sourcing and SAP Ariba Procurement fits with SAP S/4HANA in your overall solution landscape is to look at your organization's requirements and size, as well as your in-scope business processes.

Supplier management and risk, strategic sourcing, and contract negotiations are driven through SAP Ariba. The result is negotiated savings, which now need to be realized. To drive that price and contract compliance, there are two main buying channels: direct procurement, which happens in SAP S/4HANA and is plan-, replenishment-, or manufacturing resource planning-driven (MRP); and plant maintenance in SAP S/4HANA, accessing the Ariba Catalog to find materials and services. End user–driven indirect procurement of maintenance, repair, and operating supply (MRO), services, and indirect materials happens in SAP Ariba through an intuitive, policy-driven, guided buying experience to drive ease of use for all employees of a company. Supplier collaboration for all procurement scenarios coming from SAP S/4HANA or SAP Ariba will occur via the Ariba Network. This recommendation drives simplicity and fast speed to value. Cost savings from the SAP Ariba business case can self-fund digital transformation or other customer initiatives.

SAP Ariba is the go-to solution for strategic procurement requirements going beyond the traditional capabilities in SAP ERP, and this will continue to be the case in SAP S/4HANA. With the Ariba Network, SAP Ariba is also the main solution for network-supported transactions and collaboration, and the Ariba Catalog is the main solution for content management. In this hybrid approach, SAP S/4HANA supports the operational procurement side, including full purchase order–management process, as well as supplier management, with tight integration into other logistics areas.

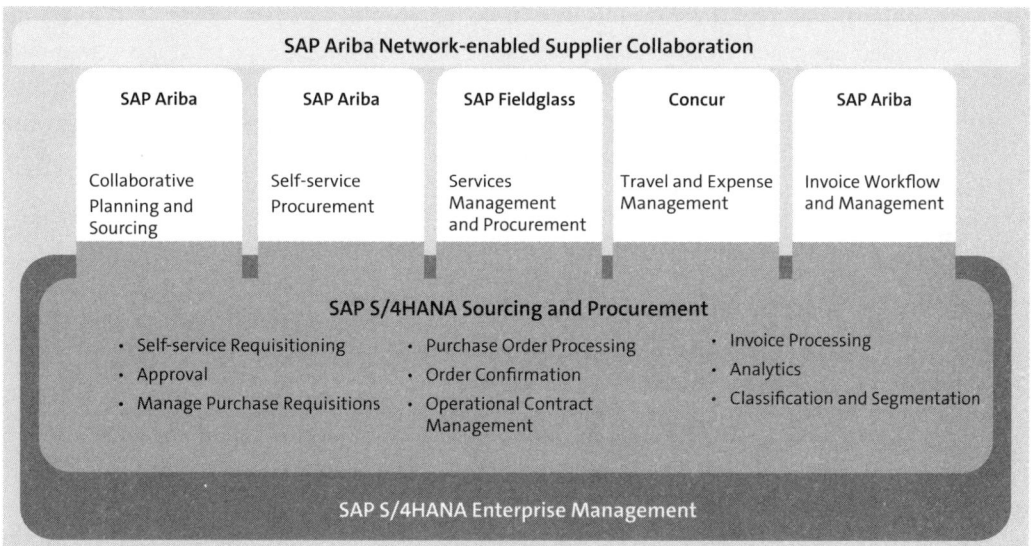

Figure 1.1 SAP S/4HANA Sourcing and Procurement Integration with SAP Ariba, SAP Fieldglass, and Concur

Figure 1.1 details the areas covered by SAP S/4HANA Sourcing and Procurement and shows where cloud solutions from SAP Ariba, SAP Fieldglass, and Concur are recommended. You can run self-service procurement, for example, in either SAP S/4HANA

1   Introduction to Sourcing and Procurement

or SAP Ariba Supply Chain Collaboration for Buyers, or in both, depending on the type of procurement. Where it makes sense, cloud options should always be evaluated, and between SAP Ariba and SAP Fieldglass, there is a cloud procurement solution for almost every scenario available. Although the focus of this book is on SAP S/4HANA, we will highlight integration opportunities in various procurement scenarios, with SAP Cloud solution counterparts noted where applicable.

1.3.2 Strategic Sourcing

One of the areas with clear advantages for the cloud is strategic sourcing. Here, a buyer needs to interact and collaborate with multiple suppliers, many of whom may not be onboarded yet. The buyer needs a platform from which to establish sourcing strategies and publish requests for pricing, quotes, information and bid responses. Auctions and other activities also need to be supported. At the end of the sourcing event, a contract and/or purchase order (PO) is typically generated, confirming the supplier and price. For contracts, the handoff from the bidding process to contract negotiation and finalization ideally should be seamless. As per Figure 1.2, the recommended approach from SAP is to leverage SAP Ariba for project/category management, sourcing, contracts, and catalogs while operationalizing the contract in SAP S/4HANA to have a source of supply for any purchasing activities initiated in the core, such as plan-driven direct procurement.

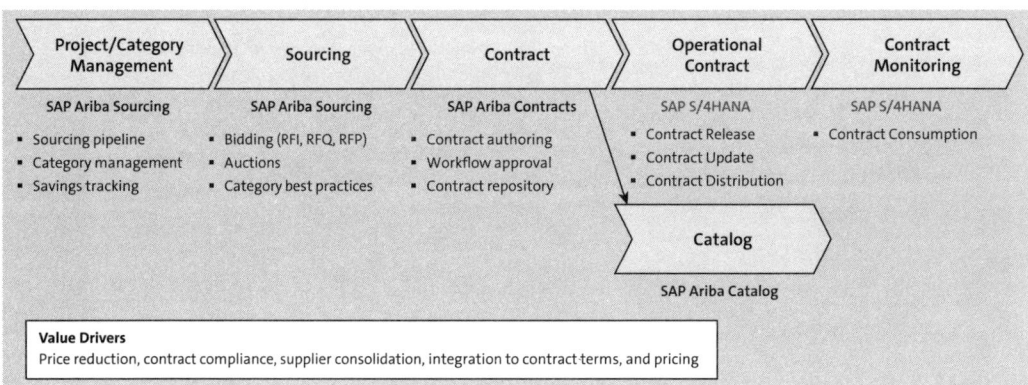

Figure 1.2 SAP Ariba and SAP S/4HANA: Strategic Sourcing

1.3.3 Procurement

For the procurement of MRO, indirect, and services, SAP Ariba's guided buying capability provides a consumer-grade guided buying experience leveraging negotiated contract pricing, company policies, and a spot marketplace for longtail spend, and it drives easy, effortless employee requisitioning through the shopping cart process using SAP Ariba Supply Chain Collaboration for Buyers and the SAP Ariba Catalog. This process then integrates with the SAP S/4HANA environment for PO execution and inventory management, backs up to the Ariba Network for Purchase Order and Invoice (PO/IV) collaboration, and finally to SAP S/4HANA for the accounts payable processing (see Figure 1.3).

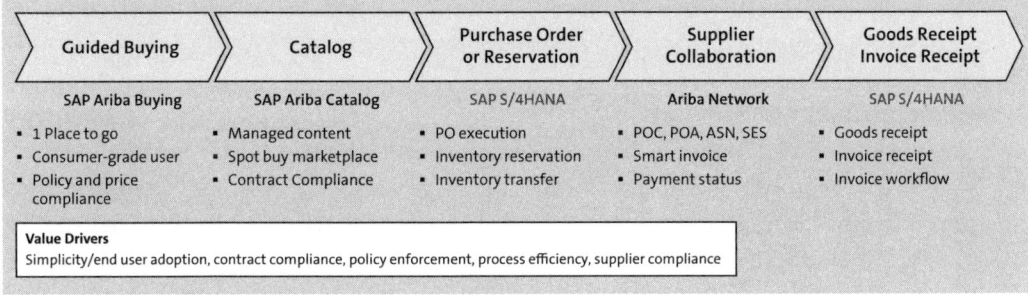

Figure 1.3 Procurement of Indirect, MRO, and Services

Guided buying is a key capability of SAP Ariba; end users require easy and simple user experiences combined with rich catalog content, which is managed and requires no maintenance from buyers. All of this is combined with deep integration with core processes in SAP S/4HANA, including operational transactions, inventory management, and plan-driven procurement. This makes the process a strong one to take advantage of the cloud.

On the direct procurement side, things are somewhat flip-flopped between SAP Ariba and SAP S/4HANA. Here, the trigger for the procurement proposal occurs during a MRP run or is created manually in response to a need in production and planning. These processes take place in SAP S/4HANA, and the requisition, source determination, and purchase order can follow in SAP S/4HANA. All supplier collaboration for direct materials happens over the Ariba Network. With SAP Ariba Supply Chain for Buyers, you now have the capability to support the more complex types of ordering such as scheduling agreements, forecasting, and contract manufacturing found in direct seamlessly at the collaboration point in the transaction in the Ariba Network, as shown in Figure 1.4.

1   Introduction to Sourcing and Procurement

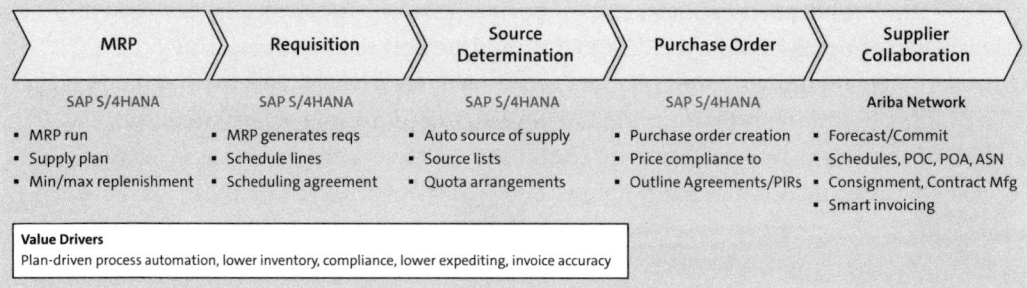

Figure 1.4 SAP Ariba and SAP S/4HANA Plan-Driven Procurement

For procurement activities originating in plant maintenance or in project management—as shown in Figure 1.5, more dynamic sourcing and content management is typically required. Here, the transaction originates in SAP S/4HANA but is then sourced by leveraging the SAP Ariba Catalog. The SAP Ariba Catalog in turn can host large MRO supplier catalogs and apply contract pricing to these items for plant maintenance requestors. Once the PO is created, the PO/IV collaboration process is supported in SAP S/4HANA via the Ariba Network as in the other scenarios, returning finally for goods receipt and invoice processing to SAP S/4HANA.

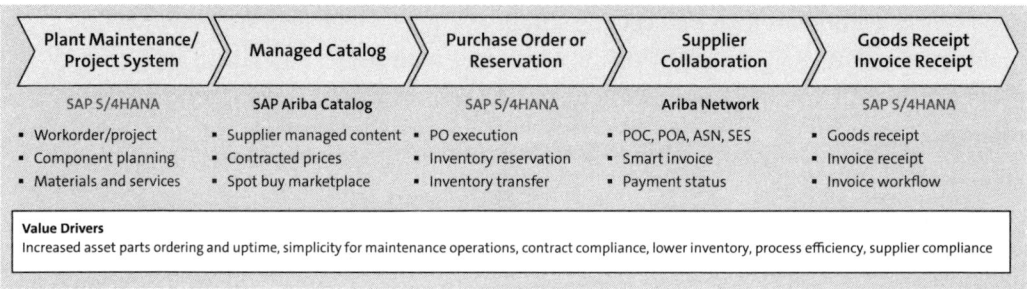

Figure 1.5 SAP S/4HANA and SAP Ariba Workorder and Project-Driven Procurement

1.3.4 Accounts Payable and Invoicing

Finally, for accounts payable and invoicing, SAP Ariba offers an array of solutions that go well beyond the simple transfer and processing of invoice documents. SAP Ariba allows all sizes of suppliers to create electronic invoices, email-based smart invoices, or B2B connections to buyers. SAP Ariba Invoice Management leverages smart invoice rules and invoices based on contracts (rate sheets) to reduce invoice errors, drive price and tax regulatory compliance, and ultimately allow buyers to receive a clean, error-free, 98 percent touchless invoice in SAP S/4HANA or SAP ERP, all to help drive automation and close the financial books faster. In addition to supporting collaboration between supplier and buyer and allowing for rules-based invoice submission, SAP Ariba also offers dynamic and self-service discounting for the suppliers and supply chain financing in SAP Ariba Payables, as shown in Figure 1.6. SAP S/4HANA serves as the digital core for accounts payable transactions, receiving an invoice and creating payment runs, but the front-end collaboration with the supplier can be significantly augmented from efficiency and discount standpoints via the inclusion of the Ariba Network and the SAP Ariba Payables solution.

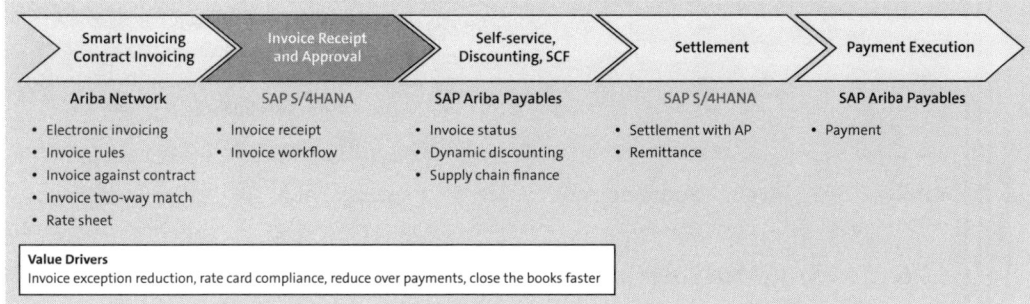

Figure 1.6 SAP Ariba and SAP S/4HANA Smart Invoicing and Contract Invoicing

SAP has embraced a cloud strategy that spans its entire solution portfolio. When assessing any SAP solution area, including procurement, you should aim to understand your options in the cloud, as well as the SAP roadmap and investment plans, from a product standpoint.

1.3.5 Sourcing and Procurement Roles within SAP S/4HANA

As with previous UIs, the concept of roles is central to SAP S/4HANA Sourcing and Procurement. The principal roles are listed in Table 1.2.

SAP S/4HANA Sourcing and Procurement Role	Description
Employee procurement—R0056-12	Manages purchase requisitions, e.g., creates purchase requisitions, confirms goods receipt and/or services performed, returns deliveries, approves supplier invoices, and evaluates suppliers

Table 1.2 SAP S/4HANA Sourcing and Procurement Roles

SAP S/4HANA Sourcing and Procurement Role	Description
Manager procurement—R0091	Approves purchasing documents, e.g., requisitions, contracts and purchase orders
Operational purchaser—R0128	Manages purchase orders, including the creation and tracking of these documents, and monitors requisitions and contracts
Strategic buyer—R0153	Manages sourcing, including supplier evaluation, manages purchase contracts and purchase orders, and monitors requisitions
Accounts payable accountant—R0005-12	Manages supplier invoices, including the creation of supplier invoices and release of blocked invoices

Table 1.2 SAP S/4HANA Sourcing and Procurement Roles (Cont.)

1.3.6 SAP S/4HANA Sourcing and Procurement SAP Fiori Apps

Perhaps equally important, the following procurement apps are available for SAP Fiori in SAP S/4HANA. These apps fall into transactional, analytical, and navigational categories.

All told, there are over 500 SAP Fiori apps already available for SAP S/4HANA Enterprise Management and over 100 roles. This provides a customer with a wide array of prebuilt options with which to tailor the user experience and process optimization. For further requirements beyond the prebuilt roles and apps, customizing apps and roles further to the customer's needs has never been easier and more mobile-ready than with the SAP Fiori-based UI.

This book's focus is on the SAP S/4HANA digital core and the SAP Ariba solutions' powerful bidirectional integration and the business scenarios available for our customers. For an in-depth look at the functionality and implementation approaches for both SAP Ariba and SAP Fieldglass, there is a dedicated title available from SAP PRESS: *SAP Ariba and SAP Fieldglass: Functionality and Implementation* (2016, www.sap-press.com/3950).

1.4 SAP S/4HANA Enterprise Management: SAP's Digital Core

SAP S/4HANA Enterprise Management is the latest ERP platform from SAP. SAP S/4HANA Enterprise Management is a new, separate product line completely rearchitected to run natively on the SAP HANA in-memory computing platform and operational database system (ODS) pioneered in-house at SAP. SAP S/4HANA is therefore not a legal successor version to the SAP Business Suite or SAP ERP; SAP ERP and SAP Business Suite products will still be available as separate product lines. SAP S/4HANA Enterprise Management thus charts a new path, but it isn't a complete break with the previous SAP ERP product lines. Much of the functionality offered in SAP S/4HANA and even the on-premise configuration approaches remain the same or similar. There is also an upgrade path on offer from SAP ERP and SAP Business Suite powered by SAP HANA to SAP S/4HANA.

SAP S/4HANA has two deployment options or editions: on-premise SAP S/4HANA and SAP S/4HANA Cloud. Similar to the SAP Business Suite products, the on-premise edition supports over 30 languages, over 60 country versions, and over 20 industry solutions. SAP S/4HANA Cloud has a more restricted scope of supported languages and industry solutions to date, with the goal of adding further supported areas in the coming quarters. SAP S/4HANA Cloud covers specific business scenarios for the marketing line of business (LOB) and for the professional services industry, as well as the most essential scenarios to run an entire enterprise in the cloud with a digital core, including finance, accounting, controlling, procurement, sales, manufacturing, plant maintenance, project system, and product lifecycle management. Marketing, professional services, and enterprise are the three main SAP S/4HANA Cloud options currently available.

The most obvious differences from previous iterations of SAP ERP and SAP S/4HANA, for either cloud or on-premise editions, are threefold. First, the improvements in speed are breathtaking, especially in the areas of in-system analytics. Second, the UI is completely reengineered for SAP Fiori. Third, the extensibility via native and almost native integrations with SAP Cloud solutions like SAP Ariba and SAP Fieldglass, as well as the optimizations and consolidations of areas requiring separate clients and interface layers, serves to further boost performance of the system and streamline the system landscape requirements.

The table structures and SAP ERP applications themselves have been completely overhauled to run optimally in an in-memory database environment. In the past, multiple indices and tables were prebuilt to minimize the impacts of calculations on system performance. These tables created inflexibility and complexity challenges of their own, however.

1.5 Summary

As a business computing concept, ERP has been around since the inception of computing itself. Up until recently, analytics and transactions had to run in separate environments because of computing constraints. Over time, computing became faster, but complexity, requirements, and data loads grew at a similar pace, moving in lockstep with the improvements in computing hardware and software speed and necessitating further separation. Now, we're at an inflection point with SAP S/4HANA Enterprise Management, in which both software and hardware advances are able to support the reunification of analytics and transactions into one unified platform.

SAP S/4HANA Enterprise Management achieves this breakthrough by leveraging simplification of the ERP data model, making quantum leaps in in-memory database technology, adding the flexibility of SAP Fiori to underpin a mobile-centric UI, and engaging in rationalization of what SAP ERP processes constitute the SAP S/4HANA core versus a separate client module requiring an interface. The platform also requires customers to reevaluate their existing SAP ERP system footprints, architectures, and processes to take full advantage of these considerable advances in ERP and business computing as a whole. Each process area will require a level of effort and strategy to achieve a comprehensive implementation of SAP S/4HANA Enterprise Management. With SAP S/4HANA Sourcing and Procurement, the procurement processes are a core part of this new platform and the focus of this book. In the following chapters, we'll attempt to provide a roadmap towards realizing a successful, comprehensive implementation of SAP S/4HANA Sourcing and Procurement.

Chapter 2
Implementation Options

SAP S/4HANA Enterprise Management is a new ERP product line from SAP, but not all upgrade paths from existing ERP systems have to be built from scratch. When embarking on a journey to SAP S/4HANA Enterprise Management, there are a number of questions to answer and areas to analyze prior to deciding on the best route.

SAP customers can choose from on-premise or cloud versions of SAP S/4HANA implementations, which have slightly different functional scopes and IT project requirements and therefore have their own pros and cons. This chapter defines processes covered by each product and the relative merits of each SAP S/4HANA implementation approach. The chapter closes with a description of the SAP Activate methodology and model company approaches and covers the project setup for each implementation scenario.

2.1 Implementation Overview

First, what does your current ERP system look like? If you're running SAP ERP, what version is it on? Are there multiple instances? A lot of custom code and processes or a pretty vanilla implementation using the standard processes of the system? Second, what are the goals of this implementation? Are you looking to upgrade on a technical level or is the mandate to reengineer processes *and* upgrade the current environment to the latest stack? Third, what areas are to be covered in this upgrade by SAP S/4HANA Enterprise Management, and what add-on solutions and interfaces are required? Can all of the business processes, transactions, and analytics run from ERP, or do you need to factor in additional modules and cloud solutions to address all of your requirements? Finally, are your design requirements or corporate initiatives such that SAP S/4HANA Enterprise Management could be deployed in the cloud?

2.1.1 Deployment Options

There are five main deployment options:

1. SAP S/4HANA or SAP HANA Enterprise Cloud
2. SAP S/4HANA Cloud, private option
3. SAP S/4HANA Cloud
4. SAP Hybris Marketing Cloud

The implementation options for on-premise systems fall largely into three primary types, as outlined in Table 2.1. A customer can convert an existing SAP ERP 6.0 EHP 7 or higher instance by following the conversion steps to on-premise SAP S/4HANA, consolidate one or multiple ERP systems into an on-premise SAP S/4HANA or SAP S/4HANA Cloud, or create a new implementation of an on-premise SAP S/4HANA or SAP S/4HANA Cloud.

SAP S/4HANA Transformation Type	Example/Benefits
System conversion	*Example:* Complete conversion of an existing SAP Business Suite system to SAP S/4HANA *Benefits:* Reevaluation of customization and existing process flows, transformation over time
Landscape transformation	*Example:* Consolidation of current regional SAP Business Suite landscape into one global SAP S/4HANA system *Benefits:* Stay with current business processes and move gradually to SAP S/4HANA innovations
New implementation	*Example:* New or existing SAP customer implementing a new or *greenfield* SAP S/4HANA system *Benefits:* Reengineering and process simplifications based on ready-to-run business processes

Table 2.1 SAP S/4HANA Transformation Options

With each option, there are both benefits and trade-offs. An organization with a lot of unnecessary processes and legacy data could elect to convert an existing system to SAP S/4HANA, but it may benefit more from rearchitecting its processes and system from the ground up in a new implementation. A relatively modern implementation on SAP ERP 6.0 with a later enhancement pack may be able to simply convert, but this is also an opportunity to evaluate a new implementation in the SAP S/4HANA

Cloud, if this is the direction the organization is moving in general. In short, deciding on a path for SAP S/4HANA involves comparing internal architecture and goals with the external options on deck and arriving at the approach that best fits the organization.

2.1.2 Cloud

Cloud computing is a general (and popular) term to describe the delivery of services hosted by a third-party cloud provider on the Internet. This option enables a customer to consume a computing resource by paying a subscription fee, versus using a traditional perpetual license and annual maintenance fees. The cloud options entail less flexibility in processes, configuration, access (web only), and governance versus on-premise implementations. However, in exchange for this, the customer also receives quarterly updates to the system, little to no internal IT overhead, and core processes on a subscription basis.

The cloud model leverages several acronym-laden concepts, including software as a service (SaaS), platform as a service (PaaS), integration platform as a service (IPaaS), and infrastructure as a service (IaaS). A PaaS provides a cloud platform and tools to help developers build and deploy cloud applications. An IPaaS is a suite of cloud services enabling development, execution, and governance of integration flows connecting any combination of on-premise and cloud-based processes, services, applications, and data within an individual organization or across multiple organizations. An IaaS lets companies "rent" computing resources such as servers, networks, storage, and operating systems on a pay-per-use basis. IaaS providers host the infrastructure and handle tasks like. Users can access all of these services from a web browser and pick and choose options on a subscription basis. SAP's cloud offerings include SaaS (application offerings in the cloud), IaaS (infrastructure via application and database services), IPaaS (integration platform options for integration of multiple cloud services and apps), and PaaS (platform for the services under the SAP Cloud Platform) options.

The main models for cloud computing are described in Table 2.2.

Cloud Computing Type	Description
Private cloud	System hosted by provider solely for a single customer. Customer accesses the system over a virtual private network (VPN).

Table 2.2 Cloud Computing Types

2   Implementation Options

Cloud Computing Type	Description
Public	System hosted by the provider for multiple customers (tenants).
Hybrid	Combines two or more distinct public cloud environments and/or on-premise providers. Integrated by standardized or proprietary technology enabling data and application portability.

Table 2.2 Cloud Computing Types (Cont.)

SAP S/4HANA Cloud falls into the public cloud type of service—that is, a true multitenant service model that includes quarterly innovation cycles and updates. SAP S/4HANA Cloud comes in several different flavors:

- *SAP S/4HANA Cloud, private option*, a bring-your-own-license (BYOL) option and therefore essentially a hosted version of an on-premise system
- *SAP S/4HANA Cloud*, the general SAP S/4HANA ERP edition for the cloud
- *SAP Hybris Marketing Cloud*, tailored for the marketing area of an organization or for a marketing-centric organization in general

Another decision matrix can be laid out for the five deployment options—on-premise, private cloud, or the three cloud variations—as in Table 2.3.

Scenario/ Deployment Option	On-Premise SAP S/4HANA	SAP S/4HANA Cloud, Private Option	SAP S/4HANA Cloud	SAP Hybris Marketing Cloud
Customer needs full control of system and functionality with ability customize and even potentially modify.	Best option for scenario, as the full functionality is available on-premise and customer owns governance of system and can customize and even modify if absolutely required.	Second-best option, as some customization and full functionality is available in private cloud. No modification permissible, however, and system governance shared between SAP and customer.	Not an option as system governance is owned by SAP and only limited customizations allowed.	Not an option due to specific functionality focus of system and cloud restriction on governance/ AMS/mods.

Table 2.3 Decision Matrix: Deployment Options

Scenario/ Deployment Option	On-Premise SAP S/4HANA	SAP S/4HANA Cloud, Private Option	SAP S/4HANA Cloud	SAP Hybris Marketing Cloud
Customer requires a subscription-based deployment option but wants full functionality and to retain some influence over governance and release updates.	Not an option, as on-premise is not a subscription.	Best option, as SAP S/4HANA private cloud allows the customer subscription model to deploy updates at its own pace and comanage governance.	Not an option as system governance/AMS is owned by SAP and only limited customizations are allowed.	Not an option due to specific functionality focus of system and cloud restriction on governance/AMS/mods.
Customer requires quarterly updates in a pure cloud environment with order-to-cash and plan-to-produce.	On-premise not an option, as updates are not quarterly and by definition it is not cloud-based.	Private cloud not an option, as it does not provide quarterly updates.	Best option, as SAP S/4HANA Cloud provides quarterly updates and also supports order-to-cash and plan-to-produce.	Not an option as it doesn't support order-to-cash and plan-to-produce.
Requires professional services, focused ERP in the cloud.	On-premise not an option, as updates are not quarterly and by definition it is not cloud-based.	Private cloud not an option, as it does not provide quarterly updates.	Best option: has professional services focus and is cloud-based.	Not an option, as it has a marketing focus and no professional services focus.
Customer requires cloud-based ERP system with marketing focus, including executive dashboard for customer analysis and planning.	On-premise not an option, as updates are not quarterly and by definition it is not cloud-based.	Private cloud not an option, as it does not provide quarterly updates.	Second-best option: is cloud-based, but doesn't have professional services focus.	Best option: has marketing focus in the cloud, with an executive dashboard for marketing analysis and planning.

Table 2.3 Decision Matrix: Deployment Options (Cont.)

Sometimes, the decision comes down to the on-premise option and one of the cloud editions from a functionality standpoint. Other times, both the on-premise option and the main cloud option are further joined by one of the specialized cloud editions; for example, if you are in a professional services company evaluating options, you might end up with three SAP S/4HANA options from which to choose.

Understanding your long-term plans for the system and your long-term approach to cloud can help balance the decision-making process with the short-term cost and effort considerations. One thing always to keep in mind is that ERP implementations are usually not something you "set and forget." An ERP platform forms the backbone of most organizations, and the decision and path to take on this upgrade journey should warrant thought and consideration.

2.1.3 On-Premise

The main options for on-premise systems moving to SAP S/4HANA are to convert to on-premise SAP S/4HANA or to set up a new implementation of either on-premise SAP S/4HANA or SAP S/4HANA Cloud. You can't convert an on-premise system directly to SAP S/4HANA Cloud.

If you're already running SAP ERP and need to figure out whether to migrate or reimplement, it helps to understand the options you have available for migration before deciding on one. If your SAP ERP level is at SAP ERP 6.0 EHP 7 or higher, you likely can upgrade to SAP S/4HANA Enterprise Management at a technical level rather than reimplementing (for a full compatibility scope to support system conversion, see SAP Note 2269324). However, this only makes sense if you aren't trying to reduce your data footprint substantially and can leverage the new SAP S/4HANA processes with your previous SAP ERP as a template for the new system. You'll also need to convert your existing database to the SAP HANA database and model as per Figure 2.1.

There are underpinning themes and infrastructure along the upgrade path from SAP ERP to SAP S/4HANA, mainly in the form of SAP NetWeaver, which remains a core infrastructure component regardless of whether you are running SAP ERP or SAP S/4HANA. Other aspects, such as SAP S/4HANA Finance, were among the first to be available on an SAP S/4HANA architecture and thus can be upgraded at an earlier enhancement pack level than some of the other components, including the sourcing and procurement functionality.

2.1 Implementation Overview

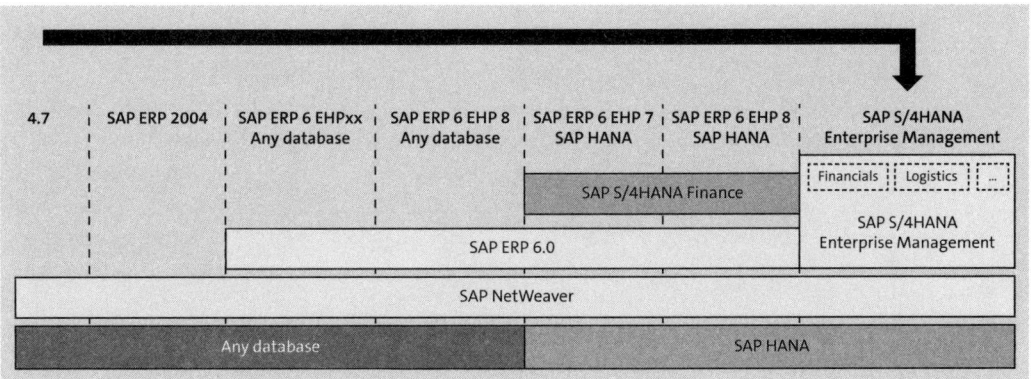

Figure 2.1 Upgrade Paths to SAP S/4HANA Enterprise Management

Another way of assessing the pros and cons of reimplementing versus converting to get to SAP S/4HANA is to build a decision matrix for the conversion and cloud decisions and weigh each category's pros and cons.

Conversion or Reimplementation Decision Matrix

In Table 2.4, some general pros and cons are detailed for typical SAP ERP assessment findings.

SAP ERP Analysis Finding	Reimplementation Pros	Conversion Pros
Heavily customized SAP ERP environment with large amounts of these customizations and legacy data no longer in used in production.	Strong opportunity to streamline SAP ERP and simplify processes based on SAP S/4HANA standards.	If some customizations and data are still required/necessary and archiving of legacy data can be performed prior to conversion, converting vs. reimplementing may save on costs and effort.
Current processes in SAP ERP mostly standard with little customization and legacy/unarchived data.	If the implementation is simple to the point at which conversion and reimplementation entail similar efforts, it may be an option to reimplement and start fresh on SAP S/4HANA.	Because less effort is required and results will be similar, conversion is a good option for implementations in SAP ERP that were already streamlined and using standard processes.

Table 2.4 SAP S/4HANA Conversion vs. Reimplementation Decision Matrix

SAP ERP Analysis Finding	Reimplementation Pros	Conversion Pros
Customer business/government model has changed significantly since SAP ERP was implemented. System no longer supports many of the required processes.	Reimplementation provides opportunity to build system processes to match new operating processes and conditions not reflected in current environment.	Feasibility assessment needs to be conducted to see if conversion and then addition of new processes is possible and more cost- and effort-effective vs. reimplementation.
Not all modules can be moved at once to SAP S/4HANA, but a conversion approach nonetheless makes sense for a business transformation and investment approach.	Reimplementation may be too costly or disruptive if a gradual migration option is feasible.	Gradual conversion/migration possible using the landscape consolidation approach in Scenario 3. Would provide managed migration vs. "big bang" cutover of SAP ERP to SAP S/4HANA.

Table 2.4 SAP S/4HANA Conversion vs. Reimplementation Decision Matrix (Cont.)

System Conversion

A system conversion to SAP S/4HANA can be done all at once, but it also allows for evaluation of existing customizations and a gradual transformation of existing process flows over time versus a new implementation. This is also an opportunity to consolidate multiple SAP ERP instances into one instance of SAP S/4HANA.

If your analysis points towards reimplementation, you can always start fresh with a new SAP S/4HANA environment. Doing so is obviously more work and investment up front, but you can still do an initial conversion/load of your legacy data, and this approach allows you take full advantage of the SAP S/4HANA functionality up front and start with a data foundation and set of processes that have been built for and on SAP S/4HANA's data/process model and architecture. There are three options in this area:

- **System conversion**
  An ERP system to an on-premise SAP S/4HANA system—for example, a complete conversion of an existing SAP Business Suite system to SAP S/4HANA. This allows for a reevaluation of customization and existing process flows, as well as transformation over time.

- **Landscape transformation**
  Hybrid scenario in which several ERP systems are moved on-premise, and some into the cloud—for example, the consolidation of a current regional SAP Business

Suite landscape into one global SAP S/4HANA system. This allows you to retain current business processes and move gradually to SAP S/4HANA innovations.

- **New implementation**
  SAP ERP system or a non-SAP system to a new SAP S/4HANA system—for example, a new or existing SAP customer implementing a new SAP S/4HANA system. This allows you to reengineer and simplify based on ready-to-run business processes.

New Implementation

For a new implementation, there are two main steps: first, install SAP S/4HANA Enterprise Management using the SAP Software Provisioning Manager; then, load your ERP data in from either SAP ERP or a third-party ERP system as part of the initial data load, as detailed in Figure 2.2.

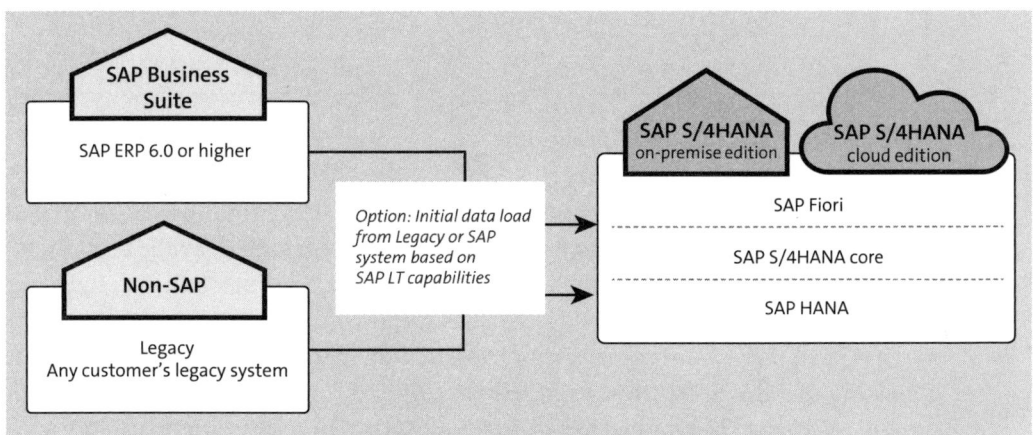

Figure 2.2 Scenario 1: New Installation of SAP S/4HANA Enterprise Management

New implementations are undertaken if there is no core ERP system to begin with or the core, underlying business processes have shifted over the years, to the point at which upgrading the SAP ERP environment brings too many legacy processes and data to be useful and/or take full advantage of SAP S/4HANA's architecture and simplifications.

Full Conversion

Another route to SAP S/4HANA is to convert an existing SAP ERP environment into SAP S/4HANA Enterprise Management. This entails three main steps: checking

2   Implementation Options

add-ons and business functions and industry-specific functionality using SAP Maintenance Planner, executing pretransition checks to validate conversion viability to SAP S/4HANA, and executing the conversion using the Software Update Manager (SUM) with the data migration option (DMO), as shown in Figure 2.3. It's important to note that the DMO is only available as of SAP ERP 6 EHP 7. If you're running an earlier release of SAP ERP or even SAP R/3, you must upgrade the SAP ERP environment to 6.0 EHP 7 via SUM and then use the DMO to convert the SAP ERP 6.0 EHP 7 environment to SAP S/4HANA Enterprise Management.

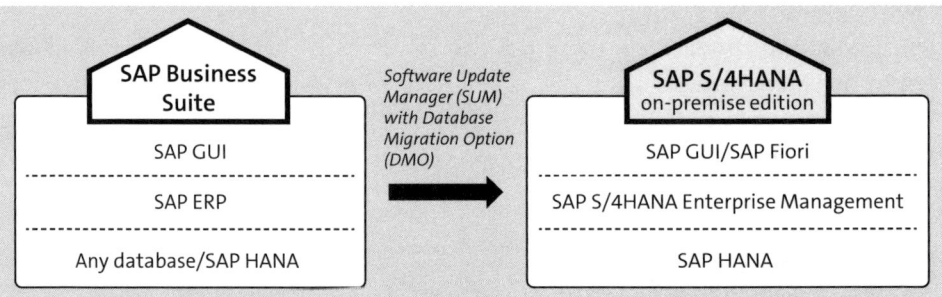

Figure 2.3 Scenario 2: System Conversion

In a full conversion to SAP S/4HANA, there may be some SAP solutions from SAP ERP that haven't been simplified in SAP S/4HANA but are still required by the customer in the new environment. Compatibility packages enable a customer to run certain classic SAP solutions on SAP S/4HANA installations in which no application simplification has been done. In many cases, SAP S/4HANA may offer a functional equivalent (reflecting the SAP S/4HANA target architecture), or the corresponding application simplification may be planned for a future SAP S/4HANA release. Compatibility packages are part of the SAP S/4HANA shipment and are supported by SAP through 2025 at this time.

Some conversions may require multiple phases and steps to reach SAP S/4HANA in the most cost-effective and least disruptive manner possible. Scenario 3 supports the consolidation of multiple legacy systems into one ERP system prior to converting to SAP S/4HANA. This can also refer to a phased migration whereby certain company codes, business units, and/or modules are migrated individually, depending on their total cost of ownership (TCO) and total cost of investment (TCI) to migrate. This way, an upgrade and a landscape consolidation can be achieved in consideration of business drivers gradually, allowing the business and IT to move areas strategically into SAP S/4HANA in a sequence rather than performing the entire migration at once.

In addition to consolidation of multiple SAP ERP systems into one SAP S/4HANA platform or a selective data transformation as necessary for company codes and business units, you also have the option to consolidate financials alone into SAP S/4HANA Finance. SAP S/4HANA Finance allows you to move multiple FI-CO modules into one SAP S/4HANA system and centralize financial postings.

2.2 On-Premise SAP S/4HANA

Users can access SAP S/4HANA Enterprise Management on-premise via either SAP GUI or using a supported web browser. This means using either a web dispatcher or load-balanced web dispatchers frontend four clients, or both an SAP Fiori and SAP S/4HANA application client with an SAP S/4HANA database client and an Adobe Document Services for the SAP NetWeaver Application Server in the backend, as shown in Figure 2.4.

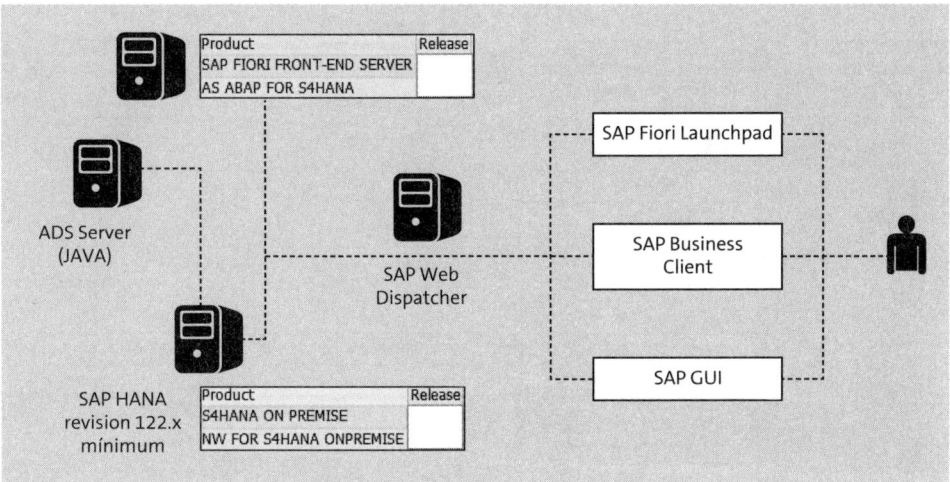

Figure 2.4 SAP S/4HANA Standard On-Premise Landscape

2.2.1 Complete Functional Scope

For organizations across industries and government sectors that need a deep and broad level of functionality combined with a high degree of flexibility in customization and system maintenance and backups, SAP S/4HANA Enterprise Management on-premise edition fits the bill. The functional scope of a typical implementation project either leverages an existing or includes a finance implementation. Without finance and controlling, few other lines of business can be managed successfully in the system. Once this is established, other areas, including sourcing and procurement, can be added to cover business processes and needs. For sourcing and procurement, self-service procurement and operational procurement, direct procurement, sourcing, contract management, supplier management, and purchasing analytics comprise the core scope for a comprehensive project in this area. Many projects focus on a more reduced scope, targeting self-service procurement for Phase 1 and then analytics during a follow-on phase.

From a development standpoint, SAP S/4HANA Enterprise Management leverages a model similar to that of previous SAP ERP platforms, with sandbox, development, quality assurance, and production environments. The development environment is further delineated with configuration and explore environments, as shown in Figure 2.5.

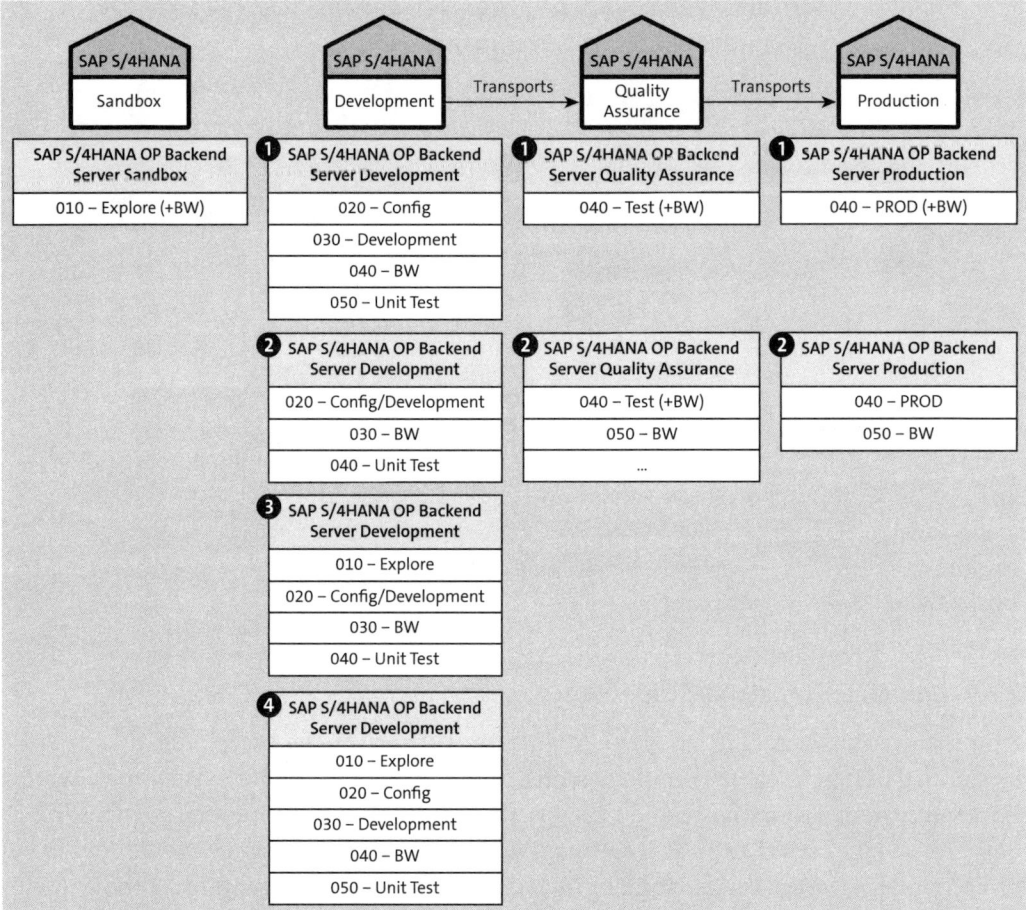

Figure 2.5 SAP S/4HANA Four-Tier Landscape

2.2.2 Installation

For the actual install of the SAP S/4HANA environment, SAP Basis resources follow these general steps:

1. Logon to SAP Maintenance Planner (available on the SAP Portal at *http://apps.support.sap.com/sap/support/mp*)
2. Select the backend system
3. Select additional systems
4. Define changes on servers
5. Select OS/DB-dependent files
6. Download selected files and install

There are two options to cover at this point in the install. One option, called the *Activated Appliance* option, will accelerate your installation of the software; the other, called *SAP Best Practices*, is the consequent implementation. SAP Best Practices will be discussed in detail in the next section of this chapter, along with some other options, like SAP Model Company. For the install, however, the Activated Appliance option would apply, as detailed in Table 2.5.

Fully Activated SAP S/4HANA Enterprise Management Appliance			
SAP S/4HANA	SAP NetWeaver for Java/Adobe Documents Service	Remote desktop (option/available via SAP Cloud Appliance Library)	SAP BusinessObjects BI platform (option/available via SAP Cloud Appliance Library)
ABAP server: with SAP S/4HANA, SAP Gateway/SAP Fiori, SAP NetWeaver, SAP Best Practices	Java server: Adobe Document Services, SAP NetWeaver Java	Windows remote desktop: Mozilla Firefox, SAP GUI 7.40, ABAP developer tools/SAP HANA studio, SAP Lumira, SAP Lumira, designer edition	SAP BusinessObjects Explorer: SAP BusinessObjects BI platform, SAP Lumira, designer edition, SAP BusinessObjects BI best practices content
SAP HANA 1.0	SAP Adaptive Server Enterprise		

Table 2.5 SAP S/4HANA Appliance Packages

2 Implementation Options

2.2.3 Activated Appliance

The Activated Appliance option includes the software to download or ship to you, provided you already have licenses for the products ordered and hardware with Linux installed (see SAP Note 2396478 for SAP partners and SAP Note 2202234 for SAP customers). This option is exclusive to SAP customers with enabled partners or SAP Services engaged. You can also go to SAP Cloud Appliance Library at *http://cal.sap.com* and enable a hosted solution with Amazon Web Services (AWS) or Azure. For this approach, you need valid credentials for using AWS/Azure.

The SAP S/4HANA appliance includes the clients described in Table 2.6.

ABAP Client	Description
Client 100—trial client	<ul><li>Preactivated SAP Best Practices configuration and sample master data (Germany, United States).</li><li>Additional configuration for end-to-end sample business process.</li><li>Transactional data and demo scenarios in US company code (1710).</li></ul>
Client 200—ready-to-activate client	<ul><li>Technical preparation activities prior to SAP Best Practices content activation.</li><li>Whitelist copy of Client 000 customizing with SAP S/4HANA Best Practices activation on top. *Whitelist* refers to a select set of tables and configuration from Client 000 needed to complement SAP Best Practices configuration in the development client.</li><li>This is the standard delivery state for SAP Best Practices (no additional configuration, no corrections applied).</li></ul>
Client 400—SAP BW client	<ul><li>For SAP Integrated Business Planning (SAP IBP) for Finance.</li></ul>
Client 500—SAP Best Practices reference client	<ul><li>Full copy of client 000 customizing with SAP S/4HANA.</li><li>This is the standard delivery state of SAP Best Practices (no additional configuration, no corrections applied).</li></ul>

Table 2.6 SAP S/4HANA Appliance Package Clients

There are numerous approaches to install SAP S/4HANA both in a hosted environment and in your own data center. If you have determined that a conversion to SAP S/4HANA is the most preferred route, this path also includes some options and decision points to consider, as discussed in the next section.

2.2.4 Information Technology Considerations

For procurement stakeholders, evaluating the current state, objectives, and SAP S/4HANA and cloud options is a key step towards successful realization and return on investment (ROI). What moves the needle in the organization from a procurement standpoint? Does the organization manufacture product and rely on a broad base of suppliers to source inputs and develop better ones? Perhaps a sourcing focus will drive the best outcomes from an impact standpoint. Are these sourcing processes largely defined, but general employees are buying things off contract and out of catalog with no approval?

Choose Your Own Procurement Adventure

Self-service procurement in SAP S/4HANA or SAP Ariba Buying can reign in this maverick spending and cut costs, as more spend moves to negotiated agreements and volumes are brought to bear. Are account payable processes out of sync with the rest of the procurement organization, leading to missed early-payment discounts and long lead times on matching POs to invoices? PO/invoice integration with the Ariba Network may offer an elegant solution for cleaning this up. In short, as with many things in life, the procurement solution you craft with the SAP S/4HANA and cloud portfolio of products is what you make it, and you will want to set directions and priorities to align with your biggest areas of opportunity.

System Administration

When choosing your implementation approach and path, understanding the system administration implications is also important. If your IT organization is running very lean, you may not have the resources onsite to support an onsite implementation of a heavy-duty ERP system such as SAP S/4HANA. On-premise SAP S/4HANA requires at minimum an SAP Basis team to support day-to-day operations and keep the hardware and software humming, as well as to implement upgrades and maintenance items for the software. You may not have enough business users in the purchasing department to support a "big bang" roll out of SAP S/4HANA functionality to suppliers. Without this helpdesk, running a bidding exercise or skills assessment may quickly overwhelm the group. These considerations will allow you to choose between cloud and on-premise approaches or hybrid versions of these approaches.

SaaS means less maintenance and administration, but you will still need technically savvy colleagues to maintain data and support issue resolution jointly with SAP. Also, in integration and platform areas, technical system administration doesn't completely go away just because you're running in the cloud. However, these areas should be much lighter; hardware-wise, though you still have to worry about maintaining and supporting the devices connecting to the cloud services, you no longer have to worry about hardware itself.

2.2.5 Integration Options

For both SAP S/4HANA Cloud and on-premise, there are a multitude of SAP and non-SAP solutions with which you can integrate, as shown in Figure 2.6.

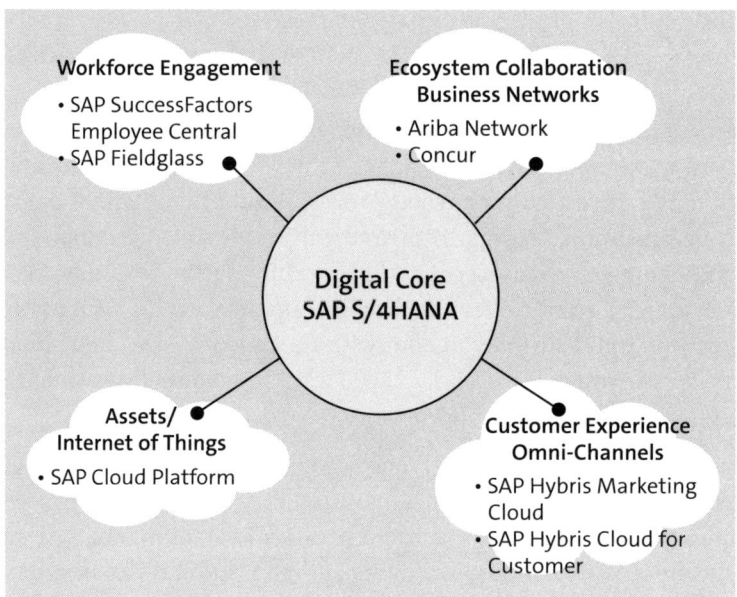

Figure 2.6 Integration Options for SAP S/4HANA

These integration areas break down into the following categories:

- *People:* SAP SuccessFactors Employee Central, SAP SuccessFactors Human Capital Management
- *Customer management:* SAP Hybris Marketing, SAP Hybris Cloud for Customer
- *Finance:* SAP Financial Services Network
- *Procurement:* SAP Ariba
- *Contingent workforce:* SAP Fieldglass
- *Travel:* Concur
- *Extensions, integrations, and custom application development:* SAP Cloud Platform

For both cloud and on-premise options, SAP S/4HANA offers prebuilt integrations, out-of-the-box integrations for areas like PO/IV collaboration between SAP S/4HANA and the Ariba Network, and extensions, integrations, and custom application development.

2.2.6 SAP S/4HANA System Conversion

For a system conversion, there is more preparation required up front and more vetting of the existing system to be converted. The main tools leveraged for a conversion are as follows:

- SUM: Allows you to update the software version or support package to the level supported for conversion.
- DMO of SUM: Upgrade an existing SAP NetWeaver-based system, perform Unicode conversion (single code page), and migrate to SAP S/4HANA in one step as part of the SUM tool.
- Software Provisioning Manager: This tool is used both to install a new SAP S/4HANA system and to migrate a system to the required software level for an SAP S/4HANA conversion. This tool can also be used to perform Unicode conversions.

The conversion process for SAP S/4HANA relies on two main phases: a preparation phase and a realization phase. Without a well-thought-out and executed preparation phase, a conversion incurs unnecessary risk that the conversion will produce a corrupted instance of SAP S/4HANA, either missing key data, components, or both. The Software Provisioning Manager and SUM tools are used right from the beginning in this preparation, whereas the DMO is used during the realization phase to activate the conversion.

Maintenance Planner

Once the system requirements an approach have been defined, the preparation steps begin in the Maintenance Planner, entering in the **Plan for SAP S/4HANA** tile, as with the install of a new environment. Here, after selecting **Plan an SAP S/4HANA Conversion of an Existing System**, define the changes based on your landscape data in your customer profile, select the files, and push all required tools, archives, and stack.xml data to the download.

Pre-Checks

The stack.xml file is recommended to be used during the prechecks, as shown in Figure 2.7.

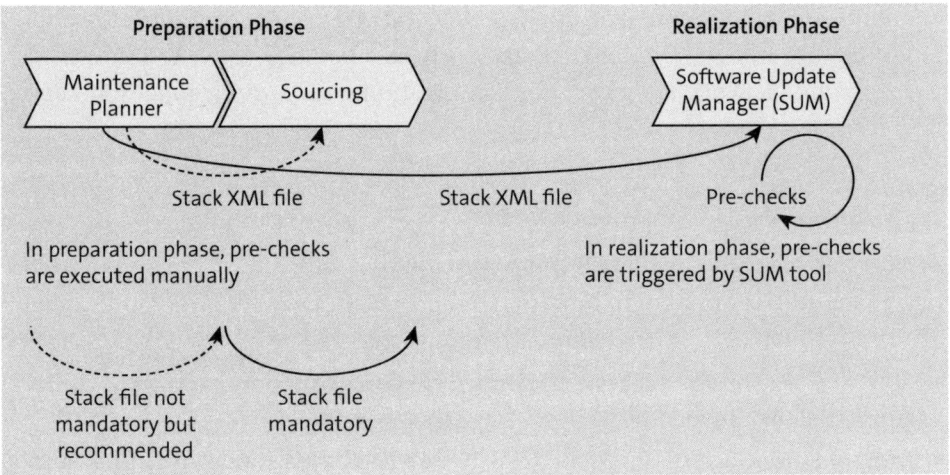

Figure 2.7 Stack XML File-Based Prechecks

Prechecks are completed as the first step in the Maintenance Planner as part of the conversion process. Prechecks are available as SAP Notes to customers that want to convert to SAP S/4HANA. These prechecks are executed on the SAP Business Suite system targeted for conversion. The precheck results list details the mandatory items to address prior to upgrading. These checks are run twice again during the conversion process in SUM, and the conversion is stopped if errors are found, as illustrated in Figure 2.8.

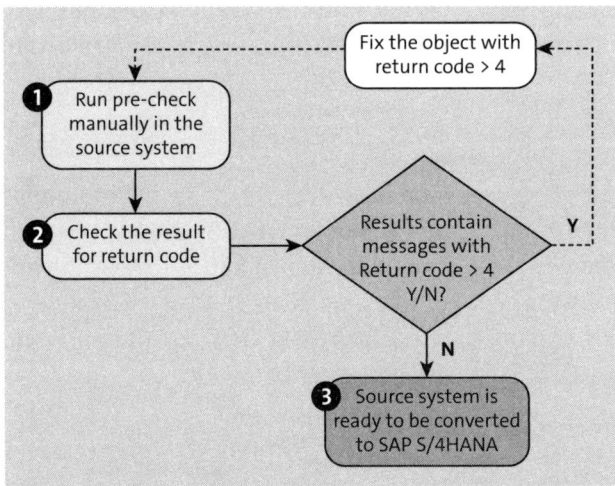

Figure 2.8 Manual Precheck before Start of System Conversion Process

During the prechecks, any objects with a return code greater than 4 must be fixed prior to starting the conversion (see Figure 2.8). SAP Note 218725 details more information about prechecks.

To perform prechecks, you must implement the reports from SAP Note 2182725. Ensure that you are using the most current SAP Note with the updated reports prior to installing it on your clients. The reports need to be run on all of the systems in scope for conversion, starting with the sandbox/development environments and then working up to quality and production. Report R_S4_PRE_TRANSITION_CHECKS should be run in the core Client 000 using Transaction SE38/SA38 with the stack XML file generated in the Maintenance Planner as per Figure 2.7. Note that though General Ledger prechecks are included in the report, to check asset accounting you'll need to implement all of the SAP Notes listed in SAP Note 2333236.

Even though you can technically move through warning messages with return code 4, these messages shouldn't be ignored entirely; they highlight issues that can cause data loss during conversion if not addressed up front.

If during the prechecks a return code of 8 or higher is issued, this is a hard-stop error; you won't be able to continue with the conversion until it's addressed.

These hard-stop error messages often refer to components that aren't supported and will need to be removed prior to conversion. Other hard-stop errors will point to SAP Notes to help address the issue identified.

During its first set of prechecks, Maintenance Planner will identify which business functions can and can't be converted and which ones will be turned off or converted in always-off mode. Likewise, strategies of business functions can change in between feature package releases. Use SAP Note 2240359 (SAP S/4HANA: Always-Off Business Functions) and the attachment contained in this note to determine the strategy changes.

If you have SAP-delivered or third-party add-ons installed on your existing system, these also will be checked. SAP Note 2214409 (SAP S/4HANA: Compatible Add-Ons) lists the compatible ones delivered by SAP for SAP S/4HANA.

Custom Code Review

With the prechecks concluded, the next step is to review the custom code in the system to be converted. For SAP NetWeaver 7.50, this involves applying SAP Notes as per Figure 2.9.

2   Implementation Options

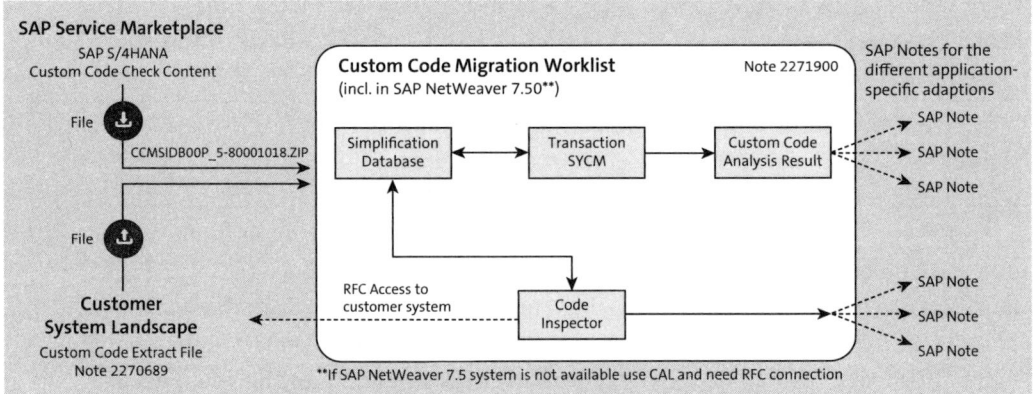

Figure 2.9 Custom Code Checks for SAP NetWeaver 7.50

The main difference between the approaches for SAP NetWeaver 7.50 and 7.51 is the custom code analysis report. This isn't required in 7.51, as shown in Figure 2.10.

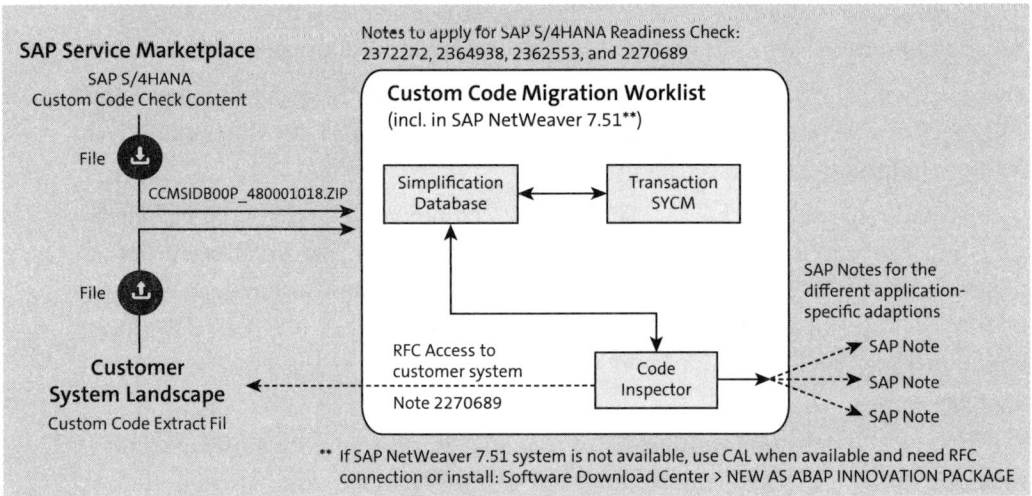

Figure 2.10 Evolution of Custom Code Checks: SAP NetWeaver 7.51

The main steps remain the same in both versions:

1. Download custom code check content.
2. Start Code Inspector (Transaction SCI).
3. Use check variant **S4HANA Readiness**.
4. Specify objects to be checked.

5. Start inspection run.
6. Analyze check results.

Once the prechecks are complete, you are ready to run the conversion in the realization phase.

The conversion of a four-tier landscape, as shown in Figure 2.11, starts with copying the production instance back to the sandbox and running the conversion of this environment. Once the sandbox has been converted, you'll have a pretty good feel for how production will stand up to the conversion process, as you have essentially just converted it.

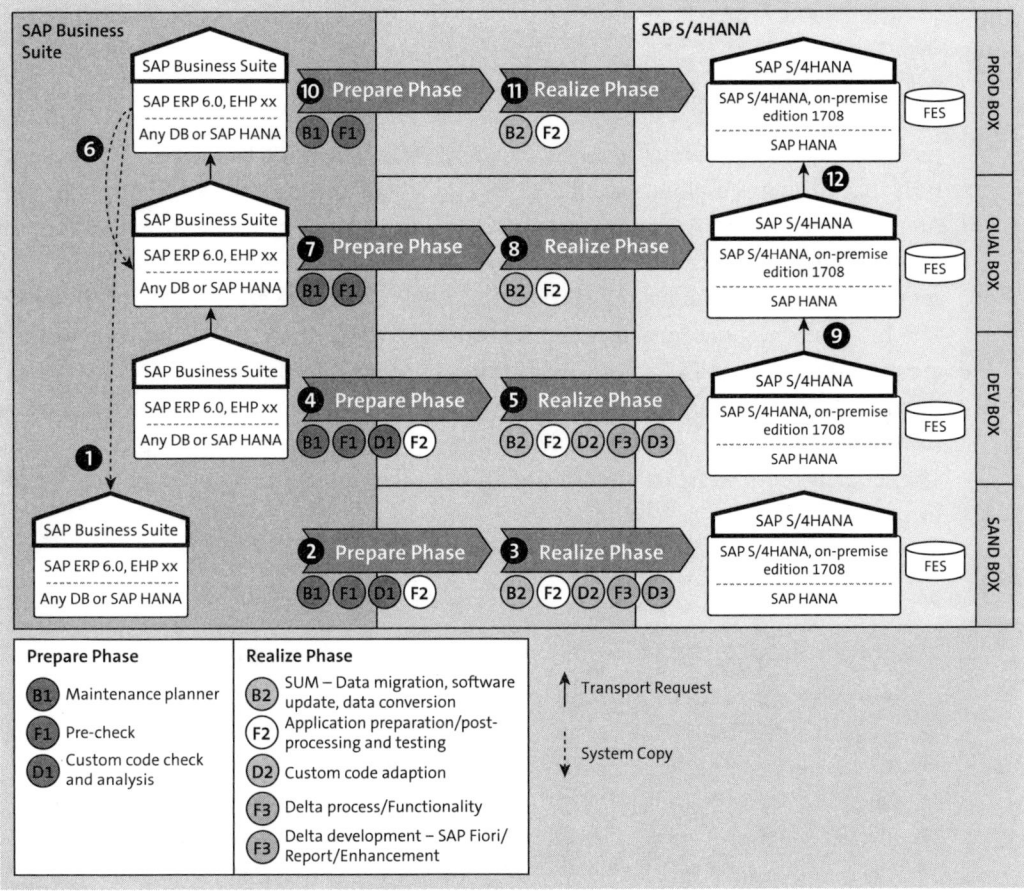

Figure 2.11 Four-Tier Landscape Conversion Overview

Next, the instances on the transport bath, beginning with the development environment, are converted. For both the sandbox and the development environment conversion, delta processes and functionality, as well as enhancements and SAP Fiori adjustments, are implemented. These changes are then promoted forward on the transport path from development, once the other instances in the landscape have been converted to SAP S/4HANA.

Once the install or conversion to SAP S/4HANA is complete, you're ready to proceed with the implementation project. Traditional plan, design, realize, test, go-live approaches are still used on occasion to implement SAP S/4HANA. However, there are a number of methodologies and tools that you can use to both accelerate and enhance your implementation, as detailed in the next section.

2.3 SAP S/4HANA Cloud

As detailed in the previous sections, SAP S/4HANA Cloud is a multitenant SaaS solution that provides a cloud-based ERP environment running on SAP HANA. Implementing SAP S/4HANA Cloud is different than implementing the on-premise version in several respects. First, there are fewer IT considerations, as the baseline equipment requirements can be as straightforward as having a device and a browser to log in. The integration approaches are more straightforward, as many of the integrations are prebuilt for other SAP solutions and cloud services; those that require customization and buildouts typically have reduced options for integrating with a cloud environment, leading to less complex decision trees and design and development cycles. The scope is reduced from that for the on-premise version, as detailed in the Hybrid Implementation box in Section 2.3.3.

2.3.1 SAP Best Practices Scope

The SAP S/4HANA Cloud scope includes the elements shown in Table 2.7.

Streamlined Procure-to-Pay	Core Finance
▪ Sourcing and contract management ▪ Operational procurement ▪ Inventory management ▪ Invoice and payables management	▪ Accounting and closing operations ▪ Cost management and profitability analysis ▪ Treasury and financial risk management ▪ Finance operations > receivables management

Table 2.7 SAP S/4HANA Cloud Options

Accelerated Plan-to-Product	Project Services
- Basic production planning - Basic production processing - Inventory management - Maintenance management	- Contract to cash - Project management - Time and expense management
Optimized Order-to-Cash	**HR Connectivity**
- Order and contract management - Inventory management - Receivables processing	- Employee central connectivity

Table 2.7 SAP S/4HANA Cloud Options (Cont.)

The principal area of concern for a sourcing and procurement project is the Streamlined Procure-to-Pay process area. However, other considerations and integration points arise with Core Finance and HR Connectivity.

2.3.2 IT Considerations

Many IT departments today face ever-increasing demands from business, as well as fragmentations of their once-centralized budgets to respond. The cloud approach has provided business decision-makers with direct access to business applications, a domain that was once brokered by, and often controlled entirely by, IT. However, just because a business unit chooses to buy a service does not mean that integration and landscape decisions, in addition to the inevitable cost and TCO decisions, shouldn't be factored in. IT needs to stay involved, even if its decision-making authority has somewhat devolved to that of an influencer rather than a driver. In purchasing SAP S/4HANA Sourcing and Procurement, a purchasing department may ignore the overall landscape of its organization from an IT standpoint, choosing an on-premise approach when core line of business processes are in the cloud, or cloud when a group such as finance has already built finance on-premise. Just as having IT make all of the business decisions in a company rarely leads to business user satisfaction, so too do business units ignore IT implications at their own peril. There are sufficient options to support a plethora of landscapes, directives, and needs from an IT standpoint in SAP S/4HANA. Inclusion of both IT and business stakeholders during the design and decision process is essential for realizing the best outcomes and ROI.

Multitenant Environment

A multitenant environment means less customization and more adoption of best practices and existing system processes by necessity. If a system is running a common code base, it can't follow the whims of every individual customer, just like a tenant living in an apartment building can't decide to remove a load-bearing wall in the building or rearchitect the plumbing without extreme consequences. Unlike in a building, in a multitenant environment you aren't at liberty to try and hack the system in this manner; the options simply aren't available. Just as living in an apartment building is not for everyone and doesn't cover everyone's needs, so too may a multitenant environment prove to be too restrictive for very large enterprises with competitive differentiation built into their systems and processes. Then again, a large enterprise may prefer a multitenant environment for the cost savings and discipline it brings in providing best practices without allowing the organization to indulge in its own unmanageable sprawl.

Automatic Upgrades

One benefit that most cloud environments have, including SAP S/4HANA Cloud, is a more frequent cadence for upgrades. Some of these upgrades may be mandatory, though most new functionality can be left turned off if required. The point is that the upgrades allow for more frequent updates to the system and are not managed directly by your organization, both saving money and preventing the familiar predicament in the on-premise world of fewer and fewer upgrades due to the effort involved as the system ages and the customization increases.

2.3.3 Standard Integration and Customization

SAP S/4HANA Cloud provides standard integration via its IPaaS approach with the SAP Cloud portfolio of products, as well as with other on-premise instances of SAP ERP. Despite having customization limitations, some customization and configuration is still quite possible in an SAP S/4HANA Cloud implementation, so it should not be interpreted as being entirely locked down to meeting business requirements that may adjust the existing processes to a degree.

> **Hybrid Implementation**
>
> As described in Table 2.3, a hybrid implementation combines two or more distinct public cloud environments and/or on-premise providers. This in turn is integrated by standardized or proprietary technology, enabling data and application portability.

> A hybrid option using the SAP S/4HANA portfolio leverages and integrates the options outlined in Section 2.2.5. For procurement, a typical hybrid implementation would include SAP Ariba solutions for procurement transformation areas connected to SAP S/4HANA (either cloud or on-premise), alongside SAP Fieldglass for contingent labor and Concur for travel and expense. From an implementation standpoint, these are multiple cloud and/or on-premise deployments connected via an integration phase and emphasis of the project, which potentially entails more interfaces and cross-system coordination but can realize further efficiency gains and business process optimization/user satisfaction as a result of using the optimal solution and environment for individual business processes and areas.

2.4 SAP Activate, SAP Best Practices, and SAP Model Companies: Quick Start Approaches and Materials for SAP S/4HANA

Traditional approaches to ERP entail five to six distinct phases. First, a preparation phase needs to be conducted to align all of the stakeholders, goals, and materials. Second, a design phase should cover all of the design considerations with the various stakeholders and juxtapose these with the system capabilities and constraints. Third, a realization phase kicks off where the system is built. A test and deploy phase (sometimes split into two separate phases) is instituted, to ensure the system works as built and meets the stakeholder requirements; during deployment, the users are trained and the system is put into production. Finally, a run phase is used to delineate continual improvements in production. Needless to say, many of these steps can take up cycles, and these cycles are expensive from time and investment standpoints.

In recent years, many firms and government entities have begun rethinking and refocusing system implementations. Some of these tuning exercises have yielded whole new approaches towards software development, such as *agile methodology*, which relies on *sprints* and *scrums* to iteratively improve upon the end product of the project, combining many mini-projects within phases rather than using a formalized, linear realization phase. SAP provides its own version of this approach in its latest project methodology, called *SAP Activate*, which will be detailed further in this chapter. SAP Activate leverages prebuilt materials and models to further jumpstart the implementation process and focus the resources and timeline on getting to value versus reinventing the basics.

2.4.1 Prebuilt Content and Templates: SAP Appliance, SAP Best Practices, and SAP Model Company

There are numerous assets available to make SAP S/4HANA implementation projects more efficient. Most implementations are for entities that share many processes in common with other entities in their industry, and general processes for manufacturing and other areas have a high degree of similarity. You don't need to reinvent the wheel for every project and create a bespoke implementation for every entity; some uniformity is necessary and even desirable—desirable because it allows implementation projects to move quickly through the commodity processes with best practice approaches and focus on the areas that truly differentiate the firm or government entity, allowing for condensed timeframes for implementations and more impactful results. These savings can amount to as much as 30 percent of the total implementation timeframe and costs. In areas like the blueprint phase, the reduction in time and investment can be as high as 90 percent.

For quick-start materials to aid in the implementation, SAP offers an SAP S/4HANA appliance option and SAP Best Practices, in addition to project methodologies in SAP Activate and SAP Model Company.

2.4.2 SAP Best Practices

The SAP S/4HANA appliance option relates more to the technical software package side of the equation on a new install approach, whereas the SAP Best Practices simplify the functional SAP S/4HANA business processes by providing core elements of each business process area and removing less common ones. SAP Best Practices are installed during the system setup. Once you have reviewed the and selected the SAP Best Practices content for your project, you build the client system and download and activate the content, which functional consultants then use as a springboard for further tailoring of the system to the customer's requirements.

SAP Best Practices content covers all of the major areas of SAP S/4HANA. The Sourcing and Procurement areas covered are as follows:

1. Supplier classification and segmentation
2. Supplier activity management
3. SAP Ariba sourcing integration
4. Purchase contract
5. Requisitioning

2.4 SAP Activate, Best Practices, and Model Companies: Quick Start Approaches and Materials

6. Procurement and consumption of consigned inventory
7. Procurement of direct materials
8. Serial number management
9. Consumables purchasing
10. Real-time reporting and monitoring of procurement
11. SAP Ariba business network integration

2.4.3 SAP Model Company

Another accelerator approach for implementing SAP S/4HANA is the SAP Model Company approach. This approach is provided as an engineered service by SAP consulting/delivery groups as a preconfigured solution, supported by handover and enablement workshops conducted by SAP consultants to jumpstart the discovery, exploration, and realization phases of the SAP S/4HANA project.

The SAP Model Company includes a business process hierarchy, end-to-end scenarios, and process diagrams sorted by role, as well as materials about configuration, test and demo scripts, and implementation tools. There are over 20 individual model company packages available for different industries and processes.

Once you've evaluated these models and tools for laying a foundation of prebuilt content to support your project, it's time to move into the SAP S/4HANA implementation. For this task, SAP has introduced a tailored project management approach for SAP ERP implementations called SAP Activate.

2.4.4 SAP Activate

SAP Activate is the successor to the Accelerated SAP (ASAP) and SAP Launch methodologies. Based on a six-phase package with agile approaches to implementation, SAP Activate leverages guided configuration, as well digital business and technology processes. The main phases of SAP Activate are discover, prepare, explore, realize, deploy, and run. As a simple, modular methodology, SAP Activate has broad coverage of SAP solutions, beginning with on-premise SAP S/4HANA and SAP S/4HANA Cloud, as well as hybrid deployments.

Discover Phase

In the *discover* phase, customers familiarize themselves with the solution to be implemented and the value it can bring their business or government entity. One of the outputs of this phase is to design an overall digital transformation strategy and an implementation approach that can realize and leverage the solution to create value for the company or government entity.

Prepare Phase

The *prepare* phase in an SAP Activate project provides for the project organization and governance planning and formation, including project schedule, budget, and project management plans. Once the prepare phase is complete, you begin the explore phase.

Explore Phase

The main goal of the *explore* phase is to net out the requirements for the implementation and the gaps using a sandbox environment; optionally, you can use this phase to design thinking workshops and prototyping, to do a hands-on validation rather than a conceptual one.

Realize Phase

In the *realize* phase, unlike in previous methodologies, both the realization of the business requirements resulting from the validation in the explore phase and the testing are combined.

Deploy Phase

Some of the final testing, such as system testing, is conducted in the *deploy* phase, in which the readiness of the solution is finalized, including end-user training, system management, and cutover activities/planning.

Run Phase

Finally, during the *run* phase, the solution is further optimized to meet the business and technical objectives of the implementation. The phases are outlined in Table 2.8.

SAP Activate Project Phase	Deliverables
Discover	Strategic planning, application value and scoping, trial system provisioning

Table 2.8 SAP Activate Phases for SAP S/4HANA Cloud and On-Premise

2.4 SAP Activate, Best Practices, and Model Companies: Quick Start Approaches and Materials

SAP Activate Project Phase	Deliverables
Prepare	Project organization and governance, schedule, budget, management plans, project standards and policies, organizatonal change management roadmap and training strategy, project team onboarding, project team infrastructure, solution scope and value determination, technical infrastructure requirements and sizing, data migration approach strategy, sandbox environment
Explore	(Note: This phase is used only in on-premise SAP S/4HANA deployments.) Project management execution, results management, results controlling, change impact analysis, communication plan, baseline build, validation workshops, gap validation, backlog prioritization, gaps and deltas design, legacy data migration design and plan, technology design and setup of DEV environment, test strategy and plan, release and sprint plan
Realize	Project management execution, management and controlling of results, organizational alignment and user enablement, technology setup for quality assurance (QA) and production environments with security and authorizations, spring execution, integrated solution and user acceptance testing, legacy data migration, value audits, technical operations setup plan including OCC for premium engagements, cutover and transition plan
Deploy	Project management execution, management and controlling of results, organizational and production support readiness check, pre go-live end-user training and delivery, technical and system testing, setup operational support, cutover to production, production support post go-live
Run	Value management, application lifecycle management, PE: operations control center, operation solution, improve and innovate solution

Table 2.8 SAP Activate Phases for SAP S/4HANA Cloud and On-Premise (Cont.)

SAP Activate in SAP S/4HANA Cloud

For SAP S/4HANA Cloud, SAP Activate's discover phase provides a preconfigured solution, value assessment, and roadmap service, as shown in Figure 2.12. With SAP S/4HANA Cloud, there is less customization possible, but business process optimization is still very much part of the implementation to take advantage of the SAP Best Practices offered for various industries.

Unlike most of the on-premise SAP S/4HANA options, licensing for SAP S/4HANA Cloud is on a subscription basis and includes infrastructure. The infrastructure preparation and customization are two areas that don't need to be covered, or can be covered less extensively than with an on-premise installation. Because there's less room to address gaps between your business processes and the underlying cloud solution, SAP S/4HANA Cloud implementations seek to verify in the discover and prepare phases whether there are any impediments to implementing in the cloud. Gaps constituting showstoppers and must-haves that can't be addressed in SAP S/4HANA Cloud may prompt evaluation of on-premise SAP S/4HANA, with which you would have greater flexibility to address these gaps.

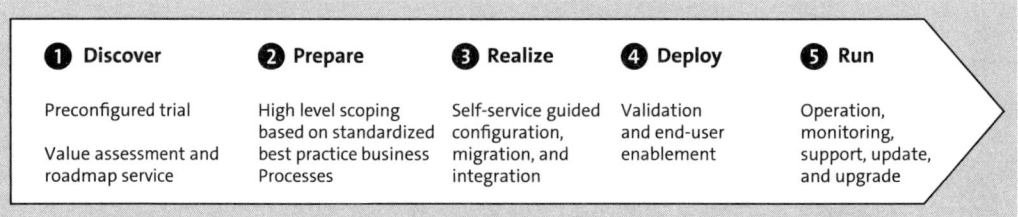

Figure 2.12 SAP S/4HANA Cloud Edition

SAP Activate Workflows

With the discover and run phases bookending, SAP Activate can be run repetitively to reach the desired outcome of the project, stringing together a number of mini-projects as shown in Figure 2.13.

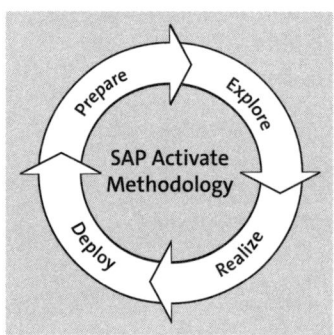

Figure 2.13 SAP Activate Methodology: Prepare, Explore, Realize, and Deploy

Further iterations are built into the SAP Activate methodology in the individual phases via the agile-driven sprints, as shown in Figure 2.14. These sprints use the prebuilt content and configuration from SAP Best Practices and SAP Model Company.

Scrum approaches work to create individual and solution elements in parallel, itemizing, prioritizing, designing, building, and validating these various product configurations and customizations as part of the scrum process during the explore and realization phases of SAP Activate. Further augmenting the agile approach in SAP Activate is the use of prebuilt content to provide modular building blocks and a platform from which to begin the explore and realize phases.

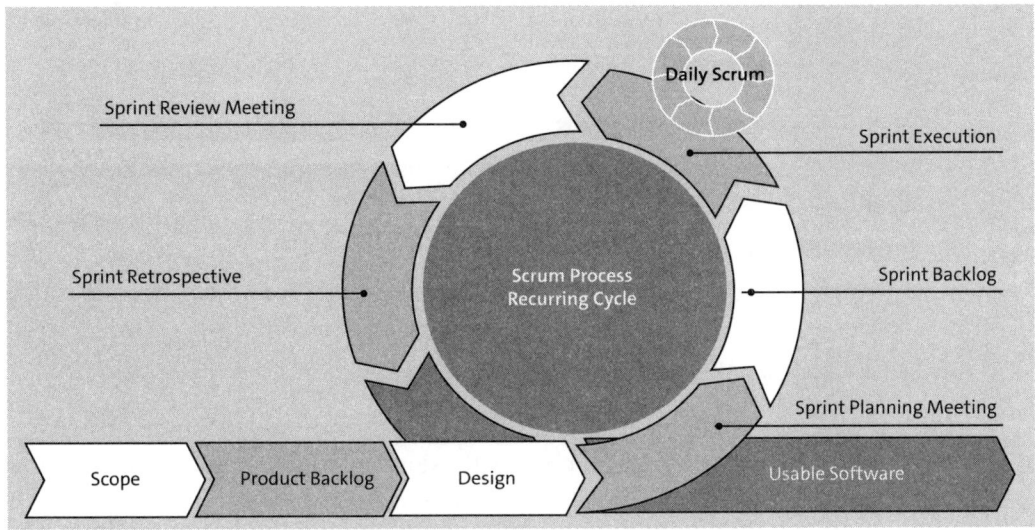

Figure 2.14 Agile Build: Use of Scrum-Based Approach in SAP Activate

Preassembly packages available via the SAP S/4HANA appliance, SAP Best Practices, and SAP Model Company are deployed during the prepare phase to jump start the explore phase and enable project participants to focus on validating the solution and identifying requirements and gaps requiring a process adjustment and/or customization within the system. These configurations and customizations in turn are built out, validated, and tested in parallel during the realization phase.

Within an agile-based approach in SAP Activate, there are two types of workshops. The first kind are solution validation workshops, in which the group validates the SAP solution and identifies and prioritizes any gaps. The gap output of this workshop is then prioritized with the other identified areas, and then a second type of workshop focused on the delta design is initiated in sequence, or sometimes in parallel, resources and scheduling permitting. During the delta design workshop, the business models and processes, as well as potential solution customizations, are reworked to address the identified gaps and then validated and accepted following the steps of solution validation and delta design.

The solution validation steps are as follows:

1. Reference value: Provide process, value, and strategic context.
2. Validation of SAP solution: Show and tell of SAP standard key design elements.
3. Identify delta and gaps: Identify delta scope and requirements, as well as document gaps.
4. Prioritize scope (delta).

The delta design steps are as follows:

1. Delta design: Update business models and process design, as well as solution visualization/UX.
2. Verify and accept: Verify process and solution design; design acceptance.
3. Document product backlog: Divide priority categories into must, should, could, and would, in order of severity.
4. Release and plan the next sprints.

During the explore and realize phases, when many of these workshops take place, there is a constant working of the product backlog, which prioritizes the work efforts and consequent workshops based on what is a must-have versus a nice-to-have. In this way, the project continually focuses on the most important and valuable items for the implementation. If the project at any time needs to move on to the next phase without addressing further log items, you can be assured that the items addressed up to this point were the most pressing, meaning the project has delivered the most value possible given resource and time constraints.

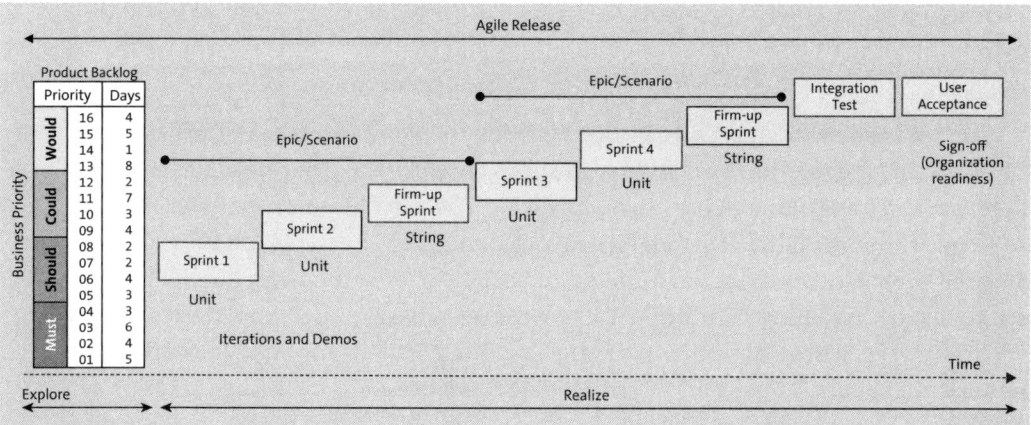

Figure 2.15 Agile Build: Iterative Realize Phase

In Figure 2.15, *epic* refers to a large user story that may take multiple sprints to build out completely. For an SAP S/4HANA project, an epic is basically a larger set of related requirements around a particular business process. The business priority product backlog is created during the explore phase to prioritize and sequence the different epics and their corresponding sprints. As an iterative process, multiple epics can run simultaneously or sequentially, drawing off the product backlog list. Finally, these epics are then validated and tested at the user level (user acceptance testing, or UAT) while gating out of the realize phase.

Quality Gates

Another safeguard in SAP Activate are *quality gates*. Quality gates ensure that a proper review and sign off takes place prior to passing to the next phase. In a quality gate, you verify that acceptance is met for the deliverables during the phase prior to gating out of the phase. For the aforementioned scenario, during the realize phase after UAT, the project would arrive at a quality gate prior to moving on to the next phase. Quality gates provide a formalized approach towards project alignment and memorialize the acceptance and understanding of participants and sponsors prior to rushing into the next phase of the project and potentially leaving critical elements of the previous phase unaddressed.

2.4.5 SAP Activate Roles

For the project team and roles involved in an SAP S/4HANA implementation, the main roles for both a migration and a new implementation of SAP S/4HANA are similar to SAP ERP role requirements in previous project scenarios, as described in Table 2.9. The main difference here is that these participants in the project team will be working within different structures and cycles than before.

Roles	Tasks and Skillsets
Project management	Align resources across various work streams and drive project to achieve milestones.
Functional expert	Determine the functional transformation capabilities enabled by SAP S/4HANA. Prioritize adoption of refined business processes to achieve and enhance business outcomes.
Technical architect	Determine the technical architecture, including security and UX requirements needed to support target solution.

Table 2.9 Project Roles: SAP S/4HANA Conversions and New Implementations

Roles	Tasks and Skillsets
OS/DB lead	Perform the technical migration of the transactional system information to the new SAP S/4HANA system. The migration approach utilized will determine the skillsets required. For a new implementation, this role focuses on structuring converted data to be loaded into the new system for optimal usage.
Development lead	Perform an evaluation of existing system for an SAP S/4HANA conversion and/or proposed customizations for a new implementation of SAP S/4HANA and determine the effort required to revert to standard and/or remediate code for SAP S/4HANA migration, or the effort required to realize the customization requirements in a new implementation.
Change management lead	Build and execute the strategy to lead the organization through the transformation underpinned by SAP S/4HANA.
End users	Perform system testing required to confirm proper operation of migrated or newly implemented SAP S/4HANA system.
Analytics	Develop analytic requirements and determine how to utilize the transformative capabilities of SAP S/4HANA, in which transactional and analytics are combined to accelerate business processes and enable end users.

Table 2.9 Project Roles: SAP S/4HANA Conversions and New Implementations (Cont.)

Each project may have specific role requirements that join the basic ones outlined in Table 2.9. Having the right individuals and roles on a project is as critical as it's been in previous methodologies.

2.5 Summary

Before diving deep into SAP S/4HANA Sourcing and Procurement, an SAP S/4HANA edition and implementation approach needs to be selected. The decision between on-premise or cloud is binary, but further decisions have to be made, such as which cloud edition to choose, which prebuilt solutions will be leveraged, and how to structure the actual implementation project. At all steps of this process, SAP provides tools, processes, and methodologies, as well as solutions. Now that we've reviewed the implementation options, we'll drill deeper in the next chapter on implementing operational procurement.

Chapter 3
Organizational Structure

As with previous SAP ERP releases, the organization structure and master data in SAP S/4HANA are fundamental elements for structured reporting, financial postings, and automating the procurement process in general. These topics warrant their own chapter and discussion.

An ill-defined organization structure can have far-reaching ramifications for procurement operations and transactions, as can poorly defined and maintained master data. Each element, whether organization structure or master data, carries maintenance efforts and potential trade-offs. This chapter will provide an overview of organization structure and master data and how they relate to sourcing and procurement in SAP S/4HANA.

3.1 SAP S/4HANA Enterprise Management Organization Structure

The SAP organization structure hierarchy is the underpinning of an SAP ERP system, and SAP S/4HANA Enterprise Management leverages this framework as well. The hierarchy supports every transaction and forms the main relationships with the master data elements in the system. As such, the SAP hierarchy comprises the management structures, markets, operational environment, geographic structures, and reporting requirements. Once established with master data and transactions associated within the system, the organizational structure is difficult to remove or rework. Therefore, special cross-module care must be taken in defining the organization structure, beyond just sourcing and procurement, and the design must have the flexibility to add more organization units as the organization grows and/or changes.

Figure 3.1 outlines the three main areas for system design and configuration. First, the organization structure has to be defined. Next, master data, such as material masters and material groups, requires definition. The master data and the organization

3 Organizational Structure

structure have dependencies and linkages with one another in most cases. General Ledger accounts, for example, are typically mapped to material groups for spend capture and analysis.

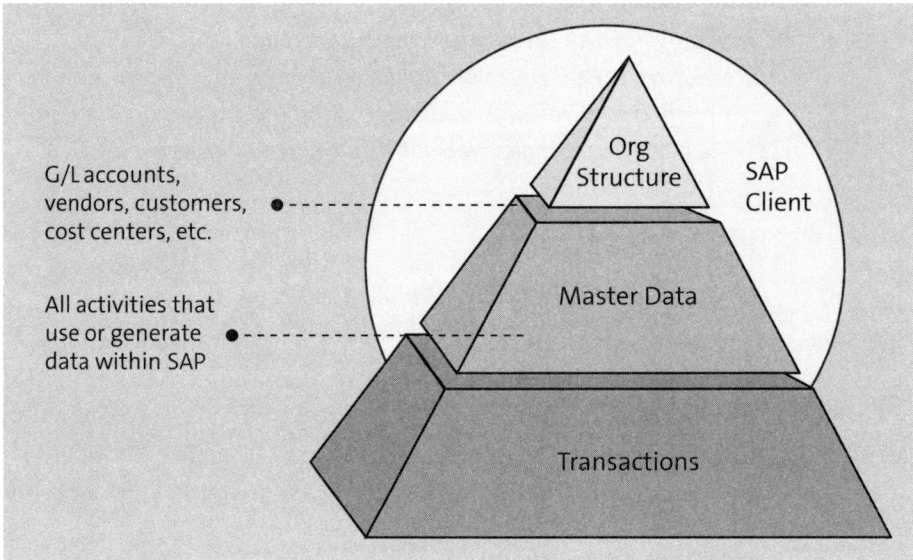

Figure 3.1 SAP Data and Organizational Hierarchy

3.1.1 Organization Structure Terminology

Many terms are used during these design phases that mean something particular in SAP. Often, consultants and long-time SAP users can sound like they're speaking their own special language. Table 3.1 outlines some of the general SAP terms used for defining the organization structure and some of the master data objects within SAP.

SAP Term	Definition
Client	The *client* is the highest level in the SAP system hierarchy, and the specifications and data that you enter cascade down the organization structure for all company codes and other objects in the organization. You make these settings at the beginning of the system setup to ensure data consistency.

Table 3.1 SAP Organization Structure Terminology

SAP Term	Definition
Controlling area	The *controlling area* represents a closed system used for cost accounting purposes and may contain one or more company codes operating in different countries and regions if required.
Company	A *company* is the smallest organizational unit for which individual financial statements are created according to the relevant legal requirements. A company can include multiple company codes; here, the company code would represent a division for the general company.
Company code	The *company code* is the smallest organizational unit of external accounting for which a complete, self-contained set of accounts can be created. This includes the entry of all posted transactions and the creation of individual financial statements, such as the balance sheet and the profit and loss statement.
Business area	A *business area* is an internal management reporting area within the company. A business area is used for additional reporting that subdivides a company code. Business areas are similar to profit center functionality.
Operating concern	The *operating concern* represents the highest reporting level in Profitability Analysis. An operating concern defines the product/market structure in an organizational unit in your company.
Credit control area	The *credit control area* is an internal hierarchy element addressing the processes of Credit Control and Credit Management.
Chart of accounts (CoA)	The *chart of accounts* is a list of all of the General Ledger (G/L) accounts used by one or multiple company codes.
Operating chart of accounts (operating CoA)	The *operating chart of accounts* contains the G/L accounts that are used for posting in your company code during daily activities. Financial Accounting and Controlling both use the operating CoA.

Table 3.1 SAP Organization Structure Terminology (Cont.)

SAP Term	Definition
Group chart of accounts (group CoA)	The *group chart of accounts* contains the G/L accounts for the entire corporate group. The group CoA enables reporting on the entire corporate group.
Country-specific chart of accounts (country-specific CoA)	The *country-specific chart of accounts* contains the G/L accounts required to meet a country's legal requirements. This allows you to provide statements for the country's legal requirements.
Profit center	The *profit center* in Controlling represents an area of responsibility within a company, typically a business unit that monitors both costs and revenues. The profit center behaves as an independent operating unit for which a separate operating statement can be calculated.
Cost center	The *cost center* is the smallest area of responsibility in which budget control is required. The cost center is used to collect expenses and is frequently used in procurement processes.
Cost element	The *cost element* is used to classify the organizations valuated consumption within a controlling area.
Activity type	*Activity types* classify the activities performed within a cost center.
Fiscal year	The *fiscal year* is typically a 12-month period that is either a calendar year or defined by the company; regular financial statements and other process cadences are defined for the fiscal year.
Currencies	*Currencies* refer to the monetary units defined at the country or currency union level.

Table 3.1 SAP Organization Structure Terminology (Cont.)

SAP S/4HANA Sourcing and Procurement leverages an organization structure beginning with the system client, controlling area, and company code and moving on through plant and down to storage location. In the case of an SAP Extended Warehouse Management (SAP EWM) implementation, you can take this one step further to the bin level. Now, let's review an example organization structure.

3.1.2 Example Organizational Structure

Using this terminology and hierarchy, a company or government entity can eventually tailor the organizational structure in the system to reflect its own organization, such as in Figure 3.2. Although this organization structure may appear to be quite complex, examples from actual customers are often far more variegated.

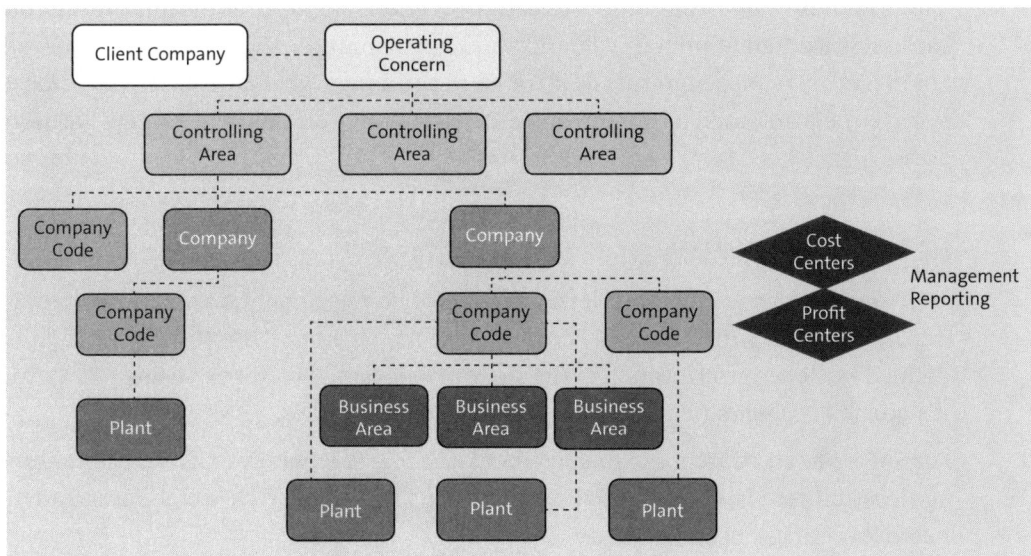

Figure 3.2 SAP Organization Structure Example

Once the general organization structure and financials have been defined and designed for SAP S/4HANA Enterprise Management, you will need to further define the purchasing-specific areas for the organization structure and master data for SAP S/4HANA Sourcing and Procurement. Underneath several of the company codes in Figure 3.2, there are plants. These plants are key to purchasing activities, as are several other linkages further down from the plant level, such as storage locations.

3.2 Organizational Structure Objects

There are several organizational structure objects in SAP S/4HANA that are either shared, such as plants and storage locations, or used solely for procurement activities, such as purchasing organizations and buyer groups.

3.2.1 Plants

The plant is always assigned to a company code and can be a manufacturing facility, a warehouse distribution center, a corporate or government headquarters, or a sales office. A plant is also, and this is important for procurement processes, where valued goods and services are produced, stored, consumed, and/or distributed. The plant allows for flexibility in the system to define procurement items at the plant level. You can assign a different price or valuation and run planning activities at the plant level. For inventory management at the plant level, you assign what are called *storage locations* to the plant, then locate the inventory from the plant in these storage location areas.

3.2.2 Storage Locations

A *storage location* is the lowest level of inventory management without implementing SAP EWM in SAP S/4HANA. For inventory management, the storage location is defined as the physical location of the stock in the plant. If you aren't using SAP EWM, it's possible to assign multiple storage locations to one plant.

For SAP EWM and warehouse management, the rule is generally to use only one storage location per plant, and then allow for the creation of multiple warehouses underneath the storage location.

3.2.3 Warehouses

Individual *warehouses* (high-rack storage, block storage, picking area, etc.) are defined as storage types within a warehouse complex and are grouped together under a warehouse number. This warehouse number is then assigned to the storage location from Inventory Management (IM). For each of these individual warehouses/storage types, you then define the bin levels for the warehouse location, creating a further level of inventory management at the warehouse level. The SAP Fiori-based frontend of SAP EWM has also changed significantly, as shown in Figure 3.3.

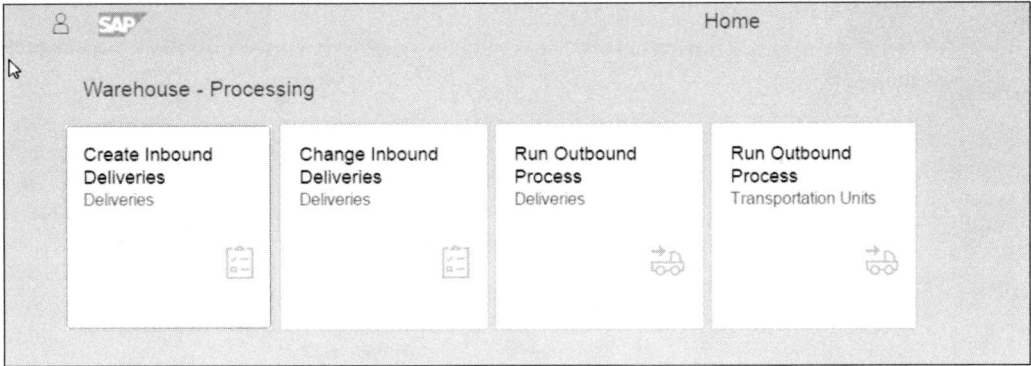

Figure 3.3 SAP EWM in SAP S/4HANA

From an organization structure standpoint, the setup of warehouse management in SAP S/4HANA is similar to its setup in other SAP ERP versions. However, from a technical standpoint, running warehouse management as part of the core SAP S/4HANA Enterprise Management system clears out a lot of redundant configuration and data loads, as the two systems become one. However, not all functionality available in previous versions of SAP EWM are available in the embedded version in SAP S/4HANA. Careful analysis needs to be conducted to determine your requirements for warehouse management and the capabilities of the current SAP S/4HANA release prior to embracing the embedded approach. More information about the inventory management aspects of SAP EWM and its setup will follow in Chapter 5.

3.2.4 Purchasing Organizations

A *purchasing organization* is responsible for procuring materials or services for one or more plants and for negotiating general conditions of purchase with suppliers. The purchasing organization is a required field and assignment for all main purchasing documents. If a plant needs to be able to procure items, it must be assigned to one or more purchasing organizations. So long as the plants are assigned a purchasing organization, the company code is optional for assignment of a purchasing organization. Assigning a company code to the purchasing organization limits the purchasing organization to the plants of the company code to which it has been assigned. Therefore, if the purchasing organization is intended to cover plants in multiple company codes, you would assign the purchasing organization at the plant level.

Purchasing organizations can be assigned as one to many, one to one, or even many to one for organization structure areas such as company codes and plants, as shown in Figure 3.4.

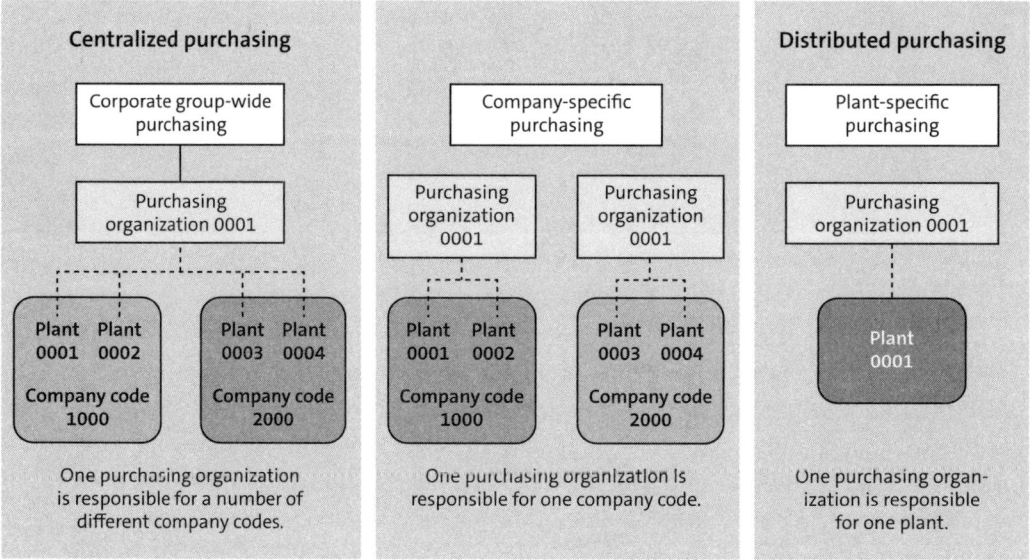

Figure 3.4 Purchasing Organization Assignments in SAP: Centralized vs. Distributed

Although purchasing organization structures can be expanded or distilled to a central organization responsible for many company codes, the general rule is that there needs to be justification for expanding the number of purchasing organizations, as these create overhead in the system. Each contact and supplier will require a reference to the purchasing organizations that use these in the system. If you create a number of unnecessary purchasing organizations, you will quickly find yourself handling a lot of unnecessary setup each time you create a new organization structure element and/or related master data item.

Similar to purchasing groups in SAP, there are setup approaches that help minimize painting yourself into a corner later on from a system standpoint. SAP purchasing groups aren't assigned to purchasing organizations in SAP S/4HANA and SAP ERP contexts, although they are set up this way in SAP SRM. Purchasing groups are named with three-character number or letter combinations. This format can be quite accommodating if the purchasing group is defined as a group and reassigned to new buyers coming on board. However, if you assign each purchasing group to an individual, each time a buyer leaves or changes organizations within the company, a new purchasing group code must be created to accommodate the new buyer replacement. This can lead to consuming the viable purchasing group codes in long term. It is also unwieldy as the purchasing documents associated with the previous purchasing group and buyer will need to be reassigned manually, rather than having a new buyer simply take over the group and the documents already in flight.

3.3 Company Code, Plant, Storage Location, Purchasing Org, and Purchasing Group Creation

This section focuses on the design and creation of organization structure objects as they pertain to procurement operations in SAP S/4HANA. Some of these objects may well be defined in system by finance and other stakeholders by the time procurement kicks off its project phase. Other times, you will have the opportunity to influence these structures during a greenfield or new implementation. In any event, procurement should always be involved in the definition and design of purchasing organizations and groups; these are completely procurement-focused entities in the system.

3.3.1 Company Code Creation

Creating a company code in SAP S/4HANA is the same as in previous SAP ERP iterations, and the guidelines for creating company codes still apply as well. You should try and minimize org structure levels and hierarchies whenever possible. Creating a large number of company codes will create system overhead. In a complex enterprise, this is sometimes unavoidable, and finance usually has a larger say in this area than procurement. The steps involved for creating a one-to-one company linked to a company code are as follows:

1. To create the company, follow IMG menu path **Enterprise Structure • Definition • Financial Accounting • Maintain Company**, or run Transaction OX15.

2. Select **New Entries**, then enter your company name and address information (see Figure 3.5).

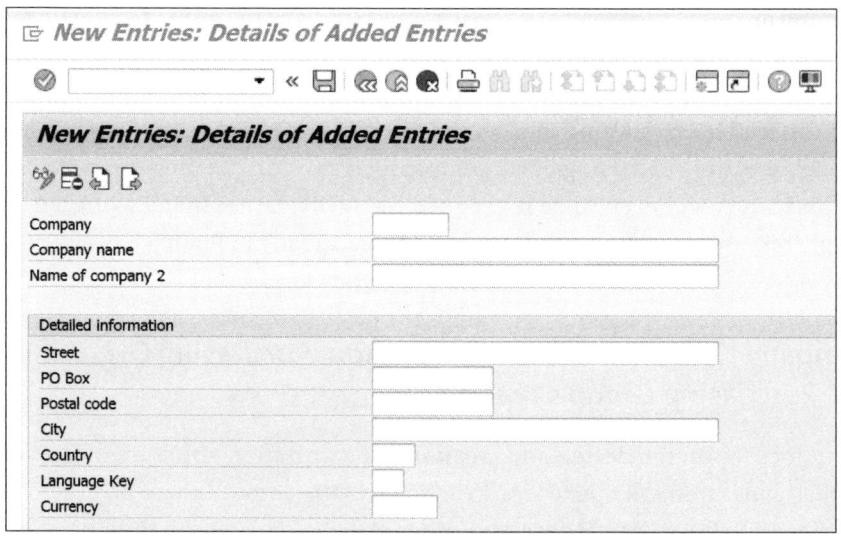

Figure 3.5 Company Creation in SAP S/4HANA

3. Next, you need to create a company code and enter address information. To create a company code in SAP S/4HANA, first enter Transaction OX02 or follow IMG menu path **Enterprise Structure • Definition • Financial Accounting • Define, Copy, Delete, Check Company Code**. Maintain the company code data at a high level as shown in Figure 3.6.

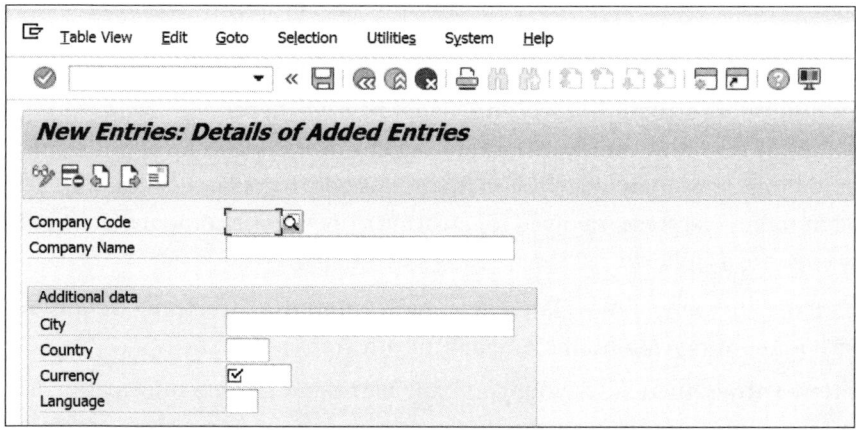

Figure 3.6 New Company Code Entry Screen

3.3 Company Code, Plant, Storage Location, Purchasing Org, and Purchasing Group Creation

On this screen, you define the number (**Company Code**), **Company Name**, **City**, **Country**, **Currency**, and **Language** for the company code. You'll define the full address in the accounting data in the next step.

4. Once you've created the company code, maintain the company code address and key accounting data in Transaction OBY6. After you create a company code, it can be assigned to a company, controlling area, and/or a financial management area, as shown in Figure 3.7. Here you can also update key areas like the CoA, tax data, fiscal year reporting settings, and other finance-driven data. Note that this is not for procurement to define in a vacuum; procurement should be working in full conjunction with finance. Just as finance shouldn't drive the purchasing org discussion, neither should procurement drive the company code definition at this level.

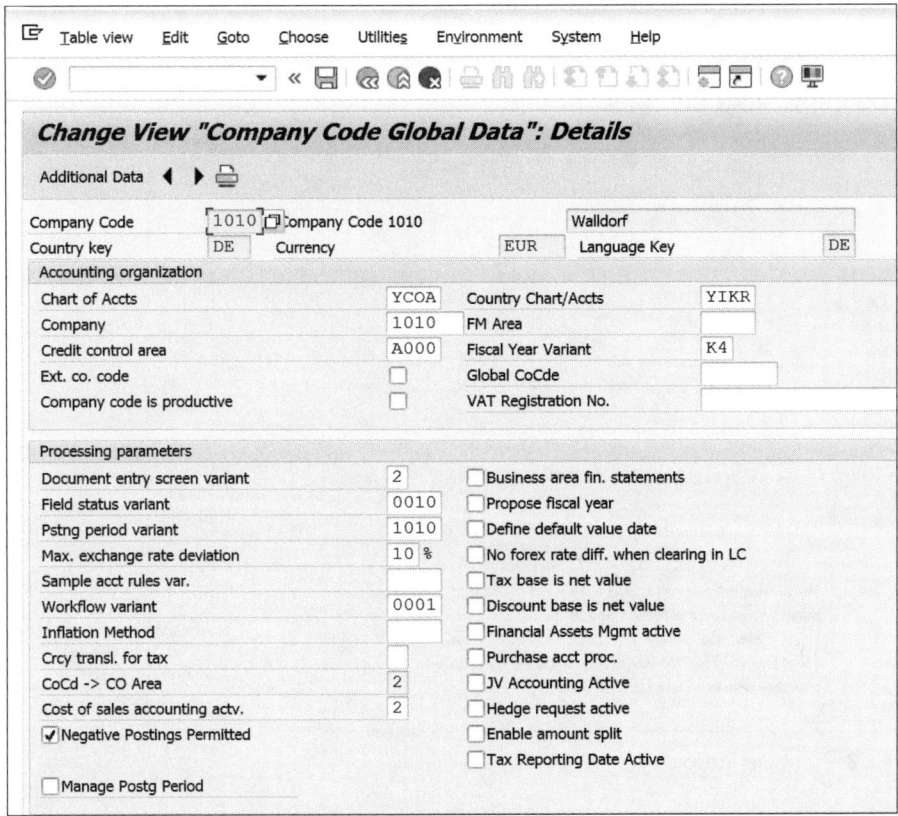

Figure 3.7 Transaction OBY6: Change Address

89

3.3.2 Plant Creation

Plant in SAP refers to a number of different things, such as a location with valuated inventory, an organization unit central in planning and production, an office, or another location type applicable to the system owner's business and activities. To create a plant, enter Transaction OX10 or follow IMG menu path **Enterprise Structure • Definition • Logistics • General • Define, Copy, Delete, Check Plant**. Here you define the **Plant**, **Name**, and address information, as well as **Factory Calendar** settings (see Figure 3.8). Different countries use different factory calendars for production, which can be very important for accurately estimating lead times in production and other areas. If the factory workers are on holiday during a time you've anticipated they would be working based on your own schedule, your supply chain calculations will be impacted.

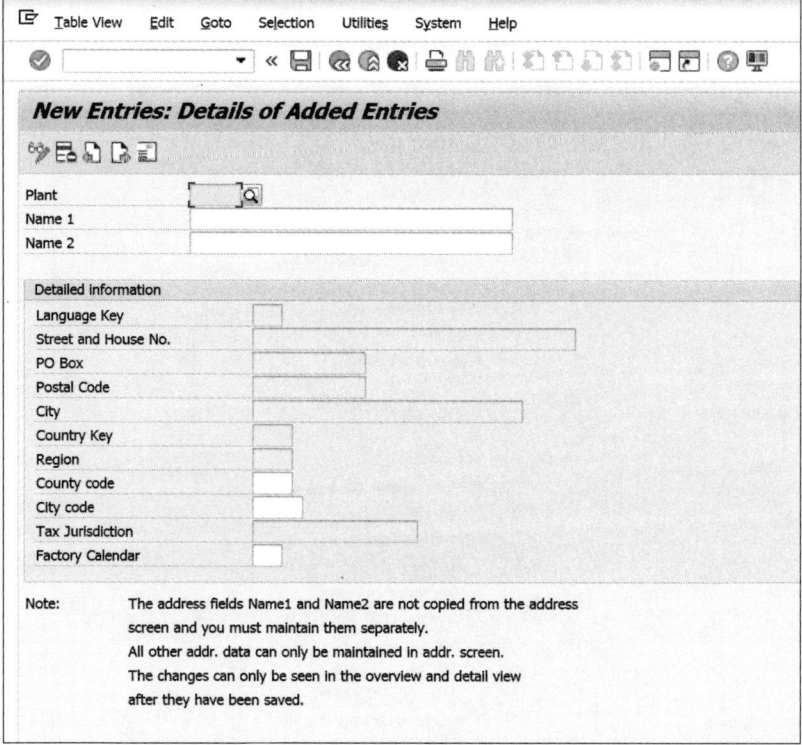

Figure 3.8 Plant Definition

A plant needs to be assigned to a company code to form part of the organization structure. A plant can't be used in the system without a company code relationship, as the key accounting settings inherited from the company code wouldn't be available. To assign a plant to a company code, enter Transaction OX18 or follow IMG path **Enterprise Structure • Assignment • Logistics—General • Assign Plant to Company Code**.

As shown in Figure 3.9, the assignment process simply consists of entering a company code number (**CoCd**) and a plant (**Plnt**) and clicking the **Save** button. A plant can be assigned to only one company code, but a company code can have many plants.

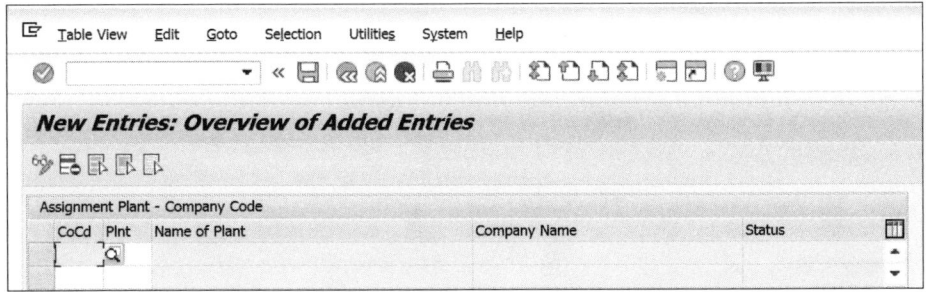

Figure 3.9 Assigning Plants to Company Code

To set up a plant, the valuation level for the system needs to be defined. This is a setting that cannot be changed easily once set and will typically involve finance determining how stock is to be valued in SAP. You can set the valuation level at the company code or plant level. If set at the company code level, a material will have the same valuation for inventory value calculations and the like across plants. If set at the plant level, you can value a material differently from plant to plant. For instance, if you have a location that is particularly remote, requiring large delivery costs to ship items there, you may want to value these items differently than at a plant with economical transportation and supply options.

3.3.3 Storage Location and Warehouse Creation

In SAP, *storage locations* allow for differentiation of the location of a material item or stock in a plant. A plant can have one or several storage locations assigned to it. Storage locations are the next level down from plant, allowing plants to have multiple storage locations for inventory management functions. Storage locations are the lowest level in Materials Management. The next level down in the organization structure after storage location is the warehouse, which is managed by the SAP EWM module in SAP S/4HANA (either embedded directly in the SAP S/4HANA system or as a sidecar module, depending on your landscape and warehouse functionality requirements).

A *warehouse* is a building or location devoted to housing inventory, whereas a plant may have multiple functions, such as production, in addition to managing inventory.

Storage locations can be linked with warehouses via IMG menu path **Enterprise Structure • Assignment • Logistics Execution • Assign Warehouse Number to Plant/Storage Location**. Here you assign the plant (**Plnt**), storage location (**SLoc**), and warehouse number (**WhN**) on one line, as shown in Figure 3.10.

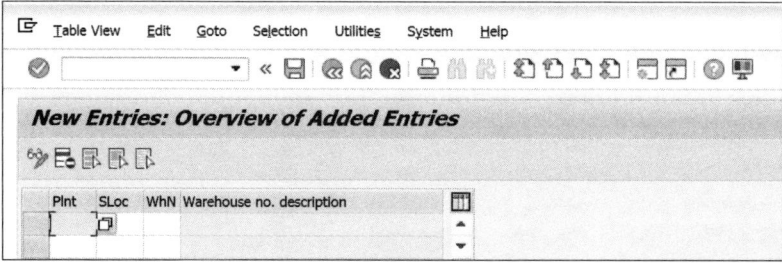

Figure 3.10 Assigning Storage Location to Warehouse

You can manage inventory directly in the storage locations without going down to a bin-level scenario necessitating a warehouse layer. Once linked, a storage location is in a parent-child relationship with SAP EWM, inheriting its settings and processes to a degree.

To create a storage location, enter Transaction OX09 or follow IMG menu path **Enterprise Structure • Definition • Materials Management • Maintain Storage Location**. Enter the plant to which the new storage location is to be assigned, as shown in Figure 3.11.

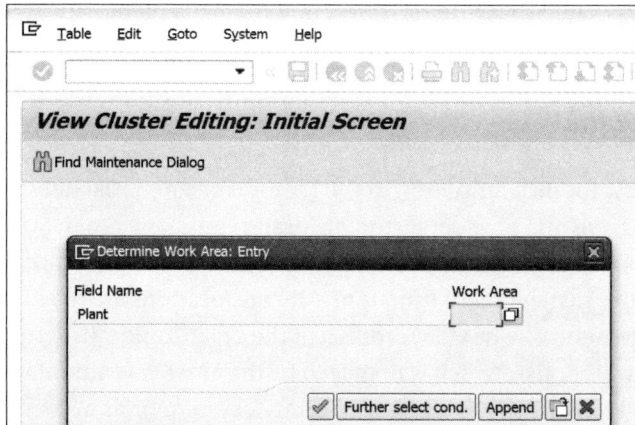

Figure 3.11 Create Storage Location in SAP S/4HANA

3.3 Company Code, Plant, Storage Location, Purchasing Org, and Purchasing Group Creation

Once you have selected the plant, select **New Entries** to create a storage location (see Figure 3.12).

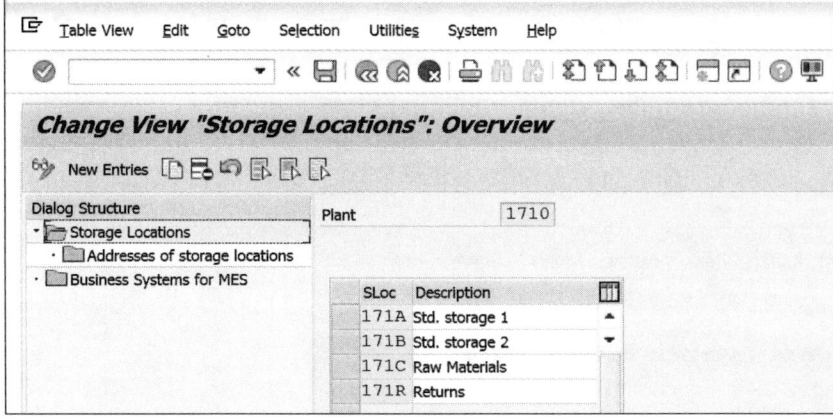

Figure 3.12 Storage Location: New Entries

Next, enter the storage location (**SLoc**) and **Description** in the fields shown in Figure 3.13 and click **Save**.

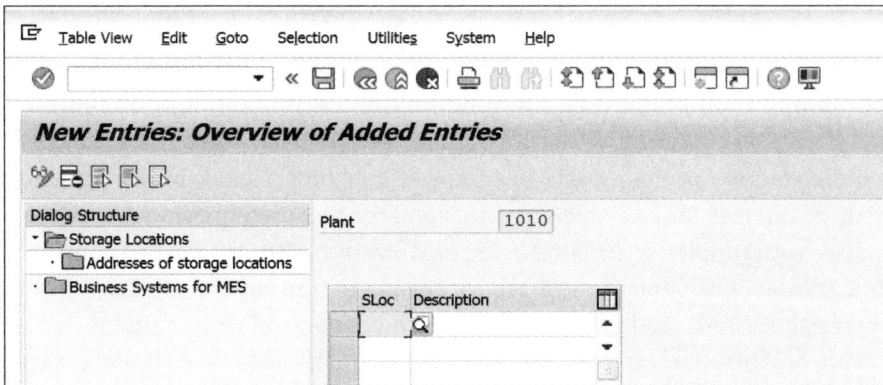

Figure 3.13 New Storage Location

3.3.4 Warehouse Creation

If you have a requirement to manage items beyond just a general area in the plant or to maintain a physical warehouse operation that supports your plants, you'll need to evaluate SAP EWM as an option for integrating your warehouse management operations with SAP S/4HANA and managing them outright. SAP EWM allows you to manage stocks at a bin level within the warehouse, providing a much more granular level of detail. This is particularly useful when manufacturing is using a large set of parts and needs to know exactly where items are in the facility and to manage them at this level in the system.

To create a warehouse number reference, follow the IMG menu path **Enterprise Structure • Definition • Logistics—Execution • Define, Copy, Delete, Check Warehouse Number**, as shown in Figure 3.14.

Figure 3.14 Creating Warehouse Number in SAP S/4HANA

Once you've defined your organization structure objects down to at least the plant level, you're ready to create your purchasing organization structure.

3.3.5 Purchasing Organization Creation

A *purchasing organization* in SAP is an organizational unit responsible for procuring materials or services for one or more plants and for negotiating general conditions of purchase with suppliers. The purchasing organization assumes legal responsibility for these transactions. A plant must always have at minimum one purchasing organization assigned to it, and must always in turn be assigned to a company code. A purchasing organization can be assigned at the company code level. If not assigned to individual company codes, a purchasing organization can lead transactions across company codes for your system. Assignment of the purchasing organization to the plant level is then required.

A purchasing organization can be assigned either centrally or in distributed fashion to individual plants. As with other organization structure elements, adding purchasing organizations means adding overhead in the system and in general. A centralized purchasing organization structure is preferable, unless there are requirements that drive a distributed purchasing organization structure in which one or more purchasing organizations are assigned at the plant level. Note that in a distributed model, in addition to creating multiple purchasing organizations, these organizations not only must be assigned to plants, but supplier records will need to be extended for each individual purchasing organization. This is where a simple master data update or change can begin to require multiple steps to assign and extend these connections to suppliers, contracts, purchase orders, and other documents. Having a single purchasing organization or a limited number for clarity and delineation is the recommended position for design.

To create a purchasing organization, use Transaction OX08 or navigate to IMG menu path **Enterprise Structure • Definition • Materials Management • Maintain Purchasing Organization**, and enter the purchasing organization (**Purch. Organization**) as shown in Figure 3.15.

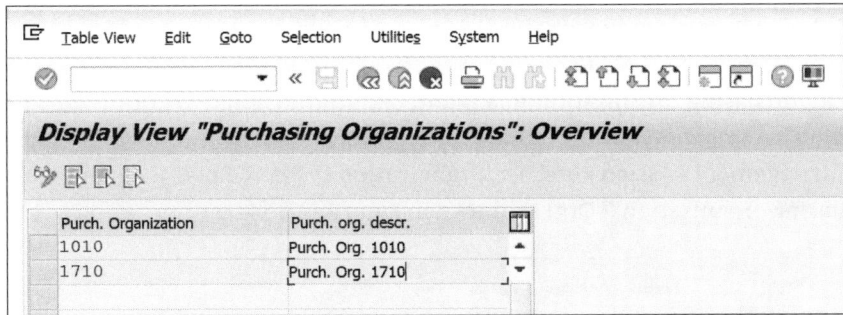

Figure 3.15 Create Purchasing Organization

Creating a purchasing organization requires simply defining a number and a description. Once you've entered this information, you can save your entries and move to the next step.

> **Note**
> Although creation of a purchasing organization is quite straightforward, remember that purchasing organizations can cover multiple countries and company codes when required and should not be created on a whim without accounting for design and maintenance considerations. As with other objects, a purchasing organization will create additional maintenance overhead in the system, so covering your requirements with the minimal amount of purchasing organizations will serve you well down the road.

3 Organizational Structure

The next step is to assign the purchasing organization to a company code using Transaction OX01 or by following the IMG menu path **Enterprise Structure • Assignment • Materials Management • Assign Purchasing Organization to Company Code**, as shown in Figure 3.16.

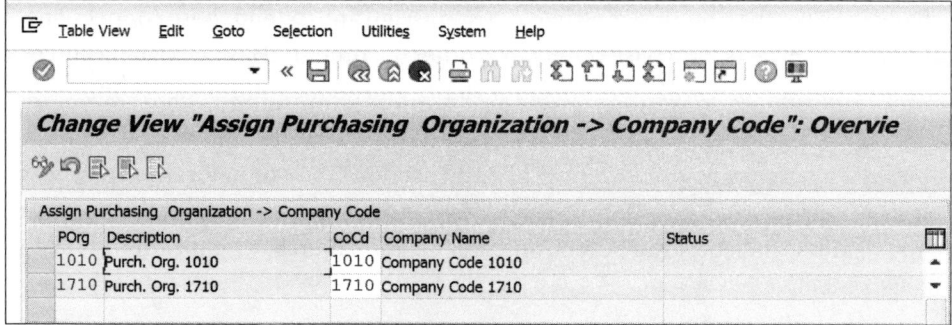

Figure 3.16 Assign Purchasing Organization to Company Code

To assign a purchasing organization to a plant, use Transaction OX17 or menu path **SAP Customizing Implementation Guide (IMG) • Enterprise Structure • Assignment • Material Management • Assign Purchase Organization to Plant**. Enter the plant (**Plnt**) and purchasing organization (**POrg**) as shown in Figure 3.17.

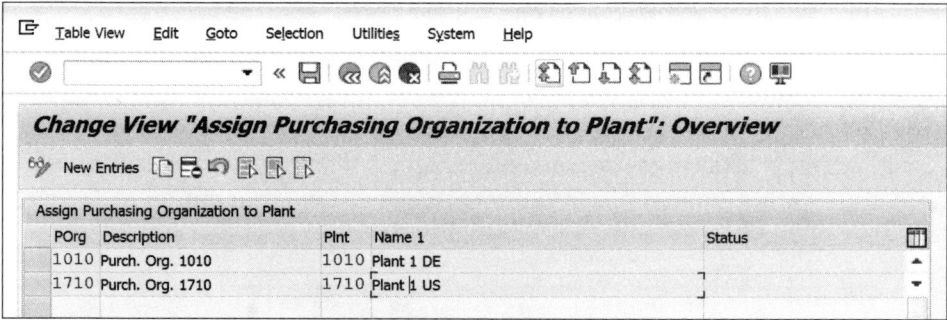

Figure 3.17 Assign Purchasing Organization to Plant

Purchasing organizations are not the only grouping and assignment available for procurement activities. You also have a further level called purchasing groups, discussed next.

3.3.6 Purchasing Group Creation

Purchasing groups are responsible for day-to-day buying activities and need not be assigned to a single purchasing organization. Purchasing groups also shouldn't be assigned to an individual buyer directly, but instead be kept generic enough to be reassigned if a new buyer or group joins the organization to cover the purchasing group in question. Once you have designed, created, and assigned your purchasing organization entities/structure, you create these buyer groups, called *purchasing groups*. To create purchasing groups, follow IMG menu path **Materials Management • Purchasing • Define Purchasing Groups** (see Figure 3.18).

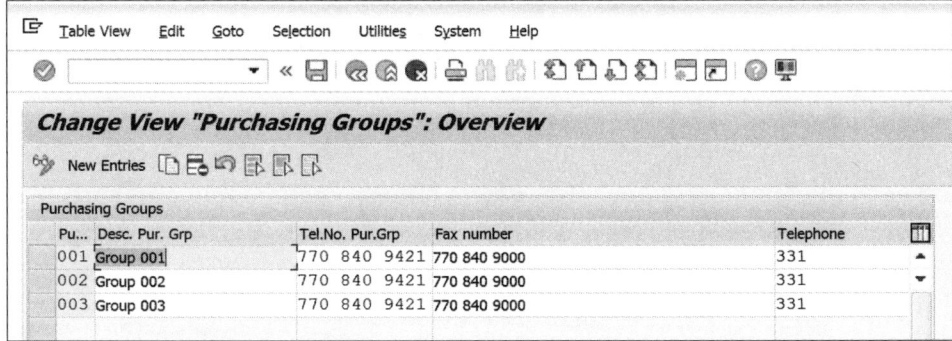

Figure 3.18 Create Purchasing Group

Enter a purchasing group number (**Pu…**), description (**Desc. Pur. Grp**), phone (**Tel.No. Pur.Grp**) and **Fax Number**, and **Save**.

You now have configured the baseline objects for an organization structure for purchasing in SAP S/4HANA.

3.4 Summary

The organization structure, master data, and transactional data designs underpin and simplify system usage in SAP ERP environments when implemented in a thoughtful manner. In all three areas, finding the optimal balance between the level of detail required and a level of simplicity to support the UX and overall volumes/footprint. Creating too many organization structures leads to redundancies and maintenance work, such as having a purchasing organization created for each company code when an overarching purchasing organization would do. Driving a level of granularity in the material masters that is not required for the business leads to user frustration in trying to find the appropriate material master to use in a transaction, as well additional maintenance to enact any changes to the material masters.

In addition, SAP S/4HANA introduces a significant change to how supplier and customer masters are managed in the system. These two types of partner functions in SAP S/4HANA are unified into a business partner concept, which has ramifications on conversions and upgrades from previous versions of SAP ERP, as well as usage of the master record in purchasing transactions in SAP S/4HANA. The next chapter shifts focus to operational procurement and the base-level types of transactions in purchasing.

Chapter 4
Master Data

Master data is defined at a system level as reusable data records supporting transactions and processes. Practically every business solution from SAP makes use of some form of master data.

For SAP S/4HANA, master data continues to play the pivotal role it has over the years in other SAP ERP environments, providing semistatic data records for suppliers, materials, material groups, units of measure, incoterms, and other data highly relevant for procurement transactions. Master data represents the building blocks of a transaction in SAP, and this data can save a significant amount of effort duplication and effort in general, when built and maintained correctly. Rather than having to create each transaction from scratch and enter in each detail, a user or automated procurement process can leverage the existing master data in SAP to create comprehensive orders using a few premaintained elements, as indicated in Figure 4.1.

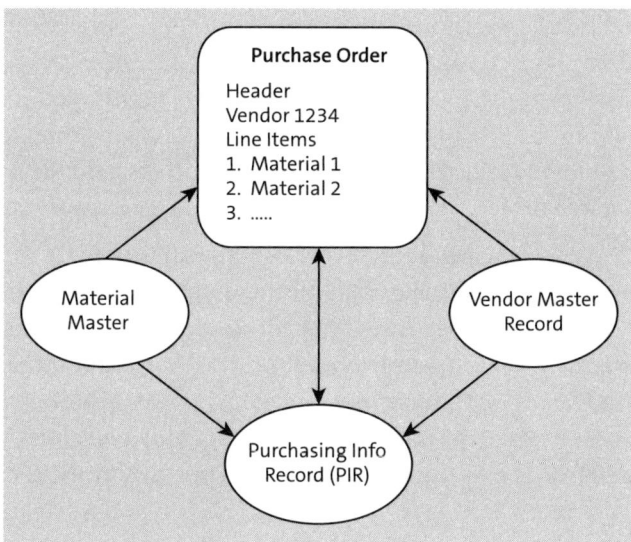

Figure 4.1 SAP Master Data

Master data in SAP refers to data that remains relatively static and is used often in transactions. Rather than recreating this data each time or storing it throughout the system in multiple records, master data is stored centrally and reused throughout the system. This makes it important to govern the creation and management of this type of data to avoid duplicate records and data redundancy.

A best practice is typically to have one group responsible for master data, rather than allowing everyone in the system to create multiple, and invariably duplicate, master data records for procurement areas such as material masters, suppliers, material groups, and purchasing info records (PIRs). Other approaches include allowing different groups to "own" different master data or even parts of the master data record. This happens frequently for payment information on a vendor master. Purchasing needs to update some areas, but payment information and verification is often the responsibility of accounting and accounts payable (AP).

4.1 Material Masters and Material Groups

A *material master record* stores a company's or government entity's material-specific data, allowing for this record to be used in all areas of logistics within the SAP ERP environment.

The information contained in a material master record may be used in a variety of activities and processes, including warehouse management (WM), purchasing, inventory management, and/or planning. As such, a centralized group often coordinates the creation of the master data "shell" and the entry of area-specific data for Purchasing, WM, and other groups as part of this record. Allowing a single group to create and manage the entire record leads to duplicate entries, with each duplicate material master containing a piece of the complete data picture.

As with previous versions of SAP ERP, you can control the user views in SAP S/4HANA to allow different departments to update only the areas pertinent to their parts of the process or business activity. You can also deputize a master data group to own the entire record and enter information centrally via a request process. Both approaches have their advantages and disadvantages. The least advantageous approach, however, is to allow for anarchy to reign in the material masters, as different groups will quickly fragment the material master records into duplicates and records with inconsistent

4.1 Material Masters and Material Groups

and divergent information. Once these fragmented material masters are used in a transaction, they become very difficult to remove from an SAP ERP system. The main point of creating and maintaining master data is to standardize and simplify usage of the system, and this discipline needs to guide the governing approach.

There are both main data and additional data screens in a material master record. Data can be maintained for the entire organization, at the plant level, or down to the storage location.

4.1.1 Creating a Material Master

A material master is a record that stores all of the information about a material that an organization procures, stores, and sells. These records can be created in SAP GUI in SAP S/4HANA via Transaction MM01 (Create), MM02 (Change), or MM03 (View), as shown in Figure 4.2, or in the SAP S/4HANA Create Material SAP Fiori app (see Figure 4.3).

When you create a material master, you must define a **Material type** and assign an industry sector. Material types include **Operating Supplies**, **Semifinished Product**, **Raw materials**, **Services**, and **Finished Product**. The material type controls whether the product is produced in house or can be procured externally and controls account postings upon receipt.

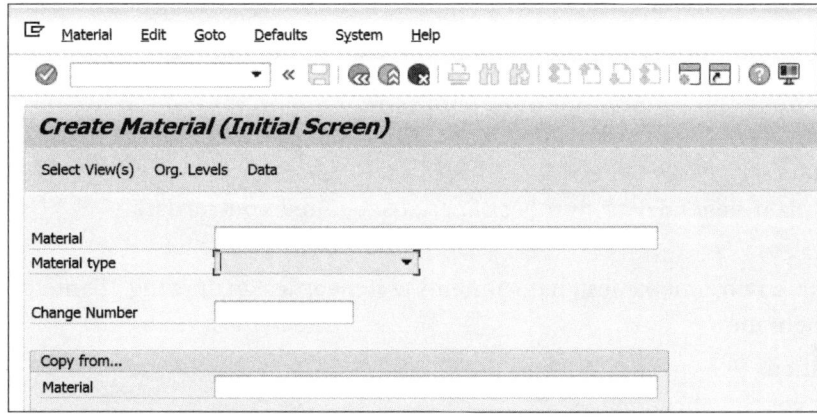

Figure 4.2 Create Material Master: SAP GUI

4   Master Data

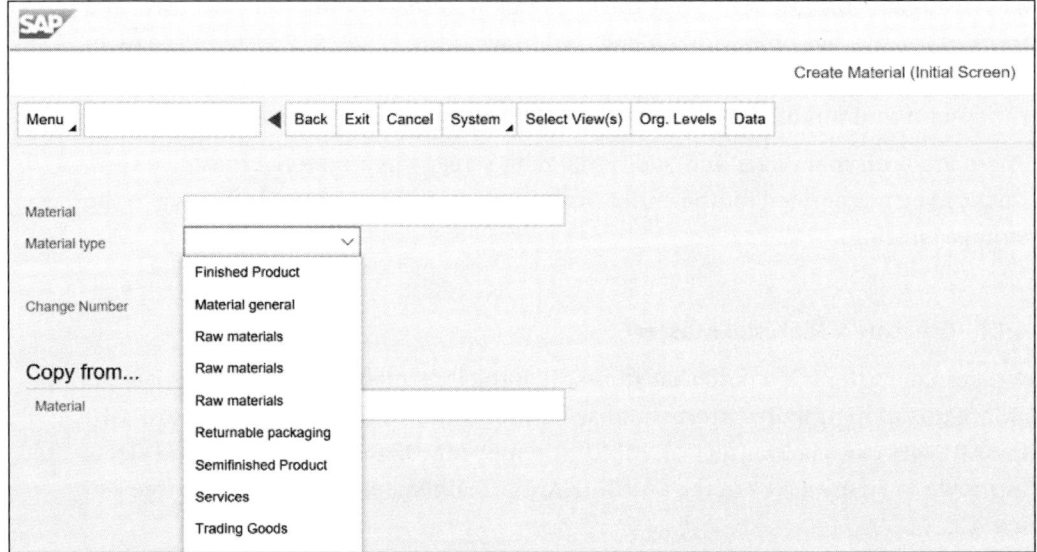

Figure 4.3 Material Master Type: SAP S/4HANA Create Material App

The industry sector type controls the screens and the order in which they can be accessed/displayed. Additional industry sector types can be configured depending upon the requirements. Once you set the industry sector type, it can't be changed by a normal user in the system.

Once you're in the material master record, there are numerous tabs available to define data for the various processes involving a material master. The main tabs are as follows:

- **Basic Data**
  Material, plant, general data, number of periods required, control data
- **Basic Data 2**
  Other data, environment, design documents assigned, design drawing, client-specific configuration
- **Classification**
  Material type classification
- **Sales Org**
  Material and general data
- **Sales Org 2**
  Material and grouping items

- **Sales General Plant**
  General data, shipping data, packaging material data, general plant parameters
- **Foreign Trade**
  Foreign trade data, origin
- **Sales Text**
  Text set at organizational level
- **MRP 1**
  General data, MRP procedure, lot size data, MRP areas
- **MRP 2**
  Procurement, scheduling, net requirements calculation
- **MRP 3**
  Forecast requirements, planning, availability check, plant-specific configuration
- **MRP 4**
  Bill of materials explosion, discontinued parts, repetitive manufacturing/assembly/deployment strategy
- **Work Scheduling**
  General data, tolerance data, in-house production time in days
- **Plant Data/Storage Area 1**
  General data, shelf life criteria
- **Plant Data/Storage Area 2**
  Weight/volume, general plant parameters
- **Accounting 1**
  Periods, future costing run, current costing run, previous costing run
- **Accounting 2**
  Determination of lowest value, last-in first-out (LIFO) data
- **Costing 1**
  General data, quantity structure data
- **Costing 2**
  Standard cost estimate, planned prices, valuation data
- **General data**
  General data, plant stocks in current period, plant stocks in previous period
- **Storage Location Stock**
  General data, storage location stock in current period, storage location stock in previous period

The main tabs for procurement are the **Basic Data** and **General** tabs, **Procurement** tabs, and **MRP** tabs. The **MRP** tabs allow for controlling the MRP process used with the material. MRP replenishments typically run, at some point, through SAP S/4HANA Sourcing and Procurement, which makes these material master tabs particularly relevant. Once you have defined these areas, you save or update the record. The record can now be used in transactions involving materials.

4.1.2 Creating a Material Group

A material group is used to categorize items being procured, stored, and sold, for reporting, taxation, and classification purposes. Following Transaction OMSF or IMG menu path **Logistics General • Material Master • Settings for Key Fields • Define Material Groups**, you define these categories as shown in Figure 4.4, maintaining a material group code (**Matl Group**), description (**Material Group Desc.**), account group (**AGrp**), default unit of weight (**DUW**), and a second description (**Description 2**) if required.

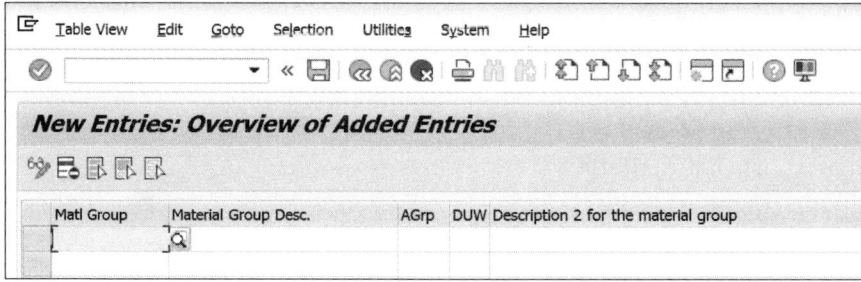

Figure 4.4 Define Material Group: SAP GUI

The material group format usually derives from an overall set of material groups selected by your organization to form the structure for managing this type of classification. United Nations Standard Product and Service Codes (UNSPSC) are popular in private sector companies, whereas federal, state, and local entities in the United States often use Federal Supply Class (FSC) codes. With any material group definition, you need to limit access to this area to avoid duplication of codes and dilution of the overall structure. Especially when it comes time to report, having a tight foundation for categorizing your purchasing spend aids enormously in reporting and analytics, not to mention in correctly classifying items during transactions.

4.2 Batch Management and Serialization

Organizations produce in a variety of ways, but each production method can be grouped largely into two categories: a company manufactures product continuously or in batches. When purchasing an item, especially one taken into inventory, understanding the batch number of the product allows for a better understanding of the product and facilitates communication with the supplier in the event a recall occurs or a follow-up issue arises with a particular batch of product. Serialization plays a similar role in making the tracking of particular products and items back to their origins easier for the end user or buyer. On the production side, batch management can be set at the client, plant (default), or material level. A serial number is given to a unique item, rather than being set at an organization level or material master level. Serial numbers are used to manage warranties on individual equipment and items in plant maintenance scenarios.

4.2.1 Batch Number Configuration

Batch and serial numbers are typically set up in conjunction with the other stakeholders of this functionality (production planning and logistics/supply chain groups) during the initial configuration of an SAP ERP environment. To configure a batch number, follow these directions: Navigate to the **Activate Internal Batch Number Assignment** screen by following menu path **Logistics General • Batch Management • Batch Number Assignment • Activate Internal Batch Number Assignment • Activate Batch Number Assignment**, or entering Transaction OMCZ (see Figure 4.5).

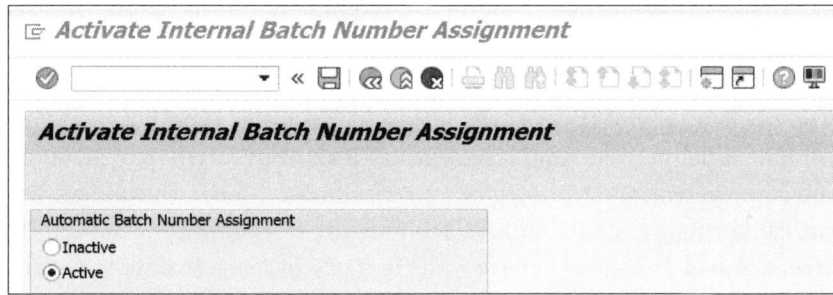

Figure 4.5 Activate Internal Batch Number Assignment

4   Master Data

If you set the batch number assignment to **Active**, you have the ability to classify your materials by batch number, allowing for tracking at the batch level. This is useful for procurement, in that you can track incoming batches in shipments. If there is a recall or an issue, you don't have to throw out or return the entire set of materials, but can have control of the batch to compartmentalize the issue, creating a kind of firebreak.

Next, if you need the system to automatically number batches on a goods receipt with an account assignment, follow the IMG menu path **Logistics General • Batch Management • Batch Number Settings • Activate Internal Batch Number Assignment • Internal Batch Number Assignment for Assigned Goods Receipt**, as shown in Figure 4.6. On this screen, you can select the batch checkbox to create and assign an internal batch number upon goods receipt automatically. If this shipment proves defective or otherwise different, you can use this batch number to quickly address the issue in your production and storage areas.

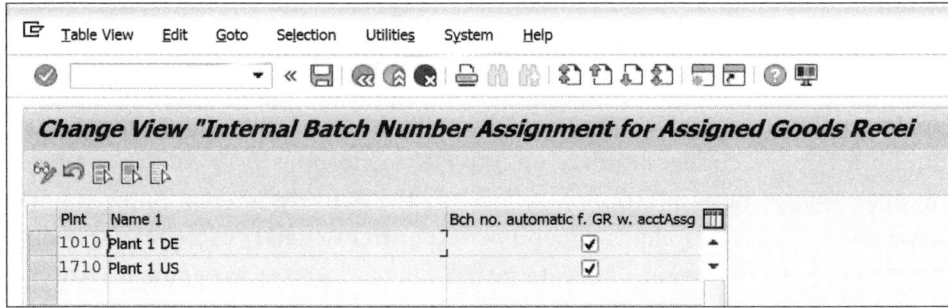

Figure 4.6 Internal Batch Number Assignment for Goods Receipts

4.2.2   Serial Number Configuration

Next up is the serial number. Master masters identify a product type, but not at the batch level or individual-item-in-stock level. The batch identifies a group of materials coming in on a goods receipt. If you require material master items to be identified uniquely, you can configure serial numbers. To configure serial numbers, navigate to **Plant Maintenance and Customer Service • Master Data in Plant Maintenance and Customer Service • Technical Objects • Serial Numbers Management • Define Serial Number Profiles • Serial Number Profile**, or use Transaction OIS2 (see Figure 4.7).

4.2 Batch Management and Serialization

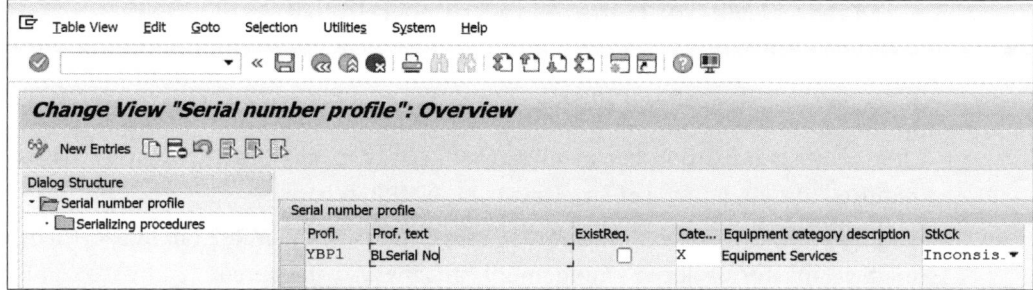

Figure 4.7 Serial Number Profile

Setting up the serial number profile and assigning it to the material master allows for a serial number to be created upon goods receipt of that particular material.

To define where serial numbers are to be used, you can use Transaction OIS2 again or follow IMG menu path **Plant Maintenance and Customer Service • Master Data in Plant Maintenance and Customer Service • Technical Objects • Serial Numbers Management • Define Serial Number Profiles • Serializing Procedures**.

The different usages for serialization are provided in the procedure codes and descriptions shown in Figure 4.8. Serialization is used in a number of areas, for which corresponding types of usage are defined (none, obligatory, automatic, optional), as well as whether or not equipment creation is required in line with the serialization.

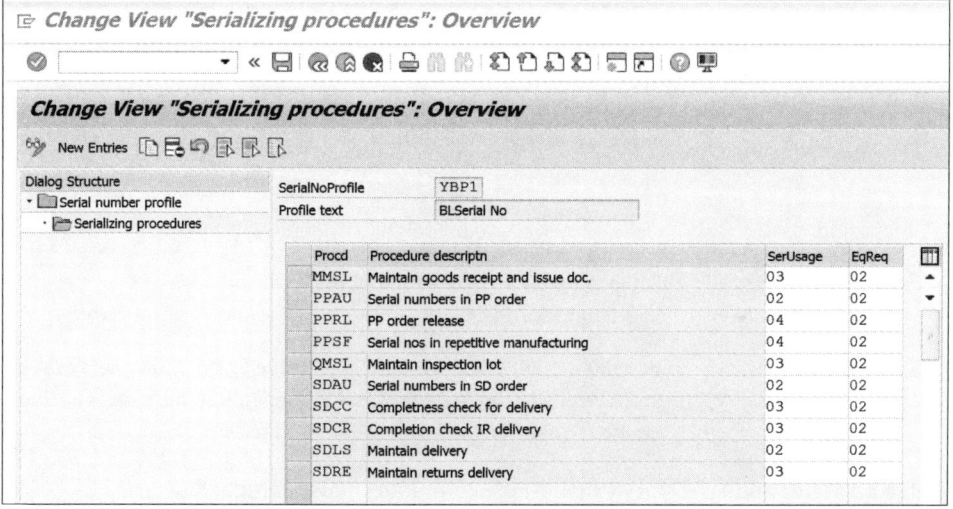

Figure 4.8 Serializing Procedures

4.3 Material Master Updates in SAP S/4HANA

Several fields and tabs have been updated in SAP S/4HANA's material master. Some of the changes to fields in Transactions MM01, MM02, and MM03 are as follows:

- **Unit of Measure Group** is considered retail-only in SAP S/4HANA, and it is not required to switch it on **Lot Size Data1** of the **MRP1** tab.
- You don't have to switch on **Quota Arrangements** in the **MRP2** tab in S/4HANA's material master, as quota arrangements are always considered.
- **BOM Explosion/Dependent Requirement** is not required in **MRP4 Selection Method**. Nor are **Action Control**, **Fair Share Rule**, **Push Distribution**, and **Deployment Horizon** in **MRP4**.
- **MRP4** also no longer has settings for **Storage Location MRP** indicator, **Spec. Procurement Type SLoc**, or **Reorder Point**, **Replenishment Quantity**.

4.3.1 SERV Product Type

SERV selected under **Product Type** classifies an item as a service material, removing several tabs and fields in the process, as noted in Table 4.1, per SAP Notes 2224251 and 2224371. These fields/tabs remain in the system tables, but aren't visible to the user.

Material Master Tab in SERV Record	Fields Impacted
Basic Data 2	ALL
Accounting 2	ALL
Basic Data 1	EAN/UPC, EAN Category, Product Allocation, Assigned vs. Effected Vals, Material Group Package Materials
Purchasing	Fields Material Group Freight, Other data
Sales General/Plant	Replacement Part, Availability Check, Material Freight Group, Shipping Data, Packaging Material Data, and General Plant
Accounting 1	**VC: Sales Order stk**, **Price Control—Value 5**, **Moving Price**, **Total Stock**, **Proj. Stk Value Class**, **Total Value**, **Valuated Un**, **Accounting Previous Year** (Button), **Std. cost estimate** (Button)

Table 4.1 Fields and Tabs Not Available in SERV Product Type Material Master

Material Master Tab in SERV Record	Fields Impacted
Sales/Sales Org 1	X-distr. Chain Status, Valid from, Dchain-spec status, Valid from, Minimum Delivery Quantity, Delivery Unit
Sales/Sales Org 2	Matl. statistics group product attributes

Table 4.1 Fields and Tabs Not Available in SERV Product Type Material Master (Cont.)

To activate **SERV** as a product type, you need to verify that delivery class G is set in table T133K for **Material Type SERV** and in **Screen Sequence Control** (Transaction OMT3E). Note that **SERV** does not replace the **Service Master DIEN**; it augments it so that items used directly with a service can be classified as such.

4.3.2 Select Material Master Configuration Options

For configuration options in purchasing, you can define the view of the material master (what tabs the user can and can't access), as well as the following:

- **Define Shipping Instructions**
  Here, you can line out instructions for the supplier, which can then be assigned for one or more material masters.

- **Define Purchasing Value Keys**
  These value keys establish rules for the issue of reminders and letters (expediters) with respect to nearly due and overdue deliveries, the admissibility of over- and underdeliveries (overages and underages), the order acknowledgment requirements for PO items, and general shipping/packaging instructions.

- **Define the manufacturer part number (MPN)**
  This is a larger topic and needs design thought prior to activation. Essentially, if you have multiple suppliers for a particular material, you can activate MPN and retain one material master with multiple suppliers. These MPNs can be further managed using source lists, PIRs, and outline agreements to provide the plant-specific logic for which ones can be ordered.

- **Define reasons for blocking approved MPN**

- **Entry aids for items without a material master**
  This configuration allows you to assign default purchasing values via a value key for PO items without a material master and info record. A valuation class assign-

ment allows the system to determine different accounts for individual material groups.

4.3.3 Material Master Field Character Expansion in SAP S/4HANA

One significant update to the material master in SAP S/4HANA is that the maximum field length of the material number has been extended to 40 characters from 18 in the **MATNR** field. The expansion to 40 characters applies for all fields and tables in SAP S/4HANA in which the material master can be stored. This means that a larger range is now available to use for material masters, but, as discussed in this section, this doesn't mean that you should necessarily use all of these numbers just because you now have them available. The character expansion also means that conversion from earlier systems will need to be analyzed for enhancements and interfaces that reference the old field length or expand the field length to ensure orderly conversion of these material masters into SAP S/4HANA. For interfaces, the material field with the new length has been added to the table or appended as a new parameter. The new 40-character-field functionality for the material master must be switched on explicitly in system to avoid inadvertent disruptions to interfaces and previous versions and their compatibility with SAP S/4HANA material master functionality. Web services already had a 60-character length for material masters and so are not impacted. Industry solutions in SAP ERP, such as Discrete Industries and Mill Products (DIMP), which had their own character-extension add-ons for material masters, will see these replaced with the standard extension now available in SAP S/4HANA.

To activate the extended material number functionality (after completing analysis of conversion impacts and interface impacts with older versions of SAP ERP or otherwise), complete the following steps:

1. First, ensure that your configuration role contains table maintenance authorization group FLE (authorization S_TABU_DIS), using Transaction FLETS or IMG menu path **Cross Application Components • General Application Functions • Field Length Extension • Activate Extended Fields**.

2. Change the material master number format using Transaction OMSL or via menu path **Logistics General • Material Master • Basic Settings**.

4.4 Supplier Master Setup and Supplier Creation

The supplier master is arguably the most vital master data for procurement. Suppliers are the core of a purchasing document; without a source of supply defined, no purchasing document can be generated. This area has also changed significantly in SAP S/4HANA. This section will both cover the initial configuration and then provide a brief tutorial on creating suppliers.

Little has changed from previous versions of SAP ERP in how we set up the organization structure in SAP S/4HANA. However, in master data there is a significant change in how vendors are set up in SAP S/4HANA Enterprise Management versus previous versions of SAP ERP. The first change is that vendors are now definitively referred to as *suppliers* in SAP S/4HANA, but not in the naming convention for *Customer/Vendor Integration* (CVI). In SAP S/4HANA, customers and vendors are now centralized into a single business partner concept. The conversion process and nuances of CVI are further explained in the next sections.

In previous versions of SAP ERP, a supplier and a customer could be the same company, but they could not share the same master data element. You had to create a supplier record and a customer record. Here, the system constraints were not reflecting the reality for many companies and government entities. A citizen today may provide the local government with services such as foster care services, submit invoices to the government, and also be a "customer" the sense that they pay their street cleaning fees or water delivery services directly of the local government. Many companies today interact both as a supplier and a customer with their business partners. A large manufacturer and an MRO distributor, for example, may buy from and sell to each other in large volumes as the manufacturer leverages the MRO distributor for plant maintenance product orders and sells to the distributor many of the items the manufacturer produces. In previous versions of SAP, both a customer and a supplier record need to be created to represent these relationships. In SAP S/4HANA Enterprise Management, only one business partner record is needed.

4.4.1 Customer/Vendor Integration

Keeping all of these data elements in sync for both the customer and the supplier falls on CVI. CVI ensures that customer and vendor master data tables, such as the core tables KN and LF, are updated automatically after a business partner is created/changed. Tables KN and LF are still populated in SAP S/4HANA as they are in SAP ERP.

Some other caveats of CVI and business partner design in SAP S/4HANA are as follows:

- The customer/vendor hierarchy remains the same as in SAP ERP.
- To create a customer or supplier record in SAP S/4HANA via an interface, the interface must call the customer/vendor creation BAPI CVI_EI_INBOUND_MAIN.
- Business partner data for retail systems such as Fashion Management System (FMS) and Customer as Consumer are not part of the conversion at this point.
- CVI is not mandatory for SAP S/4HANA Finance, on-premise.
- Mass maintenance is possible for customers and vendors via Transaction BP. Transactions XD99, XK99, and MASS are available in BP. For SAP S/4HANA 1511, implementation of SAP Note 2346269 (Mass Maintenance Functionality of Customers/Suppliers using XD99 and XK99) is required.
- DEBMAS, an IDoc used for updating customer information, and CREMAS, an IDoc used for updating supplier information, can be used in SAP S/4HANA OP 1610 and in 1511 if you implement SAP Note 2312529.
- To get nine additional customer/vendor data structures, you need to implement SAP Notes 2324208 and 2331298, then run Reports NOTE_2324208_DDIC and NOTE_2331298 to activate the DDIC structure changes. Program LSMW will need to be modified to include the input data structure.
- Custom code calls to old transactions are automatically redirected to the new versions. You don't need to change the custom code for this area. However, interfaces creating customer or vendor master data have to call CVI_EI_INBOUND_MAIN or the BusinessPartnerSUITEBulkReplicateRequest or BusinessPartnerRelationshipSUITEBulkReplicateRequest webservices rather than a previous function module (FM) and/or webservice. If you have interfaces that rely on previous FMs from ECC, the code will need to be changed to call CVI_EI_INBOUND_MAIN or the aforementioned webservice and mapping logic to new and/or custom fields may be required. To activate CVI_EI_INBOUND_MAIN, implement SAP Note 2405714 for RFC_CVI_EI_INBOUND_MAIN enhancements. You can also navigate to the Transaction BP in SAP S/4HANA by calling BUP_PARTNER_MAINTAIN from an external application.
- If you're running SAP S/4HANA alongside SAP ERP environments in your landscape, CIF interfaces to and from SAP S/4HANA for business partners are still supported, as are middleware for BP synchronization and SAP BW reporting on customers and vendors.

4.4 Supplier Master Setup and Supplier Creation

- For converting credit management data, see the IMG path **Migration to SAP S/4HANA Finance • Data Migration • Credit Management Migration**.
- For converting employees to business partners, see SAP Note 2340095 (S4TWL— Conversion of Employees to Business Partners).

4.4.2 Supplier Master Setup

Also known as the vendor master in previous versions of SAP ERP, the *supplier master* contains the core data about the supplier used to conduct transactions. The supplier master contains the following information:

- General data, such as name, address, and bank information, as shown in Figure 4.9.

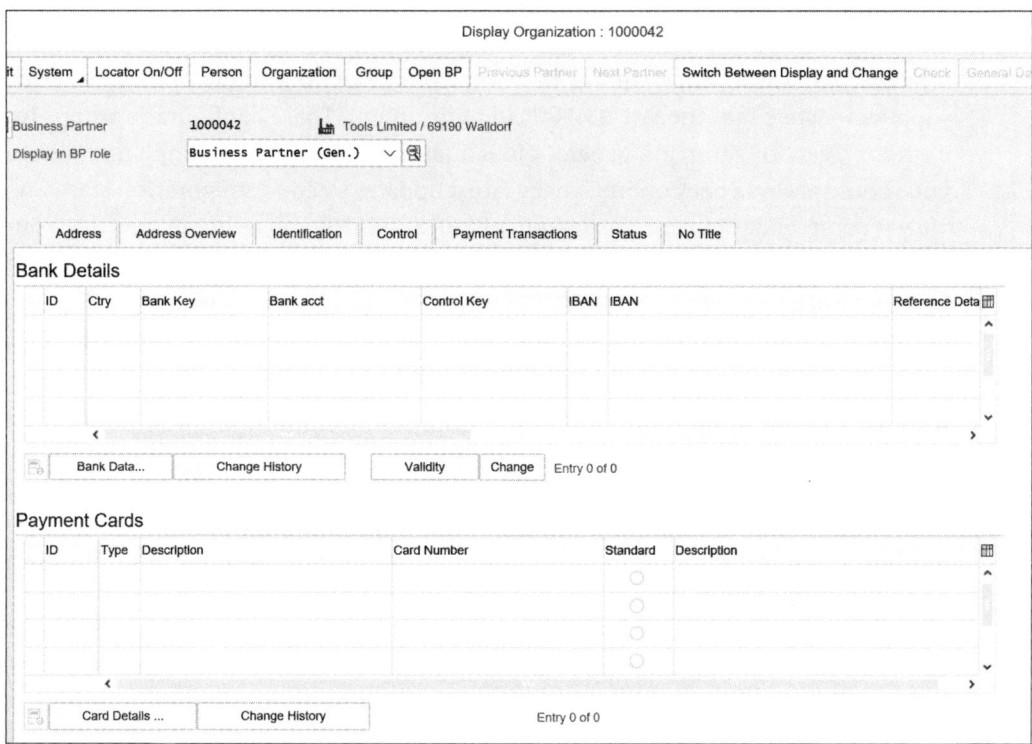

Figure 4.9 Bank Information Tab in SAP S/4HANA Transaction BP

- Purchasing data, such as the type of products supplied, the assigned purchasing organization, tax ID, incoterms/terms of payment, and several other related fields.

- Accounting data, such as reconciliation account, creditor number and payment methods. The reconciliation account number is a G/L account depicting the liabilities with regards to several vendors. The creditor number is assigned either automatically by the system or manually upon creation of the vendor master and is used as the subsidiary ledger number in financial accounting. In subledger accounting, total liabilities are calculated by vendor, rather than the process in G/L accounting, in which the liabilities are calculated for a group of vendors in that particular G/L account. The reconciliation account is derived from the vendor master record upon entry of an invoice during the payment process.

The supplier master record in SAP S/4HANA includes a customer master component now that the supplier master and customer master are unified in the BP transaction. There is some baseline configuration required to set up the supplier master in system. The business partner configuration guides and steps are updated at *service.sap.com*. These steps should be completed prior to loading and/or entering supplier masters into the SAP S/4HANA environment. These configuration steps for customer/vendor setup are general guidelines for an on-premise implementation; you should always check online for the latest updates to any configuration steps and view recommendations for the version of SAP S/4HANA you're implementing. Your project should determine customer-specific entries and steps in conjunction with Sales and Distribution stakeholders and owners in that project stream.

Substantial configuration is required for business partner setup in SAP S/4HANA, as well as the follow-on conversion scenarios for CVI. The next section outlines the business partner conversion steps in more detail, as well as the business partner set up required in each phase of the project.

4.5 Business Partner

Business partners in an SAP ERP environment, including SAP S/4HANA, are entities that transact with the SAP ERP system and your organization. Loosely defined, business partners can be suppliers who sell something to your organization, employees, and/or customers. Sometimes, an individual can represent all three categories. For example, some state and local government entities employ an individual who is maintained in the HR module of SAP ERP. This individual may sell services to the government, such as foster care services, making them a supplier in the system capable of submitting invoices or having checks cut for services rendered. Finally, this individual could be set up as a customer in the system when requesting assessment or other state government–provided services requiring a fee.

4.5.1 Business Partner Objectives

The SAP S/4HANA business partner model has the following strategic objectives:

- Share general data across different roles.
- Support different business partner categories, such as organization, person, or group.
- Allow for role versatility; one business partner can perform multiple roles, such as customer and vendor (supplier).
- Support multiple addresses for one business partner.
- Support time dependency on different subentities, such as roles, addresses, relationships, bank data, and so on.
- Support relationship flexibility, such as a supplier having a contact person.
- Provide harmonized architecture.

There were reasons for creating separate records for each of these relationships in previous versions, a principal one being that sidecar systems such as SAP SRM or SAP CRM only needed a certain type of relationship record to support their dependent transactions—a supplier record or a customer record, respectively. The SAP S/4HANA business partner approach leverages CVI to do this translation and delineation for dependent systems while synchronizing changes with the business partner in SAP S/4HANA.

Business Partner Creation Workflow

Per Figure 4.10, a business partner is created whenever a customer or supplier is created in SAP S/4HANA. The CVI contains the business partner–specific data, as well as customer and supplier data. Upon commit, the customer and/or vendor data is routed through the CVI and combined with business partner data, and the CVI link tables are maintained. Some of the vendor and customer data overlaps; for example, name and address are contained in both the customer and the vendor record and can be the same for a business partner.

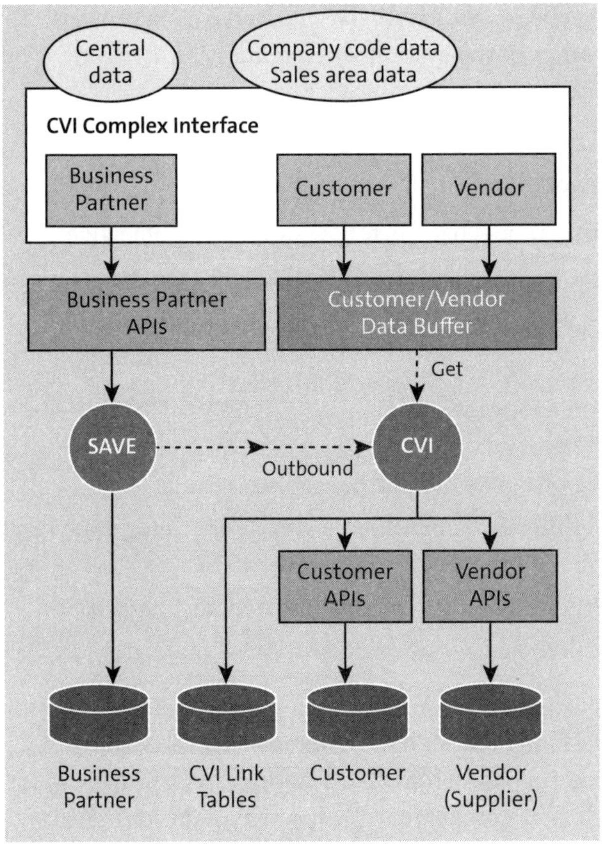

4   Master Data

Figure 4.10 Integrated Object Model: Business Partner Customer/Vendor Interface

Business Partners in SAP S/4HANA

Changing the business partner design impacts the upgrade path from SAP ERP to SAP S/4HANA. If you're looking to move suppliers and/or customers to SAP S/4HANA from a previous SAP ERP instance, you must have CVI in place to move to on-premise SAP S/4HANA. All customers, suppliers, and their contacts need to be converted to business partners. Also, whereas before in SAP ERP a user might access a supplier using Transaction XK03, this transaction—along with the others listed in the following table—no longer exist in SAP S/4HANA. In the best case, if you input a transaction code listed in the following table, you will be redirected to Transaction BP, which is the main transaction for all business partner–related transactions, including supplier and customer records:

▪ FD01	▪ FK05	▪ MK05	▪ V-06	▪ VAP1	▪ XD01	▪ XK03
▪ FD02	▪ FK06	▪ MK06	▪ V-07	▪ VAP2	▪ XD02	▪ XK05
▪ FD03	▪ MAP1	▪ MK12	▪ V-08	▪ VAP3	▪ XD03	▪ XK06
▪ FD05	▪ MAP2	▪ MK18	▪ V-09	▪ VD01	▪ XD05	▪ XK07
▪ FD06	▪ MAP3	▪ MK19	▪ V-11	▪ VD02	▪ XD06	
▪ FK01	▪ MK01	▪ V-03	▪ V+21	▪ VD03	▪ XD07	
▪ FK02	▪ MK02	▪ V-04	▪ V+22	▪ VD05	▪ XK01	
▪ FK03	▪ MK03	▪ V-05	▪ V+23	▪ VD06	▪ XK02	

Transaction BP is thus the single point of entry to create, edit, and display master data for business partners, customers, and vendors in SAP S/4HANA. The business partner number also replaces the supplier and customer numbers. This has further implications for an upgrade and/or data conversion. However, this doesn't mean that you should collapse all of the existing customer/vendor transactions in SAP ERP into Transaction BP; there is functionality in SAP ERP transactions not available in Transaction BP, and the SAP ERP help documents refer users to a variety of transactions, which could confuse users if you were to centralize on BP as a single transaction in SAP ERP.

In SAP S/4HANA, all of the previous SAP ERP transactions, reports, condition records, and forms that use the customer or vendor number as input fields require the customer or vendor number, not the BP number. Even if a new BP number has been assigned to the customer or vendor, the former customer or vendor number is required.

4.5.2 SAP S/4HANA Business Partner Implementation

The implementation process with regards to vendors and CVI is outlined in Figure 4.11. During a greenfield implementation, in which no legacy ERP system is being converted directly to SAP S/4HANA, a data conversion nonetheless would take place if you are loading supplier or customer records into SAP S/4HANA. You need to upload these supplier records via CVI if this is the case. For conversion of an existing SAP ERP environment running SAP Business Suite on SAP HANA, you need to convert the suppliers and customer records in the system to business partners first, then initiate the overall conversion to SAP S/4HANA.

4 Master Data

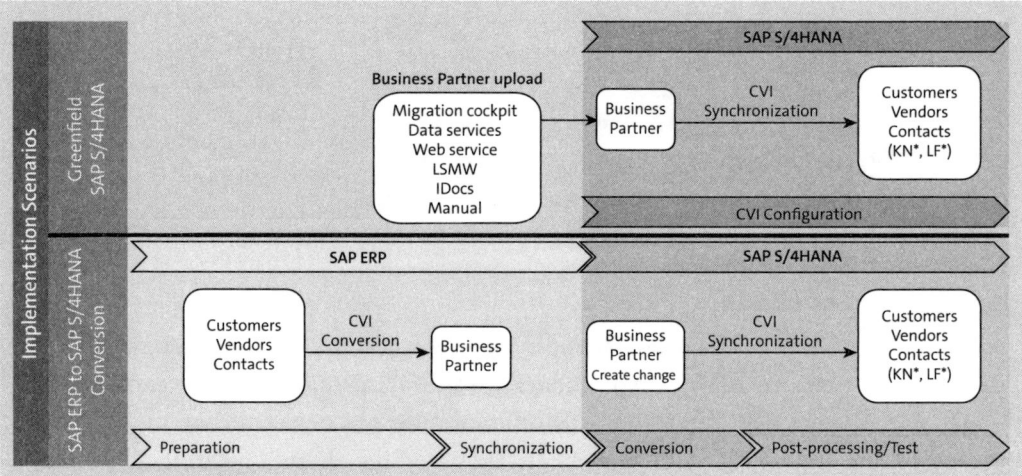

Figure 4.11 Customer/Vendor Interface: Process Scenarios

Here you verify the configuration detailed at *support.sap.com* under **Best Practice Building Block J61 for CVI Conversion** (see *https://support.sap.com/content/dam/SAAP/Sol_Pack/Library/Configuration/J61_S4HANAX_BB_ConfigGuide_EN_XX.docx*), or the corresponding version of these steps for your on-premise version of SAP S/4HANA. For SAP S/4HANA Cloud, the implementation team does not perform these steps.

4.5.3 Customer/Vendor Integration: Conversion of SAP ERP Customers and Vendors to SAP S/4HANA Business Partners

This section covers the conversion steps for SAP S/4HANA business partners. Both vendor and customer steps are included in this section. The customer record is required when initiating returns to a supplier in SAP S/4HANA. Therefore, you can't ignore the customer records in the SAP ERP environment during a conversion process to SAP S/4HANA and CVI, and some cross-business collaboration with other stakeholders on the project and in the system outside of procurement (Sales and Distribution typically owns the customer master) must take place to ensure that full master data to support certain areas, including those required for returns, is in the new SAP S/4HANA environment on go-live.

To initiate the conversion process with CVI from SAP ERP to on-premise SAP S/4HANA, there are a couple of key items to keep in mind. First, we recommend archiving the business partners (customers and vendors) marked with the **Deletion** flag. Number ranges and numbering should also remain the same in the new system, if possible, to avoid confusion and mapping exercises (note that number ranges are a nontransportable configuration item, as in previous releases of SAP ERP; you'll need to perform manual configuration in each client, including production, to set the number ranges). SAP ERP must be at version 6.0 with enhancement pack levels of 0 to 7 to begin a conversion. If you have SAP ERP 6.0 EHP 0 to 4, you'll need to apply SAP Note 2383051 if you have vendor contacts that need to be converted. For lower releases, EHP 1 to 3, you may either want to upgrade the EHP prior to conversion or create an incident message to obtain more guidance on conversion of vendor contacts.

The CVI conversion steps from SAP ERP to SAP S/4HANA and will be described in further detail ahead, beginning with the preparation phase.

CVI Preparation Phase: SAP S/4HANA Vendor/Customer Conversion to Business Partners

The first phase of a CVI conversion is *preparation*, as shown in Figure 4.12. The following tasks must be completed, many in conjunction with your technical team. As with the baseline configuration, we recommend that you check the latest conversion steps at *support.sap.com* based on the version of SAP S/4HANA to be implemented prior to proceeding with a CVI conversion.

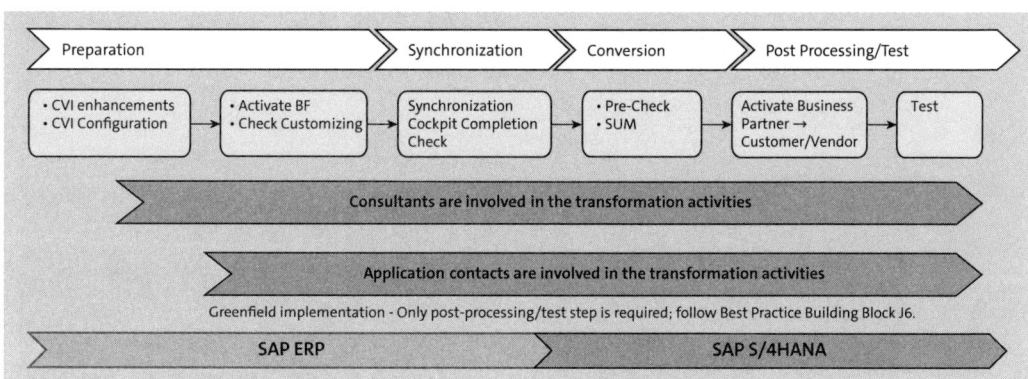

Figure 4.12 CVI Conversion for On-Premise SAP S/4HANA and Greenfield Implementations

In general, here are the steps you will follow:

1. **Check and integrate customer/vendor enhancements.** If you have any enhancements in the SAP ERP system being converted or planned in the SAP S/4HANA system, which would normally call an individual customer or vendor function

module and/or transaction, these enhancement objects will need to be rewritten for the new business partner concept and functionality.

2. Activate business function CA_BP_SOA. This is typically done by you're the technical team via Transaction SW05, as shown in Figure 4.13.

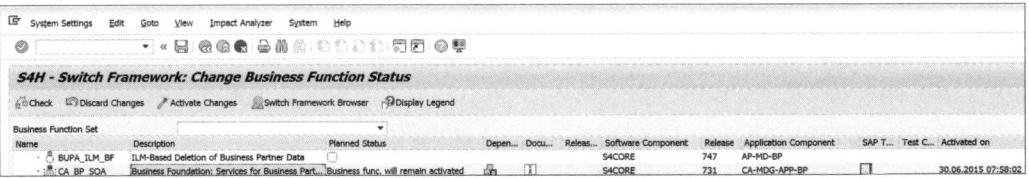

Figure 4.13 Activate CA_BP_SOA in Transaction SW05

3. Perform CVI customizing, check customizing, and trigger necessary changes as per the guides at *support.sap.com*.

4. Define number assignments according to the SAP S/4HANA conversion guide provided at *support.sap.com*.

5. Maintain BP mapping customizing and run the check report. In this step, you'll map all of the BP elements to their CVI counterparts. Follow menu path **Cross-Application Components • Master Data Synchronization • Customer • Vendor Integration • Business Partner Settings • Settings for Customer Integration • Field Assignment for Customer Integration • Assign Attributes**. After the number assignment mapping from a BP to a customer, shown in Figure 4.14, you then proceed with mapping a customer to a BP.

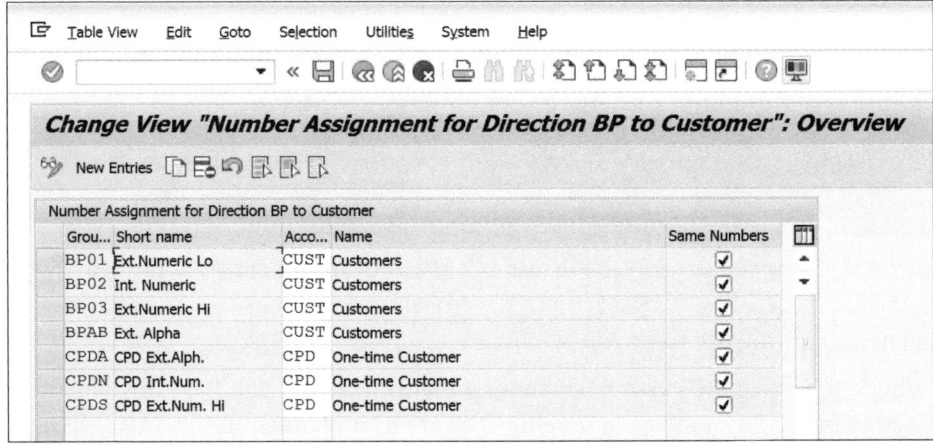

Figure 4.14 Number Assignment Direction to Customer

Finally, you map the attributes for a contact person, as shown in Figure 4.15, so that data such as legal form and legal status carry over seamlessly.

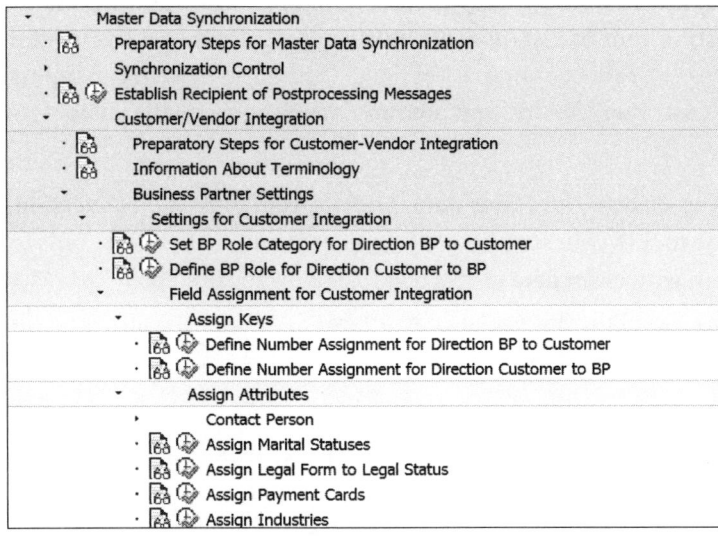

Figure 4.15 Assign Attributes Mapping for CVI to Customer

Attribute Value Mapping

Attribute value mapping must be maintained and must be equal for every existing customer instance, as in Figure 4.15. The IMG menu path is **Cross-Application Components • Master Data Synchronization • Customer/Vendor Integration • Business Partner Settings • Settings for Customer Integration • Field Assignment for Customer Integration • Assign Attributes • Contact Person •** one of the following options. For the contact person:

- Activate Assignment of Contact Persons
- Assign Department Numbers for Contact Person
- Assign Functions of Contact Person
- Assign Authority of Contact Person
- Assign VIP Indicator for Contact Person

For the customer attributes:

- Assign Marital Statuses
- Assign Legal Form to Legal Status

- **Assign Payment Cards**
- **Assign Industries**
  For this option, the industry value mapping must be maintained and should be equal for every existing vendor instance; the industry assignment for the vendor and customer shares the same configuration table. Outbound industry mapping maps the BP to the customer/vendor, and inbound mapping maps the customer/vendor to the BP.

Now, check and cleanup customer/vendor data. Prior to initiating the conversion, this is an excellent time to tidy your supplier master records and customer records to provide the new system with clean data in this regard. Follow these steps:

1. Archive vendors marked with the **Deletion** flag (optional; you can also convert these into the new system if preferred).
2. Download check reports:
   - 2216176: Pre- and postconversion check report PRECHECK_UPGRADATION_REPORT
   - 1623677: CVI customizing check report CVI_FS_CHECK_CUSTOMIZING
   - 974504: Inconsistencies in link tables of master data sync check report
   - 2399368: Excel upload option in MDS_LOAD_COCKPIT (allow for customer/vendor selection upload from Excel for BP conversion)
3. Check and integrate customer/vendor enhancement (see SAP Notes 2309153 and 1623809). The SAP Notes explain how to make customer enhancements to the customer/vendor integration (integrating additional customer/vendor fields in the business partner and using CVI synchronization to update them in the customer/vendor).
4. Activate business function CA_SUPPLIER_SOA, again using Transaction SFW5.
5. Switch to active status using Transaction SWO5 **VENDOR_SFWS_SC1** and **VENDOR_SFWS_SC2** as shown in Figure 4.16 to allow the vendor contact person data to be synchronized with the BP contact person data and ensure that they have **Global Status** set to **On**. Also, you will need to verify SAP Note 1454441 (Development of Contact Person for Vendors).

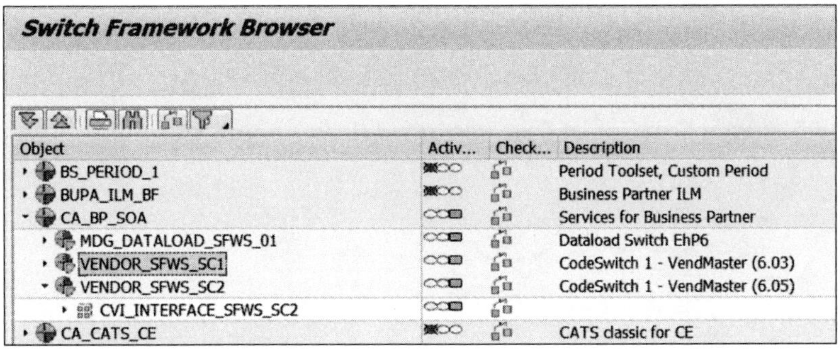

4.5 Business Partner

Figure 4.16 Vendor Sync Switches

Preparation Phase Customizing Tasks

Next, perform the customizing tasks:

1. Activate the post-processing order (PPO) request for the Business Partner synchronization object in IMG menu path **Cross-Application Components • Master Data Synchronization • Synchronization Control • Synchronization Control • Activate PPO Requests for Platform Objects in the Dialog**.

2. Activate the sync between vendor, customer, and BP under the IMG menu path **Cross-Application Components • Master Data Synchronization • Synchronization Control • Synchronization Control • Activate Synchronization Options**, as shown in Figure 4.17.

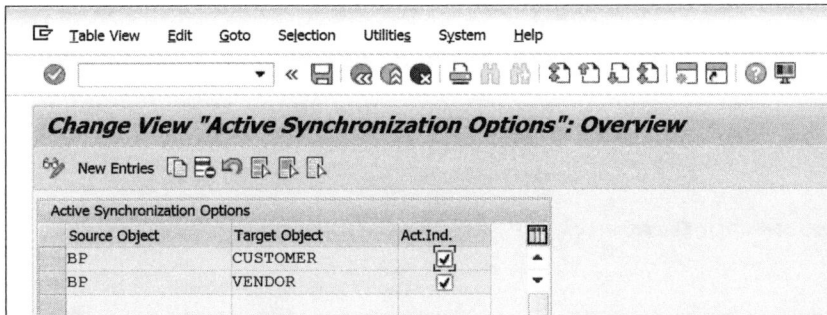

Figure 4.17 Activate Synchronization Options

3. Activate creation of postprocessing orders (PPO) for component AP-MD in IMG menu path **Cross-Application Components • General Application Functions • Postprocessing Office • Business Processes • Activate Creation of Postprocessing Orders**, as shown in Figure 4.18.

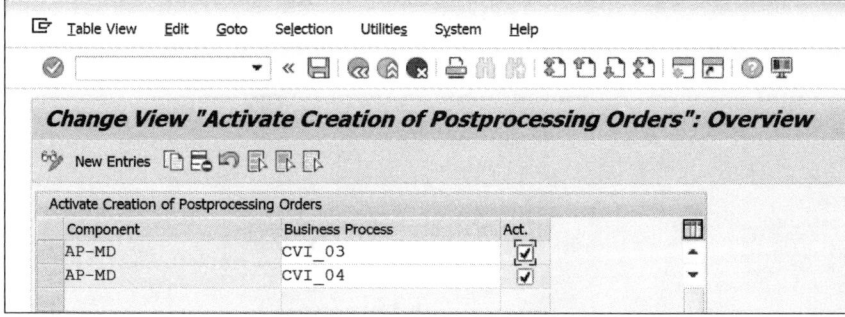

Figure 4.18 Activate Creation of Postprocessing Orders

4. Verify that the customer and vendor number ranges from the system to be converted do not overlap. If the number range settings do not overlap, they should be mirrored in the receiving system. If the number ranges do overlap, the number ranges in the receiving SAP S/4HANA system should be set so that most vendor and customer numbers can be reused.

5. If the numbers for customers and vendors should be taken into SAP S/4HANA business partner records, the number ranges in SAP S/4HANA for business partner, vendor, and customer must be set to **External** during the conversion, and then set back to **Internal** upon completion of the conversion.

The three IMG menu paths for locating the applicable number ranges are as follows:

1. Define number ranges for customer IMG menu path: **Logistics—General • Business Partner • Customers • Control • Define and Assign Customer Number Ranges** (see Figure 4.19).

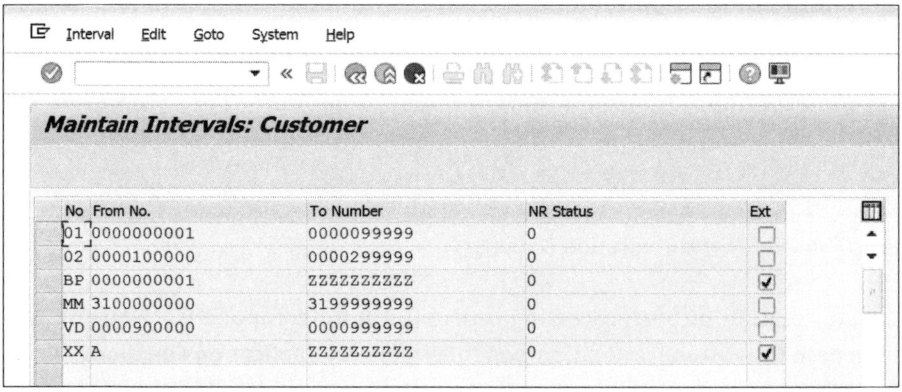

Figure 4.19 Define Customer Number Range Intervals

Once you've defined the interval, you then assign this number range to the customer records as shown in Figure 4.20.

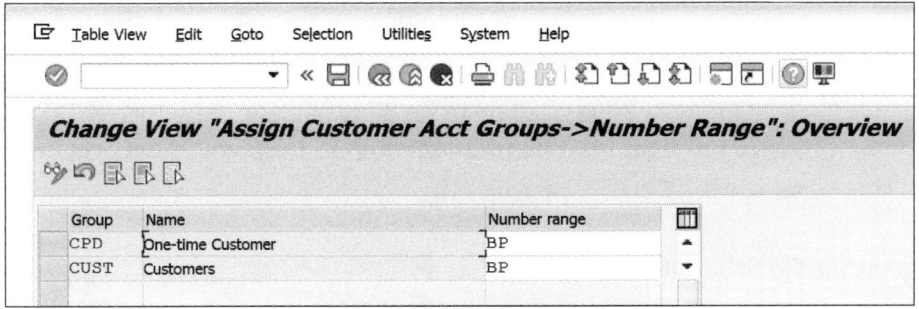

Figure 4.20 Assign Customer Account Groups to Number Range

2. Follow the same steps for vendors by defining and then assigning number ranges via the vendor IMG menu path: **Logistics—General • Business Partner • Vendor • Control • Define Number Ranges for Vendor Master Records**.
3. Define number range groupings IMG menu path: **Cross-Application Components • SAP Business Partner • Business Partner • Basic Settings • Number Ranges and Groupings • Define Number Ranges/Define Groupings and Assign Number Ranges** (see Figure 4.21).

Grouping	Short name	Description	Number range	External	Int.Std.Grping	Ext.Std Grping
BP01	Ext.Numeric Lo	External numeric numbering (lower range)	01	[x]		( )
BP02	Int. Numeric	Internal Numbering for standard use	02	[ ]	(•)	
BP03	Ext.Numeric Hi	External numeric numbering (higer range)	03	[x]		( )
BPAB	Ext. Alpha	External alpha-numeric numbering	AB	[x]		(•)
BPEE	Int.Numeric EE	Internal Numbering for Employees	EE	[ ]	( )	
CPDA	CPD Ext.Alph.	External alpha-numeric for CPD BPs	AB	[x]		( )
CPDN	CPD Int.Num.	Internal Numbering for CPD BPs	02	[ ]	( )	
CPDS	CPD Ext.Num. Hi	External num. numb. CPD (higer range)	03	[x]		( )

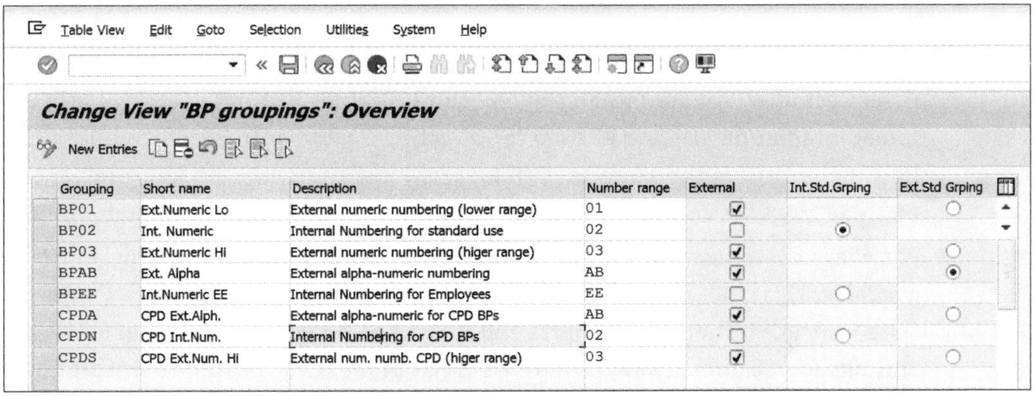

Figure 4.21 BP Groupings Overview Settings for Customer/Vendor Conversion to Business Partner

Finally, you define the contact person BP number range. This step is very important if you wish to maintain/convert contact persons successfully. The CVI conversion

Report MDS_LOAD_COCKPIT assigns an internal BP number to each contact person during conversion. The internal number range is the number range assigned to the internal standard grouping (see Figure 4.21). If the assigned internal number range conflicts with the targeted customer or vendor number ranges, the number range for the contact person will need to be changed to a new range that does not overlap with the range targeted for BP numbers. Failure to set these number ranges correctly can result in GUID error R1124: **Business Partner with GUID xxxxxxxxxxxxxxxxxxxx Does Not Exist.**

Customizing CVI Behavior with BAdIs

In the event that you need to customize the CVI behavior, there are several SAP Business Add-ins (BAdIs) provided for data assignment. Access them via IMG menu path **Cross-Application Components • Master Data Synchronization • Customer/Vendor Integration • Business Partner Settings • Business Add-Ins (BAdIs)**. For BP/customer/vendor table field extension, see SAP Note 2309153, BP_CVI: Guide for Customer Enhancements in CVI (Customer/Vendor Integration) in S4HANA Releases, as well as SAP Note 2295823, BP_CVI: Transfer of Customer/Vendor Fields to the Business Partner-Template Source Code.

Mapping is the next step in the preparation phase. The following steps need to be completed and validated prior to gating out of the preparation phase:

1. For a customer, enter BP Roles FLCU00 (company data) and FLCU01 (sales data) under IMG menu path **Cross-Application Components • Master Data Synchronization • Customer/Vendor Integration • Business Partner Settings • Settings for Customer Integration • Define BP Role for Direction Customer to BP**. For vendors, the IMG menu path is the same as path for customers, but add the following at the end: **• Settings for Vendor Integration • Define BP Role for Direction Vendor to BP**.

2. For every customer and vendor account, a business partner grouping must be available. This is set using the menu path **Cross-Application Components • Master Data Synchronization • Customer/Vendor Integration • Business Partner Settings • Settings for Customer Integration • Field Assignment for Customer Integration • Assign Keys • Define Number Assignment for Direction Customer to BP** for a customer, and the same plus **• Settings for Vendor Integration • Field Assignment for Vendor Integration • Assign Keys • Define Number Assignment for Direction Vendor to BP** for vendors.

Running Final Reports

You are now ready to run the reports prior to completing the preparation phase steps for the conversion:

1. The first report can be accessed via Transaction CVI_FS_CHECK_CUST and is used to check the customizing or by in SAP Note 1623677, BP_CVI: Check Report for Checking CVI Customizing.
As with the mapping step, this report checks the customizing in both directions: customer/vendor to BP and BP to customer/vendor. This is done in SAP S/4HANA in postprocessing or a in greenfield implementation.

2. Report FSBP_IND_SECTOR_MAPPING_CHECK is optional; it checks and creates industry mapping entries for industry assignment in the context of CVI while evaluating existing or missing assignment entries. If the number of industry values is low, this report is not required.

3. Report PRECHECK_UPGRADATION_REPORT, provided in SAP Note 2216176, is a precheck report to check if all the mappings have been completed correctly. This report can be accessed via Transaction CVI_PRECHECK_UPGRADE.

Note that the **CVI Mapping** and **Contact Person Mapping** checkboxes are checked by default in Report PRECHECK_UPGRADATION_REPORT. They are used after BP conversion to check if all customers/vendors/contact persons are converted. The report also checks whether BP roles are assigned to account groups, whether the account groups are available, and the customer/vendor value mapping.

The following SAP Notes can be used to automate the configuration steps and suppress the mandatory BP field groups check during CVI conversion. All three SAP Notes have to be applied, even if you only need part of the functions (e.g., you only need to suppress the mandatory BP field groups check during CVI conversion but don't need to use the automation feature):

1. 2336018—BP S4HANA: Suppress Mandatory BP Field Groups Checks via MDS_LOAD_COCKPIT Transaction

2. 2345087—BP_BAP: Missing Values in Required Entry Fields Cause Posting Termination in Mass Processing

3. 2344034—S/4HANA: Automation for Master Data Migration

If you want mandatory fields to throw error messages during migration, disable the mandatory field suppression feature. To disable the suppression, deactivate the implementation CVI_MIGRATION_SUPPRESS_CHK of BAdI definition CVI_CUSTOM_MAPPER.

Once all of the red light error messages have been resolved from the report and the yellow error messages are reviewed, you can proceed to the CVI synchronization phase of the conversion to SAP S/4HANA Enterprise Management.

Synchronization

Once you've completed and/or verified the preparation steps, you're ready for the *synchronization* phase, as illustrated in Figure 4.22.

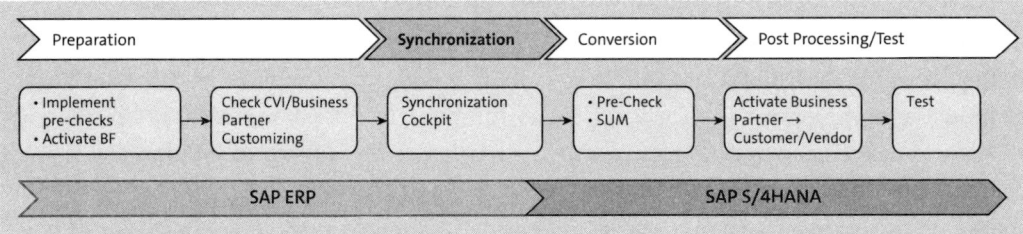

Figure 4.22 Synchronization Phase

During this phase, you will perform the following tasks:

1. Synchronize the data load according to the SAP S/4HANA Conversion Guide.
2. Review and resolve any errors due to data/customizing found in the **Monitor** tab.
3. Run PPO in the synchronization cockpit and verify the results with Report PRE-CHECK_UPGRADATION_REPORT.

To begin, run Report MDS_LOAD_COCKPIT, which creates a corresponding SAP business partner for the customer, vendor, and contact data for general data, addresses, role data, and bank details. In this report, you have the option to choose customer and/or vendor conversion to business partner or to filter by criteria such as account group and customer/vendor numbers. To expedite error analysis, we recommend running this report as a small batch initially in blocks of 10 to 50 customers/vendors.

To resolve errors, click the postprocessing object (**PPO**) icon.

The PPO displays a master data error list. You can resolve these errors within the PPO screen or outside it, but the errors must be corrected to complete the conversion of the customer/vendor and contact person. For more information on this and the synchronization cockpit, be sure to check *http://bit.ly/16410401* for the latest information and guidance.

Once you've resolved the errors, you're ready to review the conversion using the CVI_PRECHECK_UPGRADE Report PRECHECK_UPGRADATION_REPORT. Execute this report using the default selections, with the **CVI Mapping** and **Contact Person Mapping** boxes checked as shown in Figure 4.23.

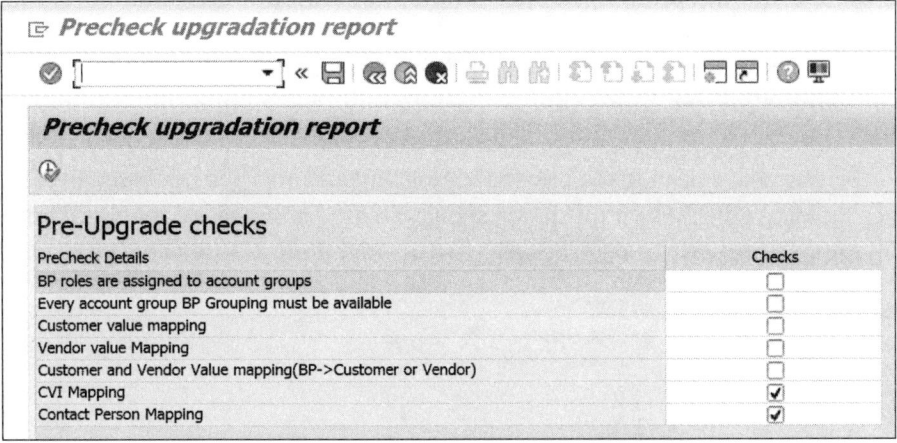

Figure 4.23 Preupgrade Checks: Default Settings

The CVI mapping checks whether all customers and vendors were mapped to a business partner, and the contact person mapping checks whether the contact persons have been converted to business partners. If you find inconsistencies, check SAP Note 974504 (Inconsistencies in Link Tables of Master Data Sync). Once you've resolved any errors, run Report MDS_LOAD_COCKPIT to complete the synchronization, then move on to the conversion phase.

Conversion Phase

The *conversion* phase (see Figure 4.24) is executed by the project's technical team as part of the overall conversion from SAP ERP to SAP S/4HANA. No CVI activities are required during this phase.

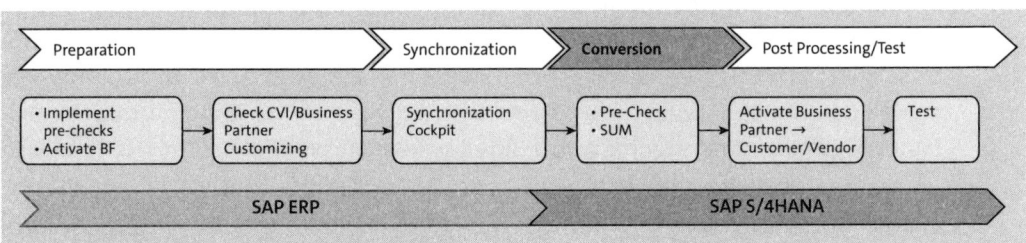

Figure 4.24 CVI Conversion Phase

4 Master Data

Postprocessing/Test Phase

Once the technical team has completed the overall upgrade, the processing/test phase is all that remains (see Figure 4.25). In this phase, you verify the configuration detailed in the Best Practice Building Block for CVI Conversion, which can be found at *support.sap.com* under **Central Configuration of Business Partners (J61)** (see *https://support.sap.com/content/dam/SAAP/Sol_Pack/Library/Configuration/J61_S4HANAX_BB_ConfigGuide_EN_XX.docx*) or the updated version hereof. Ensure that these configuration settings have been made prior to testing. If your project is not based on Best Practice Building Blocks, then this guide should be used as a general reference only. Actual configuration may be determined based on your project design considerations.

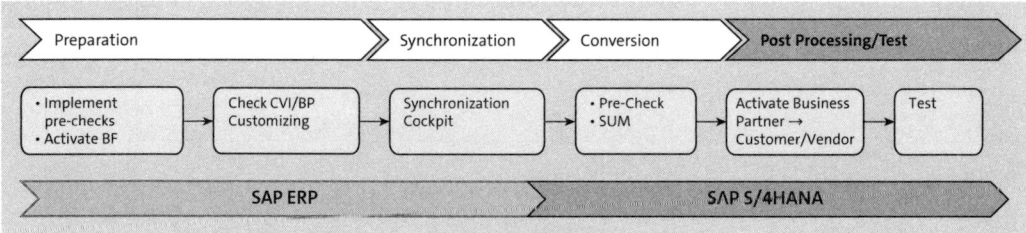

Figure 4.25 CVI Conversion: Postprocessing/Test

Once your testing is complete, you've completed the CVI conversion, which is one of the major steps in moving from SAP ERP to SAP S/4HANA Sourcing and Procurement, both from a design standpoint and in terms of conversion effort. Other master data setup/conversion, such as for material masters, isn't nearly as involved.

4.6 Summary

Master data and transactional data designs underpin and simplify system usage in SAP ERP environments when implemented in a thoughtful manner. Driving a level of granularity in the material masters that is not required for the business leads to user frustration in trying to find the appropriate material master to use in a transaction, as well additional maintenance to enact any changes to the material masters. For material groups, not designing a structured system of classification up front can lead to reporting challenges down the line as users misclassify materials and purchasing departments lack clear views into what types of items are being consumed and used in production activities.

These were all key areas in previous iterations of SAP ERP. One area that differs in SAP S/4HANA is the business partner record. SAP S/4HANA introduces a significant change to how supplier and customer masters are managed in the system. These two types of partner functions in SAP S/4HANA are unified into a business partner concept, which has ramifications for conversions and upgrades of previous versions of SAP ERP and for usage of the master record in purchasing transactions in SAP S/4HANA. The next chapter shifts focus to operational procurement and the base-level types of transactions in purchasing.

Chapter 5
Operational Procurement

Operational procurement concerns the day-to-day buying activities of a business or government entity. Much of operational procurement is unplanned or partially planned, low-value, high-volume activity. Operational procurement therefore comprises the procurement activities that keep an organization running.

Unlike in other procurement activities, which typically include a trained buyer using a tool with some degree of familiarity and training, many organizations permit any employee to create a requisition for an operational or indirect procurement item. This poses a challenge for the solution used, as the baseline training for the solution and familiarity with any process may be next to nil for the average user in operational procurement. Previous versions of SAP ERP, such as SAP ERP 6.0, supported operational procurement by leveraging existing document frameworks designed for heavy-duty buying activities between suppliers and the firm or government entity.

From the onset, this mismatch of a complex solution and simple user was sure to cause issues in operational procurement. There is nothing inherently wrong with having large amounts of detail in a **Purchase Order** or **Requisitioning** screen in a system used for heavy-duty industrial manufacturing. Often, this level of functionality is quite necessary—say, for Electronic Data Interchange (EDI) activities with a supplier or for complex items vital to the production process. Having complex, professional, buyer- and engineer-centric screens makes purchasing for the casual user a bit more cumbersome than optimal. Many of these screens can make it downright frustrating for an untrained user trying to order mundane supply items like pens and paper, as each field can issue a hard-to-understand warning message or hard-stop error, incorrect entries quickly negate the entire document's validity, and multiple tabs and steps have to be completed—all this for a simple order that costs perhaps $10 dollars. Using SAP ERP for this kind of procurement often is akin to having to use an airplane cockpit and all of its controls to steer a bicycle.

5.1 Overview

One approach to operational procurement is to take the process out of ERP systems. Cloud solutions such as SAP Ariba Buying and on-premise solutions such as SAP Supplier Relationship Management (SAP SRM) are examples of this approach. This allows a system to mask all of the complexity and the procurement options that aren't applicable to a simple transaction, distilling for the user what is necessary to find items and create orders with the fewest clicks, entries, and headaches possible. This approach, especially in cloud-based approaches, works very well for simplifying the UX and allowing even the most casual and untrained user to find what he's looking for and order it, without calls to the helpdesk or frustration. However, early in the transaction, these operational procurement systems are already dependent upon ERP, even if their UIs appear independent.

First, calls need to be made from the procurement system back to the "mothership" ERP system to find out if the user is purchasing via a correct financial object in the FI/CO system. Finance has to support a number of functions in SAP ERP, so it can't be moved into a standalone procurement solution without bringing all the other dependent modules with it or leading to an expensive, "interface spaghetti" scenario. The users themselves need to be managed in real time; terminated employees can't be allowed to continue to make purchases on behalf of a company or government entity. For this, the purchasing system requires real-time updates from the HR system or a user-management system that deactivates users throughout the landscape immediately when they leave the company or government entity.

There also is the question of efficiency and avoiding unnecessary stock to consider. What if the user is looking for an item already held and available in company or government entity warehouse? If the operational procurement system and/or buyer cannot check this prior to assigning a source of supply and issuing a PO, excess stock may be purchased instead of consuming existing stock. Excess stock causes waste, inefficiency, and, most alarmingly for a business, expense. If checking for existing stock needs to be a manual process step in a procurement system, buyers are focusing on performing manual tasks that could be automated in an integrated system, rather than strategic procurement activities that generate exponentially more savings and value for the firm or government entity. These issues pose a conundrum for operational procurement in SAP ERP: running operational procurement directly in

SAP ERP can be quite difficult for casual users and from an IT landscape perspective, but it's also the ideal place for it in many cases because all of the dependent modules and integration topics are already covered.

The main stumbling block to operational procurement in SAP ERP has always been usability and UI issues, as well as transactional volumes. An ERP system supporting operational procurement needs to be intuitive to use, minimize transaction steps while remaining flexible and capable of handling a diverse set of transactions, support catalog content, and support heavy volumes of low-dollar transactions, all while making the most of ERP's native integrations with associated modules. Incidentally, these are the driving forces behind SAP S/4HANA Sourcing and Procurement's embrace of operational procurement as a core SAP ERP process. SAP S/4HANA Sourcing and Procurement supports the operational purchaser across self-service requisitioning, requirement processing, po processing, service purchasing and entry, and purchase order collaboration. This process flow is also known as the *requisition-to-pay process*.

5.2 Requisition-to-Pay Process

Requisitions can be created directly by a user via a self-service procurement process, or from a system/business process occurring in another module in SAP ERP, such as an MRP run in which defined reorder points trigger the creation of a requisition—a bill of materials (BOM)—that requires an additional item be ordered as part of the materials list, or a project systems requirement generated from what's called a *network* in SAP Project Systems. A network in SAP Project Systems tells the user what tasks need to be performed in sequence by a certain time. Automated procurement processes typically used in the procurement of items needed in production, known as *direct procurement*, will be discussed in Chapter 6. The focus in self-service requisitioning is on user-driven requisitioning, which is more typically found in indirect procurement.

As illustrated in Figure 5.1, the requisition is the first document in the procurement chain that eventually leads to a purchase order and/or contract, as well as follow-on documents, such as order confirmations, advanced shipping notifications (ASNs), goods/service receipts (GRs), and invoices (IVs).

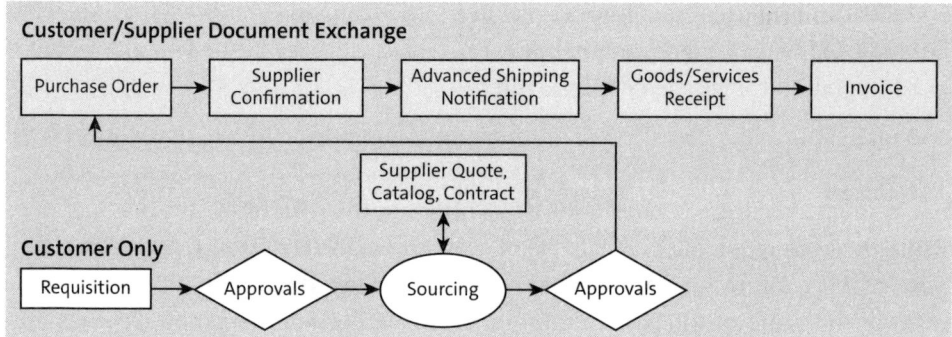

Figure 5.1 Operational Procurement: Requisition-to-Pay Process Flow

There are several item types that can be obtained as part of operational procurement, as we'll discuss in the next section.

5.3　Procurement of Stock, Consumable, and External (Service) Items

There are three main types of procurement conducted in operational procurement: stock, consumables, and external services. All of these types of procurement can be used in other procurement scenarios. Stock procurement is typically used for direct procurement activities, such as the ones discussed in the next chapter, but you can purchase and take into inventory items such as office supplies and equipment that qualify as operational indirect items as well. Consumable items are directly in the wheelhouse of operational procurement. A *consumable item* is typically an indirect item that is consumed and replenished on an ongoing basis, often by the consumers themselves. Pens, paper, coffee for the office kitchen, and other types of consumables may be ordered by the office manager or directly by an employee who notices that the office needs more of a consumable good. Consumables often do not require a goods receipt or a valuated goods receipt used primarily for inventory-management processes and valuations, as these consumable purchases are petty at an individual level. In aggregate, however, consumable purchasing can be quite significant for an organization, and a level of management in the system may thus be desirable, if not a necessity.

External services procurement is the procurement of services to be delivered by individuals or groups who are not employees of the organization, but only involved to deliver that particular scope of work. These services can support the direct side of the equation, but they can also comprise cleaning or gardening services for the grounds of the office, for example, making these external services indirect. Although an office manager may set up the purchasing documentation for external services relating to the office, a project manager may need to directly set up the purchasing framework for consultants being hired to support a project.

The defining feature for operational procurement and for stock, consumable, and external procurement is that these types of procurement do not necessarily require a trained, dedicated buyer to initiate the requisition. The demand and consequent requesting in the system may come from the employee directly. When it does, this type of procurement is squarely in the category of operational procurement, and it follows that the solution provided in system to support this activity must support its untrained and barely trained users in a way that makes self-service procurement possible and even enjoyable. This is the goal of SAP S/4HANA with self-service procurement.

5.4 Self-Service Procurement

In SAP S/4HANA Sourcing and Procurement, users can create a requisition and identify appropriate sources of supply via a consumer-grade UX; that is, a UX that users would find in their personal online shopping experiences (see Figure 5.2). Self-Service Requisitioning is completely supported with a UI built on SAP Fiori, with tiles and step simplification to enable a completely different UX from that found in traditional ERP requisitioning.

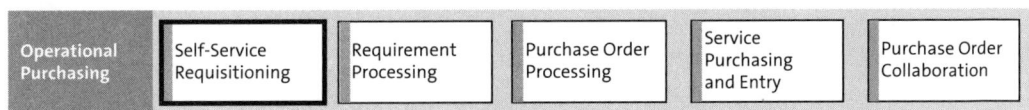

Figure 5.2 Self-Service Requisitioning in SAP S/4HANA Sourcing and Procurement

Requisitions are internal documents a corporation or government entity uses to lay claim to a service or material—essentially, a formalized request for a supply or service. Requisitions can be created with or without a source of supply and with or without a material master or service master number.

There are a number of key innovations around simplification and speed for Self-Service Procurement in SAP S/4HANA. Most importantly, one-click ordering is the predominant concept in this area, as personified in the new UI. The content search and dynamic filtering is built on SAP S/4HANA, allowing for vast performance improvements and usability over traditional ERP-based requisitioning. Catalog content is accessed like a punch-out catalog in the SAP Ariba Catalog area and/or loaded directly into SAP S/4HANA in the case of internally built catalogs. Loading and indexing catalogs in SAP S/4HANA allows for cross-catalog search directly in SAP S/4HANA.

5.4.1 Creating a Requisition or Shopping Cart in SAP S/4HANA

In Figure 5.3, the screen is simplified down to the bare essentials for creating a requisition. Either a user elects to use a catalog to find the item or, if the item isn't found in a catalog, the user can describe it. Note that the SAP Ariba Catalog solution can be embedded in this view, creating a seamless catalog experience even when the user is punching out to a catalog area.

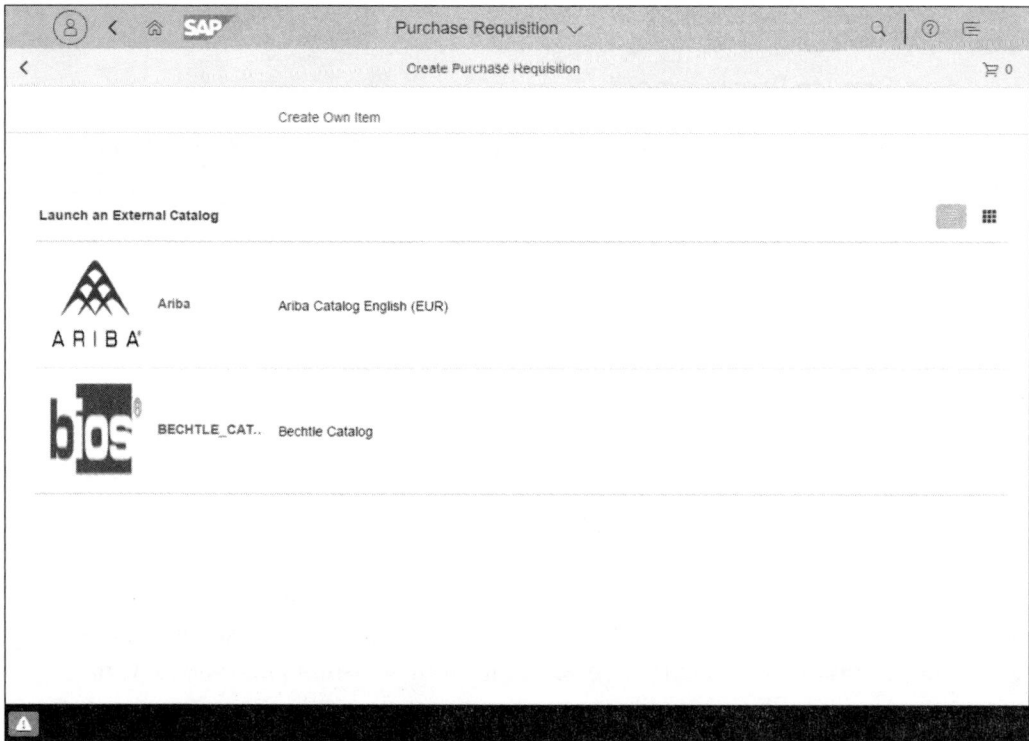

Figure 5.3 SAP S/4HANA Sourcing and Procurement: Create Requisition App

5.4 Self-Service Procurement

To create a requisition for an operational procurement item or service, a user logs into the Purchase Requisition app and types in the item in the search bar, as shown in Figure 5.4. If the desired item doesn't appear in the search results, the user can search using a different term or create a descriptive item by selecting the **Create Own Item** option (see Figure 5.4).

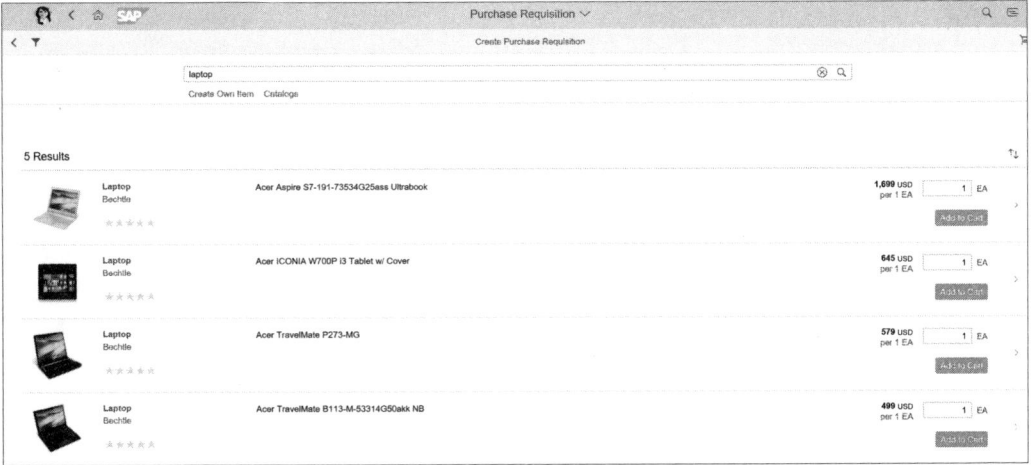

Figure 5.4 Selecting Item in Create Purchase Requisition

Once the user has selected or described an item, she is ready to order the items in the shopping cart (see Figure 5.5).

Figure 5.5 Shopping Cart Ready to Order in Purchase Requisition Create App

5 Operational Procurement

After clicking **Order**, the user receives confirmation and a requisition number (see Figure 5.6).

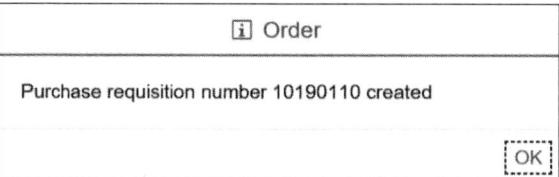

Figure 5.6 Purchase Requisition Number Created

> **Note**
>
> This requisition creation process went from a multistep, data-entry-intense process in SAP ERP to a couple of steps, with one data-entry step to define the item required and pointing to and clicking the corresponding item in the catalog—in essence achieving or exceeding parity with a consumer shopping experience online (here, the user didn't have to enter credit card information or define a shipping address).

5.4.2 Confirmation and Return Delivery

After a PO has been issued to the supplier and the goods/services have been delivered to the customer, a goods and/or services receipt often is required by the customer to process an invoice. During the goods receipt process, the customer verifies whether the correct goods/services have been delivered and whether the right quantity has been delivered, and also defines the good for inventory management if flagging, such as perishable/nonperishable, is required.

To create a goods receipt entry that can be used for a three-way match with the PO and invoice documents (see Figure 5.7), you need to reference the PO number on your goods receipt. There are two key apps in SAP S/4HANA to support goods receipts:

1. Post Goods Receipt for Purchase Order
2. Post Goods Movement

5.4 Self-Service Procurement

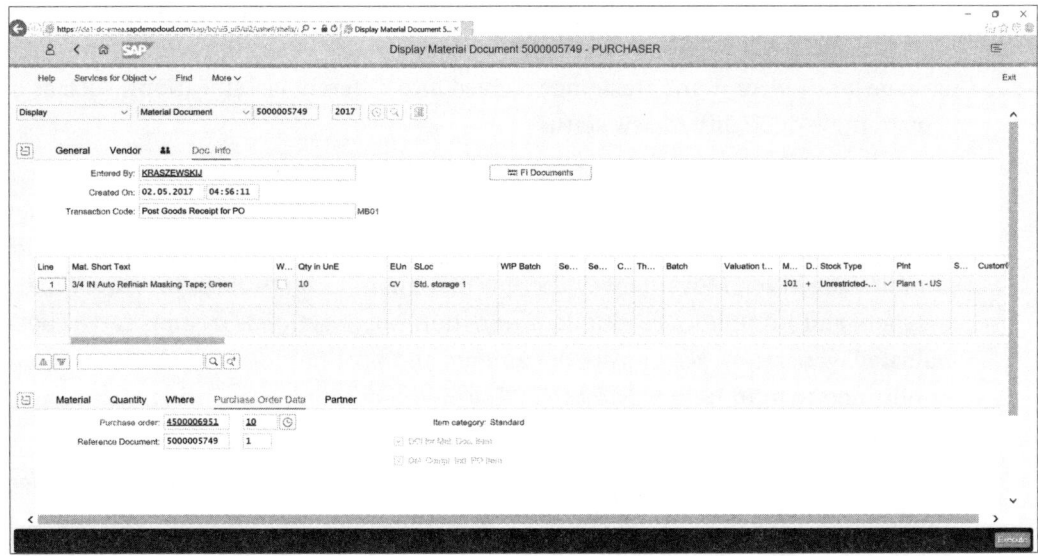

Figure 5.7 Create Goods Receipt

Goods receipts can be created in the Post Goods Receipt for Purchase Order app by searching for the PO, selecting the goods/quantity received, defining the receipt type, and then clicking **Post**, as shown in Figure 5.8.

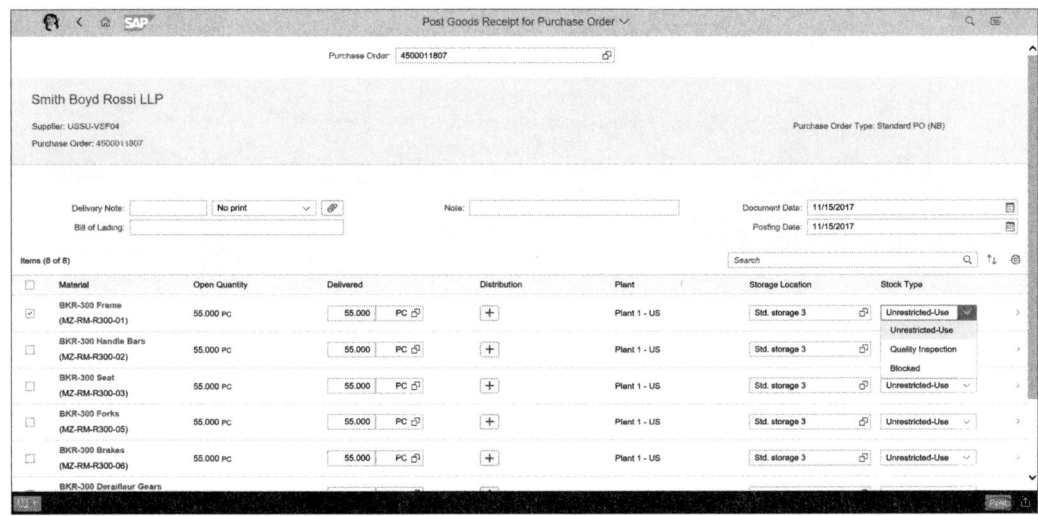

Figure 5.8 Post Goods Receipt Using SAP S/4HANA App

141

Multiple goods receipts can be entered against a single PO or even a single line item. This is typically done when items are being distributed among several plants and storage location, or items are being received into different classifications, such as in a quarantine or quality review status.

The *movement type* is a three-character key in SAP used to differentiate between goods movements, including transfer orders and issues between plants and storage locations. The most prevalent movement type is *101*, which is a basic goods receipt for purchase order. Movement types thus play an important role in inventory management and automatic account determination/posting. Goods receipts can be both valuated, generating accounting documents and postings, or nonvaluated, merely confirming that an item was received but not generating accounting documents/postings.

Valuated goods receipts are particularly relevant when purchasing assets, when depreciation runs in asset management sometimes can start the minute the good is taken into receipt. Using a valuated goods receipt approach allows for finance to realize the tax savings of depreciation in a more efficient manner, rather than waiting for the invoice posting to occur. Valuation defaults are often set at the vendor master level or for the PO type. If valuation is required—that is, if the PO is flagged for valuated goods receipt—then the goods receipt will generate an accounting document in addition to the material document (see Figure 5.9).

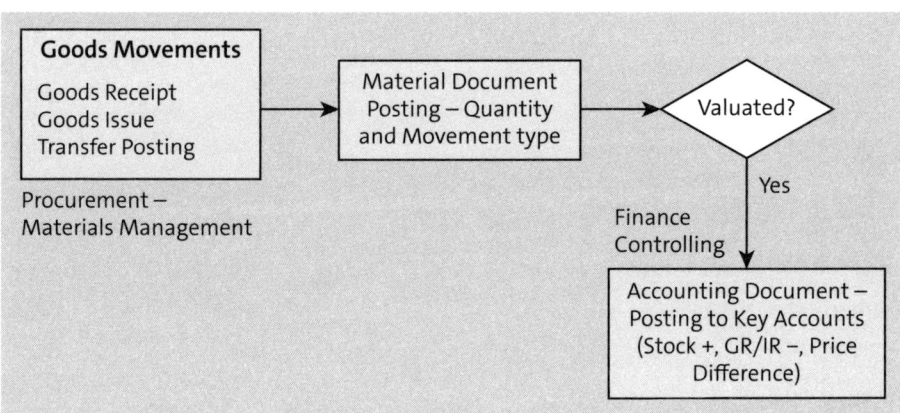

Figure 5.9 Goods Receipt: Document Postings

Creation of a goods receipt can initiate the following documents and updates in SAP ERP:

- **Update of PO and PO history**
  The goods receipt updates both the open quantities in the PO and the **PO History** tab with a **Goods Receipt Document** link.

- **Update of inventory and value**
  The goods receipt updates the stock quantities in Inventory Management areas, as well as any changes in valuation of said stock.

- **Update of stock and consumption accounts**
  The goods receipt triggers accounting updates.

- **Notification of goods receipt to the supplier**
  You can send an (optional) notification to the person ordering and/or the supplier upon goods receipt via the system.

- **Printing of a goods receipt slip**
  In some paper-oriented receiving operations, a further hard copy of the receipt is required.

- **Transfer requirement sent to warehouse management**
  If warehouse management is active, a goods receipt can also trigger a transfer request to move the newly received item into the warehouse.

- **Quality inspection**
  If the item received first needs to be inspected, prior to being placed into general availability stock, a goods receipt can trigger these activities in Quality Management (QM).

Return delivery can also be initiated directly in the Return Delivery app (see Figure 5.10). This app in particular has been enhanced as of SAP S/4HANA 1610.

Self-service requisitioning in SAP S/4HANA provides an integrated UX for requesting, reviewing, receiving, and returning. If you lose the session during the transaction, a draft of the document you were working on when you lost connectivity is created automatically and retrieved automatically upon return. This proactive connectivity extends to other parts of the process in SAP S/4HANA as well. Instead of having to click the **Refresh** button on a list or grouping, SAP S/4HANA updates these dynamically.

5 Operational Procurement

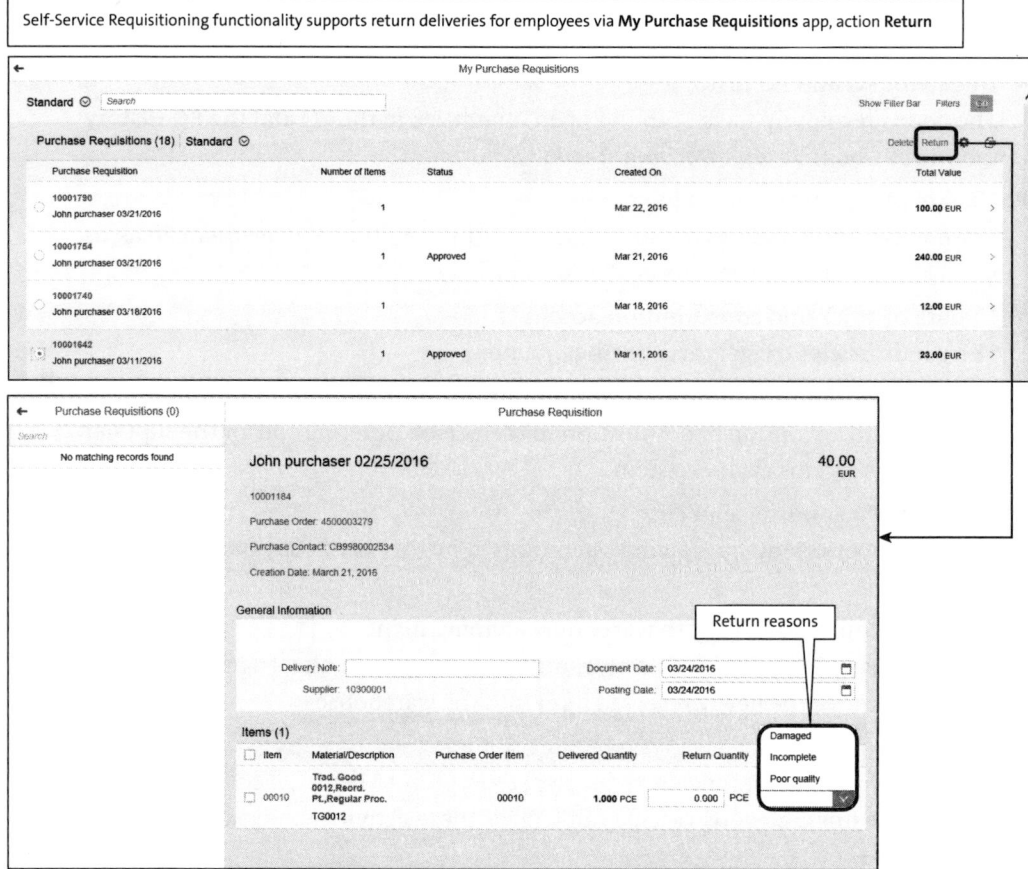

Figure 5.10 SAP S/4HANA Sourcing and Procurement Returns App: New as of 1610

5.4.3 Purchase Order Collaboration

Upon creation of a PO, the PO can be issued to a supplier via the Ariba Network and/or via EDI, email, fax, or other transmission methods supported in SAP S/4HANA. Suppliers often connect to the Ariba Network and use this as an integration layer to receive their purchase orders directly into their systems via their EDI linkage, rather than setting up a point-to-point EDI integration going out to the network to process these orders.

As mentioned in Chapter 1, PO collaboration is not something that can be done adequately in SAP ERP or even in SAP S/4HANA alone; an interaction between supplier and buyer needs to take place, and documents need to be exchanged without compromising the security of the core SAP ERP environment. Point-to-point solutions such as supplier self-services suffer from the maintenance aspects and training/change management required for the supplier base. The point-to-point model doesn't scale well, as each additional supplier represents additional calls and emails to the help desk, all of which are the onus of the buyer's organization. And yet, for a point-to-point solution to be economical, it has to scale to encompass many suppliers and high spending. This is where a network like the Ariba Network can take over the heavy lifting aspects of infrastructure, supplier onboarding, and support and allow the buyer to focus on the value-added activities within collaboration.

The Ariba Network is the main approach for true PO collaboration, as it allows the supplier to receive and work with the purchase order, confirming items or proposing changes to delivery dates and potential quantities. SAP S/4HANA provides out-of-the-box integration with the Ariba Network. The Ariba Network handles well over 1 trillion dollars in annual transactions among millions of participants. Invoicing will be covered in a later chapter, but for now, note that PO collaboration is covered with this integration to the Ariba Network, as well covered via traditional processes of document exchange such as email, fax, and EDI.

> **Note**
>
> SAP S/4HANA Cloud offers best practices for integration with the Ariba Network, which differs slightly from the on-premise standard integration and include more documents from the invoice/payment part of the process. There are also further best practice integration points with SAP Ariba Sourcing, which will be detailed further in Chapter 9.
>
> This best practice approach for SAP S/4HANA Cloud integrations also includes invoice documents from SAP Fieldglass.

5.4.4 Shopping Cart versus Requisition-to-Pay and Migrating SAP SRM Shopping Carts

Shopping carts are essentially requisitions with a more user-friendly name and, hopefully, UI. The term was first used at SAP for SAP SRM, but it's now used in SAP S/4HANA requisitions, as outlined earlier. Any requisition processes that begin to rival a commercial UX in their simplicity and usability will typically take the label *shopping cart processes*.

5.4.5 Migrating SAP SRM Shopping Carts to SAP S/4HANA

We reviewed the shopping cart/requisitioning process in SAP S/4HANA at the beginning of this chapter, but there's also a shopping cart concept in SAP SRM. Much of SAP SRM's shopping cart functionality and simplification has been replicated in SAP S/4HANA. Many SAP customers are evaluating their SAP SRM implementations during the move to SAP S/4HANA and finding this to be an opportune time to migrate from SAP SRM, given the new, streamlined functionality available in the SAP S/4HANA core and in the SAP Cloud solutions available today. This section covers the conversion process at a high level from SAP SRM shopping carts to SAP S/4HANA.

As discussed in Chapter 2, SRM functionality has been built out substantially in SAP S/4HANA Sourcing and Procurement for the self-service procurement scenario. In addition, running SAP SRM in the one-client scenario embedded with SAP S/4HANA is not an option like it was with SAP ERP. In a one-client SAP SRM scenario, your options for moving to SAP S/4HANA are to reimplement SAP SRM and connect it to SAP S/4HANA either in the classic or extended classic scenario (see Table 5.1). You can also reimplement in a standalone scenario, but this isn't typical if you already have finance running in SAP ERP.

SAP SRM Deployment Option	Classic	Extended Classic
Multiple SAP backends	Migration optional (restrictions apply)	Migration optional (restrictions apply)
Single SAP ERP backend	Migration optional	Migration optional (restrictions apply)
One client	Migration (or reimplementation on different SAP SRM scenario, such as classic) mandatory	N/A

Table 5.1 SAP SRM Deployment Scenarios and SAP S/4HANA

The other option is to use this SAP S/4HANA transition to migrate your SAP SRM users and open documents into SAP S/4HANA. SAP provides informational SAP Note 225146 for this approach.

The first step is to complete your configuration and the setup of the self-service procurement scenario in SAP S/4HANA Sourcing and Procurement (as we'll discuss in Section 5.6). Prior to shutting down your SRM environment, you would then run

Report BBP_SC_MIGRATE_TO_PR in SAP SRM. You can migrate shopping carts prior to your system conversion to SAP S/4HANA, during the conversion, or before *and* during the conversion. However, the shopping cart migration report can be run multiple times as needed, so long as SAP SRM is still up and running. This means that for a one-client SAP SRM scenario with SAP ERP, the report has to run before the conversion, because SAP SRM won't be available once the conversion begins. You can define which migration scenario you'll use during system conversion from SAP ERP/SAP SRM to SAP S/4HANA by using Report BBP_MIGRATE_SCEN in SAP SRM.

After running the report, run follow-on Report MMPUR_MIGR_EBAN in SAP S/4HANA. After this step, you can access a former SAP SRM shopping cart in SAP S/4HANA as a requisition in the self-service procurement process you have established in SAP S/4HANA and process this item further. Associated purchase orders in SAP S/4HANA also will have a linkage to the requisition created during the conversion of the shopping cart. Any PO information that wasn't transmitted to SAP ERP by the time of conversion will be unavailable in the new environment. Errors in processing shopping carts, for example, which failed to create a follow-on PO in SAP ERP, won't convert without the error being resolved first. These reports don't convert any of the SAP SRM workflows and customizations surrounding these shopping carts, and there may be manual steps to perform once the conversion is complete to process these shopping carts in SAP S/4HANA. Currently, these migration reports and approaches only apply to shopping carts. Any documents created in SAP SRM such as contracts, purchase orders, or receipts that haven't been transferred to SAP ERP at the time of conversion won't migrate automatically to SAP S/4HANA during the conversion. As with all conversions, the best approach is to close out as many open documents as possible prior to the conversion so as to convert the smallest number of open documents possible.

5.4.6 Workflow

SAP S/4HANA offers individual approval workflow apps for various procurement objects. These workflow apps rely on preconfigured release strategy procedures and business workflows. However, SAP S/4HANA also offers a generic workflow inbox that provides a holistic view across all workflow items. This inbox can be accessed in application directly or via a mobile app and filtered/sorted to prioritize workflow items. Individual workflow items can be sorted and worked on in one screen while viewing the queue (see Figure 5.11). The SAP S/4HANA workflow introduces the following improvements from previous SAP ERP versions:

5 Operational Procurement

- Execute all tasks in one screen
- Keep work items list while processing single work item
- Mobile approval possible
- Filter and sort list of work items

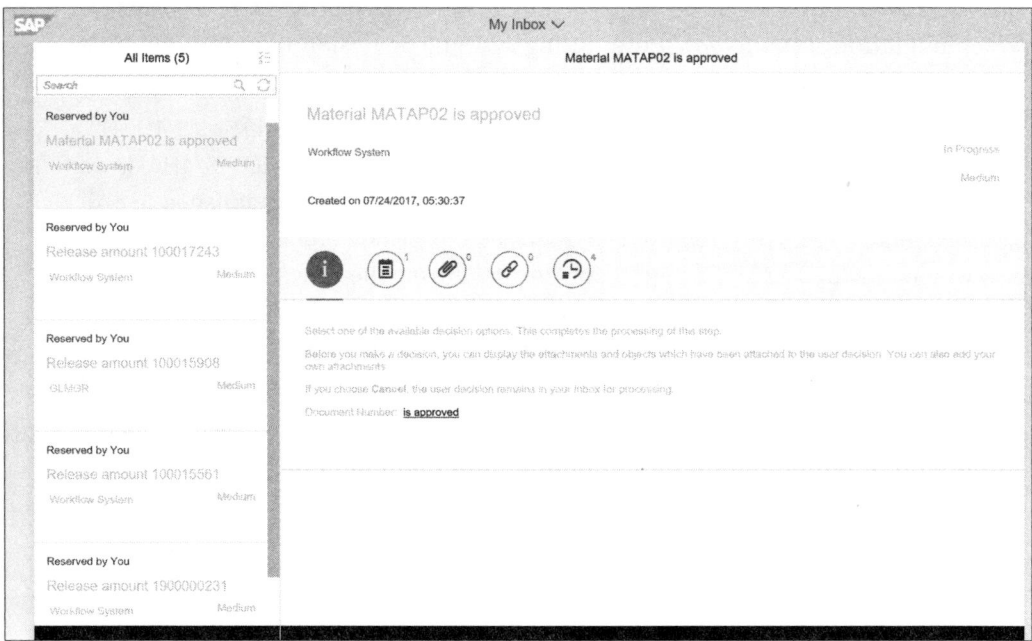

Figure 5.11 New Workflow Inbox in SAP S/4HANA

5.5 Requirement Processing in SAP S/4HANA Sourcing and Procurement

Requirements Processing (Figure 5.12) refers to the buyer activity of sorting through various requirements in need of adjustments and/or sources of supply. The main thrust in most procurement organizations is to focus requirements-processing activities on the more strategic procurement items and to automate, using intuitive designs, workflows, and catalog content to create touchless, issue-ready purchase orders.

5.5 Requirement Processing in SAP S/4HANA Sourcing and Procurement

Figure 5.12 Requirement Processing in SAP S/4HANA Sourcing and Procurement

5.5.1 Buyer-Driven and Automated Requirements Processing

Once a requisition is created, depending upon the workflow settings in the system, the requisition either is sent for approval or, if under the workflow thresholds for a given value, can be converted directly to a PO. The requisition then goes into a buyer's queue for sourcing if it contains a descriptive item or is converted to a PO directly by the buyer or automatically via a batch process if it contains only catalog items. A buyer typically takes the order from here, using one of the following SAP S/4HANA apps (see Figure 5.13) to convert the requisition to a PO:

- Automatic Creation of Purchase Orders from Requisition
- Assign and Process Purchase Requisition
- Create Purchase Order via Purchase Requisition
- Release Reminder Purchase Requisition
- Manage Purchase Requisitions—Professional

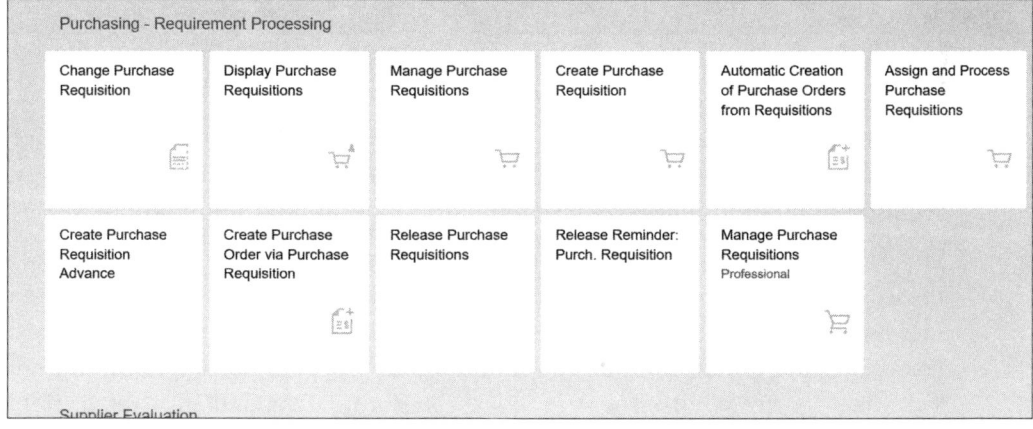

Figure 5.13 Purchasing: Requirement Processing

With the Automatic Creation of Purchase Orders from Requisitions app (see Figure 5.14), the buyer can begin converting sourced requisitions en masse to POs.

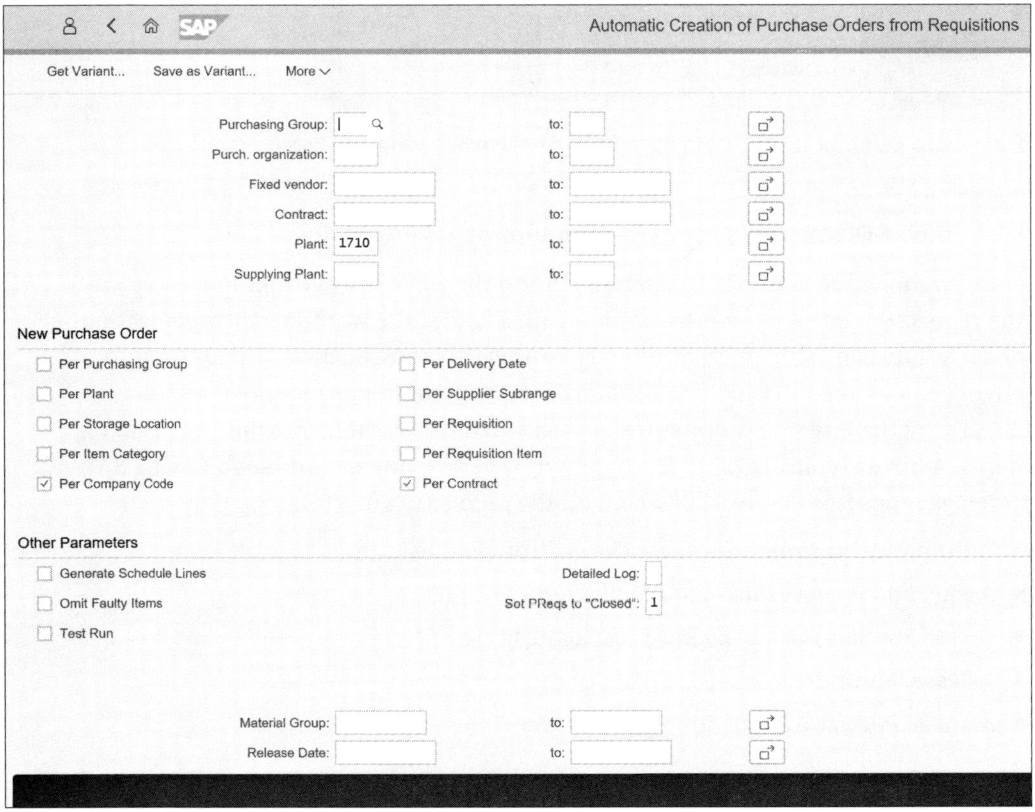

5   Operational Procurement

Figure 5.14 Automatic Creation of Purchase Orders from Requisitions

After selecting various criteria (here, **Per Company Code** and **Per Contract**), the buyer then executes the job to create purchase orders from all the available and completed requisitions matching the chosen criteria.

Traditionally in SAP ERP, a buyer has to run a search using selection criteria, review the list and manually check for sources, assign the supplier, and then move the order into a batch queue. The batch job is then run either at a set interval or manually to create an actual purchase order. The requirements processing area is streamlined in SAP S/4HANA to one screen, with prebuilt search criteria that pull in all requisitions. The options allow the buyer to dynamically change the search criteria; generate proposed sources of supply automatically based on PIRs, source lists, or contracts/agreements; and then enter direct creation of the purchase order once the source of supply has been defined—all from one screen, as shown in Figure 5.15.

5.5 Requirement Processing in SAP S/4HANA Sourcing and Procurement

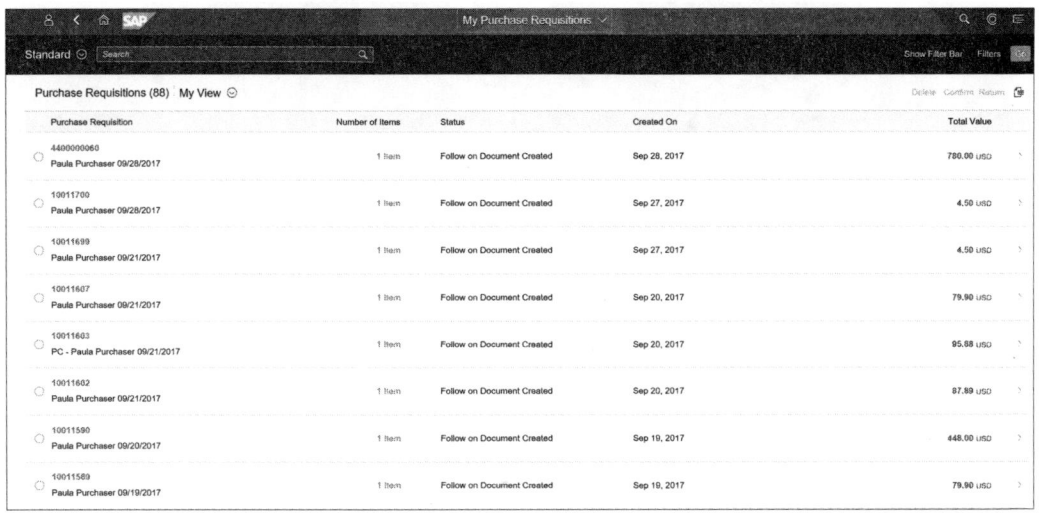

Figure 5.15 Requirements Processing Screen in SAP S/4HANA Sourcing and Procurement

5.5.2 Navigation in SAP S/4HANA Sourcing and Procurement: Requirements Processing

Requirements processing in SAP S/4HANA has the following improvements compared to previous versions of SAP ERP:

- Dynamic search and filtering and automatic proposal of search help values
- Ability to change search parameters easily in the same screen
- Automatic proposal of available info records or agreements
- Direct creation of purchase orders

If a buyer wishes to drill into any particular requisition, simply clicking a link takes you into the header of the requisition. Rather than inundating the user with a bunch of tabs and tangential information, the revised screen focuses on the essentials of item, quantity, price, material group, plant, and delivery date. If further information is required, the user can drill further into the line-item levels (see Figure 5.16). Here, **General Information**, **Quantity Date**, **Valuation**, **Account Assignment**, **Source of Supply**, **Status**, **Contact Person**, **Notes**, and **Delivery Address** links move you down the page to the applicable information area without needing to open a new tab.

5 Operational Procurement

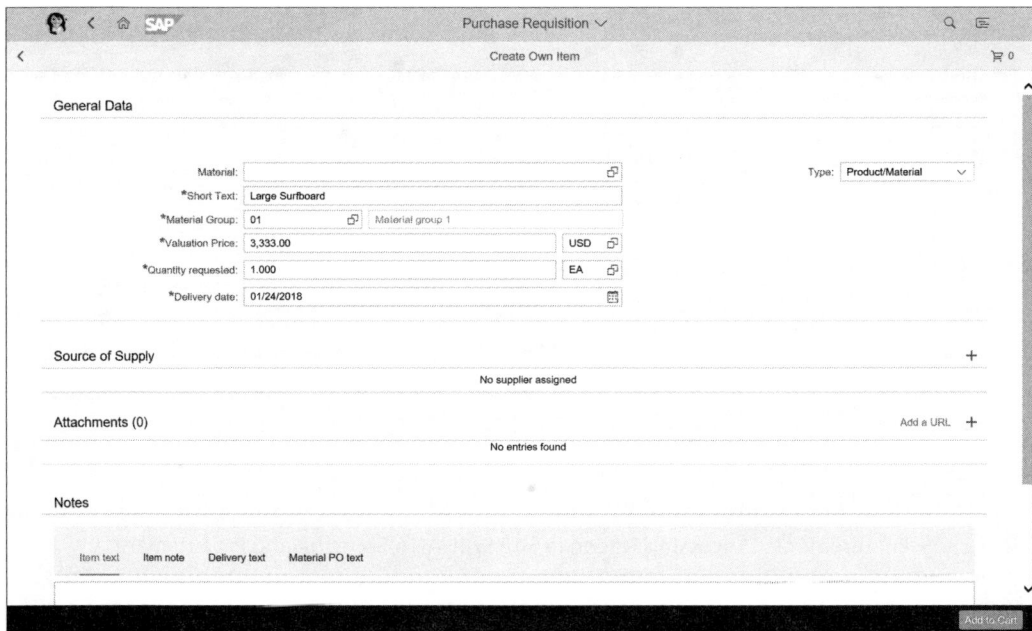

Figure 5.16 Line-Item Details in SAP S/4HANA Requisition

A buyer also has the option to create an additional purchase requisition in the Requirements Processing app. This allows a buyer to jump from the Requirements Processing app to create a new requisition, and then resume work in the Requirements Processing app seamlessly.

Next, let's discuss processing purchase orders directly in SAP S/4HANA.

5.5.3 Purchase Order Processing

Traditionally, purchase order creation and processing in SAP ERP (see Figure 5.17) involves entering numerous data points in the purchase order form, checking the document, identifying errors and further required data, tracking this missing data down, entering it and then checking again, and finally, when the document shows no further error messages, ordering. Another approach is to convert a requisition or use an existing purchase order as a template. Here too, any errors identified have to be researched and corrected prior to issuing the purchase order.

5.5 Requirement Processing in SAP S/4HANA Sourcing and Procurement

Figure 5.17 SAP S/4HANA Sourcing and Procurement Purchase Order Processing

Purchase order processing in SAP S/4HANA has been updated: there's now a centralized screen that allows for drilling down into further detail of items sequenced based on data relevance, as well as automatic population of required fields based on the materials, suppliers, and templates selected. Possible field entries are also restricted in SAP S/4HANA during the PO process. This reduces the time spent chasing down errors and entering associated data and ultimately accelerates the timeline from initiation to completion. As Figure 5.18 shows, the Create Purchase Order app in SAP S/4HANA allows the user to focus on the important and mandatory fields in the purchase order while providing tabs for the more detailed areas of the document. The top part of the screen provides the PO header information, the middle shows the items, and the bottom shows the item details.

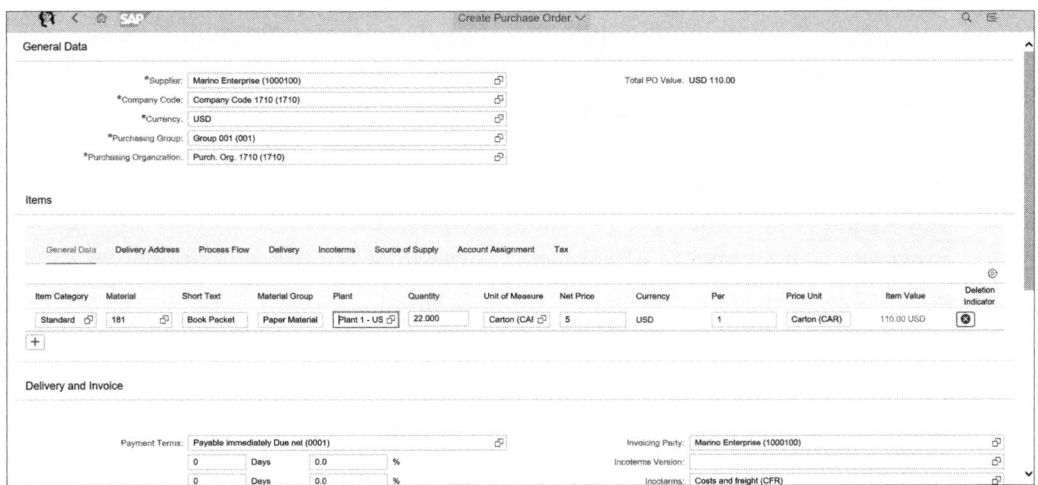

Figure 5.18 Purchase Order Header in SAP S/4HANA Sourcing and Procurement

Additional filter criteria have been added in **My Purchasing Document Items**, allowing for specifying **Purchasing Organization**, **Document Type**, **Item Category**, **Account Assignment Category**, **Delivery Date**, **Material**, **Short Text** (item), and **Supplier** name, as shown in Figure 5.19.

5   Operational Procurement

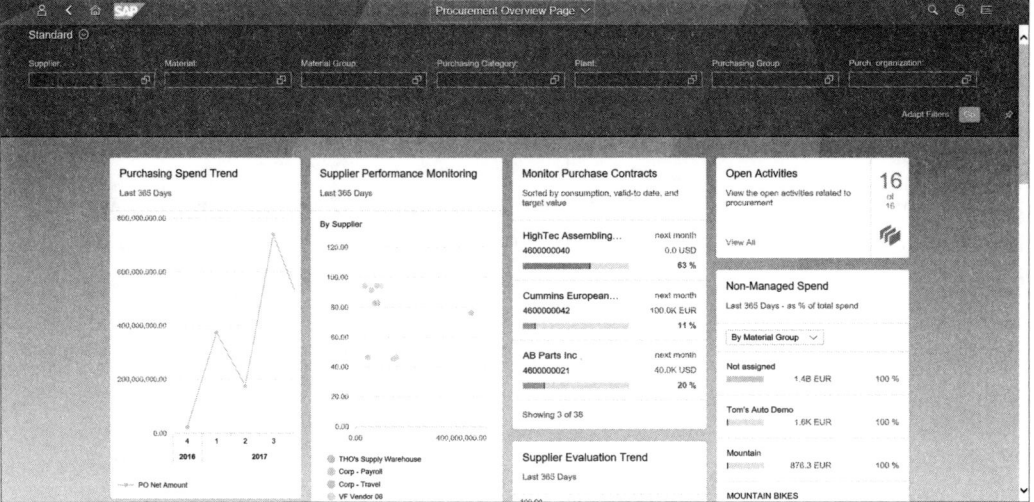

Figure 5.19 New Filter Criteria in My Purchasing Document Items

Other feature updates to the PO processing area of SAP S/4HANA Sourcing and Procurement include incoterms, short text change options, and attachments. *Incoterms* refers to payment, delivery, and other terms that define when the obligation and risk shift from supplier to customer during the transfer of goods/services. Incoterm specifications are now available at both the header and the item level. This means that if one item in a purchase order should require different incoterms than the rest, you can set this at the item level. You can also change the short text on a PO, which was previously not an option. Attachments to an SAP S/4HANA purchase order can be accessed from all of the purchase order apps in SAP S/4HANA Sourcing and Procurement.

5.6   Configuration for Self-Service Procurement

This section outlines general configuration steps required to set up self-service operational procurement processes in SAP S/4HANA Sourcing and Procurement. As discussed early in this chapter, self-service procurement can be used for stock items, consumables, and or external services. For stock items and services, this same baseline configuration for self-service procurement can support these scenarios to a degree. Stock items also require a material master, which is discussed in more detail in Chapter 4 and Chapter 6.

5.6.1 Configuration Steps: Self-Service Procurement Baseline

As with all configuration guides, this section is to be used as a reference to support your particular requirements and project. Prior to beginning configuration, you should always ensure you have researched the latest configuration and version-level guidance online and verified that you have met the requirements to begin configuration. Also, note that traditional workflow, report, interface, conversion, enhancement, and form (WRICEF) objects are beyond the scope of this configuration section and book in general; these are project-specific and typically require some development to realize. For the baseline configuration of the self-service procurement scenario, the steps are as follows in SAP S/4HANA:

1. Create employee data. For a user to access the appropriate areas of the organization structure and system functionality for self-service procurement, you must first create an employee record and assign it in the organization structure.

   In SAP Human Capital Management (SAP HCM), an employee record is comprised of *infotypes*, information units used to store specific employee master data. To create an employee, use Transaction PA30. For procurement activities, Infotypes 0001 (organizational assignment) and 0105 (system user name and communication information, such as email and address) are mandatory.

2. Create an assignment (position) for the employee in the organization structure via Transaction PPOMA.

3. Assign a business partner to the position. BP BUP003 is the employee business partner role.

4. Maintain attributes mandatory for procurement activities as per Table 5.2.

Mandatory Attributes	Default Value
Document Type: Document types can be configured in customizing under IMG menu path **Materials Management • Purchasing • Purchase Requisition • Define Document Types**	BSART
Company Code	BURKS

Table 5.2 Mandatory Procurement Activity Attributes

5   Operational Procurement

Mandatory Attributes	Default Value
Cost Center	COSTCENTER
Catalog: This allows the employee to access predefined catalogs	CATALOG
Purchasing Organization	EKORG
Purchasing Group	RESPPGRP
Account Assignment Category: Asset, Cost Center, Sales Order, Order and Network are supported	KNTTP
Material Group	MATKL
Currency	WAERS
Plant	WERKS

Table 5.2 Mandatory Procurement Activity Attributes (Cont.)

5.6.2   Configure Catalogs (Optional)

To set up a catalog, you need to configure the web service in order to access the catalog. To create a catalog link (web service), go to **Materials Management • Purchasing • Environment Data • Web Services: ID and Description**. For typical web service configuration values, see Table 5.3.

Sequence Number	Name of Parameter for Web Service	Value of Parameter for Web Service
10		https://s1.ariba.com/Buyer/Main/ad/contentPunchin/OCIPunchinDirectAction
20	PunchinId	NAME/USER ID
30	PunchinPassword	PASSWORD
40	Realm	APCProduction-T
50	Full Name	S4 HANA Catalog

Table 5.3 Web Service Configuration Values

Sequence Number	Name of Parameter for Web Service	Value of Parameter for Web Service
50	UniqueName	S4HANA
	EmailAddress	EMAIL ADDRESS
60	DefaultCurrency	USD
70	UserLocate	US
80	ModifyURL	FALSE
90	User.Address.UniqueN	OCI_DEFAULT
100	Hook_URL	Return URL

Table 5.3 Web Service Configuration Values (Cont.)

SAP S/4HANA requires a *hook URL* to be maintained with the type set as `Return URL`. If you wish to keep some parameters secure from catalog vendors, you can leverage the `MMPUR_OCI_PARAMETERS` BAdI.

5.6.3 Cross-Catalog Search (Optional)

SAP S/4HANA now allows for cross-catalog search in the **Search** bar of the Create Requisitions app without going into each individual catalog. If you plan to use this functionality, there are some setup steps required.

As prerequisites, verify that catalog data is available in OCI 5.0 format and that your catalog suppliers can provide this as a JSON file or through HTTP service. Catalogs and their corresponding webservice IDs, as well as content management services (CMSs; for loading images and attachments), must be set up and configured in the system.

To set up cross-catalog search, complete the following steps:

1. Replicate catalog data and any required material master data to Materials Management staging tables.
2. Index the data for cross-catalog search.
3. Define number ranges for catalog items by entering "01" as the catalog item number range. Follow IMG menu path **Materials Management • Purchasing • Purchase Requisition • Self Service Procurement • Define Number Ranges for Catalog Items**.

4. Enter a number range for search items. Follow IMG menu path **Materials Management • Purchasing • Purchase Requisition • Self Service Procurement • Define Number Ranges for Search Items**. Enter "01" as the attachment key number range for MMPUR_ATT.

5. Maintain a common **Currency** to enable a price filter on items. Follow IMG menu path **Materials Management • Purchasing • Purchase Requisition • Self Service Procurement • Define Settings for Cross Catalog Search** as per Figure 5.20.

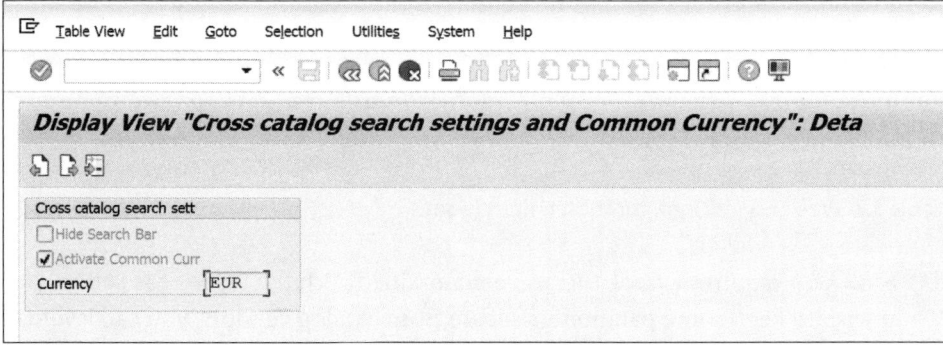

Figure 5.20 Cross-Catalog Search Settings and Common Currency

Note that after the data is extracted, if you change this setting to another common currency, you'll need to reindex and run Program MM_PUR_CTLG_EXT_COM_CUR_UPD.

6. If you've enabled catalogs using OCI 4.0, you'll have to activate the ICF service OCI_CATALOG using Transaction. To do so, first select menu option **Service • Host**, then select **Activate Service**. Second, ensure that every node path is set to active in /SAP/BC/REST/SAP/OCI_CATALOG. For more information, check SAP Note 2376996.

7. Maintain additional attributes for catalogs. You can control whether a catalog is visible and whether it is used for OCI 5.0 extraction by following IMG menu path **Materials Management • Purchasing • Purchase Requisition • Self Service Procurement • Define Additional Attributes for Product Catalog Categories**. Enter a web service and maintain the attributes. Select the **Don't Show** checkbox if you don't wish to display the catalog. Select the **OCI Extraction** checkbox if you want to import data from this catalog using the catalog data import (see Figure 5.21).

5.6 Configuration for Self-Service Procurement

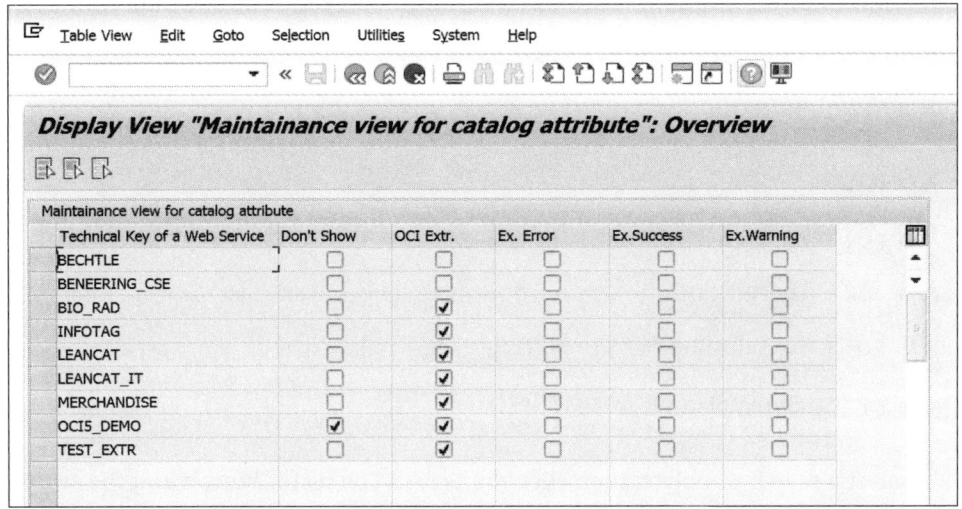

Figure 5.21 Maintaining Catalog Attributes for Display and OCI Extraction

8. Indexing and embedded search configuration is typically conducted by a technical resource with SAP Basis–level access to the system. Embedded search in SAP S/4HANA Sourcing and Procurement leverages SAP NetWeaver Enterprise Search, a search solution providing unified and secure real-time access to enterprise data and data from within and outside of an organization. SAP NetWeaver Enterprise Search returns data from SAP systems and other search providers and allows direct access to the associated applications and actions. Embedded search is the Enterprise Search component for SAP NetWeaver Application Server (AS) ABAP and serves as the search platform using the SAP HANA engine, connecting via RFC destinations, URLs, and/or repository addresses to outside search providers and data sources. Refer to SAP Note 1164979 and *help.sap.com* for configuration guidelines. For self-service requisitioning, SAP NetWeaver Enterprise Search includes business templates and indexes via search object connectors to enable search and access of both supplier catalogs and material master data from MM.

9. For search templates, the SAP S/4HANA administrator needs to create one search template for each business connector, which then delivers the result data in a predefined form as per the attributes in the template. These templates are not delivered by default in an SAP S/4HANA environment and require activation on the admin's part. You can mass-activate search templates using Transaction ESH_COCKPIT. To do so, select **Switch to Modeler** and go to the software component MM-PUR-REQ. Under this component you will find the templates listed in Table 5.4.

Search Template	Description
MM_PUR_CTLG_SRH	Search Results Model (Catalog Item Data)
MM_PUR_CTLG_ATTCH	Images and Attachments
MM_PUR_CTLG_ATTRB	Attributes
MM_PUR_CTLG_CUST_FLD	Customer Fields
MM_PUR_CTLG_PRC_CON	Converted Price Data (Prices in different exchange rates)
MM_PUR_CTLG_SRCHTRM	Search Terms

Table 5.4 Search Templates in MM-PUR-REQ

10. Select a search template, then click the **Create Connector** button and the search object connector will be created.

5.6.4 Importing Catalog Data and Images

Cross-catalog search is enabled in SAP S/4HANA by importing and syndicating data from catalog items and material masters into a single repository of SAP S/4HANA tables for search, indexing the data, and then leveraging embedded search APIs to drive the item-search queries. For more information on the tables, see package VDM_MM_PUR_CATALOG. As shown in Table 5.5, key tables include:

Table	Description
MMPUR_CAT_ITM	Main data for catalog items
MMPUR_CAT_PRCONV	Price converted to common currency
MMPUR_CAT_LNGTXT	Long text
MMPUR_CAT_DSCTXT	Description
MMPUR_CAT_PRCSCL	Price scales
MMPUR_CAT_ITM_SRH	Search items description
MMPUR_CAT_MGPTXT	Material group text
MMPUR_CAT_ATMAIN	Attachments main

Table 5.5 MMPUR_CAT Tables

Table	Description
MMPUR_CAT_ATTCHM	Attachments
MMPUR_CAT_ATTHMB	Thumbnail attachment
MMPUR_CAT_ATHTXT	Attachment text
MMPUR_CAT_ATTRB	Attributes for catalog items

Table 5.5 MMPUR_CAT Tables (Cont.)

Figure 5.22 shows the steps involved in preparing data for cross-catalog search.

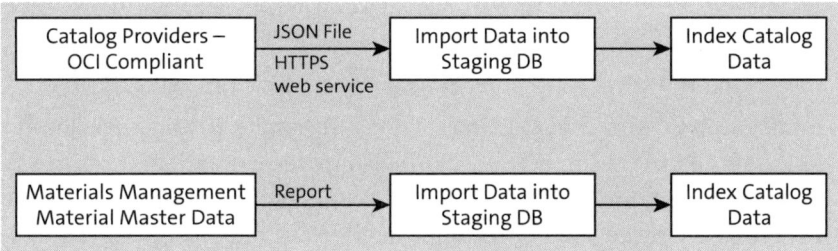

Figure 5.22 Preparation for Cross-Catalog Search in SAP S/4HANA

Open catalog interface-compliant (OCI) data maintained by catalog providers can be imported as a JSON file or HTTPS webservice, while MM material master data can be extracted using reports. Starting with OCI 5.0, multiple customer fields are supported for import. You can maintain the customer fields in INCLUDE structure MMPUR_CA_INCL_CAT_ITM of table MMPUR_CAT_ITM.

The CMS must be configured to extract and store images in an SAP S/4HANA catalog scenario. This is cross-client configuration and requires appropriate authorization. The content management repository is MMPUR_CAT_CONTENT and the contents are maintained in table MMPUR_CAT_CNTNT. Following these steps to maintain a physical storage path and the HTTPS requirement for loading images:

1. Follow IMG menu path **SAP NetWeaver • Knowledge Management • Settings in Knowledge Warehouse System • Content Management Service • Define Content Repositories**.
2. In the **Content Repository** field, select **MMPUR_CAT_CONTENT** and click **Edit**.

3. In the **Phys. Path** field, enter the physical path determined for storing the files in your system landscape, and select the HTTPS requirement in the fields for both the frontend and backend.

4. The ABAP server or other servers hosting images need to be configured in the web dispatcher. The system administrator needs to configure the system in such a way that any URL containing the term *imageloader* should be redirected to where the images are loaded. For importing OCI 5.0–compliant catalogs via JSOM or a report/webservice approach, you must have the MMPUR_CAT_CONTENT_MGMT role assigned.

5.6.5 Import JSON File

To import a file via JSON, follow these steps:

1. Enter Transaction MMPUR_CAT_EXT. A catalog importer screen will appear.
2. Add the catalog web service ID or existing catalog web service ID and select **Import Action Applicable File**. In the **Import File/URL** field, provide the path of the file to be imported. Select the **Import Image** checkbox if images are to be imported. In the **Image Folder** field, enter the path for the folder containing images. Click the **Schedule Job** button.
3. Define the start time for the load to begin, and execute.

5.6.6 Import Catalog via Web Service

To import a catalog via web service, follow these steps:

1. Enter Transaction MMPUR_CAT_EXT. A catalog importer screen will appear.
2. Add the catalog web service ID or existing catalog web service ID and select **Import Action Applicable HTTP/HTTPS**. Provide the **URL**, **User Name**, and **Password** to be imported. You can also provide a transaction ID and requested page, if you would like to resume a stalled transaction.
3. Select the **Import Image** checkbox if you want to import images, and provide the folder path to the folder containing the images. If using a proxy server, the MMPUR_CAT_PROXY_INFO BAdI needs to be implemented.
4. Click the **Schedule Job** button. Define the start time for the load to begin, and execute.
5. Select the **Reschedule Delta** indicator for activating a delta import. The indicators are described further in Table 5.6.

5.6 Configuration for Self-Service Procurement

Importing Type	Value of Indicator	Remarks
Full or initial load	**Reschedule Delta**: OFF	Use when you're importing data into a catalog the first time. All catalog items are added to tables.
Delta load	**Reschedule Delta**: ON	Use when you want to change data or add additional items to an already imported catalog.

Table 5.6 Reschedule Delta Indicators

6. Table 5.7 contains some user-exit BAdI options to support meeting requirements outside of the standard content-management capabilities in SAP S/4HANA.

SAP S/4HANA BAdI (Enhancement)	Description
MMPUR_CATALOG_ENRICH_DATA	The ENRICH_ITEM_DATA enhancement spot provides access to catalog item data, search terms, attributes, price scales, images, and customer fields.
MM_PUR_CTLG_BDI_SRH	Influence search behavior using this BAdI. Standard search behavior searches more relevant columns first and then organizes these in the results.
MMPUR_CATALOG_ENRICH_DATA	The MMPUR_CATALOG_TRANSFER enhancement spot allows items selected in a catalog to be enriched when transferring to the user's requisition in SAP S/4HANA Sourcing and Procurement.
MMPUR_CAT_PROXY_INFO	You can use the MM_PUR_CAT_PROXY_INFO enhancement spot to specify proxy server settings to access the Internet.
MMPUR_CAT_CLL_ENRICH	You can use the MMPUR_CAT_CLL_ENRICH enhancement spot to transfer additional parameters to a webservice, such as a product catalog or a vendor list.
BD_MMPUR_REQ_APPR_PRV	You can use the ES_MMPUR_REQ_APPR_PRV enhancement spot to modify the approver data, such as displaying the approver name on the user interface of the My Purchase Requisition app.

Table 5.7 Available BAdIs for Influencing Purchasing in SAP S/4HANA Sourcing and Procurement

5.7 Integration with Cloud Applications

Let's explore several integration scenarios with cloud applications. First, we'll examine service purchasing and entry with SAP S/4HANA and SAP Fieldglass. Next, SAP S/4HANA Cloud services procurement integration. Then, integration with the Ariba Network for PO/invoice automation with SAP S/4HANA and SAP S/4HANA Cloud. Finally, we'll examine SAP SuccessFactors Employee Central integrations.

5.7.1 Service Purchasing and Entry with SAP S/4HANA and SAP Fieldglass

Service purchasing in Figure 5.23 doesn't refer solely to SAP S/4HANA Sourcing and Procurement functionality in this process. Although the user still has services procurement capabilities similar to those used when purchasing a material in SAP S/4HANA Sourcing and Procurement, there is also SAP Fieldglass integration. SAP Fieldglass is a cloud-based vendor-management system (VMS) used to manage services procurement and external workforce programs. For external service procurement and services supplier management, SAP Fieldglass invoices are integrated as of SAP S/4HANA 1610, and further integration is planned in later releases of SAP S/4HANA.

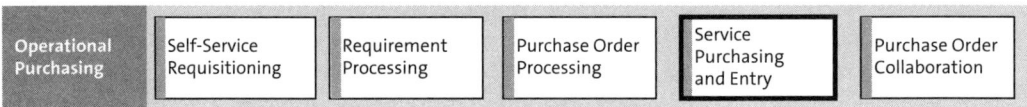

Figure 5.23 Service Purchasing and Entry

As of SAP S/4HANA 1709, further improvements to the service procurement capabilities within the SAP S/4HANA core include simplified service procurement, with SAP Fiori apps for Service Entry Sheet and Service Confirmation (see Figure 5.24).

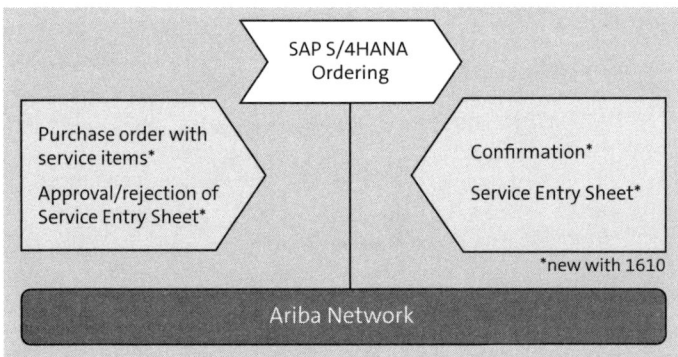

Figure 5.24 Ariba Network Integration with SAP S/4HANA Sourcing and Procurement: Services

5.7.2 SAP S/4HANA Cloud: Services Procurement Integration

SAP S/4HANA Cloud is a natural integration candidate for SAP Fieldglass. As shown in Figure 5.25, SAP S/4HANA Cloud leverages best practices integration approaches to integrate and extend SAP S/4HANA Cloud with the Ariba Network and SAP Fieldglass, primarily on the invoicing side for SAP Fieldglass for now and the significant documents in a P2P process for the Ariba Network (PO, confirmation, ship notice, goods receipt, and invoice). Future releases of SAP S/4HANA and SAP S/4HANA Cloud are expected to build on the standard integration of document types for SAP Fieldglass.

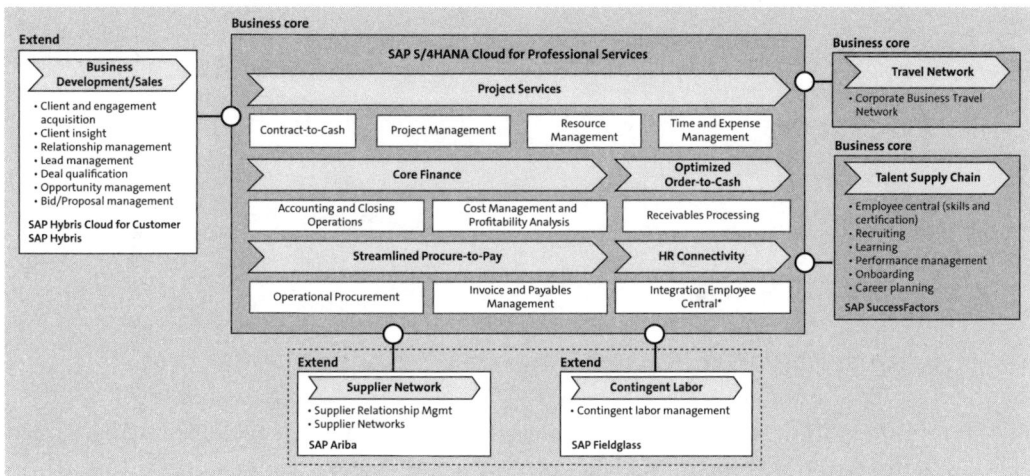

Figure 5.25 SAP Fieldglass and SAP Ariba Integration with SAP S/4HANA Cloud for Professional Services

5.7.3 SAP Ariba

For SAP S/4HANA operational procurement integration with SAP Ariba, the main applicable scenario is the natively supported purchase order/invoice integration with the Ariba Network. There are a number of resources available to support you with the install and deployment of this integration for SAP S/4HANA Cloud and on-premise.

SAP S/4HANA Integration with the Ariba Network for PO/Invoice Automation

The process flow in Figure 5.26 details the integration elements between SAP S/4HANA and the Ariba Network.

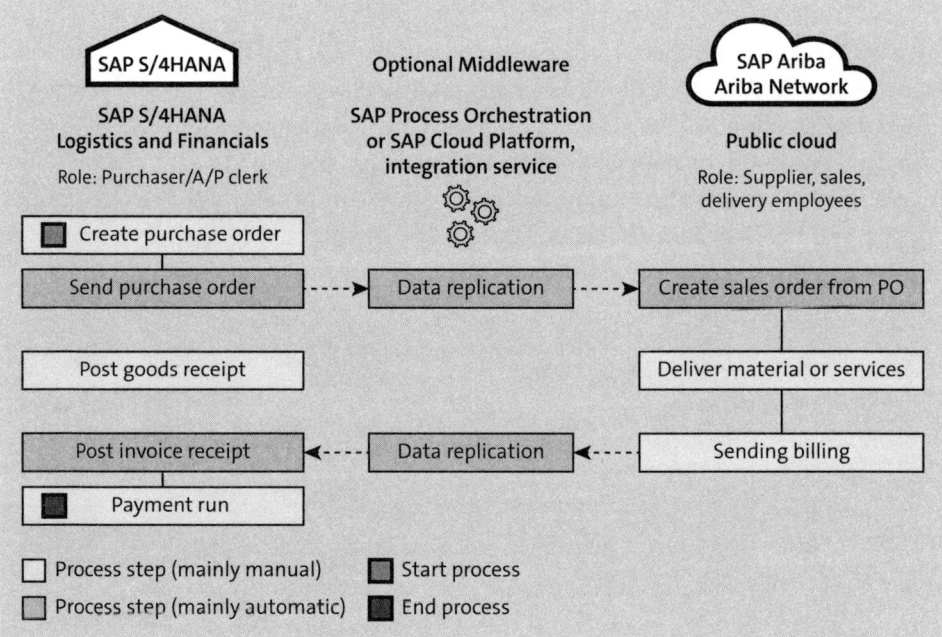

Figure 5.26 Process Flow: Purchase Order Invoice Integration with Ariba Network

The integration is native within SAP S/4HANA and can be established using guided configuration within SAP Activate or via the SAP Ariba account settings. These best practices are available at *https://rapid.sap.com/bp/#/RDS_S4_ARI*. The building block to implement for the self-service procurement scenario in SAP S/4HANA is **Ariba— Purchase Order to Invoice Integration with Procurement (J82)**. This building block contains the following:

- Scope-item simulation, with which you can test run the scope to understand where the configuration guide steps will cover your requirements or leave gaps
- Process model BPMN2, providing a business process representation of how the software works, which you can use in process-modeling applications
- Prebuilt test scripts you can use to ensure the system has been integrated as designed
- A process model, a representation of the business process to show how the software works as standard

- The Ariba Network Configuration Guide (J81), providing configuration of logon credentials to the Ariba Network and mapping of org structure elements such as company codes to Ariba Network IDs.

Once you've configured the logon credentials and mappings from SAP S/4HANA to your Ariba Network (J81) subscription, you'll invite and (in the event that they aren't already transacting on the network) onboard your suppliers in the Ariba Network to begin transacting in your SAP S/4HANA instance.

SAP S/4HANA Cloud Integration with the Ariba Network for PO/Invoice Automation

As with the SAP S/4HANA integration with the Ariba Network, this integration leverages guided configuration, best practices, and SAP Activate to support the solution depicted in Figure 5.27. For SAP S/4HANA Cloud, the solution approach uses native direct web services for integrating to and from the Ariba Network. The J82 building block materials are available at *https://support.sap.com/content/dam/SAAP/Sol_Pack/Library/FactSheets/J82_S4CLD1608_EN_US.htm*, including:

- Process model, outlining the process between SAP S/4HANA Cloud and Ariba Network
- Test script, for validation for integration implementation
- Process model BPMN2, providing a business process representation of how the software works, which you can use in process-modeling applications

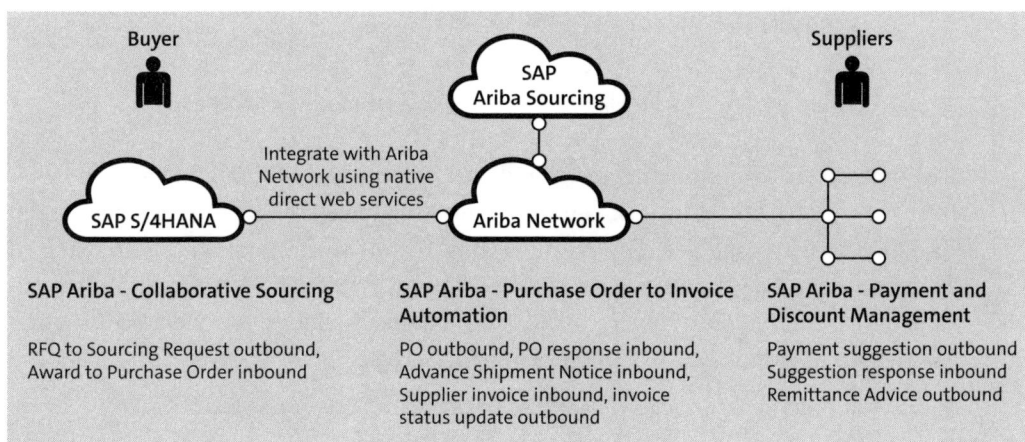

Figure 5.27 SAP S/4HANA Cloud Integration with SAP Ariba

5.7.4 SAP SuccessFactors

SAP SuccessFactors integration with both SAP S/4HANA and SAP S/4HANA Cloud has a similar integration framework and approach as that for SAP Ariba, based on predefined integration scenarios that you evaluate, activate, and deploy in your environment.

SAP S/4HANA Integration with SAP SuccessFactors Employee Central

SAP S/4HANA integrates with SAP SuccessFactors by leveraging predefined configuration and integration scenarios (see Figure 5.28). An overview of the integration materials is available at *http://bit.ly/16410501*. This integration is web service-based and can be scheduled as a middleware job.

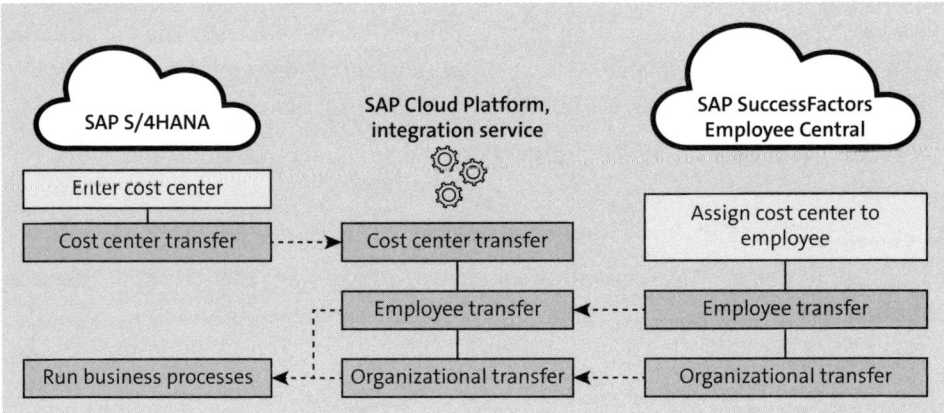

Figure 5.28 Integrating SAP S/4HANA with SAP SuccessFactors Employee Central

The manual process entails creating or identifying a cost center first in SAP S/4HANA. This is a manual step. The cost center is then transferred to SAP SuccessFactors and assigned to the employee. The employee and/or organizational data is transferred back to SAP S/4HANA automatically via batch processing. The configuration is available at *https://rapid.sap.com/bp/#/RDS_EC_S4*. This includes overview documentation, scope documentation, and the following accelerators:

- Sales supplement, an overview of the package and business value
- Customer presentation, slides on the scope of integration

- Demo script, for communicating the scope and functionality
- Delivery supplement, providing important information about the delivery of the solution
- Service and one-page slides, slides defining the solution and scope (one-pagers)
- Software and delivery requirements, a list of prerequisites for the deployment of the solution
- Solution scope, scope documents
- Project schedule, a schedule for the project including roles/skills required
- SAP Notes, providing additional documentation for package and implementation

SAP S/4HANA Cloud Integration with SAP SuccessFactors Employee Central

SAP SuccessFactors can also integrate with SAP S/4HANA Cloud using the same approach of best practices, building blocks, and SAP Activate. The required efforts are slightly more varied, and therefore involved, than with the Ariba Network packages. Upon completion of the integration, the employee from SAP SuccessFactors is realized as a business partner (BP) in SAP S/4HANA. Data from SAP SuccessFactors can be used to populate the employee data in SAP S/4HANA, such as the following:

- Basic employee information (person, name, employee)
- Communication information, such as email, phone, and fax
- Payment information with payment method and bank account
- Employee status
- Employment percentage
- Working hours per week
- Job title
- Job information, business unit, division, and department
- Cost center assignment

As with on-premise SAP S/4HANA integrations, from a process standpoint, you first establish or identify the cost center in SAP S/4HANA, then transfer this cost center to SAP SuccessFactors Employee Central and assign an employee, and then transfer the employee record back over to SAP S/4HANA (see Figure 5.29). The transfer processes are automated process steps, whereas the cost center assignment is manual.

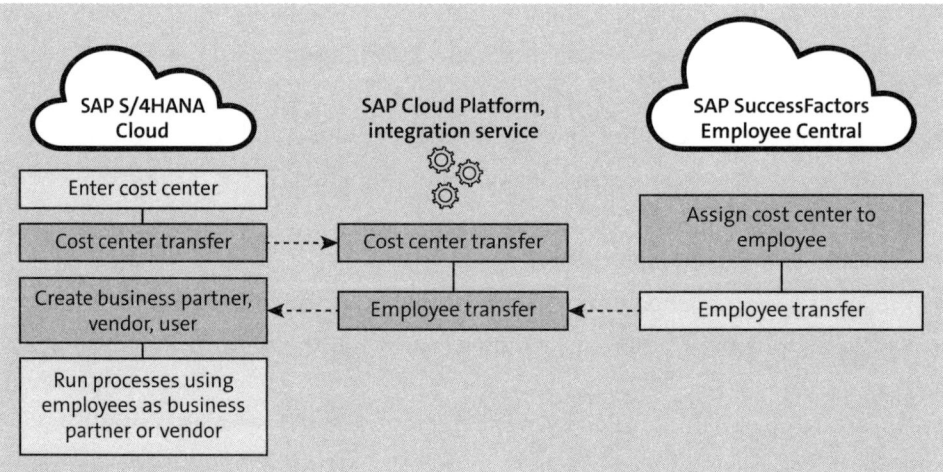

Figure 5.29 Integrating SAP S/4HANA Cloud with SAP SuccessFactors Employee Central

More on SAP SuccessFactors Employee Central integration building blocks and integration information is available at *https://support.sap.com/content/dam/SAAP/Sol_Pack/Library/FactSheets/JB1_S4HANAX_EN_US.htm*, where you'll find the latest integration information, as well as the following:

- Process diagram, which outlines the integration approach
- Test script, for verification of implementation
- Process model BPMN2

5.8 Summary

Operational procurement has been updated in SAP S/4HANA Sourcing and Procurement, both at the UI level with the SAP Fiori app-based approach for key transactions and views, and in terms of internal catalog emphasis. Although many of the core requisitioning transactions are simplified for the casual user, SAP S/4HANA Sourcing and Procurement retains some of the old favorites for PO creation in the advanced options of the apps to support complex ordering processes created by professional buyers with multiple data points and references. Many of these processes and options are required by direct procurement for their types of purchase orders. The next chapter will dive deeper into automated and direct procurement topics.

Chapter 6
Automated and Direct Procurement

This chapter outlines direct and automated procurement approaches and simplifications/changes in SAP S/4HANA, providing an overview of the main processes and related solution areas, configuration steps, and design considerations.

In manufacturing, it's easier to make a clear distinction between indirect procurement of office supplies supporting day-to-day business operations and direct procurement of parts and items going into the end product(s) produced by the organization. Direct procurement is often separated into its own area from an organizational standpoint. Direct procurement also is a leading candidate for automation in procurement operations due to its high volumes, predictability, and longer lead times.

The main thrust of automating procurement is to identify sources of supply up front for materials and then allow for the forecasting processes and approaches in MRP to generate procurement proposals that already have a source of supply assigned to the requisition or a schedule line item for an existing scheduling agreement with a supplier. Once the source of supply is assigned automatically for a particular material, automation of the entire transaction, from demand generation to proposal to purchasing document to transmission, is possible.

Much of direct procurement and other reoccurring types of procurement can be automated in SAP S/4HANA, leveraging tried-and-true, ERP-based approaches such as MRP, source lists, reorder points, information records, and scheduling agreements. However, in SAP S/4HANA, not all direct procurement processes and functionality is like-for-like with previous versions of SAP ERP, and a new cloud solution called SAP Ariba Supply Chain Collaboration bridges the network collaboration needs for SAP ERP-based direct-purchasing scenarios.

6.1 Automated and Direct Source-to-Pay Processes

In SAP environments, the direct procurement department often operates autonomously or only loosely aligned with the rest of the procurement organization. Direct procurement may only have a few buyers working directly with the product teams to procure the desired mix of products and raw materials from the optimal mix of suppliers. Direct buyers may be "embedded" with the product groups or company's plants, with razor-sharp focus on their particular areas of procurement to ensure proper cost-effective supply at all times and avoid disruption to the business. Products and goods purchased as direct procurement items by an organization may have long lead times, require special handling, and involve deep partnerships with the suppliers.

Indirect procurement items are typically more straightforward; where indirect versus direct procurement flips is on the user side. User management and workflows are typically more complex on the indirect side than the direct side. Direct buyers may number in the single digits and be responsible for an enormous amount of spend. The job of these buyers is to know and understand their procurement systems and tools so to create optimal orders based on demand and forecasts from the areas they cover. Indirect buyers may push most of the up-front ordering process via self-service requisitioning onto lightly trained employees ordering items for themselves or their offices. Indirect procurement users, therefore, may number in the thousands and have little to no training, purchasing once every quarter rather than every day or week.

SAP S/4HANA Enterprise Management, like its predecessor SAP ERP platforms, offers a wide array of functionality and processes to support and automate direct procurement processes (*automated procurement*). Some of these automation techniques are also applicable to frequently bought indirect items and/or indirect items with longer lead times and a regular purchasing cadence. There are two main planning approaches for these procurement scenarios: consumption-based planning and materials requirements planning (MRP). *Consumption-based planning* is driven by previous material consumption. As in Figure 6.1, consumption-based planning leverages reorder point, forecast-based, and time-phased planning, which can be defined as follows:

- *Reorder point planning:* Sets a stock threshold; if the planned available stock falls below this point, an order is issued. The reorder point is set to cover average material requirements during the replenishment lead time. Manual reorder point planning entails the MRP controller, an employee tasked with optimizing MRP processes and order volumes, creating the reorder point manually and automatic, where the system determines the reorder point using the forecast.

- *Forecast-based planning:* Creates forecast requirements at regular intervals using the historical values in the material forecast.
- *Time-phased planning:* Also uses historical values in the material forecast using predefined intervals in a particular cadence.

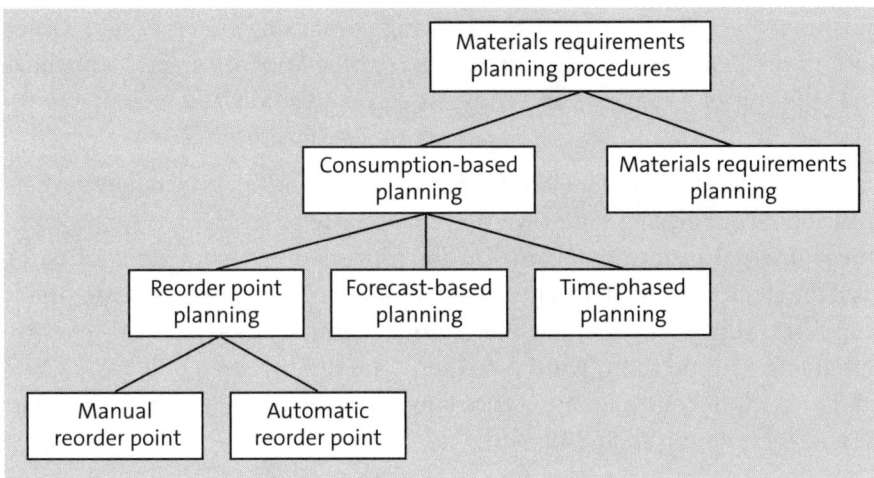

Figure 6.1 Overview of MRP Procedures

Current demand drivers for materials, such as sales orders and dependent and manual reservations, display in the current stock requirements list to help consumption-based planning approaches take these elements into account, in addition to the historical consumption patterns. If the demand for materials in production is relatively static, then low-value item, consumption-based planning approaches may suffice for creating sufficient stock on hand. If the item is high value with fluctuating demand, then MRP provides more accurate provisioning of materials than consumption-based planning. In the next section, we'll review MRP as it relates to procurement activities, as well as the changes to MRP in SAP S/4HANA.

6.2 Materials Requirements Planning

MRP aggregates the demand from various production, inventory, and forecast processes to secure and/or procure materials and have them available when needed for the production process. These materials can be in inventory at the plant/storage/warehouse level. If sufficient materials are not in stock, or by drawing down the stock certain reorder point thresholds are crossed, the MRP run can generate procurement proposals, such as planned orders, requisitions, or scheduling agreement line items. A planned order is reviewed first by the MRP controller and then converted into a requisition, whereas a requisition is immediately available for purchasing to review and source. Some organizations prefer to review the requisition and designate MRP run requisitions for a review step prior to having purchasing convert them. Other organizations prefer a more formal process whereby the MRP run creates a planned order, the MRP controller reviews and converts to a requisition, and only then does purchasing get involved.

As illustrated in Figure 6.2, once the MRP controller and the other stakeholders in this process, including purchasing, have reviewed the proposed items/orders for procurement, these internal planning documents are converted to reservations or stock transfers if the stock is on hand or, if not, to actual purchase orders and releases them to the suppliers. MRP thus generates the internal planning and proposed procurement line items automatically, which are then typically reviewed and adjusted (if required) by the MRP controller and other employees involved in the process and then released for ordering and fulfillment.

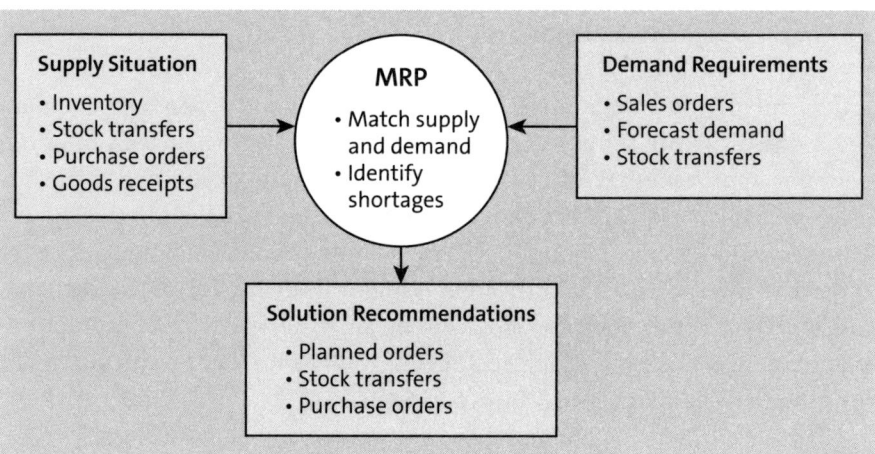

Figure 6.2 MRP General Flow

MRP-specific information is maintained in the material master, and it follows that MRP approaches require material masters as a core master data element in this process. Material masters have multiple tabs for maintaining MRP information, including:

- General data that must be defined for a planning material
- Data dependent on the MRP procedure
- Data requirement scheduling
- Data required for lot-size calculation

The material type defined in the material master also controls the types of procurement that are permissible for the material master, whether in-house only, external procurement only, or both. Defining the material types and understanding the procurement ramifications for a particular material type is thus key to establishing a coherent MRP strategy and procurement strategy in general. For example, if your material master type defines the material as requiring in-house-only procurement and you occasionally need to source it from an external supplier, then you'll need to create a duplicate material with a material type that allows for external procurement. In addition to nuances of material settings and MRP, there are significant changes between SAP ERP and SAP S/4HANA when it comes to MRP. We'll cover these differences ahead and outline both MRP improvements and limitations in SAP S/4HANA.

6.2.1 MRP in SAP ERP versus SAP S/4HANA

Executing the traditional MRP run transaction in previous versions of SAP ERP is not without its challenges:

- MRP is resource-intensive and sometimes requires batch runs spanning several hours/days.
- New demand and supply changes impact the MRP plan, leaving you with an outdated MRP plan or a need to rerun MRP to take the changes into account.
- There's no real-time view of material information and needs across sites.
- Multiple transactions are required to navigate shortages and solutions in MRP scenarios.

These shortcomings in traditional SAP ERP environments impact MRP and lead to suboptimal decision-making, as well as unnecessary efforts to arrive at these decisions. Fortunately, SAP S/4HANA is well-positioned to address shortcomings in MRP in traditional ERP systems by leveraging significant improvements in speed and simplifications. Some of the key advantages of and advances in MRP Live include:

6   Automated and Direct Procurement

- MRP runs are exponentially faster—up to 10 times faster—in SAP S/4HANA, which leads to MRP controllers having more timely and accurate information.
- There's a single, real-time view of material shortages across sites.
- You have the ability to pinpoint critical demands and supplies, such as overdue orders, in SAP S/4HANA.
- You can simulate a solution's viability in real time and then implement it in an expedient manner.
- The MRP planning scope has been expanded in SAP S/4HANA, allowing for planning sets of materials with all components, materials for which a certain production planner is responsible for one material across all plants.
- The main transaction for the MRP run in previous SAP ERP versions was MD01 (see Figure 6.3).

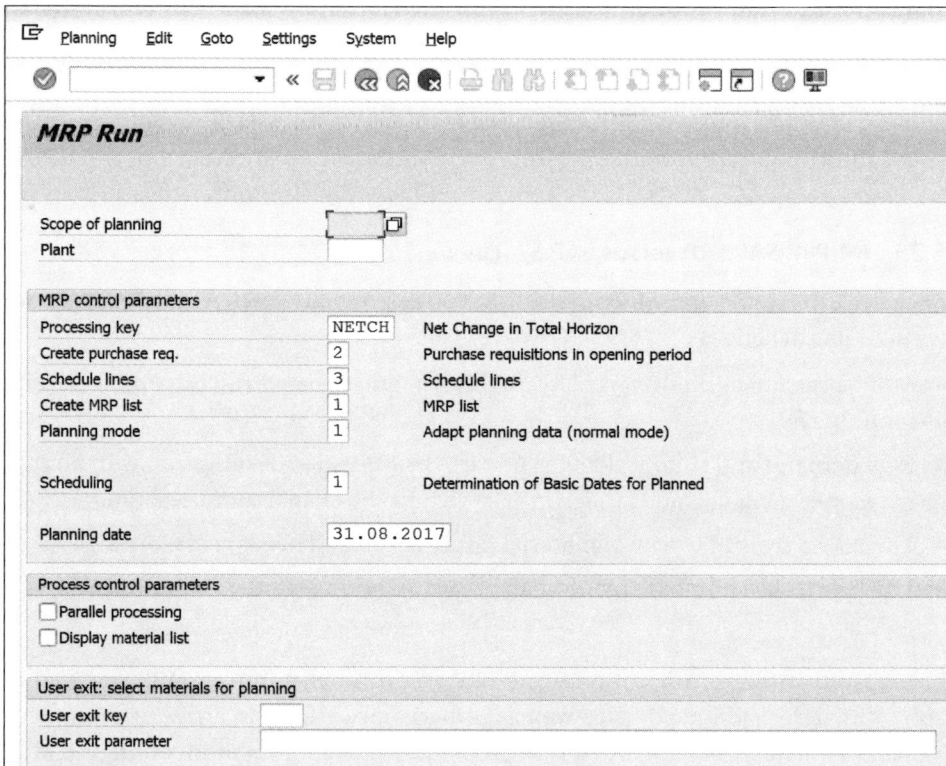

Figure 6.3 Transaction MD01 MRP Run

The new transaction in SAP S/4HANA is called MRP Live (see Figure 6.4).

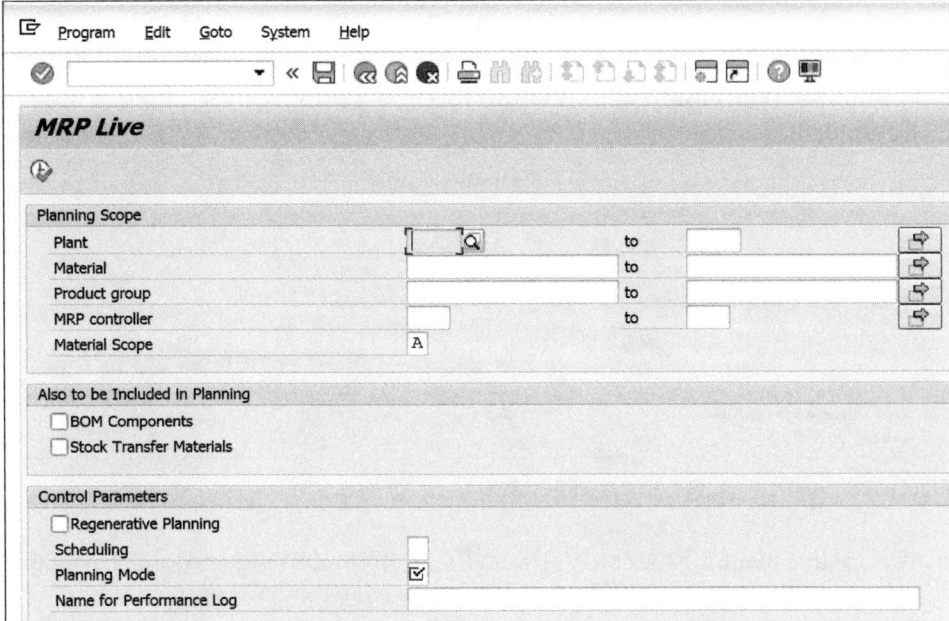

Figure 6.4 Transaction Code MD01N MRP Live

Some further differences in MRP Live versus the MRP run include the following:

- MRP Live always considers quota arrangements; there's no need to switch this on in the material master as there was for traditional MRP (flagging material master attribute MARC-USEQU).
- If you want to source a purchase requisition from a particular supplier, you no longer need to define a source list entry. It's sufficient to flag **Auto Source** in the PIR. Flagging an item for automatic sourcing in the PIR allows MRP Live to automatically assign the supplier as the source of supply.
- Production versions are the main source of supply for MRP Live. If you want a BOM, phantom assembly, subcontracting, or routing item to be considered by MRP Live, you need to create a production version.
- Forecast-based planning and planned independent requirements are not differentiated in the SAP Fiori UI in SAP S/4HANA for MRP.

- Report PPH_SETUP_MRPRECORDS (shown in Figure 6.5) replaces Reports RMMDVM10 and RMMDVM20; to display variants for the new report, use Transaction PPH_MDAB instead of Transactions MDAB and MDRE. The long-term planning report is now Report PPH_SETUP_MRPRECORDS_SIMU rather than Reports RMMDVM10 and RMMDVM20. However, Transaction MD21 is still used to display planning file entries.

Figure 6.5 Report PPH_SETUP_MRPRECORDS

- The original planning files MDVM/MDVL and DBVM/DBVL are no longer available in SAP S/4HANA. They were replaced by the new planning file PPH_DBVM.
- SAP S/4HANA MRP plans for the plant and MRP area. Planning at the storage location level isn't possible.

MRP areas define where the product is to be stored, whereas MRP groups define parameters for MRP. MRP groups are discussed in more detail in Section 6.4.4. Note that once an MRP area is created in the system via **Production** • **Materials Requirements Planning (MRP)** • **Master Data** • **MRP Areas** • **Define MRP Areas**, it can't be undone easily. Careful consideration and coordination with production planning and stakeholders of MRP is thus required prior to implementing MRP areas.

6.2.2 MRP SAP Fiori Apps

There are many available apps for monitoring and working with MRP in SAP S/4HANA. Two of the apps, Monitor Production Orders (Figure 6.6) and Picking Components for Process Orders (Figure 6.7), are assigned to the production planning users of the system.

6.2 Materials Requirements Planning

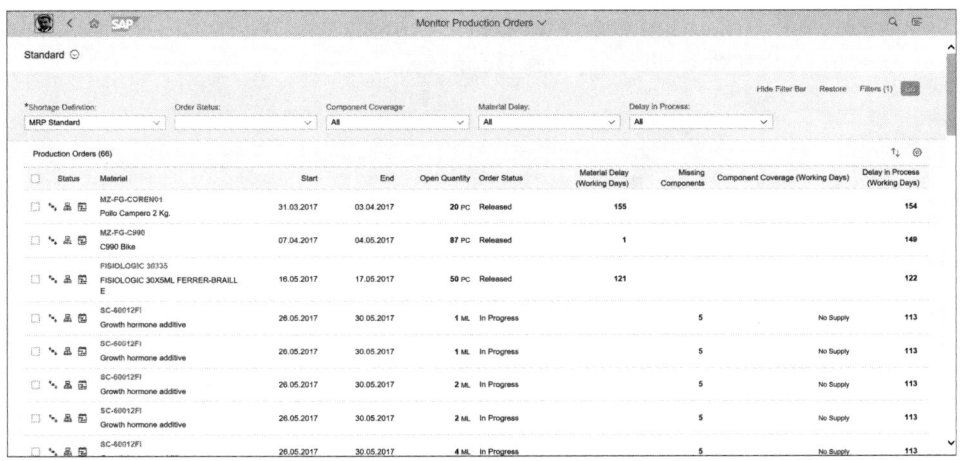

Figure 6.6 Monitor Production Orders App

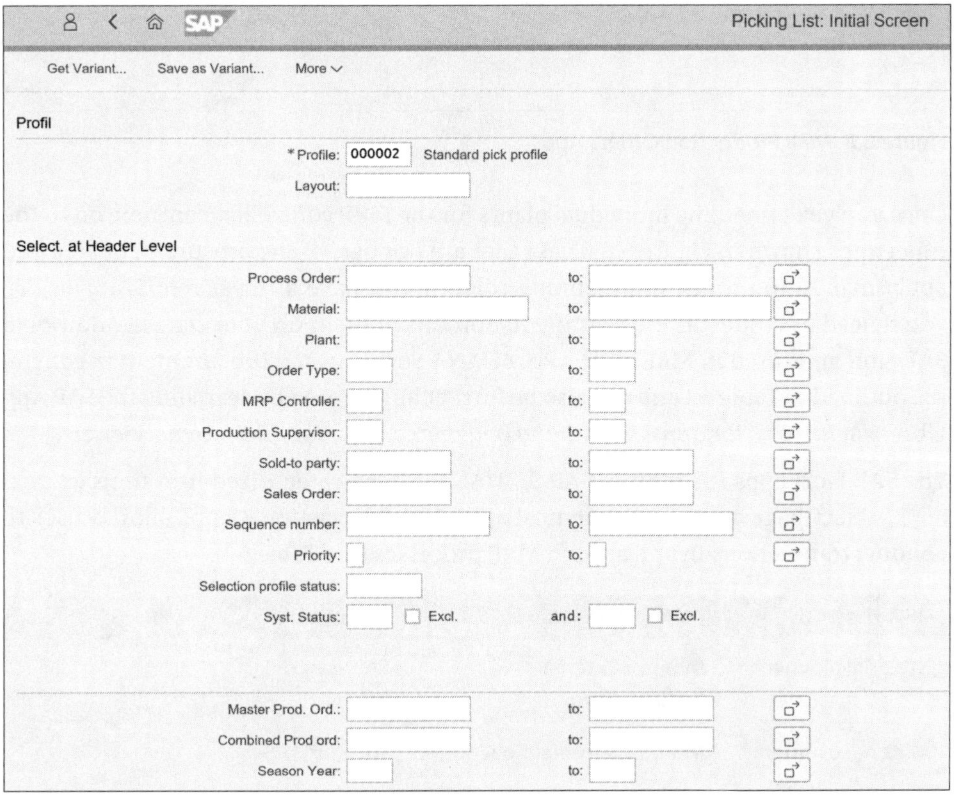

Figure 6.7 Picking Components for Process Order App

6   Automated and Direct Procurement

To navigate the production orders area, first define your MRP controllers by using the Maintain MRP Controllers app (see Figure 6.8).

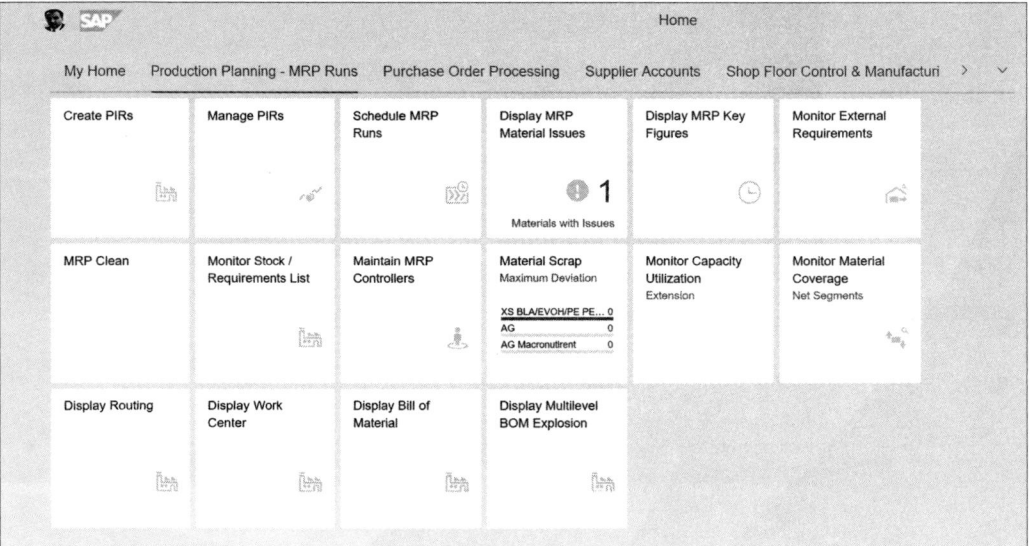

Figure 6.8 MRP Production Orders Apps

Once you've defined the individual plants for the MRP controller, continue on to the other apps shown in Figure 6.8. These tiles are not part of the procurement area and apply mainly to production planning roles. If you have a buyer role/SAP Fiori UI, you'll need to request these tiles if you don't have them on your screen. Additional SAP Fiori apps used in MRP and SAP S/4HANA Sourcing and Procurement in general are outlined in Table 6.1 and can also be further augmented by searching the SAP App Library at *https://fioriappslibrary.hana.ondemand.com/sap/fix/externalViewer/*.

The SAP Fiori apps for MRP in SAP S/4HANA can be categorized into transactional apps, object page apps, and analytical apps. The transactional apps allow a user to conduct transactions in and around MRP processes (see Table 6.1).

Role Name	SAP Fiori App Name	UI Technology	Comments
Material planner	Monitor External Requirements	SAP Fiori UI5	
Material planner	Monitor Material Coverage	SAP Fiori UI5	

Table 6.1 MRP SAP Fiori Apps: Transactional

Role Name	SAP Fiori App Name	UI Technology	Comments
Material planner	Manage External Requirements	SAP Fiori UI5	
Material planner	Manage Material Coverage	SAP Fiori UI5	
Material planner	Monitor Internal Requirements	SAP Fiori UI5	
Material planner	Monitor Production Orders or Process Orders	SAP Fiori UI5	
Material planner	Manage Internal Requirements	SAP Fiori UI5	
Material planner	Manage Production Orders or Process Orders	SAP Fiori UI5	
Purchaser	My Inbox—Approve POs	SAP Fiori UI5: Smart Template	
Purchaser	My Purchasing Document Items	SAP Fiori UI5	
Material planner	Manage Change Requests	SAP Fiori UI5	
Purchaser	Manage Sources of Supply	SAP Fiori UI5	
Purchaser	Manage POs	SAP Fiori UI5	
Material planner	MRP Cockpit Reuse Component	SAP Fiori UI5	
Purchaser	Manage Purchase Requisitions	SAP Fiori UI5	
Inventory manager	Manage Stock	SAP Fiori UI5	
Material planner	Manage PIRs	SAP Fiori UI5	
Material planner	Schedule MRP Runs	Generic UI5 Job Scheduling Framework	
Material planner	Maintain MRP Controllers	Generic UI5 Config. Framework	

Table 6.1 MRP SAP Fiori Apps: Transactional (Cont.)

Role Name	SAP Fiori App Name	UI Technology	Comments
Material planner	Display MRP Material Issues	Generic UI5 Config. Framework	
Material planner	Display MRP Key Figures	Generic UI5 Config. Framework	
Purchaser	Manage Purchase Contracts	SAP Fiori UI5	
Purchaser	Schedule Purchasing Jobs	Generic UI5 Job Scheduling Framework	Cloud only
Production planner	Schedule Order Conversion Runs	Generic UI5 Job Scheduling Framework	
Purchaser	Manage Source Lists	SAP Fiori UI5	Cloud only
Purchaser	Manage Purchasing Info Records	SAP Fiori UI5: Smart Template	Cloud only
Purchaser	Procurement Overview Page	SAP Fiori UI5: Overview Page	Cloud only
Purchaser	Manage Supplier Quotation	SAP Fiori UI5: Smart Template	Cloud only

Table 6.1 MRP SAP Fiori Apps: Transactional (Cont.)

The object page apps in SAP for MRP are listed in Table 6.2.

Role Name	SAP Fiori App Name	UI Technology	Comments
Purchaser	Purchase Order	SAP Fiori UI5: Smart Template	
Purchaser	Purchase Requisition Item	SAP Fiori UI5: Smart Template	
Purchaser	Purchase Contract	SAP Fiori UI5: Smart Template	
Purchaser	Purchasing Info Record	SAP Fiori UI5: Smart Template	

Table 6.2 MRP SAP Fiori Apps: Object Pages

Role Name	SAP Fiori App Name	UI Technology	Comments
Purchaser	Supplier	SAP Fiori UI5: Smart Template	
Purchaser	Purchase Requisition	SAP Fiori UI5: Smart Template	Cloud only
Purchaser	Purchase Contract Item	SAP Fiori UI5: Smart Template	
Inventory manager	Material Document	SAP Fiori UI5: Smart Template	

Table 6.2 MRP SAP Fiori Apps: Object Pages (Cont.)

The SAP S/4HANA analytical apps for MRP are listed in Table 6.3.

Role Name	SAP Fiori App Name	UI Technology	Comments
Inventory manager	Stock—Single Material	SAP Fiori UI5	
Inventory manager	Material Inventory Values—Balance Summary	Web Dynpro	
Inventory manager	Material Inventory Values—Line Items	Web Dynpro	
Inventory manager	Stock—Multiple Materials	SAP Fiori UI5	Cloud only
Material planner	Analyze PIR Quality	Web Dynpro	On-premise only
Inventory manager	Inventory Turnover Analysis	SAP Fiori UI5	Cloud only

Table 6.3 MRP SAP Fiori Apps: Analytical

Rather than digging through transaction codes or finding the correct IMG menu path, an SAP S/4HANA MRP controller simply needs to be assigned the aforementioned apps to do her work, accessing these apps via the tiles in a dashboard-like setting.

To make settings for an MRP controller to manage material shortages in the MRP apps, follow IMG menu path **Production • Material Requirements Planning • Apps for Material Requirements Planning • General Settings • Define Material Shortage Profiles**. Here, you define what constitutes a material shortage via assigning a profile, as in Figure 6.9.

6   Automated and Direct Procurement

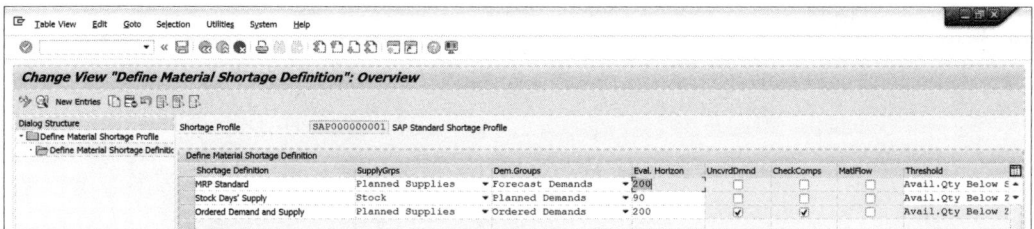

Figure 6.9 Material Shortage Profile: MRP App

In tandem with MRP, you typically need some approach to estimate future requirements. Setting a reorder point is useful in some instances, but knowing what future demand for a component or material will be with some degree of accuracy may provide a better understanding of the sourcing and ordering requirements, ultimately achieving greater efficiencies in direct procurement operations. Fortunately, SAP S/4HANA MRP combines reflexive demand indicators such as reorder points with proactive forecasting approaches and historical analysis to drive precision and alignment in the material quantities ultimately ordered.

SAP S/4HANA provides an app view in Monitor Material Coverage (see Figure 6.10). Once in the app, you have an overview of the coverage with availability details as in Figure 6.10, where you see the net and individual segments of materials with MRP analysis of supply.

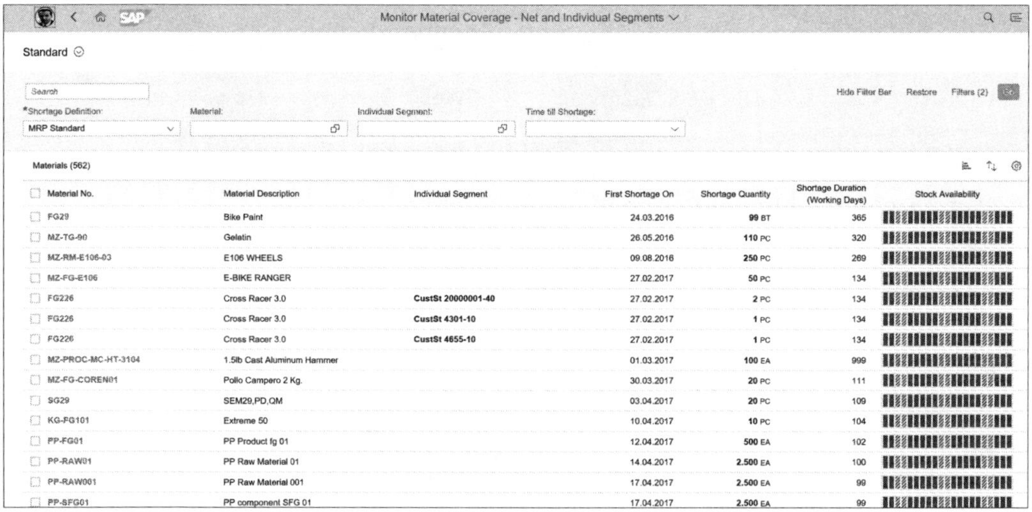

Figure 6.10 Monitor Material Coverage: Net and Individual Segments

This section outlined the tools available for understanding MRP requirements in SAP S/4HANA from a materials-on-hand standpoint. The next section will cover augmenting this planning understanding with further forecasting and predictive capabilities in SAP S/4HANA to drive a comprehensive picture of historical consumption, existing stocks, and future predictive consumption for MRP controllers.

6.3 Forecasting and Planning

At its core, MRP is a prediction of upcoming needs and requirements. To drive accuracy in this prediction, forecasting and planning for future demand is required. There are several different forecasting scenarios to consider, such as forecasting for ongoing production operations, for which you have history and current stock counts; expansions of production areas, for which you are making changes to existing products that may require additional components and stock, but the overall product line is established and has historical data and some of the stock to support the forecast; and new product and production areas, for which you don't have history or existing stock upon which to base your forecast.

With regards to stock counts, having real-time analysis in SAP S/4HANA provides tactical information on potential supply shortages for materials. If consumption history for an item exists in the system, you can also carry out a forecast process. Alternatively, if you don't have consumption data for a particular item, you can carry out forecast planning using an alternate material with historical consumption data available. You also can enter historical consumption data for a material manually. This section covers forecasting and planning in SAP S/4HANA MRP, beginning with forecasting.

> **Note**
> MRP Live on SAP S/4HANA doesn't perform forecast-based planning, so this type of planning reverts to the classic MRP-run transaction.

6.3.1 Forecast Planning

Forecast planning uses material consumption patterns, both planned and unplanned, to derive future requirements and align stocks and orders with anticipated demand. Forecast planning can't be planned in the new MRP Live transaction in SAP S/4HANA (Transaction MD01N). To execute forecast planning, forecast parameters must be maintained in the material record under the **Forecast** tab and the **MRP3** tab, under **Forecast Requirements**, as shown in Figure 6.11.

6   Automated and Direct Procurement

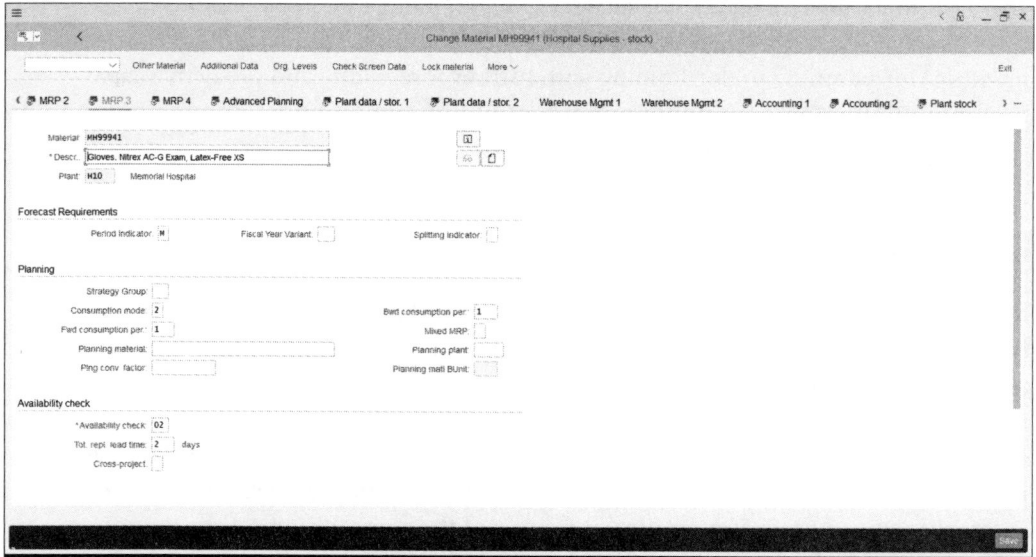

Figure 6.11 Forecast Planning Parameters

You can execute a forecast at the at the plant level via Transaction MP30. You can also select **MP38** (foreground) or **MPBT** (background) as an option on this menu path, for forecasting at the MRP area total level.

To carry out the forecast, you must first select a model to be applied. General patterns typically can be discerned by analyzing the historical consumption of a material. The main models in SAP forecasting are as follows:

- *Constant model:* Consumption values vary statistically over time by a mean value.
- *Trend model:* Consumption values rise or fall over a period of time with only minor fluctuations.
- *Seasonal model:* Consumption values rise and fall according to time period or events occurring annually.
- *Seasonal trend model:* Consumption values rise or fall continuously from the mean in a seasonal manner (fluctuating, but trending upwards or downwards).

The MRP controller can choose one of these models in the material master in the **Forecasting** tab, as shown in Figure 6.12; have the system make an automatic selection; or select one manually and have the system verify the selection. The system will automatically apply the constant model if it's unable to discern another model pattern while analyzing the data.

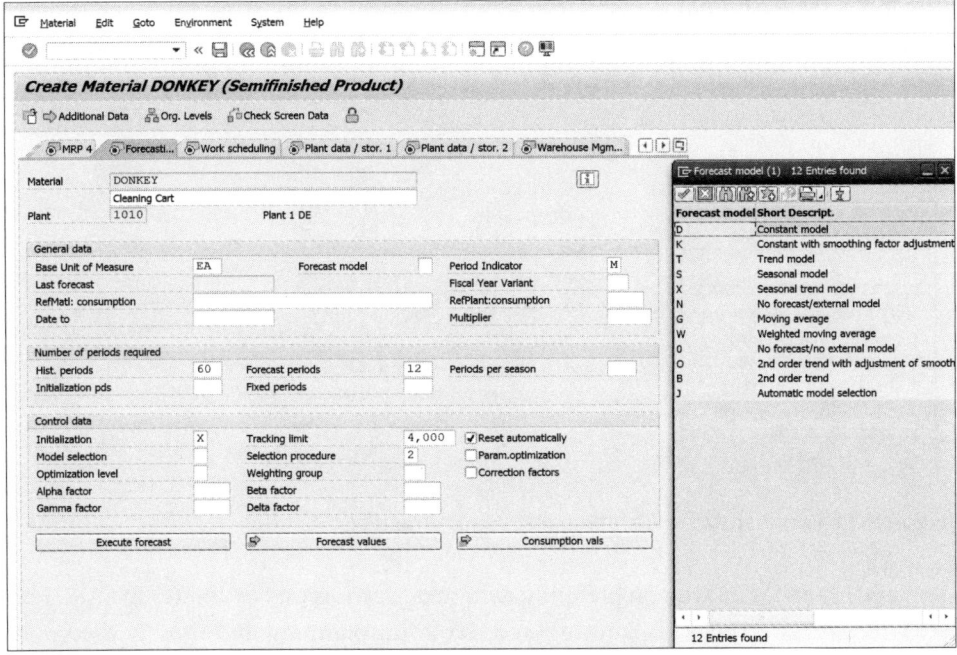

Figure 6.12 Forecast Model Selection: Forecasting Tab in Material Master

You can set the forecast model to be used directly in the material master or via a forecast profile in Transaction MB80. Here, you define the defaults and settings for the forecast profile, including the model, as shown in Figure 6.13.

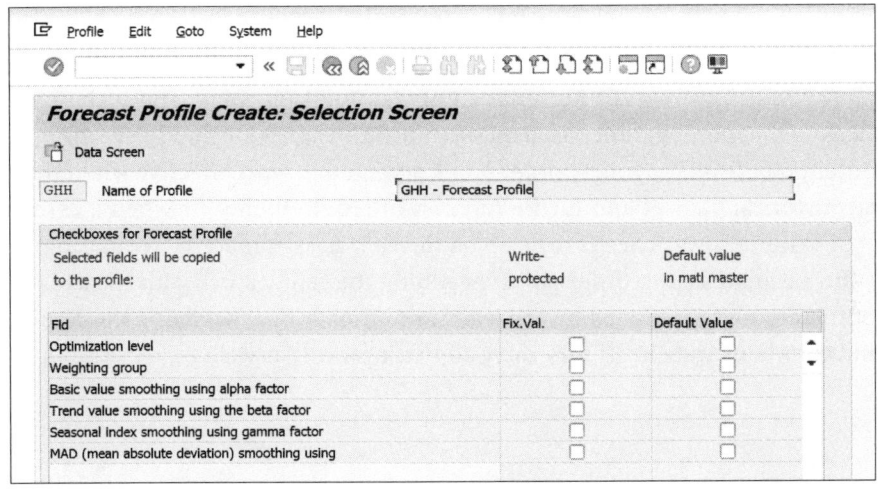

Figure 6.13 Forecast Profile Settings

The forecast requirements calculation then compares the existing stock and ordered outstanding for a material with the amounts required per the forecast and creates purchasing proposals to cover any deltas/shortages, as shown in Figure 6.14.

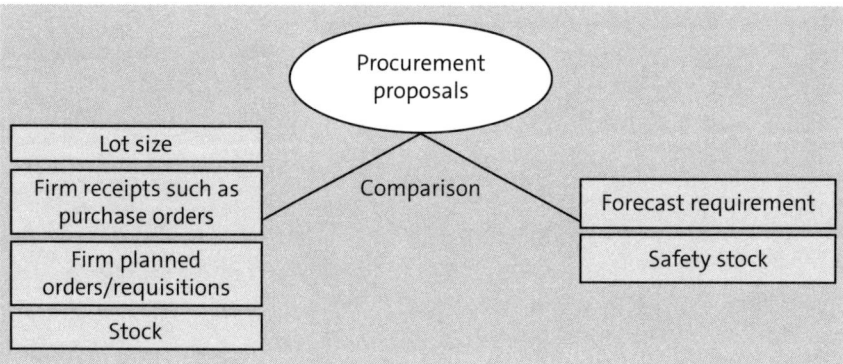

Figure 6.14 Forecast-Based Planning: Net Requirements Calculation

Forecasting relies heavily on planning data to derive forecast estimates in SAP. Next, we'll discuss two types of planning: reorder point planning and time-phased planning.

6.3.2 Reorder Point Planning

For manual reorder point planning, you can make settings directly in the **MRP 1** tab of the material master. Here, you can set the **MRP Type/controller**, as well as maximum stock permissible, as shown in Figure 6.15 in the **MRP procedure** section.

You can also have the system calculate reorder points in an automated fashion by selecting the MRP type **VM** for **Automatic Reorder Point Planning**. The system will then calculate the reorder point based on historical consumption and select the optimal reorder point level for you. Reorder point planning is most effective when there is a clear historical dataset and future forecast of requirements, or when a certain amount of material always needs to be on hand, regardless of material requirements. The system calculates the reorder point by adding the safety stock with the average usage of the product multiplied by the lead time. If lead times are high, the reorder point and commensurate inventory carry adjusts upwards as well.

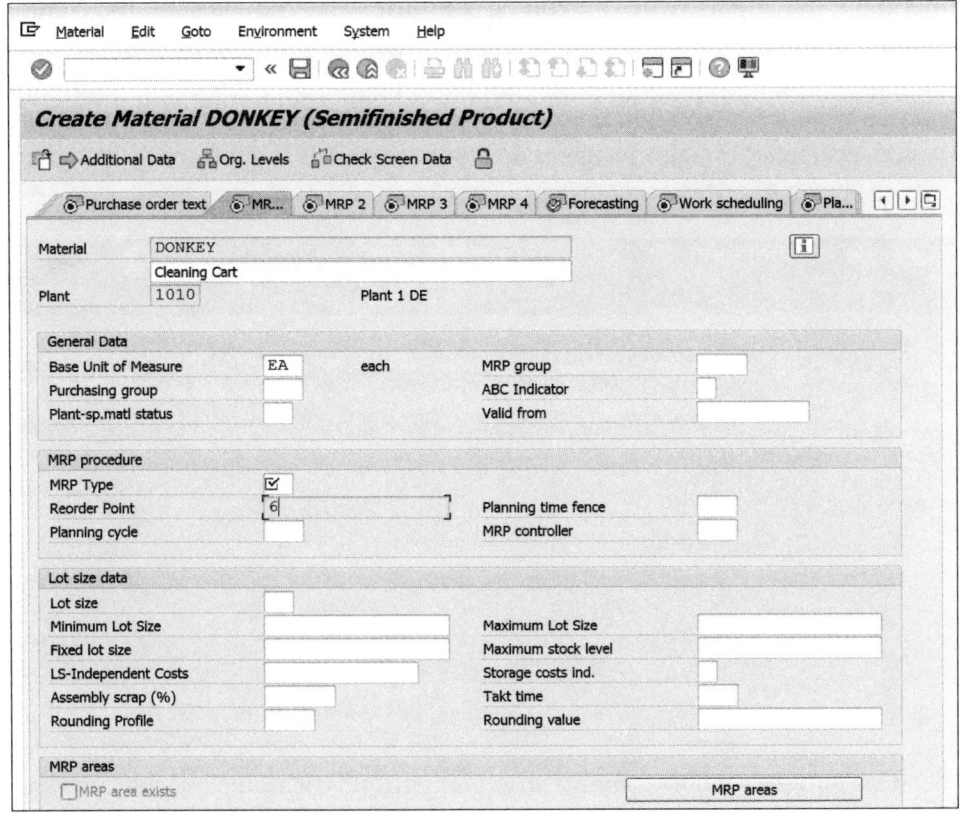

Figure 6.15 MRP 1 Tab: Reorder Point

6.3.3 Time-Phased Planning

Time-phased planning is based on a specific time interval, often based on the supplier delivery schedule to align the orders better with the delivery time. Time-phased planning can be combined with reorder point planning. If a reorder point is crossed, the material is planned from the point of shortage to the next MRP run, and for this time interval the ordered quantity must cover the shortage. Beginning with the next MRP run, time-phased planning again plans the material at the regular intervals.

6.3.4 Forecast Collaboration

Once an MRP controller has derived an internal forecast, a reality check with the supplier often is required. Determining requirements far in advance is good, but ensuring that there is a supply base with contracts in place and knowledge of the coming demand to adequately fulfill the orders in the expected time is better. An MRP controller and/or buyer can always reach out to suppliers to confirm readiness and discuss upcoming demand outside of the system. Using SAP Ariba Supply Chain for Buyers, a supplier can also review and commit materials forecasts and share them with the buyer in system, as shown in Figure 6.16.

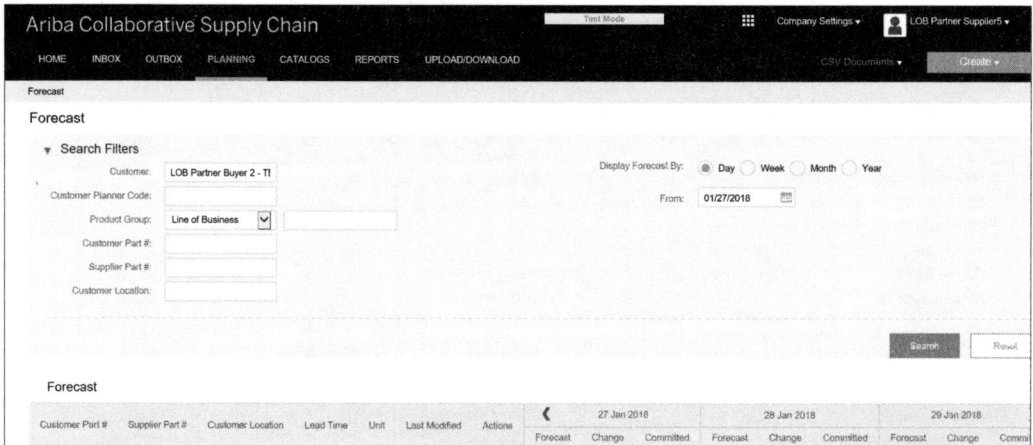

Figure 6.16 Forecast Review in SAP Ariba Supply Chain Collaboration for Buyers

In Figure 6.17, the supplier commits an amount in SAP Ariba Supply Chain Collaboration for Buyers. If the amount doesn't match the forecasted amount required, a buyer knows to begin looking at alternate sources of supply for the remainder or all of his order.

In addition to forecast commit on the supplier side, the buyer also has a forecast dashboard at her disposal (see Figure 6.18), which allows the buyer to view what was shared with the supplier for the forecast, not just what currently exists in the SAP S/4HANA planning areas. Leveraging the dashboard, the buyer is able to obtain real-time status information, measure supplier performance, and prevent potential supply chain disruptions.

Via the Supply Chain Monitor, further alerts and overview analysis is possible in SAP Ariba Supply Chain Collaboration for Buyers.

Once you've created the forecast and verified with your supply base that it should be possible on both sides to realize, the next step is to underpin the MRP requirements with agreements and suppliers, which is the topic of the next section.

6.3 Forecasting and Planning

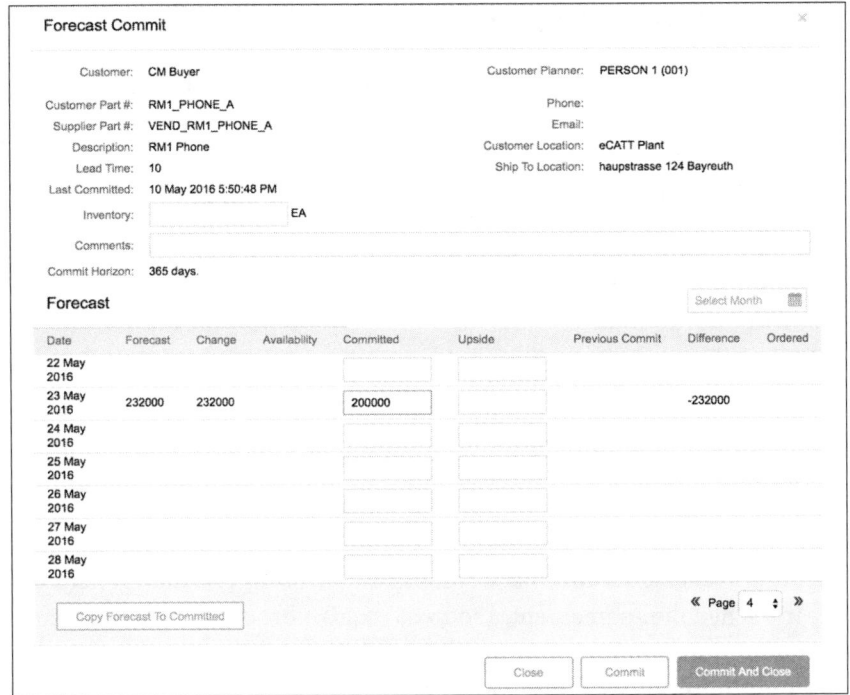

Figure 6.17 Forecast Commit in SAP Ariba Supply Chain Collaboration for Buyers

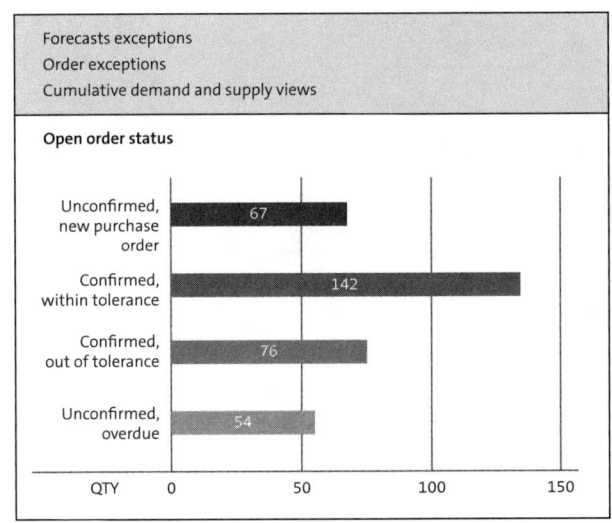

Figure 6.18 Forecast Dashboard in SAP Ariba Supply Chain Collaboration for Buyers

6.4 Contract and Source Determination

Once the material requirements have been determined in an MRP run, the source of supply needs to be identified to determine whether a procurement proposal is to be generated or a reservation or other in-house transaction made to secure the material. SAP S/4HANA supports the following sources of supply, prioritizing these options in descending order:

1. Production versions (in-house)
2. Delivery schedules (external)
3. Purchasing contracts (external)
4. Purchasing info records (external)
5. Source list (available as of SAP S/4HANA OP 1709; previous versions do not support source lists)

Once a source of supply has been identified and assigned, or it's determined that no source of supply is available for automatic assignment, the MRP run then generates a schedule line in a scheduling agreement, a sourced requisition, or an unsourced requisition (see Figure 6.19). Upon review of the requisitions, the source of supply is confirmed, and these requisitions are then converted to purchase orders and transmitted to the suppliers.

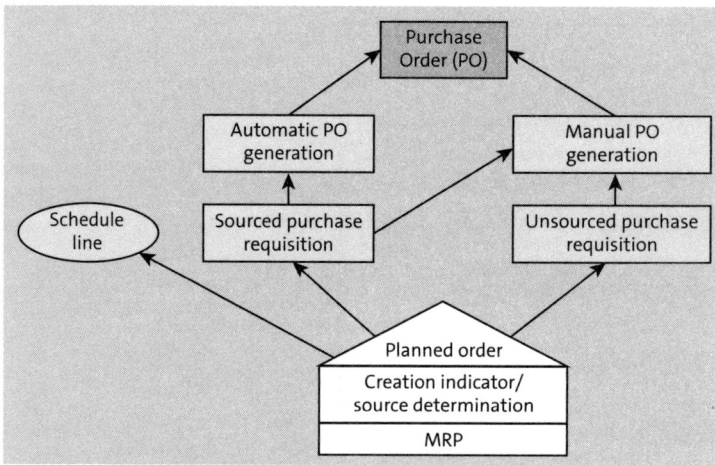

Figure 6.19 Planned Orders: Sources of Supply

Now, let's discuss the ways in which you can assign a source of supply (or multiple sources) up front.

6.4.1 Purchasing Information Record

The PIR contains additional information for a material purchased from a specific supplier and can apply either at the purchasing organization or plant level. The PIR contains a source of supply for the material, as well as a purchasing group, invoice verification indicators, net price, delivery tolerances, and other purchasing-specific data. The pipeline and consignment PIRs can store prices for different validity periods to assist in purchasing planning. There are four main PIR categories:

- **Standard PIR**
  Used for standard purchase orders, the standard PIR can be used for materials and services with and without master records.

- **Pipeline PIR**
  Used for purchasing liquids that are delivered via a pipeline from supplier.

- **Consignment PIR**
  Used for consignment, in which the supplier maintains stock on your premises at their cost, only billing after consumption.

- **Subcontracting PIR**
  Used for subcontract orders and can contain information on component assembly prices from the supplier.

In SAP S/4HANA, numerous apps support PIR transactions and analysis, including the following:

- **Purchasing Info Record**
  Displays individual PIRs.

- **Create Purchasing Info Record**
  App version of Transaction ME11.

- **Manage Purchasing Info Records**
  You can view, manage, change, and create PIRs using this app, as shown in Figure 6.20. Here, you can create a PIR, which includes tabs for **General Information**, **Conditions**, **Invoice**, **Delivery and Quantity**, and **Supplier**.

- **Mass Change to Purchasing Info Records**
  You can change multiple fields in multiple records simultaneously using this app.

- **Monitor Purchasing Info Records Price History**
  Allows for monitoring price history and details (date, price, and units), based on filter criteria you set.

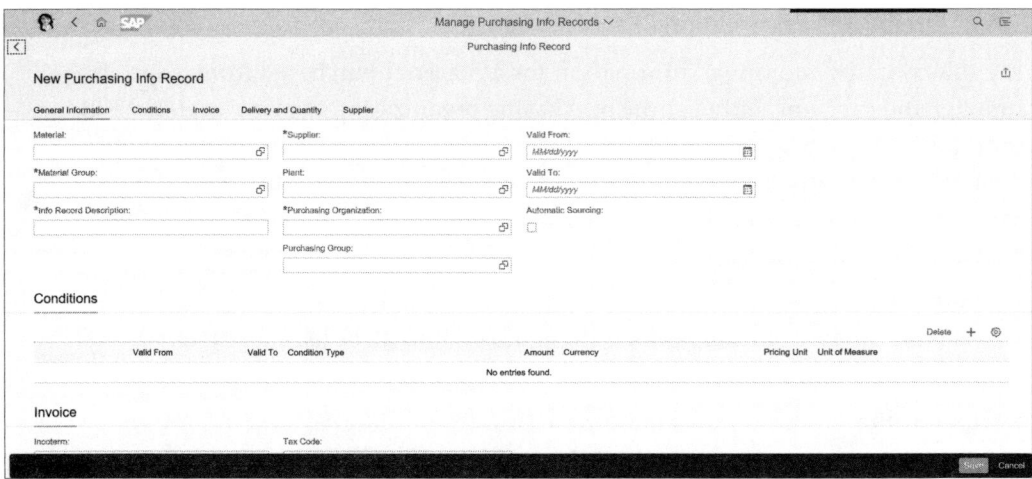

Figure 6.20 Manage Purchasing Info Records: Create PIR

Going directly to SAP GUI, the main PIR transaction codes are listed in Table 6.4.

Transaction Code	Description
ANZE	Display Purchasing Info Record
ME11	Create Purchasing Info Record
ME12	Change Purchasing Info Record
ME13	Display Purchasing Info Record

Table 6.4 Purchasing Info Record Transaction Codes

6.4.2 Source List

The source list specifies suppliers for a material by time period. You can create an entry in a source list directly from the PIR and define a source of supply as fixed (preferred), planning (used for MRP), or blocked. For the planning indicator, in SAP S/4HANA 1709 and beyond, if you set the source of supply with the MRP 1 indicator, this source of supply is automatically assigned to purchase requisitions and planned orders in MRP. If you set MRP 2 for the scheduling agreement, scheduling agreement lines created to order the material will contain the supplier as the source of supply. The blocked indicator can be set with a validity range, preventing ordering with a particular supplier for a set period of time.

Source lists can also be maintained directly, via an outline agreement, or automatically for each PIR or outline agreement in which the material is referenced. You can set a source list requirement for a plant, which requires each material procured for the plant to have a source list entry. You can also set a source list requirement at the material master level, requiring the material to have a source list entry prior to ordering.

Although source lists are integral to many plant-specific direct procurement activities, they aren't supported in SAP S/4HANA versions 1511 and 1610 for MRP. Later versions beginning with SAP S/4HANA 1709 will take source lists into account during MRP runs. For older versions of SAP S/4HANA, quota agreements are recommended as a workaround. MRP in SAP S/4HANA considers quota arrangements automatically; no switch activations are required in the material master.

6.4.3 Quota Arrangement

Quota arrangements are used in MRP processes to allocate purchasing between two or more suppliers. Quota arrangements are used to hedge supply chain risks and ensure purchasing allocation in a formalized manner. Quota arrangements are often used in MRP scenarios and allow for an automated procurement proposal generation to allocate procurement proposals among designated suppliers in a defined fashion.

For MRP, you can use allocation quota arrangements and splitting quota arrangements. Allocation quota arrangements allocate the entire lot to a particular supplier, whereas splitting arrangements allow for lots to be split between suppliers.

To create a quota agreement, you can log into the SAP S/4HANA Manage Quota Arrangement app available from the SAP App Library. Here, you can search for quota arrangements and create, maintain, analyze, and view them, as well as maintain base quantities so that a minimum quantity is assigned even if further suppliers are added. You also can navigate to a supplier/material fact sheet to further inform the settings of the quota arrangement.

For maintaining quota arrangements in SAP GUI directly, enter Transaction MEQ1 (Figure 6.21), use Transaction MEQ2 to change one, Transaction MEQ3 to display an arrangement, and Transaction MEQ4 to view changes in SAP GUI. If you wish to analyze quota arrangements, use Transaction MEQ6.

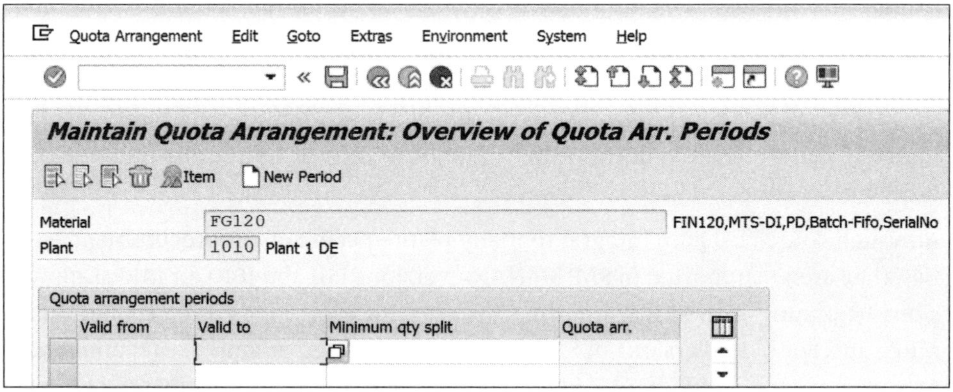

6   Automated and Direct Procurement

Figure 6.21 Maintain Quota Arrangements

6.4.4 Scheduling Agreement

A *scheduling agreement* is an outline agreement with a supplier defining the timeframe and delivery dates when certain materials and services are to be delivered over a period of time. Quantities to be delivered can be divided among schedule lines to feed production appropriately and optimize inventory during the process. Rather than carry all the inventory up front for the production process, the materials can be planned and ordered in the appropriate quantities at the applicable times. One scheduling agreement can replace a significant number of purchase orders and the administrative overhead associated with managing each of these PO document flows to invoice in the system. In SAP S/4HANA, the following apps are available for scheduling agreement creation and management:

- Manage Scheduling Agreements
- Mass Changes to Scheduling Agreements
- Manage Workflows for Scheduling Agreements

A scheduling agreement can have an additional release step prior to being issued to the supplier (document type LPA), or a scheduling agreement can be issued directly to the supplier (document type LP). Using scheduling agreements without release documentation requirements, as in the latter option, in conjunction with MRP, allows for material requirements for scheduling line items to be created and issued directly to the supplier during the MRP run. A scheduling line agreement thus can be fixed, unlike a requisition or a planned order, making scheduling agreement line items a direct approach towards procuring items from an MRP run. There is no second conversion step to a PO, in other words; the scheduling agreement line item constitutes an additional order.

196

Scheduling agreements cover the following procurement types:

- Standard
- Subcontracting, which can specify when components are to be delivered to the subcontractor for assembly/work for each scheduled line item
- Consignment, for scenarios in which the supplier only invoices after consumption of provided stock on-premise at customer
- Stock transfer, for internal orders of items from other plants/warehouses

The creation of scheduling agreement lines during MRP runs can be assigned in the MRP group and plant parameters. To maintain parameters either by plant or by MRP group, follow the IMG menu path **Materials Management • Consumption Based Planning • Master Data**, then either **Plant Parameters • Carry Out Overall Maintenance of Plant Parameters**, or **MRP Groups • Carry Out Overall Maintenance on MRP Groups** (see Figure 6.22 and Figure 6.23).

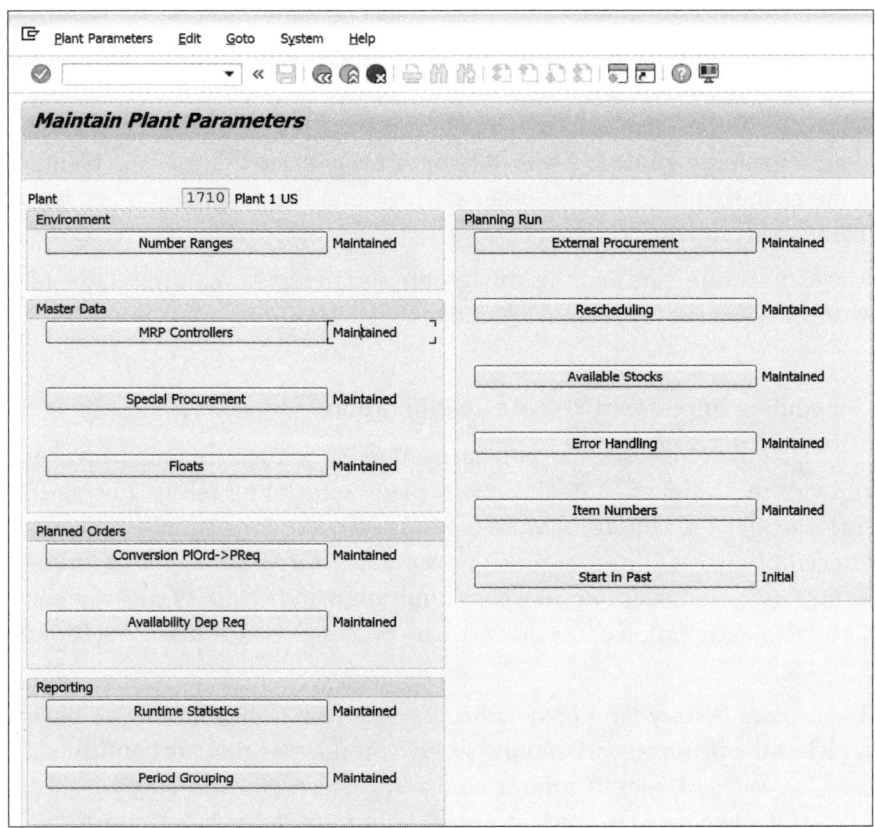

Figure 6.22 Maintain Plant Parameters

6 Automated and Direct Procurement

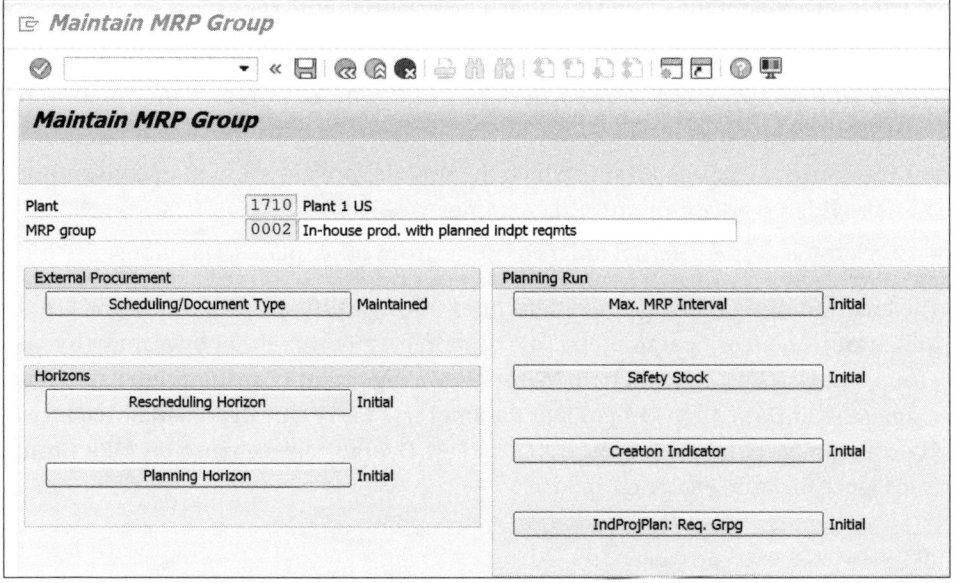

Figure 6.23 Maintain MRP Group

Here, you can maintain your MRP controllers and other master data items, planning run parameters, reporting, planned order settings, and the general number ranges for the plant environment.

If both the plant parameters and the MRP group parameters have been set, the MRP group settings have priority over the plant ones.

6.4.5 Scheduling Agreement Release Collaboration

Scheduling agreement releases, like purchase orders, sometimes require some back-and-forth with the supplier to finalize. With many scheduling releases being triggered automatically via MRP runs, often the only recourse for a supplier looking to finalize or clarify a release line is to pick up the phone. SAP Ariba Supply Chain Collaboration for Buyers provides two-way communication and visibility with suppliers, as well as further automation of the downstream processes on the invoice side of the process.

Under the **Release History** tab in SAP Ariba Supply Chain Collaboration for Buyers, you can review the firm zone-scheduling agreement releases that are confirmed for production, as well as trade-off zone releases—for which you will only be out the material costs if you have to cancel—and planning zone releases (see Figure 6.24).

6.4 Contract and Source Determination

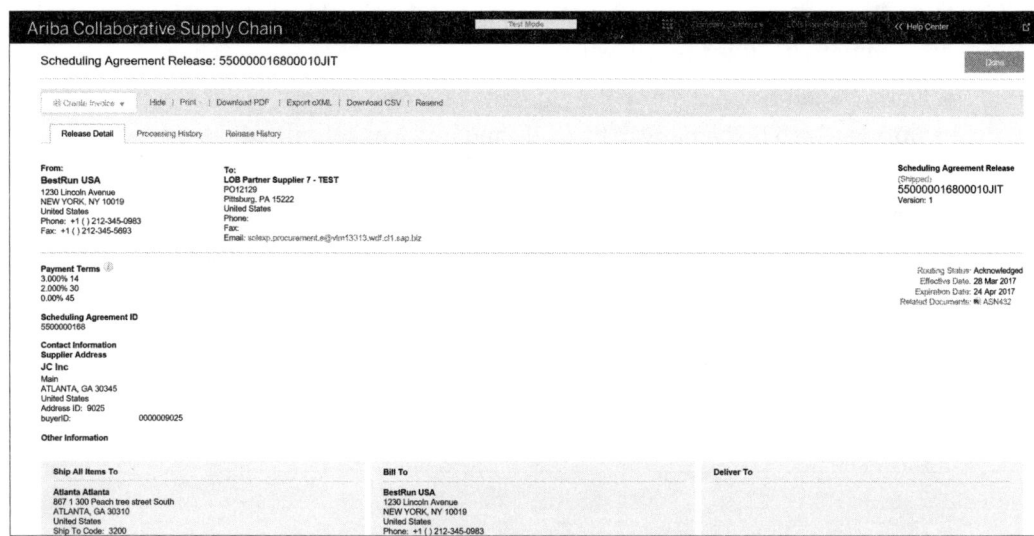

Figure 6.24 Scheduling Agreement Release History in SAP Ariba Supply Chain Collaboration for Buyers

Scheduling agreements are a core direct procurement process and an oft-used alternative to purchase orders in MRP scenarios; scheduling agreements can cut straight to the order if necessary and leverage an existing agreement, versus creating a completely new order. Yet this abridged manner of creating a scheduling agreement release also makes this approach more prone to confusion if the supplier needs to clarify or adjust something. SAP Ariba Supply Chain Collaboration for Buyers supports the end-to-end scheduling agreement process between supplier and buyer, mitigating potential confusion in these areas and helping to fully realize the efficiencies provided by a scheduling agreement ordering approach.

6.4.6 Blanket Purchase Order

Blanket purchase orders are typically used for ordering low-value, high-volume items delivered in an ad hoc manner, sometimes per the customer's request or per an agreement. Rather than create a separate PO for each delivery/order, a blanket PO is established as a kind of bucket with a set amount/quantity and time period. The supplier then delivers and invoices on this blanket PO accordingly. Blanket POs are at the other end of the spectrum from MRP in automating procurement. Rather than automating high-value direct procurement, blanket POs are mostly used for automating

199

low-value indirect procurement. Advantages of using blanket POs for automating procurement include the following:

- Period validity versus one-time order. A blanket PO can cover a period of time during which deliveries can be made and invoices submitted.
- No goods receipt or service entry sheet is required normally for a blanket PO, which cuts down on the process cycles and costs for low-value items.
- Monthly invoices are generally used to further cut down on the processing costs and steps.

Creating a blanket PO or framework order in SAP S/4HANA is much like it was in SAP ERP. In the Create PO app, in advanced mode, select **Framework Order** as the PO type (see Figure 6.25). This is the same as in Transaction ME21N in SAP GUI.

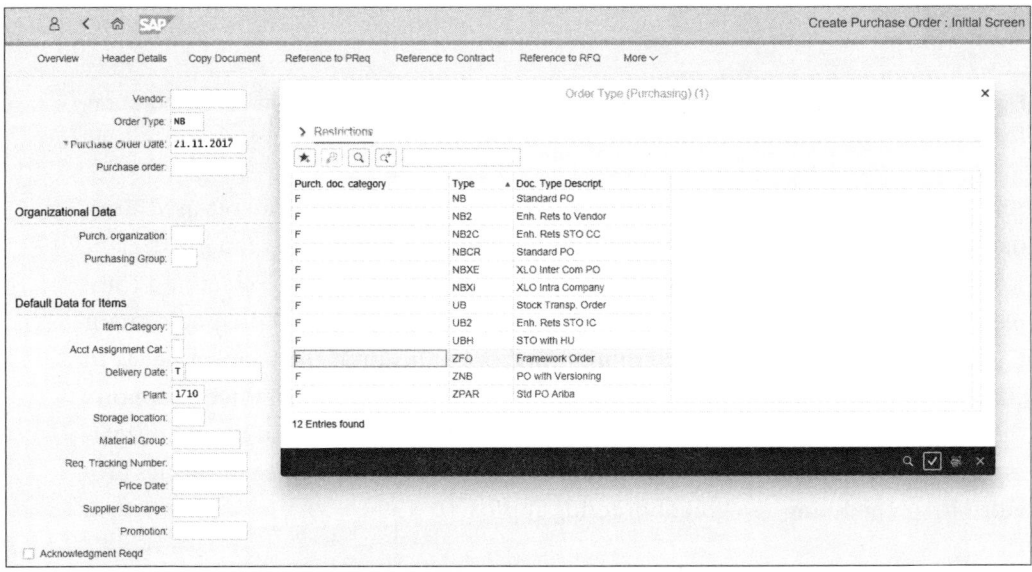

Figure 6.25 Framework PO in SAP S/4HANA

Selecting item type **B** for limit item allows a date range and value to be defined. You don't have to define the account assignment up front as with other orders. It can be set to **Unknown—U** to allow the invoice to perform the correct account assignment at the end of a transaction. In a framework order, you can set multiple delivery dates and a bucket of money from which the supplier invoices as it makes deliveries. The system validates the invoice against the blanket PO's limit and validity period and deducts the amount from the total.

6.4.7 Purchase Orders and Multitier Purchase Orders

SAP Ariba Supply Chain Collaboration for Buyers supports standard purchase orders, as does the Ariba Network in general. However, for direct procurement, there are several variations on the PO process that are the focus of SAP Ariba Supply Chain Collaboration for Buyers. The first is the multitier order. Although rare in indirect procurement, multitier orders can be common in direct procurement. Multitier orders pose challenges to standard purchasing systems. In a multitier order, the order is placed with a contract manufacturer, which then gives the go-ahead to a further supplier.

The multitier order capability allows for both drop-shipping and inbound shipment and receipt visibility, as shown in Figure 6.26.

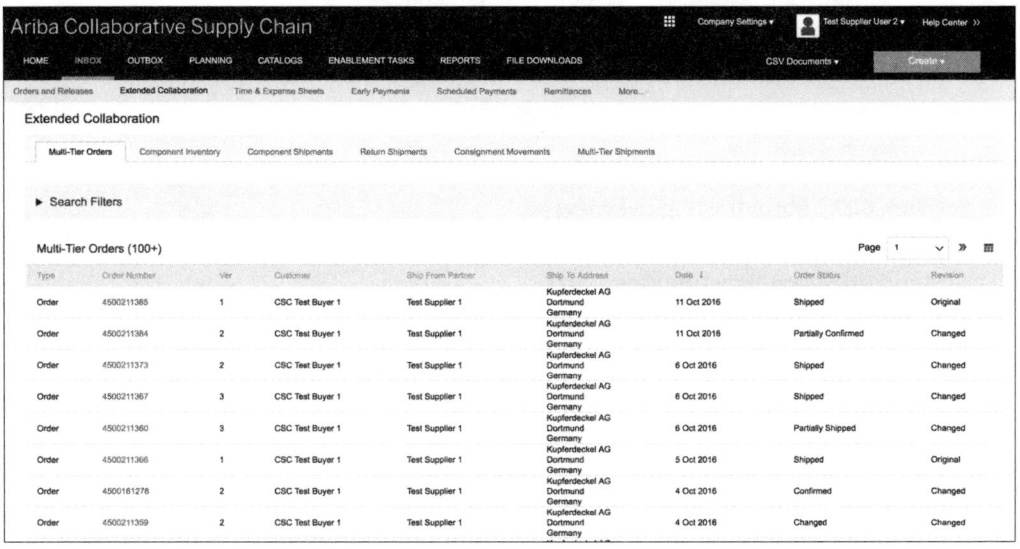

Figure 6.26 Multitier Orders: Drop-Shipping Visibility

This type of collaboration would not be possible directly in SAP S/4HANA because the suppliers need an area to login to and interact within. The Ariba Network effectively creates this space and the functionality to allow both the buyer and suppliers to share data across each other's respective internal systems, even when multiple suppliers are involved in fulfilling the same order.

6.4.8 Subcontracting

Some supplier relationships require you as the purchasing organization to provide the supplier with the components used in their part of the value creation. A typical example in manufacturing would be assembly. Here, the manufacturer places an order with an assembly provider for a certain number of finished goods, then provides the parts that the assembly supplier is to use for the putting the finished product together. These components are usually associated with a BOM (see Figure 6.27).

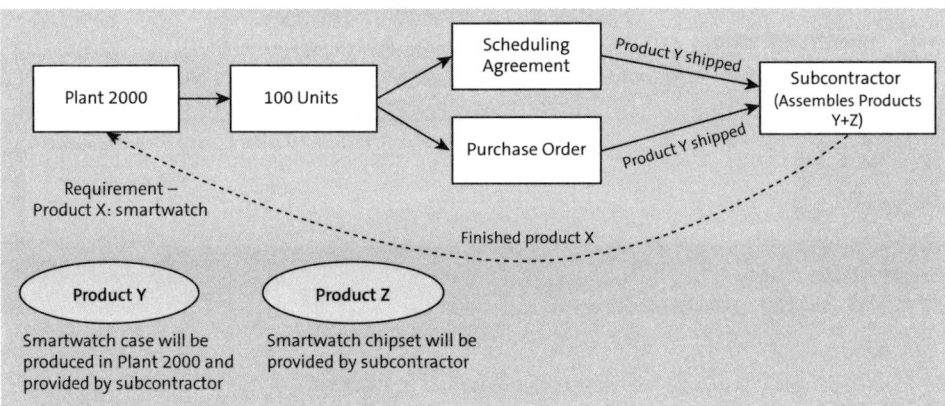

Figure 6.27 Subcontracting Overview

Standard Subcontracting Approach

In SAP, there are multiple ways of setting up this transaction, but many approaches add more complexity than they are worth. For example, you can choose to create plants that are technically the supplier's locations and track your inventory as you move it to these locations for finishing. For each transaction requiring subcontracting, you then have to issue a PO and create multiple goods movements and accounting entries internally to support the process. This approach requires more manual effort and accounting acrobatics than is optimal. The most straightforward way to support subcontracting processes is to use the standard subcontracting approach in the system. The process is as follows:

1. Select PO type **L** when creating the purchase order for a subcontracted item. L is the subcontracting PO type and allows you to create subitems manually or via a BOM explosion automatically for the components to be provided to the subcontractor. Although the final product doesn't necessarily require a materials master, the components do require a material master record for this process in SAP.

2. For the MRP to pick up the subcontracting order correctly, you must maintain a subcontracting entry for the associated material in its MRP area assignment, an MRP-relevant source of supply/quota agreement with the subcontracting setting (again, source lists are not supported in SAP S/4HANA before version 1709 for

6.4 Contract and Source Determination

MRP, so you would need to use a quota agreement as a workaround in these versions), and a BOM containing the components. During the MRP run, the system explodes the BOM requirements and classifies dependent, subcontracting elements as such.

To flag a material master directly for subcontracting, choose a half finished (**HALB**) or finished (**FERT**) material, and in the **MRP** tab maintain the **Special Procurement** field with option **30** for the plant, as shown in Figure 6.28.

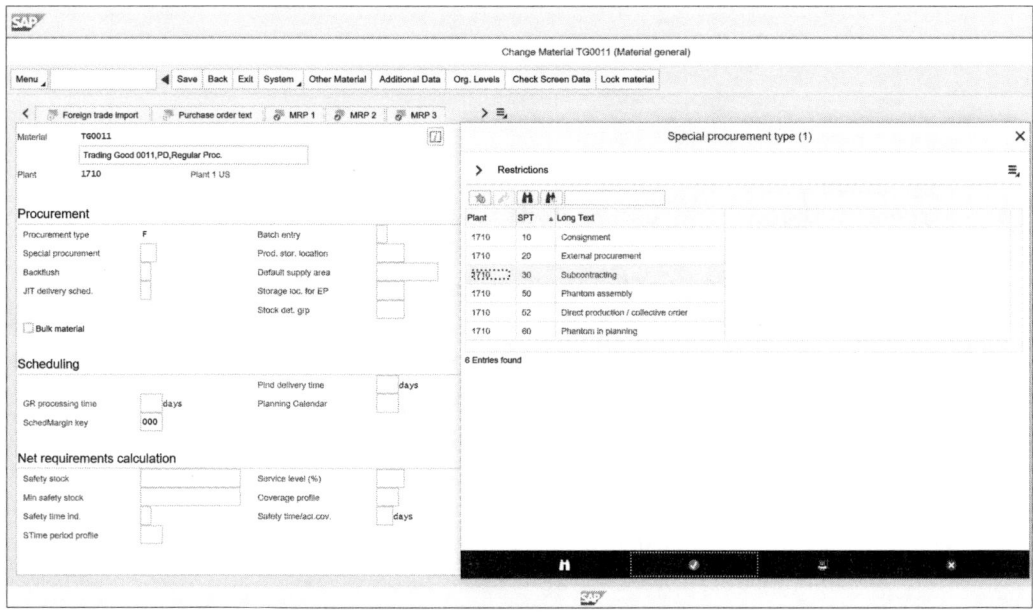

Figure 6.28 Procurement Settings for Subcontractor in Material Master

Subcontracting in SAP S/4HANA

In previous versions of SAP ERP, component materials to be provided to the subcontractor could be planned as a separate stock. However, with SAP S/4HANA, a subcontracting MRP area is the default option for subcontracting planning. Subcontracting will appear under the general plant stock if there is no MRP area maintained for the supplier.

Also, in previous versions of SAP ERP, you could check subcontracting stocks by supplier by running reports from a specific IMG menu path. This transaction is now available as an app in SAP S/4HANA, as shown in Figure 6.29.

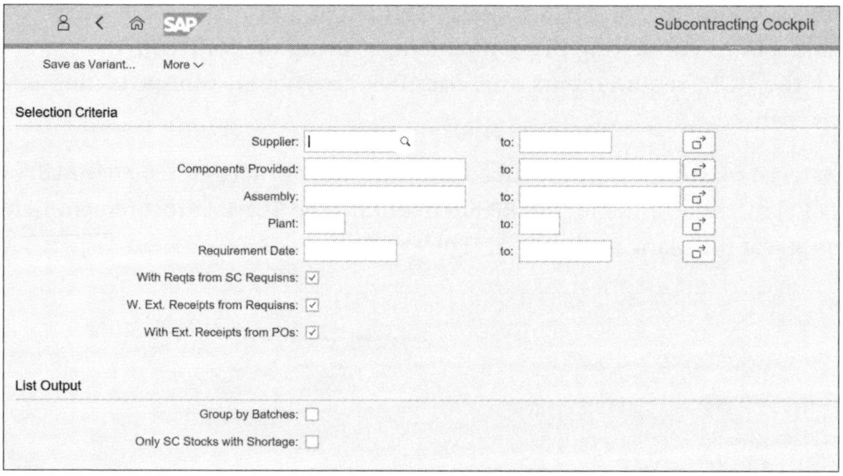

6   Automated and Direct Procurement

Figure 6.29 Display Subcontracting Stocks by Supplier

In SAP S/4HANA, MRP areas have to be created for every subcontractor; if MRP area–specific material master records don't exist, MRP uses default planning parameters. This differs from classic SAP ERP for subcontracting, in which you could plan either with or without MRP areas. If you elected to plan without MRP areas, you weren't able to use the full functionality around lot sizing and were only able to order full lot sizes. If you chose the MRP area route, material data on an MRP area was required for all components. These two options are now combined into one driven by MRP areas, but it doesn't require material data on all components and can support full-lot sizing and sourcing functionality.

Upgrading MRP Subcontracting to SAP S/4HANA

To upgrade MRP subcontracting processes in SAP ERP to SAP S/4HANA, you need to take stock of your existing subcontracting suppliers and processes and identify any gaps, execute a standard upgrade to SAP S/4HANA, and then at postprocessing proceed as follows:

1. Maintain subcontracting MRP areas for all subcontracting suppliers requiring provision stocks to be planned separately from requirements. The customizing entry in the supplier master is sufficient to trigger stock transfers and reservations from the plant to the subcontracting MRP area. You only have to maintain entries in the material masters if special situations exist for lot sizing, purchase requisitions/orders, and/or third-party order processing.

2. Run regenerative MRP and test.

Subcontracting Order Collaboration

As detailed in this chapter, the standard subcontracting process in SAP entails a leap of faith to a degree, which some MRP controllers and their ilk are unwilling to make. Upon issuing a subcontracting PO and shipping out the components to the supplier, the buyer doesn't technically receive updates on the production of the order until the final product or subassembly with the components is shipped back from the supplier to the buyer. Tracking the materials and valuations, which technically still belong to the buying organization, becomes difficult using the standard process. This often is used as justification by finance and other stakeholders on the buyer side for setting up phantom plants to represent the supplier and then moving and tracking the materials in these plants. This creates a host of additional transactions for each subcontracting order and does scale well.

SAP Ariba Supply Chain Collaboration for Buyers provides an extra layer of visibility that has been sought in the subcontracting process, including component receipt and consumption notices from the supplier, as well as full B2B-level manufacturing visibility into the supplier's progress.

Using the supplier portal on the Ariba Network, a supplier can login and confirm the consumption of subcontracting components into the assembly, as shown in Figure 6.30.

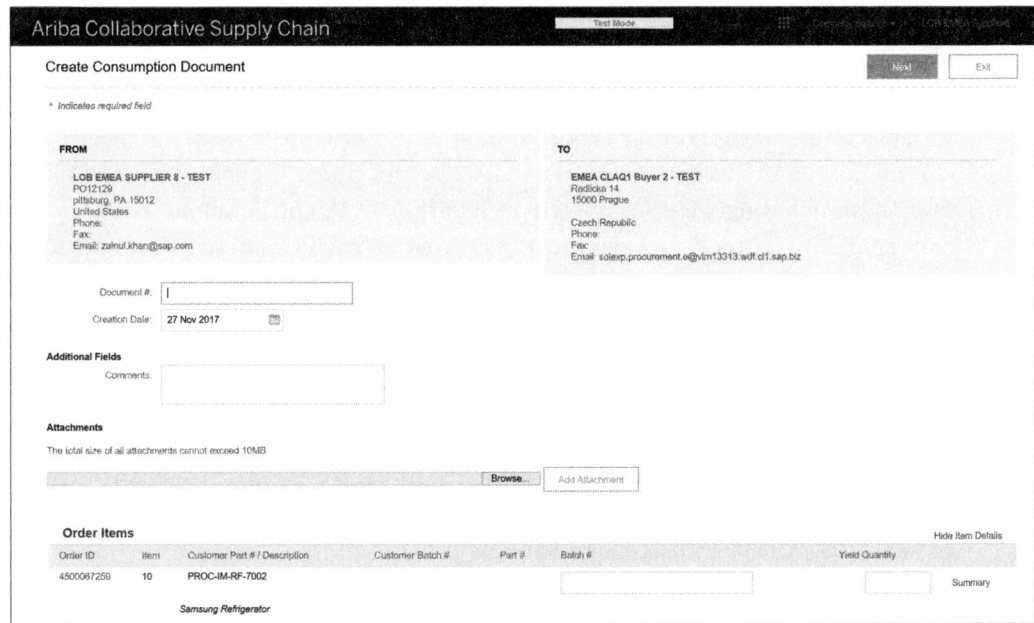

Figure 6.30 Subcontracting Supplier Dashboard: Components Consumed

Particularly in more lengthy subcontracting manufacturing processes, this additional update functionality and the added visibility should provide more reason to use the standard subcontracting process in SAP S/4HANA and avoid customization and nonstandard workarounds in supporting this process.

6.4.9 Consignment Stock

Consignment stock is stored on the buyer's premises but is owned by the supplier until consumed. Typically, consignment stock can be returned to the supplier after an agreed-upon time period if not consumed. The trigger for ownership transfer and consequent payment liability to the supplier is when you transfer a consignment stock item out of your consignment stock. Invoicing is typically conducted on a monthly basis, or potentially at the point of stock transfer if an Evaluated Receipt Settlement (ERS) approach has been defined for vendor invoice payment and/or if the supplier is notified immediately of the transfer.

You can manage multiple consignment stocks from various suppliers and in various currencies. Consignment stock can be allocated to unrestricted, quality-inspection, or blocked-use types as your regular stock materials. You can transfer consignment stock between these three use types, but only the unrestricted use type allows for withdrawals. Using consignment purchasing info records, you can also apply discounts, price quantity scales, and other PIR functionality to consignment stock.

Creating a consignment purchase order is similar to a blanket PO or limit item. In the item category, you select **K** for **Consignment**, as shown in Figure 6.31.

As far as setup for supporting a consignment order, you must assign the special procurement type key **10** in the material master record under the **MRP 2** tab and maintain the purchasing view, as shown in Figure 6.32. A consignment PIR and any corresponding source list entries must be created to link the material master with the purchasing information.

Many of the orders created in MRP in manufacturing scenarios are for components that are so numerous from a parts and/or volume standpoint that managing these orders and sources of supply can quickly overwhelm buyers with larger procurement scenarios and sourcing activities to worry about. In Section 6.4.12, we'll preview a solution called SAP Supply Base Optimization, which covers this area of spend from price negotiation and sourcing standpoints, using nascent technologies and approaches in artificial intelligence and linear programming.

6.4 Contract and Source Determination

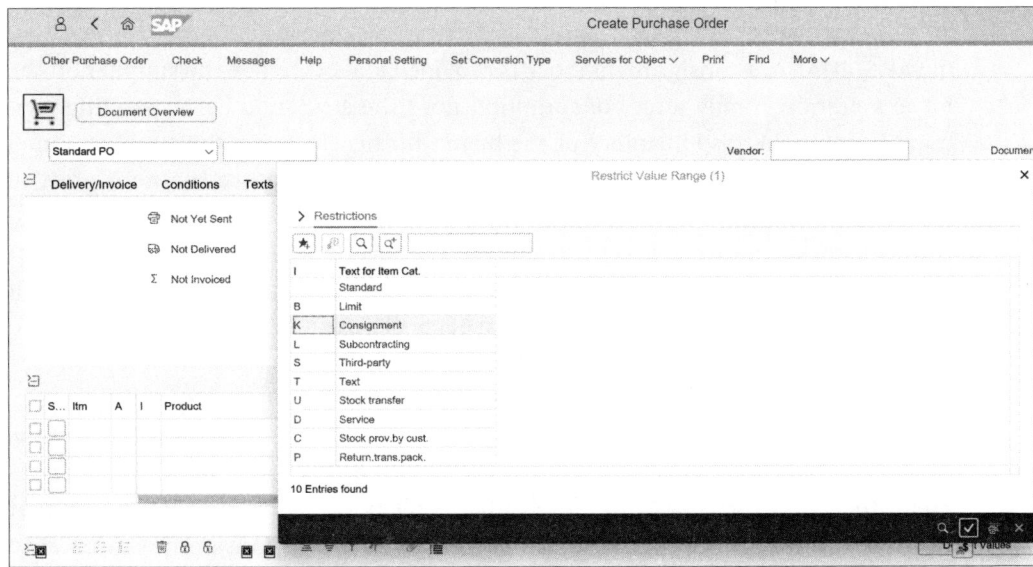

Figure 6.31 Consignment Purchase Order

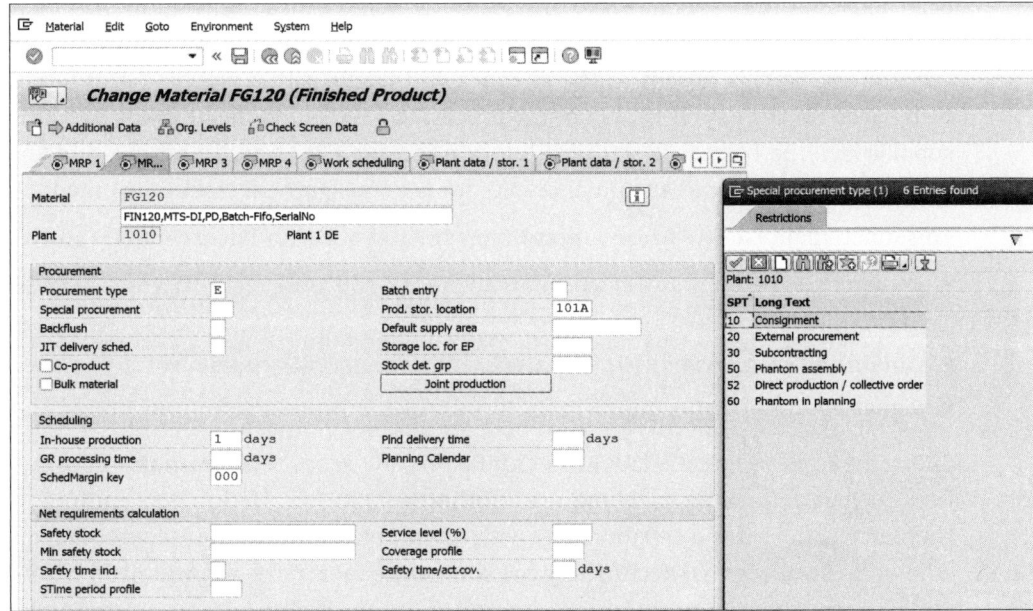

Figure 6.32 Consignment Material Master Setting in MRP 2 Tab

6.4.10 Consignment Orders

In SAP S/4HANA, a consignment stock is provided and owned by the supplier on the buyer's premises; only after consumption does the stock and corresponding payment become the responsibility of the buyer. In this situation, the supplier sometimes has to go onsite to a customer and physically inventory the item prior to submitting an invoice. There may also be incomplete processes for ordering replenishment stock in between inventory cycles in the event the stock is consumed prior to the supplier taking inventory and replenishing automatically. These types of issues run counter to the overarching goal of consignment, which is for the buyer to have real-time access to stock that isn't carried on the buyer's books and for the supplier to have a beachhead at the customer from which the supplier can deepen relationships with and relevance in the customer's supply chain. As with subcontracting, this issue starts with communication, visibility, and management of the consignment stock. Here too, SAP Ariba Supply Chain Collaboration for Buyers provides that last mile of track to bridge these challenges and allow for the consignment process to perform as intended.

The communication focus is from buyer to supplier. Once the consignment stock has been delivered, the buyer needs to provide the supplier with a notification that it has been received and take the items into consignment stock. Upon consumption, another notification is sent to the supplier. In the event that self-billing or ERS is being used for the payment area of the process, a payment is then expedited to the supplier. Alternatively, with the consumption consignment transfer notification, the supplier can now submit a manual invoice for the consignment stock consumed.

This functionality in SAP Ariba Supply Chain Collaboration for Buyers enables you to:

- Replenish and receive consignment inventory and transfer it to your stock as needed
- Obtain and share visibility into material movements with suppliers
- Signal change of ownership of inventory and settle payments to suppliers

SAP Ariba Supply Chain Collaboration for Buyers allows for faster turnaround times in areas that don't technically require another SAP ERP transaction but require further notification to and collaboration with the supplier to close gaps. These are gaps where the customer has technically consumed the inventory and will need billing and possible replenishment from the supplier, but the supplier isn't yet aware of the consumption.

6.4.11 Quality Management Collaboration in SAP Ariba Supply Chain Collaboration for Buyers

Another core topic in direct procurement—which is only tangential in indirect procurement, for the most part—is quality management. For indirect procurement, if an order arrives in subpar quality or with damage, it can be shipped back. If the quality deficiencies aren't caught until the items are consumed, the supplier doesn't get further orders from the customer, typically. On the direct side, deficiencies in quality can have catastrophic ramifications, as faulty components are included in finished products, bad batches of pills fill buyer-provided pill packaging and are shipped out, and so on. Inventory management with the Quality Management module allows for some inspection and management of quality for incoming orders, but the in-system communication with and visibility of the supplier is somewhat limited beyond the receipt of the delivery. Often, the supplier may not quite understand why the order was returned. Other times, the supplier is notified too late, after it has already produced and shipped further replications of the defect to the buyer and other customers/partners. SAP Ariba Supply Chain Collaboration for Buyers provides a platform for handling the quality-management aspects of the order process, from notification to deviation response/request in real time, allowing suppliers to recognize and correct issues faster, thus lessening the damage to the buyer's and the supplier's production and operations.

In addition to providing the structure for the quality communications, this approach also allows for the entire communication stream to be captured in one area, rather than in several individual emails. This makes the overall transaction flow and issue resolution much clearer from a quality-management standpoint, and it allows the buyer and supplier to learn how these issues were resolved previously from older interactions.

6.4.12 SAP Supply Base Optimization

SAP Supply Base Optimization is a cloud-based decision-management tool that incorporates market benchmark data and applies predictive analytics to optimization and simulation methods to enable intelligent negotiation and business-award decisions with suppliers.

SAP Supply Base Optimization focuses on driving the price of higher-volume components used in manufacturing BOMs and has a strong value proposition in industries in which component prices continuously fluctuate or decrease, such as tech manufacturing and aerospace. In these industries, the components are numerous and prices trend down as the technology ages and newer versions and general advances are released.

Many buying organizations can't devote full-time employees to these types of components, other than on a quarterly or annual basis when it comes time to review and renegotiate. As a result, suppliers can reap a kind of "rent" between the actual, current cost of the component and the price (usually higher) that was initially agreed upon with the customer. The customer is too busy to focus on these lower-priority areas, which require significant analysis and time investment, with only modest potential savings amounts per individual component.

The SAP Supply Base Optimization solution seeks to automate the tedious parts of such analysis and derive actionable insight, target prices, and optimal award splits among suppliers. The high-level business process covered by SAP Supply Base Optimization is as follows:

1. **Scope**
   Propose and refine components for negotiation. Set the target price for negotiation using historic and market benchmark data.

2. **Negotiate**
   Initiate iterative "always-on" negotiations with suppliers. See status of all negotiations at any point in time.

3. **Analyze and award**
   Input business rules and decision logic for optimization. Apply simulation methods to analyze different supplier award scenarios and make final award decision. Auto award for low-priority parts.

4. **Update and report**
   Notify suppliers of updated award decisions. Update master data in the backend ERP. Provide summary reports by project, supply base manager, commodity group, and so on.

There are two main outputs from SAP Supply Base Optimization for the negotiation and consequent award: target price and award split. The target price is used by the supply base manager to negotiate with suppliers in order to get the negotiated price as close to the target price as possible. SAP Supply Base Optimization uses predictive analytics libraries to provide a generated target price based on historic and market benchmarking data. The generated target price can be overridden by the supply base manager.

The split calculation provides the supply base manager with a demand quantity share, which can be provided to each supplier based on constraints assigned to the supplier and award process. The split calculation is derived based on linear programming, which in turn leverages machine learning.

As shown in Figure 6.33, SAP Supply Base Optimization provides the supply base manager with a tool to automate analysis and negotiations at the component level, leveraging both advances in SAP S/4HANA with real-time availability of both data and analytics, and machine learning and linear programming. Expect these types of solutions and approaches to grow in the future as more procurement processes and operations utilize this confluence of technology and applications to automate and refine procurement efficiencies and effectiveness.

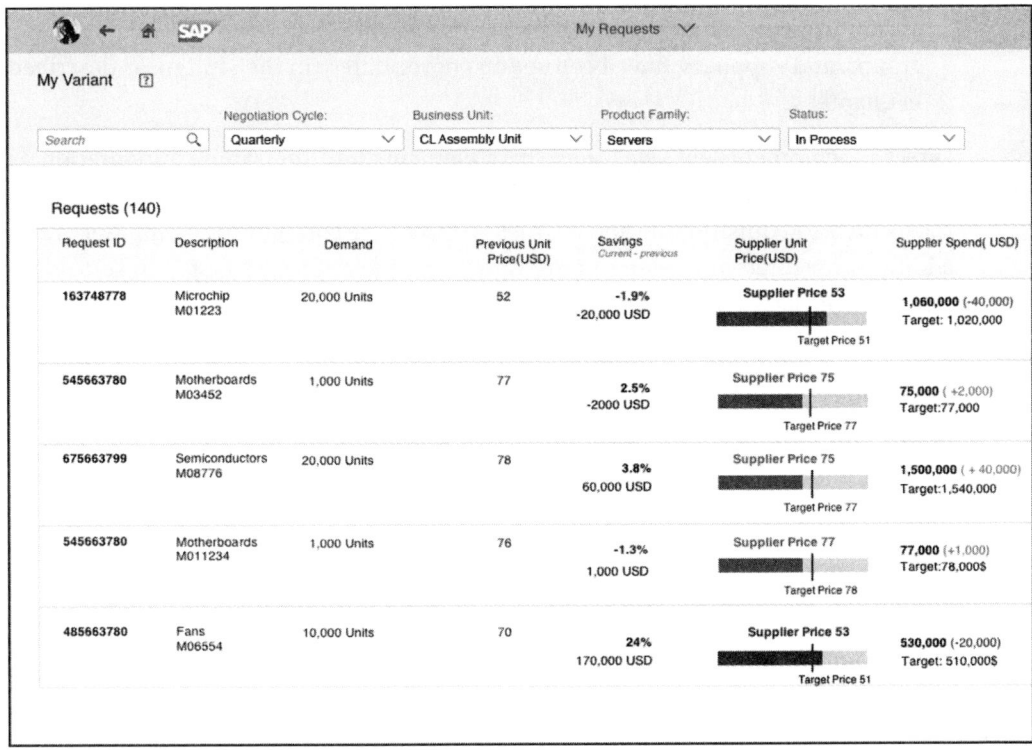

Figure 6.33 SAP Supply Base Optimization: My Requests App

6.5 Configuration

There are enough parameters in automated and direct procurement that you can configure your setup in an infinite variety of ways to realize your internal business processes and goals. This section covers the main baseline configuration and setup steps required to realize direct material procurement.

6.5.1 Defining Master Data

The prerequisites for direct and automated procurement configuration and execution are as follows:

1. Company Code, Plant, Storage Location, Purchasing Org, and Purchasing Group have been defined as described in Chapter 3. Without the organization structure, procurement is not possible in the system.
2. Master data objects, including units of measure, material masters, material groups, and suppliers, have been set up appropriately in the system, as described in Chapter 4.

Direct procurement leverages these data elements and the same configuration as defined in Chapter 5. A user can create a PO for either an indirect item or direct material using the Requisitioning app in SAP S/4HANA. The configuration differences and additions for direct procurement are mostly on the automation side in setting up MRP, and the usage of different document and item types, such as scheduling agreements and subcontracting. This is the focus of the next section.

6.5.2 Configuring Automated and Direct Procurement

Now, we'll cover setting up document types, then setting up the MRP and automation configuration settings.

Document Type Configuration

The first step for setting up purchase orders and purchase requisitions is to define the number ranges and document types. For requisitions, you typically just need one range and one document type, as discussed ahead. The requisition then can be used to create different document types at the PO level as required.

Define Requisition Number Range

First, follow the IMG path **Materials Management • Purchasing • Purchase Requisition • Number Range**, then define a number range to be used for your requisitions (see Figure 6.34).

6.5 Configuration

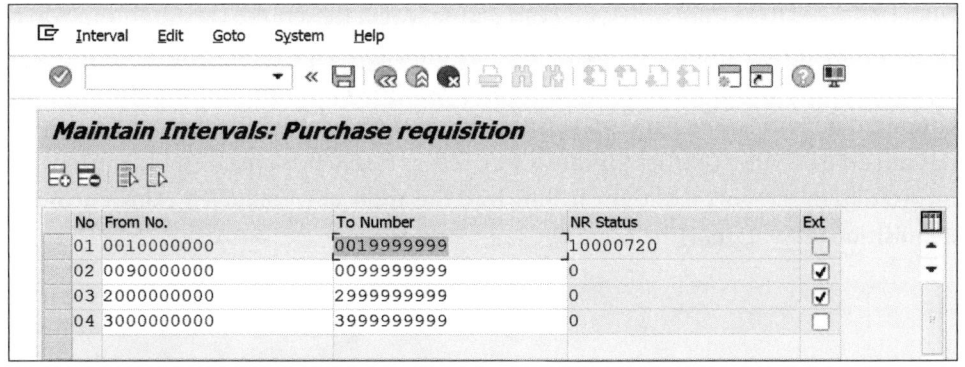

Figure 6.34 Define Number Range for Requisitions

If you have external systems creating requisitions in SAP S/4HANA, this is where you would define these number ranges and flag them as external, as well as the 2- and 3-series number ranges above. Once saved, these number ranges can be assigned to document types.

Define Document Types for Requisition

Next, you define the document type and use the number range created in the previous step. Follow IMG path **Materials Management • Purchasing • Purchase Requisition • Document Type**, then set the document type (default is NB), along with the ranges for both internal and external if required (see Figure 6.35).

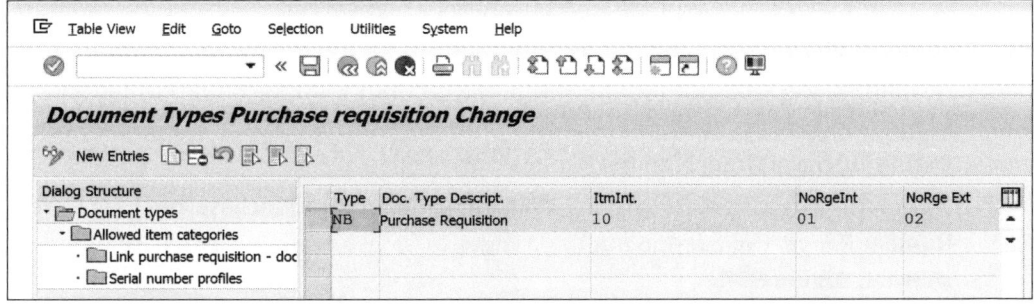

Figure 6.35 Document Type Setting for Requisition

In Figure 6.35, **ItmInt.** refers to the item interval. Setting this to **10** means that each additional item will be spaced 10 digits from the previous item (10, 20, 30…).

213

Under **Allowed Item Categories**, you can define which item types can be entered on a requisition. This is where standard, service, limit (blanket), and consignment item types can be maintained to support these processes for direct and automated procurement activities (see Figure 6.36). You can also link further document types and define serial number profiles for these item categories in this area by highlighting the targeted item category and then drilling into the applicable folder (e.g., **Link Purchase Requisition—Document**).

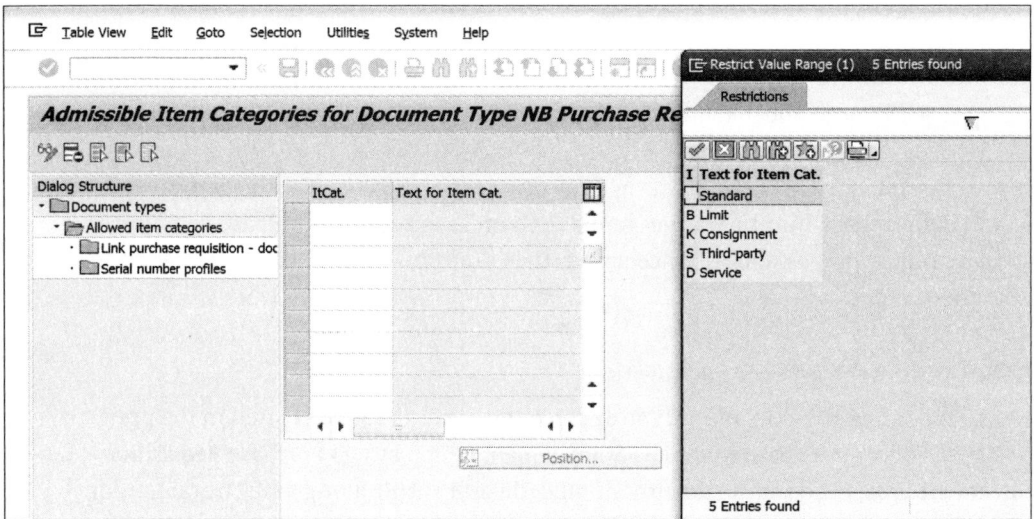

Figure 6.36 Maintaining Item Categories for Requisition Document Type

Now that you've configured the baseline requisition, you can move onto configuring the purchase order.

Define Purchase Order Number Ranges

Follow the IMG path **Materials Management • Purchasing • Purchase Purchase Order • Number Range**, then define number ranges to be used for your purchase orders as shown in Figure 6.37.

If you have external systems creating purchase orders in SAP S/4HANA, this is where you would define these number ranges and flag them as external, as well as the 41-, 44-, 56-, and 61-series number ranges above. Once saved, these number ranges can now be assigned to document types.

6.5 Configuration

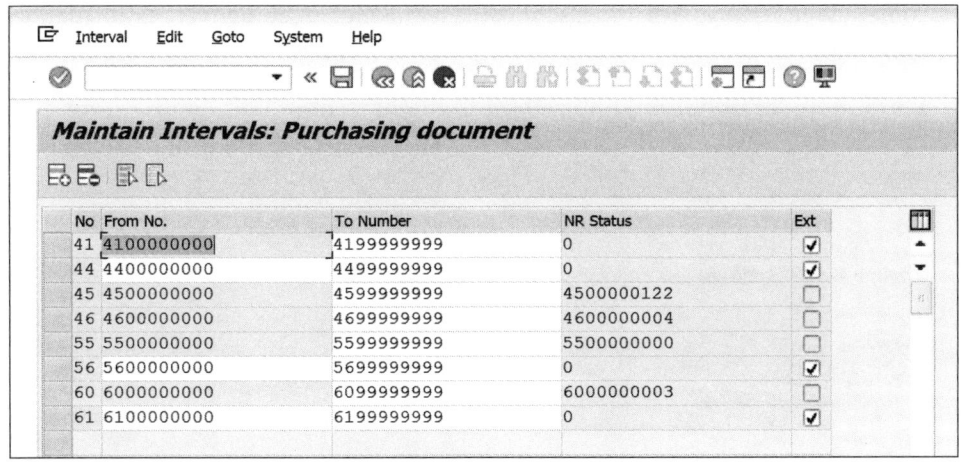

Figure 6.37 Define Purchase Order Number Ranges

Define Document Types for Purchase Order

Next, you define the document type and use the number range created in the previous step. Follow IMG path **Materials Management • Purchasing • Purchase Order • Document Type**, then set the document type (default is NB), along with the ranges for both internal and external if required (see Figure 6.38).

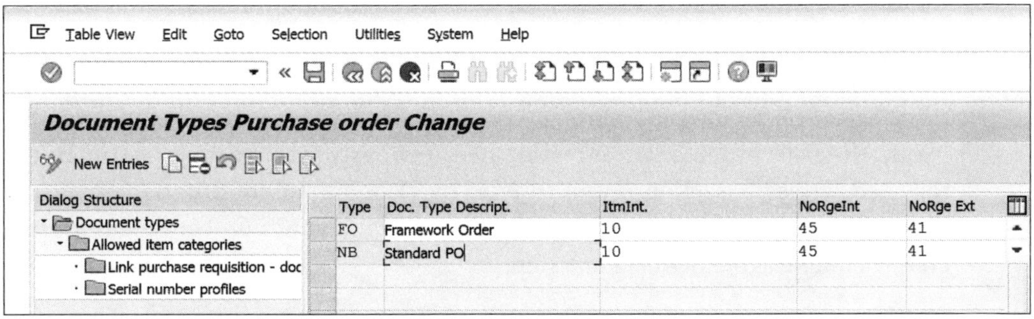

Figure 6.38 Purchase Order Document Type Definition

As with requisitions, under **Allowed Item Categories**, you can define which item types can be entered on a purchase order. This is where standard, service, limit (blanket), and consignment item types can be maintained to support these processes for direct and automated procurement activities. You want to keep these in alignment with the settings you made for requisitions where possible, to avoid scenarios in which a requisition is using an item type unsupported by your purchase order document type settings. You can also link the requisition document types and define serial number profiles for these item categories in this area by highlighting the targeted item category and then drilling into the applicable folder (e.g., **Link Purchase Requisition—Document**; see Figure 6.39).

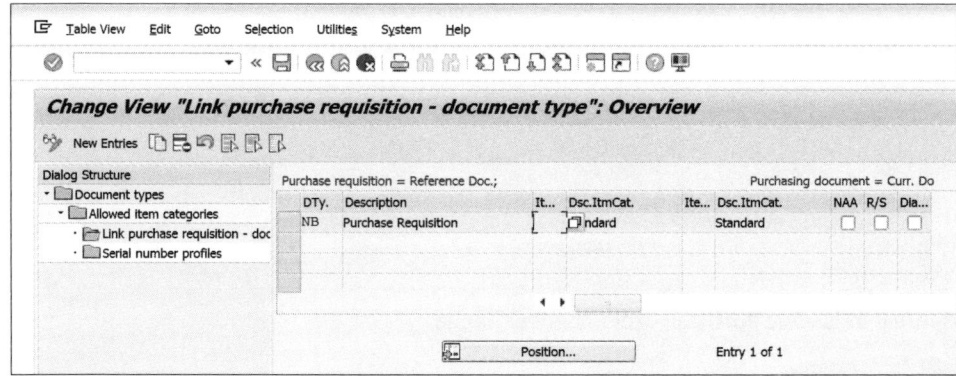

Figure 6.39 Link Purchase Requisition Document Types to PO Doc Type

Now that you've configured the baseline requisition settings and purchase order settings, you're ready to move onto configuring the scheduling agreement document type.

Define Scheduling Agreement Number Ranges

Follow the IMG path **Materials Management • Purchasing • Scheduling Agreement • Number Range**, then define number ranges to be used for your scheduling agreements. Note that number ranges maintained previously to set up purchase orders are reflected in this transaction as well, to avoid overlapping and confusion when setting up further ranges. This also means that you can set up your number ranges for POs and scheduling agreements in one step.

Define Document Types for Scheduling Agreement

Next, define the document type and use the number range created in the previous step. Follow IMG path **Materials Management • Purchasing • Scheduling Agreement • Document Type**, then set the document type (default is LP), along with the ranges for both internal and external if required (see Figure 6.40).

As with requisitions and purchase orders, under **Allowed Item Categories**, you can define which item types can be entered on a purchase order. This is where standard and consignment item types can be maintained to support these processes for scheduling agreements. You can also link the requisition document types to these item categories in this area by highlighting the targeted item category and then drilling into applicable folder (e.g., **Link Purchase Requisition—Document**).

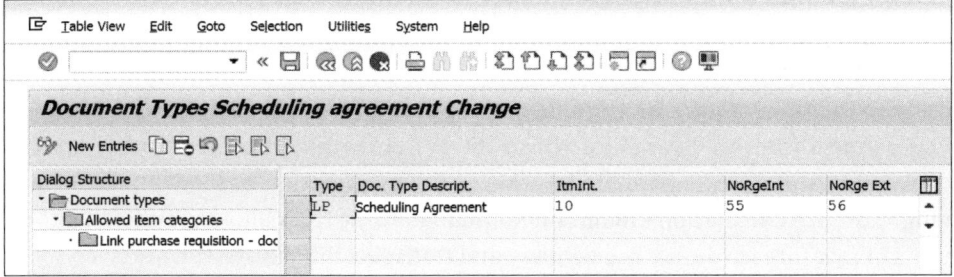

Figure 6.40 Scheduling Agreement Document Type Definition

Now that you've configured the baseline scheduling agreements and the core document types for requisitions and purchase orders, you're ready to configure further areas for MRP.

Forecast Planning Configuration

For a forecast to be used for MRP, you must configure the forecast indicator for the corresponding MRP type in IMG menu path **Materials Management • Consumption-Based Planning • Master Data • Check MRP Types**, as shown in Figure 6.41.

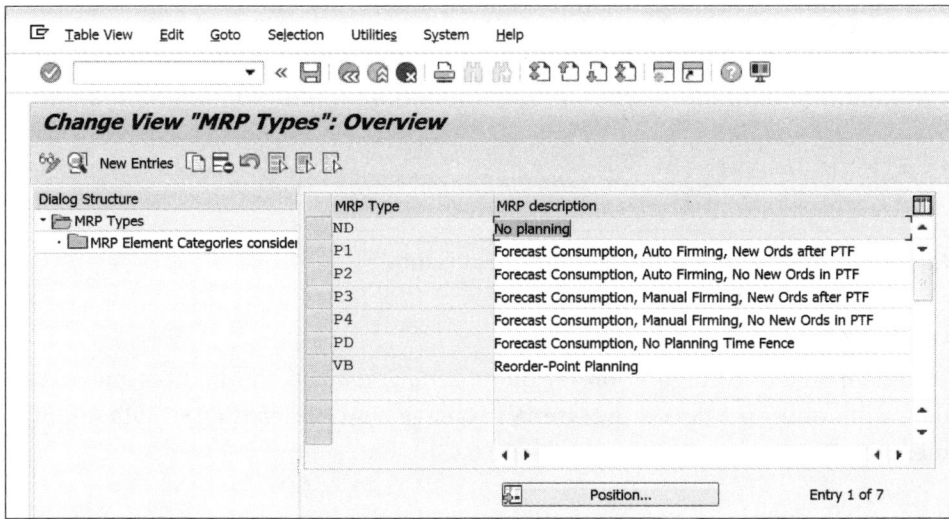

Figure 6.41 Forecast: MRP Types

217

6 Automated and Direct Procurement

Option forecast configuration can be set following the IMG menu path **Materials Management • Consumption-Based Planning • Forecast**. Here, you can define weighting groups for moving average, split forecast requirements for MRP, and assign forecast errors to error clauses.

Purchase Info Record Configuration

You can maintain a rounding profile in the PIR or in general customizing, in which you define a threshold value for which the system will round the number up to a deliverable unit. For the latter, follow IMG path **Consumption-based Planning • Planning • Lot-Size Calculation • Maintain Rounding Profile**. This allows you to adapt the units of measure in MRP to the delivery and transport units.

Source Lists Configuration

Under IMG path **Materials Management • Purchasing • Source List**, you can identify which plants require a source list as shown in Figure 6.42.

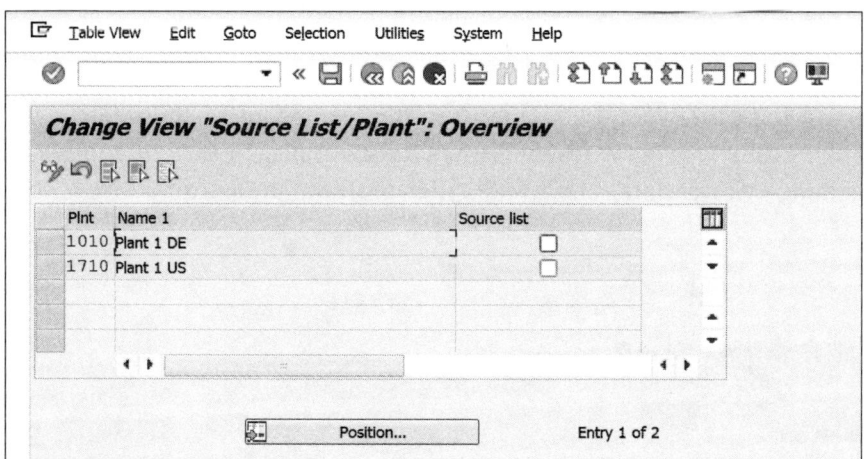

Figure 6.42 Source List Requirement Setting at Plant

Quota Arrangements Configuration

The main area of configuration for quota arrangement is the number range. You define this under the IMG path **Materials Management • Purchasing • Quota Arrangement • Define Number Ranges** (see Figure 6.43).

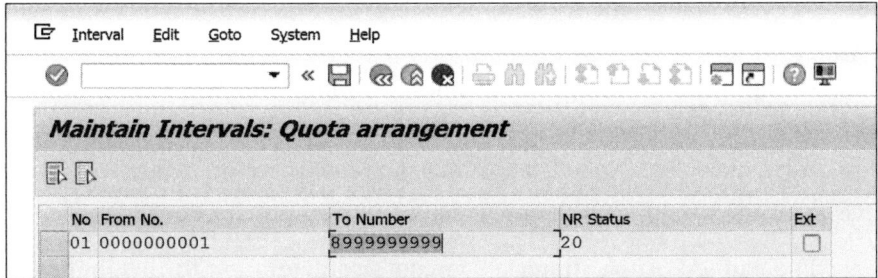

Figure 6.43 Number Range Configuration for Quota Arrangement

This is an overview of baseline configuration in support of direct procurement and automated procurement activities in SAP S/4HANA systems. Direct procurement is embedded in SAP ERP due to the tight linkages with other modules that reside in this area, such as Production Planning, Sales and Distribution, and Finance. These areas and stakeholders will provide further requirements for a project to seamlessly configure a cross-module direct procurement process.

6.6 Integration with SAP Ariba

Let's examine two SAP Ariba integration scenarios: SAP Ariba Supply Chain Collaboration and SAP Ariba Supply Chain Collaboration for Buyers and SAP S/4HANA.

6.6.1 SAP Ariba Supply Chain Collaboration

Formerly known as Collaborative Supply Chain (CSC), Supply Chain Collaboration has evolved to support direct procurement processes on the supplier side in the Ariba Network.

The main direct procurement transactions supported now include schedule releases, subcontract orders, consignment inventory checks, and quality notifications/responses on the buyer side. On the supplier side, leveraging the power of the Ariba Network, a supplier can now collaborate on forecasts, confirm POs and component receipts/consumption, provide manufacturing visibility, advise of order deviations, and submit an invoice back to the buyer. With SAP Ariba Supply Chain Collaboration for Buyers and SAP Ariba Strategic Sourcing, there is coverage for all of the following processes in SAP S/4HANA:

- Product Lifecycle Management (PLM), Sourcing, Contracts: SAP Ariba Strategic Sourcing
- Forecast to Commit in SAP Integrated Business Planning (SAP IBP): SAP Ariba Strategic Sourcing
- Request, order, make: SAP Ariba Supply Chain Collaboration for Buyers
- Receive, manage, pay: SAP Ariba Supply Chain Collaboration for Buyers

Chapter 9 will detail SAP Ariba Strategic Sourcing's configuration further, but we'll delve deeper into the setup for SAP Ariba Supply Chain Collaboration for Buyers in the next section.

6.6.2 SAP Ariba Supply Chain Collaboration for Buyers and SAP S/4HANA

To establish basic connectivity between the SAP S/4HANA environment and SAP Ariba Supply Chain Collaboration for Buyers, verify the applicability of these steps in the Configuration Guide for Business Network Collaboration at *http://bit.ly/16410601*. Similar instructions are available for connecting SAP Integrated Business Planning (IBP), which replaces Advanced Planning and Optimization, and SAP Ariba Supply Chain Collaboration for Buyers. SAP IBP is the planning tool of choice used in SAP S/4HANA and in conjunction with SAP Ariba Supply Chain Collaboration for Buyers on forecast collaboration topics. Now, execute the (high-level) steps described next.

To begin, verify access to an SAP Ariba Buyer account/SAP Ariba Supply Chain Collaboration for Buyers account by logging in using the credentials provided. If you can't login, you'll need to request this access from SAP Ariba and your account team.

Once verified, invite suppliers to the Ariba Network via menu path Launchpad Navigation. These suppliers are those that will be conducting direct procurement transactions and confirmations with your organization. To invite suppliers, navigate to **Business Network • Integration Configuration • Invite Suppliers to Ariba Network**.

The next step requires setting up a *shared secret*. This is a security step to ensure that your suppliers are who they say they are upon login. To maintain a shared secret, proceed as follows:

1. Log in to your SAP Ariba Supply Chain Collaboration for Buyers account.
2. Choose **Administration • Configuration • cXML Setup**.
3. Under **Authentication Method**, select **Shared Secret** and enter your shared secret.

Once you have the security settings in place with the shared secret, it's time to enable your suppliers:

1. Log into your SAP Ariba Buyer account and go to the **Supplier Enablement** tab.
2. Go to the **Active Relationships** tab. If your supplier is in the **Active Relationships** table, jump to step 5 below and assign a private ID. If the supplier isn't in the **Active Relationships** table, search for the suppler and add it to **Selected Suppliers**. Via **Selected Suppliers**, click the supplier and choose **Request a Relationship**. The supplier must accept the request prior to proceeding to step 5 in these instructions.

In the next steps, you'll create a private ID for a supplier so that the supplier can log in:

1. Log on to SAP Ariba Supply Chain Collaboration for Buyers with your SAP Ariba Buyer account.
2. In the **Supplier Enablement Tab**, choose **Supplier Relationships** • **More Actions** • **Edit** • **Edit Preferences for Supplier** • **Enter Supplier Identifiers for Procurement Application** • **Add**.
3. If tying the supplier to only one ERP, enter the supplier ID in the first field.
4. If tying the supplier to multiple ERP backends, choose each system and enter the supplier ID.
5. Save.

You've now set up your suppliers for SAP Ariba Supply Chain Collaboration for Buyers.

> **Note**
> An additional setting is available for suppliers in the **Forecast** area to further define whether a supplier can view and forecast data, which is set as a default. In the **Forecast** area, you can override the default forecast rules and determine whether a supplier is allowed to view and commit forecast data. Save your preferences for the supplier by clicking the **Save** button on the screen.

6.7 Summary

Automated and direct procurement processes continue to evolve in SAP S/4HANA while leveraging core SAP ERP approaches such as MRP and reorder point planning. Although MRP remains as a unifying automation engine for procurement in SAP

S/4HANA, there are simplifications and updates both to the MRP cockpit and to the overall support of different sourcing protocols and forecast methodologies. Scheduling agreements, subcontracting, and consignment procurement processes all continue as viable vehicles for automating purchasing and facilitating direct procurement, in particular in SAP S/4HANA; now these processes have the added option of integrating with the Ariba Network via SAP Ariba Supply Chain Collaboration for Buyers. Long considered a differentiator and an argument for ERP-based procurement, direct procurement integrated with core production and planning modules in SAP S/4HANA embodies this history while expanding towards a future state of integrated and automated direct procurement processes, as well as real-time information exchange with suppliers.

Chapter 7
Inventory Management

Proper management and minimization of working capital held in physical stocks is a key need for all enterprises. SAP S/4HANA provides many capabilities in Inventory Management to perform goods movements and to report on historical and current stock balances and values.

Inventory Management is a core component of SAP S/4HANA Enterprise Management, supporting SAP S/4HANA Sourcing and Procurement with the receipt of goods. This component also integrates tightly with other integrated end-to-end logistics business processes, such as order and contract management for sales, service management, product planning, and production orchestration and execution. Inventory management also integrates with internal and external accounting functions, recording the financial impact of goods movements as they happen. Figure 7.1 illustrates how inventory management integrates with other core SAP S/4HANA logistics and financial functions.

Inventory Management covers the following core areas of functionality in the SAP S/4HANA system:

- Stock management on both a quantity and value basis
- Planning, entry, and recording of material movements
- Physical inventory processes
- Reporting of goods movements, stock balances, and physical inventory results

7 Inventory Management

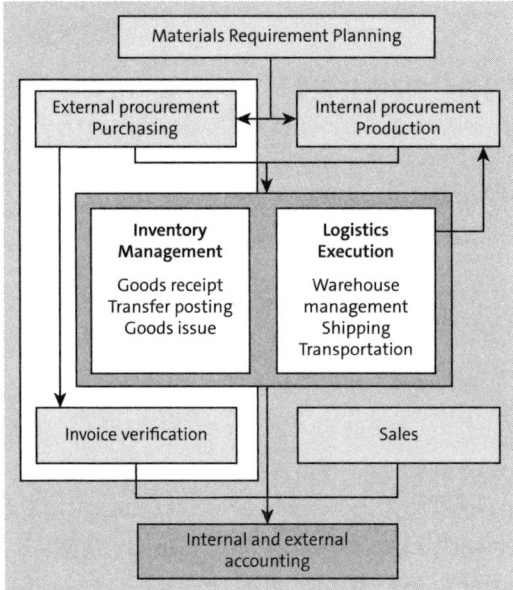

Figure 7.1 Inventory Management Integration

7.1 Inventory Management in SAP S/4HANA

The inventory management component manages and records all movements of goods in the system. It also has capabilities to manage the quantities of physical stocks in all plants in the enterprise. Integration with Financial Accounting means that financial impacts to general ledgers are posted immediately upon recording the goods movement in the SAP S/4HANA system. Inventory Management has extensive reporting capabilities so that stock balances and goods movements can be made visible to the enterprise, facilitating end-to-end process harmonization.

Inventory Management in the SAP S/4HANA system has the following solution capabilities:

- Goods receipt
- Goods issue
- Stock transfers
- Transfer postings
- Basic warehouse management
- Basic shipping

For the purposes of this book, we'll focus on the solution capabilities of Inventory Management that impact SAP S/4HANA Sourcing and Procurement business processes, which are goods receipt, goods issue, stock transfers, and transfer postings.

7.1 Inventory Management in SAP S/4HANA

7.1.1 Inventory Management Data Model

The inventory management data model for stocks in prior versions of SAP ERP was quite complex.

Each material document, which is the system record for goods movements, was represented in the system in two tables: a header record containing date, time, and user information, and one or more line items containing information about movement type, material, quantities, units of measure, and so on. Using these tables involved joining the two to obtain a unified dataset for the application or query at hand. Figure 7.2 shows both the SAP Business Suite powered by SAP HANA and the SAP S/4HANA inventory management data models in more detail.

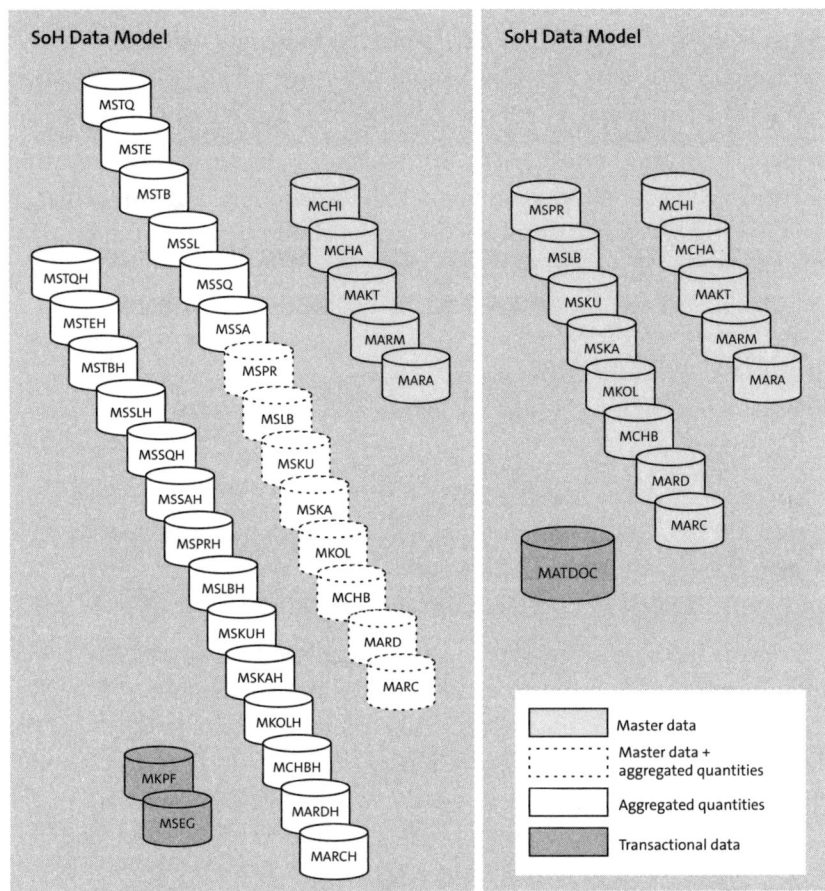

Figure 7.2 Comparison of SAP Business Suite Powered by SAP HANA and SAP S/4HANA Inventory Management Data Models

7.1.2 Material Master

The material master was involved in inventory management as well. Two tables used for holding material master control attributes—table MARC, for plant-level material attributes, and table MARD, for storage-location-level material attributes—were used to hold stock quantities and values at the plant and storage-location-data levels, respectively. This meant that inserts into the database for goods movements required locking the material master at the respective level being transacted. This was quite problematic for SAP clients with high volumes of goods movements at peak periods because locking issues sometimes prevented these movements from taking place in a timely manner.

In addition, other tables were used to store quantities and values that were specific to the kind of stock being processed. These tables needed to be updated during goods movement postings as well, which further complicated the updates. These included tables MCHB (Stocks at Batch Level), MKOL (Special Stocks from Supplier), and others.

Several aggregate tables were also present in the data model for use in reporting applications. These aggregate tables summarized the stock movement and balance data into time-phased buckets. Lastly, historical stock balance tables were also architected into the data model for use in reporting and costing.

7.1.3 SAP S/4HANA Simplifications

The inventory management data model has been completely rearchitected for the SAP HANA in-memory platform.

The material document has been reduced to one table, table MATDOC, which contains header and line item data for goods movements. The stock quantity and amount fields, which were previously stored in the hybrid tables, have been eliminated. The stock aggregate and historical stock tables have also been eliminated.

This simplification reduces the total data footprint required to maintain Inventory Management data and therefore increases the transactional throughput of the system because transactions now do not need to update nearly as many tables as before. It also means that only main tables are needed; redundancy in the database is eliminated. The master data is now clearly separated from the transactional data in the data model. Less data means a smaller memory footprint, increasing throughput.

All stock calculations now harness the power of the SAP S/4HANA database and read table MATDOC directly. This enables stock balances, both current and historical, to be calculated in real time, without use of aggregate tables. Analytics can now be calculated in real time and go to the most granular level. This capability enables inventory managers to react to operational situations and eliminate bottlenecks in material flow through the enterprise.

This architecture also eliminates the need for material master locking during `INSERT` operations on the database, thus improving transactional throughput by a factor of 10 to 25 times. Analytics now run natively and avoid the overhead involved in `JOIN` operations on the underlying data tables.

Twenty-one tables were eliminated in the new Inventory Management data model, and stock aggregate columns in eight additional tables were removed as well.

Material valuation data was previously housed in the accounting tables of the material master. Now, the material ledger is required in SAP S/4HANA and is used to house material valuation data. This allows inventory valuation in multiple currencies to be maintained consistently. The valuation tables in the classic SAP ERP data model (table `MBEW`, etc.) have been eliminated from the data model. Note that SAP does provide CDS views for those customers who are converting to SAP S/4HANA and who need to preserve their investment in legacy developments to run their business processes. The previous hybrid, aggregate, and historical views of the database are available via CDS views in the system.

7.2 Stock Management in SAP S/4HANA

Stock management is the core purpose of Inventory Management. The functions of the system allow all goods movements affecting physical stocks to be documented. This allows stock balances to be instantly obtainable, both for the present or for points in the past. If the material type assigned to the material permits valuation, then the appropriate financial documents are posted in the system when the goods movements are recorded.

It's useful to consider stock management as an amalgam of multiple data elements. Each data element used reflects one aspect of the stock—for example, the condition, location, and physical and logistical attributes of the stock itself:

- Material
- Location
- Usability
- Ownership
- Batch management
- Serialization

7.2.1 Material

Stocks are primarily identified with a material number. Each material is represented in the system with a unique identifier. Each material contains an attribute known as the *material type*, which defines control features for a grouping of materials.

7.2.2 Location

The location information in Inventory Management consists of two attributes:

- The plant, the physical location where logistics activities in support of the enterprise are transacted
- The storage location, a subset of a plant used for stock-management purposes

All stock managed in an enterprise must be assigned to a plant. The plant provides the linkage to Financial Accounting via the company code assigned to that plant.

If the stock is managed in a facility that the enterprise owns or controls, then the stock is assigned to a storage location upon receipt. However, there are other types of stocks in an enterprise that may not have a storage location identified. A good example of this is stock being transferred between two facilities. If goods being transferred have been issued from the supplying plant but haven't yet arrived in the receiving plant, then the stock in SAP S/4HANA is designated in-transit to the receiving plant and doesn't list a storage location. A storage location must be specified on the goods receipt into stock at the physical location.

7.2.3 Usability

Stock type is the term used in SAP to designate the disposition or usability of the stock for materials planning and execution purposes. There are four main stock types supported in SAP S/4HANA:

- Unrestricted use stock
- Quality inspection stock
- Blocked stock
- Customer returns stock

Each stock type is described ahead.

Unrestricted Use

The *unrestricted use* stock type is used to designate inventory quantities that are free to be considered for materials planning or execution purposes, such as deliveries to customers or consumption for production. Unrestricted use stocks can be freely transferred between plants and storage locations.

Quality Inspection

The *quality inspection* (QI) stock type is used for identifying quantities of goods that are undergoing processing by the quality department at the current time. QI stocks are considered *available* from a materials planning point of view. However, these stocks can't be shipped to a customer or consumed internally until a decision has been made about their usability. They can be transferred between storage locations in a plant but can't be transferred between plants.

QI stocks may be under the control of the Quality Management (QM) module. If QM is active for that material in that plant, then Quality Management processes control the postings of material into and out of the QI stock type. If QM isn't active for that material in that plant, then transfer postings are used to post stocks out of QI stock into unrestricted use stock.

Blocked

The *blocked* stock type is used when a material becomes unusable for planning and execution purposes. Blocked stocks generally aren't considered during materials planning. Blocked stocks can't be used for fulfilling customer or production demands. Blocked stocks can be transferred between storage locations within a plant.

Note that unrestricted use, quality inspection, and blocked stocks are considered valuated stocks if the stock type assigned to the material is valuated in the valuation area assigned to the plant.

Customer Returns

The *customer returns* stock type is a less commonly used stock type. It can be used to manage goods that have been delivered back into a storage location from a customer when a decision hasn't been made as to whether the goods will be accepted back into stock. Customer returns stock is always nonvaluated stock. Once a decision is made to accept the goods, a transfer posting from customer returns to either unrestricted use, quality inspection, or blocked stock is made. This transfer posting posts the quantities into valuated stock and creates an accounting document.

7.2.4 Ownership

Most stocks in an SAP S/4HANA system are owned by the enterprise and are reflected in the appropriate stock accounts in Financial Accounting. However, it's possible to represent stocks that are owned by an external party in the system. Special stock indicators are used to represent these ownership scenarios in Inventory Management. Each special stock has a unique one-letter identifier in the database.

The following are examples of special stocks that are owned by the enterprise and physically stored at an external location:

- Component stocks provided to supplier for subcontracting (special stock O)
- Finished goods consigned to a customer (special stock W)
- Returnable transport packaging at customer (special stock V)

Note that these special stocks can be in either unrestricted use or quality inspection stock types.

The following are examples of special stocks owned by an external party and physically stored in a plant and storage location:

- Supplier consignment stock (special stock K)
- Supplier-owned returnable transport packaging (special stock M)

7.2.5 Batch Management

Many industries, such as food or pharmaceuticals, require stock management based on the attributes of a manufacturing lot of a material. SAP S/4HANA provides the Batch Management component to fill these needs. A *batch* is defined as a subset of a material with a set of attributes that have common values.

If you need a material to be batch-managed in the SAP S/4HANA system, set the batch management indicator on a material master view at the plant level, such as the purchasing view.

A batch can contain one or more characteristics, which are equivalent to the attributes being measured. Each characteristic in a batch can contain one or more values that differentiate one batch from another for that material. Typically, the characteristic values are recorded upon the initial goods receipt of a batch-managed material from production or procurement.

All goods movements for batch-managed materials must identify the unique batch of the material being transacted.

Note that it's very difficult to change the batch management indicator on a material once material movements have been recorded in the system. Therefore, consider carefully before setting the batch management indicator on the material master.

7.2.6 Serialization

Some industries need to identify individual units of a material—for example, consumer electronics or medical devices, for which it's important to track units for customer servicing and warranty purposes. Serial Number Management is used in SAP S/4HANA for these requirements.

Making a material relevant for serialization involves the assignment of a serial number profile in the storage view of the material master. The serial number profile is set up in system configuration and designates the types of business transactions for which serial numbers need to be recorded.

If serialization is active for Inventory Management for a material in a plant, then serial numbers must be recorded for each unit of material in a goods movement.

7.2.7 Goods Movements

Goods movements are transactions in SAP S/4HANA that result in a change in stock.

There are four main types of goods movements:

- **Goods receipts**
  These are goods movements that result in an increase in quantities of stock.
- **Goods issues**
  These are goods movements that result in a decrease in quantities of stock.
- **Stock transfers**
  These are goods movements that result in quantities of stock moving between two logistics organizational elements. For instance, you can transfer stock between two plants in an enterprise or between two storage locations in a plant.
- **Transfer postings**
  These are goods movements that result in a change in identity, disposition, or ownership of a material. Transfer postings can be done in conjunction with stock transfers in some cases.

Each goods movement in the SAP S/4HANA system is recorded as a material document. A material document contains information on the type of goods movement, the date and time of posting, the user identifier who created the goods movement, the materials transacted, quantities and units of measure, and associated details. The details are recorded in table MATDOC in SAP S/4HANA.

Many goods movements reference other SAP S/4HANA documents. For instance, a goods receipt can reference a purchasing document and line item. This information is recorded in the material document as well.

Each material document line item contains a movement-type code. The movement type in the SAP S/4HANA system is a three-character field that identifies the type of goods movement to be recorded (goods receipt, goods issue, transfer posting). Movement types play an important control function in determining what data is required to successfully post the goods movement and to pass information into other system components, such as Financial Accounting. Special stock indicators are used for some movement types depending on the situation.

Movement types are paired with a reversal movement type. These reversal movement types are used to undo a movement already posted in the system. It is typical to have the reversal movement type be the movement type number.

Examples of movement types important for Sourcing and Procurement include the following:

- 101: Goods Receipt for a Purchasing Document
- 543 O: Goods Issue from Component Stock Provided to Supplier

7.3 Goods Receipts

Goods receipts are goods movements that result in an increase in stock. They are important goods movements for Sourcing and Procurement, as they form an important process link between purchasing and financial accounting. Goods receipts usually reference other SAP S/4HANA documents, such as purchase orders or inbound deliveries. This streamlines the entry of the goods receipt data, which can be copied directly from the reference document. However, there are goods receipts that can be entered without any reference, such as when initial stocks are entered into the system at startup.

Goods receipts can be entered into the SAP S/4HANA system in two ways: a material document can be posted directly in the system using the Post Goods Movement app, or, alternatively, if the supplier of the goods transmits an advanced shipping notification to you, you can then convert this communication into an inbound delivery document in SAP S/4HANA. Inbound delivery documents can be used when available to plan inbound receipts needs with much more precision because the quantities and dates are firmer than at the time of purchase order entry or purchase order acknowledgement.

The inbound delivery can be created in the SAP S/4HANA system with reference to one or more purchasing documents. As an alternative, these documents can also be created via the receipt of an advance shipping notification (ASN) from the supplier of the goods prior to the actual receipt. EDI or the Ariba Network can be utilized to transmit ASNs to an SAP S/4HANA system. Inbound deliveries allow for more precise planning of the inbound movements and provide up-to-date firm supply data to materials planning.

The confirmation control key entered on the purchasing document line item controls the method by which a goods receipt is posted. If the confirmation control key includes inbound deliveries, then the following documents must be referenced to receive the goods. Otherwise, the purchase order or scheduling agreement line item can be referenced directly at goods receipt.

- Movement types for goods receipts with reference to documents:
    - 101: Goods Receipt with reference to Purchase Order/Production Order
- Movement types for goods receipts without reference:
    - 561: Initial Stock Entry for Unrestricted Use Stock
    - 563: Initial Stock Entry for Quality Inspection Stock
    - 565: Initial Stock Entry for Blocked Stock

Goods receipts can be posted using apps that post goods movements directly into Inventory Management. Some goods receipts also can be posted using integration with shipping documents, such as inbound deliveries. Both types of goods receipts are described in the following sections.

7.3.1 Posting Goods Receipts Using Inventory Management Apps

There are a variety of SAP Fiori apps for Inventory Management that can be used to record the arrival of goods at your facility. These apps are described in more detail in the sections ahead.

The following SAP Fiori apps are available in SAP S/4HANA for processing goods receipts:

- Post Goods Receipt for Purchase Order
- Manage Stock
- Material Documents Overview

In addition, the following WebGUI apps are also available for processing goods receipts:

- Post Goods Movement
- Output Material Documents

Post Goods Receipt for Purchase Order

The Post Goods Receipt for Purchase Order app is used to record the physical receipt of goods into a facility. This app requires the receipt of these goods to be made with reference to an existing purchasing document. It is vital that goods receipts reference the correct purchasing documents used to order them in order for the procure-to-pay business process to work efficiently.

The Post Goods Receipt for Purchase Order app (Figure 7.3) lets you do the following:

- Post the receipt of goods with reference to a purchasing document that contains order items for stock material (procurement for stock)
- Post the receipt of goods with reference to a purchasing document that contains order items with account assignments (procurement for direct consumption)
- Post the receipt of goods into supplier consignment stock
- Assign batches on the item level during goods receipt processing for those materials that require them

This app cannot process purchase orders that use non-SAP-delivered purchase order document types.

This app also cannot process purchase order items which fulfill at least one of the following conditions:

- The **Delivery Completed** indicator is set on the line item.
- The material is serialized.

If all items of a purchase order fulfill at least one of these two conditions, the purchase order is not able to be processed in this app. Use the Goods Movement App as an alternative for processing purchase orders meeting these criteria.

7.3 Goods Receipts

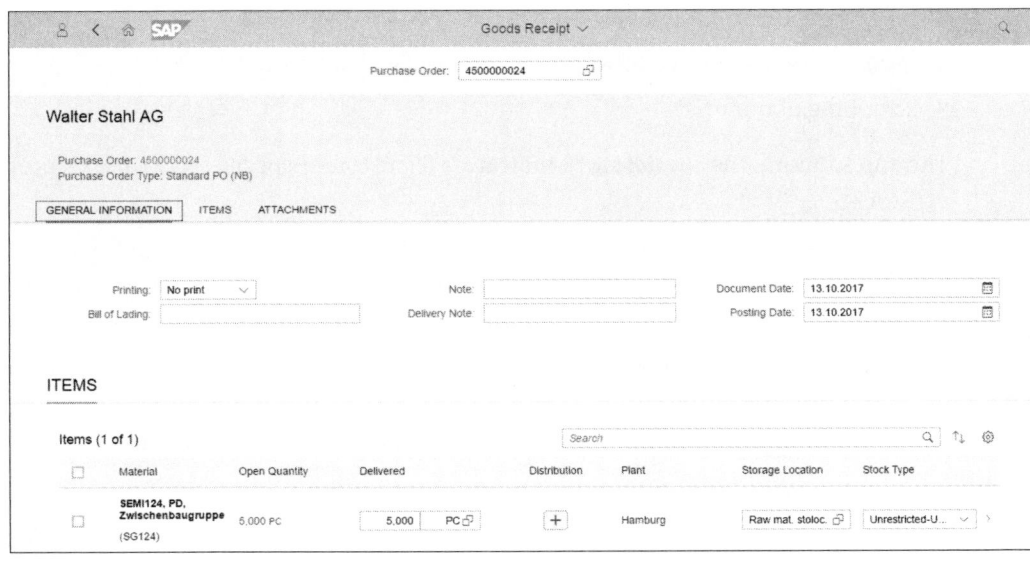

Figure 7.3 Post Goods Receipt for Purchase Order App

The app supports goods receipts for the following account assignments:

- A: Asset
- C: Sales order
- F: (Production) order
- K: Cost center
- P: Project
- S: Third party

The following special stocks are also supported:

- Project stock
- Sales order stock

The Post Goods Receipt for Purchase Order app is assigned to the inventory manager and warehouse clerk standard authorization roles.

Manage Stock

The Manage Stock app (Figure 7.4) lets you perform stock changes in the SAP S/4HANA system.

This app can perform the following types of goods movements:

- Initial entry of stock balances for unrestricted use or blocked stocks
- Scrapping of material

The app supports the special stock indicators E (customer special stock) and Q (project stock).

This app supports movement-type-dependent reason codes. Reason codes let you add a short explanation for the underlying purpose of a specific goods movement, such as poor quality.

If you notice that you've made an error in posting stock changes, you can correct the error by reversing the material document and posting the stock changes again. To reverse the material document, use the Material Documents Overview app.

Note that serialized materials cannot be managed via this app.

The Manage Stock app is assigned to the inventory manager standard authorization role.

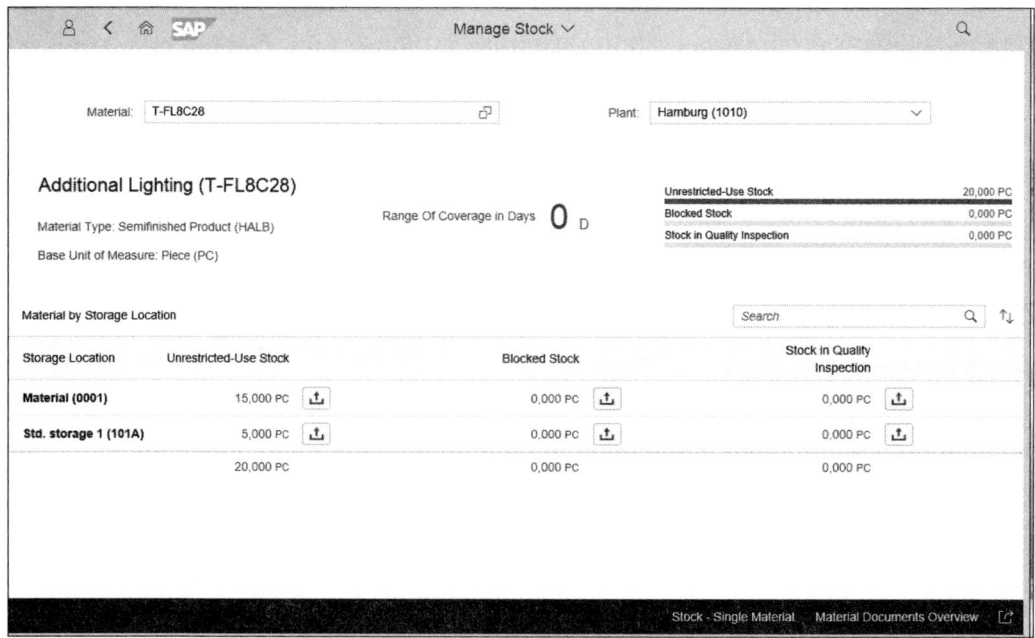

Figure 7.4 Manage Stock App

Material Documents Overview

The Material Documents Overview app (Figure 7.5) provides the capability to show a list of material document items based on filter criteria and display the details for a selected material document item. You can also reverse a material document.

This app can be used to do the following:

- Display a material document item list based on filter criteria
- Display the material document details for a specific material document item
- Display the document flow for a material document with the relevant preceding and follow-on documents
- Get an overview of material documents, such as goods issue, goods receipt, and material movements with document date, movement type (e.g., goods issue for delivery), and document items
- Add attachments to a material document
- Output a material document, such as to a printer or to EDI
- Reverse a selected material document

The Material Documents Overview app is assigned to the inventory manager, warehouse clerk, and employee—procurement standard authorization roles.

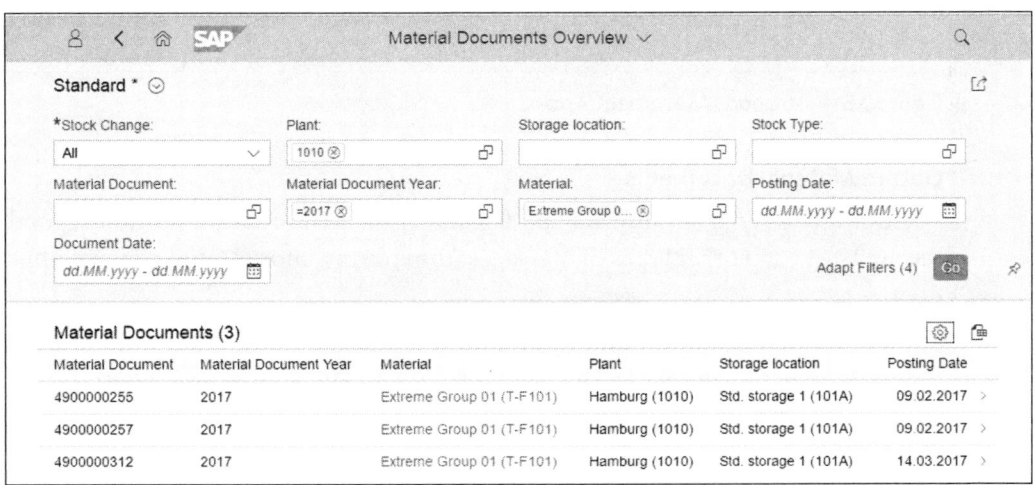

Figure 7.5 Material Documents Overview App

Post Goods Movement

The Post Goods Movement app (Figure 7.6) is used to perform goods movements, including goods receipts in the SAP S/4HANA system. It can also be used to review a specific material document and its associated documents.

This app is used when the simplified goods receipts SAP Fiori apps don't support all aspects of the type of goods receipt needed for your enterprise.

The Post Goods Movement app runs directly on the backend SAP S/4HANA system and is functionally equivalent to the classic SAP ERP Transaction MIGO.

The Post Goods Movement app is assigned to the inventory manager and warehouse clerk standard authorization roles.

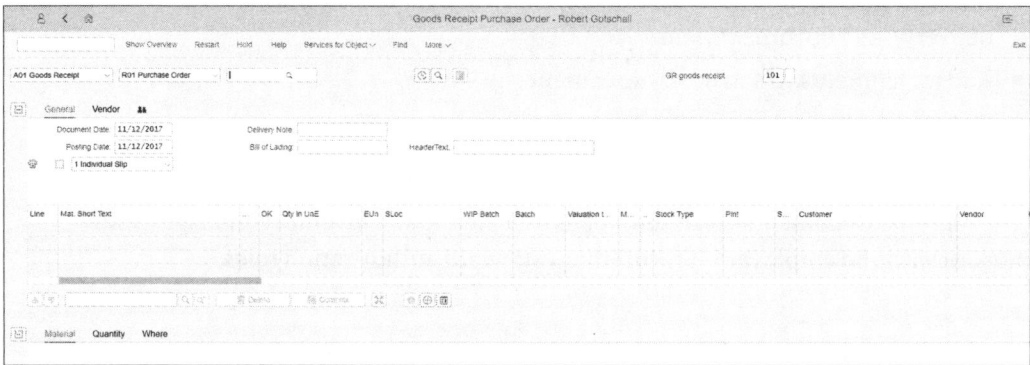

Figure 7.6 Post Goods Movement App

Output Material Documents

The Output Material Documents app (Figure 7.7) is used to create printouts, goods receipt labels, and other types of messages from the Inventory Management component.

The Output Material Documents app runs directly on the backend SAP S/4HANA system and is functionally equivalent to the classic SAP ERP Transaction MB90.

The Output Material Documents app is assigned to the inventory manager and warehouse clerk standard authorization roles.

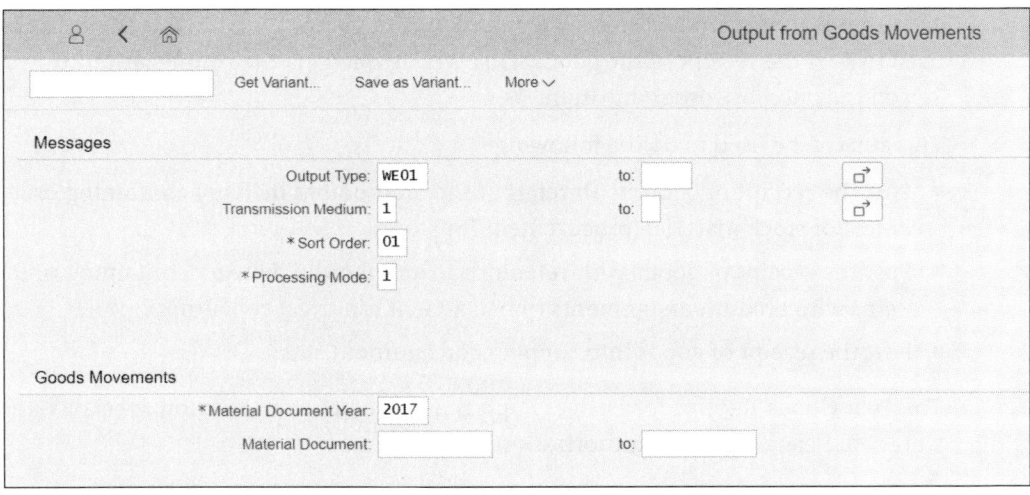

Figure 7.7 Output Material Documents App

7.3.2 Apps Used for Processing Goods Receipts via Inbound Deliveries

There are a variety of SAP Fiori apps that can be used to record the arrival of goods at your facility if your supplier transmits details to you via an advanced ship notification. These apps are described in more detail in the following sections.

The Post Goods Receipt for Delivery SAP Fiori app is available in SAP S/4HANA for processing goods receipts via inbound deliveries. In addition, the following WebGUI apps are also available:

- Inbound Deliveries for Purchase Orders
- Create Inbound Delivery
- Change Inbound Delivery
- Display Inbound Delivery
- My Inbound Delivery Monitor

Post Goods Receipt for Delivery

The Post Goods Receipt for Delivery app enables a user to record goods receipts with reference to an inbound delivery document. The app displays a selection of inbound deliveries from the supplier that can be posted.

7   Inventory Management

Note that if an inbound delivery is required for the purchase order, this app must be used to post the receipt of the goods. This is controlled via the confirmation control key on the purchase order line item.

This app can be used to do the following:

- Post the receipt of goods with reference to an inbound delivery containing order items for stock material (procurement for stock)
- Post the receipt of goods with reference to an inbound delivery containing order items with account assignments (procurement for direct consumption)
- Post the receipt of goods into supplier consignment stock

The Post Goods Receipt for Delivery app is assigned to the receiving specialist and warehouse clerk standard authorization roles.

Inbound Deliveries for Purchase Orders

The Inbound Deliveries for Purchase Orders app (Figure 7.8) is used to list purchase orders which are approved but do not have inbound deliveries created. Users can select the purchase orders for which they wish to create inbound deliveries.

The Inbound Deliveries for Purchase Orders app runs directly on the backend SAP S/4HANA system and is functionally equivalent to the classic SAP ERP Transaction VL34.

The Inbound Deliveries for Purchase Orders app is assigned to the receiving specialist standard authorization role.

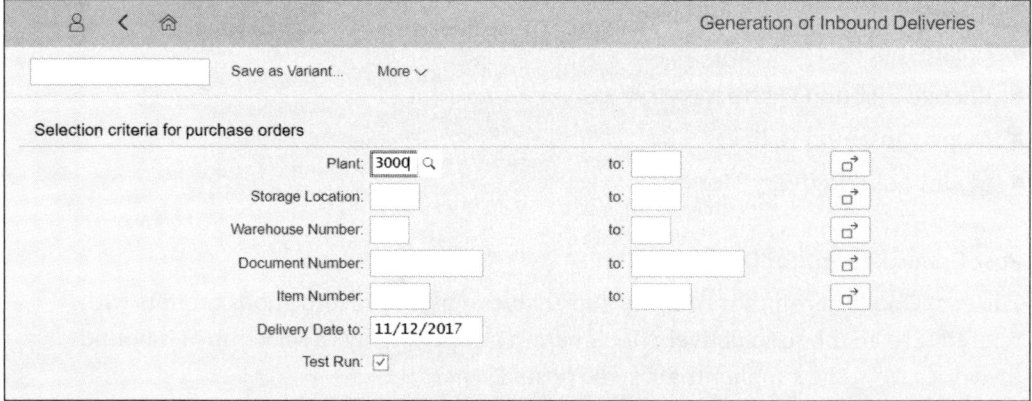

Figure 7.8 Inbound Deliveries for Purchase Orders App

7.3 Goods Receipts

Create Inbound Delivery

The Create Inbound Delivery app (Figure 7.9) is used to create an inbound delivery that references an individual purchase order.

The Create Inbound Delivery app runs directly on the backend SAP S/4HANA system and is functionally equivalent to the classic SAP ERP Transaction VL31N.

The Create Inbound Delivery app is assigned to the receiving specialist standard authorization role.

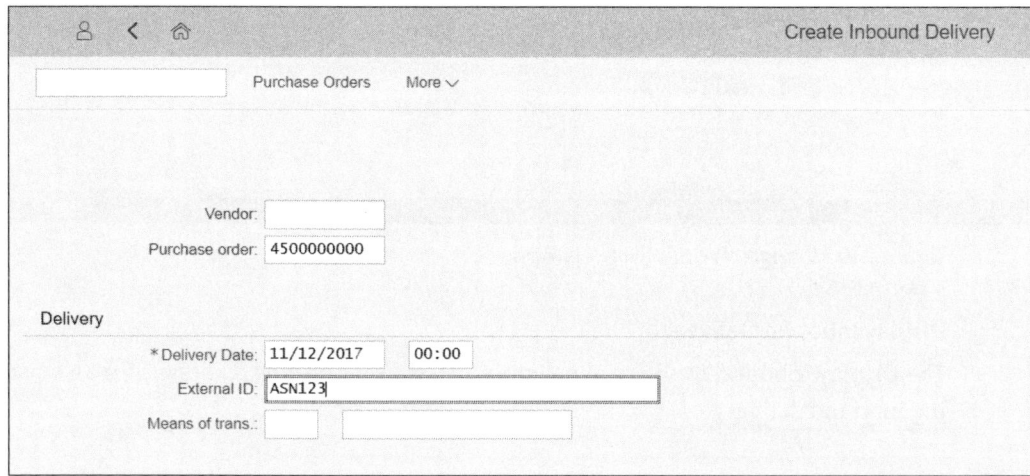

Figure 7.9 Create Inbound Delivery App

Change Inbound Delivery

The Change Inbound Delivery app (Figure 7.10) is used to make changes to an existing inbound delivery. The types of changes that can be made depend on the status of the document.

The Change Inbound Delivery app runs directly on the backend SAP S/4HANA system and is functionally equivalent to the classic SAP ERP Transaction VL32N.

The Change Inbound Delivery app is assigned to the receiving specialist standard authorization role.

7 Inventory Management

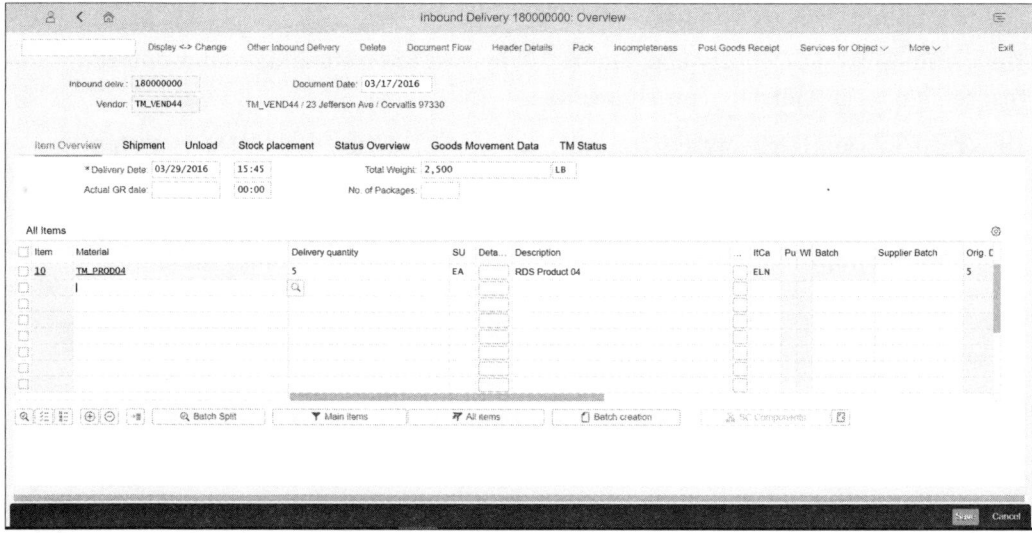

Figure 7.10 Change Inbound Delivery App

Display Inbound Delivery

The Display Inbound Delivery app (Figure 7.11) is used to show all details for an existing inbound delivery.

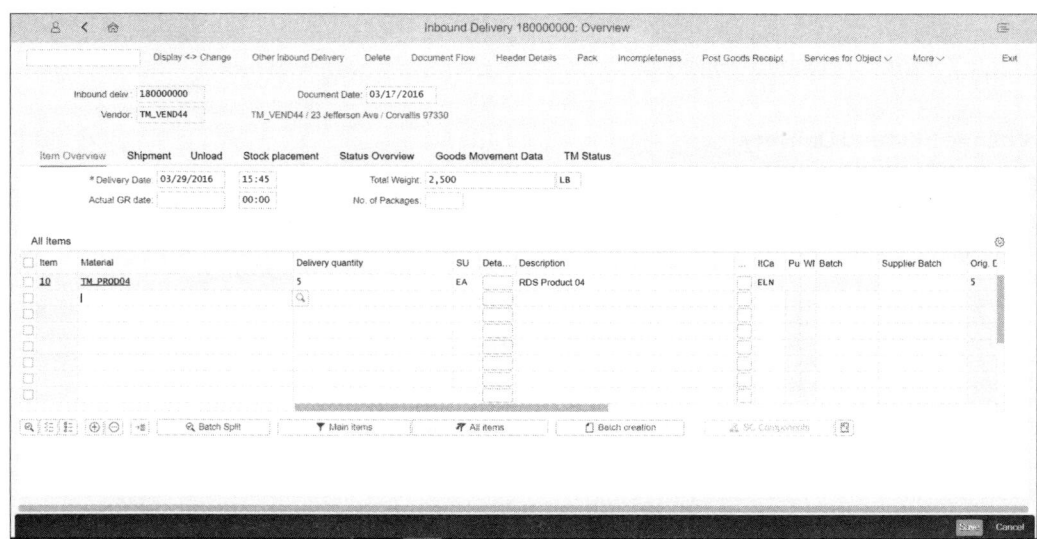

Figure 7.11 Display Inbound Delivery App

7.3 Goods Receipts

The Display Inbound Delivery app runs directly on the backend SAP S/4HANA system and is functionally equivalent to the classic SAP ERP Transaction VL33N.

The Display Inbound Delivery app is assigned to the receiving specialist standard authorization role.

My Inbound Delivery Monitor

The My Inbound Delivery Monitor app (Figure 7.12) is used to generate worklists of current inbound deliveries and to take appropriate action on the deliveries displayed. Worklists can be created that allow update of putaway quantities on line items and to post goods receipts against inbound delivery documents. General lists of inbound deliveries that meet entered criteria can also be generated.

The My Inbound Delivery Monitor app runs directly on the backend SAP S/4HANA system and is functionally equivalent to the classic SAP ERP Transaction VL06I.

The My Inbound Delivery Monitor app is assigned to the receiving specialist standard authorization role.

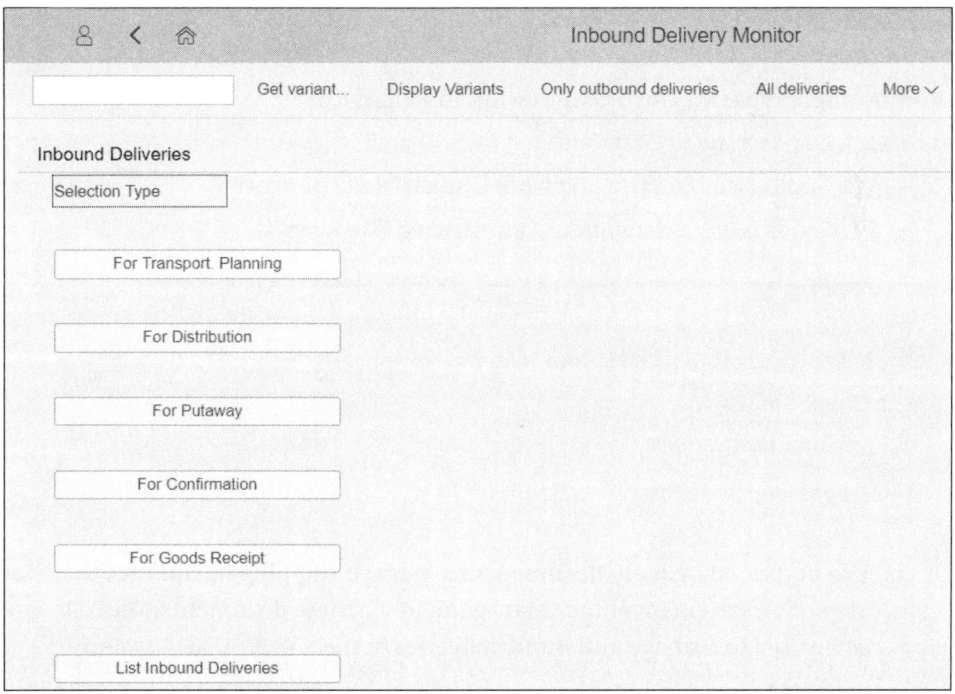

Figure 7.12 My Inbound Delivery Monitor App

7.4 Goods Issues

Goods issues are classified as goods movements that result in a decrease in stock quantities. Goods issues can be planned in the SAP S/4HANA system or can be unplanned.

Planned goods issues are issued with reference to an existing document, such as an outbound delivery to a customer or a reservation. Those customers requiring shipping integration with their goods issue processes will generally reference outbound delivery documents created by the warehouse.

Unplanned goods issues are issued without any reference. Examples are scrapping or goods issue to samples.

Here are the movement types for goods issues with and without reference documents:

- Movement types for Goods Issues with Reference to Documents:
  - 261: Goods Issue to Production Order
  - 601: Goods Issue to Outbound Delivery to Customer
  - 641: Goods Issue to In-Transit Stock between Plants in Same Company Code
  - 643: Goods Issue to In-Transit Stock between Plants in Differing Company Codes
- Movement types for Goods Issues without Reference:
  - 201: Goods Issue to Cost Center
  - 333: Goods Issue to Sampling from Unrestricted Use Stock
  - 551: Goods Issue to Scrap from Unrestricted Use Stock

> **Note**
>
> Apps used for goods issues without reference include:
>
> - Manage Stock
> - Post Goods Movement
>
> These apps were described in Section 7.3.

If you use outbound delivery documents to manage shipping operations, then you can post goods issues in Inventory Management via these documents. The following apps can be used to manage outbound deliveries in the SAP S/4HANA system:

7.4 Goods Issues

- Create Outbound Deliveries
- My Purchase Orders—Due for Delivery
- Manage Outbound Deliveries

We'll describe these apps in the following sections.

7.4.1 Create Outbound Deliveries

The Create Outbound Deliveries app (Figure 7.13) can be used to create one or more outbound delivery documents from eligible sales documents. Once the delivery creation run occurs, a log is available that shows the outbound deliveries created and error information for those sales orders that didn't convert correctly.

The Create Outbound Deliveries app can do the following:

- Search for sales documents that are due for delivery
- Sort your table entries by ascending or descending order
- Create outbound delivery documents from the sales orders selected
- Display a log that provides you with information about the deliveries created and any errors encountered during the delivery creation run

The Create Outbound Deliveries app is assigned to the shipping specialist standard authorization role.

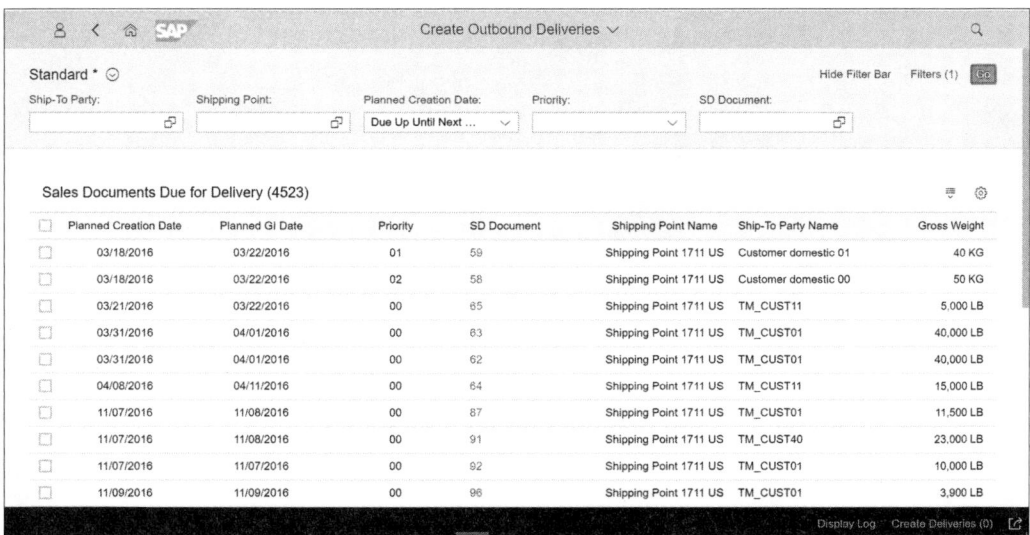

Figure 7.13 Create Outbound Deliveries App

7 Inventory Management

7.4.2 My Purchase Orders—Due for Delivery

The My Purchase Orders—Due for Delivery app (Figure 7.14) is used to create outbound deliveries for those purchase orders that involve outbound movements of material. These types of purchase orders include returns of material to suppliers or the provisioning of component materials to a subcontractor out of storage location stock. Specific selection criteria are entered, and a list of eligible purchase orders is shown. Outbound deliveries then can be created for the selected orders.

The My Purchase Orders—Due for Delivery app runs directly on the backend SAP S/4HANA system and is functionally equivalent to the classic SAP ERP Transaction VL10B.

The My Purchase Orders—Due for Delivery app is assigned to the shipping specialist standard authorization role.

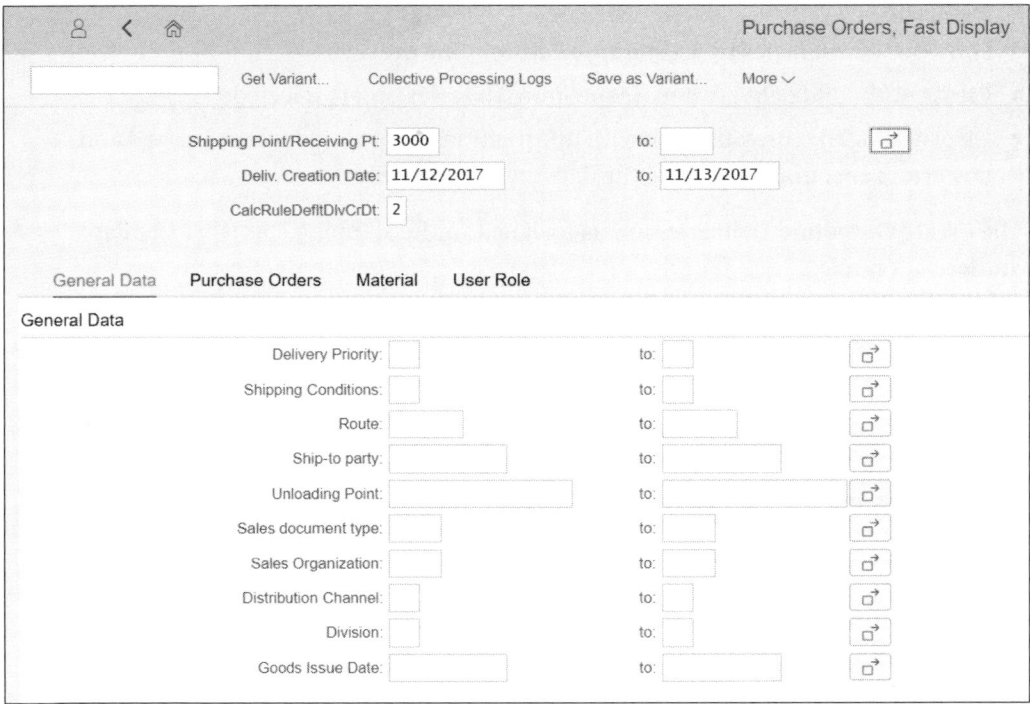

Figure 7.14 My Purchase Orders—Due for Delivery App

7.4.3 Manage Outbound Deliveries

The Manage Outbound Deliveries app (Figure 7.15) produces a list of outbound deliveries to your specifications. You can click a specific outbound delivery to see details about the document, such as the ship-to customer, weights, or volumes. You can then process the documents, depending on the status of the delivery. For instance, you can post a goods issue for a delivery from this app if it has been completely picked. If you subsequently need to change a delivery document, you can use the app to reverse the goods issue posting and then edit the document.

The Manage Outbound Deliveries app is used to do the following:

- Search for outbound deliveries using provided filter criteria
- Sort your table entries in ascending or descending order
- Pick the outbound delivery by transferring to the Pick Outbound Delivery app
- Post goods issues for one or more outbound deliveries
- Reverse goods issue postings for one or more outbound deliveries

The Manage Outbound Deliveries app is assigned to the shipping specialist standard authorization role.

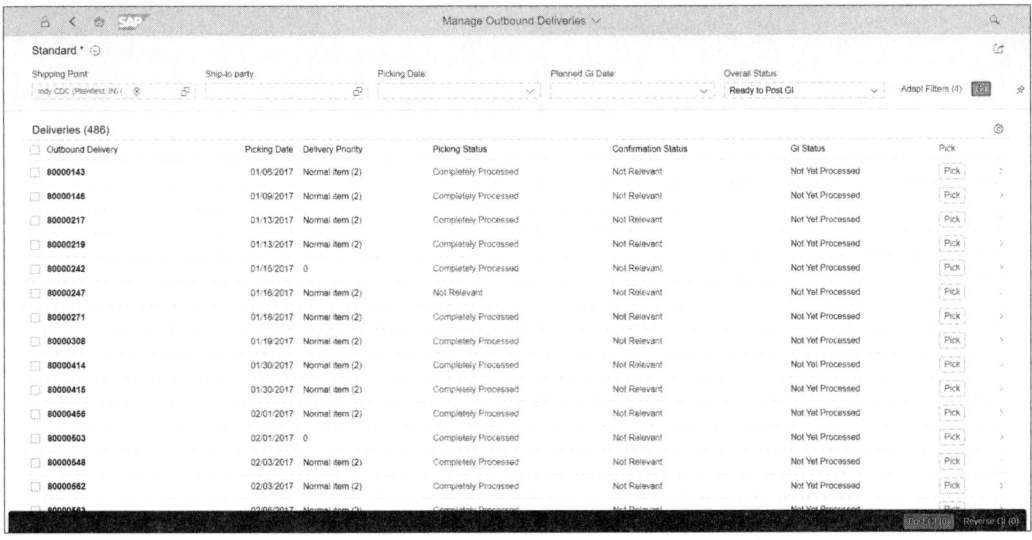

Figure 7.15 Manage Outbound Deliveries App

7.5 Stock Transfers

Stock transfers are goods movements in Inventory Management that result in a change in location. This can be between storage locations in a plant or between two distinct plants. There are three types of stock transfers:

1. Plant to plant within one company code
2. Plant to plant between two company codes
3. Storage location to storage location

Stock transfers can take place in either one-step or two-step processes.

7.5.1 One-Step Stock Transfers

In one-step stock transfers, the material moves from the issuing plant and storage location to the receiving plant and storage location immediately upon posting. One-step stock transfers are typically used when goods movements are performed in the system after the physical transfer takes place.

The following movement types are used for one-step stock transfers:

- 301: Plant to Plant
- 311: Storage Location to Storage Location

We'll describe these apps in the following sections.

7.5.2 Two-Step Stock Transfers

Two-step transfers are used to record the goods issue from the issuing plant and storage location separately from the goods receipt into the receiving plant and storage location. This two-step process has the benefit of providing visibility into in-transit stock quantities between the two locations.

The following movement types are used for two-step stock transfers:

- 303: Plant to Plant—Goods Issue from Shipping Plant
- 305: Plant to Plant—Goods Receipt in Receiving Plant
- 313: Storage Location to Storage Location—Goods Receipt in Receiving Plant
- 305: Plant to Plant—Goods Receipt in Receiving Plant

Note that these movement types only work with unrestricted use stock.

Simple movements of stock can be recorded in the SAP S/4HANA system with just a material document. The following apps can be used to perform stock transfers using Inventory Management goods movements:

- Transfer Stock—In-Plant
- Transfer Stock—Cross-Plant
- Manage Stock

We'll describe these apps in the following sections.

> **Note**
> The Manage Stock app is described in Section 7.3.1.

7.5.3 Transfer Stock—In-Plant

The Transfer Stock—In Plant app (Figure 7.16) is used to make transfer postings within a plant.

Utilize this app to make storage location to storage location stock transfers. You can transfer unrestricted, quality inspection, or blocked stocks. You can move supplier consignment, sales order, or project special stocks between storage locations as well.

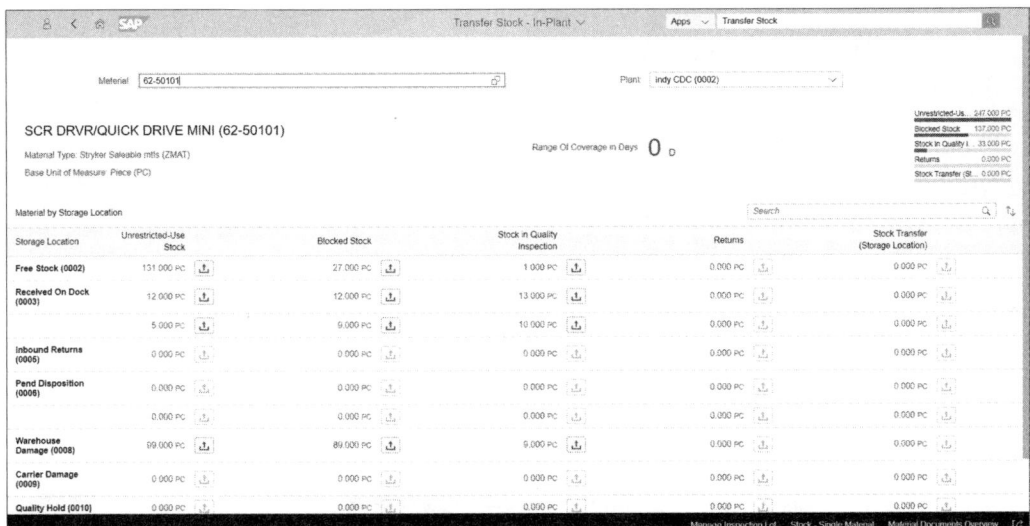

Figure 7.16 Transfer Stock—In-Plant App

7   Inventory Management

This app also lets you transfer from one stock type to another. In addition, it allows transfers of ownership from supplier consignment stock to unrestricted use stock.

You can also check the range of coverage for the existing stocks based on the consumption of unrestricted use stock materials in the last 30 days.

You can branch from this app to other apps, such as Stock—Single Material and Material Documents Overview.

The Transfer Stock—In-Plant app is assigned to the inventory manager and warehouse clerk standard authorization roles.

7.5.4   Transfer Stock—Cross-Plant

Use the Transfer Stock—Cross-Plant app (Figure 7.17) to create transfer postings from one plant to another.

You can also transfer stock from one stock type to another using this app.

You can branch from this app to other apps, such as Manage Stock, Transfer Stock—In-Plant, and Material Documents Overview.

The Transfer Stock—Cross-Plant app is assigned to the inventory manager and warehouse clerk standard authorization roles.

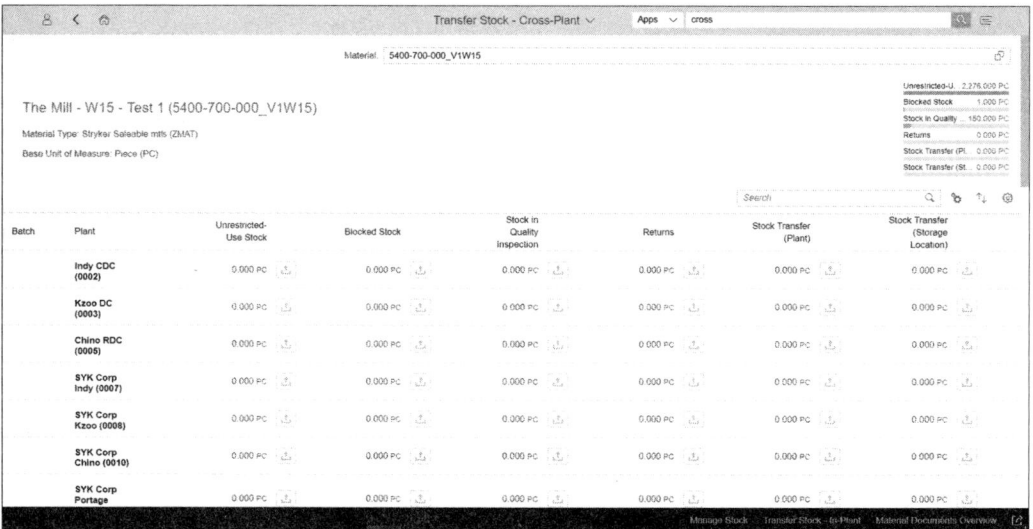

Figure 7.17 Transfer Stock—Cross-Plant App

7.5.5 Stock Transfer Execution Using Shipping Integration

It's common to use the shipping component of SAP S/4HANA to transact stock transfers through your facilities. The same apps described earlier for handling goods receipts with inbound deliveries (e.g., Post Goods Receipt for Purchase Order) also can be used for performing receipts for inbound stock transport purchase orders.

7.5.6 Stock Transfer Reporting

It's important to monitor the status of stock transfers in the system, especially those that involve a two-step process. This will ensure that all physical stock transfers are posted in a timely manner and that up-to-date stock information is available for materials planning.

SAP S/4HANA provides the following apps to obtain reports for in-process stock transfers:

- Overdue Materials—Stock in Transit
- Display Stock in Transit

We'll describe these apps in the following sections.

Overdue Materials—Stock in Transit

The Overdue Materials—Stock in Transit app (Figure 7.18) provides information on materials for which a stock transport order has been created and issued, but which have not been received to date. You can identify these materials to complete the stock transfer process or to investigate potential issues with the transfers.

Use the Overdue Materials—Stock in Transit app to do the following:

- Review the stock transport orders for which materials are scheduled to arrive in a plant
- Display a list of stock transport orders for which the stock transfer process hasn't yet been completed
- Follow up on the results by choosing a purchase order or a material from the list, and then choosing one of the following apps: Post Goods Receipt for Purchase Order, Stock—Single Material, or Stock—Multiple Materials

The Overdue Materials—Stock in Transit App is assigned to the shipping specialist, receiving specialist, warehouse clerk, and inventory manager standard authorization roles.

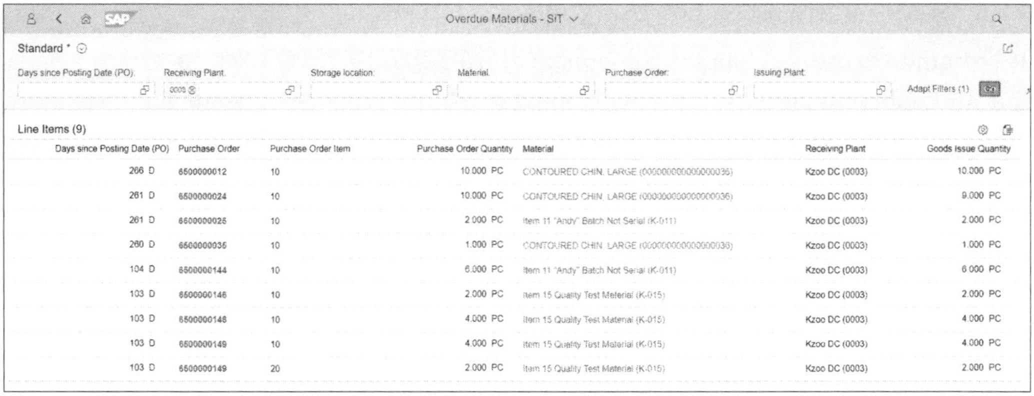

7 Inventory Management

Figure 7.18 Overdue Materials—Stock in Transit App

Display Stock in Transit

The Display Stock in Transit app (Figure 7.19) is used to show all stocks that have been issued from one plant and are currently in transit to another plant. It also shows stock transport purchase order references and the value of the goods transferred.

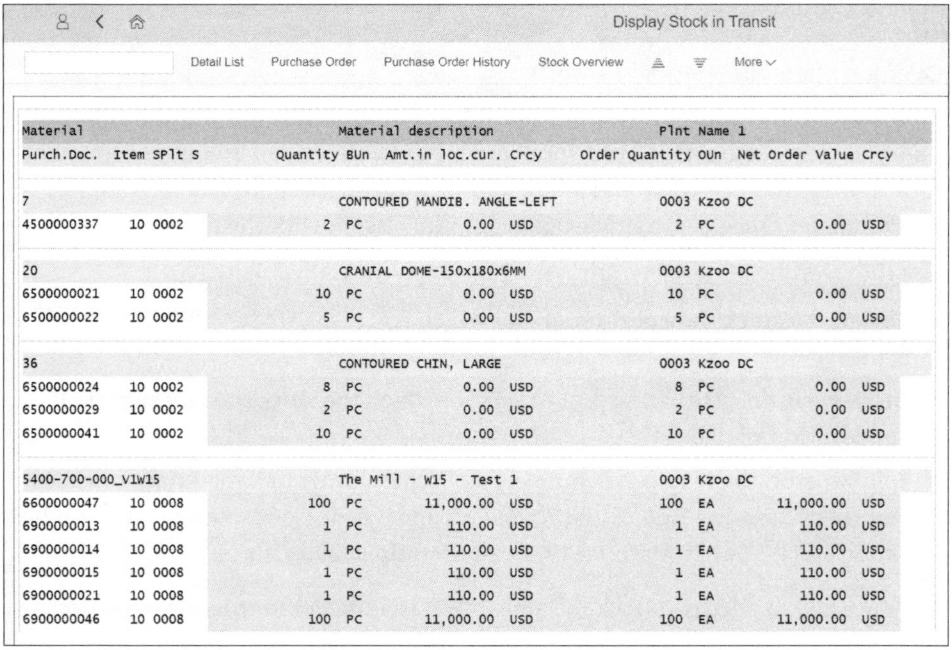

Figure 7.19 Display Stock in Transit App

The Display Stock in Transit app runs directly on the backend SAP S/4HANA system and is functionally equivalent to the classic SAP ERP Transaction MB5T.

The Display Stock in Transit app is assigned to the inventory manager standard authorization role.

7.6 Transfer Postings

Transfer postings are goods movements that result in a change in identity, usability or ownership for a quantity of stock. Typically, the stock does not physically move in the system during a transfer posting. However, it's possible to combine some types of transfer postings with changes in location as well.

7.6.1 Changes in Stock Identity

Transfer postings that result in a change in stock identity involve changes in material. Note that a material can only to transferred to the stock of another material if both materials share the same base unit of measure.

If a material is batch-managed in the SAP S/4HANA system, a change in batch identity can also be posted. Both the material and batch can be changed at the same time.

The 309 movement type is used to change material or batch quantities in stock.

7.6.2 Changes in Stock Usability

Transfer postings that result in a change in stock usability involve a change in the stock type. In general, most stock types can be transferred interchangeably. However, if Quality Management is active for a material in a plant, then transfers into or out of quality inspection stock must be done in conjunction with a QM process, such as inbound inspection.

Movement types used to transfer stock from one stock type to another are shown in Table 7.1.

From Stock Type	To Stock Type	Movement Type
Quality inspection	Unrestricted use	321
Unrestricted use	Quality inspection	322

Table 7.1 Stock Transfer Movement Types for Usability Changes

253

From Stock Type	To Stock Type	Movement Type
Blocked	Unrestricted use	343
Unrestricted use	Blocked	344
Blocked	Quality inspection	349
Quality inspection	Blocked	350
Customer returns	Unrestricted use	453
Customer returns	Quality inspection	457
Customer returns	Blocked	459

Table 7.1 Stock Transfer Movement Types for Usability Changes (Cont.)

7.6.3 Changes in Stock Ownership

If you have stocks delivered to your facility by a supplier on a consignment basis and you wish to take financial ownership of these stocks, you enter a transfer posting to recognize that fact. Similarly, if you return stock that was delivered on a consignment basis to your customer, you post a transfer posting as well. Movement type 411 K is provided for this purpose.

7.6.4 Apps Used for Transfer Postings

The following SAP Fiori apps are used to post transfer postings in the SAP S/4HANA system:

- Transfer Stock—In-Plant
- Manage Stock

The Post Goods Movements WebGUI app also can be utilized to create transfer posting goods movements.

Descriptions of these apps can be found in Section 7.5.

7.7 Physical Inventory

Good accounting practices require periodic reconciliation of the stock balances found in the SAP S/4HANA system to the physical stocks in the warehouse. These assets need to be reflected accurately on the company's financial statements. Accurate stock balances also optimize the benefits of MRP in assuring availability of material for production and sales processes.

The system provides a variety of physical inventory methods to accomplish this requirement. Regardless of the method used, all physical inventory processes encompass the following three phases (see Figure 7.20):

❶ Creation of the physical inventory documents

❷ Entry of the physical counts into SAP S/4HANA

❸ Posting of physical inventory differences

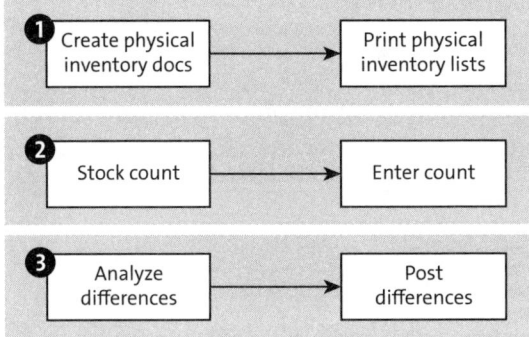

Figure 7.20 Phases of Physical Inventory

7.7.1 Creation of Physical Inventory Documents

A physical inventory document is needed to begin the process. These documents contain a header, which holds information on the count event itself, such as the document number, the person responsible for the count, and the planned count date. Line items on the physical inventory document contain the materials being counted and hold the system and actual count information.

Stocks are counted in Inventory Management based on the following:

- Material
- Plant
- Storage location
- Stock type
- Valuation type/batch
- Special stock

Each combination of these elements will be counted separately during a physical inventory.

The method of creating physical inventory documents is dependent on the technique used for the count. SAP S/4HANA supports the following techniques:

- Manual physical inventory (spot inventory)
- Annual physical inventory
- Continuous physical inventory
- Cycle counting
- Sample-based physical inventory

For more information on the physical inventory methods available, consult the SAP Help website.

Once the documents are created, it's common to print the physical inventory count sheets. These are then distributed to the counters, who record the physical quantities on the sheet. Count sheets can be transferred to a mobile application for counting as well.

7.7.2 Entry of Physical Counts

After the physical count is recorded, this information is entered into the SAP S/4HANA system. The system can provide feedback to the entry clerk if the quantity recorded during the count exceeds the system count based on a defined threshold percentage. This helps prevent data-entry errors.

Once the counts are entered, they can be analyzed by authorized personnel. This analysis may result in a recount of the material in that storage location.

7.7.3 Posting of Physical Inventory Differences

Once the physical inventory counts are confirmed, any differences detected need to be posted to Inventory Management so that the physical and system counts are reconciled.

This action results in a goods movement posting either incrementing or decrementing the quantity of goods in stock. Financial postings are also made at the same time.

7.7.4 Physical Inventory Apps

SAP S/4HANA supplies apps for use in managing the physical inventory processes supported by the system. There are apps to support the execution of a physical inventory, and others for monitoring the physical inventory processes and reporting.

7.7.5 Physical Inventory Execution Apps

The following WebGUI apps are available for execution of physical inventory processes:

- Create Physical Inventory Document
- Change Physical Inventory Document
- Enter Inventory Count
- Change Physical Inventory Count
- Enter PI Count w/o Document
- Enter and Post PI Count w/o Document
- Request Physical Inventory Recount
- Process Physical Inventory Count Results
- Print Physical Inventory Documents
- Create Physical Inventory Documents – Regular Stock
- ABC Analysis for Cycle Counting

These apps are described in more detail in the following sections.

Create Physical Inventory Document

You use the Create Physical Inventory Document app (Figure 7.21) to manually create a physical inventory document. You use this app when you want to perform a physical inventory for a specified set of materials of your choosing. These are also known as *spot inventories*. You can activate this document at the same time if you wish.

The Create Physical Inventory Document app runs directly on the backend SAP S/4HANA system and is functionally equivalent to the classic SAP ERP Transaction MI01.

The Create Physical Inventory Document app is assigned to the warehouse clerk and inventory manager standard authorization roles.

7 Inventory Management

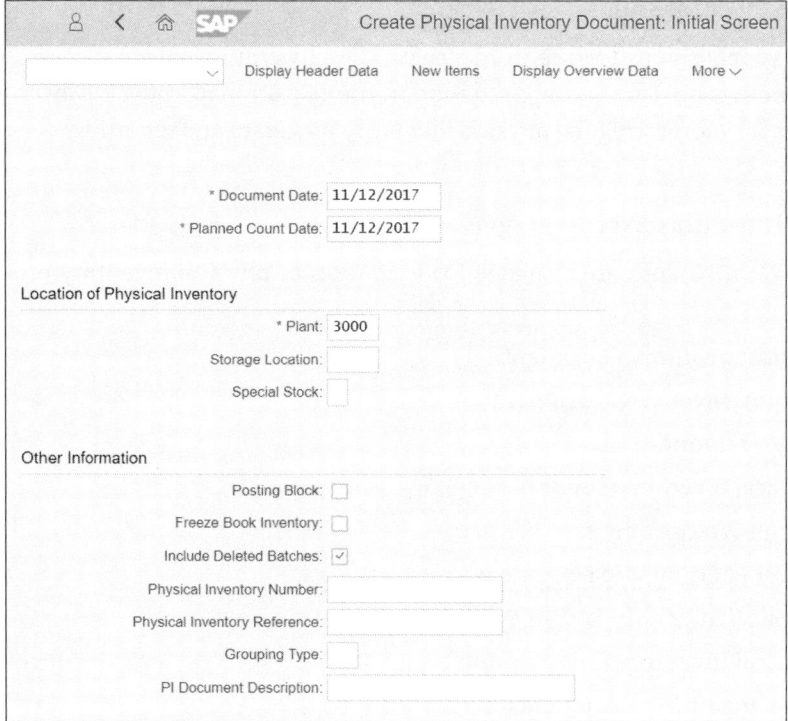

Figure 7.21 Create Physical Inventory Document App

Change Physical Inventory Document

You use the Change Physical Inventory Document app (Figure 7.22) to change an existing physical inventory document. You use this app when you want to add or change materials that need to be counted. You can activate physical inventory documents using this app as well.

The Change Physical Inventory Document app runs directly on the backend SAP S/4HANA system and is functionally equivalent to the classic SAP ERP Transaction MI02.

The Change Physical Inventory Document app is assigned to the warehouse clerk and inventory manager standard authorization roles.

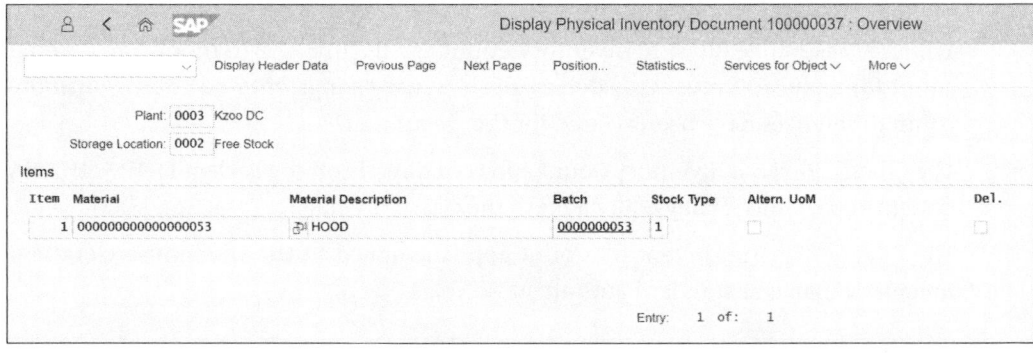

Figure 7.22 Change Physical Inventory Document App

Enter Inventory Count

You use the Enter Inventory Count app (Figure 7.23) to enter the count results that have been recorded by the inventory counter on the physical inventory count sheet. Messages will appear if the entered counted inventory quantities exceed the book quantities by a predefined threshold.

The Enter Inventory Count app runs directly on the backend SAP S/4HANA system and is functionally equivalent to the classic SAP ERP Transaction MI04.

The Enter Inventory Count app is assigned to the warehouse clerk and inventory manager standard authorization roles.

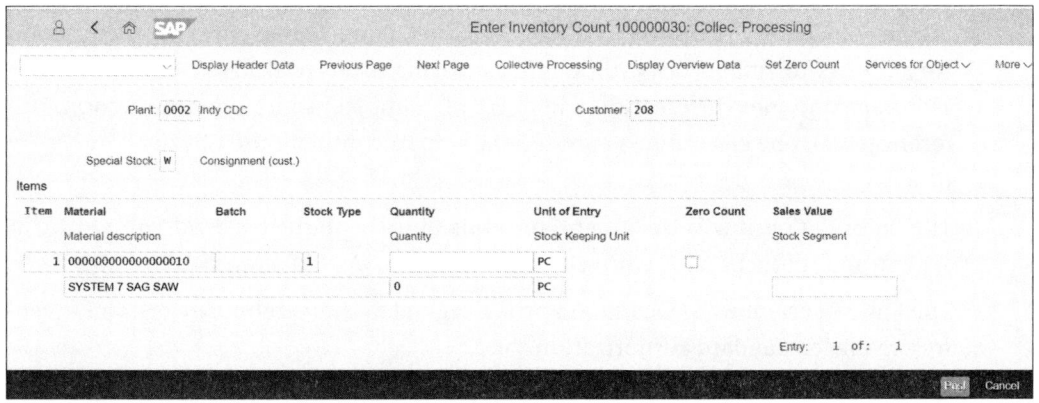

Figure 7.23 Enter Inventory Count App

Change Physical Inventory Count

You use the Change Physical Inventory Count app (Figure 7.24) to modify an entered count for a physical inventory document. You use change entered counts until the count differences have been cleared for this document.

The Change Physical Inventory Count app runs directly on the backend SAP S/4HANA system and is functionally equivalent to the classic SAP ERP Transaction MI05.

The Change Physical Inventory Count app is assigned to the warehouse clerk and inventory manager standard authorization roles.

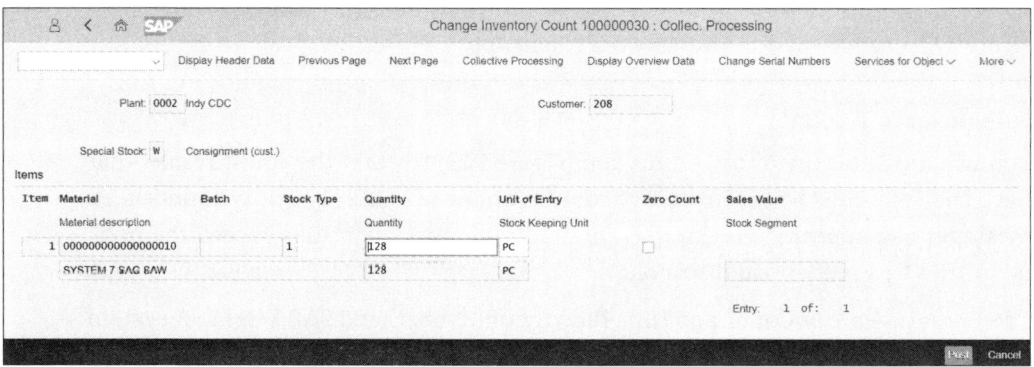

Figure 7.24 Change Physical Inventory Count App

Enter PI Count w/o Document

You use the Enter PI Count w/o Document app (Figure 7.25) to enter physical inventory counts for materials without first creating a physical inventory document. This app combines the creation and entry of count steps into one transaction. Differences must be cleared in a subsequent step to complete the physical inventory process.

The Enter PI Count w/o Document app runs directly on the backend SAP S/4HANA system and is functionally equivalent to the classic SAP ERP Transaction MI09.

The Enter PI Count w/o Document app is assigned to the warehouse clerk and inventory manager standard authorization roles.

7.7 Physical Inventory

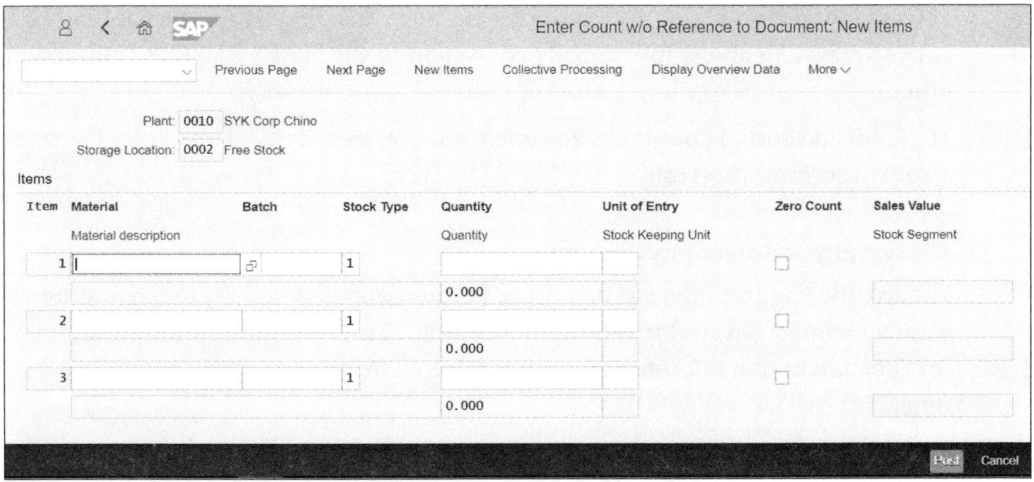

Figure 7.25 Enter PI Count w/o Document App

Enter and Post PI Count w/o Document

You use the Enter and Post PI Count w/o Document app (Figure 7.26) to enter physical inventory counts and post differences for materials without first creating a physical inventory document. This app combines creation, entering, and clearing of differences steps into one transaction.

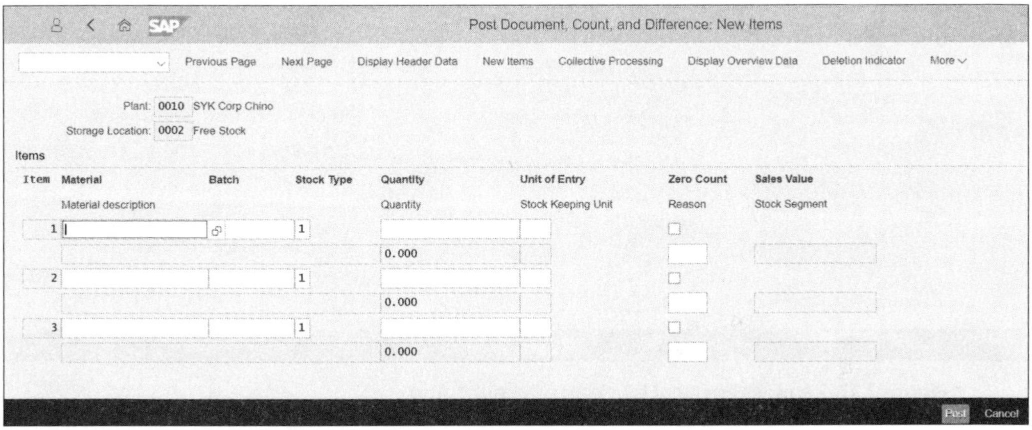

Figure 7.26 Enter and Post PI Count w/o Document App

7 Inventory Management

The Enter and Post PI Count w/o Document app runs directly on the backend SAP S/4HANA system and is functionally equivalent to the classic SAP ERP Transaction MI10.

The Enter and Post PI Count w/o Document app is assigned to the inventory manager standard authorization role.

Request Physical Inventory Recount

You use the Request Physical Inventory Recount app (Figure 7.27) to recount items from a counted physical inventory document. This creates a new physical inventory document that references the items selected for recount from the original document.

The Request Physical Inventory Recount app runs directly on the backend SAP S/4HANA system and is functionally equivalent to the classic SAP ERP Transaction MI11.

The Request Physical Inventory Recount app is assigned to the inventory manager standard authorization role.

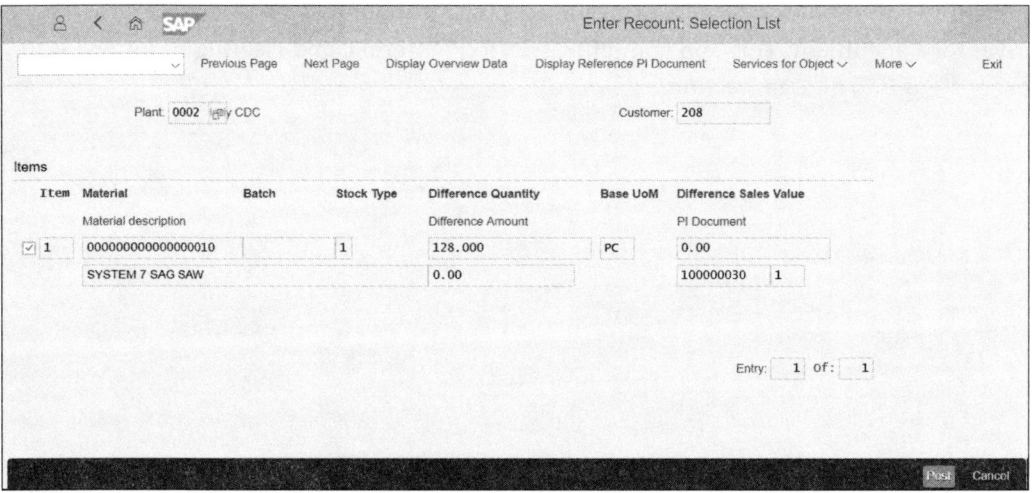

Figure 7.27 Request Physical Inventory Recount App

Process Physical Inventory Count Results

You use the Process Physical Inventory Count Results app (Figure 7.28) to create a list of physical inventory differences in the system based on entered selection criteria. A list of physical inventory items meeting the criteria is displayed. You can clear the differences directly from this list, or you can enter or change count results.

The Process Physical Inventory Count Results app runs directly on the backend SAP S/4HANA system and is functionally equivalent to the classic SAP ERP Transaction MI20.

The Process Physical Inventory Count Results app is assigned to the inventory manager standard authorization role.

PhysInvDoc	Item	Material	Batch	Plant	SLoc	Book Quantity	Qty Counted	Difference Quantity	Unit
100000022	1	000000000000000007	0000000051	0002	0002	5.000	7.000	2.000	PC
100000022	2	000000000000000007	0000000053	0002	0002	14.000	14.000	0.000	PC
100000022	3	000000000000000007	0000000055	0002	0002	14.000	14.000	0.000	PC
100000022	4	000000000000000007	0000000060	0002	0002	61.000	61.000	0.000	PC
100000022	5	000000000000000007	0000000074	0002	0002	15.000	12.000	3.000-	PC
100000022	6	000000000000000007	0000000079	0002	0002	5.000	7.000	2.000	PC
100000022	7	000000000000000007	0000000084	0002	0002	73.000	75.000	2.000	PC
100000030	1	000000000000000010		0002		0.000	128.000	128.000	PC
100000045	1	000000000000000027	0000000048	0002		4.000	27.000	23.000	PC

Figure 7.28 Process Physical Inventory Count Results App

Print Physical Inventory Documents

You use the Print Physical Inventory Documents app (Figure 7.29) to print activated, uncounted physical inventory documents that can be distributed to the persons performing the count. The system tracks that the physical inventory documents have been printed because these documents are typically controlled documents in an enterprise.

The Print Physical Inventory Documents app runs directly on the backend SAP S/4HANA system and is functionally equivalent to the classic SAP ERP Transaction MI21.

The Print Physical Inventory Documents app is assigned to the warehouse clerk and inventory manager standard authorization roles.

7   Inventory Management

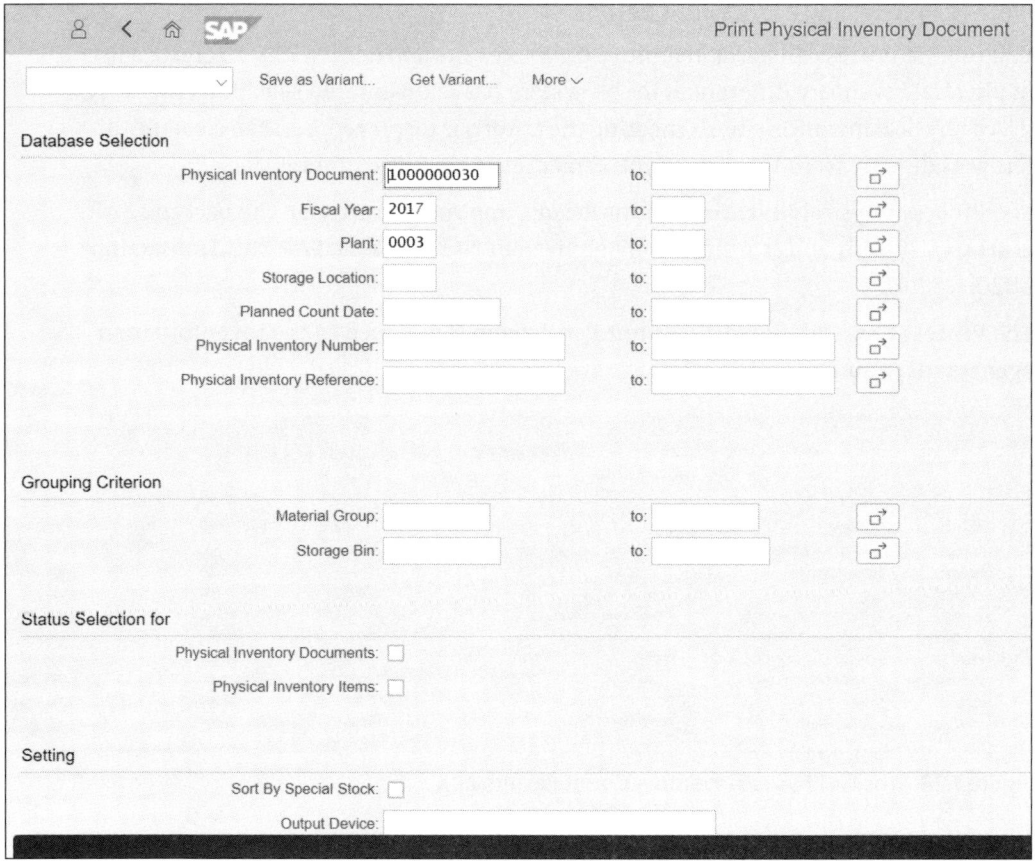

Figure 7.29 Print Physical Inventory Documents App

Create Physical Inventory Documents—Regular Stock

You can use the Create Physical Inventory Documents—Regular Stock app (Figure 7.30) to create several physical inventory documents at one time, based on entered selection criteria. The physical inventory documents are then created in a batch run and are available for counting.

Note that this app creates documents for normal storage location stocks only; there are other apps for creating physical inventory counts for special stocks.

The Create Physical Inventory Documents—Regular Stock app runs directly on the backend SAP S/4HANA system and is functionally equivalent to the classic SAP ERP Transaction MI31.

The Create Physical Inventory Documents—Regular Stock app is assigned to the warehouse clerk and inventory manager standard authorization roles.

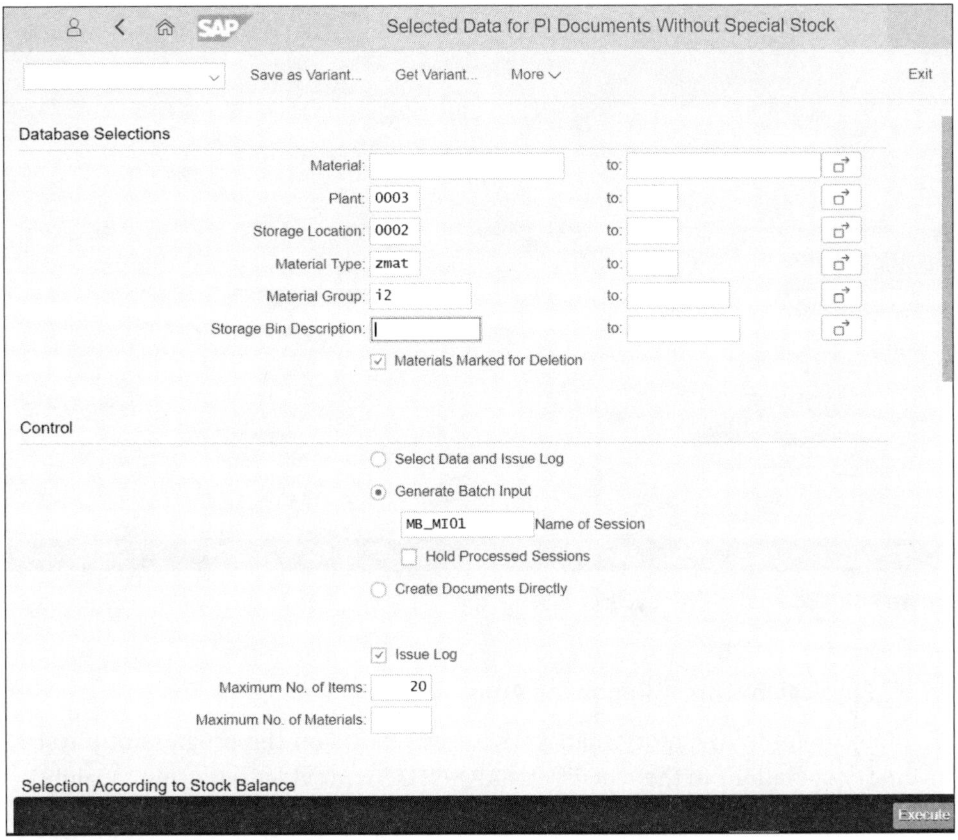

Figure 7.30 Create Physical Inventory Documents—Regular Stock App

ABC Analysis for Cycle Counting

You can use the ABC Analysis for Cycle Counting app (Figure 7.31) to set cycle count indicators on the material master for those materials subject to the cycle counting method of physical inventory. The cycle count indicator determines the frequency per year with which a material needs to be counted per the settings in configuration. The system analyzes consumption or forecast data for that material and plant in the system and sets the cycle count indicator accordingly.

The ABC Analysis for Cycle Counting app runs directly on the backend SAP S/4HANA system and is functionally equivalent to the classic SAP ERP Transaction MIBC.

7 Inventory Management

The ABC Analysis for Cycle Counting app is assigned to the inventory manager standard authorization role.

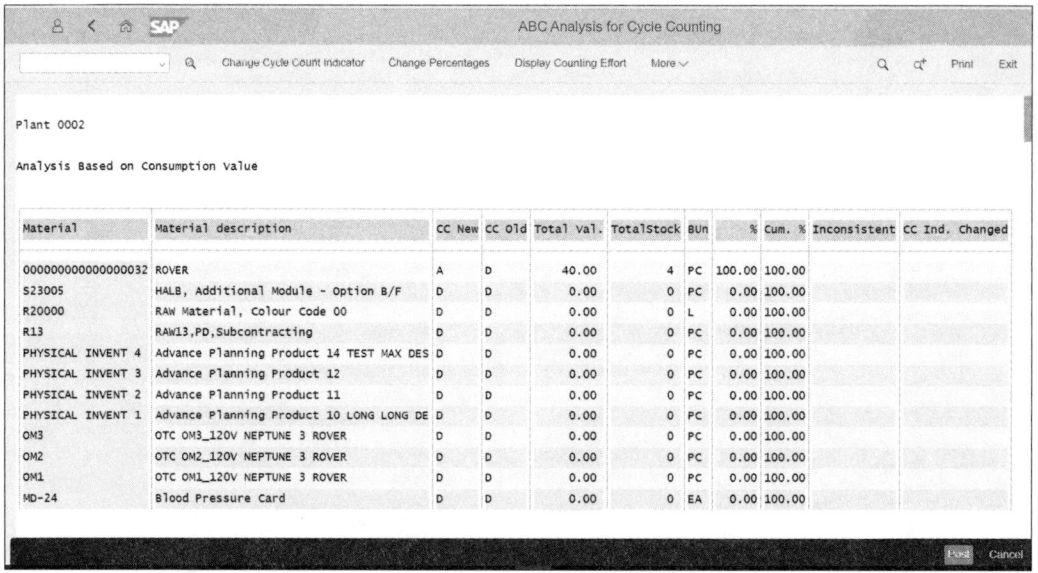

Figure 7.31 ABC Analysis for Cycle Counting App

7.7.6 Physical Inventory Reporting Apps

It's often useful to inventory managers to see reports on the progress of physical inventory operations in their facilities. SAP S/4HANA provides reporting capabilities for physical inventory processes to fulfill this need.

The following SAP Fiori apps are available for the inventory manager to monitor the physical inventory processes in their facilities:

- Physical Inventory Document Overview
- Physical Inventory Analysis

In addition, the following WebGUI apps are available for physical inventory process monitoring:

- Display Physical Inventory Progress
- Display PI Document Items for Materials

These apps are described in more detail in the following sections.

7.7 Physical Inventory

Physical Inventory Document Overview

The Physical Inventory Document Overview app (Figure 7.32) is used to manage the physical inventory process regardless of the physical inventory method used. You can use specific search criteria such as storage location, specific count status, or planned count date to filter results. The search result shows detailed information to the item level of a specific material.

The Physical Inventory Document Overview app can perform the following tasks:

- Obtain an overview of physical inventory documents meeting entered criteria
- Display key facts about the selected physical inventory documents, including the following:
  - Information about specific physical inventory documents, such as count status (**Not Counted**, **Partially Counted**)
  - Lists of physical inventory document items, materials, and batches
  - Counting progress and posting progress, shown as a bar chart
- Define defaults for the fiscal year, plant, and storage location filters

The Physical Inventory Document Overview app is assigned to the inventory manager and warehouse clerk standard authorization roles.

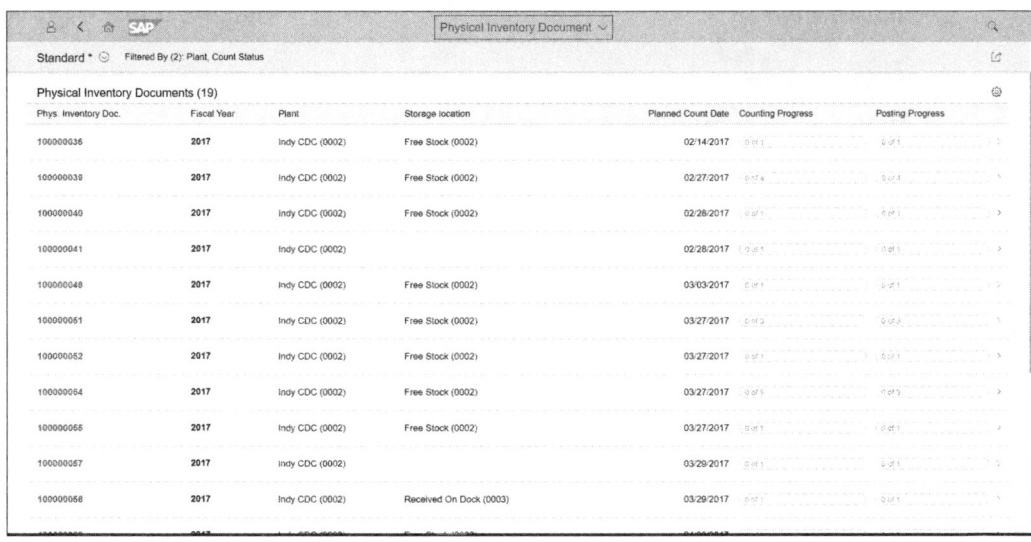

Figure 7.32 Physical Inventory Document Overview App

Physical Inventory Analysis

The Physical Inventory Analysis app is used by inventory managers to analyze physical inventory results in their company and identify opportunities for process improvement.

The Physical Inventory Analysis app lets you do the following:

- Drill down to an individual physical inventory document item
- Define filters to narrow your search scope
- Choose from many different available dimensions and key figures

In addition, this app supports sorting, totaling, and subtotaling, as well as export to Excel. Default filters can be set for fiscal year, plant, storage location, and material.

The Physical Inventory Analysis app is assigned to the inventory manager standard authorization role.

Display Physical Inventory Progress

You can use the Display Physical Inventory Progress app (Figure 7.33) to display a report on the progress of physical inventory activity based on entered selection criteria.

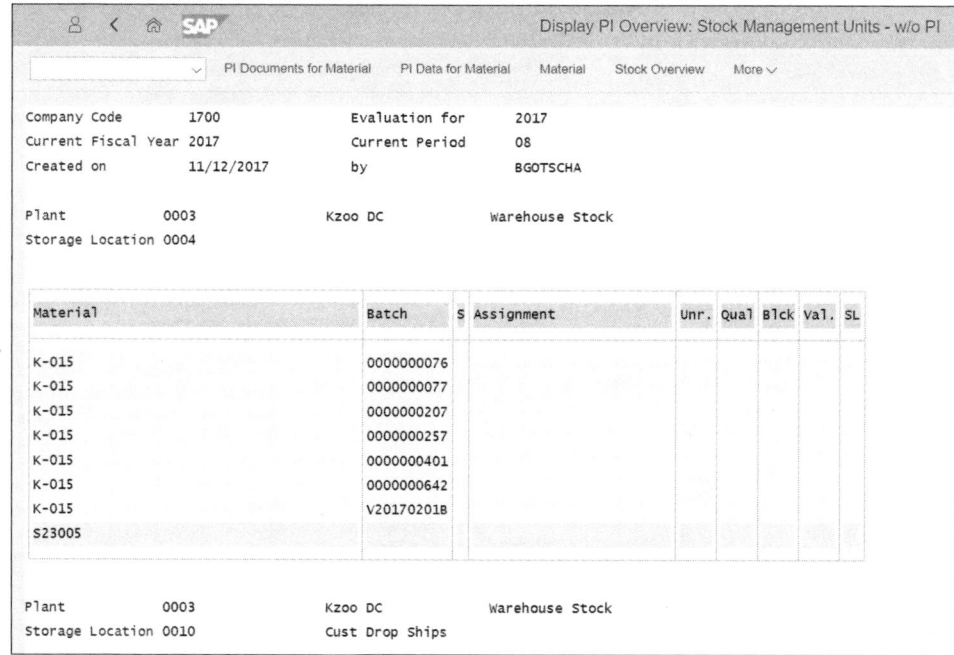

Figure 7.33 Display Physical Inventory Progress App

You can drill into the resulting list of materials and batches to obtain lists of physical inventory documents created.

The Display Physical Inventory Progress app runs directly on the backend SAP S/4HANA system and is functionally equivalent to the classic SAP ERP Transaction MIDO.

The Display Physical Inventory Progress app is assigned to the inventory manager standard authorization role.

Display PI Document Items for Materials

You can use the Display PI Document Items for Materials app (Figure 7.34) to list physical inventory items for materials based on entered selection criteria. A list of materials is shown, along with the physical inventory document items for that material.

The Display PI Document Items for Materials app runs directly on the backend SAP S/4HANA system and is functionally equivalent to the classic SAP ERP Transaction MI22.

The Display PI Document Items for Materials app is assigned to the inventory manager standard authorization role.

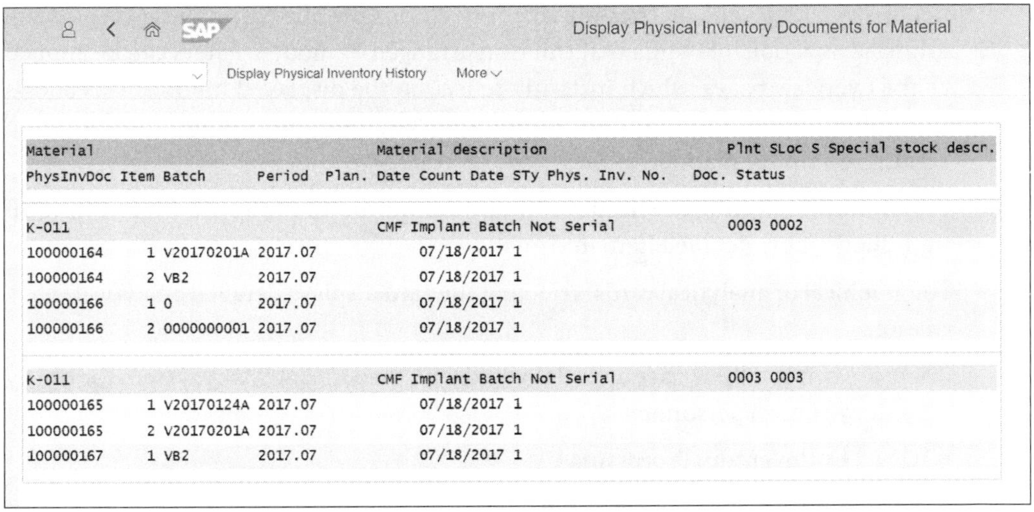
SAP
Display Physical Inventory Documents for Material
Display Physical Inventory History
More
Material Material description Plnt SLoc S Special stock descr.
PhysInvDoc Item Batch Period Plan. Date Count Date STy Phys. Inv. No. Doc. Status
K-011 CMF Implant Batch Not Serial 0003 0002
100000164 1 V20170201A 2017.07 07/18/2017 1
100000164 2 VB2 2017.07 07/18/2017 1
100000166 1 0 2017.07 07/18/2017 1
100000166 2 0000000001 2017.07 07/18/2017 1
K-011 CMF Implant Batch Not Serial 0003 0003
100000165 1 V20170124A 2017.07 07/18/2017 1
100000165 2 V20170201A 2017.07 07/18/2017 1
100000167 1 VB2 2017.07 07/18/2017 1

Figure 7.34 Display PI Document Items for Materials App

7.8 Reporting in Inventory Management

Proper control of physical stocks requires a robust set of inventory management reports. SAP S/4HANA builds on SAP ERP's stock balance reporting capabilities by adding new capabilities to visualize the current stock situation, thus enabling fast action in the case of logistics bottlenecks. These capabilities include inventory analytics, which show key performance indicators in real time, and the inventory overview pages, new in SAP S/4HANA, which show multiple key analytics on a single screen.

There are several inventory management reporting apps that come delivered with the SAP S/4HANA system. These can be broadly grouped into four types:

1. Inventory overview pages
2. Goods movements reporting apps
3. Stock balances reporting apps
4. Inventory analytics

7.8.1 Inventory Overview Pages

Inventory overview pages allow inventory managers and warehouse clerical personnel to see all relevant metrics for their operations on one page. These metrics are arranged as actionable cards that can be rearranged or hidden. Filters can be applied to the overview pages, which instantly reflect on the displayed metrics. This allows the user to focus on important items, enabling decision-making and follow-on actions in a timely manner.

For list cards, selecting the header of a card brings you to the app itself; selecting an item shows more detailed item information.

For graphical or analytical cards, selecting the card displays detailed analytical information.

There are two overview page apps delivered with the SAP S/4HANA system for use by inventory-control personnel:

- Overview Inventory Processing
- Overview Inventory Management

We'll discuss these apps in the following sections.

Overview Inventory Processing

The Overview Inventory Processing app shows the current and most important information and tasks relevant for a warehousing clerk. The information is displayed on a set of actionable cards. You can therefore focus on the most important tasks, enabling faster decisions and immediate action.

The following cards are available in the Overview Inventory Processing app:

- Recent Inventory Counts
- Warehouse Throughput History
- Recent Material Documents
- Monitor Purchase Order Items
- Overdue Materials—GR Blocked Stock
- Outbound Delivery List
- Inbound Delivery List

The Overview Inventory Processing app is assigned to the warehouse clerk standard authorization role.

Overview Inventory Management

The Overview Inventory Management app is used by inventory managers to show the most important information and tasks relevant at the current time.

The following cards are available in the Overview Inventory Management app:

- Recent Material Documents
- Overdue Material—GR Blocked Stock
- Stock Value by Special Stock Type
- Warehouse Throughput History
- Monitor Purchase Order Items
- Stock Value by Stock Type

The Overview Inventory Management app is assigned to the inventory manager standard authorization role.

7.8.2 Goods Movement Reporting

It's often useful to determine how the stock balances in the system were derived. This is especially true when trying to reconcile physical inventory counts with book inventories. Goods movement reports in SAP S/4HANA allow you to list goods movements that meet user-entered selection criteria for analysis and action.

SAP S/4HANA features two apps to report on goods movements recorded in the system:

- Material Documents Overview
- Display Material Documents List

These will be discussed in the following sections.

Material Documents Overview

The Material Documents Overview app is described in detail in Section 7.3.1.

Display Material Documents List

The Display Material Documents List app (Figure 7.35) is used to display material documents that meet entered selection criteria.

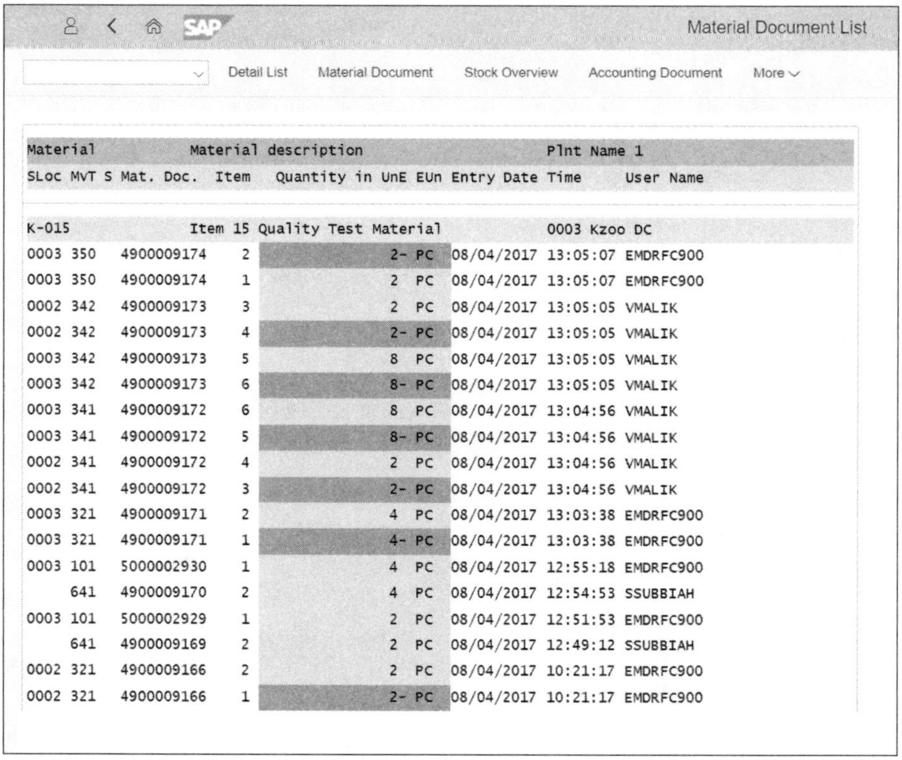

Material | Material description | Plnt Name 1

SLoc	MvT	S	Mat. Doc.	Item	Quantity in UnE	EUn	Entry Date	Time	User Name
K-015				Item 15 Quality Test Material			0003 Kzoo DC		
0003	350		4900009174	2	2-	PC	08/04/2017	13:05:07	EMDRFC900
0003	350		4900009174	1	2	PC	08/04/2017	13:05:07	EMDRFC900
0002	342		4900009173	3	2	PC	08/04/2017	13:05:05	VMALIK
0002	342		4900009173	4	2-	PC	08/04/2017	13:05:05	VMALIK
0003	342		4900009173	5	8	PC	08/04/2017	13:05:05	VMALIK
0003	342		4900009173	6	8-	PC	08/04/2017	13:05:05	VMALIK
0003	341		4900009172	6	8	PC	08/04/2017	13:04:56	VMALIK
0003	341		4900009172	5	8-	PC	08/04/2017	13:04:56	VMALIK
0002	341		4900009172	4	2	PC	08/04/2017	13:04:56	VMALIK
0002	341		4900009172	3	2-	PC	08/04/2017	13:04:56	VMALIK
0003	321		4900009171	2	4	PC	08/04/2017	13:03:38	EMDRFC900
0003	321		4900009171	1	4-	PC	08/04/2017	13:03:38	EMDRFC900
0003	101		5000002930	1	4	PC	08/04/2017	12:55:18	EMDRFC900
	641		4900009170	2	4	PC	08/04/2017	12:54:53	SSUBBIAH
0003	101		5000002929	1	2	PC	08/04/2017	12:51:53	EMDRFC900
	641		4900009169	2	2	PC	08/04/2017	12:49:12	SSUBBIAH
0002	321		4900009166	2	2	PC	08/04/2017	10:21:17	EMDRFC900
0002	321		4900009166	1	2-	PC	08/04/2017	10:21:17	EMDRFC900

Figure 7.35 Display Material Documents List App

The Display Material Documents List app runs directly on the backend SAP S/4HANA system and is functionally equivalent to the classic SAP ERP Transaction MB51.

The Display Material Documents List app is assigned to the warehouse clerk and inventory manager standard authorization roles.

7.8.3 Stock Balances Reporting Apps

There are several SAP-supplied SAP Fiori apps to monitor the current quantities of stocks in the SAP S/4HANA system. These include the following:

- Stock—Single Material
- Stock—Multiple Materials
- Batch Overview

In addition, several WebGUI transactions are also supplied by SAP for stock monitoring:

- Batch Information Cockpit
- Display Stock Overview
- Display Warehouse Stock

We'll discuss these apps in the following sections.

Stock—Single Material

The Stock—Single Material app (Figure 7.36) provides an overview of all stocks for one material. You can review your stock by specific plants and storage locations for which you are responsible. The app can display the stock information as a table or a diagram.

The Stock—Single Material app has the following capabilities:

- Display a stock overview for a single material by plant and storage location as a table or a bar graph
- Display the stock history of the material for the last 12 periods as a curve diagram (Figure 7.37)

7 Inventory Management

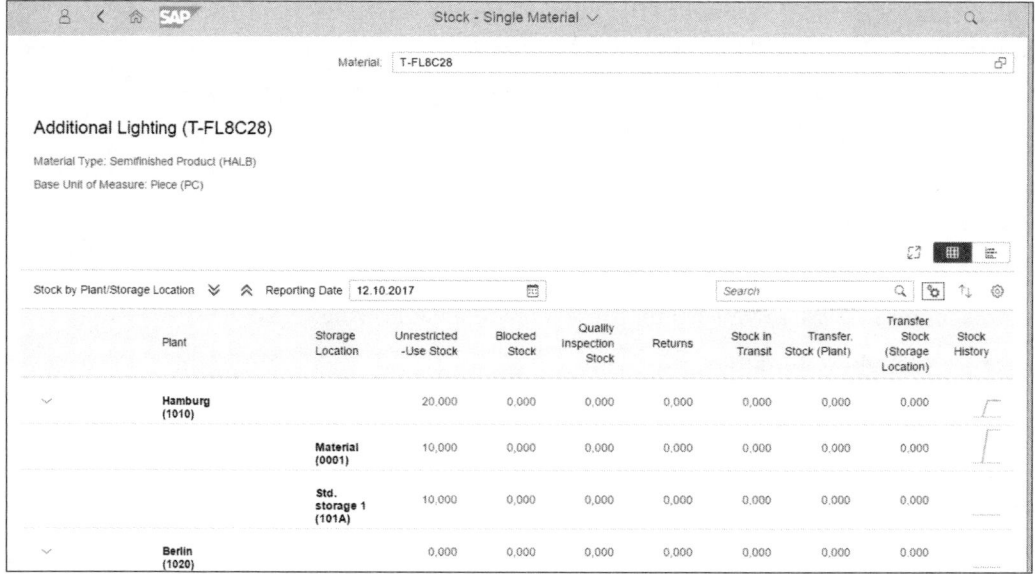

Figure 7.36 Stock—Single Material App

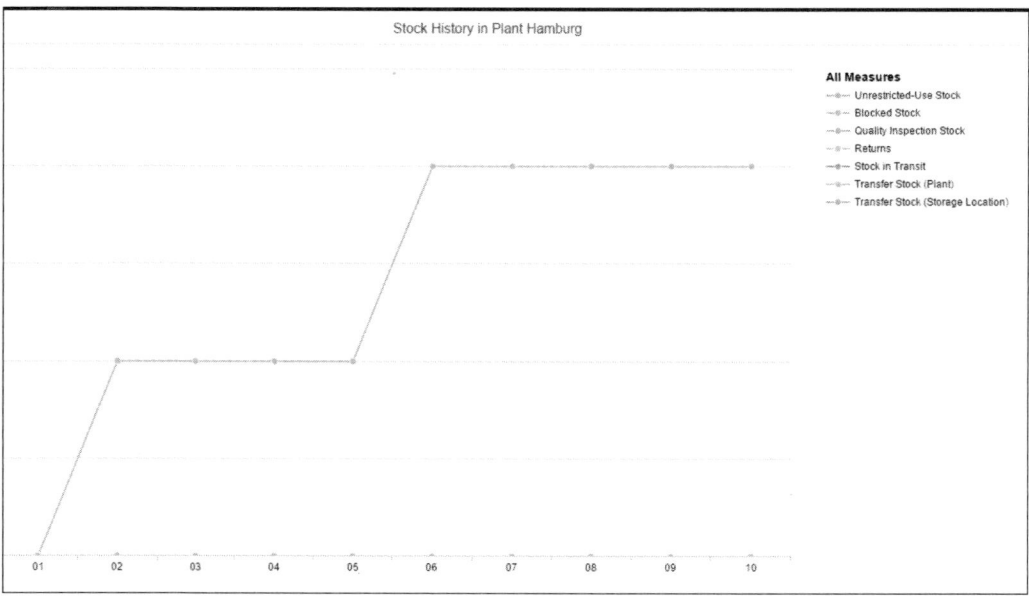

Figure 7.37 Stock—Single Material App: Stock History Curve Map

- Compare the stock information with the safety stock and minimum safety stock values defined for that material
- Transfer to other apps, such as:
  - Manage Stock
  - Transfer Stock—In-Plant
  - Transfer Stock—Cross-Plant
  - Material Documents Overview
  - Stock—Multiple Materials

The Stock—Single Material app is assigned to the shipping specialist, receiving specialist, warehouse clerk, and inventory manager standard authorization roles.

Stock—Multiple Materials

The Stock—Multiple Materials app (Figure 7.38) provides an overview of stocks for one or more materials. You can review your stock by specific plants and storage locations for which you are responsible. The app can display the stock information as a table or a diagram.

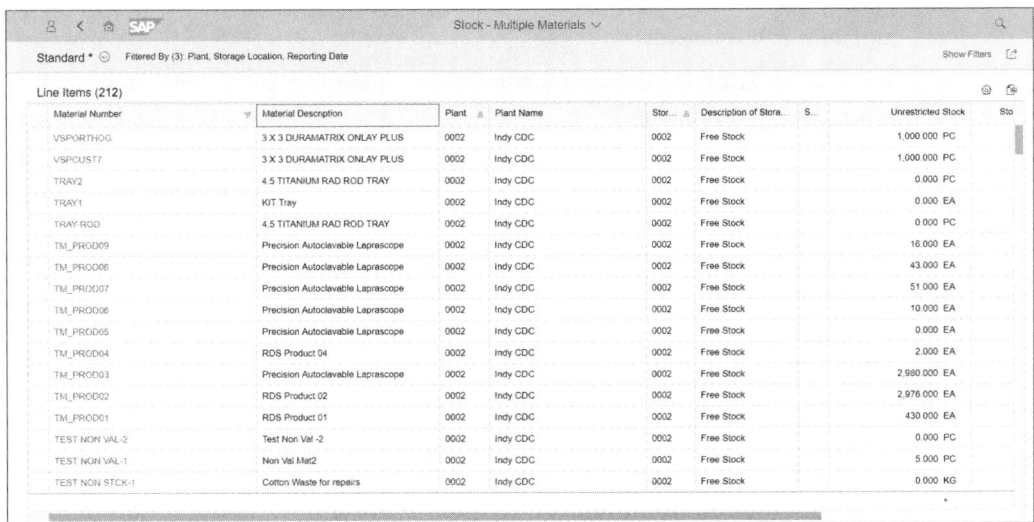

Figure 7.38 Stock—Multiple Materials App

The Stock—Single Material app has the following capabilities:

- Display a stock overview of one or more materials
- Display the value of your stock
- Export the results to a spreadsheet

The Stock—Multiple Materials app is assigned to the shipping specialist, receiving specialist, warehouse clerk, and inventory manager standard authorization roles.

Batch Overview

The Batch Overview app lets you create, edit, and display batches in your SAP S/4HANA system. This app gives you quick and easy access to batch-relevant information.

New or changed batch records can be stored as draft versions. This allows others to locate and review these draft versions using the search or the filter options to complete the work.

The Batch Overview app allows you to:

- Search for existing batches or ranges of batches
- Edit existing batch masters
- Create new batch masters
- Obtain information about other business documents related to the batch, such as inspection lots or deliveries
- Save new or changed batches as drafts for others to work on
- Transfer to the Stock—Single Material or Transfer Stock—In-Plant app

The Batch Overview app is assigned to the warehouse clerk and inventory manager standard authorization roles.

Batch Information Cockpit

You can use the Batch Information Cockpit app (Figure 7.39) for further analysis and control options, such as calling up the batch master for changing and displaying mater data, classification data, and the batch where-used list, containing information about the lifecycle of a batch.

The Batch Information Cockpit app runs directly on the backend SAP S/4HANA system and is functionally equivalent to the classic SAP ERP Transaction BMBC.

The Batch Information Cockpit app is assigned to the quality technician standard authorization role.

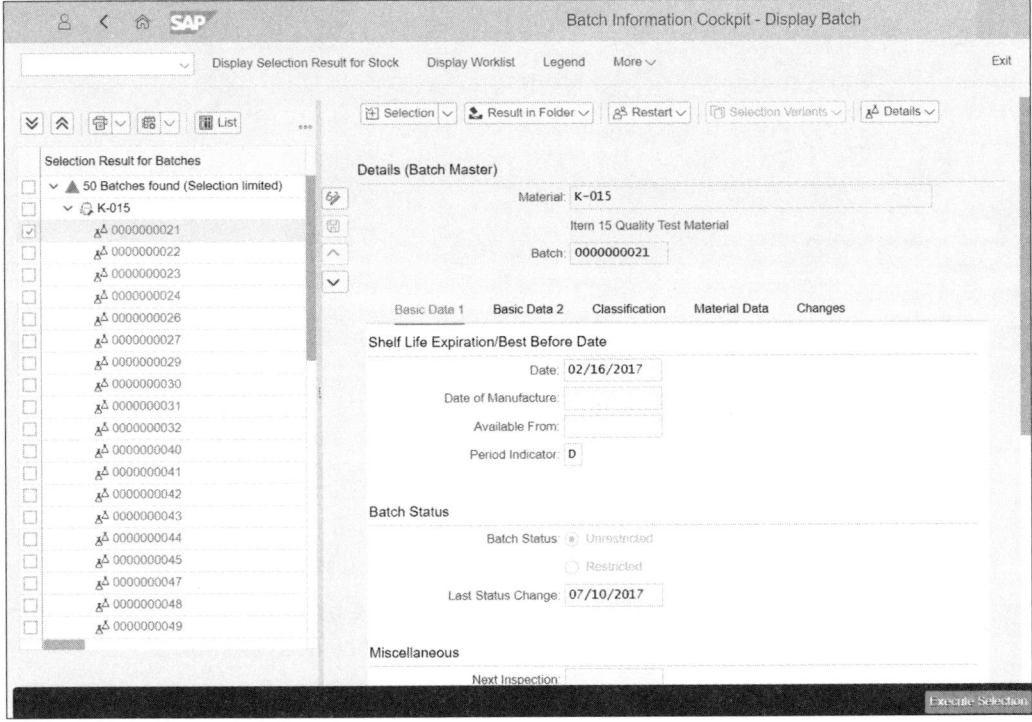

Figure 7.39 Batch Information Cockpit App

Display Stock Overview

The Display Stock Overview app (Figure 7.40) is used to display current stock balances for a single material in all plants, storage locations, and special stock types across the enterprise.

The Display Stock Overview app runs directly on the backend SAP S/4HANA system and is functionally equivalent to the classic SAP ERP Transaction MMBE.

The Display Stock Overview app is assigned to the inventory manager and warehouse clerk standard authorization roles.

7   Inventory Management

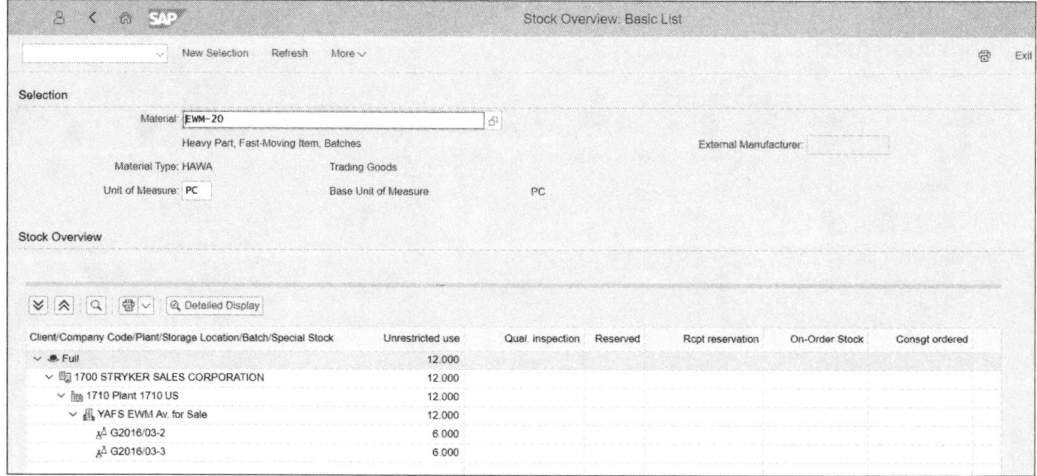

Figure 7.40 Display Stock Overview App

Display Warehouse Stock

The Display Warehouse Stock app (Figure 7.41) is used to display current stock balances for one or more materials in selected plants and storage locations.

The Display Warehouse Stock app runs directly on the backend SAP S/4HANA system and is functionally equivalent to the classic SAP ERP Transaction MB52.

The Display Warehouse Stock app is assigned to the inventory manager standard authorization role.

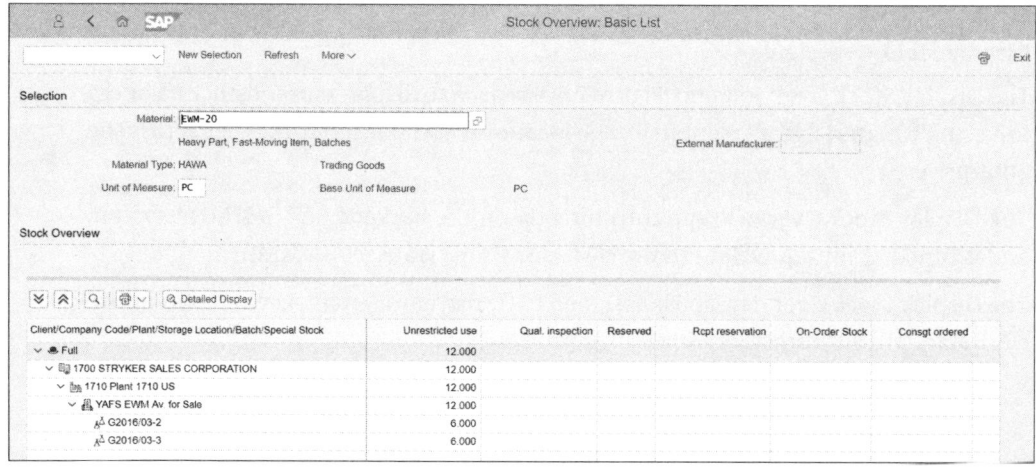

Figure 7.41 Display Warehouse Stock App

7.8.4 Apps for Monitoring Financial Inventory Values

The monetary value tied up in physical stocks in your facility is a key metric by which inventory managers are measured. Therefore, SAP S/4HANA provides several standard reports to help manage and control inventory values.

In addition, the following apps can be used to monitor the financial inventory values in the system:

- Material Inventory Values—Balance Summary
- Material Inventory Values—Line Items

We'll discuss these apps in the following sections.

Material Inventory Values—Balance Summary

Use the Material Inventory Values—Balance Summary app (Figure 7.42) to understand the quantities and values of your material inventories on a specific date, which can be current or in the past.

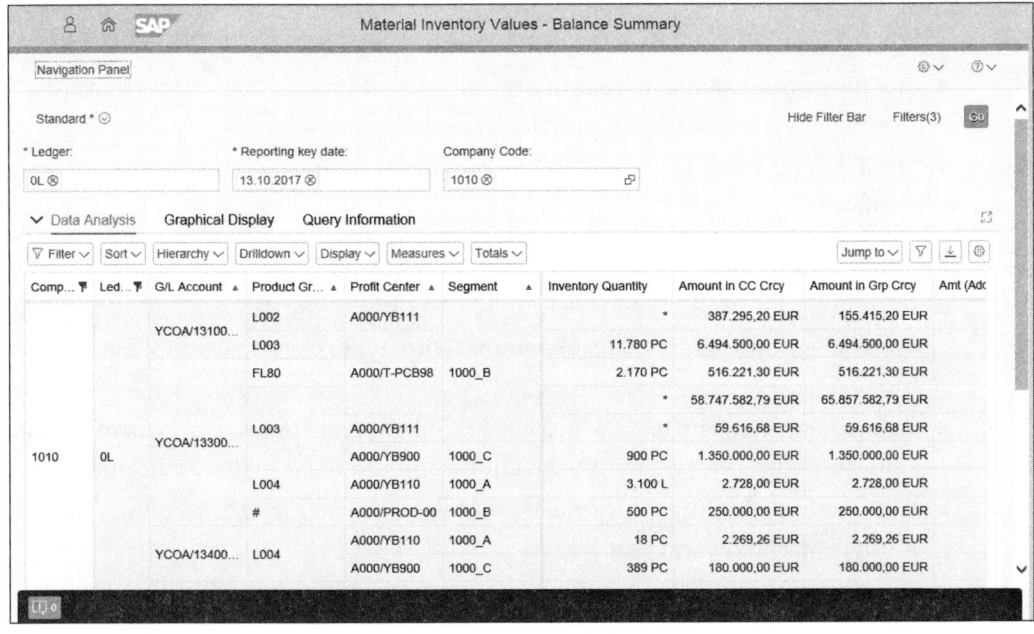

Figure 7.42 Material Inventory Values—Balance Summary App

The Material Inventory Values—Balance Summary app allows you to do the following:

- View inventory values and quantities sorted by company code, G/L account, material group, material, business transaction type, posting date, and document number
- Analyze line items in detail with a wide number of attributes (plant, material) and key figures (inventory quantity, inventory amount in up to three currencies
- Filter and analyze inventories using dimensions such as G/L account, material, profit center, and fiscal year
- Show the analysis of the line items using graphics, tables, or a combination of both

The Material Inventory Values—Balance Summary app is assigned to the inventory manager standard authorization role.

Material Inventory Values—Line Items

The Material Inventory Values—Line Items app (Figure 7.43) is used to understand quantities and values of your material inventories at the line-item level.

This app displays the following information about material inventory values:

- The inventory value and quantity of the journal entries that affect the value of material inventories during a particular period
- The date of the source document, the proposed posting date, and the actual posting date

The Material Inventory Values—Line Items app allows you to do the follwing:

- View inventory values and quantities sorted by company code, G/L account, material group, material, business transaction type, posting date, and document number
- Analyze line items in detail with a wide number of attributes (plant, material) and key figures (inventory quantity, inventory amount in up to three currencies)
- Filter and analyze inventories using dimensions such as G/L account, material, profit center, and fiscal year
- Show the analysis of line items using graphics, tables, or a combination of both

The Material Inventory Values—Line Items app is assigned to the inventory manager standard authorization role.

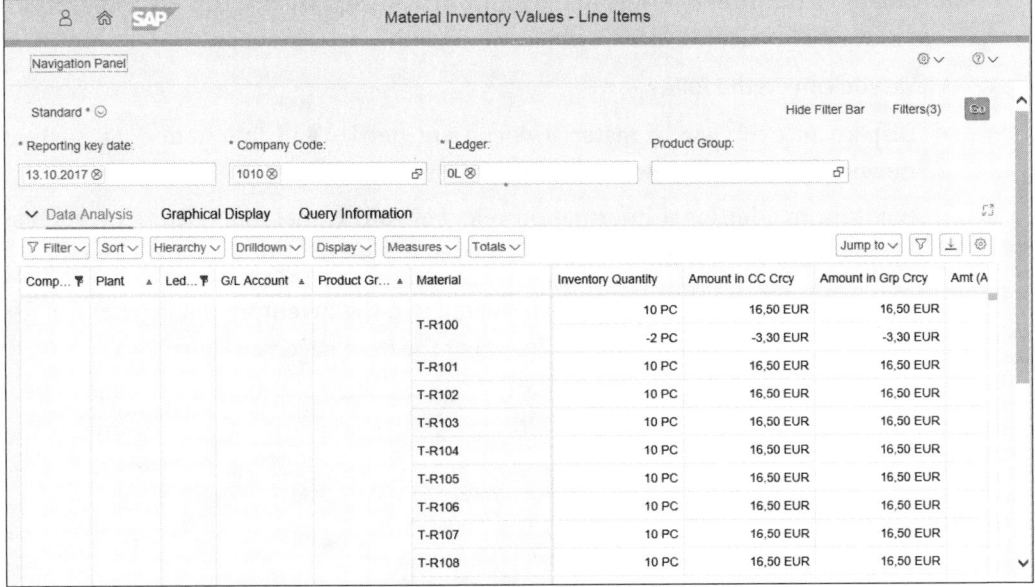

Figure 7.43 Material Inventory Values—Line Items App

7.8.5 Inventory Management Object Pages

There are several object pages available when using Inventory Management in SAP S/4HANA:

- Material Document
- Material
- Supplier
- Customer
- Inbound Delivery
- Outbound Delivery

We'll discuss these object pages in the following sections.

Material Document Object Page

The **Material Document** object page (Figure 7.44) displays useful information about the material document posted in the SAP S/4HANA system. Via this object page, you can navigate to related business objects and to transactional apps.

Here, you can do the following:

- Display an overview of material document header and line item data, such as movement type, document date, and materials transacted
- Navigate to additional information relevant to this material document, such as details for related business partners, related master data, or related documents

The **Material Document** object page is assigned to the inventory manager and warehouse clerk standard authorization roles. For the item page, see Figure 7.45.

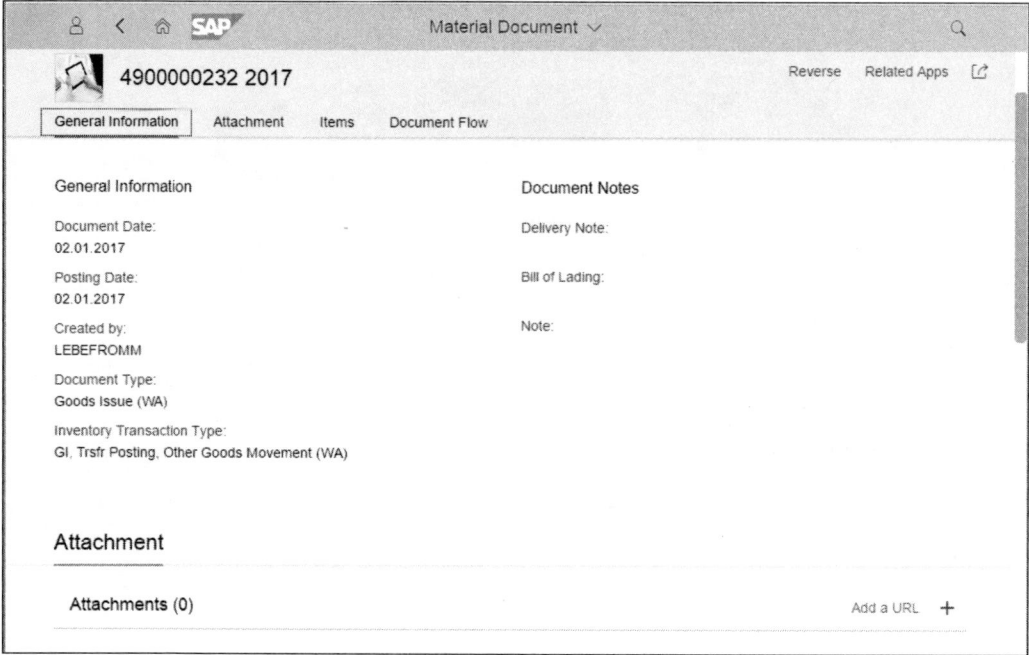

Figure 7.44 Material Document: General Information

7.8 Reporting in Inventory Management

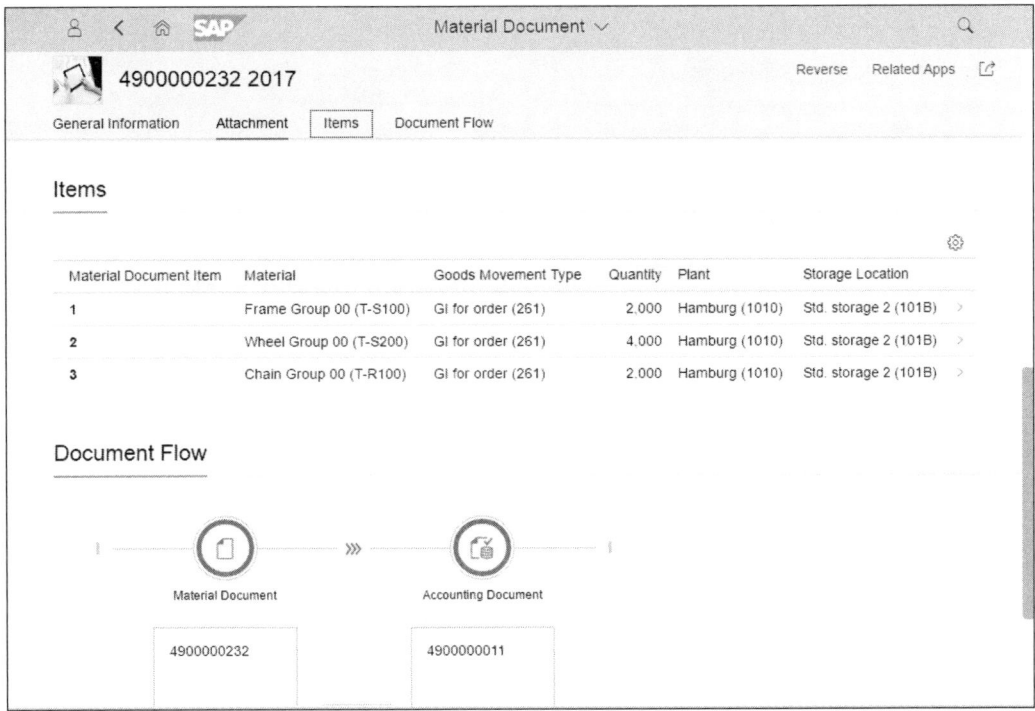

Figure 7.45 Material Document: Items

Material Object Page

The **Material** object page (Figure 7.46) is used to display an overview of a specific material.

You navigate to this object page from other SAP Fiori apps, or you can navigate to additional information related to this material, such as detailed information about related master data or related documents.

The **Material** object page can also show the following:

- Suppliers of the material, using the purchasing view
- Purchase orders for the material, using the purchasing view
- Sales orders, using the sales view

The **Material** object page is assigned to the purchaser, warehouse manager, warehouse clerk, and accounts payable accountant standard authorization roles.

7 Inventory Management

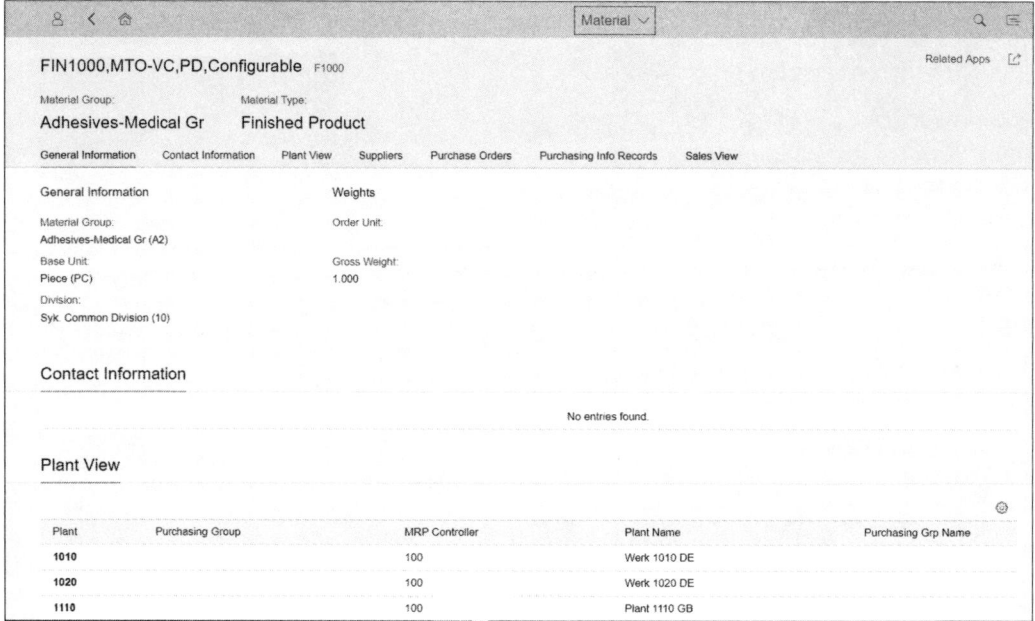

Figure 7.46 Material Object Page

Supplier Object Page

The **Supplier** object page (Figure 7.47) is used to display an overview of a specific supplier.

You navigate to this object page from other SAP Fiori apps, or you can navigate to additional information related to the individual supplier, such as detailed information about related business partners, related master data, or related documents.

The **Supplier** object page can also show the following:

- Company code data for the supplier
- Communication and blocking data for the supplier
- Materials provided to your company by the supplier
- Annual spend for the supplier

The **Supplier** object page is assigned to the strategic buyer standard authorization role.

7.8 Reporting in Inventory Management

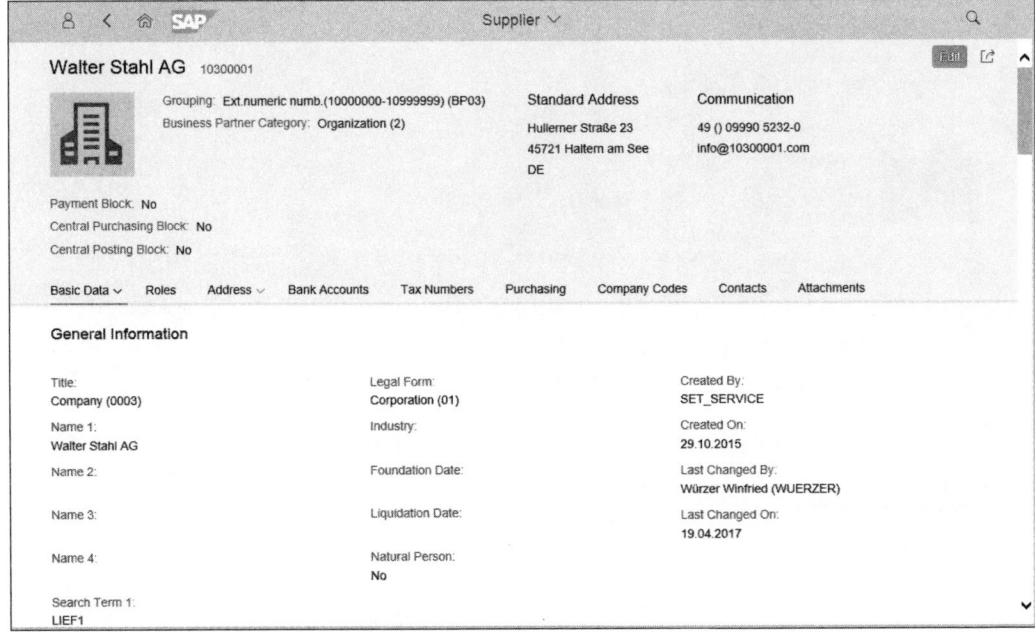

Figure 7.47 Supplier Object Page

Customer Object Page

The **Customer** object page (Figure 7.48) is used to display an overview of a specific customer.

You navigate to this object page from other SAP Fiori apps, or you can navigate to additional information related to the individual customer, such as detailed information about related business partners, related master data, or related documents.

The **Customer** object page can also show the following:

- Company code data for the customer
- Sales area data for the customer
- Related sales orders and billing documents for the customer
- Communication data and blocking data for the customer

The **Customer** object page is assigned to the customer master specialist and accounts receivable accountant standard authorization roles.

7 Inventory Management

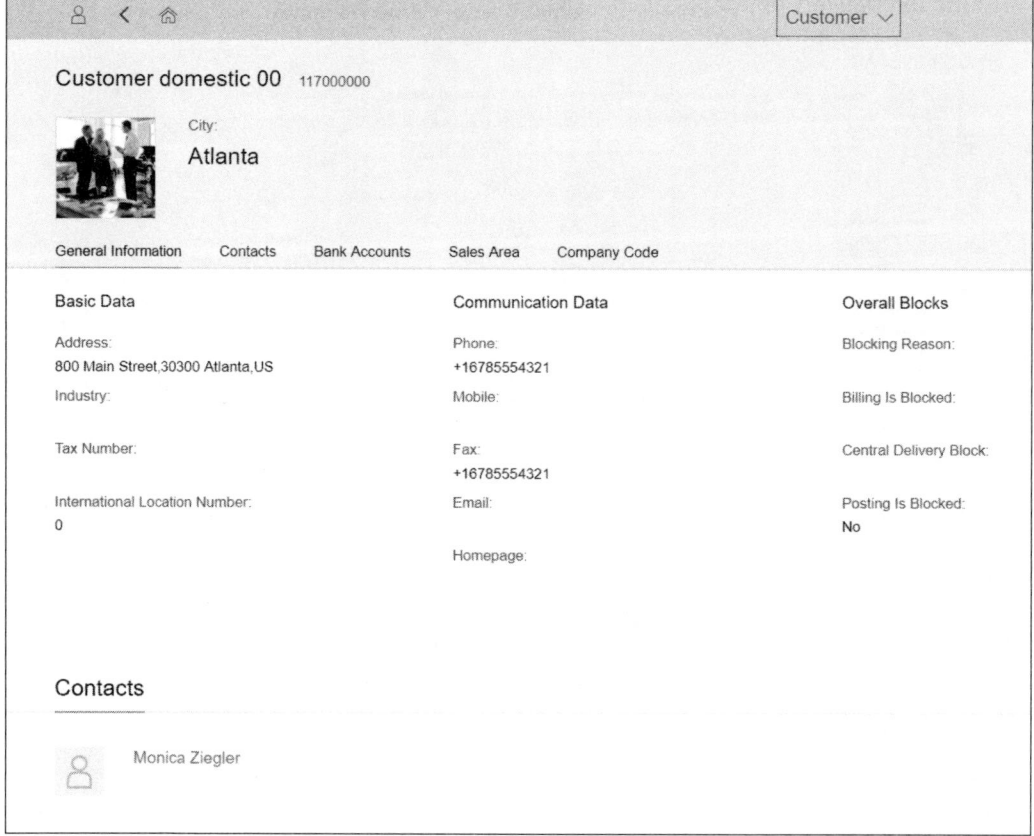

Figure 7.48 Customer Object Page

Inbound Delivery Object Page

Use the **Inbound Delivery** object page to display details about a specific inbound delivery document. You can also easily access related documents and master data related to this inbound delivery document, such as business partners.

You can navigate this app by searching for inbound deliveries from the **Enterprise Search** area of the SAP Fiori launchpad. You can search for inbound deliveries using key fields such as receiving point, material number, or supplier. The results are shown in a worklist from which you can easily retrieve details for each inbound delivery document listed.

The **Inbound Delivery** object page can be used to:

- Display attributes of the inbound delivery document, such as receiving point, overall status, and delivery date.
- Display the materials to be received, along with quantity and receiving plant and storage location.
- Display the contact details of the business partners involved in the outbound delivery.
- Display the process flow, which is a graphical overview of the chain of connected process steps and corresponding business documents (document flow). For example, you can see the sales order that preceded the outbound delivery or the material document that recorded the goods issue posting for the outbound delivery.

The **Inbound Delivery** object page is assigned to the receiving specialist, inventory manager, and warehouse clerk standard authorization roles.

Outbound Delivery Object Page

Use the **Outbound Delivery** object page to display details about a specific outbound delivery document. You can also easily access related documents and master data related to this outbound delivery document, such as business partners.

You can navigate to this app by searching for outbound deliveries from the **Enterprise Search** area of the SAP Fiori launchpad. You can search for outbound deliveries using key fields such as shipping point, material number, or customer. The results are shown in a worklist from which you can easily retrieve details for each outbound delivery document listed.

The **Outbound Delivery** object page can be used to:

- Display attributes of the outbound delivery document, such as shipping point, overall status, and delivery date.
- Display the materials to be shipped, along with quantity and shipping plant and storage location.
- Display the contact details of the business partners involved in the outbound delivery.
- Display the process flow, which is a graphical overview of the chain of connected process steps and corresponding business documents (document flow). For example, you can see the sales order that preceded the outbound delivery or the material document that recorded the goods issue posting for the outbound delivery.

The **Outbound Delivery** object page is assigned to the shipping specialist standard authorization role.

7.8.6 Inventory Management Analytics

Managing the myriad of stock items in a typical warehouse can be a daunting task. Warehouse and inventory managers need information to understand how goods are moving in, through, and out of a facility. They also need to understand the velocity of materials, so that materials that are moving slowly can be addressed in terms of storage space and placement within the warehouse.

SAP S/4HANA supplies the following analytic apps for use by inventory managers.

- Goods Movement Analysis
- Inventory Turnover Analysis
- Slow or Non-Moving Materials

We'll discuss each app in the following sections.

Goods Movement Analysis

The Goods Movement Analysis app allows you to investigate goods movements in your enterprise.

The Goods Movement Analysis app has the following features:

- Define filters to narrow your search scope, such as plant, material, and material group.
- Choose from a variety dimensions for analysis, such as plant, storage location, material, year/month, calendar week, and day of year.
- Choose from a variety of key figures, such as stock change quantity, stock change amount, consumption quantity, consumption amount, movement count, issue count, and receipt count.
- Drill down to an individual material document item if required.
- Sorting, totaling, and subtotaling are supported.
- Export to Excel is supported.

The Goods Movement Analysis app is assigned to the inventory manager standard authorization role.

7.8 Reporting in Inventory Management

Inventory Turnover Analysis

The Inventory Turnover Analysis app (Figure 7.49) assists you in monitoring the turnover of material in a plant.

Turnover is defined as the relation between goods issue quantities and stock quantities within a set time period.

This app provides you with detailed information on materials that have turnover issues based on a specified time horizon.

The Inventory Turnover Analysis app lets you do the following:

- Perform research on turnover-related issues down to individual materials
- Display detailed turnover analysis results using different representations—for example, as a scatter or bubble chart

The Inventory Turnover Analysis app is assigned to the inventory manager standard authorization role.

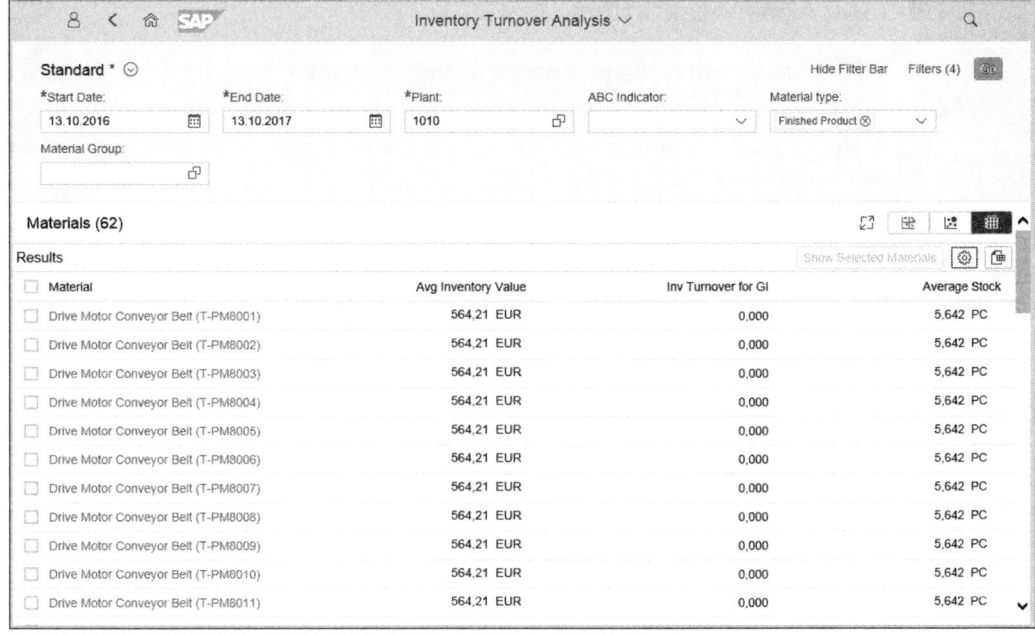

Figure 7.49 Inventory Turnover Analysis App

Slow or Non-Moving Materials Analysis

Use the Slow or Non-Moving Materials Analysis app to monitor and investigate those materials for which the velocity through the warehouse is slower than normal. Based on this, you can then initiate follow-on actions, such as scrapping.

The Slow or Non-Moving Materials Analysis app has the following features:

- Allows monitoring of slow-moving materials
- Monitors how much working capital is tied up by the slow-moving items
- Execution of follow-up activities based on the analysis results
- Inform colleagues about the slow-moving stock situation

The Slow or Non-Moving Materials Analysis app is assigned to the inventory manager, receiving specialist, shipping specialist, and warehouse clerk standard authorization roles.

7.9 SAP Ariba Integration

In a collaborative, connected procurement supply chain, it's important to inform a supplier when the physical receipt of goods that they shipped to you has occurred. The receipt of this information may trigger the billing process by the supplier, for example. The Ariba Network supports this requirement with the ability to exchange goods movement data from SAP S/4HANA with the network.

Goods receipts confirmation will act as a proof of delivery for the supplier. If suppliers are managing their stocks at your enterprise, as is the case in a supplier-managed inventory scenario, these confirmations are useful for calculating stock balances.

Receipt confirmations are transmitted from SAP S/4HANA to SAP Ariba as a `Receipt Request` message. The supplier can then see the goods receipts in the SAP Ariba portal.

Other goods movements, such as goods issues to subcontracting stock or transfer postings from supplier consignment to own stock, can be transmitted as a `Product ActivityMessage` message type from SAP S/4HANA to SAP Ariba. This is useful for letting suppliers know that parts are on their way to their facilities or that a payment will be coming for items on a consignment program.

7.10 Summary

You now know that SAP S/4HANA provides many apps for recording the receipt, placement, and issue of goods in your facilities. There are many apps that allow you to report, both at a tactical and a strategic level, the impacts of those goods movements, both on the logistics supply chain and on the financials of your company.

Chapter 8
Contracts Management

Purchasing contracts are agreements made by a buying organization with a supplier for supply of materials and services. Contract management in purchasing is the process of managing such contracts, which include creation, execution, monitoring, analysis, and renewal of contracts in SAP S/4HANA.

This chapter explains the contract management process and the SAP Fiori apps relevant to contract management and related analytics. We have also provided the detailed configuration steps required in SAP S/4HANA to run contract management. In addition, this chapter covers the Legal Content Management solution offered within SAP S/4HANA.

Businesses are increasingly becoming competitive- and success-driven in today's digital economy. To be a successful organization, it's essential that the procurement process, which is one of the core lines of business for any industry, is run with high efficiency and low costs. Most companies use the concept of longer-term purchasing agreements with suppliers to achieve procurement process optimization and improved financial performance. Such agreements are defined as *outline purchase agreements*, which may be referred to as *blanket* or *umbrella agreements* outside SAP systems. Outline purchase agreements within SAP comprise contracts, centrally agreed-upon contracts, distributed contracts, scheduling agreements, and scheduling agreements referencing a centrally agreed-upon contract. The solution addressing these agreements is referred to as Operational Contract Management under the Collaborative Sourcing and Contract Management stream in SAP S/4HANA, as shown in Figure 8.1.

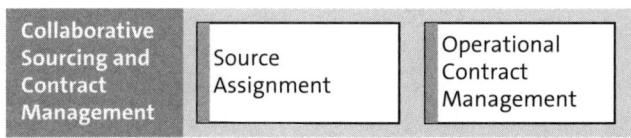

Figure 8.1 Collaborative Sourcing and Contract Management

8 Contracts Management

8.1 Contract Creation

A contract is a document created and maintained in the SAP S/4HANA system. This document holds all the information relevant to the purchasing agreement between the organization and the supplier. Once the quantities, prices, terms, and conditions are finalized, the contract is created in the system. The different types of contracts and how they're created in the system are explained in this section.

8.1.1 Types of Contracts

A *contract* is a type of outline agreement with suppliers in SAP S/4HANA, which allows for the issue of release orders (a.k.a., call-off orders) for the agreed-upon materials or services of the contract. These purchase contracts in SAP S/4HANA consist of *items*, which are materials, material groups, or services. It's possible to create the following contracts, depending on the business requirements:

- **Quantity Contract**
  This type of contract stipulates the quantity, negotiated price, and conditions for purchase of materials or services from the supplier with whom the contract is established. This allows the purchaser to issue multiple release orders to the supplier with reference to the contract until the total quantity reaches the value defined in the contract.

- **Value Contract**
  These contracts are generally used for purchasing materials or services that belong to certain material groups defined in materials management. These contracts stipulate the total value of the contract—which is also known as the *target value*—the material groups, and the supplier. Specific materials or services are not listed as line items in the contract, but the contact allows purchase of materials or services that belong to the material groups that are listed as line items in the contract. Purchasers can create release orders for materials or services that belong to the material groups identified in the contract.

- **Contract Release Order**
  It's possible to create a release order, which is simply a PO referencing a contract, using SAP GUI Transaction ME21N. In this transaction, if you enter the contract number in the **Outline Agreement** field under the **Items** pane, the system will populate all the information from the contract and expect you to input the quantity and delivery date. After creating the release order, it's possible to edit and display the document using Transactions ME22N and ME23N, respectively. With the introduction of SAP Fiori apps in SAP S/4HANA, the UI has moved away from the old

8.1 Contract Creation

SAP GUI–based transactions to the new SAP Fiori UX, which is explained in the next section.

8.1.2 Manage Purchase Contracts

Contracts can be created either directly by entering all the data manually or by referencing purchase requisitions, RFQs/quotations, or existing contracts. The SAP GUI Transaction ME31K is used for creating a contract, and this transaction is also available from the SAP Fiori launchpad. With the introduction of SAP Fiori apps for SAP S/4HANA, the Manage Purchase Contracts SAP Fiori app is used for creating or editing contracts. Logon to the SAP Fiori launchpad and click the **Manage Purchase Contracts** tile to open the app. Click the **+** button to create a contract. The header screen, shown in Figure 8.2, is presented for entering header information.

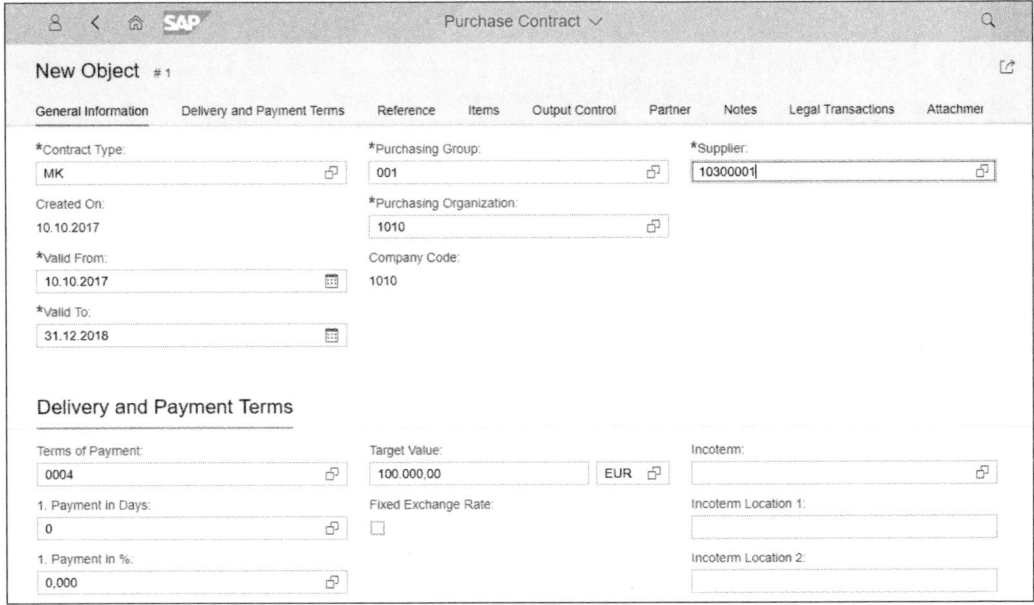

Figure 8.2 Create Contract: Header

After entering the contract type, P. Org, P. Group, and so on in the **General Information** tab, navigate to the other header tabs and fill out relevant information. It's possible to add attachments, include notes, add partner function information, and provide reference information, such as quotation number, sales person, and so on, as shown in Figure 8.3.

8 Contracts Management

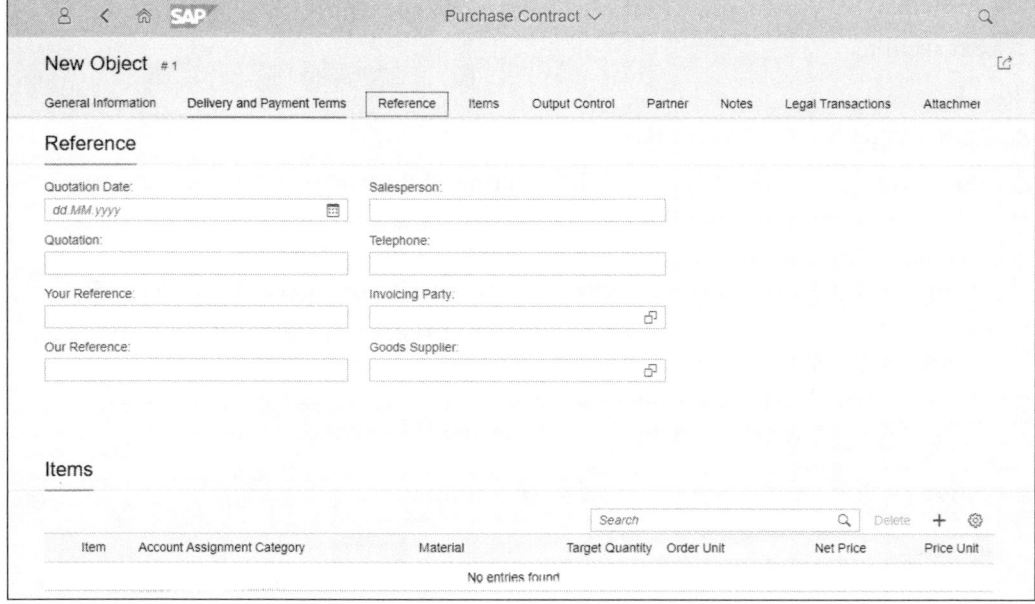

Figure 8.3 Create Contract: Reference

Once you've entered all the header information, choose the **Item** tab and click **+** (**Add**) to add item details for the contract. Input the material number, plant, and storage location in the **General Information** tab, as shown in Figure 8.4.

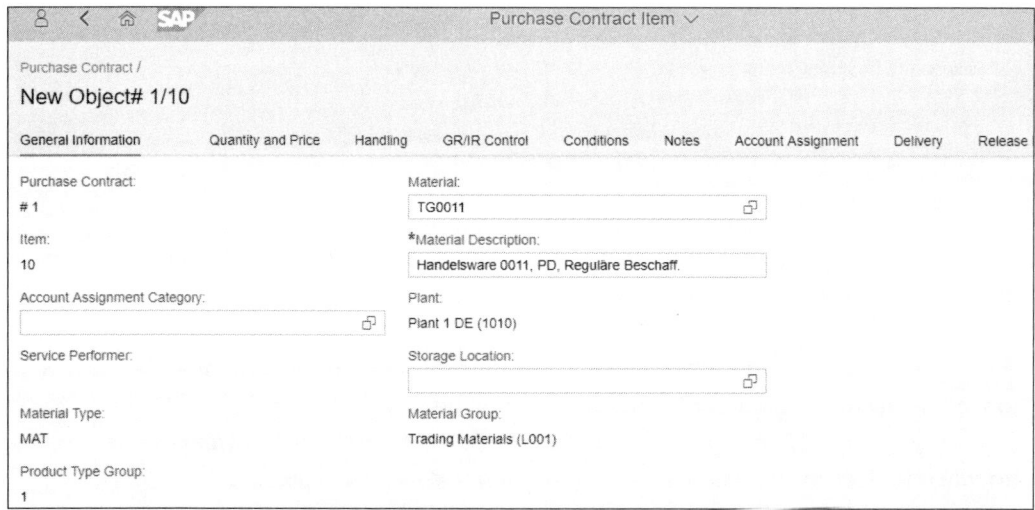

Figure 8.4 Create Contract Item: General Information

On the item detail screen, after entering quantity and price, go to the **GR/IR Control** tab and add relevant information, as in Figure 8.5.

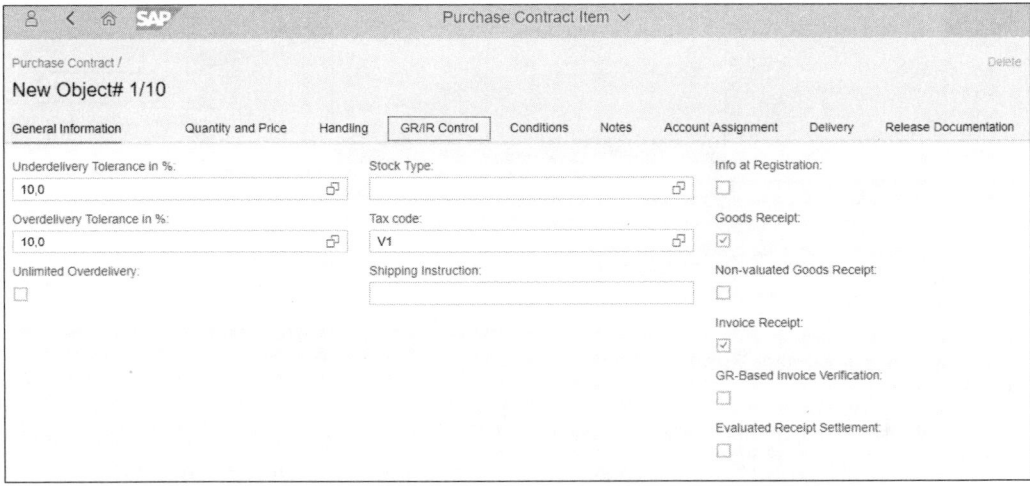

Figure 8.5 Create Contract Item: GR/IR Control

Then, go to the **Conditions** tab and add (**+**) conditions, as shown in Figure 8.6.

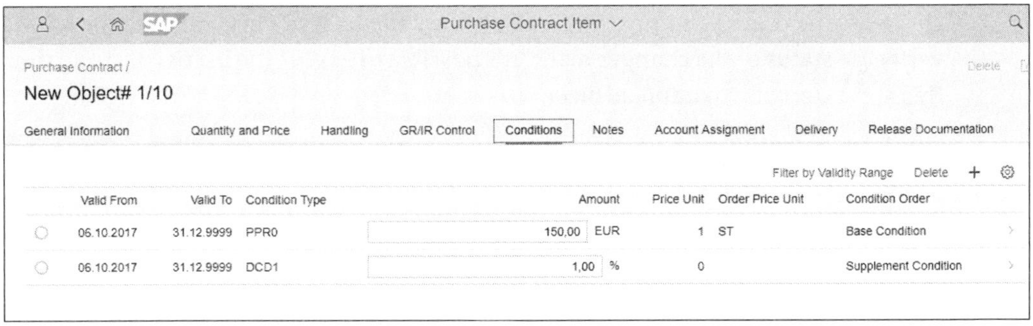

Figure 8.6 Create Contract Item: Conditions

Check all the entries and click the **Apply** button to apply the conditions; then save the contract. This completes the process of creating a contract.

This app also provides the capability to search for contracts based on a wide range of criteria, including supplier, purchasing organization, purchasing group, approval status, creation date, validity status, and so on. It's also possible to navigate to the contract in display mode and edit it from there, as shown in Figure 8.7.

8 Contracts Management

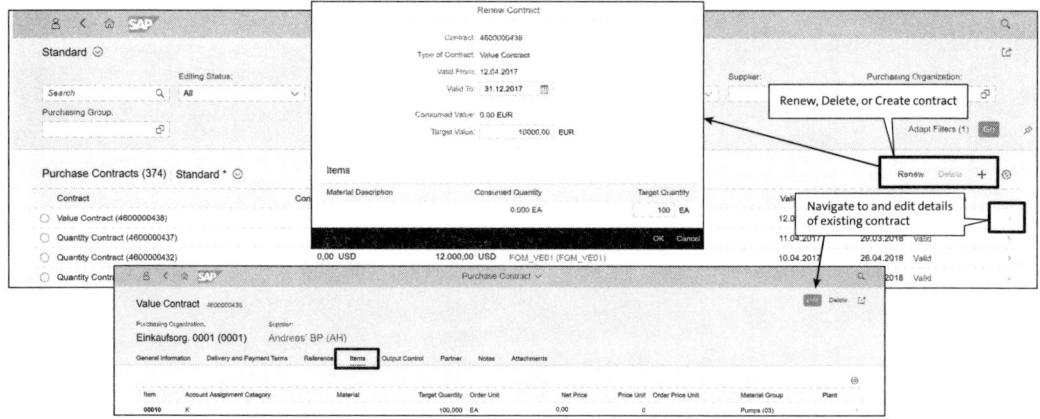

Figure 8.7 Manage Purchase Contract

Selecting a contract from the list and clicking the **Renew** button allows the user to extend the validity period, target quantity, or target value of the contract.

8.1.3 Mass Change to Purchase Contract

This app (see Figure 8.8) enables the purchaser to change the fields of multiple purchase contracts at the same time. It also allows the user to check the change logs to verify the status of the changes made. It's possible to export the list of contracts from this app externally to a spreadsheet.

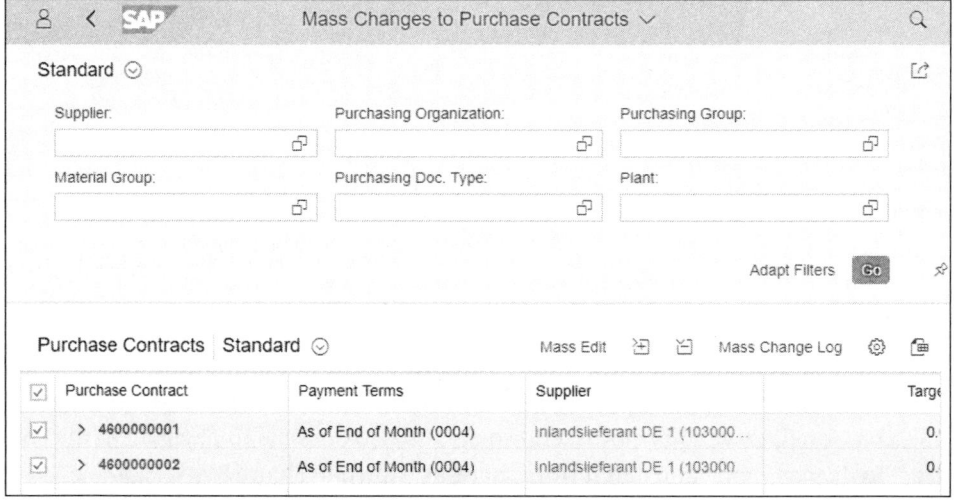

Figure 8.8 Mass Changes to Purchase Contracts

8.2 Contract Consumption

Purchase managers and buyers want to monitor existing contracts in the system and analyze consumption patterns. They also want to obtain advance information about both planned and predicted expiry dates of contracts. This information helps the purchasing organization regulate consumption and initiate contract renewal or the renegotiation process. This section describes the SAP Fiori apps available in SAP S/4HANA to both analyze and predict contract data.

8.2.1 Value Contract Consumption

This SAP Fiori app analyses the value contracts in the system and displays target and released amounts and the consumption percentage over the last 365 days. It's possible to display the KPIs by supplier, purchasing group, purchasing organization, document, and trend. The output can be filtered by **Purchase Contract**, **Calendar Week/Month/Quarter/Year**, **Purchasing Group/Organization**, **Supplier**, **Currency**, **Company Code**, and **Created By**, as shown in Figure 8.9.

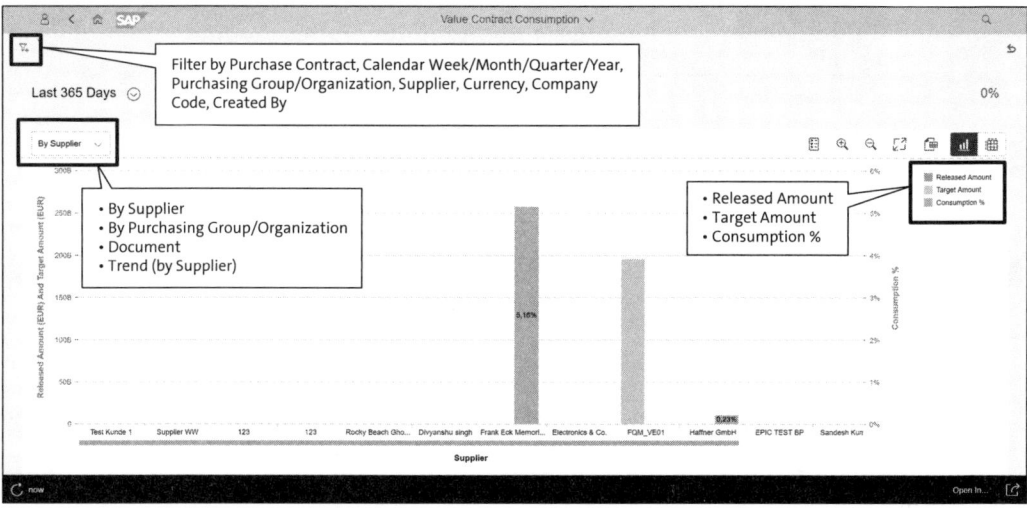

Figure 8.9 Value Contract Consumption

8.2.2 Quantity Contract Consumption

This SAP Fiori app determines the percentage of consumption of quantity type contracts. It also displays the target and released quantities of contracts. The results can be viewed by supplier, purchasing group, purchasing organization, document, and trend. It's also possible to filter the output by **Purchase Contract**, **Calendar Week/Month/Quarter/Year**, **Purchasing Group/Organization**, **Supplier**, **Currency**, **Company Code**, **Created By**, **Cost Center**, **Purchasing Category**, **Material Group**, **Material**, **Plant**, and **Purchase Order Unit**.

The Quantity Contract Consumption app (Figure 8.10) provides an additional measure for predicted contract consumption in trend view, based on historical data from closed contracts.

In document view, the predicted contract consumption and the predicted expiry date based on 100 percent consumption for individual contracts are provided.

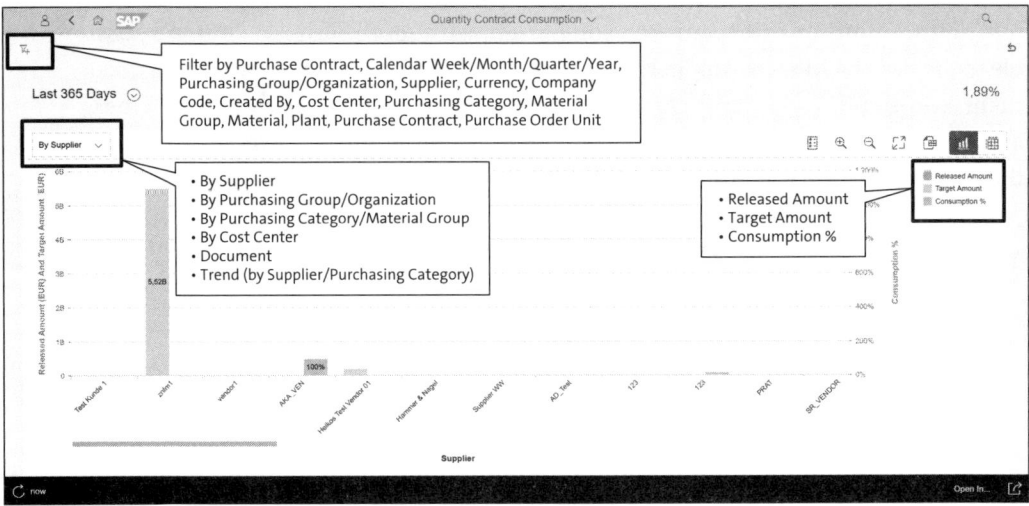

Figure 8.10 Quantity Contract Consumption

8.3 Contract Dashboard Reporting and Expiry Notification Setting

Reporting in contract management has undergone major changes in SAP S/4HANA. The capability that comes with the in-memory technology of SAP S/4HANA and the SAP Fiori UI has made it possible to offer a number of innovations in the areas of reporting and analytics. This section provides a detailed explanation of all the SAP Fiori apps that come with SAP S/4HANA. It's also important to note that SAP has embarked on a new journey to introduce more innovative apps as part of every new release.

SAP Fiori provides its role-based, consumer-grade UX across all lines of business. SAP Fiori 2.0 is the latest evolution of UX for SAP S/4HANA and provides a harmonized UX for both on-premise and cloud solutions with a new visual theme called *Belize*. SAP Fiori 2.0 enriches UX with intuitive, easy-to-use apps that run on both mobile devices and computers. SAP Fiori apps help zero-in on key functions, tasks, and activities for the user. SAP Fiori overview pages are the latest app type, and they allow users to get live KPIs and action items, including lists of contracts that will expire in the near future. SAP Fiori apps are categorized as transactional, analytical, and object page types. Transactional apps run business transactions, and object page apps display master data and documents. Analytical apps, as the name suggests, are used to analyze live data for instant business insight. These apps also provide capability to act based on insights. Detailed information on all the apps is available at *https://fioriappslibrary.hana.ondemand.com/sap/fix/externalViewer/*.

The new visual theme, Belize, is also available for SAP GUI transactions. In other words, wherever SAP Fiori apps aren't available yet, the SAP GUI transactions can be accessed from SAP Fiori launchpad through these SAP GUI apps. These apps run in the backend as SAP GUI applications but are presented to the user in the Belize theme. This helps users access the system from a central SAP Fiori launchpad, enjoy the new UX, and avoid the need to logon to SAP GUI. It is worth mentioning that SAP is replacing additional SAP GUI transactions with SAP Fiori apps in each SAP S/4HANA release. The SAP Fiori apps discussed in the following sections are available within the Contract Management solution in SAP S/4HANA.

8.3.1 Unused Contracts

This app (Figure 8.11) identifies all the contracts that are not used within the last 365 days from the current date and displays the target and released amounts. The output can be displayed by supplier, purchasing group, or purchasing organization, in tabular format or as a chart. It is possible to drill down and be able to view the related documents.

This app allows you to view releases compared to target amounts graphically and determine whether you're consuming your existing contracts appropriately.

8 Contracts Management

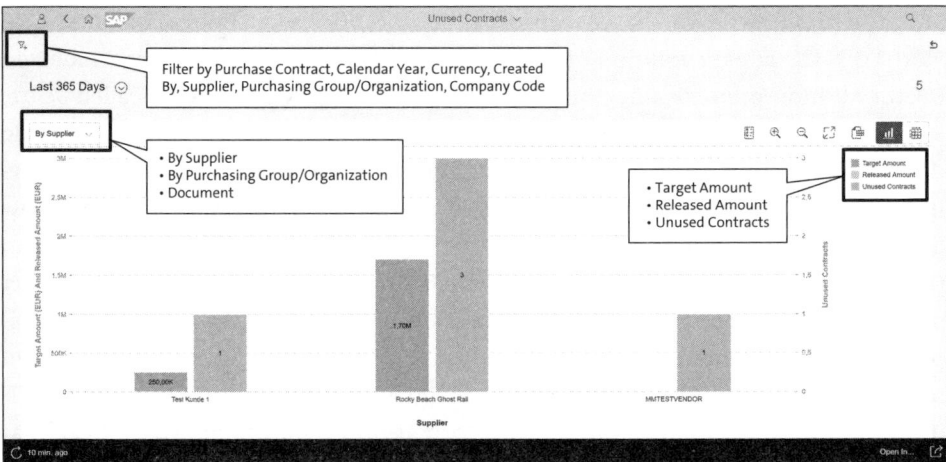

Figure 8.11 Unused Contracts

8.3.2 Off-Contract Spend

Often, purchases are made without a negotiated price for materials or services. Procurement managers always want to know how much or what percentage of materials are procured outside of negotiated contracts. Analyzing this information helps buyers determine the types of products and areas in need of further contracts and negotiated prices. The Off-Contract Spend app (Figure 8.12) enables the buyer to analyze and control such purchases, resulting in improved procurement processes and reduced costs.

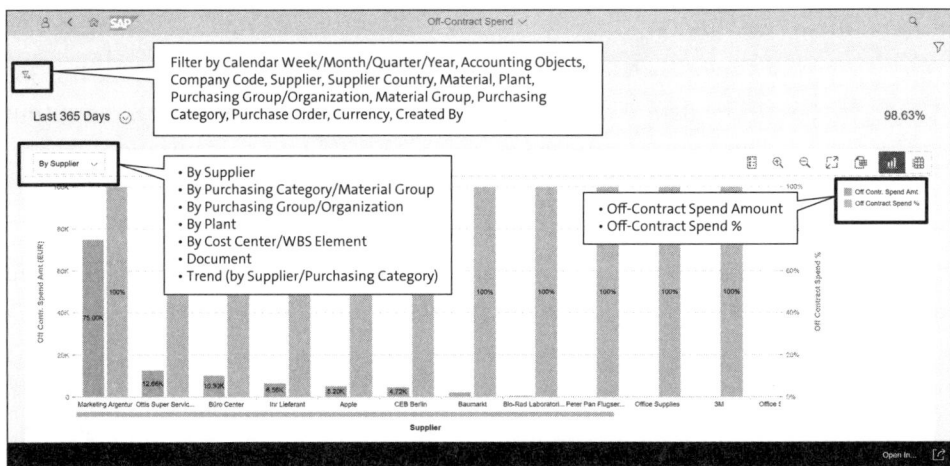

Figure 8.12 Off-Contract Spend

8.3 Contract Dashboard Reporting and Expiry Notification Setting

This app provides the total spend amount and percentage of purchase orders that don't reference a contract. The values can be displayed by supplier, purchasing group, purchasing organization, purchasing category, or material group, in tabular format or as a chart. The app can display all documents that contribute to the spend. It's also possible to analyze the trend of the spend by purchasing category or by supplier.

8.3.3 Contract Leakage

The Contract Leakage app (Figure 8.13) is used to identify purchase order spend on items procured without referencing an existing contract. Such a buying pattern is likely to increase costs and decrease efficiency. The Contract Leakage app helps monitor such spending happening outside contracts despite having a contract. It's possible to analyze the data by supplier, purchasing group, purchasing organization, purchasing category, or material group. For each view, the list of documents that contribute to the spend amount can be displayed as well.

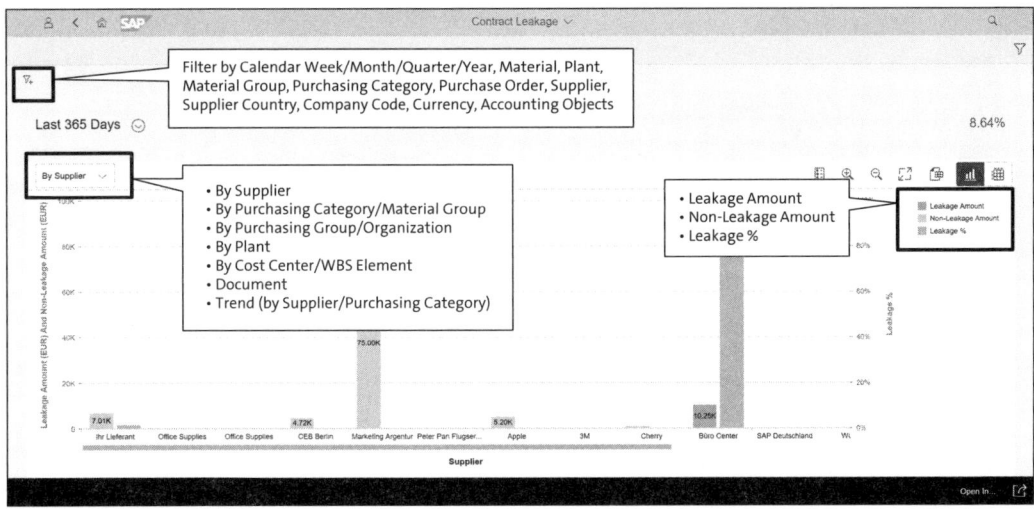

Figure 8.13 Contract Leakage

8.3.4 Purchase Contract Items by Account Assignment

This app displays purchase contract items grouped by their cost centers, using filter criteria such as **Purchase Contract**, **Cost Center**, **Order**, **WBS Element**, **Asset**, and so on. Clicking any cost center of the result output lets you view details such as material, supplier, account assignment category description, net value, and account assignment

8 Contracts Management

quantity for each purchase contract item assigned to that cost center. The app allows you to drill down further to view the corresponding purchase orders and general information. It also allows navigation to object pages for material and supplier.

8.3.5 Monitor Purchase Contract Items

This app (Figure 8.14) initially displays a chart and table view with aggregated values of purchase contract items for material groups with EUR as the currency. Purchase contract items can be displayed based on filter criteria such as **Display Currency**, **Purchase Contract**, **Material Group**, **Material**, **Supplier**, **Cost Center**, and so on. It's possible to drill down further to view detailed information for any dimension. In the chart, the Y-axis represents the measure and the X-axis represents the dimension. It's possible to click any purchase contract item and view the corresponding purchase orders and general information. This app allows for navigation to contextual information related to a purchase contract, a purchase contract item, and a material.

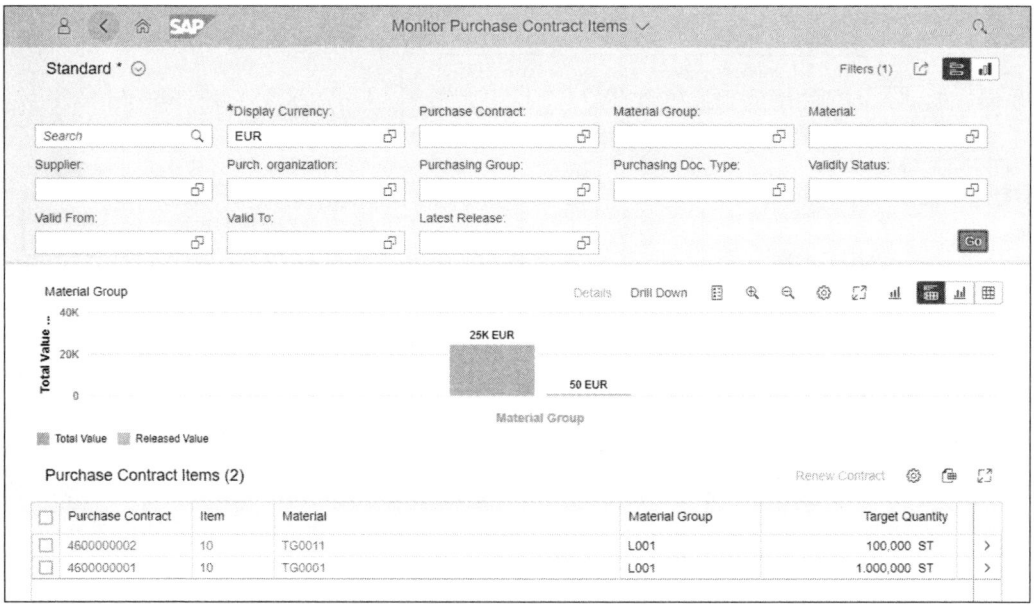

Figure 8.14 Monitor Purchase Contract Items

8.3.6 Contract Expiry

This app (Figure 8.15) identifies contracts that are expiring within a certain time period and can display the number of expiring contracts, target amount, and released amount. The output can be displayed by supplier, purchasing group, purchasing organization, purchasing category, or material group, in tabular format or as a chart. It's also possible to filter the data by **Purchase Contract**, **Validity Start/End**, **Created By**, **Currency**, **Purchasing Group/Organization**, **Supplier**, and **Company Code**.

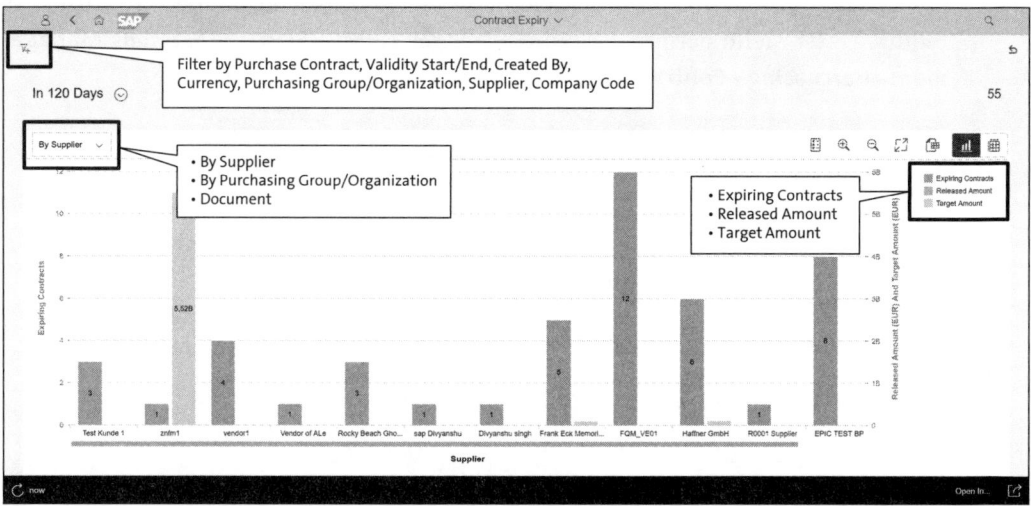

Figure 8.15 Contract Expiry

8.4 Configuration

To realize the features and functionalities of contract management, the system needs to be configured based on business requirements. This section provides the details of standard SAP-recommended configuration steps for contract management. These settings are made in the SAP S/4HANA system by following the customizing path provided in the following sections for each step.

8.4.1 Configuring Contracts

With SAP S/4HANA, it's possible to take advantage of the SAP Best Practices activation approach for customizing, as explained in Chapter 2. However, if you use the traditional customizing approach, this section can help. This information also helps validate the SAP standard configuration.

Define Document Types

To define document types, navigate to **IMG (SPRO) • Materials Management • Purchasing • Contract • Define Document Types**. Table 8.1 provides the SAP-standard settings; it's possible to define additional contract document types depending on business requirements. New number ranges may also be defined and used as required. The menu path to set number ranges is **IMG (SPRO) • Materials Management • Purchasing • Contract • Define Number Ranges** (see Figure 8.16).

Field Name	Value (First Entry)	Value (Second Entry)
Type	MK	WK
Doc. Type Description	Quantity Contract	Value Contract
Item Number Interval	10	10
Number Range—Internal	46	46
Number Range—External	44	44
Update Group Statistics	SAP	SAP
Field Selection Key	MKK	WKK

Table 8.1 Define Document Types

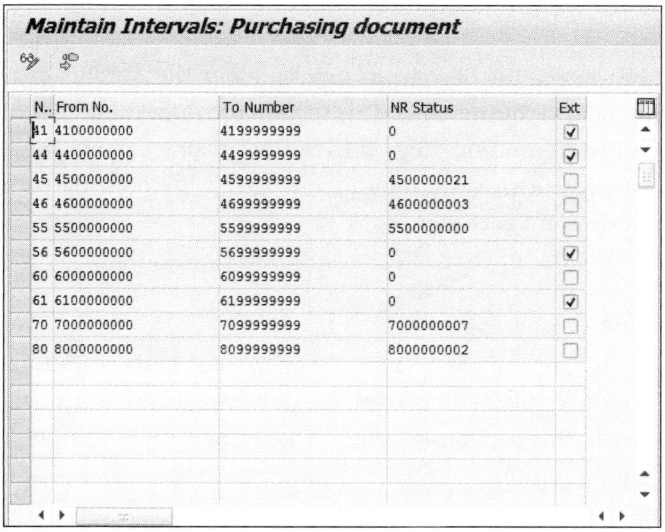
Maintain Intervals: Purchasing document

N..	From No.	To Number	NR Status	Ext
41	4100000000	4199999999	0	✓
44	4400000000	4499999999	0	✓
45	4500000000	4599999999	4500000021	
46	4600000000	4699999999	4600000003	
55	5500000000	5599999999	5500000000	
56	5600000000	5699999999	0	✓
60	6000000000	6099999999	0	
61	6100000000	6199999999	0	✓
70	7000000000	7099999999	7000000007	
80	8000000000	8099999999	8000000002	

Figure 8.16 Define Number Ranges: Contract

Define Item Categories

After defining the document types, select the line for the **Doc Type** defined in the previous step and double-click **Allowed Item Categories**. On the admissible item categories for the document type, the item categories listed in Table 8.2 can be configured depending on business requirements.

Item Category	Description	Use Case
Blank	Standard	
M	Material unknown	Used when similar materials are negotiated for same price but with different material number
W	Material Group	Only for value contract with material groups but without item price or quantity
D	Service	When contract is created for performance of services
K	Consignment	When contract is created for consignment materials
L	Subcontracting	When contract is created for subcontracting activities

Table 8.2 Item Categories in Contracts

Then, select the line for each **Item Category** and double click **Link Purchase Requisition Document Type**. On the **Change View "Link purchase requistion-document type": Overview** screen, define the allowed follow-on documents.

Release Procedure for Contracts

A *release procedure* is used for the contract approval process. If the value of a contract exceeds $10,000, for example, it may have to be approved by a manger before the contract can be processed further. The approver in this process uses a predetermined release code to approve (release) the document. *Release* in this context refers to approving contracts in the system. The procedure is set up in a series of configuration steps:

1. Navigate to **IMG (SPRO)** • **Materials Management** • **Purchasing** • **Contract** • **Release Procedure for Contracts**, as shown in Figure 8.17.

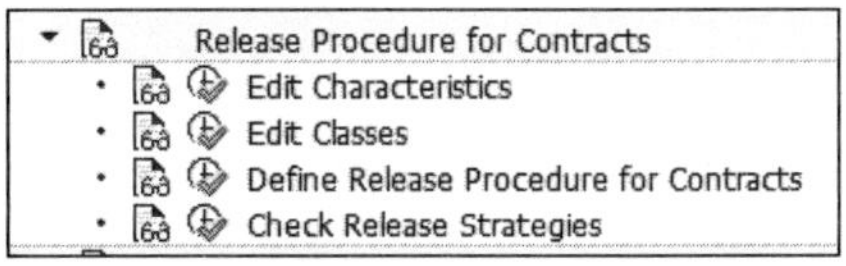

Figure 8.17 Release Procedure for Contracts

8 Contracts Management

2. Create characteristics.
3. Create classes.
4. Set up the release procedure for contracts.
5. Create release group.
6. Create release code.
7. Create release indicator.
8. Create release strategy.
9. Check release strategies.

Texts for Contracts

Text types are used while creating contracts, and text maintained under each text type is generally used to provide additional information either at the header level or item level within the contract. For this functionality to work, text types must be defined. In this customizing step, it's possible create new text types or to use the existing (standard) text types and define copying rules for adopting texts from other objects, such as RFQ, quotation, contract, and so on. To begin, navigate to **IMG (SPRO)** • **Materials Management** • **Purchasing** • **Contract** • **Texts for Contracts**, as shown in Figure 8.18.

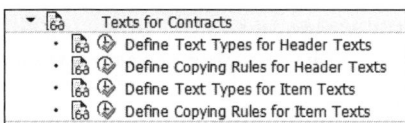

Figure 8.18 Texts for Contracts

Now, you need to define text types for header texts.

After the text types are defined, open the **Define Copying Rules for Header Texts** node, select the text type for which copying rules need to be defined, and choose **Text Linkages** for **Display Text Types: Header Text Contract**.

On the **Maintain Text Linkages: Header Text Contract** screen, enter the source object from which the text can be copied and the source text type. It's possible to set the copying rule to any of the following options:

- Text automatically adopted in target object
- User can have text adopted in target object
- Text can't be adopted in target object

This customizing activity is repeated for item text types.

Set Up Authorization Check for G/L Accounts

In this step, you set the G/L account authorization check to **Active** in contracts. Navigate to **IMG (SPRO)** • **Materials Management** • **Purchasing** • **Contract** • **Set Up Authorization Check for G/L Accounts**. This indicator is set at the company code level. Whenever a contract is created with an item requiring account assignment, the system checks whether the creator of the contract has the necessary authorization for the G/L account entered. This setting is used as a control mechanism based on the business requirements per company code.

8.4.2 Configuring Contract Workflow

New SAP Fiori apps are provided for managing workflows for purchasing documents. This is planned for contracts as well in upcoming releases. This app allows for workflow configuration without the need to write any code. It's possible to define workflow preconditions to start the workflow. This app provides the capability to assign approvers who are either specific users or managers or cost center managers. Multi-step approvals are also included in this design.

8.5 Scheduling Agreement

Scheduling agreements are another form of outline purchase agreement in SAP S/4HANA. These agreements are used to procure materials over a specified period of time following a set schedule of delivery. The predetermined delivery schedules in the agreement indicate quantities of the items and dates of delivery. Conditions can be maintained at the header level, which applies to all the items, or at the item level, which applies only to a specific item. These agreements have the account assignment function, which allows the buyer to allocate costs by maintaining details of controlling objects at the item level within the document at the time of creation.

The benefits of using scheduling agreements include the following:

- Shorten processing times and reduce the amount of paperwork required otherwise
- Delivery schedule can replace a large number of discrete purchase orders or contract release orders
- Reduced inventory
- Possible to run manufacturing operations on the just-in-time principle

- Suppliers require shorter lead times with smaller deliveries spread over a long period, resulting in better planning and efficient resource allocation for suppliers
- Scheduling agreement can work in conjunction with MRP, especially in repetitive manufacturing involving large quantities

8.5.1 Scheduling Agreement with Release Document

This type of agreement is created by choosing scheduling agreement document type LPA. In this case, the schedule lines entered within the agreement aren't transmitted to the supplier at the time of creation of the agreement and are internal to the system. The schedule lines maintained in this agreement can be changed at any time during the life of the agreement, which allows some level of flexibility in scheduling procurement. Whenever a scheduling agreement release is created, the information stored in the schedule lines are used to create and transmit the releases to the supplier. Two types of releases available with this type of scheduling agreement (LPA) are forecast delivery schedule (FRC) and JIT delivery schedule. The release documentation generated in this process provides information on the releases transmitted to the supplier over a set period.

8.5.2 Scheduling Agreement without Release Document

This type of agreement is created by choosing scheduling agreement document type LP. The scheduling lines created in this type of agreement are external and official. This means that the scheduling lines are transmitted to the supplier as soon as they're created. Also, there is no release documentation associated with this agreement.

8.5.3 Stock Transport Scheduling Agreement

If a company is procuring materials internally from another plant on a regular basis, it's possible to set up a stock transport scheduling agreement by choosing document type LU at the time of creation. SAP standard uses item category U, Stock Transfer, for this type of agreement.

8.5.4 Creating Scheduling Agreements

Scheduling agreements can be created manually or by referencing purchasing documents such as purchase requisitions, RFQ/quotations, other scheduling agreements, or centrally agreed-upon contracts. It's possible to create a scheduling agreement by copying any one of the purchasing documents and then making changes before saving the agreement.

8.5.5 Manage Scheduling Agreement

This SAP Fiori app provides the capability to search scheduling agreements by purchasing organization, agreement type, supplier, status, and validity period. It allows the user to display, edit, create, and delete scheduling agreements. It's possible to maintain schedule lines within scheduling agreements. It also highlights those scheduling agreements that are expiring soon and allows the user to renew or create a new scheduling agreement, as shown in Figure 8.19.

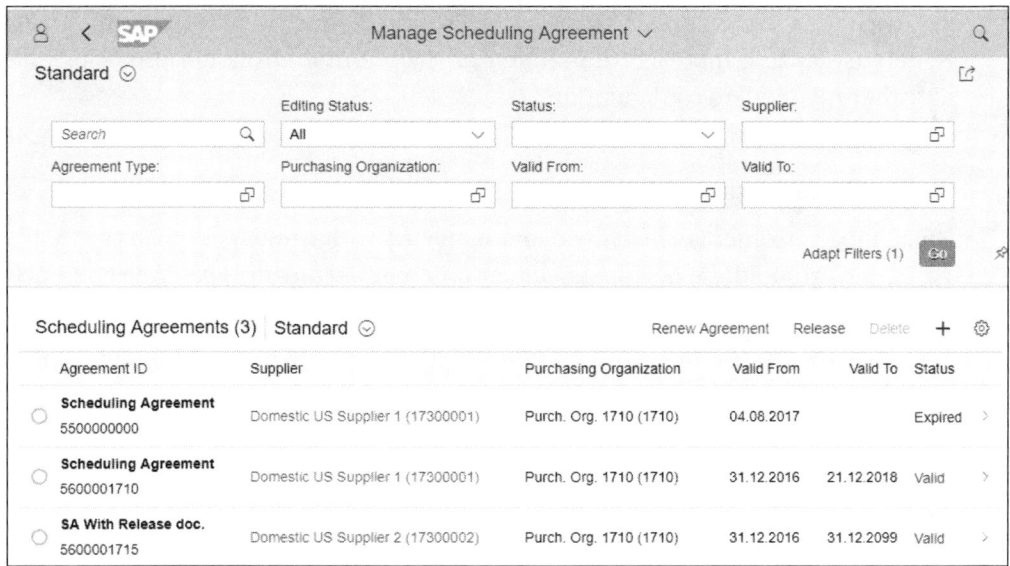

Figure 8.19 Manage Scheduling Agreement

> **Note**
>
> The following is the list of transactions available for scheduling agreements in the SAP Fiori Belize theme:

8   Contracts Management

- Display Scheduling Agreement (Transaction ME33L)
- Create Scheduling Agreement (Transaction ME31L)
- Display Scheduling Agreement Schedule (Transaction ME39)
- Change Scheduling Agreement (Transaction ME32L)
- Print Scheduling Agreement (Transaction ME9L)
- Print Scheduling Agreement Releases (Transaction ME9L)
- Create Scheduling Agreement Releases (Transaction ME84)
- Create Transport Scheduling Agreement (Transaction ME37)
- Release Scheduling Agreement (Transaction ME35L)

8.6   Customizing Scheduling Agreements

With SAP S/4HANA it's possible to take advantage of the SAP Best Practices activation approach for customizing, as explained in Chapter 2. However, if you use the traditional customizing approach, this section can help. This information also helps validate the SAP standard configuration.

8.6.1   Define Document Types

Scheduling agreements are defined and managed as documents in the system. It's possible to group these documents under different document types based on business requirements. First, you need to define document types and their attributes.

Table 8.3 provides the SAP-standard settings; it's possible to define additional scheduling agreement document types depending on business requirements, via **IMG (SPRO)** • **Materials Management** • **Purchasing** • **Scheduling Agreement** • **Define Document Types**.

Field Name	Value (First Entry)	Value (Second Entry)	Value (Third Entry)
Type	LPA	LP	LU
Doc. Type Description	SA With Release Doc.	Scheduling Agreement	Stock Trans. Sch. Agreement
Item Number Interval	10	10	10

Table 8.3 Define Document Types

Field Name	Value (First Entry)	Value (Second Entry)	Value (Third Entry)
Number Range—Internal	55	55	55
Number Range—External	56	56	56
Update Group Statistics	SAP	Blank	SAP
Field Selection Key	Lpl	Blank	
Control	Blank	Blank	T
Time-Dependent Conditions	Checked	Unchecked	Checked
Release Document	Checked	Unchecked	Unchecked

Table 8.3 Define Document Types (Cont.)

New number ranges may also be defined and used as required. This step generally is required if new document types are defined in the previous step. The menu path for creating number ranges is **IMG (SPRO)** • **Materials Management** • **Purchasing** • **Scheduling Agreement** • **Define Number Ranges**.

8.6.2 Define Item Categories

After defining the document types for scheduling agreements, select the line for the **Doc Type** and double-click **Allowed Item Categories**. Maintain the item category as listed in Table 8.4. These can be configured depending on business requirements.

Item Category	Description	Use Case
Blank	Standard	
K	Consignment	When scheduling agreement is created for consignment materials
L	Subcontracting	When scheduling agreement is created for subcontracting activities
U	Stock Transfer	This item category can be used only with Document Type LU (Stock Transfer Scheduling Agreement)

Table 8.4 Item Categories in Scheduling Agreements

Now, select the line for each **Item Category** and double-click **Link purchase requisition-document type**. On the **Change View "Link purchase requisition-document type": Overview** screen, define the allowed follow on documents.

8.6.3 Maintain Release Creation Profile

A *release creation profile* is used to determine the period in which releases (types of delivery schedule) are generated against a scheduling agreement and transmitted to the vendor. This also controls the creation periodicity of the releases; the aggregation of scheduled quantities, starting from the day after release creation; and the implementation of a tolerance check. In this step, a release creation profile is maintained for scheduling agreements with a release document. This profile determines the release creation strategy and how backlog and immediate requirements are considered in the release creation. To maintain the release creation profile, navigate to **IMG (SPRO)** • **Materials Management** • **Purchasing** • **Scheduling Agreement** • **Maintain Release Creation Profile for SA with Release Document**.

The following criteria also can be set up in the profile:

- Aggregation and release horizon: If and how delivery schedules are to be aggregated with the release creation
- Release creation periodicity: The frequency with which SA releases are generated
- Tolerance profile: For releases that need to be generated because of changed delivery schedules, a tolerance check is carried out
- Last goods receipts: If and how last inbound deliveries and goods receipts are determined and outputted during the release creation
- Internet release: If, during the release creation, Internet releases are to be generated
- Printing with Smart Forms: Which additional information in SA releases is outputted if you use the print form ISAUTO_ESCR_FRC_JIT, based on SAP Smart Forms
- Criteria for dynamic stopping: On the basis of which criteria SA releases are subject to dynamic stopping

> **Note**
>
> For more customizing steps such as the following, see the Customizing—Contracts section:

- Release Procedure for Scheduling Agreements
- Define Screen Layout at Document Level
- Texts for Scheduling Agreements
- Set Up Authorization Check for G/L Accounts

8.7 Legal Content Management

Legal content in SAP S/4HANA includes contracts, agreements, security policies, and other documents with legal significance in an organization. Such content is generated throughout an enterprise as part of different business processes, including procurement and sales and distribution. Legal content could include company policies and intercompany agreements as well. The objective of this solution is to make legal departments of organizations become *information-enabled*. This means that an organization has complete control over all the legal content relevant to the company. Some of the challenges faced by businesses today in legal content management include distributed repositories for storage of legal content, lack of comprehensive search capabilities, unstructured content in multiple formats, no consistent risk and compliance management, inefficient or unclear workflow in document processing, and content management in silos within the organization.

8.7.1 Legal Content Management in SAP S/4HANA

The new approach with Legal Content Management in SAP is to provide a central layer for legal content within SAP S/4HANA. The concept is to use legal content as master data and allow all information to follow the same data structure and be categorized semantically. This makes it possible to create and reuse text blocks and adapt to changing regulations and business needs.

The new features offered within Legal Content Management are as follows:

- Central repository for all contractual obligations with extensive search and reporting capabilities
- Machine-based, discoverable, reusable, and adaptable content
- Fully structured, standardized, and digitized content
- Supports all legal content–related processes with easy task management and flexible workflows; fully digitized end-to-end process within Legal Content Management

315

8 Contracts Management

- Intelligent Legal Content Assembly and easy (re)use of standard clauses
- Flexible solution to build, monitor, and, if needed, adjust legal transactions
- Latest technology and user-friendly UI available in the cloud and on-premise

Legal Content Management provides the following SAP Fiori applications designed for creation and management of legal content in enterprises that can be integrated into all core business processes:

- Manage Contexts for Legal Content
- Request Legal Content
- Manage Legal Transactions
- Categories

We'll discuss these apps in the following sections.

8.7.2 Manage Context for Legal Content

This SAP Fiori app can be started from the SAP Fiori launchpad by going to the **Legal Content Management** group and clicking the **Manage Context** tile. This app helps create and manage context used as a template when creating a legal transaction. Context covers a particular business scenario, such as procurement or sales and distribution processes, and provides a foundation for how a legal transaction is processed and what kind of information needs to be provided.

This app displays existing contexts and allows for filtering/search by **Context** ID, **Owner**, **Status**, **Editing Status**, and validity, as shown in Figure 8.20.

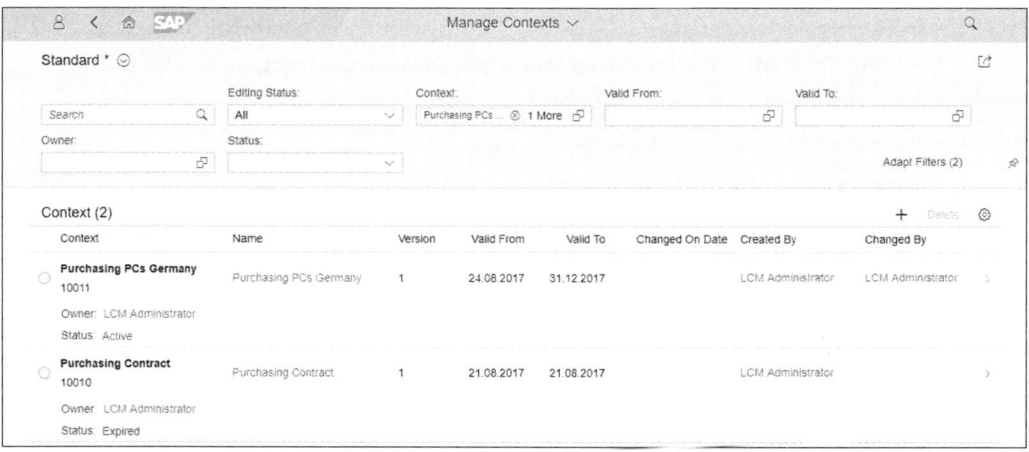

Figure 8.20 Manage Contexts

The following functions are provided in the app:

1. *Live update function*: The list of contexts in the content area is updated immediately when a user changes the filter criteria.
2. *Deleting contexts*: Select a context and delete it directly from the list. The deletion of a context is possible only if it isn't yet assigned to a legal transaction.
3. *Personalization of the table settings*: Display additional columns and rearrange the order of the displayed columns.
4. *Creating contexts*: From this app, create a new context by clicking the **+** sign (**Create Object**). As shown in Figure 8.21, first the header and general information are filled in, and then the required information is provided in all the tabs:
    - Under the **Categories** tab enter the categories that describe the business scenario, which are covered by the context.

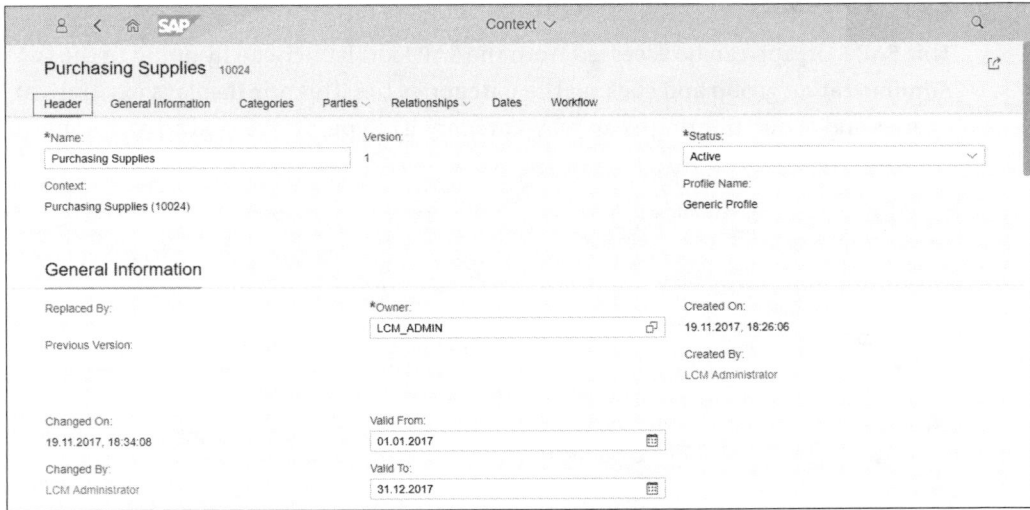

Figure 8.21 Create Context

   - In the **Parties** section, define the parties involved in the business scenario represented by this context. Parties can be entities such as suppliers or purchase organizations, internal contacts, and external contacts. Entities marked as **Main Entity** in the context are mandatory and can't be deleted in the legal transaction process.
   - In the **Relationships** section, define the legal transactions used in the business scenario covered by this context. For example, in a context for a supplier

contract, a legal transaction for the purchase order may be considered a relationship.
  - In the **Dates** tab, enter timelines and milestones for the business scenario covered by this context.
  - It's possible to define a simple release or even a complex workflow process under the **Workflow** tab.
5. *Editing contexts*: From the list of contexts displayed in the Manage Contexts app, you can navigate to the item details and review or edit the context. Here, you can add, display, edit, or remove categories, parties, relationships, workflow steps, and dates. Depending on the type of change, a new version of the context can be created.

8.7.3 Categories for Legal Content

This SAP Fiori app can be accessed from the SAP Fiori launchpad by going to the **LCM Administration** group and clicking the **Categories** tile. This app displays existing categories and allows filtering/search by **Category** ID, **Type**, **Status**, and so on, as shown in Figure 8.22.

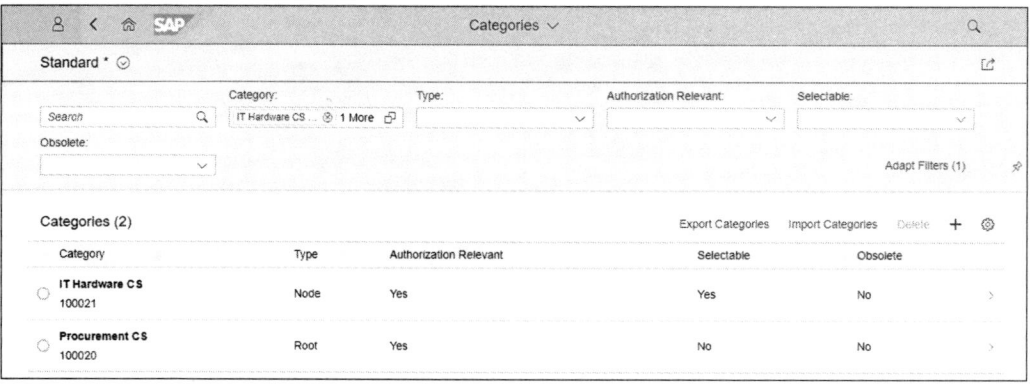

Figure 8.22 Categories for Legal Content

The following functions are provided in the app:

- Create and edit categories
- Add, display, edit, or remove children categories, thus creating a hierarchical tree structure

- Export categories into an Excel file and import categories from an Excel file
- Delete categories that aren't assigned to a context or a legal transaction
- Personalize the list output table settings—for example, display additional columns and rearrange the order of the displayed columns

The categories created in this app can be used in the Manage Context, Request Legal Content, and Manage Legal Transactions apps.

8.7.4 Request Legal Content

This SAP Fiori app can be started from the SAP Fiori launchpad by going to the **Legal Content Management** group and clicking the **Request Legal Content** tile. This app allows a user to submit a request for a legal content. The app comes with an intuitive wizard to take the user through a multistep process of providing necessary information and submitting a request for legal content. Based on the information provided by the user through this app, a legal transaction is created and sent to the responsible person or team for further processing.

The steps involved in submitting a request for legal content are as follows:

1. **Basic Data**: Enter a **Name** and choose a **Context ID** (as shown in Figure 8.23). This should have already been created in the Manage Contexts app. The context selected here provides information for the following steps based on the template of the context.

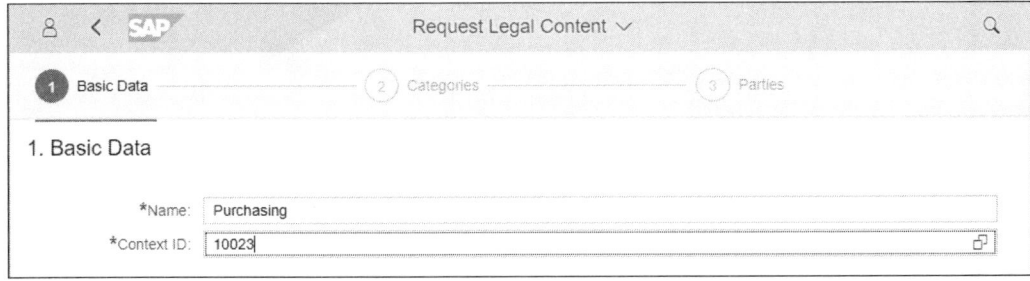

Figure 8.23 Request Legal Content Step 1

2. **Categories**: The **Group**, **Path**, and **Category** are filled in based on the context (see Figure 8.24). If the category is marked as **Required**, it can't be removed or changed. However, the user can add additional categories if needed.

8 Contracts Management

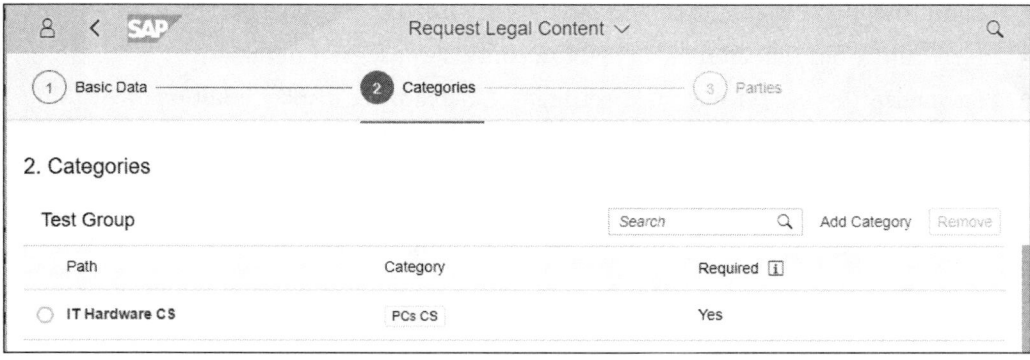

Figure 8.24 Request Legal Content Step 2

3. **Parties**: Parties are entities such as customers or vendors, internal contacts such as purchase manager or legal counsel, or external contacts such as contact person or signing authority (see Figure 8.25). If the context selected in Step 1 has predefined parties, the system already adds those parties. It isn't possible to remove main or required entities, but it's possible to add additional parties.

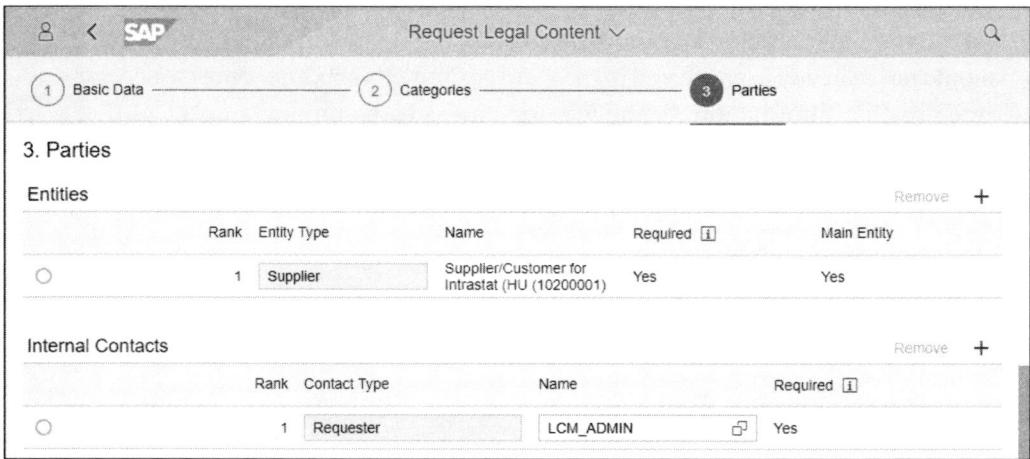

Figure 8.25 Request Legal Content Step 3

4. **Relationship**: Add relationships in this step.
5. **Dates**: Add dates in this step.
6. **Review**: In this step, the information entered in the previous steps is reviewed and edited if necessary.

Depending on the context selected in Step 1, the overall number of steps can vary. If, for example, no relationships are predefined in the context, Step 4 won't be shown in the wizard. It's possible to add relationships if needed at a later stage after the legal transaction is created from this legal request.

Now, the legal content request is submitted. At this point, the system creates a legal transaction based on the request. This legal transaction will be available in the worklist of the Manage Legal Transactions app.

8.7.5 Manage Legal Transactions

This app is used to manage the legal transaction through its life cycle. The app displays existing legal transactions and allows filtering/search by **Legal Transaction Number**, **Context**, **Editing Status**, **Created By**, **Changed By**, **Health** (status), and so on, as shown in Figure 8.26.

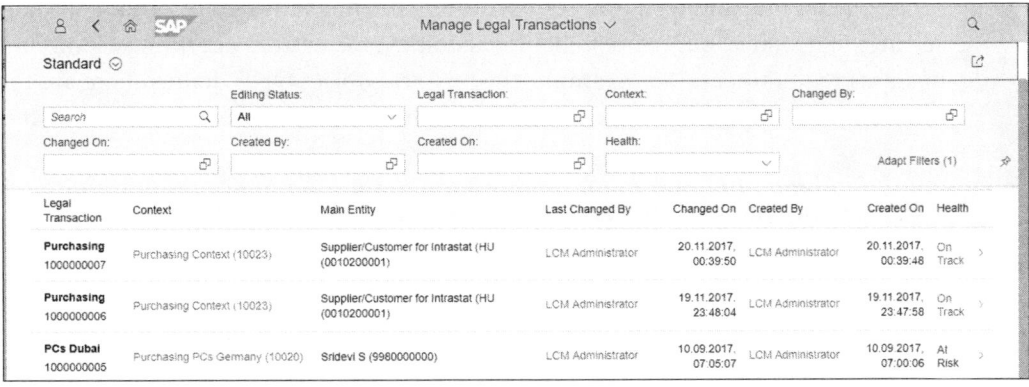

Figure 8.26 Manage Legal Transactions

The display columns of the results can be personalized by rearranging columns or showing additional columns. From the list displayed, it's possible to navigate to individual legal transactions and edit them as well. From within the legal transaction, it's possible to create a task and start the workflow. A **History** function to display the change log for the legal transaction is also provided in this app. Figure 8.27 shows the **Edit** view of an existing legal transaction; it allows the user to navigate to tabs for **Categories**, **Parties**, **Relationships**, **Dates**, **Reminders**, and **Tasks** and to edit data. From the **Documents** tab, it's possible to add documents to the legal transaction.

8 Contracts Management

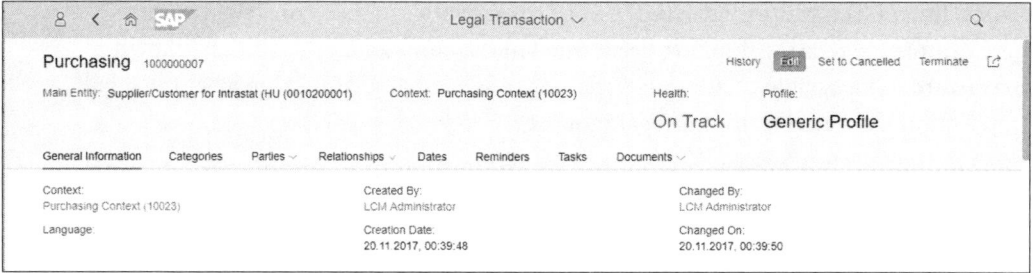

Figure 8.27 Edit Legal Transaction

8.8 Customizing Legal Content Management

Legal Content Management requires some basic customizing to be done in the SAP S/4HANA system. The functionalities explained in the previous section work based on the values maintained in this section. We've provided the details of the standard settings and values, but it's possible to customize the system according to varying business requirements. For example, the business object types defined here are for the purpose of classifying object types to meet business requirements and context.

8.8.1 Define Number Ranges

At the time of creation of legal transactions, contexts, categories, and documents, the system assigns IDs. These IDs are assigned base on the range maintained in this customizing step. SAP-standard number ranges are shown in Table 8.5 these values are maintained via the following menu path: **IMG (SPRO) • Legal Content Management • General Settings • Number Ranges • Maintain Number Ranges for Legal Transactions/ Maintain Number Ranges for Contexts/Maintain Number Ranges for Categories/ Maintain Number Ranges for Documents**.

Object	Number Range Number	From Number	To Number
Legal transactions	01	1000000000	9999999999
Contexts	01	10000	99999
Categories	01	100000	999999
Documents	01	1000000000	9999999999

Table 8.5 Maintain Number Ranges for Legal Content Management

8.8.2 Define Reminder Types

Reminder emails are used to manage legal transactions. In this customizing step, reminder types are defined (see Figure 8.28), and it's possible to assign email templates for each reminder type. A few basic reminder types are provided in Table 8.6. The customizing values are maintained in the system via the following menu path: **IMG (SPRO) • Legal Content Management • General Settings • Define Reminder Types**.

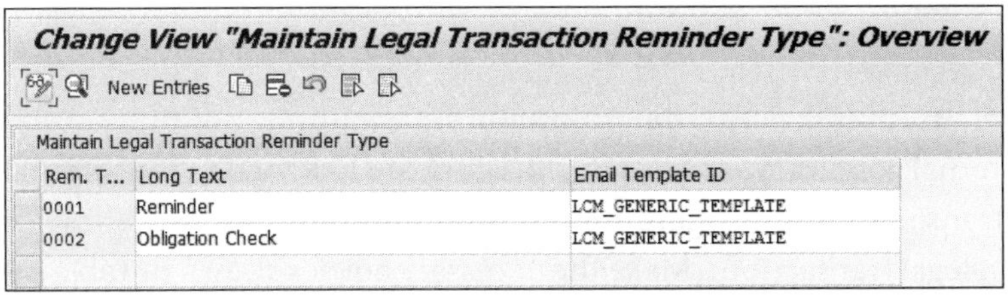

Figure 8.28 Define Reminder Types

Field Name	Entry 1	Entry 2
Reminder Type	0001	0002
Long Text	Reminder	Obligation Check
Email Template ID	LCM_GENERIC_TEMPLATE	LCM_GENERIC_TEMPLATE

Table 8.6 Define Reminder Types

8.8.3 Define Date Types

Different date types are used in legal transactions, and those dates types are defined in this customizing activity. It's possible to define the date as a single date or a period by marking the **True** checkbox, as shown in Figure 8.29. Set the values provided in Table 8.7 at the following menu path; the values shown in the table are only representative: **IMG (SPRO) • Legal Content Management • General Settings • Define Date Types**.

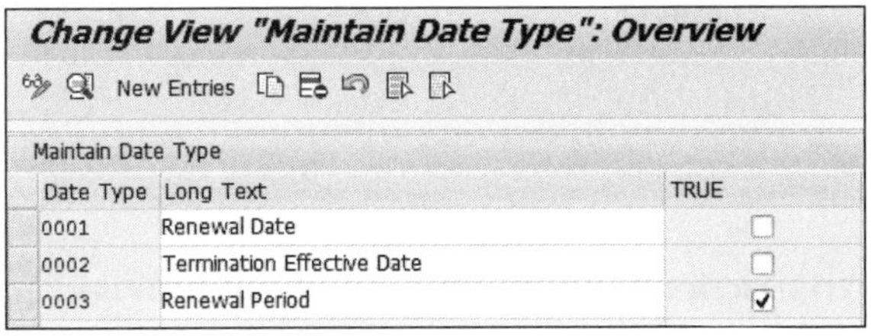

Figure 8.29 Define Date Types

8 Contracts Management

Field Name	Value 1	Value 2	Value 3
Date Type	0001	0002	0003
Long Text	Renewal Date	Termination Effective Date	Renewal Period
True	Unchecked	Unchecked	Checked

Table 8.7 Define Date Types

8.8.4 Define Internal Contacts

In this step, the internal contact types are defined, which are assigned to the internal contacts in legal transactions (see Figure 8.30). These types determine the role of internal contacts in legal transactions. Make the necessary entries shown in Table 8.8 at the following menu path: **IMG (SPRO)** • **Legal Content Management** • **General Settings** • **Define Internal Contacts**.

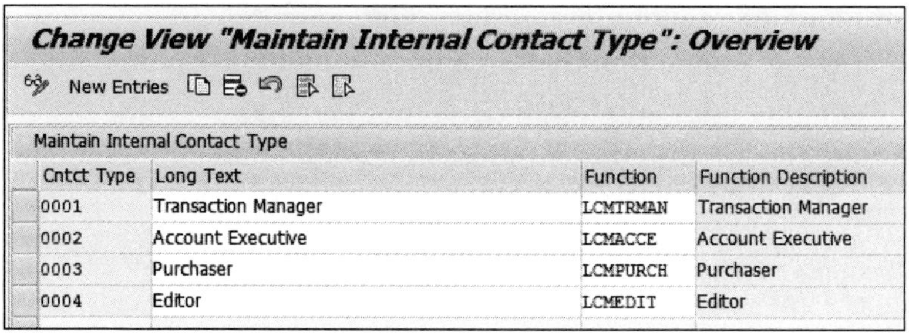

Figure 8.30 Define Internal Contact Types

Field Name	Value 1	Value 2	Value 3	Value 4
Contact Type	0001	0002	0003	0004
Long Text	Transaction Manager	Account Executive	Purchaser	Editor
Function	LCMTRMAN	LCMACCE	LCMPURCH	LCMEDIT

Table 8.8 Define Internal Contacts

8.8.5 Define Entity Types

An organization involved in a legal transaction in Legal Content Management is identified as an *entity* in the system. In this customizing activity, the entity types are defined, and these types are assigned to entities in a legal transaction (see Figure 8.31). The types defined here determine the role of an entity within a legal transaction. Make the necessary settings shown in Table 8.9 at the following menu path: **IMG (SPRO)** • **Legal Content Management** • **General Settings** • **Define Entity Types**.

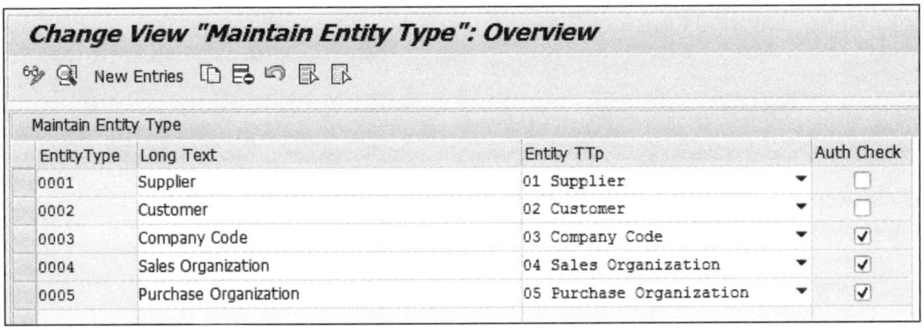

Change View "Maintain Entity Type": Overview

EntityType	Long Text	Entity TTp	Auth Check
0001	Supplier	01 Supplier	☐
0002	Customer	02 Customer	☐
0003	Company Code	03 Company Code	☑
0004	Sales Organization	04 Sales Organization	☑
0005	Purchase Organization	05 Purchase Organization	☑

Figure 8.31 Define Entity Types

Field Name	Entity Type	Long Text	Entity Technical Type	Authorization Check
Value 1	0001	Supplier	Supplier	Unchecked
Value 2	0002	Customer	Customer	Unchecked
Value 3	0003	Company Code	Company Code	Checked
Value 4	0004	Sales Organization	Sales Organization	Checked
Value 5	0005	Purchase Organization	Purchase Organization	Checked

Table 8.9 Define Entity Types

8.8.6 Define External Contacts

External contact types are defined in this activity, and these types are assigned to external contacts in legal transactions. The type defined here determines the role of external contacts in legal transactions. Standard and basic values are provided in Table 8.10. Follow this menu path to complete this customizing activity: **IMG (SPRO)** • **Legal Content Management** • **General Settings** • **Define External Contacts** (as seen in Figure 8.32).

8 Contracts Management

Field Name	Value 1	Value 2	Value 3	Value 4
Contact Type	0001	0002	0003	0004
Long Text	Main Contact	Signer	Legal Contact	Account Manager

Table 8.10 Define External Contacts

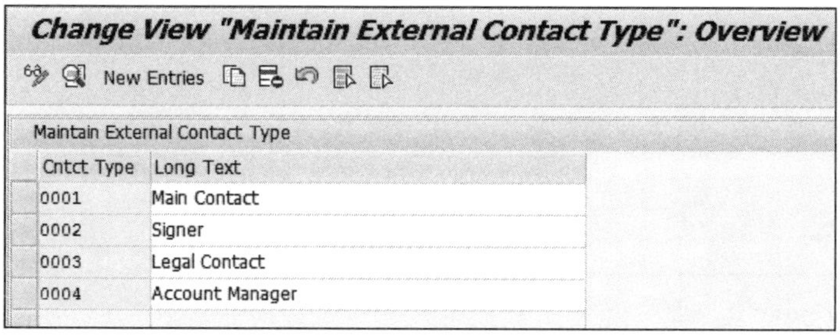

Figure 8.32 Define External Contact Types

8.8.7 Define Technical Types for Linked Object Types

Linked object types are defined as described in Section 8.8.8 ahead. In this section, the technical types are defined for the linked object types. Linked objects are business objects linked through a legal transaction. Table 8.11 shows the standard technical object types. To complete this step, go to **IMG (SPRO)** • **Legal Content Management** • **General Settings** • **Define Technical Types for Linked Object Types** (as seen in Figure 8.33).

Field Name	Value 1	Value 2	Value 3	Value 4	Value 5
Lnk.Obj.Tech. Type	PC	PO	SO	SQ	RFQ
Lnk.Obj.Tech. Cat.	Internal SAP	Internal SAP	Internal SAP	Internal SAP	Internal SAP
Business Entity	I_PURCHASE-CONTRACT	I_PURCHASE-ORDER	I_SALES-ORDER	I_SALES-QUOTATION	I_REQUEST-FORQUOTATION
Semantic Object	Purchase-Contract	Purchase-Order	SalesOrder	SalesQuotation	RequestForQuotation

Table 8.11 Technical Types for Linked Object Types

8.8 Customizing Legal Content Management

Field Name	Value 1	Value 2	Value 3	Value 4	Value 5
Semantic Object Attr.	PURCHASE-CONTRACT	PURCHASE-ORDER	SALES-ORDER	SALE-SQUOTATION	REQUEST-FORQUOTATION

Table 8.11 Technical Types for Linked Object Types (Cont.)

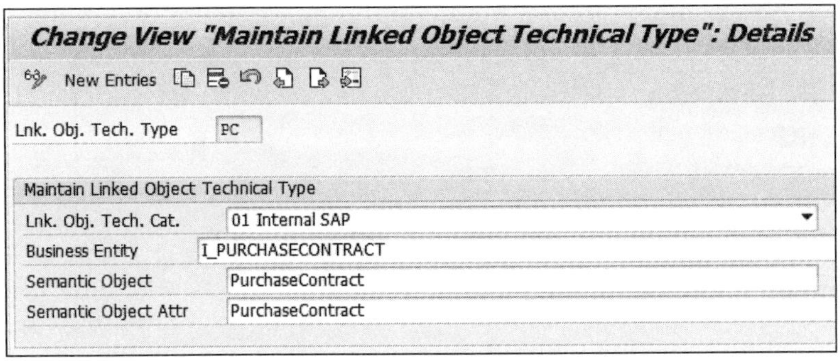

Change View "Maintain Linked Object Technical Type": Details

- Lnk. Obj. Tech. Type: PC
- Maintain Linked Object Technical Type
- Lnk. Obj. Tech. Cat.: 01 Internal SAP
- Business Entity: I_PURCHASECONTRACT
- Semantic Object: PurchaseContract
- Semantic Object Attr: PurchaseContract

Figure 8.33 Define Technical Types for Linked Object Types

8.8.8 Define Linked Object Types

A linked object is a business object in the system that is linked to a legal transaction. For example, purchase orders or sales orders may be considered linked business objects for a given legal transaction. The linked object types defined here determine the purpose of the linked object within the legal transaction. The values provided in Table 8.12 are generally used for linked objects. To make the necessary settings in customizing, go to **IMG (SPRO)** • **Legal Content Management** • **General Settings** • **Define Linked Object Types** (as seen in Figure 8.34).

Field Name	Linked Object Type	Long Text	Lnk.Obj.Tech. Type	Integration Link
Value 1	0001	Purchase Order	PO	Blank
Value 2	0002	Purchase Contract	PC	Purchase Contract
Value 3	0003	Request for Quotation (RFQ)	RFQ	Reference for Quotation

Table 8.12 Define Linked Object Types

8 Contracts Management

Field Name	Linked Object Type	Long Text	Lnk.Obj.Tech. Type	Integration Link
Value 4	0004	Sales Order	SO	Blank
Value 5	0005	Sales Quotation	SQ	Blank

Table 8.12 Define Linked Object Types (Cont.)

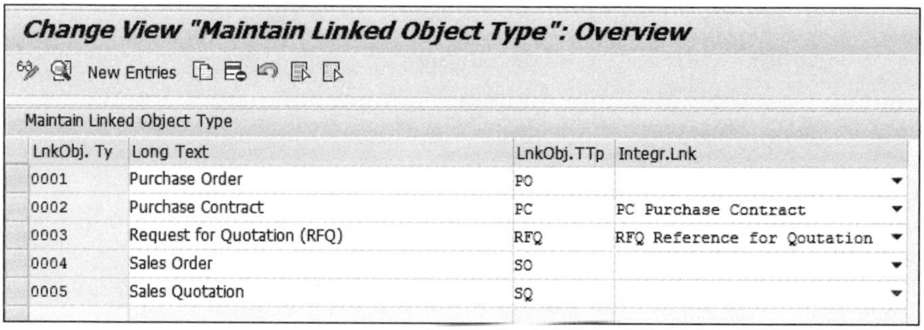

Change View "Maintain Linked Object Type": Overview

LnkObj. Ty	Long Text	LnkObj.TTp	Integr.Lnk
0001	Purchase Order	PO	
0002	Purchase Contract	PC	PC Purchase Contract
0003	Request for Quotation (RFQ)	RFQ	RFQ Reference for Qoutation
0004	Sales Order	SO	
0005	Sales Quotation	SQ	

Figure 8.34 Define Linked Object Types

8.8.9 Define Content Types

The *content type* describes the purpose of the documents such as an amendment or master agreement used in legal transactions. The content types defined in this customizing step are assigned to documents from within the Manage Documents app. Enter the values provided in Table 8.13 at the following menu path: **IMG (SPRO) • Legal Content Management • Documents • Define Content Types**.

Field Name	Value 1	Value 2	Value 3
Content Type	AMD	MC	NDA
Long Text	Amendment	Master Contract	Nondisclosure Agreement

Table 8.13 Define Content Types

8.8.10 Define Document Stamps

Document stamps indicate the status of documents in Legal Content Management. Stamps defined in this customizing step can be assigned to documents in the application. Maintain the values provided in Table 8.14 under menu path **IMG (SPRO)** • **Legal Content Management** • **Documents** • **Define Document Stamps**.

Field Name	Value 1	Value 2
Stamp Name	0001	0002
Long Text	Published	Reviewed Externally

Table 8.14 Define Document Stamps

8.8.11 Define Profiles

The profiles defined in this step can be assigned to contexts and legal transactions in the Manage Contexts and Manage Legal Transactions apps. The profiles predefine the values that can be selected for the different data types, such as entities, internal contacts, dates, and so on, for a legal transaction. Customizing profiles and profile sets helps reduce the number of values presented for selection in the UI to the ones that are relevant for a specific business scenario.

This customizing activity has three steps to complete. In the first step, a profile set is maintained for the entity type, internal contact type, external contact type, and so on by maintaining the values provided in Table 8.15 at the following menu path: **IMG (SPRO)** • **Legal Content Management** • **Profiles** • **Define Profiles** (as seen in Figure 8.35).

Field Name	Profile Set	Set Type	Long Text
Value 1	G1	1 Entity	Generic Entities
Value 2	G2	2 Internal Contact	Generic Internal Contacts
Value 3	G3	3 External Contact	Generic External Contacts
Value 4	G4	4 Date	Generic Dates
Value 5	G5	5 Linked Object	Generic Linked Objects
Value 6	G6	6 Reminder	Generic Reminders
Value 7	G7	7 Document Content	Generic Document Contents

Table 8.15 Define Profile Set

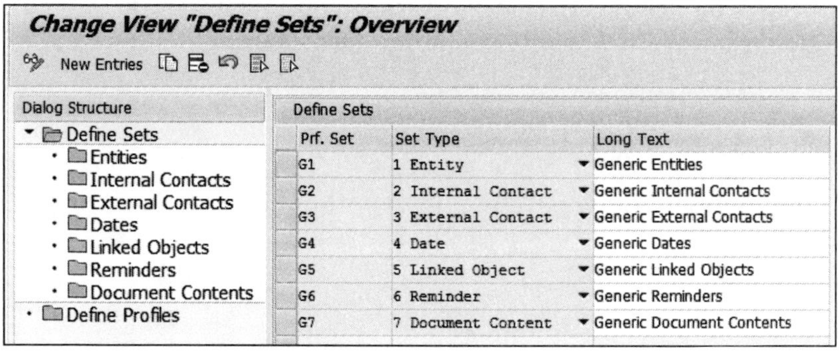

8 Contracts Management

Figure 8.35 Define Profile Sets

In the second step, for each profile set created—for example, G1 Entity—a list of entity types is maintained. This is achieved by selecting **Profile Set G1** and double-clicking the **Entities** node under **Define Sets** in the dialog structure (see Figure 8.36) and then maintaining the values provided in Table 8.16.

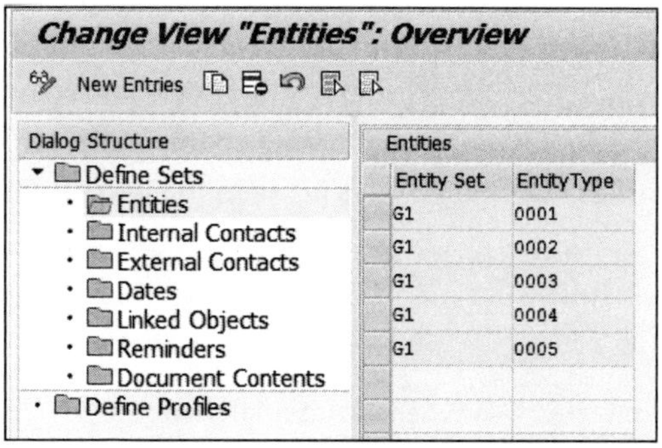

Figure 8.36 Define Entity Set

Field Name	Entity Set	Entity Type	Long Text
Value 1	G1	0001	Supplier
Value 2	G1	0002	Customer
Value 3	G1	0003	Company Code
Value 4	G1	0004	Sales Organization
Value 5	G1	0005	Purchase Organization

Table 8.16 Define Entity Set

This step is repeated for **Internal Contact Set** (Table 8.17), **External Contact Set** (Table 8.18), **Date Set** (Table 8.19), **Linked Objects Set** (Table 8.20), **Reminders Set** (Table 8.21), and **Document Contents Set** (Table 8.22).

Field Name	Internal Contact Set	Internal Contact Type	Long Text
Value 1	G2	0001	Transaction Manager
Value 2	G2	0002	Account Executive
Value 3	G2	0003	Purchaser
Value 4	G2	0004	Editor

Table 8.17 Define Internal Contact Set

Field Name	External Contact Set	Contact Type	Long Text
Value 1	G3	0001	Main Contact
Value 2	G3	0002	Signer
Value 3	G3	0003	Legal Contact
Value 4	G3	0004	Account Manager

Table 8.18 Define External Contact Set

Field Name	Date Set	Date Type	Long Text
Value 1	G4	0001	Renewal Date
Value 2	G4	0002	Termination Effective Date
Value 3	G4	0003	Renewal Period

Table 8.19 Define Date Set

Field Name	Linked Obj. Set	Linked Obj. Type	Long Text
Value 1	G5	0001	Purchase Order
Value 2	G5	0002	Purchase Contract

Table 8.20 Define Linked Object Set

8 Contracts Management

Field Name	Linked Obj. Set	Linked Obj. Type	Long Text
Value 3	G5	0003	Request for Quotation (RFQ)
Value 4	G5	0004	Sales Order
Value 5	G5	0005	Sales Quotation

Table 8.20 Define Linked Object Set (Cont.)

Field Name	Reminder Set	Reminder Type	Long Text
Value 1	G6	0001	Reminder
Value 2	G6	0002	Obligation Check

Table 8.21 Define Reminder Set

Field Name	Document Content Set	Content Type	Long Text
Value 1	G7	AMD	Amendment
Value 2	G7	MC	Master Contract
Value 3	G7	NDA	Nondisclosure Agreement

Table 8.22 Define Document Content Set

The third step in this customizing activity is to define profiles, which consist of the profile sets defined in the first step. The profiles defined here can be assigned to contexts and legal transactions. This third step is completed by double-clicking **Define Profiles** in the dialog structure, as shown in Figure 8.35. Then, maintain the values provided in Table 8.23.

Field Name	Value
Profile	GENERIC
Long Text	Generic Profile
Entity Set	G1
Internal Contact Set	G2

Table 8.23 Define Profiles

Field Name	Value
External Contact Set	G3
Date Set	G4
Linked Object Set	G5
Reminder Set	G6
Document Content Set	G7

Table 8.23 Define Profiles (Cont.)

8.8.12 Define Document Types

A *document* is defined as an instance of legal content tailored to a specific transaction or activity in a certain business context. In this customizing step, a new document type, LCM, is defined for Legal Content Management. To define a document type for Legal Content Management, first navigate to **IMG (SPRO)** • **Cross-Application Components** • **Document Management** • **Control Data** • **Define Document Types**, then enter the values provided in Table 8.24 as shown in Figure 8.37.

Field Name	Value
Document Type	LCM
Document Type description	Legal Content Mgmt
Use KPro	X
Version Assignment	
Archiving Authorization	
Internal Number Range	02
External number range	01
Number exit	MCDOKZNR
Vers. No. Incr.	2
Document Status	+
Document Desc.	+

Table 8.24 Define Document Type

8 Contracts Management

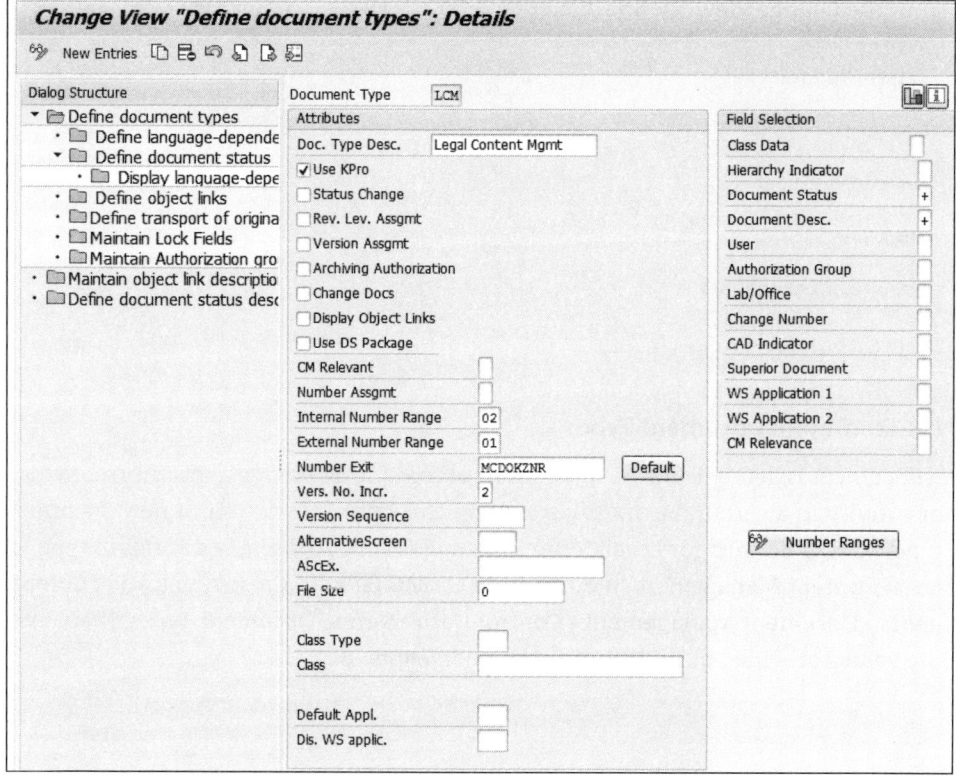

Figure 8.37 Define Document Type LCM

Click the green arrow to go back, select document type **LCM**, and double-click **Define document status** from the dialog structure (see Figure 8.38).

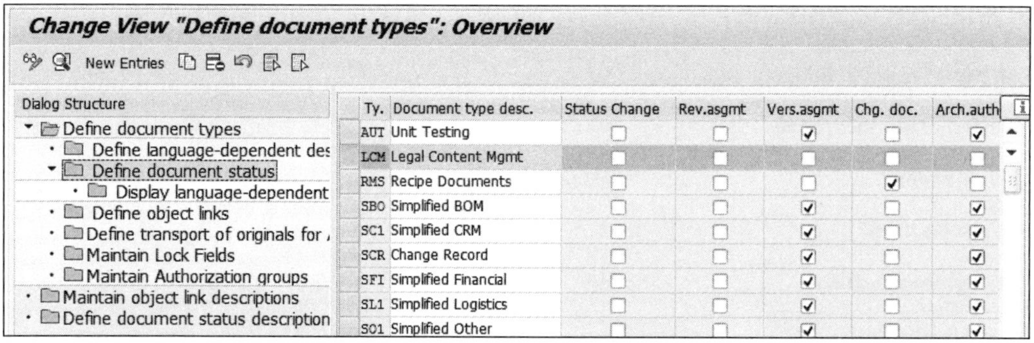

Figure 8.38 Define Document Status

8.8 Customizing Legal Content Management

Now, the **Change View "Define document status": Overview** screen appears, as shown in Figure 8.39. On this screen, select the new entries and maintain the values shown in Table 8.25.

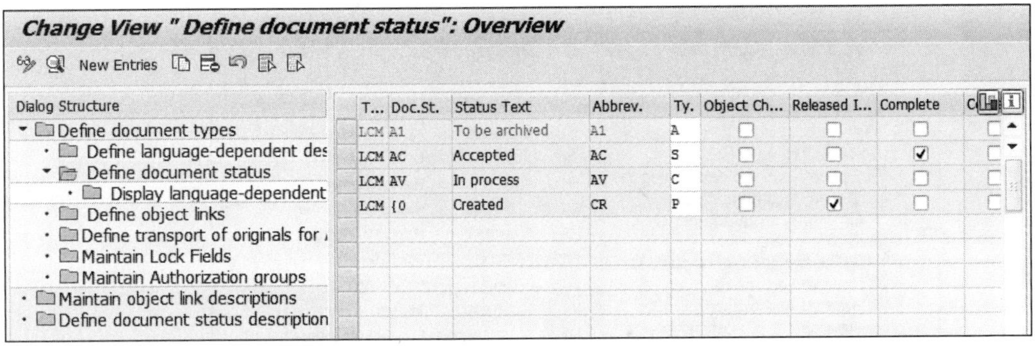

Figure 8.39 Define Document Status Overview

Field Name	Value 1	Value 2	Value 3	Value 4	Value 5
Document Status	{0	AV	AC	A1	{2
Status	CR	AV	AC	A1	IW
Status Text	Created	In process	Accepted	To be archived	In Work
Status Type	P	C	S	A	O
Status Type Description	Primary status	Check-in status	Locked status	Archive status	Original processing status
Prev. 1		{0	AV	AC	AV
Prev. 2		AC		AV	{0
Prev. 3		A1			
Prev. 4		{2			
Complete for ECM			Checked		

Table 8.25 Define Document Status

Now, go back to the overview screen, open the **Maintain Object Links** folder, and maintain the following values, as shown in Figure 8.40:

335

- Language: **EN**
- Object: **LCMDOC**
- Object Description: **Lgl Content Mgmt Doc**

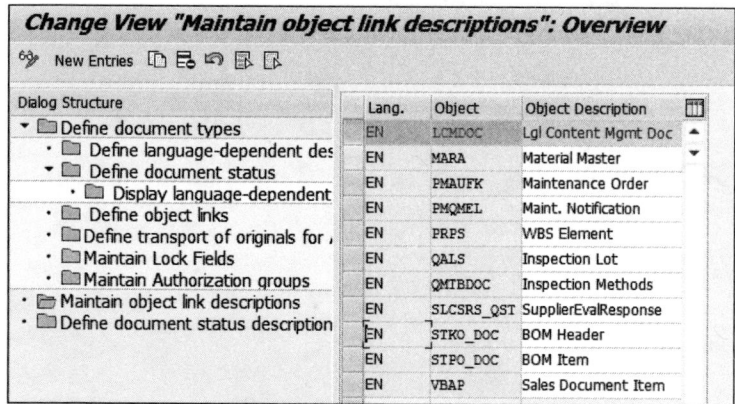

Figure 8.40 Maintain Object Link Descriptions

Return again to the overview screen, select document type **LCM**, open the **Define Object Links** folder, and maintain the following values, as shown in Figure 8.41:

- Document Type: **LCM**
- Object: **LCMDOC**
- Screen No.: **500**

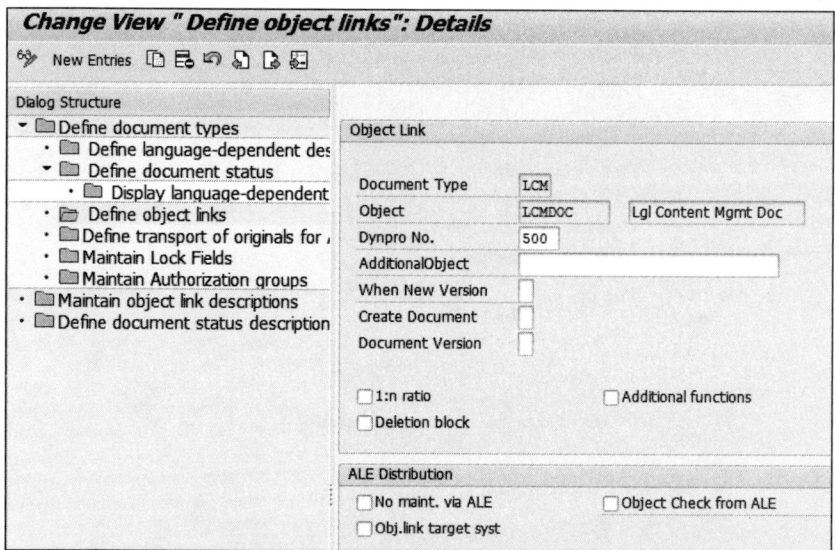

Figure 8.41 Define Object Links

8.8.13 Background Job Definitions

SAP S/4HANA comes with a jobs repository for scheduling technical background jobs (as seen in Table 8.26). Scope-dependent jobs need to be defined in this repository before they can be activated. The application components to which these jobs belong need to be active in the system before maintaining the related table, table STJR_JOBD_SCOPE. For this activity, go to **IMG (SPRO)** • **SAP NetWeaver** • **Application Server** • **System Administration** • **Activation of Scope-Dependent Background Job Definitions (S/4HANA)**.

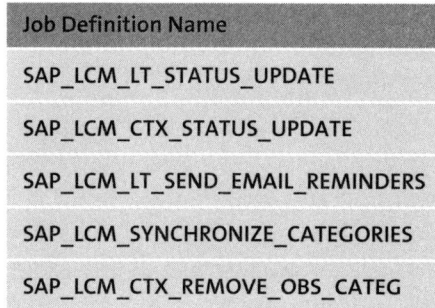

Job Definition Name
SAP_LCM_LT_STATUS_UPDATE
SAP_LCM_CTX_STATUS_UPDATE
SAP_LCM_LT_SEND_EMAIL_REMINDERS
SAP_LCM_SYNCHRONIZE_CATEGORIES
SAP_LCM_CTX_REMOVE_OBS_CATEG

Table 8.26 Scope-Dependent Background Job Definitions

8.9 Summary

Contract management is a core area for procurement organizations. Without an existing agreement in place, it's difficult to drive disciplined pricing and terms. Contracts can be tied to catalog items to underpin a clear ordering process and UX, representing a model way to conduct corporate purchasing. SAP S/4HANA updates many older transaction codes and screens with SAP Fiori apps, but much of the setup and configuration remains the same. However, there are now shortcuts in the form of SAP Best Practices activation, which automatically sets up standard functionality in the system.

Having the functionality to craft agreements with suppliers is half of the equation. The other half is finding the right supplier for each these agreements. The next chapter will focus on the sourcing functionality in both SAP S/4HANA and SAP Ariba, which is used to drive the correct source of supply for each contract.

Chapter 9
External Sourcing

Procurement of materials and services is one of the main functions of most business organizations. Identifying the best sources for those materials and services in terms of price, timeliness, quality, and so on is one of the important tasks of a purchasing organization.

Whether fulfilling a one-time requirement of high-value items or a continuous requirement of any item, a buyer engages in a strategic process of finding one or more sources to fulfill the requirement from a pool of competing suppliers. This process is generally known as *strategic sourcing* and sometimes known as *external sourcing*.

Sourcing within a procurement function by definition is the process of finding suppliers of goods and services for an organization. Sourcing in SAP S/4HANA uses the request for quotation process, which begins with a purchase requisition and ends with an award and creation of a purchase order or a contract. This process involves communication between the purchasing organization and suppliers who are external to the SAP S/4HANA system. SAP traditionally offered SAP Supplier Relationship Management (SAP SRM) along with Supplier Self-Service (SUS) for sourcing solutions using the RFx process. This approach required an organization to implement SAP SRM/SUS applications, including a dedicated supplier portal. With the introduction of SAP S/4HANA, this sourcing solution is offered as an extended solution with SAP Ariba's cloud applications, which enables external communication and interaction with the suppliers. SAP provides standard integration between SAP S/4HANA and the SAP Ariba solutions required for this sourcing process. Because SAP Ariba solutions are used by both buyers and suppliers, this approach eliminates the need for every purchasing organization to create a dedicated portal for the suppliers to interact.

In this chapter, we'll cover the complete end-to-end business process, including variations available within sourcing in SAP S/4HANA. All the SAP Fiori apps offered in this solution are explained and illustrated with screenshots. We've also provided the configuration steps and illustrative screenshots to help you implement the entire solution.

9 External Sourcing

9.1 Sourcing Strategies

A sourcing solution was offered in SAP ERP along with SAP SRM, but now in SAP S/4HANA the solution is offered along with SAP Ariba. The new strategy is more efficient and simpler because SAP S/4HANA is tightly integrated with SAP Ariba Sourcing and Ariba Network. Ariba Network helps establish easy and quick connections to millions of suppliers worldwide who are already in the network. In this new approach, the sourcing process is initiated in SAP S/4HANA, from where you reach out to suppliers in Ariba Network, identify the sources through SAP Ariba Sourcing, award the suppliers in SAP Ariba Sourcing, and bring the data back to SAP S/4HANA to create a purchase contract or purchase order to complete the process.

9.1.1 Sourcing Process Flow

The process flow is shown in Figure 9.1. Within SAP Best Practices, this scope item is known as Ariba—Sourcing Integration.

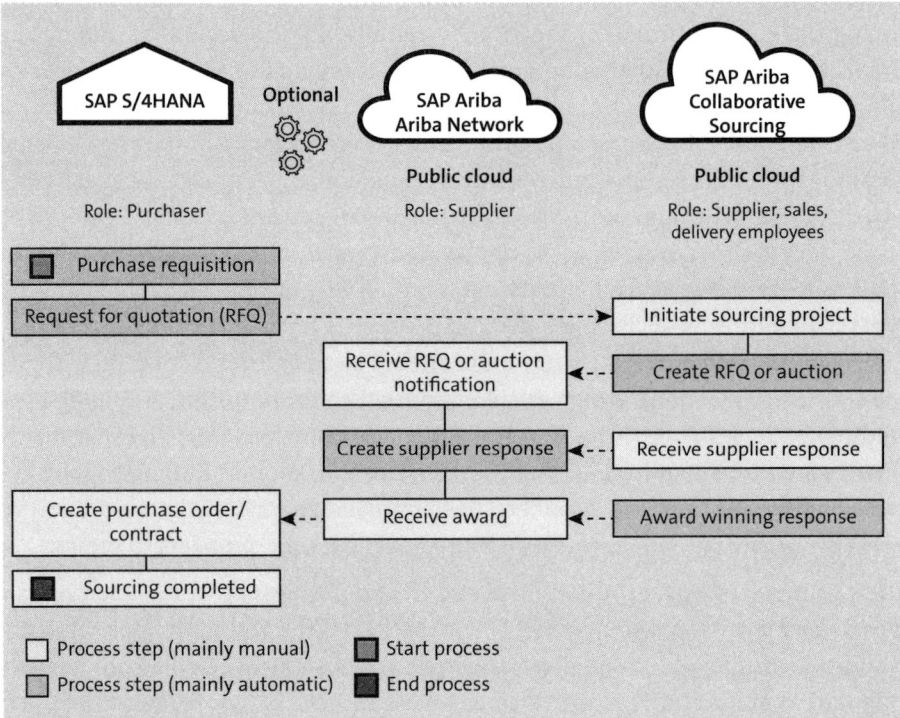

Figure 9.1 Process Flow

9.1.2 Sourcing Optimization

Sourcing optimization is achieved in SAP S/4HANA with the help of the new SAP Fiori apps described in the next section, as well as the features and functionalities available within SAP Ariba solutions. The sourcing solution helps achieve the following:

- Provide visibility and identify savings opportunities
- Standardize source-to-contract processes across business units
- Drive materials cost savings and optimization across all spend categories
- Increase speed and efficiency across different teams
- Reduce risk by finding better suppliers and innovation partners

9.2 Request for Quotation

A request for quotation is a request from a purchasing organization of a company that's sent to suppliers, soliciting them to submit a quotation for the supply of materials or services. Request for Quotation (RFQ) is a purchasing document created in the SAP S/4HANA system either from a purchase requisition or by copying an existing RFQ. RFQs also can be created manually without referencing any other document. RFQs for lean services can be created by selecting **Services** as the **Product Type Group** at the item level.

It's possible to create a single RFQ that contains both material and service items. It's important to note that the RFQs created in the new SAP Fiori app can't be viewed or processed in the SAP GUI environment and vice versa. The RFQ and Quotation (MM-PUR-RFQ) solution offered using SAP GUI processes and transactions in SAP ERP isn't a strategic choice in SAP S/4HANA. Support for this solution is likely to end at some point in the future.

9.2.1 Collaborative Sourcing

Collaborative sourcing is the ability of the purchasing organization to work in collaboration with the millions of suppliers available in the Ariba Network. The buyers together with the suppliers can improve efficiency and meet compliance requirements across the entire sourcing process. This approach incorporates seamless processes, transparent communications between the buyers and suppliers, and trust between the parties involved in the sourcing process. Collaborative sourcing capability is achieved through SAP Ariba Sourcing. This section explains the process steps on the SAP S/4HANA side. In this process, once the RFQ is created and published in SAP S/4HANA, it's sent to SAP Ariba Sourcing, in which a sourcing request is created based on the RFQ received from SAP S/4HANA. The RFQ type used for this process in SAP S/4HANA is external sourcing request.

The buyer then creates a sourcing project in SAP Ariba Sourcing with reference to the sourcing request and publishes the project. This sourcing project results in RFQs in the SAP Ariba Sourcing application for the suppliers to respond to. The suppliers can access these RFQs and submit their responses or quotations through their SAP Ariba accounts in SAP Ariba Sourcing. After the RFQ closing time, the buyer can review all the responses from different suppliers, compare them, and award one or more suppliers in SAP Ariba Sourcing. The awarded quotations are automatically sent to SAP S/4HANA, in which purchase orders or contracts are created, depending on the document type selected in SAP Ariba Sourcing while awarding.

9.2.2 Quote Automation for Procurement

If a purchasing organization is interested in requesting only price and quantity information or shipping costs, it's possible to use the external price request RFQ type. This RFQ type, once saved and published in SAP S/4HANA, is sent to the Ariba Network, where the suppliers can create their responses. These bids submitted by suppliers through their SAP Ariba accounts are sent back to SAP S/4HANA, where they can be processed. The buyer can compare the bids (quotations) received, award one of those in the SAP S/4HANA system, and create a purchase order or contract. Within SAP Best Practices, this scope item is known as Ariba—Quote Automation Integration for Procurement.

9.2.3 Request for Price

This RFQ process helps the buyer to create price requests in SAP S/4HANA and send them directly to suppliers by email or send a printed version by mail. The internal sourcing request RFQ type is used for this process. Suppliers respond to the RFQ by providing their quotations via email or mail. The buyer manually creates quotations in the SAP S/4HANA system using the Manage Supplier Quotations app based on the quotations received from the suppliers. The quotations created in the SAP S/4HANA system are compared, and the best one is awarded. It's possible to award the best quotation in one of the following ways: directly within the quotation by clicking **Award**, from the list in the Manage Supplier Quotations app, or from the list in the Compare Supplier

Quotations app. After awarding the quotation, the follow-on document, either a purchase order or a contract, is created in SAP S/4HANA. Quotations that do not meet the requirements should be set to **Rejected** or **Completed** manually. After completion of this process, the RFQ may be set to **Completed** as well. The process flow is shown in Figure 9.2. Within SAP Best Practices, this scope item is known as Request for Price.

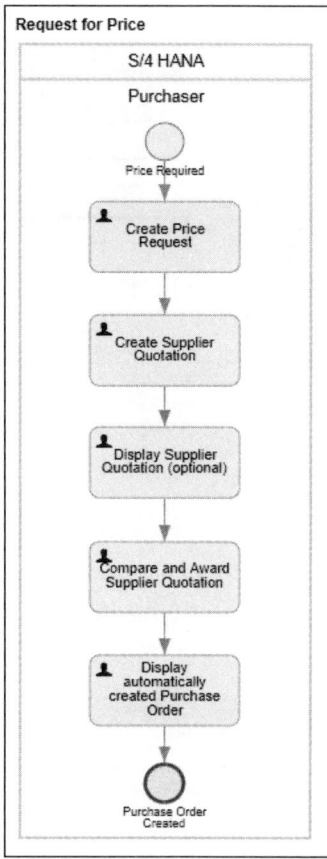

Figure 9.2 Request for Price

9.2.4 Manage Request for Quotation

This SAP Fiori app provides the capability to display the list of all existing RFQs and to search for RFQs by **RFQ Number**, **RFQ Type**, **Status**, **Company Code**, **Purchasing Org.**, **Purchasing Group**, **Quotation Deadline**, and so on. This app also helps copy an existing RFQ, create a new RFQ from scratch, and delete an RFQ. It's possible to customize the filters and display columns shown in Figure 9.3. From this app, you also can display an existing RFQ by clicking any of the listed RFQs. This allows the user to review all the information within the RFQ, including output details/status, legal transactions associated with the RFQ, and process flow.

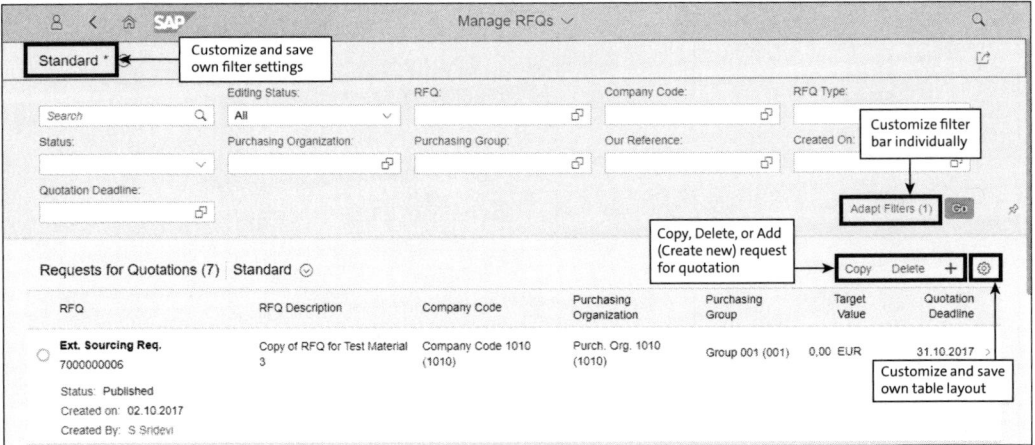

Figure 9.3 Manage RFQ

9.2.5 Create Request for Quotation

To create an RFQ from an existing purchase requisition, access the Manage Purchase Requisitions SAP Fiori app, select the purchase requisition, and click the **Create RFQ** button, as shown in Figure 9.4.

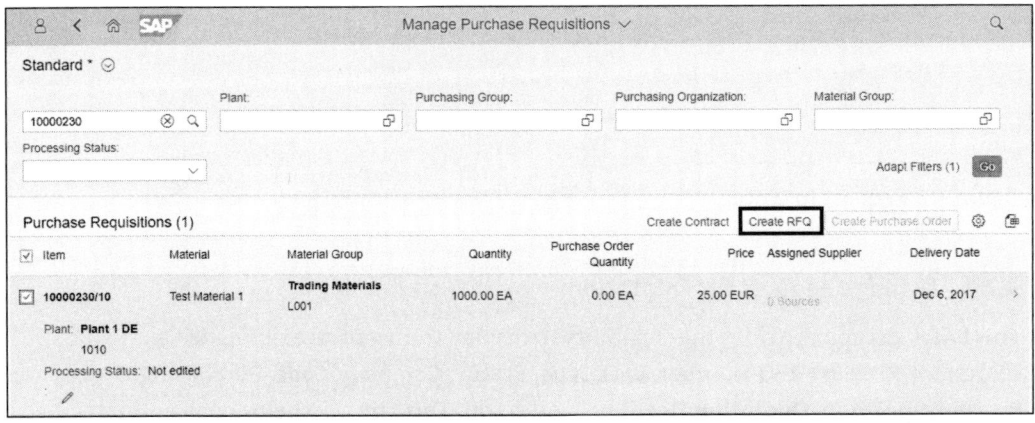

Figure 9.4 Manage Purchase Requisitions

9.2 Request for Quotation

This action will take you to the create **Request for Quotation** creation screen (Figure 9.5), where RFQ type, quotation deadline, and organizational information such as company code and purchasing organization are entered.

The system adds all this information, including item details, from the purchase requisition. It's also possible to specify the follow-on document, either a purchase order or contract, for the RFQ here on this screen. This app allows the user to maintain delivery and payment terms, add bidders if desired, and add attachments. Once all values are entered, the RFQ is published. At this point, the RFQ is sent from SAP S/4HANA to SAP Ariba Sourcing.

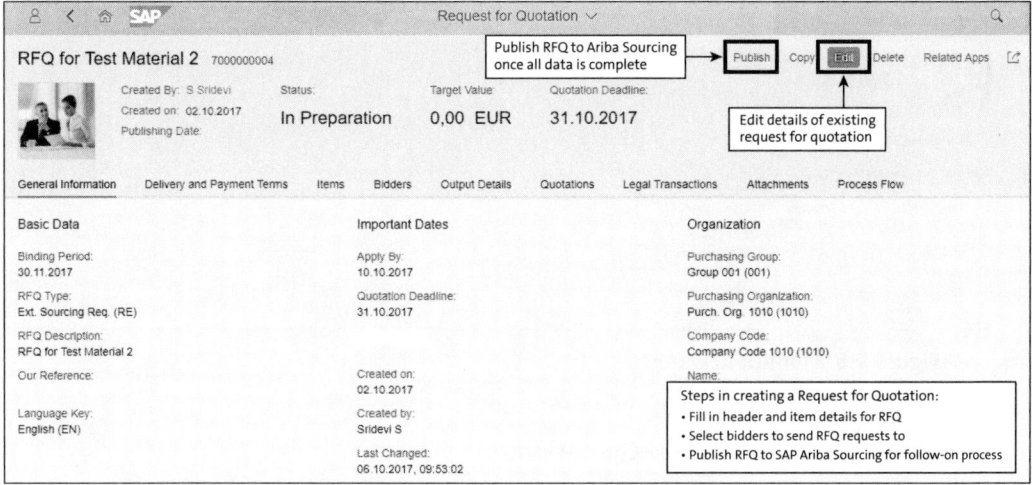

Figure 9.5 Create/Edit Request for Quotation

9.2.6 Monitor Request for Quotation Items

This app, shown in Figure 9.6, enables the strategic purchaser to monitor RFQ items. It allows the user to display the list of all the RFQ items in a table view, along with a chart for awarded quotation value and submitted quotation value. By default, the chart is displayed per suppliers; you can change the settings to display the chart per company code, plant, purchasing organization, and many more options. The app provides options to choose the chart type from a variety of types, such as bar chart, line chart, pie chart, and more. The output results can be filtered by RFQ number, RFQ type, quotation deadline, purchasing category, material group, company code, plant,

9 External Sourcing

purchasing org., and so on. The user can select any RFQ item to view the corresponding quotes and general information and navigate to view contextual information related to a supplier or material.

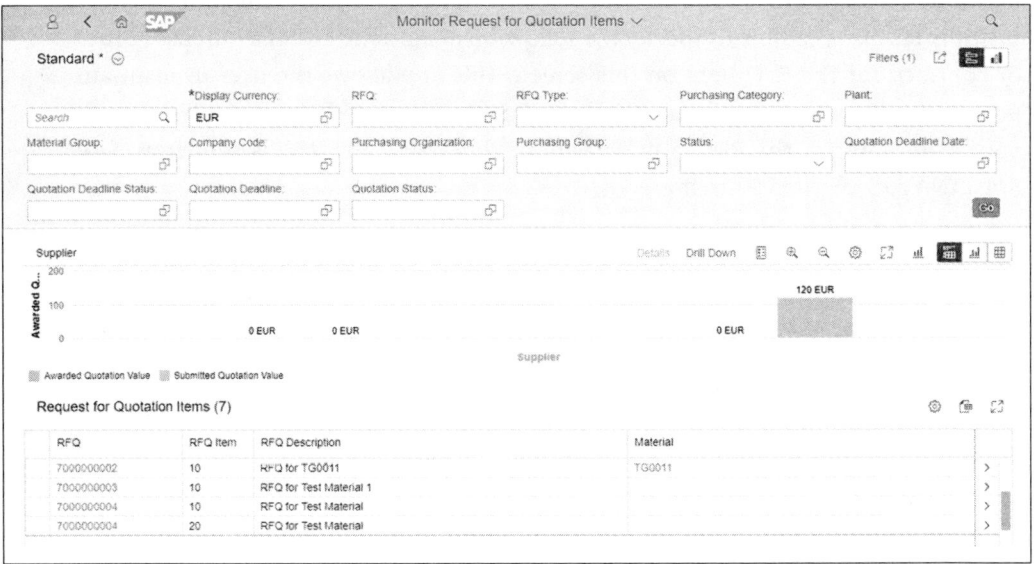

Figure 9.6 Monitor RFQ Items

9.2.7 Compare Supplier Quotations

This app (Figure 9.7) enables the purchaser to compare supplier quotations received against an RFQ and to find the best offer. It allows the user to search for a specific RFQ and display all quotations received for this RFQ; it also allows the user to check whether all the invited suppliers have submitted their quotations.

It displays an overview of all quotations for a selected RFQ, providing information such as basic supplier data, total net value (which reflects the complete net costs for the goods or services, including transportation costs), and fully quoted items (fully quoted items are items that the supplier can deliver in the requested quantity).

This app identifies the lowest-priced item as the best-priced item. Other factors, such as supplier evaluation score, are not included in the calculation. The purchaser can award the best quotation directly from this app and create a PO or contract.

9.2   Request for Quotation

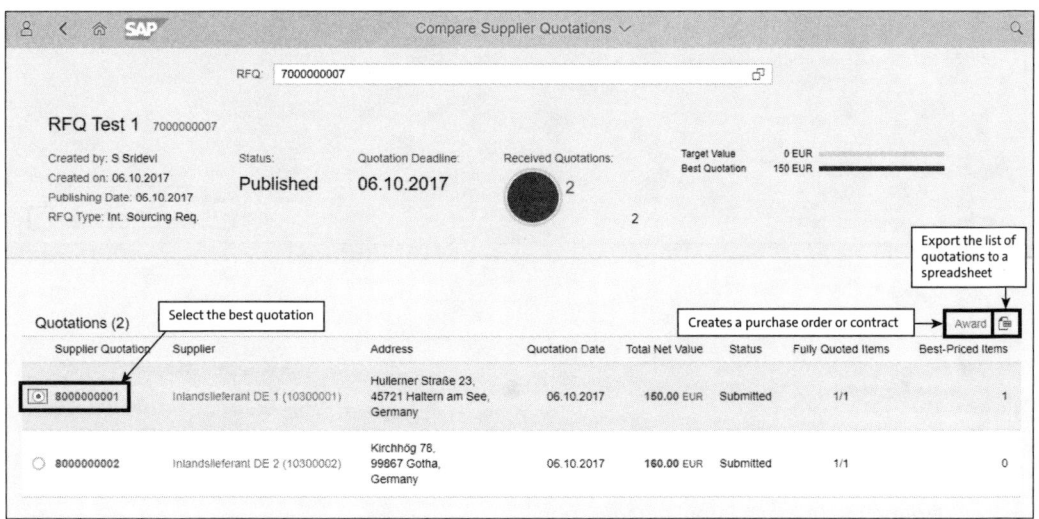

Figure 9.7 Compare Supplier Quotations

9.2.8   Manage Supplier Quotation

This app (Figure 9.8) enables the user to display all supplier quotations that have been received for different RFQs. It also allows the user to select any quotation and view its detailed information. The app features include the following:

- Search for a quotation by quotation number, type, status, submission date, supplier, RFQ number, RFQ type, and more
- Display detailed information for a quotation by selecting the quotation from the search result list
- Display item details, such as the actual item, quantity, and pricing details
- Submit quotations that are in the **In Preparation** status
- Edit quotations that are in the **In Preparation** or **Submitted** status
- Delete quotations that are in the **In Preparation** status
- Award quotations
- Set quotations to **Completed**
- Navigate to detailed information about suppliers and RFQs

347

9 External Sourcing

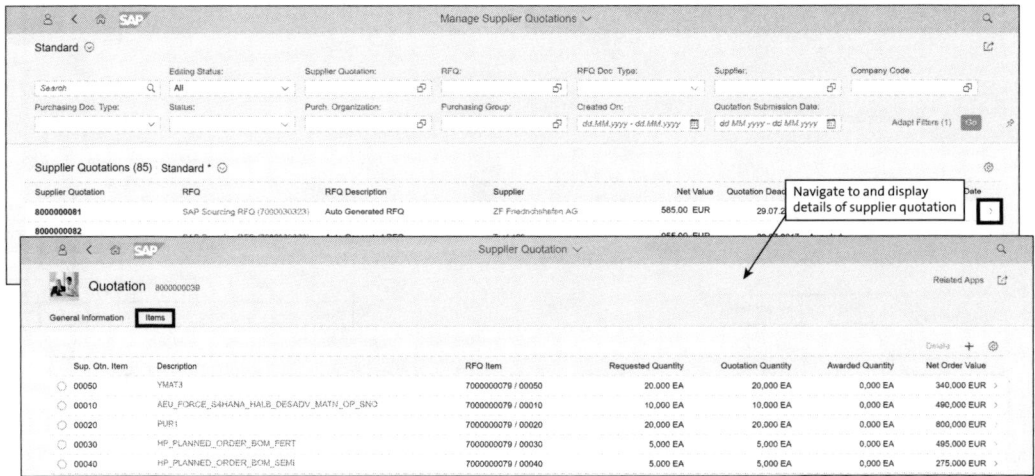

Figure 9.8 Manage Supplier Quotations

9.2.9 Manage Workflows for Supplier Quotation

This app enables the user to define an approval process for supplier quotations, which allows the approver to check the awarded quotations before a follow-on document is created. The awarded quotation can be approved or rejected.

For external quotation (RE) types of quotations, the workflow process isn't relevant, because these quotations are approved and awarded in SAP Ariba Sourcing. The default setting for quotations of the price quotation (RSI) and internal quotation (RQ) types is automatic approval. This app helps the user define a workflow process based on the business requirements for these quotation types. Both one-level approval by the manager of the workflow initiator and multilevel approval by the manager of the workflow initiator and by the higher-level managers are possible.

This app comes with the following standard features:

- Display the list of existing workflow definitions
- Display the details of an existing workflow definition
- Create new workflows by defining preconditions and step sequence
- Copy an existing workflow to create a new one
- Activate or deactivate workflows

Setting up a workflow for quotations using this app doesn't require any development skills. This app helps the business user to set up a workflow by following the steps described ahead. Figure 9.9 shows the steps involved. Start the Manage Workflows for Supplier Quotation app and click the **Add** button to create a workflow. Enter a name for the workflow, and provide a description if necessary. You can set up a validity period for this workflow. Choose one or more preconditions for the workflow to start. The workflow will start only if the selected preconditions are met. Standard preconditions available are as follows:

- **Quotation Follow-On Document Category**
- **Quotation Follow-On Document Type**
- **Initiator of Workflow**
- **Quotation Document Currency**
- **Quotation Document Type**
- **Supplier Quotation Creator**
- **Quotation Total Net Amount is greater than**
- **Quotation Total Net Amount is less than or equal to**

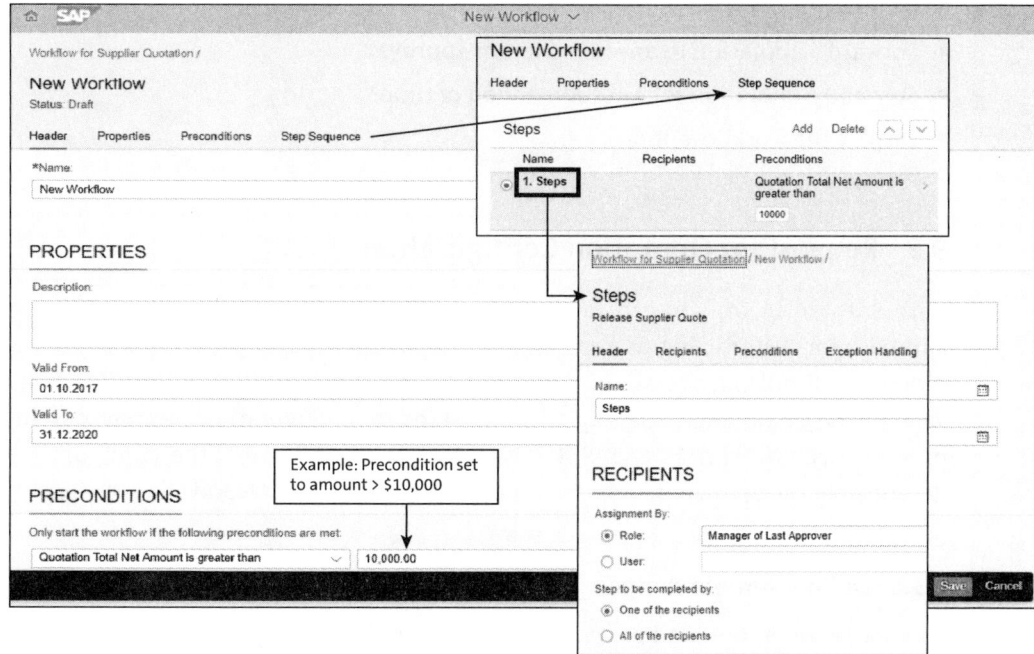

Figure 9.9 Create Workflow for Quotations

The next step in setting up the workflow is to add a step sequence as listed in Table 9.1.

Step Sequence Type	Precondition	Recipient	Exception Handling
Automatic Release of Supplier Quote	Allowed/ Selectable	N/A	Allowed/ Selectable
Release Supplier Quote	Allowed/ Selectable	Allowed/ Selectable	Allowed/ Selectable

Table 9.1 Workflow Step Sequence

9.2.10 My Inbox

This app displays the list of all quotations that have been sent for approval. The user can perform the following actions through this app:

- Approve quotations
- Reject quotations
- Claim a quotation so that only he/she can approve or reject it
- Forward a quotation to another user for approval
- Suspend a quotation for a certain period of time
- Display the workflow or task log

9.3 Request for Quotation Configuration

With SAP S/4HANA, you can take advantage of the SAP Best Practices activation approach for customizing, as explained in Chapter 2. However, if you choose the traditional customizing approach, this section can help. This information also helps validate the customer settings against SAP-standard configuration. For the sourcing process (RFQ) to work in SAP S/4HANA along with SAP Ariba, the configuration described in the following sections needs to be done in the SAP S/4HANA system.

9.3.1 Define Number Ranges

Request for quotation and *supplier quotation* are the two types of documents that need to be configured for the sourcing solution in SAP S/4HANA. These documents are assigned a unique number at the time of creation for identification. The system will use a number from within the number range defined in this step. Number ranges, which include starting and ending numbers and assignment type (external or internal), are defined using the values shown in Table 9.2 at menu path **IMG (SPRO)** • **Materials Management** • **Purchasing** • **Supplier Quotation Process** • **Define Number Ranges**.

No	From No	To Number	NR Status	External Assignment
70	7000000000	7099999999	0	Unchecked
80	8000000000	8099999999	0	Unchecked

Table 9.2 Define Number Ranges

9.3.2 Define Document Types for RFQ

The SAP system manages RFQs as documents, and this customizing step allows for creation of document types necessary for the business. The standard customizing settings can be made by following menu path **IMG (SPRO)** • **Materials Management** • **Purchasing** • **Supplier Quotation Process** • **Define Document Types for RFQ**.

This menu path will bring up the **Document Types RFQ Change** screen; here, you can create new entries. The values required for creating the three standard document types are shown in Table 9.3.

Type	Doc. Type Description	No. Range Int.	External Processing	Awarding
RE	Ext. Sourcing Req.	70	Ariba Sourcing Request	External
RQ	Int. Sourcing Req.	70	Blank	Internal
RSI	Ext. Price Request	70	Ariba Quote Automation	Internal

Table 9.3 Document Types for RFQ

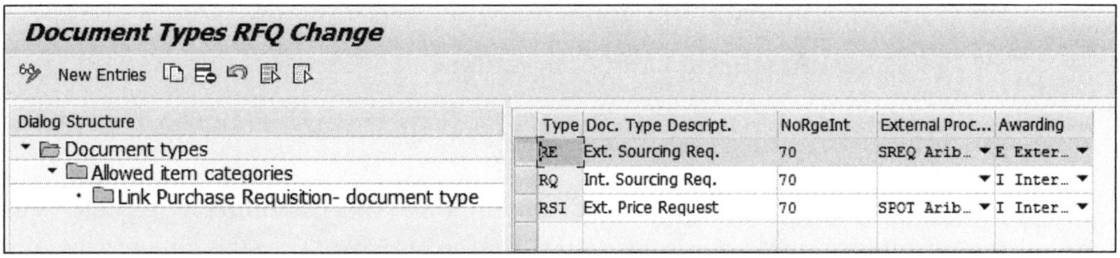

Figure 9.10 Define Document Types for RFQ

Then, select each document type and double-click **Allowed Item Categories** in the dialog structure area, as shown in Figure 9.10. This brings up the **Admissible Item Categories for Document Type** screen; on this screen, create entries as shown in Table 9.4.

Entry	Item Cat.	Text for Item Cat.
Admissible Item Categories for Document Type RE Ext. Sourcing Req.	Blank	Standard
Admissible Item Categories for Document Type RQ Int. Sourcing Req.	Blank	Standard
Admissible Item Categories for Document Type RSI Ext. Price Request	Blank	Standard

Table 9.4 Admissible Item Categories for RFQ Document Type

Return to the **Document Type RFQ Change** screen. Select each document type and double-click the **Link Purchase Requisition** document type in the **Dialog Structure** area. This brings up the **Change View "Link Purchase Requisition - document type": Overview** screen. On this screen, create new entries as shown in Table 9.5.

Entry	DTy.	Description	Item Cat	Dsc. Item Cat.	Item Cat.	Dsc. Item Cat
For Doc. Type RE	NB	Purchase Requisition	Blank	Standard	Blank	Standard
For Doc. Type RQ	NB	Purchase Requisition	Blank	Standard	Blank	Standard
For Doc. Type RQ	NBS	Purchase Req. NBS	Blank	Standard	Blank	Standard
For Doc. Type RSI	NB	Purchase Requisition	Blank	Standard	Blank	Standard

Table 9.5 Link Purchase Requisition Document Type

9.3.3 Define Document Types for Quote

The SAP system manages quotes as documents, and this customizing step allows for creation of document types as necessary for the business. The standard customizing settings can be made by following **IMG (SPRO) • Materials Management • Purchasing • Supplier Quotation Process • Define Document Types for Quote**.

9.3 Request for Quotation Configuration

This menu path will bring up the **Document Types Quote Change** screen; here, create new entries, as shown in Table 9.6.

Type	Doc. Type Description	No. Range Int.
RE	External Quotation	80
RQ	Internal Quotation	80
RSI	Price Quotation	80

Table 9.6 Define Document Types for Quote

Now, select each document type and double-click **Follow-On Document Categories** in the **Dialog Structure** area, as shown in Figure 9.11. This will open the **Change View "Follow-on Document Categories": Overview** screen, on which you can create new entries, as shown in Table 9.7.

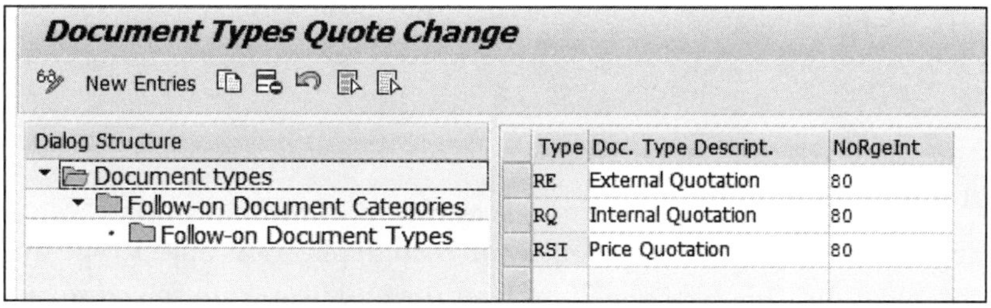

Figure 9.11 Define Document Types for Quote

	Target Document Category	Description
For Doc. Type RE	F	Purchase Order
For Doc. Type RE	K	Contract
For Doc. Type RQ	F	Purchase Order
For Doc. Type RQ	K	Contract
For Doc. Type RSI	F	Purchase Order

Table 9.7 Follow-On Document Categories

Select **F** for **Target Document Category** and double click **Follow-On Document Types** in the **Dialog Structure** area. This will bring up the **Change View "Follow-on Document Types": Overview** screen and on this screen, create the new entries shown in Table 9.8.

Target Doc. Type	Target Doc. Type Description
NB	Standard PO

Table 9.8 Follow-On Document Type for Category F

Now, select **K** for **Target Document Category** and double-click the **Follow-On Document Types** in the **Dialog Structure** area. This will bring up the **Change View "Follow-on Document Types": Overview** screen. Here, create new entries as shown in Table 9.9.

Target Doc. Type	Target Doc. Type Description
MK	Quantity Contract
WK	Value Contract

Table 9.9 Follow-On Document Type for Category K

9.3.4 Assign Output Channels

In this activity, output channels are assigned for each application object type and output type combination. This setting will prevent the end user from selecting output channels that aren't available for a certain application object or output type. In other words, only those output channels that actually can be used are displayed in the applications.

Start by navigating to **IMG (SPRO) • Cross-Application Components • Output Control • Assign Output Channels**. Then, maintain the recommended settings as shown in Table 9.10.

Application Object Type	Output Type	Channel
REQUEST_FOR_QUOTATION	EXTERNAL_REQUEST	XML
REQUEST_FOR_QUOTATION	INTERNAL_REQUEST	EMAIL
REQUEST_FOR_QUOTATION	INTERNAL_REQUEST	PRINT

Table 9.10 Assign Output Channels

9.3 Request for Quotation Configuration

9.3.5 Assign Form Templates

In this activity, the predefined and custom form templates are assigned to specific application object types and output types. This setting will enable the end user to choose from the selection of form templates assigned here.

To assign a form template, first navigate to **IMG (SPRO) • Cross-Application Components • Output Control • Assign Form Templates** (as in Figure 9.12).

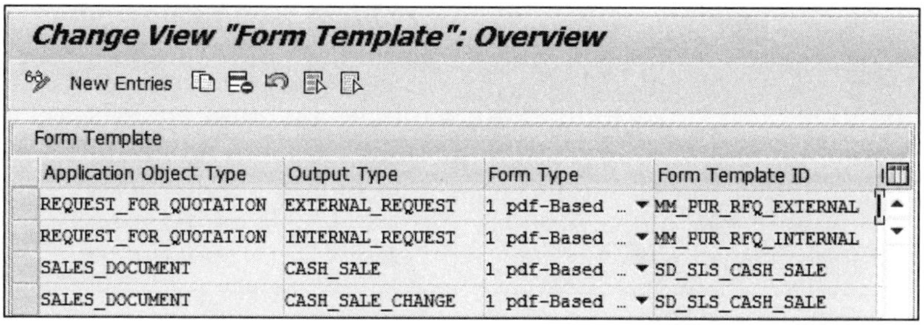

Change View "Form Template": Overview

Application Object Type	Output Type	Form Type	Form Template ID
REQUEST_FOR_QUOTATION	EXTERNAL_REQUEST	1 pdf-Based ...	MM_PUR_RFQ_EXTERNAL
REQUEST_FOR_QUOTATION	INTERNAL_REQUEST	1 pdf-Based ...	MM_PUR_RFQ_INTERNAL
SALES_DOCUMENT	CASH_SALE	1 pdf-Based ...	SD_SLS_CASH_SALE
SALES_DOCUMENT	CASH_SALE_CHANGE	1 pdf-Based ...	SD_SLS_CASH_SALE

Figure 9.12 Assign Form Templates

This will bring up the **Change View "Form Template": Overview** screen; on this screen, maintain the standard template assignments as shown in Table 9.11.

Application Object Type	Output Type	Form Type	Form Template ID	Program
REQUEST_FOR_QUOTATION	EXTERNAL_REQUEST	PDF-Based Print Form with Fragments	MM_PUR_RFQ_EXTERNAL	Blank
REQUEST_FOR_QUOTATION	INTERNAL_REQUEST	PDF-Based Print Form with Fragments	MM_PUR_RFQ_INTERNAL	Blank

Table 9.11 Assign Form Templates

9.3.6 Map Application and Output Type to cXML Message

RFQs are sent from SAP S/4HANA to SAP Ariba, and for this SAP S/4HANA Output Management with the cXML message type is used. In this customizing activity, the cXML message type for the output type used for RFQ documents is defined by following menu path **IMG (SPRO) • Integration with Other SAP Components • Business**

Network Integration • Integration with the Ariba Network • Application-specific Settings • Define Message Output Control • Method 2: Use SAP S/4HANA-Based Output Management • Map Application and Output Type to cXML Message (for Output Management).

This will open the **Change View "New Output Mgt: Map Application and Output Type to cXML M"** screen, as shown in Figure 9.13; on this screen, make the assignment shown in Table 9.12.

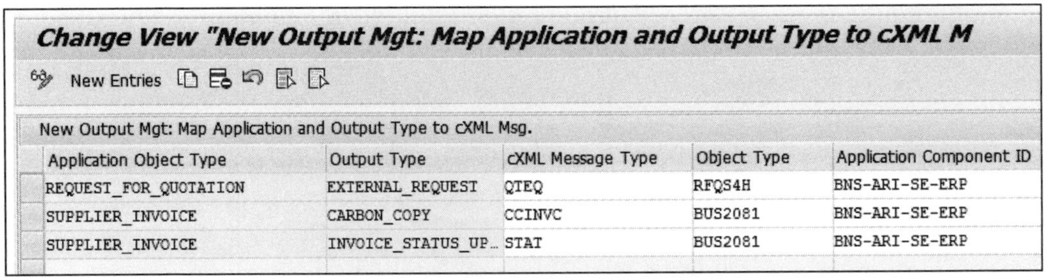
Change View "New Output Mgt: Map Application and Output Type to cXML M

New Entries

New Output Mgt: Map Application and Output Type to cXML Msg.

Application Object Type	Output Type	cXML Message Type	Object Type	Application Component ID
REQUEST_FOR_QUOTATION	EXTERNAL_REQUEST	QTEQ	RFQS4H	BNS-ARI-SE-ERP
SUPPLIER_INVOICE	CARBON_COPY	CCINVC	BUS2081	BNS-ARI-SE-ERP
SUPPLIER_INVOICE	INVOICE_STATUS_UP...	STAT	BUS2081	BNS-ARI-SE-ERP

Figure 9.13 Map Application and Output Type to cXML Message

Application Object Type	Output Type	cXML Message Type	Object Type	Application Component ID
REQUEST_FOR_QUOTATION	EXTERNAL_REQUEST	QTEQ	RFQS4H	BNS-ARI-SE-ERP

Table 9.12 Map Application and Output Type to cXML Message

9.3.7 Activation of Scope-Dependent Background Job Definitions

SAP S/4HANA comes with a jobs repository for scheduling technical background jobs. Scope-dependent jobs need to be defined in this repository before they can be activated. The application components to which these jobs belong need to be active in the system before maintaining the related table, table STJR_JOBD_SCOPE.

Begin by navigating to **IMG (SPRO) • SAP NetWeaver • Application Server • System Administration • Activation of Scope-Depend. Background Job Definitions (S/4HANA).**

This will open the screen shown in Figure 9.14. On this screen, maintain job definition names as listed in Table 9.13.

9.3 Request for Quotation Configuration

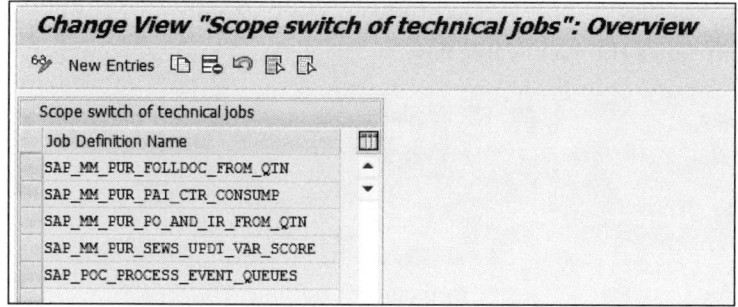

Figure 9.14 Scope-Dependent Background Job Definition

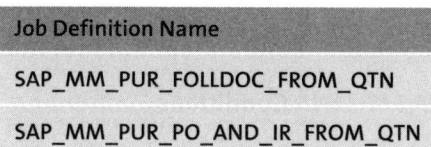

Table 9.13 Scope-Dependent Background Job Definition

9.3.8 Define Document-Specific Message Customizing

In this activity, settings are made to define whether to enable the transfer of attachments with business objects. Definitions are made both for inbound and outbound messages. For enabling the transfer of attachments, select **Document Management System** under **Attachment Transfer**. If no entry is made, attachments are not transferred.

Begin by navigating to **IMG (SPRO)** • **Integration with other SAP Components** • **Business Network Integration** • **Integration with the Ariba Network** • **Application-Specific Settings** • **Define Document-Specific Message Customizing**.

This will open the screen shown in Figure 9.15.

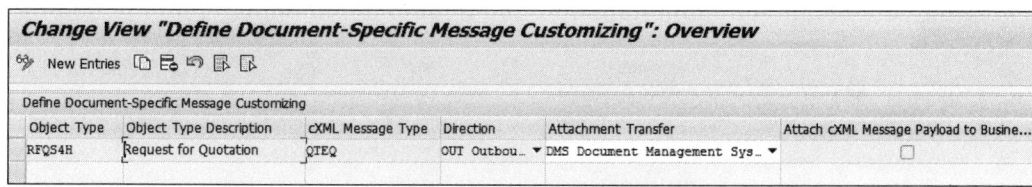

Figure 9.15 Define Document-Specific Message Customizing

On the **Change View "Define Document-Specific Message Customizing": Overview** screen, create new entries as shown in Table 9.14.

Object Type	Object Type Description	cXML Message Type	Direction	Attachment Transfer	Attach cXML Message Payload to Business Object
RFQS4H	Request for Quotation	QTEQ	Outbound	Document Management System	No

Table 9.14 Enable Transfer of Attachments with Business Objects

9.3.9 Map cXML Price Modifications to SAP S/4HANA Conditions

In the sourcing process via SAP Ariba Sourcing, bidders are allowed to make price modifications (discounts and surcharges). In the quote-automation process (quotes are submitted directly on the Ariba Network), bidders can modify the shipping costs. These price modifications are transferred to SAP S/4HANA in the Quote Message cXML message. In this Customizing activity, map the cXML price modifications to the price conditions that exist in SAP S/4HANA.

Begin by navigating to **IMG (SPRO) • Integration with Other SAP Components • Business Network Integration • Integration with the Ariba Network • Application-Specific Settings • Integration with Ariba Sourcing • Map cXML Price Modifications to S/4HANA Conditions**.

This will open the screen shown in Figure 9.16.

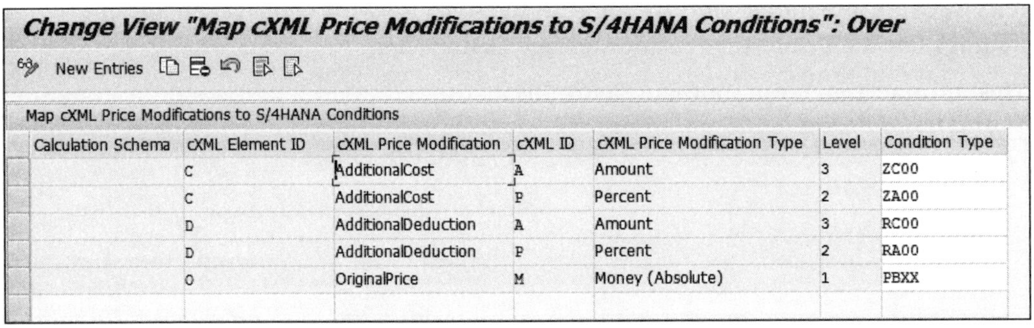

Calculation Schema	cXML Element ID	cXML Price Modification	cXML ID	cXML Price Modification Type	Level	Condition Type
	C	AdditionalCost	A	Amount	3	ZC00
	C	AdditionalCost	P	Percent	2	ZA00
	D	AdditionalDeduction	A	Amount	3	RC00
	D	AdditionalDeduction	P	Percent	2	RA00
	O	OriginalPrice	M	Money (Absolute)	1	PBXX

Figure 9.16 Map cXML Price Modifications to SAP S/4HANA Conditions

On the **Change View "Map cXML Price Modifications to S/4HANA Conditions: Over"** screen, create new entries as shown in Table 9.15.

cXML Element ID	cXML Price Modification	cXML ID	cXML Price Modification Type	Level	Condition Type
C	AdditionalCost	A	Amount	3	ZC00
C	AdditionalCost	P	Percent	2	ZA00
D	AdditionalDeduction	A	Amount	3	RC00
D	AdditionalDeduction	P	Percent	2	RA00
O	OriginalPrice	M	Money (Absolute)	1	PBXX

Table 9.15 Map cXML Price Modifications to SAP S/4HANA Conditions

9.4 Flexible Workflow

In SAP S/4HANA, the process owners—for example, the one responsible for the sourcing process—are provided with the tools necessary to configure the approval workflow relevant to the business processes they own. They can configure the workflow needed for the business processes themselves without needing to go to the IT department. This strategy empowers the process owner and eliminates costs associated with development. The Manage Workflows SAP Fiori app allows process owners to use this new flexible workflow procedure in SAP S/4HANA. This approach also provides the flexibility to change the workflow as and when required to meet changing requirements.

This section describes the configuration steps required for the Manage Workflows for Supplier Quotation app to work.

9.4.1 Scenario Activation

Workflow IDs are provided in the system for each scenario, such as release purchase order, release supplier quotation, and so on. To activate the scenario relevant to the business process in question, follow menu path **IMG (SPRO)** • **SAP NetWeaver** • **Application Server** • **Business Management** • **SAP Business Workflow** • **Flexible Workflow** • **Scenario Activation** (see Figure 9.17).

The supplier quotation workflow scenario is activated by creating an entry as shown in Table 9.16. This setting makes the scenario visible in the Manage Workflows for Supplier Quotation app.

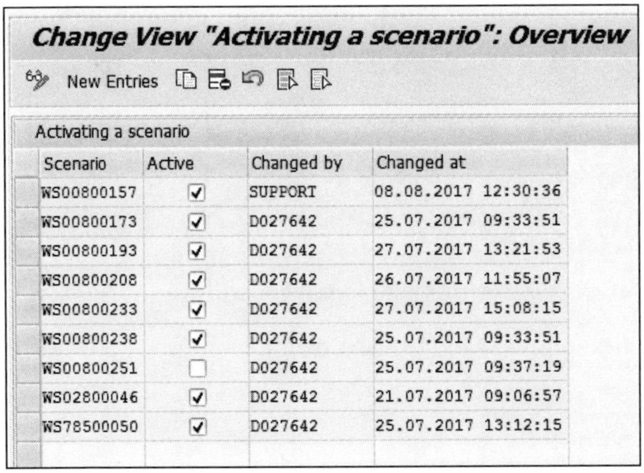

Change View "Activating a scenario": Overview

Scenario	Active	Changed by	Changed at
WS00800157	✓	SUPPORT	08.08.2017 12:30:36
WS00800173	✓	D027642	25.07.2017 09:33:51
WS00800193	✓	D027642	27.07.2017 13:21:53
WS00800208	✓	D027642	26.07.2017 11:55:07
WS00800233	✓	D027642	27.07.2017 15:08:15
WS00800238	✓	D027642	25.07.2017 09:33:51
WS00800251	☐	D027642	25.07.2017 09:37:19
WS02800046	✓	D027642	21.07.2017 09:06:57
WS78500050	✓	D027642	25.07.2017 13:12:15

Figure 9.17 Scenario Activation

Scenario	Active
WS00800193	select

Table 9.16 Scenario Activation

9.4.2 Register Event for Subsequent Workflow

For triggering a subsequent workflow, further triggering events need to be determined in addition to the event ASSIGNED. To do this, a check function module is implemented. To start, follow menu path **IMG (SPRO) • SAP NetWeaver • Application Server • Basis Services • Archive Link • Customizing Incoming Documents • Workflow Scenarios • Register Event for Subsequent Workflow**.

This will open the **Change View "Event Type Linkages": Overview** screen; on this screen, create the entries shown in Table 9.17. Then configure the receiver call as seen in Table 9.18.

Customizing settings made in this step are shown in Figure 9.18.

9.4 Flexible Workflow

Object Category	Object Type	Event	Receiver Type
ABAP Class	CL_MM_PUR_WF_OBJECT_QTN	SUBMITTED_FOR_APPROVAL	WS00800193

Table 9.17 Register Event for Subsequent Workflow

Receiver Call	Receiver Function Module	Event Delivery	Linkage Activated	Behavior Upon Error Feedback	Receiver Status
Function Module	SWW_WI_CREATE_VIA_EVENT_IBF	Using tRFC (Default)	select	System defaults	No errors

Table 9.18 Receiver Configuration

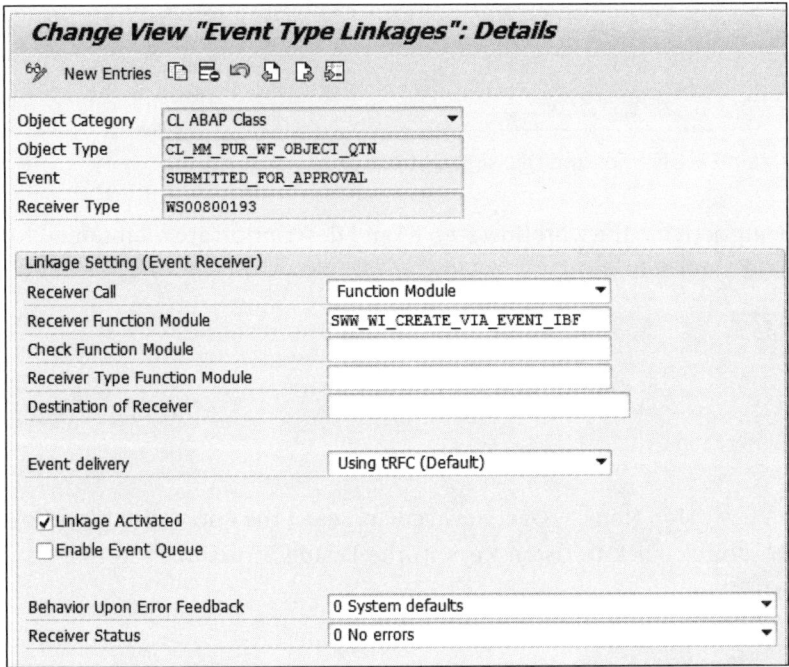

Figure 9.18 Event Type Linkages

9 External Sourcing

9.4.3 Maintain Task Names and Decision Options

Each workflow ID is assigned a step ID, and the possible decision keys such as approve and reject need to be maintained. The step ID determines the task, and the decision keys determine the possible decisions within the workflow.

Begin by navigating to **IMG (SPRO)** • **SAP NetWeaver** • **SAP Gateway Service Enablement** • **Content** • **Workflow Settings** • **Maintain Task Names and Decision Options**. This opens the screen shown in Figure 9.19.

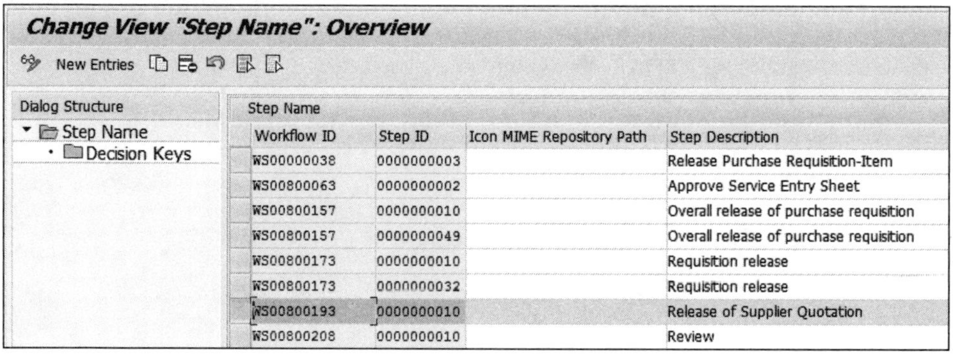

Figure 9.19 Maintain Task Names and Decision Options

In this customizing activity, the workflow step ID and description are maintained for the workflow ID as Table 9.19.

Workflow ID	Step ID	Step Description
WS00800193	10	Release of Supplier Quotation

Table 9.19 Workflow Step

On the **Change View "Step Name": Overview** screen, select the entry with **Workflow ID WS00800193**, double click **Decision Keys** in the **Dialog Structure**, and maintain entries as Table 9.20.

Key	Decision Text	Nature
1	Approve	POSITIVE
2	Reject	NEGATIVE

Table 9.20 Decision Keys

9.4.4 Visualization of SAP Business Workflow

The metadata required for visualization of SAP Business Workflow is defined in this step. The metadata for each task type relevant to the workflow scenario is defined here.

Begin by navigating to **IMG (SPRO)** • **SAP NetWeaver** • **Application Server** • **Business Management** • **SAP Business Workflow** • **Visualization of SAP Business Workflow Metadata** • **Client-Dependent Configuration**.

On the **Change Visualization Metadata for Work Items and Objects** screen (see Figure 9.20), select **SAPUI5 My Inbox** for the **Worklist Client** field. Then, select the **Task** tab and create the following entry as Table 9.21.

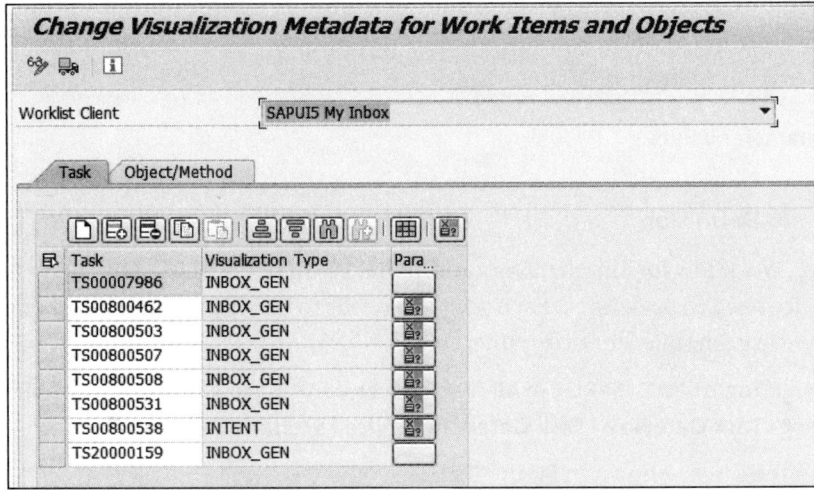

Figure 9.20 Visualization of SAP Business Workflow

Task	Visualization Type
TS00800462	INBOX_GEN

Table 9.21 Visualization Type

Then, select the **Parameters Available** button for task **TS00800462**; on the **Parameter for TS00800462** screen, maintain the following values as parameter values (as Table 9.22).

9 External Sourcing

Parameter Name	Visualization Parameter Value
APPLICATION_PATH	N/A
COMPONENT_NAME	cross.fnd.fiori.inbox.annotationBasedTaskUI
QUERY_PARAM00	service=/sap/opu/odata/sap/MM_PUR_QTN_MAINTAIN_SRV
QUERY_PARAM01	entity=/C_SuplrQuotationEnhWD(SupplierQuotation='{&_WI_Object_ID.MS_SUPPLIER_QUOTATION.SUPPLIERQUOTATION&}', DraftUUID=guid'00000000-0000-0000-0000-000000000000', IsActiveEntity=true)
QUERY_PARAM02	annotations=/sap/opu/odata/IWFND/CATALOGSERVICE;v=2/Annotations(TechnicalName='MM_PUR_QTN_MAINTAIN_ANNO_MDL',Version='0001')/$value/
SCHEME	SAPUI5

Table 9.22 Parameter Values

9.4.5 Scenario Definition

Scenarios (e.g., Workflow for Supplier Quotation) that are to be consumed by the Task Gateway service need to be defined. Each scenario needs to be assigned to at least one consumer type (e.g., mobile, desktop, tablet).

Begin by navigating to **IMG (SPRO)** • **SAP NetWeaver** • **SAP Gateway Service Enablement** • **Content** • **Task Gateway** • **Task Gateway Service** • **Scenario Definition**.

This will open the screen shown in Figure 9.21.

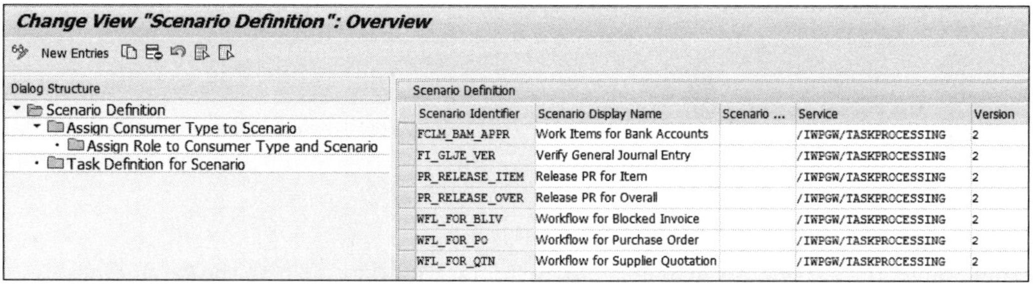

Figure 9.21 Scenario Definition

On the **Change View "Scenario Definition": Overview** screen, create the following new entries (as Table 9.23).

Scenario Identifier	Scenario Display Name	Technical Service Name	Version	EntitySet External Name	Property External Name
WFL_FOR_QTN	Workflow for Supplier Quotation	/IWPGW/TASKPROCESSING	2	Task	TaskDefinitionID

Table 9.23 Scenario Definition Values

On the **View "Scenario Definition": Overview** screen, select the entry for **Scenario Identifier: WFL_FOR_QTN**, double-click **Assign Consumer Type to Scenario** in the **Dialog Structure** area, and create the following entry: TABLET.

Return to the overview screen, select **WFL_FOR_QTN**, choose **Task Definition for Scenario** in the **Dialog Structure** area, and create the following entry (as Table 9.24).

SAP System Alias	Task Type
LOCAL_TGW	TS00800462

Table 9.24 SAP System Alias

9.4.6 Maintain Attribute for Workflow Task

There are two levels of agent assignment in SAP Business Workflow: determining possible agents and determining responsible agents. The work item is only sent to the responsible agents, but the responsible agents must also be possible agents. We recommend that all employees in the company be possible agents. By classifying the task as a general task, we guarantee that the responsible agents are also always possible agents.

Begin by navigating to **IMG (SPRO)** • **SAP NetWeaver** • **Application Server** • **Basis Services** • **ArchiveLink** • **Customizing Incoming Documents** • **Workflow Scenarios** • **Determine Possible Agents for a Task**.

On the **Task: Maintain** screen, fill in following entry as Table 9.25.

Task Type	Task
Standard Task	00800462

Table 9.25 Task Maintain Values

9 External Sourcing

Choose **Display** to see the screen shown in Figure 9.22.

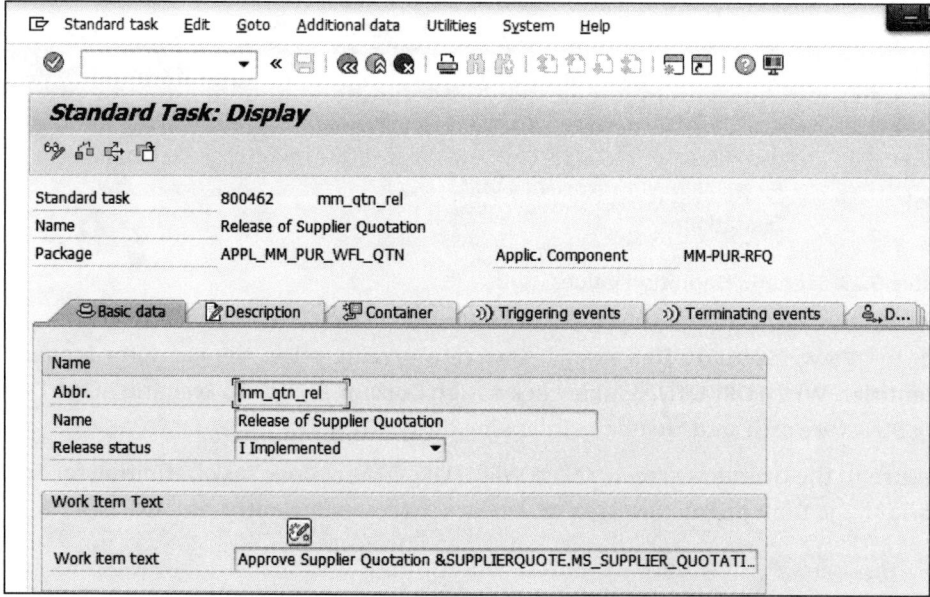

Figure 9.22 Maintain Attribute for Workflow Task

On the **Standard Task: Display** screen, go to **Additional Data** • **Agent Assignment** • **Maintain**.

On the **Standard task: Maintain Agent Assignment** screen (see Figure 9.23), select the following row (as Table 9.26):

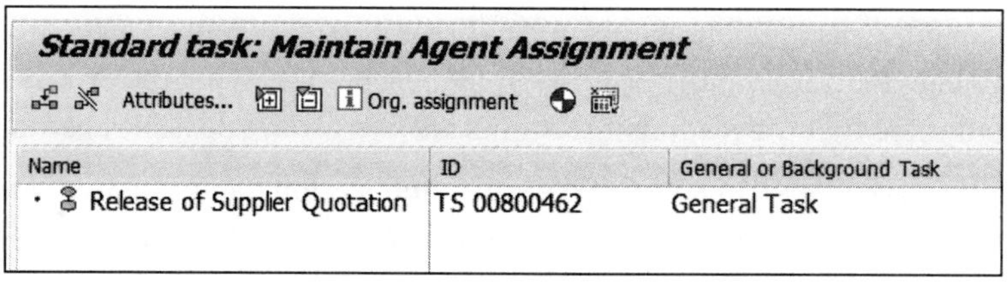

Figure 9.23 Maintain Agent Assignment

Name	ID
Release of Supplier Quotation	TS 00800462

Table 9.26 Agent Assignment

Click **Attributes**, then, on the **Task** screen, choose **General Task** and click **Transfer**. Then, go back twice and complete the activity.

9.5 Integration with SAP Ariba

SAP provides three integration options between SAP S/4HANA and SAP Ariba's cloud solutions. The following integration options are available as of the time of writing:

- SAP HANA Cloud Platform, integration service
- SAP Process Orchestration
- Direct connectivity via SAP S/4HANA web services

However, SAP's strategic approach for SAP Ariba integration is SAP Ariba Cloud Integration Gateway. This solution is enabled by SAP Cloud Platform Integration, which provides a fast and simple way to connect SAP Ariba solutions with backend systems and trading partners. This approach eliminates the need for multiple adapters for different solutions and scenarios. SAP Ariba Cloud Integration Gateway comes with intuitive self-service tools that enable quick and easy configuration and testing. The self-service wizard provides the following features:

- Automated testing and scenarios
- Real-time monitoring and alerts
- Automatic upgrades
- Alignment with SAP
- Security safeguards

9.6 Summary

Sourcing—more specifically, external sourcing—involves collaboration with suppliers outside the organization. SAP has strategically used SAP Ariba solutions as the extended solution to achieve this external communication and collaboration. Tight integration optimizes the overall solution capability. In this chapter, we focused on the SAP S/4HANA side of the solution. The SAP Fiori apps and the flexible workflow explained in this chapter are key differentiators of the solution.

Chapter 10
Invoice and Payables Management

Entry of a supplier invoice, matching this information with data from Purchasing and Receiving, and the subsequent processing of invoice data to facilitate payment completes the procure-to-pay process cycle enabled by SAP S/4HANA.

Invoice Management and Payables Management are essential end-to-end processes delivered with SAP S/4HANA Sourcing and Procurement. The entry and validation of a supplier's invoice into the system records the billing details and enables the matching and approval processes. Once the invoice is entered, matched, and optionally approved, the process to pay a supplier for the goods and services rendered is performed. These two processes complete the procure-to-pay end-to-end business process.

In Invoice Management, all pertinent details of a supplier invoice are entered into the system, which are then verified against both the purchasing documents to which it is referenced and the quantities of goods or services that have been received to date. If the document details, such as the prices and quantities in the entered invoice, matches the information contained in the SAP S/4HANA system, then the supplier invoice document is accepted and posted to the system. If discrepancies are found, then the documents can be held or parked and the discrepancies addressed with the supplier and with the purchasing and receiving departments. Once the information is matched, then the supplier invoice document can be successfully posted in the system, with appropriate accounting documents created to reflect the general ledger impact of the invoice entry.

In Payables Management, the accepted invoice becomes eligible for payment. A payment proposal is generated by the system, and once reviewed and approved it's then included in a subsequent payment run. Funds are then transferred from the customer to the supplier's banking accounts via a variety of payment methods.

The SAP S/4HANA system contains integrated capabilities to handle the complete invoice verification and payables processes. There are three main solution capabilities available in SAP S/4HANA:

1. **Invoice Processing**
   Entry and validation of supplier invoices into the system
2. **Accounts Payable**
   Processing of payments due to suppliers
3. **Invoice Collaboration**
   Working with suppliers to integrate invoices and payables via the Ariba Network

We'll describe each solution's capabilities in detail in the following sections.

10.1 Invoice Processing

The Invoice Processing capability of Sourcing and Procurement is focused on the entry, validation, and posting of supplier invoice details into the SAP S/4HANA system. The information contained in the invoice presented by the supplier is checked for accuracy against the customer's referenced purchasing documents and the goods receipts that have been logged into the system. Price, quantity, tax, and accounting information are all checked.

If the total invoice amount is in balance with the reference documents, then the invoice document can be posted successfully in the system. The appropriate financial postings are also posted at the same time due to the integration of Invoice Processing with Financial Accounting.

If the total invoice amount isn't found to be in balance or additional information or expertise is needed to process the invoice document, then the invoice entry can be held or parked by the invoice entry processor for later processing by knowledgeable personnel.

Entry of supplier invoices that reference purchasing documents is supported, as are financial invoices (FI only) without a specific purchase document reference.

10.1.1 Innovations in Invoice Processing in SAP S/4HANA

SAP S/4HANA brings many innovations to Invoice Processing. Managing supplier invoices in classic SAP ERP involved a good deal of transferring back and forth between multiple screens. First, selection criteria had to be entered on an invoice listing screen. The resulting report listed all invoice documents that satisfied the entered selection criteria. Detecting issues and resolving them involved moving back and forth between the invoice list screen and the invoice details screen. If you needed to change the selection criteria of the invoice list, you needed to fully regenerate the invoice list first.

With SAP S/4HANA, the dynamic search capabilities in the Supplier Invoices List app provide a streamlined way of selecting and managing invoices of concern.

The many apps available to support Invoice Processing make the job of entering supplier invoices streamlined and simple. The following native SAP Fiori apps for Invoice Processing are available:

- Create Supplier Invoice
- Supplier Invoices List
- Display Supplier Balances

> **Note**
> The following WebGUI transactional apps for Invoice Processing are also available from SAP:
> - Create Supplier Invoice (Advanced)
> - Display Supplier Invoice (Advanced)
> - Release Blocked Invoices
> - Clear GR/IR Clearing Account
> - Display/Cancel Account Maintenance
> - Create Consignment and Pipeline Settlement
> - Create Evaluated Receipt Settlement

10.1.2 Supplier Invoice Documents

The supplier invoice document in SAP S/4HANA is a representation of the presentation and acceptance of a bill from a supplier to a customer. It also passes information needed to complete the procure-to-pay cycle to Financial Accounting. Entry of a supplier invoice document is a necessary step in most procure-to-pay processes; it ensures that a supplier will be paid for the goods or services provided.

10 Invoice and Payables Management

There are four types of supplier invoice documents supported by the SAP S/4HANA system:

1. Supplier invoice
2. Credit memo
3. Subsequent credit
4. Subsequent debit

Supplier Invoice

A *supplier invoice* is a document presented by a supplier for reimbursement of goods or services rendered. It contains details about the supplier, bank information, identification of items and quantities purchased, supplier pricing, unplanned delivery costs, and tax and account determination information.

Credit Memo

A *credit memo* is a document used to record the entry of an invoice for a credit claimed from the supplier. This document arises from a return of defective goods, a reduction of an invoice, or for other reasons.

These documents can be considered debits for the vendor. The accounting postings for credit memos typically are the reverse of a normal supplier invoice posting.

Credit memos can be entered directly into the system or can be generated automatically via Evaluated Receipt Settlement (ERS).

Subsequent Credit

A *subsequent credit* invoice document is posted when you've entered and settled an invoice for which the supplier has billed you at too high a price. The subsequent credit memo entered is a value-only document and doesn't affect the quantities originally invoiced. It's valuable to enter subsequent credits when needed in the system to preserve the invoice history.

Subsequent Debit

A *subsequent debit* invoice document is posted when you've entered and settled an invoice for which the supplier has billed you at too low a price. The subsequent debit memo entered is value-only as well and doesn't affect the quantities originally invoiced.

Automatic Settlements

Invoice documents can be created automatically in the system, based on regularly scheduled settlements of procurement processes. These include ERS, consignment or pipeline settlement, or billing based on invoicing plans. These processes produce invoice documents based on data in your SAP S/4HANA system, rather than relying on a bill submitted by the supplier directly.

10.1.3 Results of Invoice Processing

The following actions take place on successful posting of an invoice document in SAP S/4HANA:

- A logistics invoice document is created to reflect the supplier billing details.
- One or more financial documents are created based on the data entered. These FI documents reference and are traceable to the logistics invoice document. These documents post the amounts entered for the invoice lint items to the appropriate G/L accounts.
- The purchase order history in the referenced purchasing document line items is updated, which provides a complete audit trail of activities linked to line items.
- If required, the prices on the material master are adjusted.

10.1.4 Types of Supplier Invoice Verification

There are two types of supplier invoice verification supported by the SAP S/4HANA system. They differ in the data that is proposed during the entry of the invoice document. These two types are purchase order-based invoice verification and goods receipt-based invoice verification.

Purchase Order-Based Invoice Verification

In this technique, illustrated in Figure 10.1, the system generates one invoice line for each referenced purchase order item. The quantities proposed during invoice entry are determined by the difference between the total delivered quantity and the total invoiced quantity. If the quantities and amounts on the supplier invoice differ from those proposed, as in the case of a partial goods receipt, these items will need to be adjusted by the invoice processor.

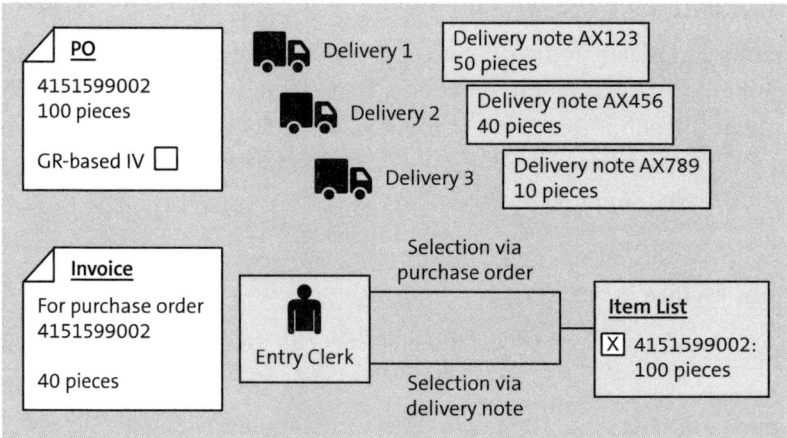

Figure 10.1 Purchase Order-Based Invoice Verification

Goods Receipt-Based Invoice Verification

In this technique, illustrated in Figure 10.2, the quantities and amounts proposed on the invoice entry must match one or more goods receipts recorded in the SAP S/4HANA system. With goods receipt–based invoice verification, the invoice can't be entered without a goods receipt reference. This procedure is useful if you want to assure that goods have been received prior to posting a supplier's invoice.

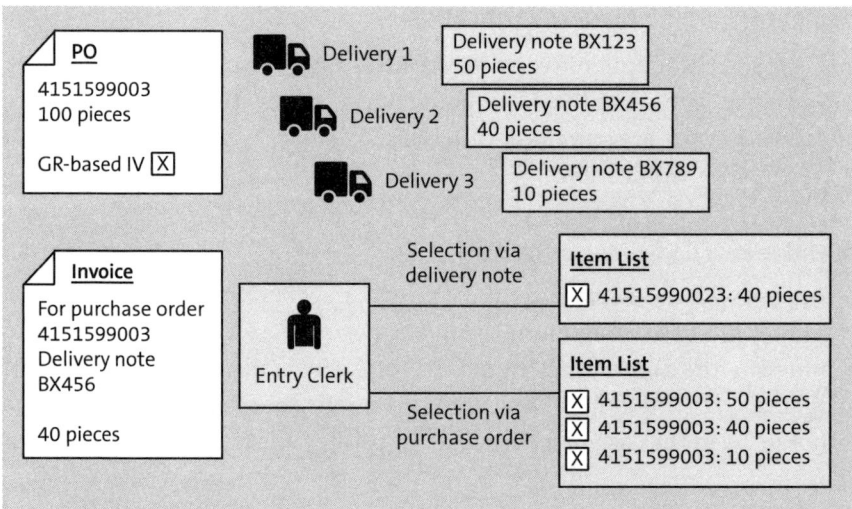

Figure 10.2 Goods Receipt-Based Invoice Verification

The invoice lines created are proposed from each partial delivery connected to the referenced purchasing documents or delivery notes. This allows goods receipts and invoice receipts to be aligned in the purchase order history.

This function is controlled by setting the GR-based **Invoice Verification** indicator on the purchasing organization views for the supplier business partner role. The value here is adopted into the purchasing document. If desired, this same setting can be made at the purchasing organization and plant levels as well by maintaining alternate purchasing data for the business partner. The setting at the plant level supersedes the value from the purchasing organization view.

The GR-based **Invoice Verification** indicator can be set or unset on a PIR as well. This setting for a PIR is adopted into the purchasing document preferentially over the settings maintained in the supplier master.

10.1.5 Entry of Invoice Documents

A supplier's invoice can be entered via a variety of techniques into the SAP S/4HANA system. It's possible to utilize all types of invoice entry techniques, depending on the supplier and your business requirements:

- Invoice entry online, using SAP Fiori apps
- Invoice entry via EDI
- Invoice entry via the Ariba Network

Online Invoice Entry Using SAP Fiori Apps

Use the available online SAP Fiori apps to enter a supplier invoice when the document is presented to you via normal delivery methods, such as the postal service or email. The SAP S/4HANA system automatically adopts referenced documents to minimize data entry, and it verifies that the prices and quantities presented by the supplier match the information in your system.

Basic header data about the invoice is entered into the system, such as the invoice date, invoice reference from the supplier, and total invoice amount. A tax code can be entered here if needed.

References to purchasing documents such as purchase orders, scheduling agreements, or service entry sheets are then entered. The system will adopt key information from these documents such as quantities, prices, and tax information, therefore speeding up invoice data entry and reducing errors.

The system checks that the invoice data from the supplier matches the information in the reference documents. If the total amount doesn't balance or is outside of configured tolerances, then the system will flag the invoice and won't allow posting until corrections are made.

Sometimes freight charges passed onto you from the supplier are present on an invoice. If these weren't planned for in the purchase order itself, this amount can be added to the invoice in the form of unplanned delivery costs.

The invoice can be held, parked, or posted by the invoice processor as needed. Figure 10.3 shows these invoice statuses.

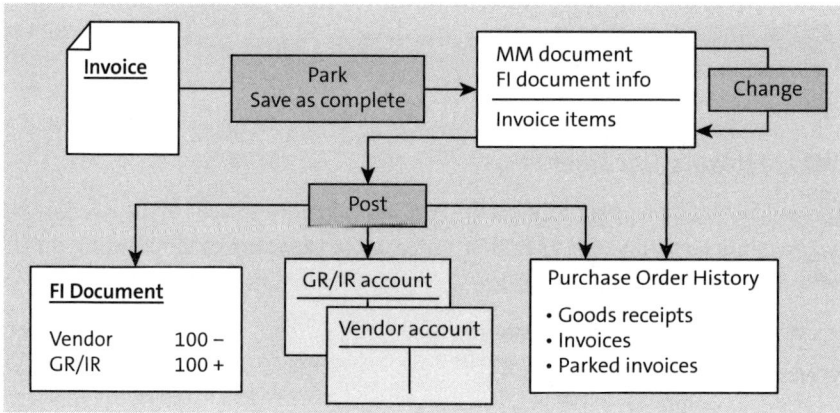

Figure 10.3 Supplier Invoice Statuses

Holding a document lets you save the invoice document in its current state, with only the minimum amount of validation. The system only checks for the existence of the company code and supplier. A logistics invoice document is created during hold, but no financial documents are posted, and no updates to purchase order history are performed. Held invoices need to be monitored and subsequently processed for the procure-to-pay process to continue.

Parking an invoice document is useful if you're missing data needed for posting and you don't want to have to reenter the data. The invoice document doesn't have to be in balance to be parked. A logistics invoice document is created, and the purchase order history is updated as well. An open, parked supplier line item is also generated and FI document numbers assigned. A duplicate invoice check also occurs at this time. Parking a document can trigger a workflow to commence further processing on the invoice document.

Save as complete is another option that you can use if you have a complete, balanced document but don't want to post the document at that point. Like parked documents, a logistics invoice document is created, and the purchase order history is updated as well. An open, parked supplier line item also is generated and FI document numbers assigned. A duplicate invoice check also occurs at this time.

The SAP Fiori apps used to enter an invoice into the SAP S/4HANA system are described in more detail in the following sections.

If required, entered invoices can go through an approval process. There are standard workflows available in the SAP S/4HANA system which route a supplier invoice document to approvers based on your company's requirements.

Posting a supplier invoice in SAP S/4HANA will typically result in the following postings:

- Debit to the supplier subaccount of the invoicing supplier partner on the invoice
- Credit to the GR/IR account

Invoice Entry using Electronic Data Interchange

EDI can be used between two trading partners to facilitate the exchange of documents. Transmitting a supplier invoice and the subsequent posting of that document in the system is a key process often enabled via this technique. The system validates the data sent by the supplier and, if acceptable, posts the invoice into the system without the need for human intervention. SAP S/4HANA supports multiple EDI protocols for the transmission and acceptance of supplier invoice documents.

Invoice Entry via the Ariba Network

The Ariba Network is a cloud-based business-to-business marketplace where buyers and suppliers can connect and do business on a single, networked platform. Exchange of supplier invoices is just one of the standard integrations built into SAP Ariba that can be integrated into the SAP S/4HANA system. See Section 10.3 for additional information.

Invoice Reduction

If you dispute the values or quantities on the supplier invoice presented, you can reduce the invoice entered to match what you think is correct. This is known as *invoice reduction* in SAP S/4HANA (see Figure 10.4). To reduce an invoice, take the following steps:

- Mark the line item as **Vendor Error: Reduce Invoice**.
- Enter the reduced value or quantity (or both) into the reduction fields provided.
- Verify the values and quantities given on the supplier invoice and enter them in the fields provided.

The system posts two documents when invoice reduction is used. First, an invoice document for the invoiced quantities and values is created. Second, a credit memo is generated for the difference quantities and values. Optionally, you can also generate a complaint document that can be transmitted back to the supplier in this situation.

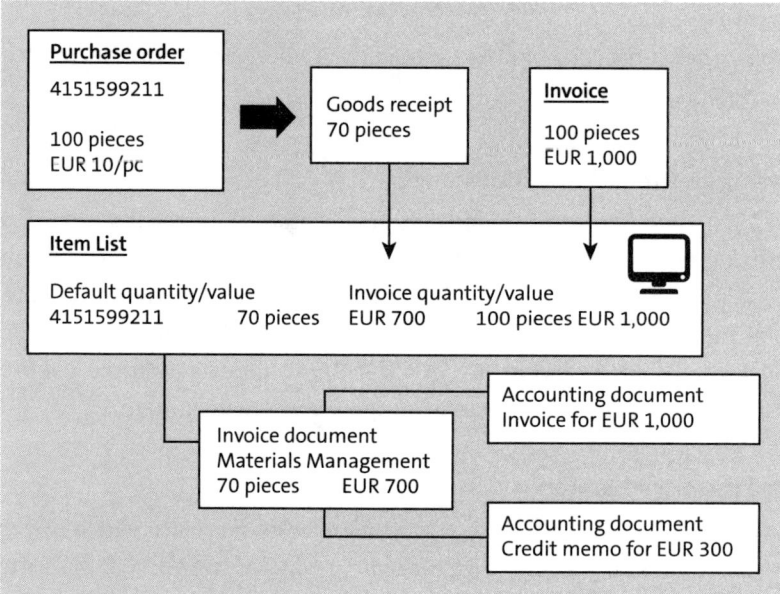

Figure 10.4 Invoice Reduction

Simulation of Invoice Postings

SAP S/4HANA can simulate the accounting postings for an invoice prior to the actual posting of the invoice document. This capability allows the invoice processor to observe the G/L account postings based on the entered data.

Click the **Simulate** button to see the resulting simulated postings. You can also post the invoice directly from the simulation if you wish.

10.1.6 Invoice Processing

There are a variety of SAP Fiori transactional apps available to enter and process supplier invoice documents in SAP S/4HANA:

- Create Supplier Invoice
- Create Supplier Invoice—Advanced

Create Supplier Invoice

This native SAP Fiori app allows you to create and display a supplier invoice based on information received from your supplier. You can note one or more purchase order items to which this invoice refers. Once entered, SAP S/4HANA compares the quantity and amount data for each supplier invoice item with the data of the related purchase order item. If goods receipt-based invoice verification has been defined for a purchase order item, the system compares the supplier invoice data with the related goods receipt data as well. If the quantities or amounts lie outside defined tolerances, the invoice is posted is automatically blocked for payment. An approval process also can be triggered by the system. When looking at the details, you can reverse a posted supplier invoice or release a blocked invoice. These features are available in the Create Invoice app (as seen in Figure 10.5 and Figure 10.6):

- Create a new supplier invoice document; you can create credit memos, subsequent credits, and subsequent debits as well.
- Edit fields on the invoice document, which the system then transfers to Financial Accounting.
- Change the currency exchange rate displayed, if allowed by customization.
- Relate all entered invoice items for one or multiple purchase order references for which the invoice was received. You can deselect items that are not relevant.
- It's possible to create a supplier invoice without a purchase order reference. In this case, additional data will need to be entered manually in the invoice document, such as currency, baseline date, terms of payment, and invoicing party.
- Create additional G/L account items as required.
- Enter and check tax data for the invoice.
- Edit payment terms if the payment terms pulled from the purchase order need to be altered.
- Enter unplanned delivery costs presented on the supplier's invoice.
- Add one or more attachments to the invoice document.
- Simulate, hold, or post the supplier invoice.

10 Invoice and Payables Management

- Reduce the invoice, which generates a credit memo alongside the invoice document.
- Output specific business documents, such as letters of complaint to the invoicing party arising due to invoice reduction.

The Create Supplier Invoice app is assigned to the accounts payable accountant—procurement standard authorization role.

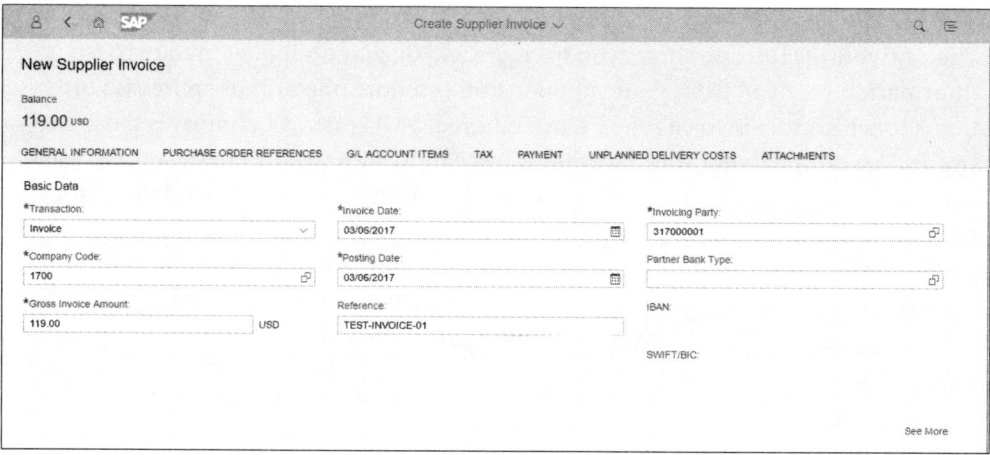

Figure 10.5 Create Supplier Invoice App: Header Data

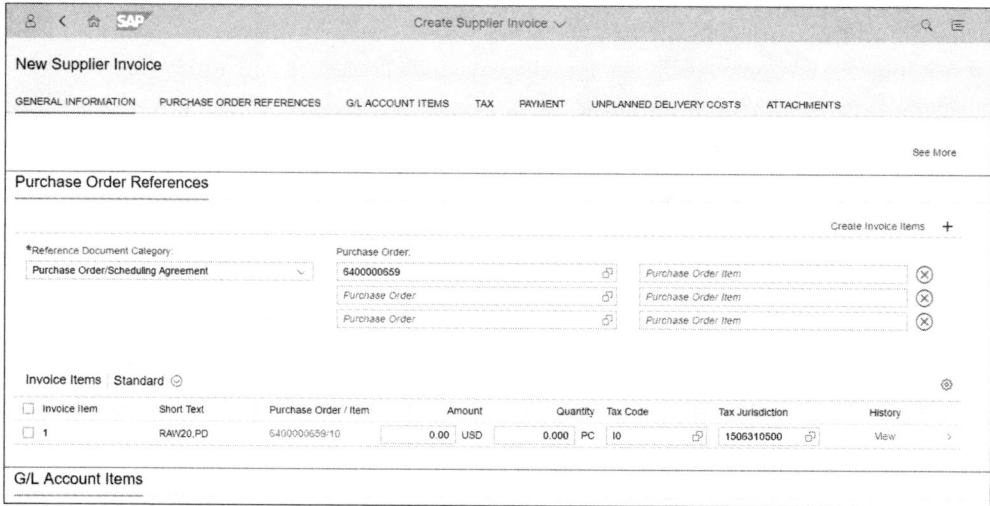

Figure 10.6 Create Supplier Invoice App: Purchase Order Reference

Create Supplier Invoice—Advanced App

The Create Supplier Invoice—Advanced app (Figure 10.7) is used when the supplier invoice is too complex to enter using the Create Supplier Invoice native SAP Fiori app. This situation can occur, for example, if you need to register multiple account assignments for the same line item on the invoice. The Create Supplier Invoice—Advanced app runs directly on the backend SAP S/4HANA system and is functionally equivalent to the classic SAP ERP Transaction MIRO.

The Create Supplier Invoice—Advanced app is assigned to the accounts payable accountant-procurement standard authorization role.

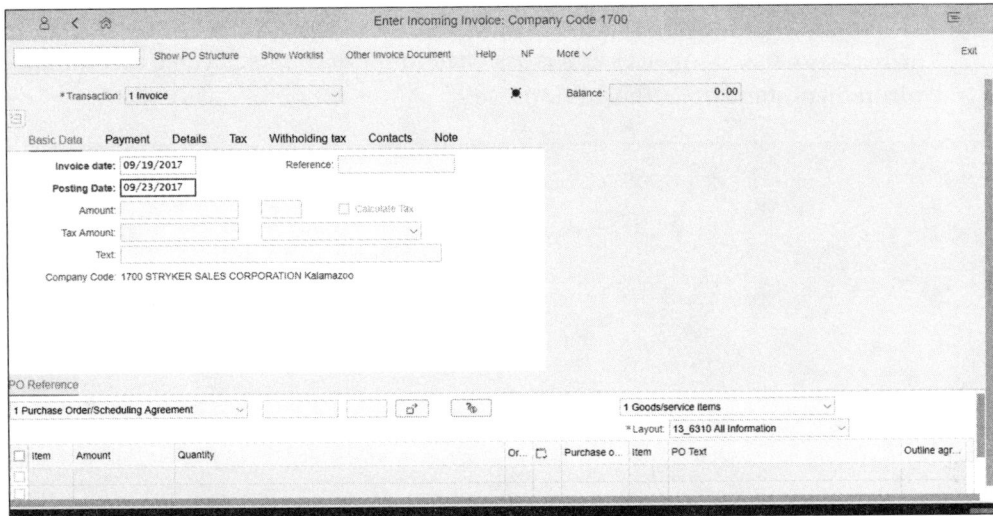

Figure 10.7 Create Supplier Invoice—Advanced App

10.1.7 Other Invoice Processing Apps

Several other invoice processing apps are available within the SAP S/4HANA system:

- Release Blocked Invoices
- Print Supplier Invoices
- Clear GR/IR Clearing Account
- Display/Cancel Account Maintenance
- Create Consignment and Pipeline Settlement
- Create Evaluated Receipt Settlement

We'll discuss these in the following sections.

10   Invoice and Payables Management

Release Blocked Invoices

Invoices may be blocked in SAP S/4HANA for a variety of reasons, such as exceeding invoice tolerances or a stochastic (random) block.

The Release Blocked Invoices app allows you to obtain a list of all blocked invoice documents and selectively release any documents that were blocked and for which the root cause of blocking (e.g., a missing goods receipt) has been addressed. Invoices that were manually blocked during invoice entry can be released using this app as well (as seen in Figure 10.8 and Figure 10.9).

This app runs on the backend SAP S/4HANA system and is functionally equivalent to the classic SAP ERP Transaction MRBR.

The Release Blocked Invoices app is assigned to the accounts payable accountant—procurement standard authorization role.

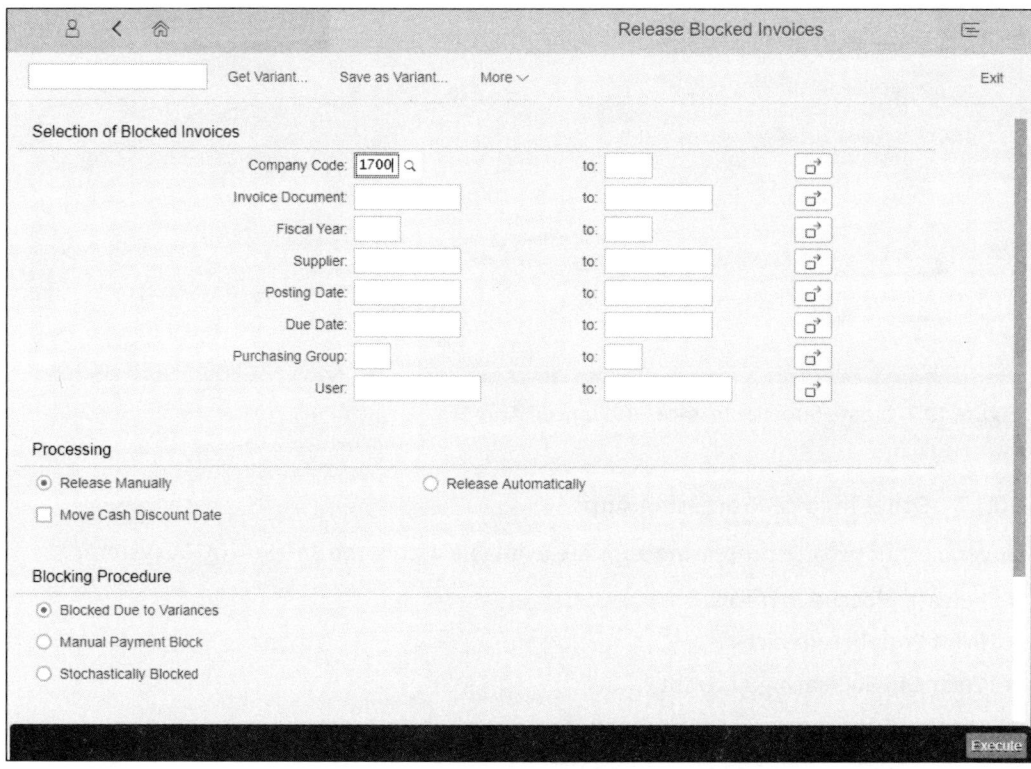

Figure 10.8 Release Blocked Invoices: Selection Screen

10.1 Invoice Processing

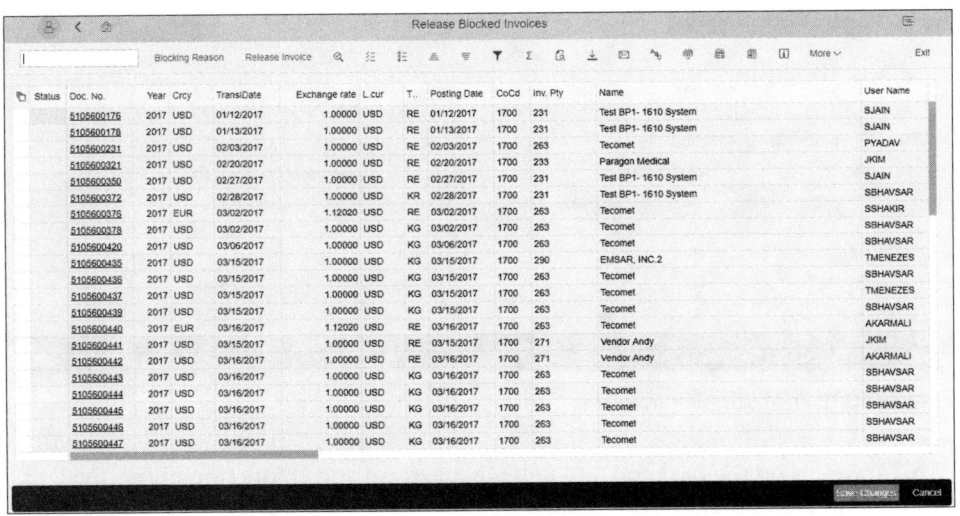

Figure 10.9 Release Blocked Invoices: Worklist Screen

Print Supplier Invoices

This native SAP Fiori app allows you to print outputs from Invoice Processing in real time (see Figure 10.10 and Figure 10.11). These outputs include complaint communications from invoice reduction and ERS documents.

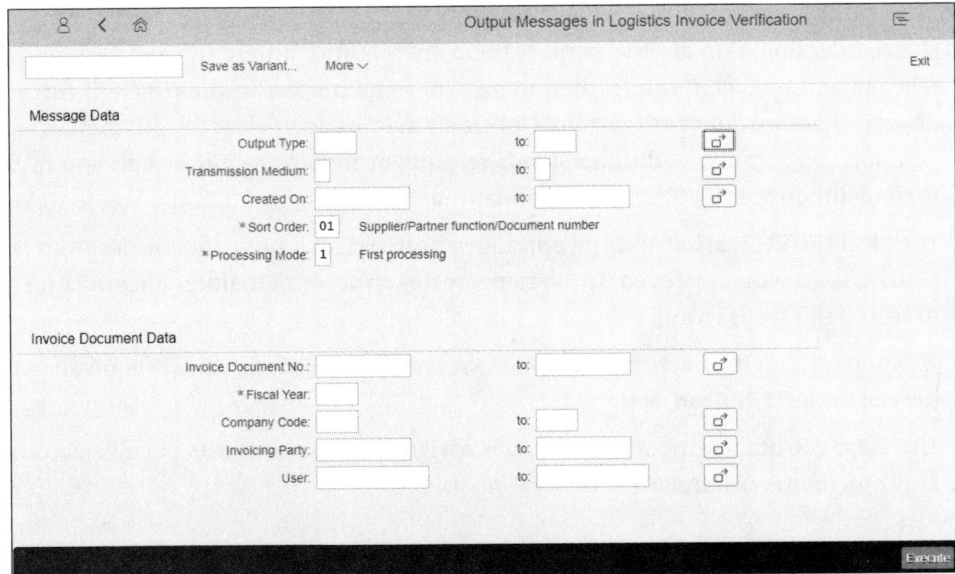

Figure 10.10 Print Supplier Invoices: Selection Screen

10   Invoice and Payables Management

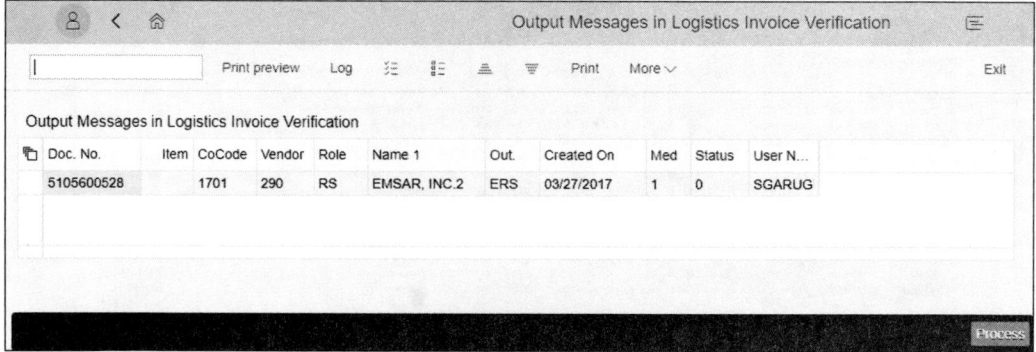

Figure 10.11 Print Supplier Invoices: Messages Worklist Screen

This app runs on the backend SAP S/4HANA system and is functionally equivalent to the classic SAP ERP Transaction MR90.

The Print Supplier Invoices app is assigned to the accounts payable accountant—procurement standard authorization role.

Clear GR/IR Clearing Account App

The goods receipt/invoice receipt (GR/IR) clearing account is a G/L account used for clearing quantities and amounts from goods receipts and supplier invoices. The GR/IR account is cleared if the delivered quantity and the invoiced quantity for a purchase order line item are the same. If there are quantity differences between goods receipts and invoice receipts, then items will remain open in the GR/IR. If further deliveries, return deliveries, invoices, or credit memos don't clear the differences and you don't expect any additional goods receipts or invoice receipts, then you must then maintain the GR/IR account manually (as seen in Figure 10.12 and Figure 10.13).

The Clear GR/IR Clearing Account app allows you to clear leftover quantities from the GR/IR G/L account as needed. The system creates an account maintenance document to record this transaction.

This app runs on the backend SAP S/4HANA system and is functionally equivalent to the classic SAP ERP Transaction MR11.

The Clear GR/IR Clearing Account app is assigned to the accounts payable accountant-procurement standard authorization role.

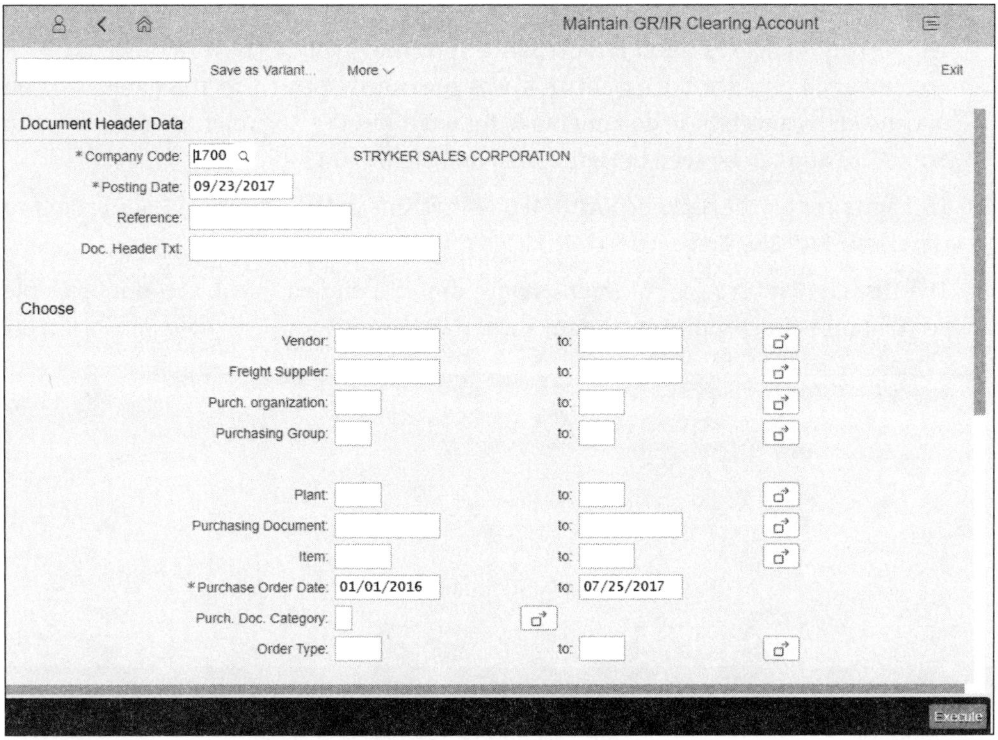

10.1 Invoice Processing

Figure 10.12 Clear GR/IR Clearing Account: Selection Screen

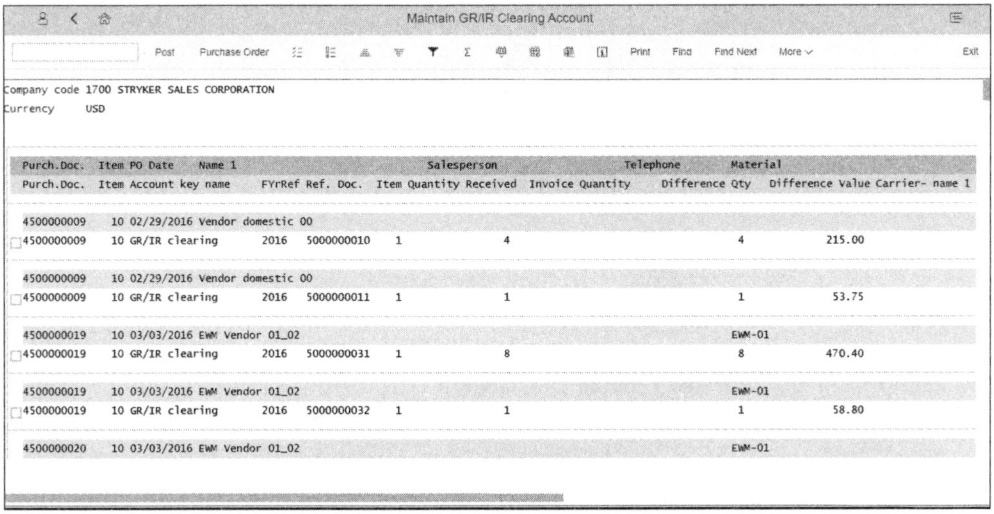

Figure 10.13 Clear GR/IR Clearing Account: Worklist Screen

385

10 Invoice and Payables Management

Display/Cancel Account Maintenance

The Display/Cancel Account Maintenance app allows you to show or cancel a GR/IR account maintenance document that was previously posted to the database. You may need to cancel these documents if, for example, the documents were posted in error. This app can be seen in Figure 10.14 and Figure 10.15.

This app runs on the backend SAP S/4HANA system and is functionally equivalent to the classic SAP ERP Transaction MR11SHOW.

The Display/Cancel Account Maintenance app is assigned to the accounts payable accountant—procurement standard authorization role.

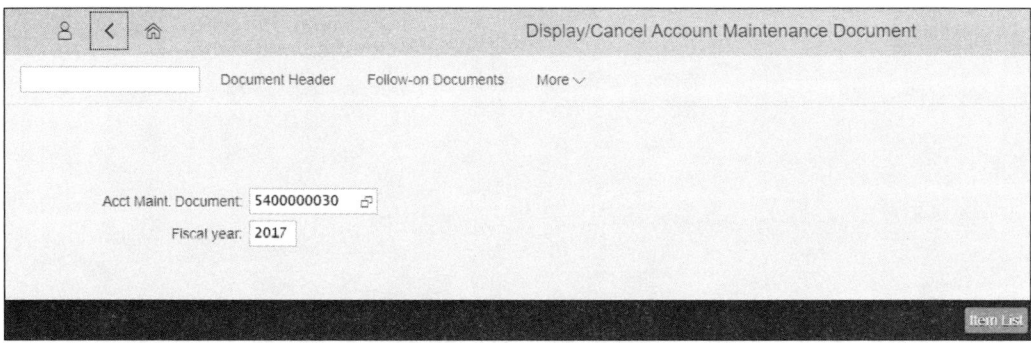

Figure 10.14 Display/Cancel Account Maintenance: Selection Screen

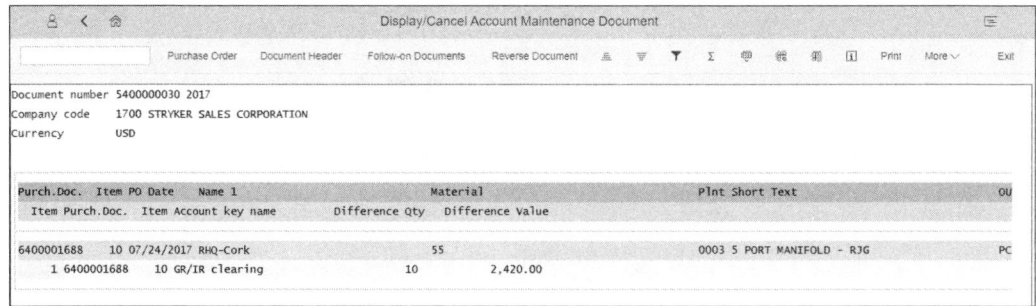

Figure 10.15 Display/Cancel Account Maintenance: Details Screen

Create Consignment and Pipeline Settlement

The Create Consignment and Pipeline Settlement app allows you to periodically settle consignment and pipeline liabilities that occur during normal business. This app can be seen in Figure 10.16 and Figure 10.17.

Because consignment and pipeline withdrawals are made in the system in Inventory Management, a supplier liability record is recorded in the system with a price that's valid at the date of withdrawal. This price isn't on record in the referenced purchase order; it's obtained from the consignment or pipeline PIR.

This settlement function will post an invoice document in the system automatically for any supplier consignment or pipeline liabilities that it finds based on the selection criteria entered into the SAP S/4HANA system.

This app runs on the backend SAP S/4HANA system and is functionally equivalent to the classic SAP ERP Transaction MRKO.

The Create Consignment and Pipeline Settlement app is assigned to the accounts payable accountant—procurement standard authorization role.

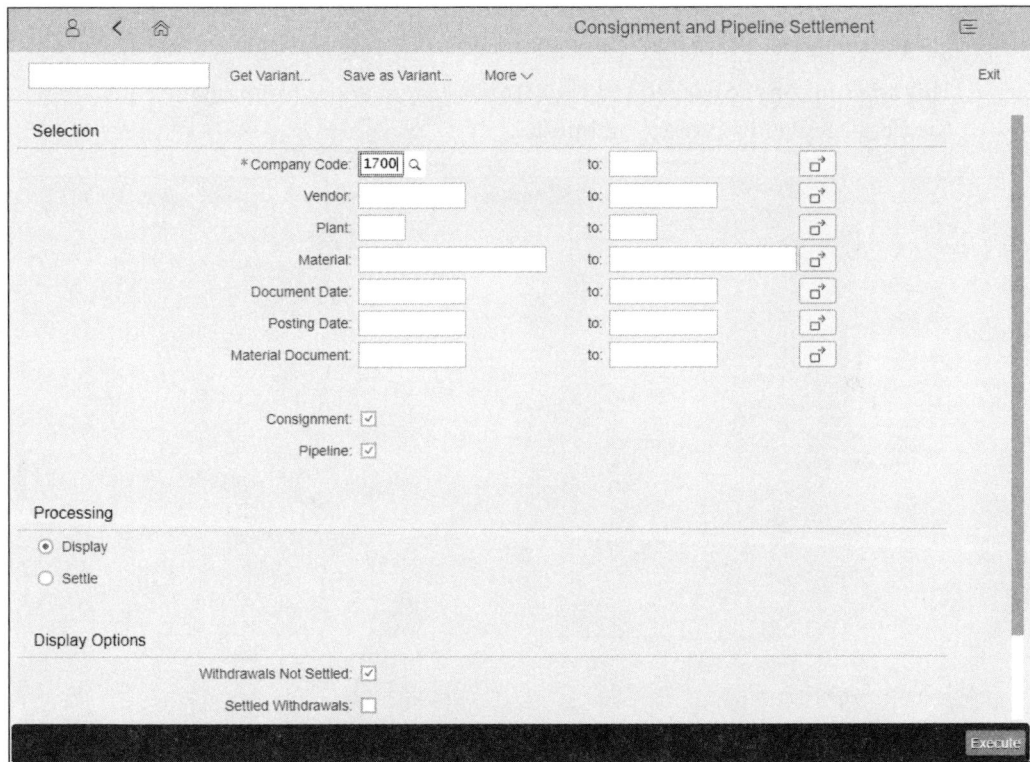

Figure 10.16 Create Consignment and Pipeline Settlement: Selection Screen

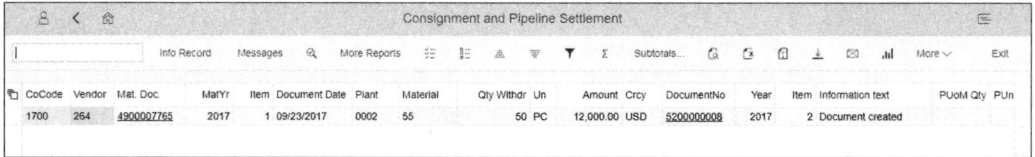

Figure 10.17 Display Create Consignment and Pipeline Settlement: Worklist Screen

Create Evaluated Receipt Settlement

The Create Evaluated Receipt Settlement app allows you to automatically create invoice documents for purchase order items that have been received from specified suppliers. The supplier doesn't send an invoice for its shipments; rather, you create invoices based on the goods receipt quantities and the purchase price found on the purchase order line items. You can generate a message to the supplier informing it of the invoices generated via this procedure. This app can be seen in Figure 10.18 and Figure 10.19.

This app runs on the backend SAP S/4HANA system and is functionally equivalent to the classic SAP ERP Transaction MRRL.

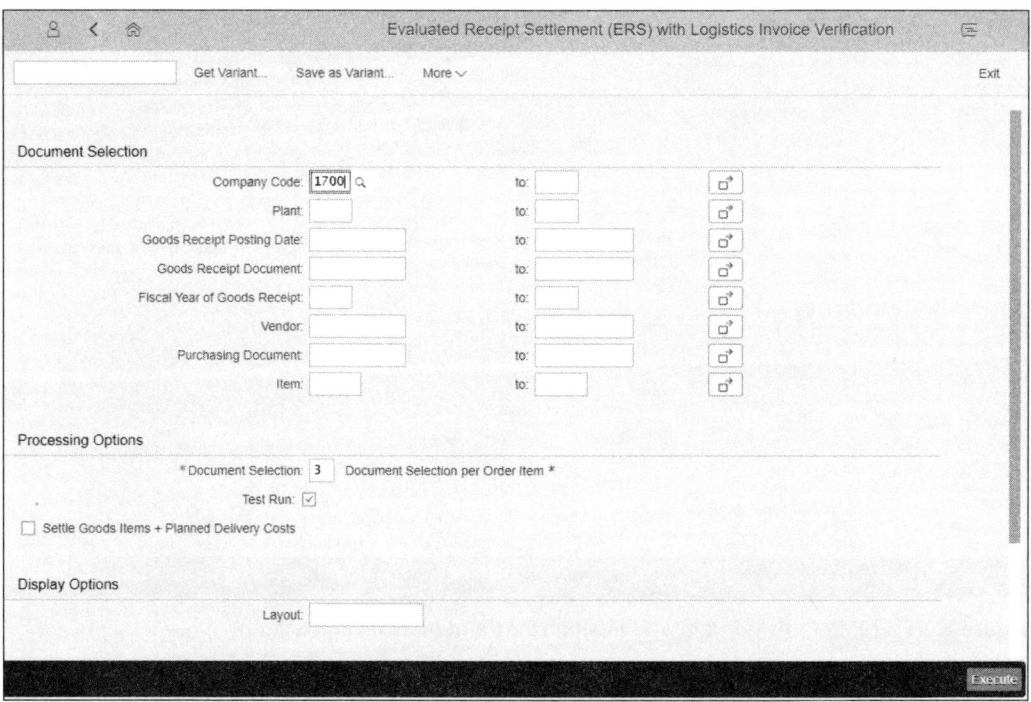

Figure 10.18 Create Evaluated Receipt Settlement: Selection Screen

10.1 Invoice Processing

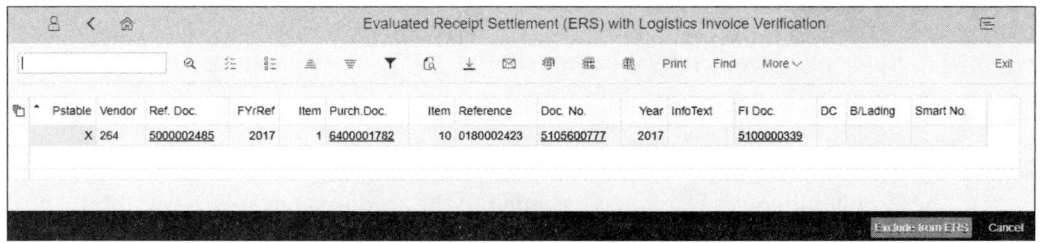

Figure 10.19 Create Evaluated Receipt Settlement: Worklist Screen

The Create Evaluated Receipt Settlement app is assigned to the accounts payable accountant—procurement standard authorization role.

10.1.8 Reporting in Invoice Processing

There are two tactical reporting apps delivered with SAP S/4HANA for use in Invoice Processing:

- Supplier Invoices List
- Display Supplier Invoice—Advanced

We'll discuss each app in the following sections.

Supplier Invoices List

The Supplier Invoices List app (Figure 10.20) allows you to search for supplier invoices and use the resulting search result as a worklist to display and process details for these invoices. This is very useful for day-to-day invoice management because you can, for example, display a list of blocked supplier invoices and release or reverse these documents easily.

Once you've selected a document, you can drill into that supplier invoice document to see all the details for that transaction. The system automatically knows if the invoice can be displayed via the native SAP Fiori app or if the Display Invoice Document—Advanced app is required. Certain complex invoices can't be rendered in the native SAP Fiori app. SAP S/4HANA automatically detects these documents and displays them in the appropriate app.

In the header section of the worklist, you can filter invoices in the list by entering filter values in the selection fields. You can also create your own variants or hide the filter bar if you wish.

389

You can also do the following:

- Sort supplier invoices by different criteria
- Hide or show columns in the worklist
- Navigate to the details for a specific supplier invoice

The Supplier Invoices List app is assigned to the accounts payable accountant—procurement and accounts payable accountant standard authorization roles.

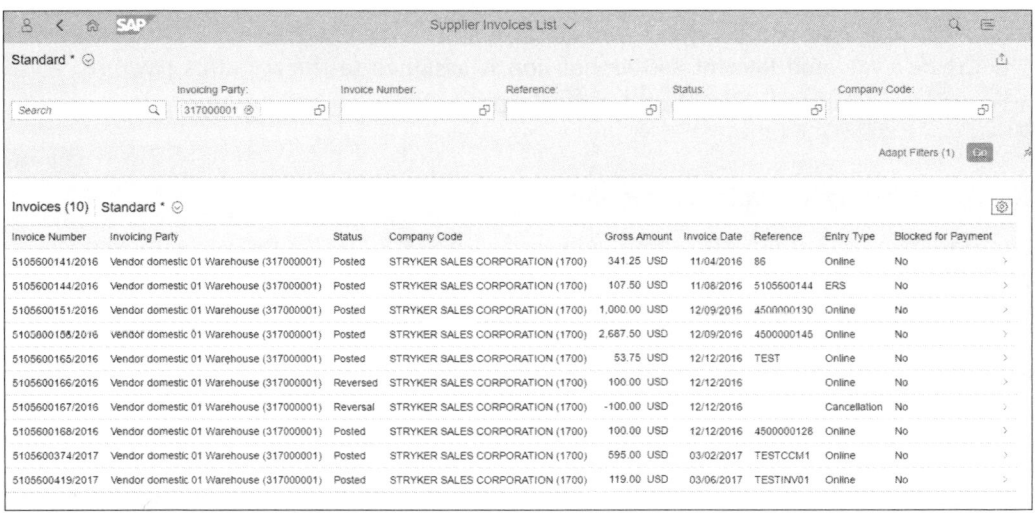

Figure 10.20 Supplier Invoices List

Display Supplier Invoice—Advanced

The Display Supplier Invoice—Advanced app shows all details available for a supplier invoice document in the system. This app is useful for viewing invoices that were created in both the Create Supplier Invoice and Create Supplier Invoice—Advanced apps, or through Supplier Collaboration via the Ariba Network (as seen in Figure 10.21 and Figure 10.22).

The Display Supplier Invoice—Advanced app runs directly on the backend SAP S/4HANA system and is functionally equivalent to the classic SAP ERP Transaction MIR4.

The Display Supplier Invoice—Advanced app is assigned to the accounts payable accountant—procurement standard authorization role.

10.1 Invoice Processing

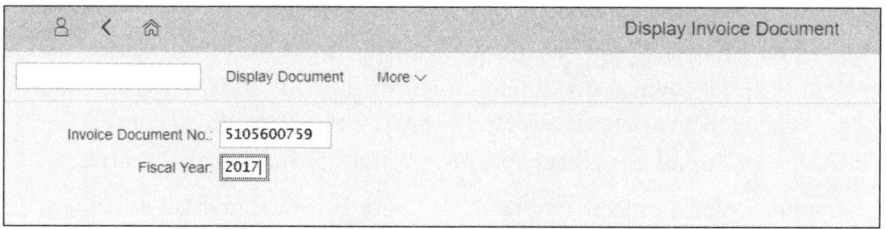

Figure 10.21 Display Supplier Invoice—Advanced: Selection Screen

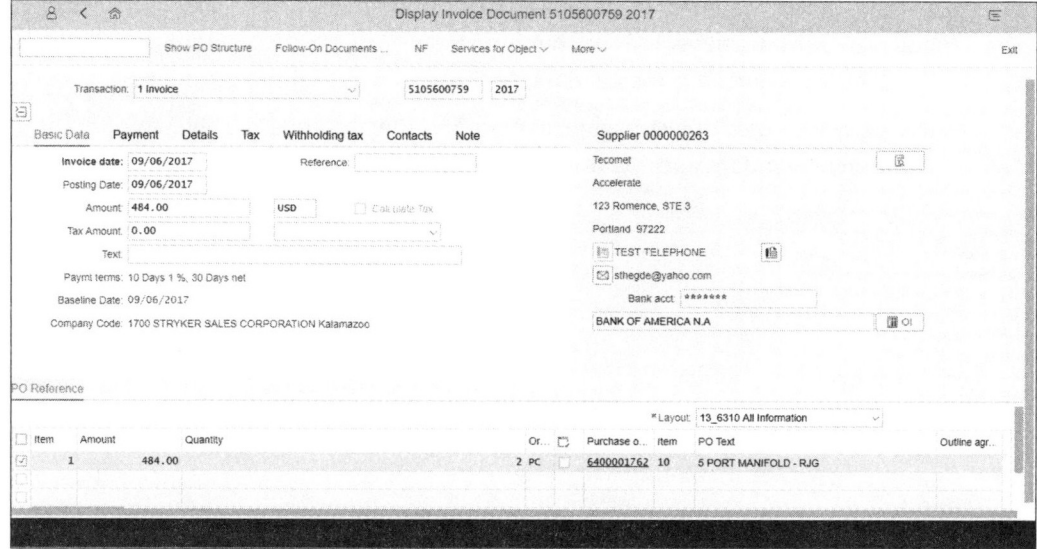

Figure 10.22 Display Supplier Invoice—Advanced: Details Screen

10.1.9 Object Pages

There are two object pages available in the Invoice Processing capability of the Invoice and Payables Management area:

- Supplier Invoice
- Supplier Accounting Document

Many of the transactional SAP Fiori apps allow you to click a supplier invoice document or a supplier accounting document to obtain details for these items.

391

Supplier Invoice Object Page

The Supplier Invoice object page (Figure 10.23) displays detailed information about an individual supplier invoice document stored in the SAP S/4HANA system. This object page is called in a variety of ways in the SAP Fiori system: from context-sensitive links in the List Supplier Invoices app, for example, or from Global Search.

Use the Supplier Invoice object page to obtain details for an invoice document of interest. You can also link to the Purchase Order object page from this app.

You can display an overview of the supplier invoice header data, such as the supplier and bank details, referenced purchasing documents, and key facts, such as gross invoice amount, fiscal year, and payment status. You can also obtain details about related business partners, master data, and related purchasing documents.

The Supplier Invoice object page is assigned to the accounts payable accountant—procurement standard authorization role.

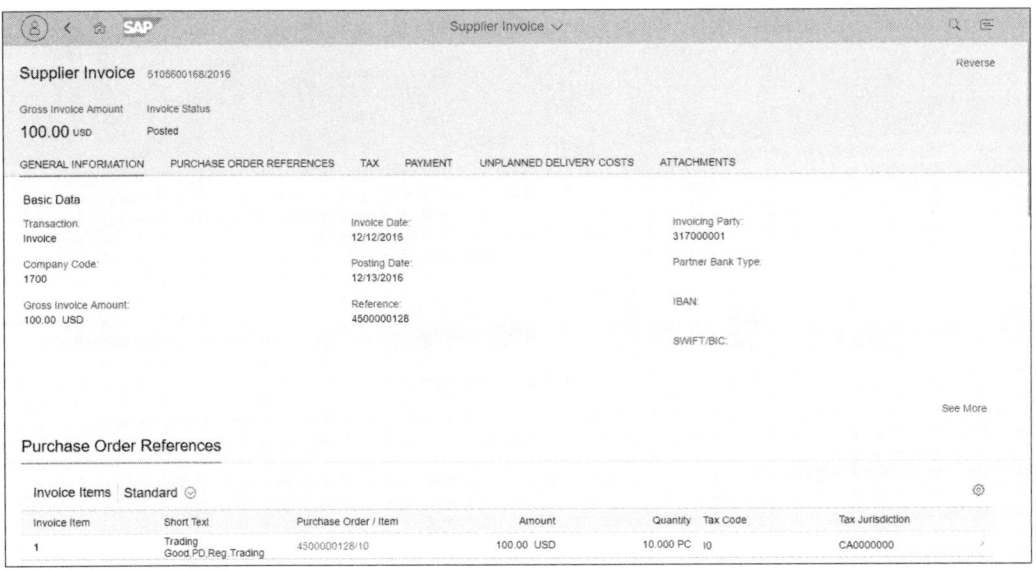

Figure 10.23 Supplier Invoice Object Page

Supplier Accounting Document Object Page

The Supplier Accounting Document object page displays information about supplier accounting documents. These documents are produced when accounting postings are made during supplier invoice document processing in SAP S/4HANA.

You can display an overview of the accounting document data, including the supplier, amount, document status, and document posting date. You also can navigate to its related business objects, such as purchase order, supplier, or journal entry.

The Supplier Accounting Document object page is assigned to the accounts payable accountant, accounts payable manager, warehouse clerk, and inventory manager standard authorization roles.

10.2 Accounts Payable

Accounts Payable is the second capability provided by the Invoicing and Payables functionality in Sourcing and Procurement.

Accounts payable departments handle invoice entry and payment processes so that an enterprise's suppliers are paid while optimizing cash flow. There is tight integration between the Invoice Processing and Payables Processing components of Sourcing and Procurement: one feeds the other.

There are three major areas of Accounts Payable that the SAP S/4HANA system supports:

1. Supplier Payment Processing
2. Supplier Account Management
3. Correspondence

10.2.1 Supplier Payment Processing

Supplier Payment Processing apps assist the accounts payable accountant in running the operational payables function and assure that payments are made to the suppliers at the optimal time.

The following native SAP Fiori apps for Supplier Payment Processing are available:

- Post Outgoing Payments
- Clear Outgoing Payments (Manual Clearing)
- Manage Payment Blocks
- Manage Automatic Payments
- Revise Payment Proposals
- Manage Supplier Down Payment Requests

- Create Single Payment
- Manage Payment Media
- Approve Bank Payments
- Monitor Batches and Payments

> **Note**
>
> The following WebGUI transactional apps for Supplier Payment Processing are also available:
>
> - Create Supplier Down Payment Requests (Transaction F-47)
> - Post Supplier Down Payments (Transaction F-48)
> - Schedule Automatic Payments (Transaction F110)
> - Post Supplier Outgoing Payments (Transaction F-58)

We'll discuss these apps in the following sections.

Post Outgoing Payments

The Post Outgoing Payments app (Figure 10.24) allows you to post and clear a single outgoing payment in one step. Normally, enterprises process outgoing payments automatically based on payment proposals. However, if you want to perform a payment to a supplier immediately, you need to enter the payment data manually. You can clear these outgoing payments with open supplier line items. You can also post an outgoing payment to a G/L account or on account.

The following features are available in the Post Outgoing Payments app:

- List open items that can be cleared with the outgoing payment.
- Add or change the discount to be applied to each invoice.
- Create residual items by entering a residual amount and assigning one or more reason codes and reference information about the business partner. You can define in configuration if a new item is to be posted to the business partner account or if the difference is to be cleared.
- Post an outgoing payment to a G/L account, if required with account assignment.
- Post an outgoing payment *on account*, which means to a customer or supplier account without reference to a specific item if clearing isn't possible.
- Search for open items of selected suppliers or of all suppliers via fuzzy logic.

- Create notes and affix attachments while posting the clearing document.
- Enter characteristics for profitability-related postings to assign profitability segments in CO-PA.
- Arrange open items using an invoice reference.
- Simulate the resulting journal entry.
- Clear the payment with the selected open items.

The Post Outgoing Payments app is assigned to the accounts payable accountant standard authorization role.

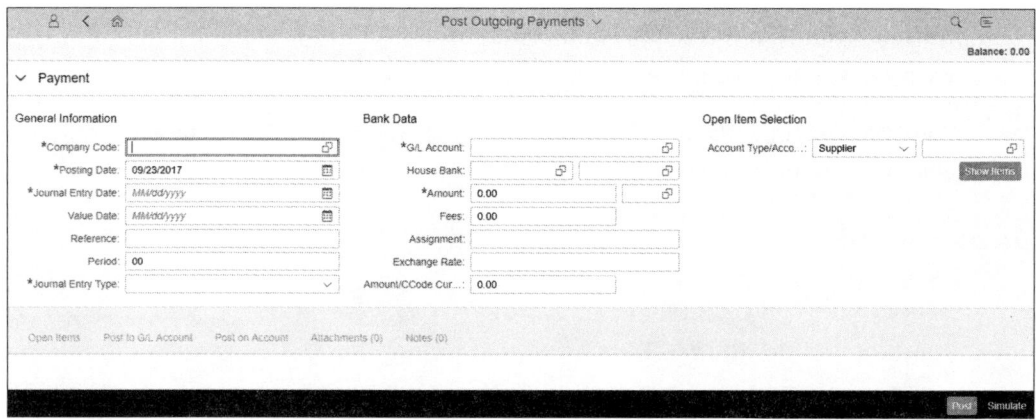

Figure 10.24 Post Outgoing Payments App

Clear Outgoing Payments (Manual Clearing)

Normally, the system will clear outgoing payments automatically. However, if you've paid your supplier manually without reference to an open item, you can use this app to find the matching items and clear the payment manually.

The Clear Outgoing Payments (Manual Clearing) app (Figure 10.25) can provide the following functions:

- View open outgoing payments in your area of responsibility in My Worklist.
- List open items to clear the open payments.
- Apply or change the discount to be applied to each invoice.
- Create residual items by entering a residual amount and assigning one or more reason codes and reference information about the business partner.
- Post an outgoing payment to a G/L account, if required with account assignment.

- Post an outgoing payment on account—that is, to a customer or supplier account without reference to a specific item—if clearing isn't possible.
- Search for open items of selected suppliers or of all suppliers via fuzzy logic.
- Enter characteristics for profitability-related postings to assign profitability segments in CO-PA.
- View the withholding tax posted for each open item.
- Create notes and attachments while posting the clearing document.
- Simulate the resulting journal entry.
- Clear the open payment with the selected open items that match the payment.
- Clear open items for a supplier account instead for a payment.
- Clear open items for down payments.

The Clear Outgoing Payments (Manual Clearing) app is assigned to the accounts payable accountant standard authorization role.

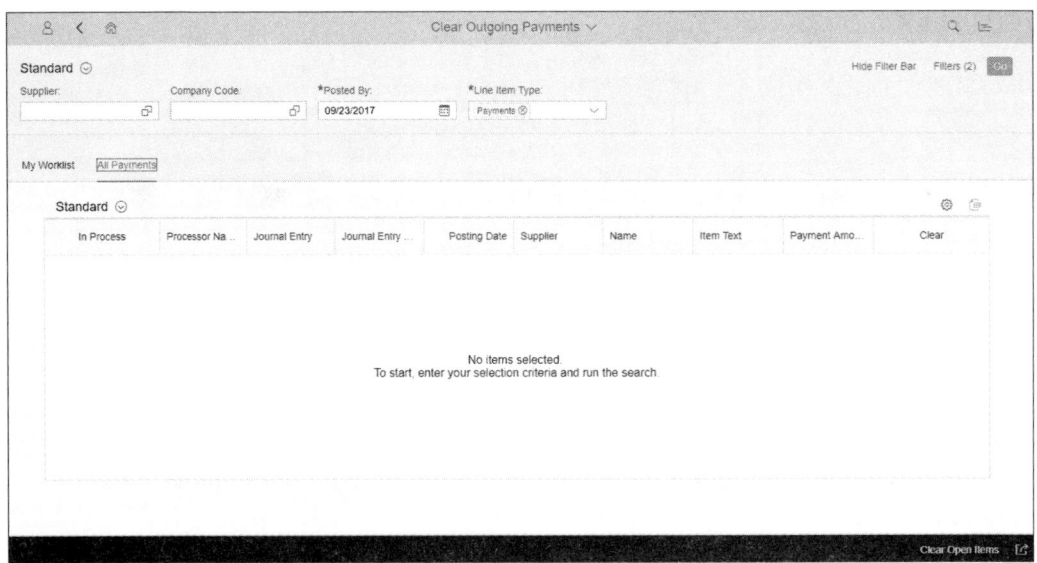

Figure 10.25 Clear Outgoing Payments (Manual Clearing) App

Manage Payment Blocks

Payment blocks on invoices or supplier accounts can be set or removed using the Manage Payment Blocks app (Figure 10.26). You can use the search and sort functions to select and display invoice documents that are blocked.

The Manage Payment Blocks app provides the following functions:

- Search for open invoices by supplier, purchase order, invoice number, or journal entry.
- Display supplier accounts and open invoices and view their blocking status.
- Display open invoices with payment details and related documents.
- View the status of invoices and supplier accounts.
- Select supplier accounts and invoices to block them for payment or unblock them.
- Enter payment block reasons and comments.

The Manage Payment Blocks app is assigned to the accounts payable accountant standard authorization role.

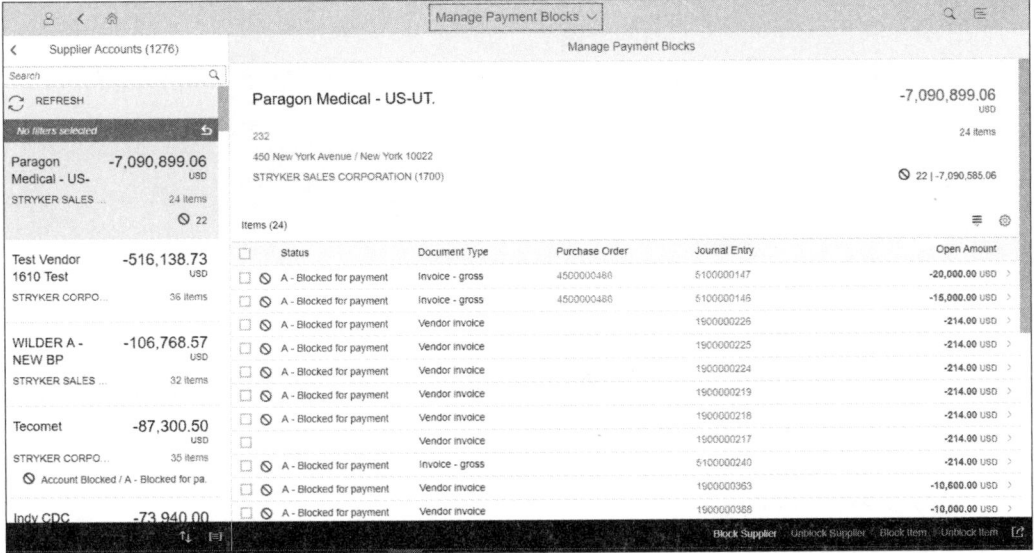

Figure 10.26 Manage Payment Blocks App

Manage Automatic Payments

The Manage Automatic Payments app (Figure 10.27) allows you to schedule payment proposals or payments. You then can obtain an overview of the status of the proposals or payments.

The Manage Automatic Payments app has the following features:

10 Invoice and Payables Management

- Schedule payment proposals or payments directly.
- Automatically create payment media after scheduling payment runs. You can find the created payment media in the Manage Payment Media app.
- Create payment advices.
- Search proposals and payments by identifier, run date, user ID, and company code.
- Check for completeness via the log.

The Manage Automatic Payments app is assigned to the accounts payable accountant standard authorization role.

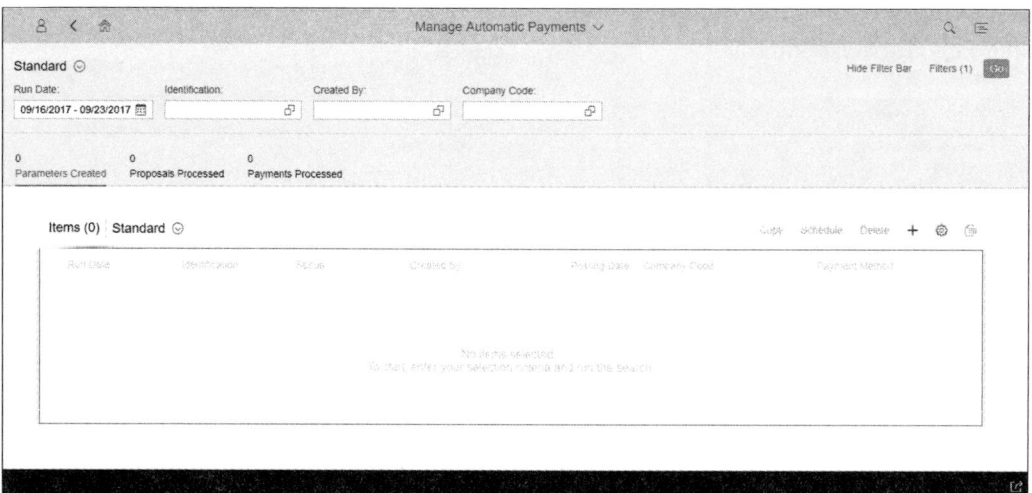

Figure 10.27 Manage Automatic Payments App

Revise Payment Proposals

The Revise Payment Proposals app (Figure 10.28) allows you to check and revise payment proposals and the details of open items. This assures that all supplier payments are made in a timely and accurate manner and that these payments remain compliant with company policies.

You can perform the following using the Revise Payment Proposals app:

- Display open payment proposals.
- Edit payment proposals to change payment methods, partner bank account, or other payment-related information if needed.

- Block and unblock items in payments and reallocate items among payments.
- Mass block items in payments.
- Calculate the total payment amount by payee, currency, and other criteria.
- Check the exceptions log.
- Navigate to the Manage Payment Proposals app.

> **Note**
>
> The key performance indicator on the **Revise Payment Proposals** tile displays only the number of outgoing payments; it doesn't include incoming payments that could be part of a payment proposal.
>
> The Revise Payment Proposals app is assigned to the accounts payable accountant standard authorization role.

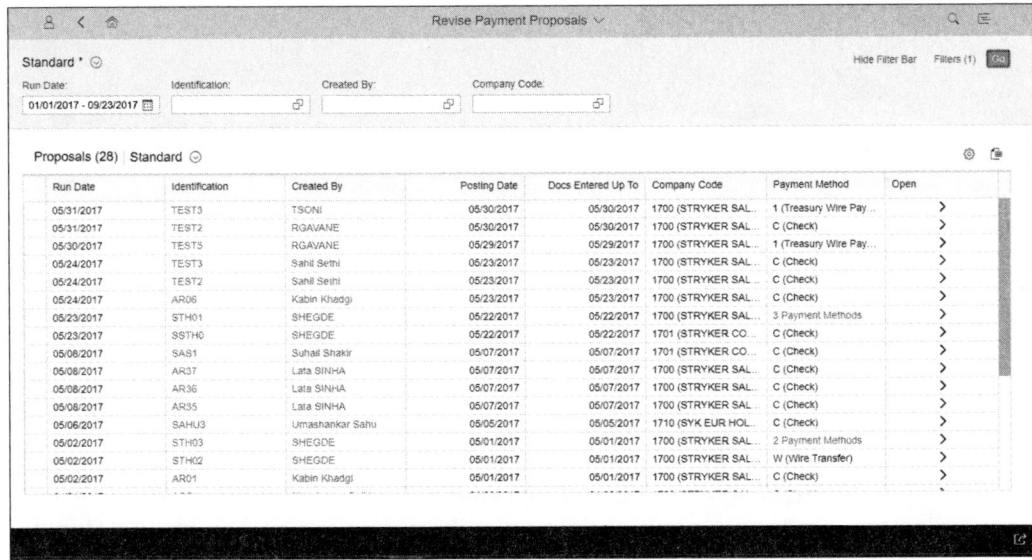

Figure 10.28 Revise Payment Proposals App

Manage Supplier Down Payment Requests

Ordinarily, down payment requests are generated in the SAP S/4HANA system based on information entered in the purchase order document. However, there are times when you may need to create a down payment request manually. Use the Manage Supplier Down Payment Requests app (Figure 10.29) in these cases to create down payment requests as needed. Once the payment run has made the down payment, the payment run also automatically clears the corresponding down payment request. In some cases, you may need to clear the down payment request manually.

The Manage Supplier Down Payment Requests app allows you to perform the following tasks:

- View existing down payment requests from suppliers.
- Change existing down payment requests.
- Create new down payment requests.
- Add notes and attachments to down payment requests.
- Export the table of existing down payment requests to a spreadsheet.

The Manage Automatic Payments app is assigned to the accounts payable accountant standard authorization role.

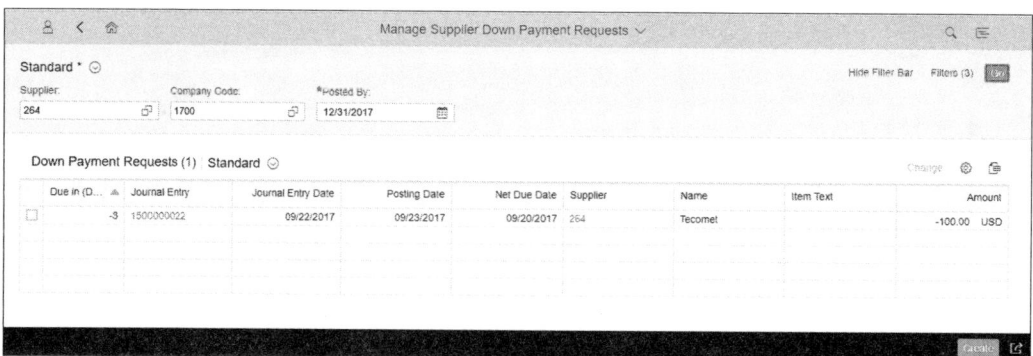

Figure 10.29 Manage Supplier Down Payment Requests App

Create Single Payment

The Create Single Payment app (Figure 10.30) lets you make direct payments to suppliers that have open supplier line items and haven't presented an invoice. Supplier and bank information and amounts to be paid are entered, and a payment is created. This payment posts as a down payment request. This document is used to trigger a payment run. The open items selected are cleared when the payment run completes.

This app allows you to perform the following tasks:

- Execute one-off payments in one step without an invoice.
- Trigger the payment process for specified open supplier line items.

- Add attachments to the payment.
- Get a log of the results when payment is made.

The Create Single Payment app is assigned to the accounts payable accountant standard authorization role.

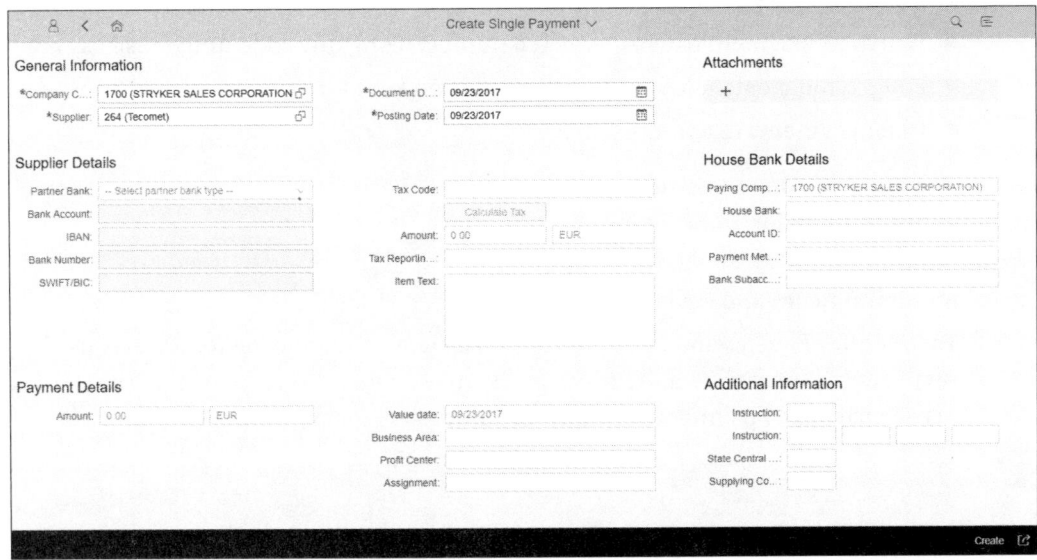

Figure 10.30 Create Single Payment App

Manage Payment Media

The Manage Payment Media app enables you to transfer data required for electronic payment transactions to banks via a data medium. A payment medium is created with each successful payment run.

The Manage Payment Media app allows you to perform the following tasks:

- View existing payment media along with their processing statuses.
- Download payment media.
- Delete payment media.
- Display and analyze payment summary information.

The Manage Payment Media app is assigned to the accounts payable accountant standard authorization role.

10 Invoice and Payables Management

Approve Bank Payments

The Approve Bank Payments app lets an accounts payable manager review and process payment batches. You can check the payments contained in the batch and approve, reject, or defer individual payments or entire batches if you wish.

This app lets you perform the following tasks:

- Search for payment batches by batch number, company code, and house bank.
- Edit payment batch due dates and instruction keys for payments.
- Defer payments to a future date.

The Approve Bank Payments app is assigned to the accounts payable manager standard authorization role.

Monitor Batches and Payments

The Monitor Batches and Payments app (see Figure 10.31 and Figure 10.32) is used to review details of batches and the payments they contain. You can observe the statues of each batch and payment in a batch at all stages of the payment process.

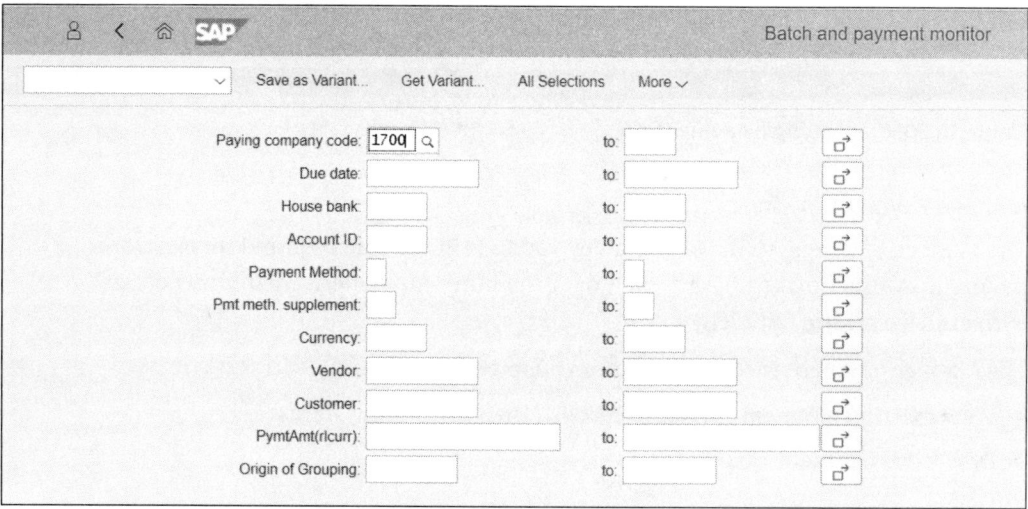

Figure 10.31 Manage Batches and Payments: Selection Screen

This monitoring app is useful for performing the following tasks:

- View the history of a payment batch.
- Edit payment batch due dates and instruction keys for payments.

- Review all payment batch approvers and their contact information.
- View the payment medium file details associated with the batch.

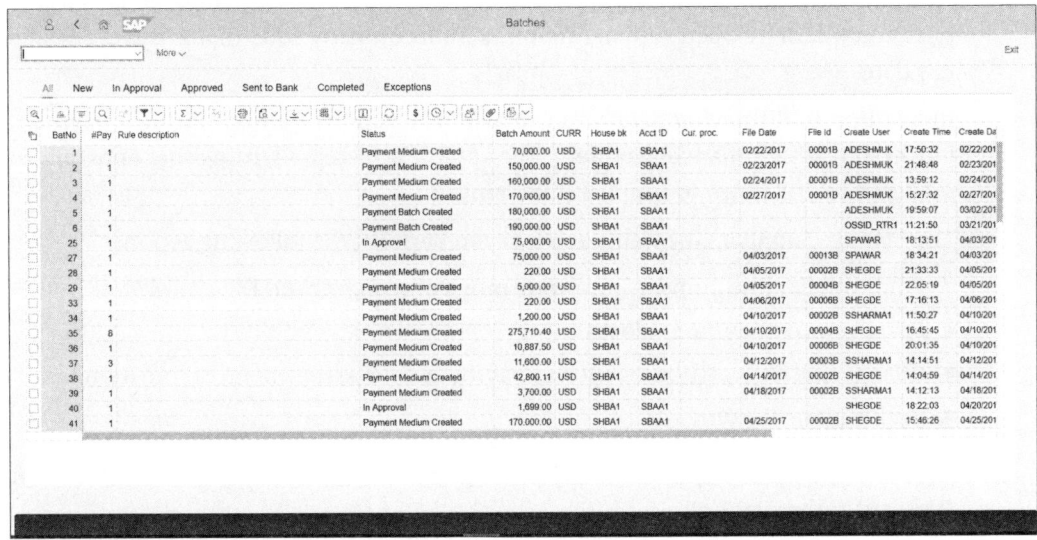

Figure 10.32 Manage Batches and Payment: Report Screen

The Monitor Batches and Payments app is assigned to the accounts payable accountant standard authorization role.

This app runs on the backend SAKP S/4HANA system, and is functionally equivalent to the classic SAP ERP Transaction BNK_MONI.

10.2.2 Supplier Account Management

The Accounts Payable department periodically needs to review supplier account data to assure that all transactions for those suppliers are correctly represented in the system and that payments are being made at the optimum time.

The following transactional apps support the accounts payable accountant in managing supplier accounts:

- Manage Supplier Line Items
- Display Supplier Balances

We'll discuss these apps in the following sections.

10   Invoice and Payables Management

Manage Supplier Line Items

The Manage Supplier Line Items app (Figure 10.33) is used to find supplier line items using a wide range of search criteria. For example, you can see all line items of a supplier account or all open supplier invoices for a company code that are overdue at a key date.

In addition to displaying data, you can also take actions such as setting a payment block or creating a manual payment. The app is also accessed from other apps, allowing users to drill down to supplier line items.

The Manage Supplier Line Items app lets you perform the following actions:

- Find supplier line items using a wide range of search criteria.
- Set or remove payment blocks.
- Change line item attributes such as payment data, assignment, or line item text.
- Create manual payments.

The Manage Supplier Line Items app is assigned to the accounts payable accountant standard authorization role.

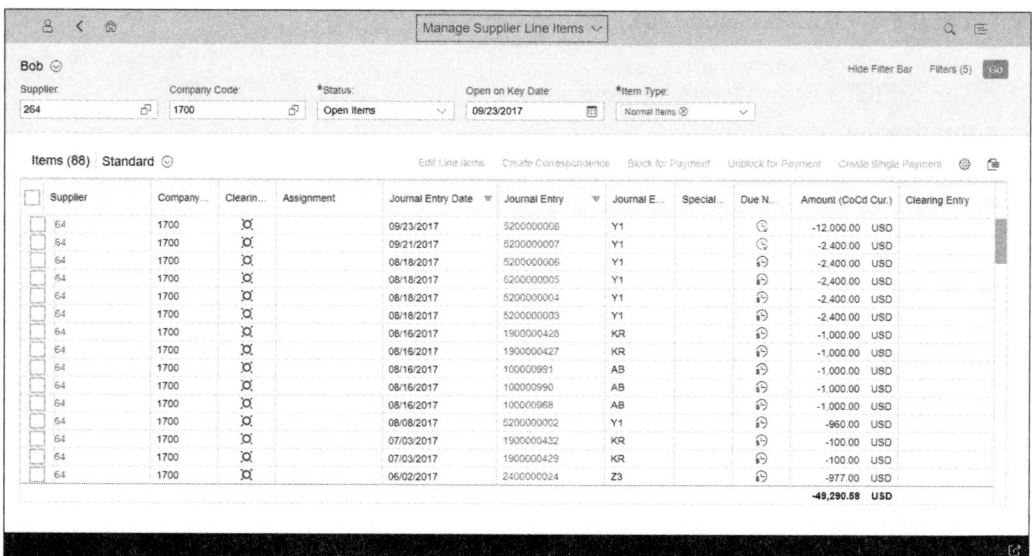

Figure 10.33 Manage Supplier Line Items App

Display Supplier Balances

The Display Supplier Balances app (Figure 10.34) can be used to view debits, credits, and balances on supplier accounts by company code, fiscal year, and supplier. The app allows you to further analyze amounts by drilling down to related line items. Furthermore, you can compare purchases between two fiscal years.

The Display Supplier Balances app is useful for the following:

- Displaying balances, debits, credits and imputed interest on supplier accounts.
- Searching for supplier balances by company code, fiscal year, and supplier.
- Comparing purchases from the current and the previous year.

The Display Supplier Balances app is assigned to the accounts payable accountant standard authorization role.

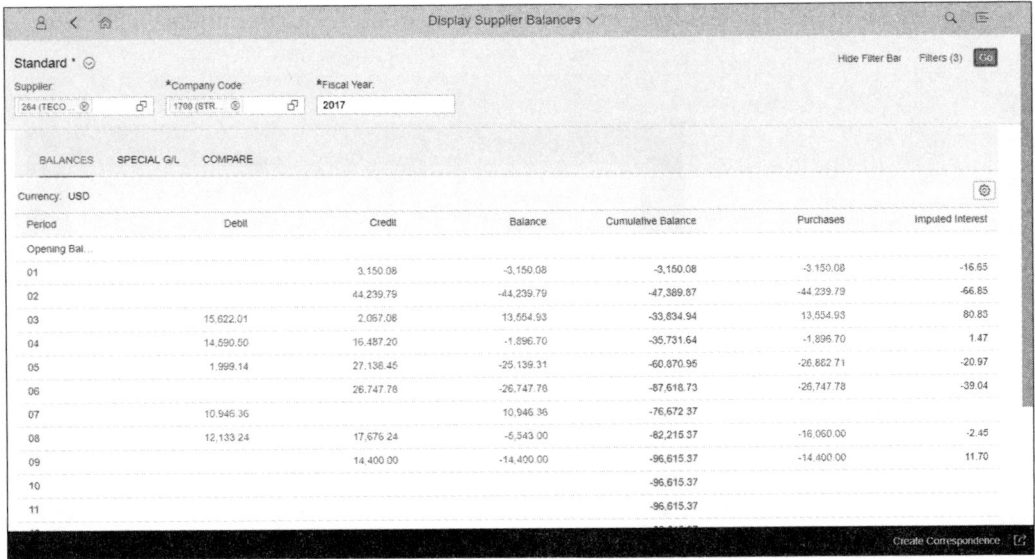

Figure 10.34 Display Supplier Balances App

10.2.3 Create Correspondence

Sometimes, you'll need the SAP S/4HANA system to issue a formal communication to a supplier. The Create Correspondence app (Figure 10.35) facilitates these types of requests. Correspondence can include issuing a supplier statement or a dunning notice for late delivery.

> **Note**
>
> In addition, there are multiple WebGUI apps available in SAP S/4HANA to produce correspondence as well. These apps include the following:
>
> - Create Balance Confirmations (for Suppliers): Transaction F.18/F18P
> - Create Periodic Account Statements: Transaction F.27
> - Create Dunning Notices: Transaction F150
> - Create Standard Letters (for Suppliers): Transaction F.66
> - Create Correspondence (for Internal Documents): Transaction F.62
> - Print Correspondence Requests: Transaction F.61
> - Delete Correspondence Requests: Transaction F.63

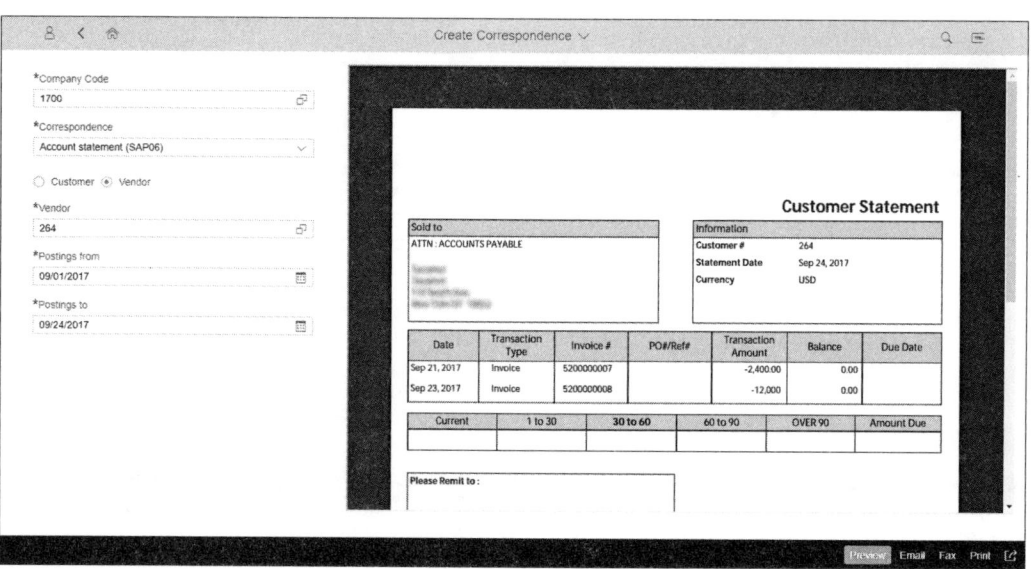

Figure 10.35 Create Correspondence App

The Create Correspondence app lets you manage many types of correspondence with your suppliers. You can review, email, print, fax, or download individual items. This is a standalone app, but it's also called from a number of other Accounts Payable apps, such as Display Supplier Balances.

The app lets you do the following:

- Create correspondence for a supplier.
- Preview the correspondence prior to transmission.
- Email, fax, print, or download correspondence in PDF format.

> **Note**
>
> This app is also used by accounts receivable personnel to create correspondence to customers.
>
> The data required for generating documents depends on whether they're intended for a customer or a supplier and on the type of correspondence being transmitted.

The Create Correspondence app is assigned to the accounts payable accountant standard authorization role.

10.3 Invoice Collaboration with the Ariba Network

There are multiple integrations between SAP S/4HANA and the Ariba Network for invoice and payment documents that come delivered with the SAP S/4HANA system. These integrations use the Output Management capabilities of SAP S/4HANA, which can format and send cXML messages.

The following Invoicing and Payables Management message types are natively integrated from SAP S/4HANA to the Ariba Network:

- **Supplier Invoice (Inbound from Supplier)**
  Invoices that are sent to SAP S/4HANA via the Ariba Network are shown as draft invoices in the Supplier Invoice List app and can be processed into complete invoice documents.

- **Invoice Status Update (Outbound to Supplier)**
  Once the invoice is balanced and posted to SAP S/4HANA, a message can be sent back to the supplier via the Ariba Network to provide notification that the invoice has been entered and is being processed by accounts payable.

- **Carbon Copy Invoice (Outbound to Supplier)**
  A copy of an invoice generated in the SAP S/4HANA system can be generated and sent to your supplier.

- **Payment Proposal (Outbound to Supplier)**
  Because payment proposals are created in accounts payable, these proposals can be communicated to your suppliers via the Ariba Network.
- **Payment Proposal Update (Inbound from Supplier)**
  Payment proposals can be modified by the supplier and returned to the customer. You can receive these changes from your suppliers via the Ariba Network.
- **Payment Remittance Advice (Outbound to Supplier)**
  A payment advice can be generated from the accounts payable payment run and sent via the Ariba Network to the supplier. This notifies the supplier that a payment has been made.
- **Cancel Payment Remittance Advice (Outbound to Supplier)**
  If the payment is subsequently cancelled, the supplier can be notified of that cancellation via a payment advice cancellation document. This can be automatically generated and sent via the Ariba Network to the supplier. This notifies the supplier that the cancellation has been made.

10.4 Summary

You've learned that SAP S/4HANA provides a complete solution for managing the entry of invoice data into the SAP S/4HANA system. Once these invoices are entered and verified in the system, control passes to accounts payable for supplier payment. There are many reporting apps that allow accounts payable personnel to monitor the invoicing and payment process from end to end.

Chapter 11
Supplier Management

Managing suppliers and the relationships between suppliers and the buying organization is at the heart of procurement. Some organizations strive to have tight relationships with their strategic suppliers, coinnovating and building new products and markets in tandem with their core supply base.

This type of strategy is deployed in a variety of scenarios, even in counterintuitive ones like fast food. McDonalds is widely cited as having deep relationships with its suppliers and working on products jointly with these suppliers to obtain a signature flavor or product.

Others look at purchasing as a commodity-acquisition activity and seek to obtain the lowest prices and best quality; they choose the supplier who currently can provide this, switching whenever necessary to the lowest price. This type of approach works well in procurement situations with low switching costs and commodity-type materials and services.

Whatever the approach, supplier management is a must for a procurement organization if it's to contribute to the success of a company in the long term. Buying from the wrong supplier can have disastrous consequences for the buyer. Not managing the supply base to obtain competitive pricing based on your volumes and negotiating can mean success or failure in the marketplace.

Supplier Management and Evaluation functionality in SAP S/4HANA has been augmented with additional, subjective criteria and survey capabilities that were previously the domain of SAP Supplier Relationship Management (SAP SRM). This chapter will detail supplier management from qualification to classification/segmentation to onboarding to evaluation, highlighting new functionality and nuances in SAP S/4HANA.

11 Supplier Management

11.1 Supplier Discovery, Qualification, and Onboarding

Supplier discovery, qualification, and onboarding are not in scope for SAP S/4HANA Sourcing and Procurement and SAP S/4HANA in general. These areas are best handled using the SAP Ariba Discovery and SAP Ariba Supplier Lifecycle and Performance cloud solutions from SAP Ariba. Alternatively, you can also implement SAP Supplier Lifecycle Management if you require an on-premise version of this capability. The following is a high-level overview of each solutions' capabilities.

11.1.1 SAP Ariba Discovery and SAP Ariba Supplier Lifecycle and Performance

SAP Ariba Discovery allows you to create a posting for your desired item or service, post it to the Ariba Network, have suppliers submit proposals, review the proposals, and select the best one. You can also post more generic requests to identify category suppliers or search from 1.5 million suppliers in 233 countries covering over 20,000 commodity codes (material groups) on the Ariba Network worldwide. Once you've selected a supplier, you can enter it into SAP S/4HANA directly and begin transacting, or further qualify it and have the supplier maintain its own record using SAP Ariba Supplier Lifecycle and Performance.

SAP Ariba Supplier Lifecycle and Performance provides the following capabilities:

- Vendor data model with two-way sync between the solution and SAP S/4HANA
- Registration and onboarding with supplier portal
- Supplier-managed information
- Supplier 360-degree view
- Reports and analysis
- Supplier performance management (scorecards, questionnaires, KPIs)
- Reports and analysis (based on category, location, and business unit)
- Supplier segmentation, qualification, and development
- Supplier lifecycle and performance management
- Risk assessments and due diligence intelligence
- Risk-exposure monitoring (reputational, compliance, financial, sustainability, and operational risks)
- Engagement-level inherent risk and residual risk calculation to drive actions for sourcing and contracts
- Risk mitigation (flexible workflows for procurement and risk management teams)

11.1.2 SAP Supplier Lifecycle Management

Customers occasionally can't leverage a cloud solution due to control sensitivities in their supply base or a need to customize the system beyond a multitenant, public cloud solution's abilities to accommodate. SAP Supplier Lifecycle Management is an on-premise solution that integrates with SAP S/4HANA and provides the following capabilities:

- **Onboarding and registration**
  SAP Supplier Lifecycle Management provides automated workflows and supplier self-services for registration and maintenance of supplier records.
- **Qualification**
  Including questionnaires, reusable libraries, and weighted scoring.
- **Classification and segmentation**
  Creates a searchable, collaborative classification system for suppliers.
- **Portfolio management of suppliers**
  Provides industry reports and promotion processes.
- **Performance management**
  KPI-driven analysis capabilities.

If your organization requires qualification capabilities, onboarding, and/or supplier-driven maintenance of supplier records, it may be preferable to leverage the aforementioned functionalities in SAP Ariba Supplier Lifecycle and Performance, foregoing the duplication of these in SAP S/4HANA. This means having SAP Ariba Supplier Lifecycle and Performance drive the supplier qualification, onboarding, and evaluation processes, with SAP S/4HANA receiving the updated supplier record outputs from this process. Similarly, if you elect to implement SAP Supplier Lifecycle Management as part of your SAP S/4HANA landscape, you can focus the supplier registration, qualification, evaluation, and classification in this system rather than mixing supplier-management processes in SAP Supplier Lifecycle Management and SAP S/4HANA.

11.2 Supplier Management

SAP S/4HANA Sourcing and Procurement separates Supplier Management into two distinct areas: Classification and Segmentation, and Supplier Evaluation, as shown in Figure 11.1. First, a user can leverage capabilities to classify suppliers and create segments or groups of similar suppliers. Once the suppliers have been organized in this manner from an analysis standpoint, the user can begin conducting objective and subjective exercises to determine the optimal suppliers and supplier mixes to support the organizational procurement objectives.

11 Supplier Management

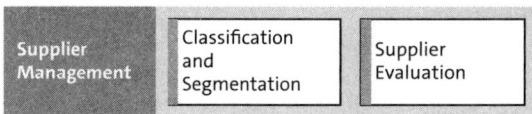

Figure 11.1 SAP S/4HANA Sourcing and Procurement: Supplier Management

The most comprehensive solution for supplier management should include a network approach to facilitate supplier self-services and collaboration. The next section will cover supplier management with the Ariba Network.

11.2.1 Supplier Management with the Ariba Network

SAP S/4HANA doesn't have functionality or plans to replace the supplier-side approaches supported in the Ariba Network and SAP Ariba Supplier Lifecycle and Performance's supplier management and onboarding solutions. It makes sense to onboard a supplier via a network, as the suppliers don't need to register repeatedly at their customers' individual supplier portals and maintain their commercial details for conducting business. Having a network at the size and feature depth of the Ariba Network, via which over a trillion dollars in transactions take place annually between millions of suppliers and customers, means that a supplier can register on the Ariba Network, maintain its information in a centralized location, and have this information curated and up-to-date for a majority of its customers in one area. This includes customers running SAP S/4HANA as their digital core, as SAP S/4HANA comes with prebuilt linkages and a roadmap for further deepening of these integration points in future releases.

In short, SAP S/4HANA Sourcing and Procurement doesn't plan to encompass self-registration or self-service data maintenance by suppliers directly, but focuses only on supplier classification and supplier evaluation. These supplier onboarding activities are instead conducted directly by the buyer in SAP S/4HANA, who registers the supplier internally and updates the data on the supplier record or via an integration with the Ariba Network to allow for supplier self-service.

11.2.2 Buyer-Side Processes in SAP S/4HANA

Although sell-side processes for supplier self-registration and supplier self-maintenance are not currently available in SAP S/4HANA and not planned, on the buyer side, SAP S/4HANA supports the following:

- Supplier Data Creation and Maintenance
- Supplier Hierarchies
- Supplier Classification
- Supplier Evaluation
- Supplier Risk with Dun & Bradstreet
- Supplier Qualification via Activity Management
- Certificate Management via Attachments
- Activity Management
- Category Management and Purchasing Categories

On the buyer side, therefore, SAP S/4HANA supports qualification, portfolio management, visibility, and performance management for the customer's supply base.

The basic steps in the supplier lifecycle are registration and onboarding, classification and segmentation, analysis, and supplier-performance management. The next section reviews the segmentations and classification approaches in SAP S/4HANA for supplier management.

11.2.3 Classification and Segmentation

SAP S/4HANA Sourcing and Procurement has new functionality and a new focus for Classification and Segmentation. With Classification and Segmentation, the procurement organization groups similar expenditure items into purchasing categories of spend. Apply further analysis and reporting, and an organization can begin to see which categories of spend are strategic to the organization, where the most money is being spent by category, and possible areas for expansion and consolidation of spend. Once this insight is gleaned from Classification and Segmentation, suppliers can be evaluated based on their performance and the types of materials and services they provide.

Suppliers are managed in SAP S/4HANA using attributes in their master data, as well as continuous activity and task management based on their objective and subjective performance metrics. Activity and task management are new concepts and features in SAP S/4HANA Sourcing and Procurement, as is the integration with Dunn & Bradstreet for data. Unlike previous versions of SAP ERP, SAP S/4HANA supports additional functionality for supplier management, including the ability to classify suppliers and conduct analysis in the system using Dunn & Bradstreet data overlays. These additional features provide an integrated overview that's leveraged directly in procurement transactions in real-time, enabling a user to move from insight to action seamlessly in SAP S/4HANA.

11.2.4 Supplier Segmentation and Classification Apps

The main apps in SAP S/4HANA Sourcing and Procurement for the segmentation and classification area include the following (these apps can be found in the SAP Fiori App Library under *https://fioriappslibrary.hana.ondemand.com/sap/fix/externalViewer/#*):

- **Manage Purchasing Category**
  Create/maintain/view purchasing categories
- **Translate Purchasing Category**
  Maintain a translation for a purchasing category in another language
- **Manage Activities**
  Review purchasing activities touching suppliers in the system
- **Monitor Tasks**
  Monitor purchasing activities and tasks assigned in the system
- **Process Tasks**
  View worklist of tasks assigned to you and display or edit the tasks

Previous versions of SAP ERP and the segmentation and classification area for supplier evaluation focused on classifications existing in the systems. Material groups were used to create categories for classification of the type of supplier. Using this classification, you could then use objective criteria available in the system from transactions and subjective criteria from creating surveys system riding sidecar to the ERP instance, such as SAP SRM. This has changed in SAP S/4HANA; now, both survey and objective data converge in the core ERP, as do the analytics and reporting themselves. The next section focuses on a new concept in SAP S/4HANA: *purchasing categories*.

Purchasing Categories

SAP S/4HANA leverages a purchasing category approach for segmentation and classification that extends beyond a single material group to capture all of the spend and suppliers in a particular area of the business for procurement-centric analysis. Accessed via the aforementioned Manage Purchasing Category app, a *purchasing category* can be used group to several material groups into one purchasing category, essentially providing a meta-layer capability to allow purchasing departments to connect otherwise unrelated and related material groups into a larger set for the classification and segmentation of suppliers. This is also a key feature for purchasing departments to classify and segment materials as you can use an aggregate, business-centric view without having to rely on UNSPSC roll-ups or other approaches.

11.2 Supplier Management

Once the suppliers have been logically grouped into purchasing categories, buying departments can organize work around these categories and drive efficiencies in key areas of the organization's activities and business. With the addition of certification data in attachments, as shown in Figure 11.2, qualified suppliers can be grouped by their certifications, purchasing category, and evaluations/feedback on performance.

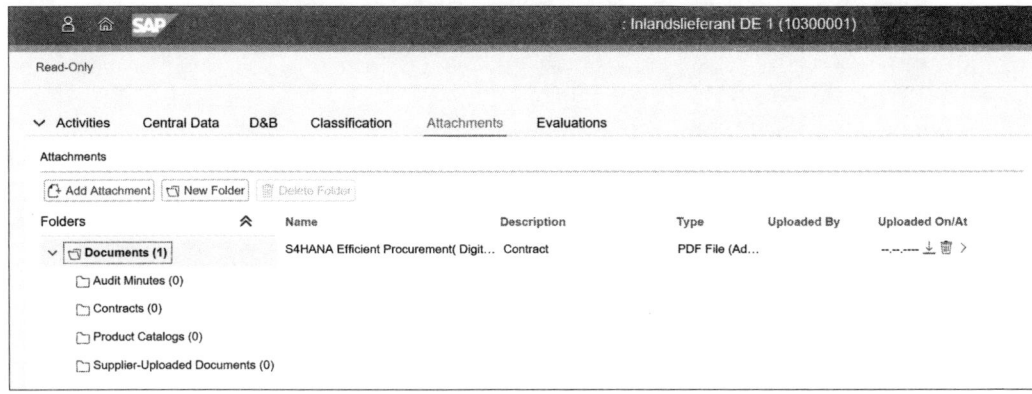

Figure 11.2 Attachments Tab in S/4HANA Supplier Record

Both the buying departments and supplier groups are flexible in the system, allowing for dynamic adjustments. SAP S/4HANA Sourcing and Procurement isn't a pure transactional system from this standpoint, but a system capable of providing in-system overviews and analytics to aid in the purchasing process. To create, manage, and translate purchasing categories in SAP S/4HANA, you simply click the corresponding app's tile (see Figure 11.3). Once created, a purchasing category can be further managed and translated.

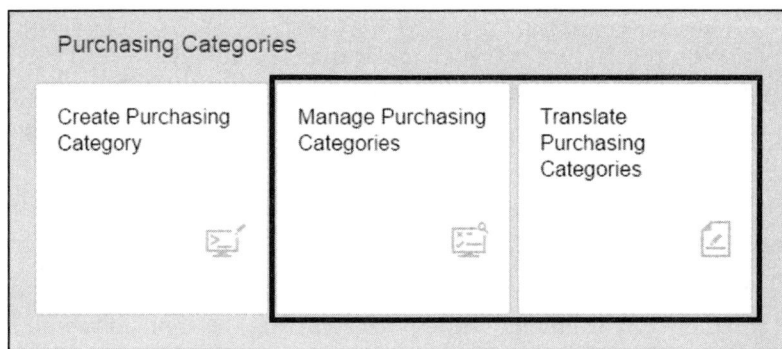

Figure 11.3 Purchasing Category Apps

11 Supplier Management

To create a purchasing category, open the Purchasing Category SAP Fiori app, as shown in Figure 11.4, and enter both the applicable material groups and suppliers, as well as applicable activities.

Figure 11.4 Creating Purchasing Category

One-to-many suppliers, activities, and material groups can be assigned to one purchasing category, further enabling aggregated purchasing spend analytics and efficient commodity management.

> **Note**
>
> Although many material groups can be assigned to one purchasing group, a material group can only be assigned to one purchasing group.

The data entered in the purchasing category updates at the supplier-record level, facilitating analysis as in Figure 11.5. Here, users can review classification data, scorecards, spend and revenue information, and risk, further informing their transaction decisions and strategies.

In the **Central Data** tab of a supplier record, the buyer can review the assigned purchasing categories this supplier, as in Figure 11.6.

Access to supplier records typically is limited to maintain the quality of the master data in the SAP S/4HANA environment. The app for accessing the supplier record is the Manage Supplier Data app, and this app is typically assigned to the supplier master data manager/owner, rather than to the extended buyer population.

11.2 Supplier Management

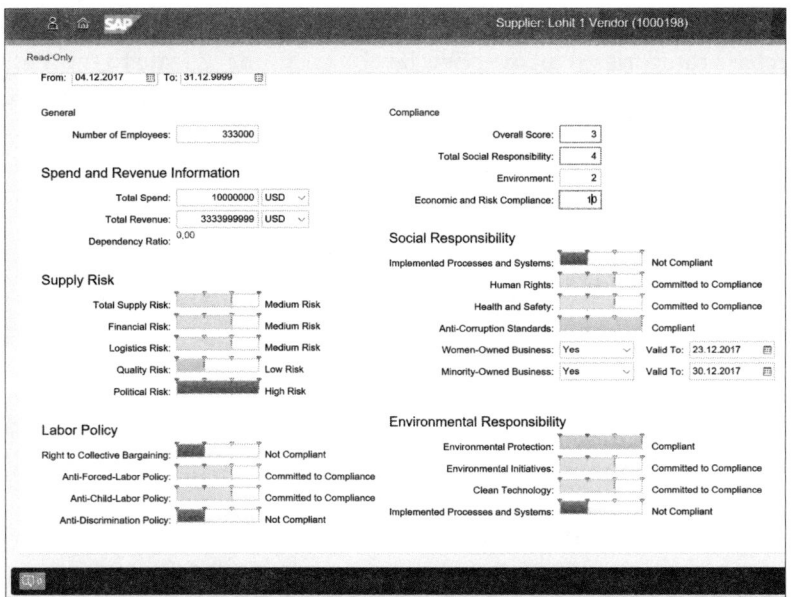

Figure 11.5 Supplier Record with Analysis and Classification Data

Figure 11.6 Central Data Tab: Supplier

11   Supplier Management

Managing a Purchasing Category

To manage purchase categories at an overview level, a user can navigate to the Manage Purchase Categories app and search or filter on specific purchasing categories, as in Figure 11.7.

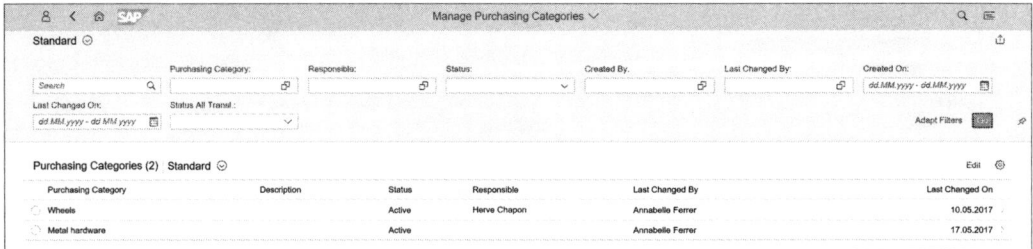

Figure 11.7 Manage Purchasing Categories App

Translating a Purchasing Category

If you're running a global system with global procurement operations, you may also be managing the purchasing categories at an international level, requiring translations for the various supported system languages and regions. In the Translate Purchasing Categories app, a user can review purchasing categories that have been translated into other languages, as well as the status of in-process translations, as shown in Figure 11.8.

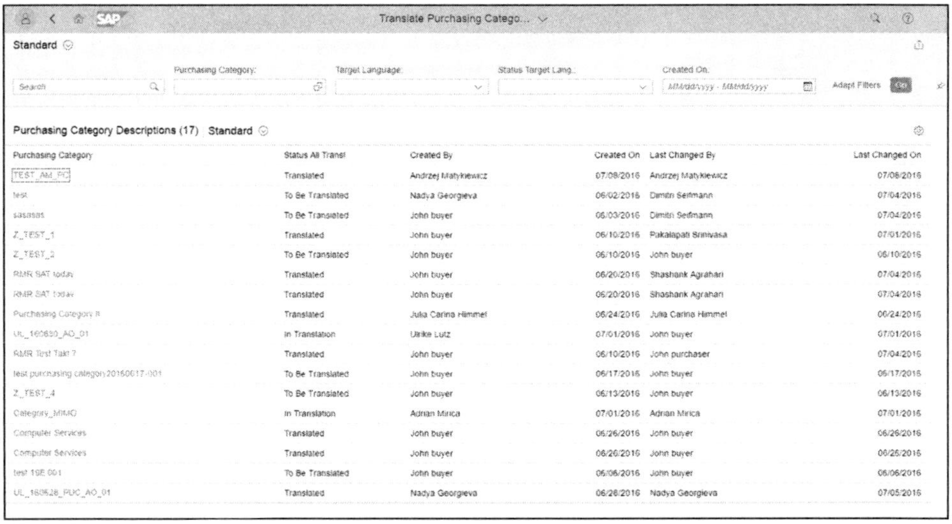

Figure 11.8 Translate Purchasing Categories App

11.2 Supplier Management

Supplier Activities and Tasks

Suppliers can be assigned activities and tasks assigned to these activities in SAP S/4HANA Sourcing and Procurement. To make an assignment, open the Manage Activities app from the **Purchasing Activities** section in SAP S/4HANA (see Figure 11.9).

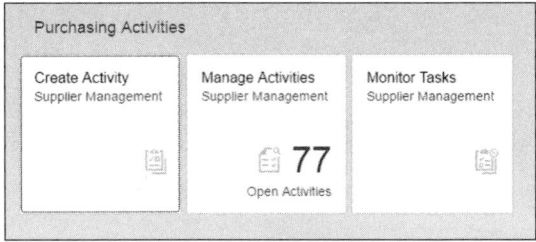

Figure 11.9 Purchasing Activities

You create purchasing activities in this app by selecting **Create** and filling out the fields for **Description**, **Status**, and who is **Responsible** for this activity. Purchasing activities and tasks are created using Web Dynpro transactions in SAP S/4HANA. Once an activity's been created, you can search for and manage activities in the SAP Fiori-based Manage Activities app (see Figure 11.10).

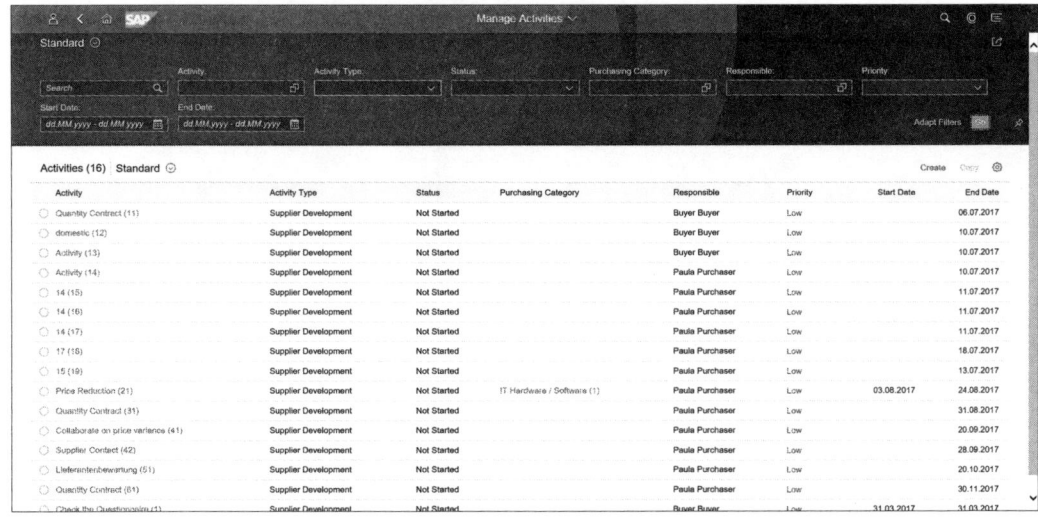

Figure 11.10 Manage Activities App

Once a task has been created, it too can be monitored in the Monitor Tasks app (see Figure 11.11). You can assign an internal employee to a task, for example, and then

11 Supplier Management

navigate to the task in the monitor and drill into it by clicking it, which then sends you to the Web Dynpro transaction.

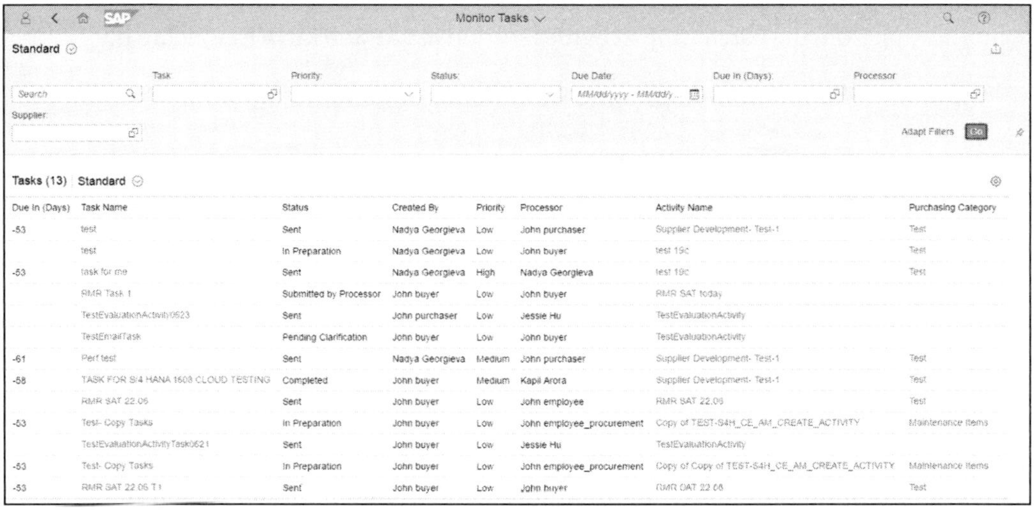

Figure 11.11 Monitor Tasks App

If you're assigned a task in a purchasing activity, you can process the task by going to the Process Tasks app and selecting the task you wish to process, as shown in Figure 11.12.

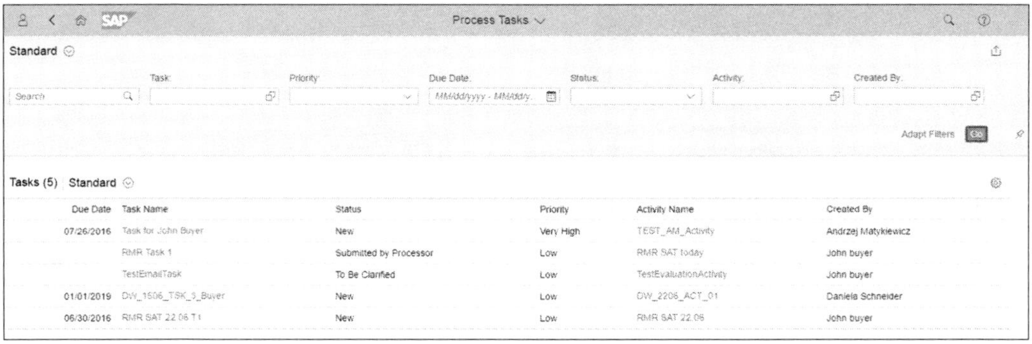

Figure 11.12 Process Tasks App

This section covered the first step in the supplier management process in SAP S/4HANA, which is to segment and classify your suppliers in system. In the following section, we'll review the second area of supplier management, supplier evaluation.

11.3 Supplier Evaluation

Supplier evaluation in SAP S/4HANA Sourcing and Procurement leverages the classification and segmentation overlay an organization establishes in the system, the objective transaction and performance metrics generated during the transactions of the supplier with the organization in the system, and the subjective user feedback from evaluation surveys and questionnaires to establish a comprehensive view of the supplier. All of these activities and feedback data points roll into a unified score for the supplier. Based on these scores, it's possible to further group and segment your suppliers into performance categories and identify low performers in need of improvement or high performers deserving of further business and spend volumes.

In classic SAP ERP, users had to use SAP SRM, SAP Supplier Lifecycle Management, or another platform to create supplier evaluations and questionnaires. Alternatively, a user could manually score a supplier in SAP ERP. Supplier evaluation for soft facts using questionnaires wasn't available in SAP ERP directly.

SAP S/4HANA Sourcing and Procurement has the code set from SAP Supplier Lifecycle Management embedded, which means the following capabilities are now native:

- Questionnaire definition directly in SAP S/4HANA
- Evaluation requests and distribution to appraisers
- Consolidated evaluation results review in evaluation scorecards
- Monitoring and searching for evaluation responses and details

Bringing increased speed and real-time capabilities to bear on supplier management means that users can consume these supplier evaluation views embedded in their transactions and processes. New innovations in supplier evaluation functionality in SAP S/4HANA include the following:

- Functionality to define questionnaires in SAP S/4HANA directly
- Creating evaluation requests and distributing to appraisers
- Consolidated evaluation results in evaluation scorecards
- Monitor and search flexibility for evaluation responses and navigation to response details

There are numerous supplier evaluation apps, which center on two main areas (see Figure 11.13). First, there are questionnaire-focused apps like Manage Questions, Translate Questions, Manage Templates, Monitor Responses, and Manage Questionnaires. The second area are the scorecard apps, such as Supplier Evaluation by Quantity, Time, and Price, as well as Overall Supplier Evaluation Score. In many of these evaluation apps, you can set KPIs, which are displayed in green, yellow, or red on the tiles for an individual supplier or metric, allowing a user to understand up front how the supplier or area is tracking to targets.

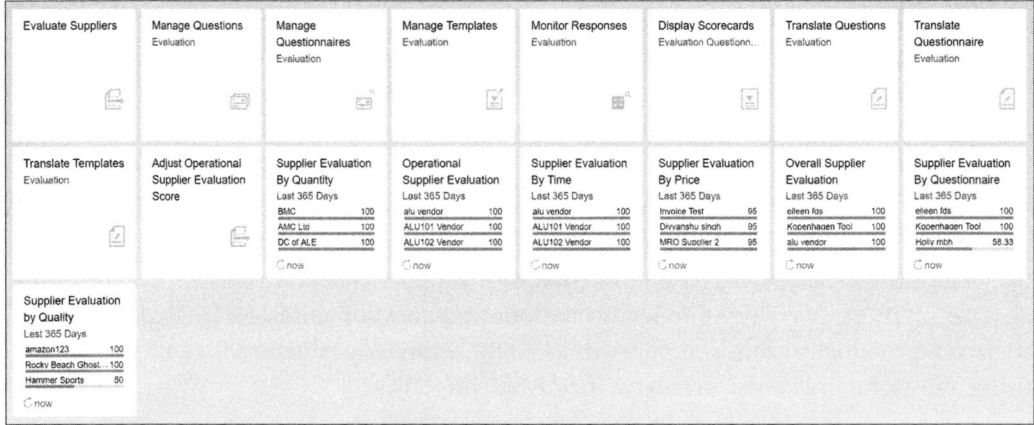

Figure 11.13 Supplier Evaluation Apps

These apps can be obtained from the SAP Fiori App library by searching for "supplier evaluation" as shown in Figure 11.14.

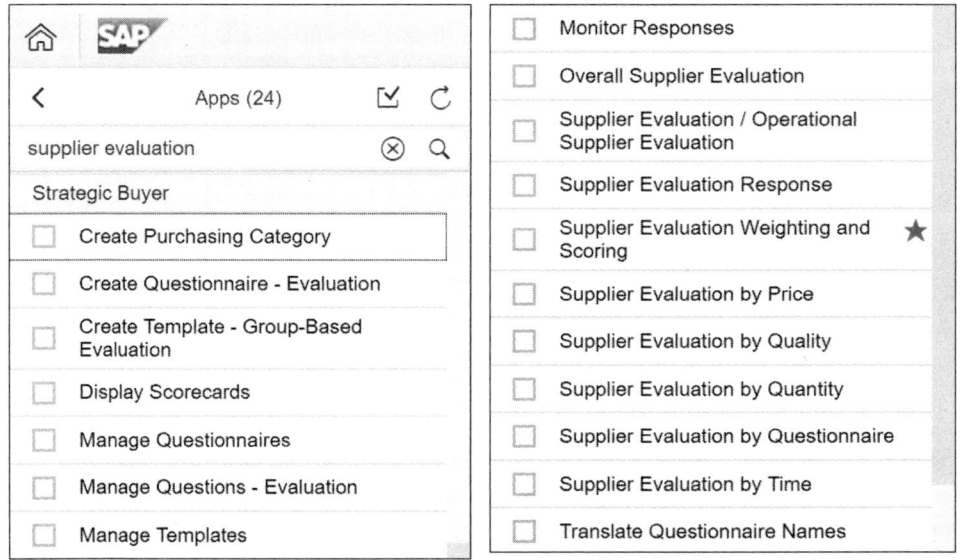

Figure 11.14 Supplier Evaluation App Search in Library

11.3.1 Supplier Evaluation Scorecard

Another app from the SAP Fiori App library search is the Manage Scorecards app. In SAP S/4HANA, the performance of suppliers is updated continuously, comparing purchase order data with goods receipt and invoice data. Employees and purchasers also rate performance by filling out questionnaires periodically. The KPI shows the scores across both hard and soft ratings and data points. As you can see in Figure 11.15, the scorecard itself provides an overall score, but it also provides details about both the objective and subjective ratings, as well as survey responses and survey response rates.

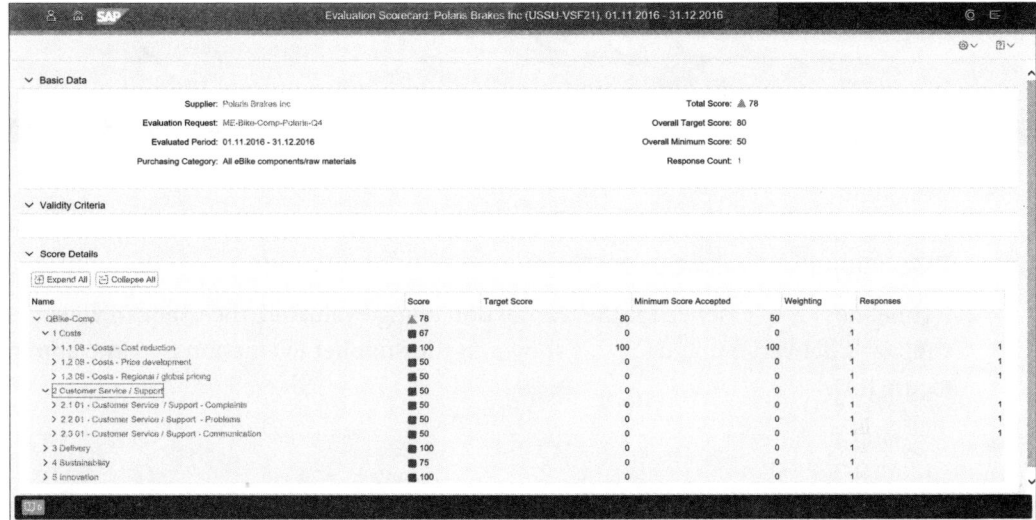

Figure 11.15 Supplier Evaluation Scorecard

The scorecard also lists a target score for the supplier, essentially a KPI setting, so that a user can understand what the organization feels is a reasonable rating to have in this purchasing category. You also have the option of maintaining validity criteria in order to timebox the scorecard and assign guidance about applicability.

11.3.2 Individual Supplier Evaluation

Individual supplier evaluation apps provide specific views into performance, such as the Supplier Evaluation by Quantity app shown in Figure 11.16. Here, variances in quantities ordered versus quantities delivered can be viewed by a supplier, allowing a user to understand the accuracy of each supplier in terms of order fulfillment.

11 Supplier Management

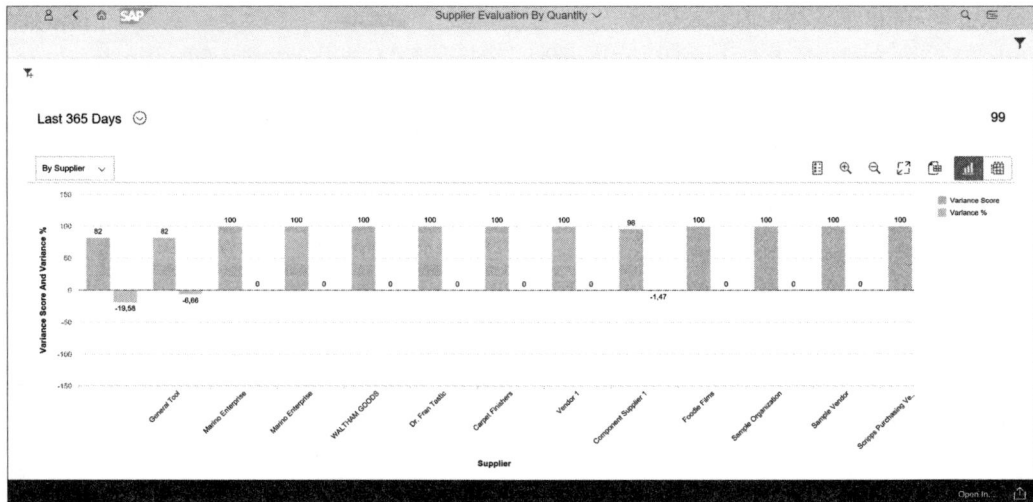

Figure 11.16 Supplier Evaluation by Quantity

11.3.3 Supplier Evaluation by Time

If timeliness is of essence for the transaction being evaluated, the user can view the supplier's delivery punctuality, as shown in the Supplier Evaluation by Time app in Figure 11.17.

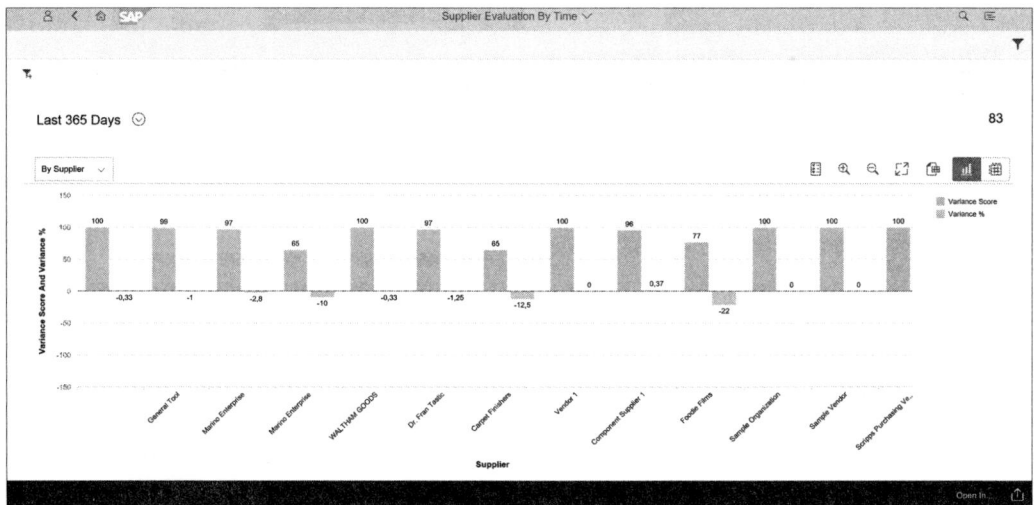

Figure 11.17 Supplier Evaluation by Time

Here, adherence to the delivery date is shown graphically, allowing a user to understand whether a supplier is a suitable candidate for a just-in-time (JIT) process, for example. If a supplier routinely misses its delivery dates based on this report, a user would want to think twice about including them in a mission-critical manufacturing process running in a JIT fashion.

11.3.4 Supplier Evaluation by Price

Perhaps most importantly in some commodity-procurement situations, how faithfully a supplier adheres to the quoted price in the PO can be assessed by selecting the Supplier Evaluation by Price app. As shown in Figure 11.18, if a supplier has wide variance in its quoted price, this may warrant further investigation to determine if there are transportation/logistics costs not being quoted up front or even a more nefarious bait-and-switch problem with the supplier.

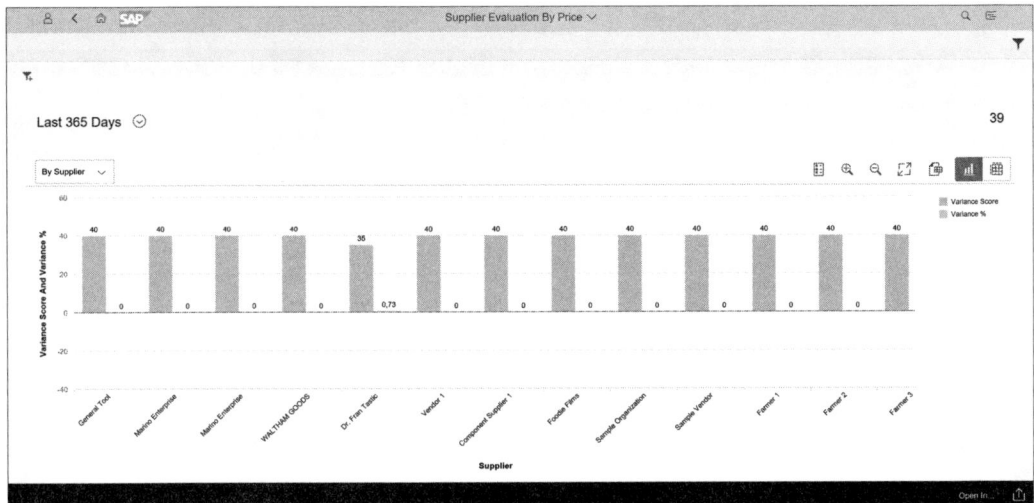

Figure 11.18 Supplier Evaluation by Price

11.3.5 Supplier Evaluation by Questionnaire

Statistics is a slippery slope if the data isn't there in sufficient volumes to underpin a correlation, much less causation. One survey or sample does not a statistical analysis make, and it would be premature to pass judgement too quickly or harshly based on sparse data, no matter how tempting. Ideally, you should have over 35 samples to begin analysis. The Supplier Evaluation by Questionnaire app, shown in Figure 11.19, shows which suppliers have reached such a level in the survey response area and which ones require more follow up.

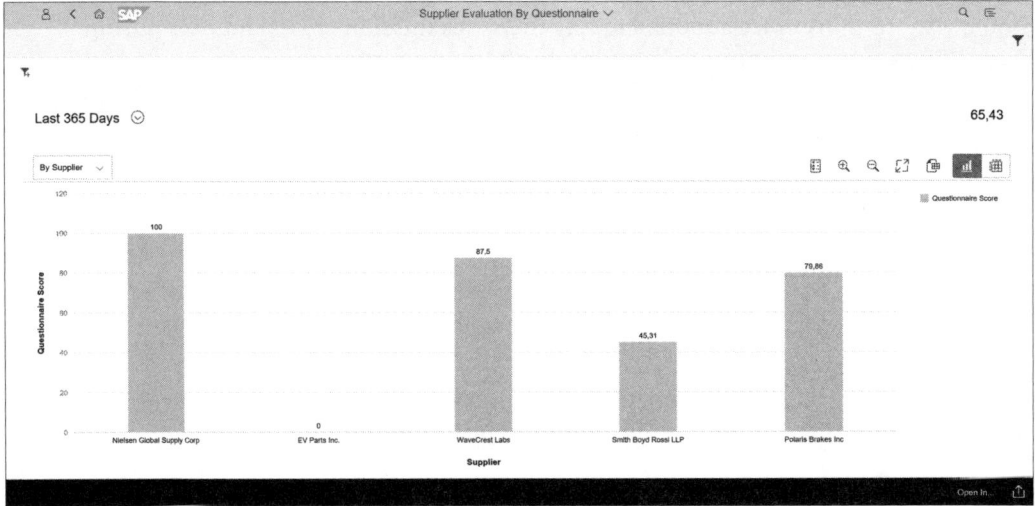

Figure 11.19 Supplier Evaluation by Questionnaire

To create a questionnaire, go to the Create Questionnaire app in SAP S/4HANA and fill out the information in the **Add Evaluation** screen, as shown in Figure 11.20.

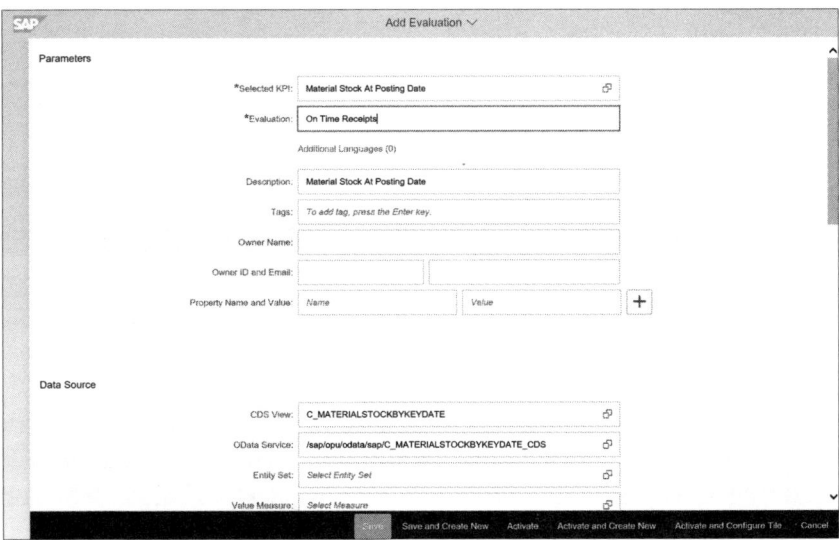

Figure 11.20 Add Supplier Questionnaire

11.3.6 Combined Scorecard

Combined operational and questionnaire scores can be viewed in a graphical format by drilling into the scorecard as shown in Figure 11.21. Similarly, you can drill further into the purchasing documents that underpin the operational score—without having to change systems, as in days of yore.

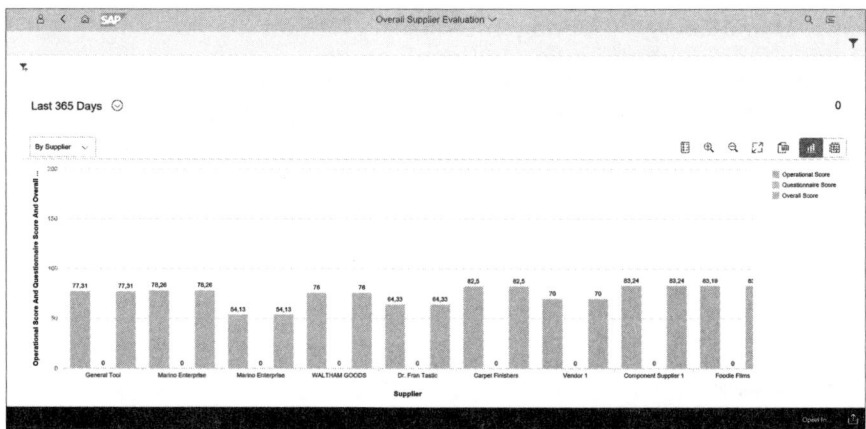

Figure 11.21 Combined Scorecard: Operational and Questionnaire Scores

11.3.7 Operational Supplier Evaluation

Supplier scores can also be reviewed in a graphical fashion side by side in the Supplier Evaluation/Operational Supplier Evaluation app, shown in Figure 11.22. Here, the operational scores and weighted averages for time, price, and quantity are displayed, along with an overall operational score.

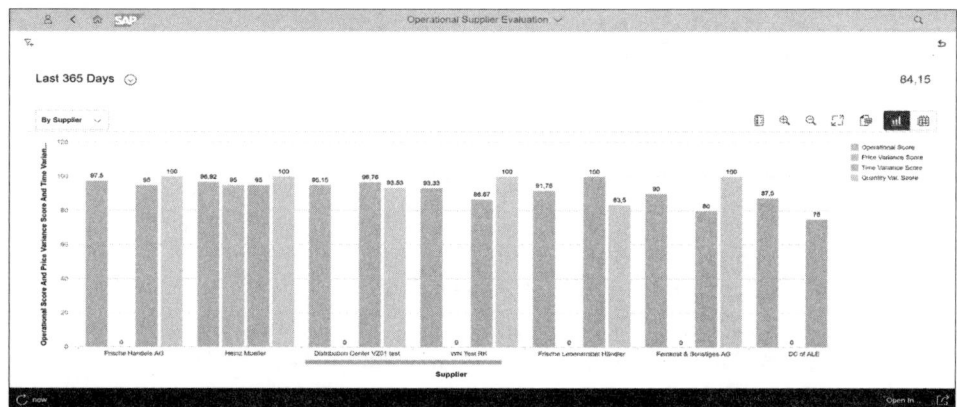

Figure 11.22 Operational Supplier Evaluation

11 Supplier Management

11.4 Configuration

In addition to installing the supplier evaluation apps outlined in Figure 11.14, you need to complete some basic configuration to enable both Supplier and Category Management in the SAP S/4HANA system.

11.4.1 Supplier and Category Management Configuration

First, follow IMG menu path **Materials Management • Purchasing • Supplier and Category Management • Purchasing Categories**, as shown in Figure 11.23.

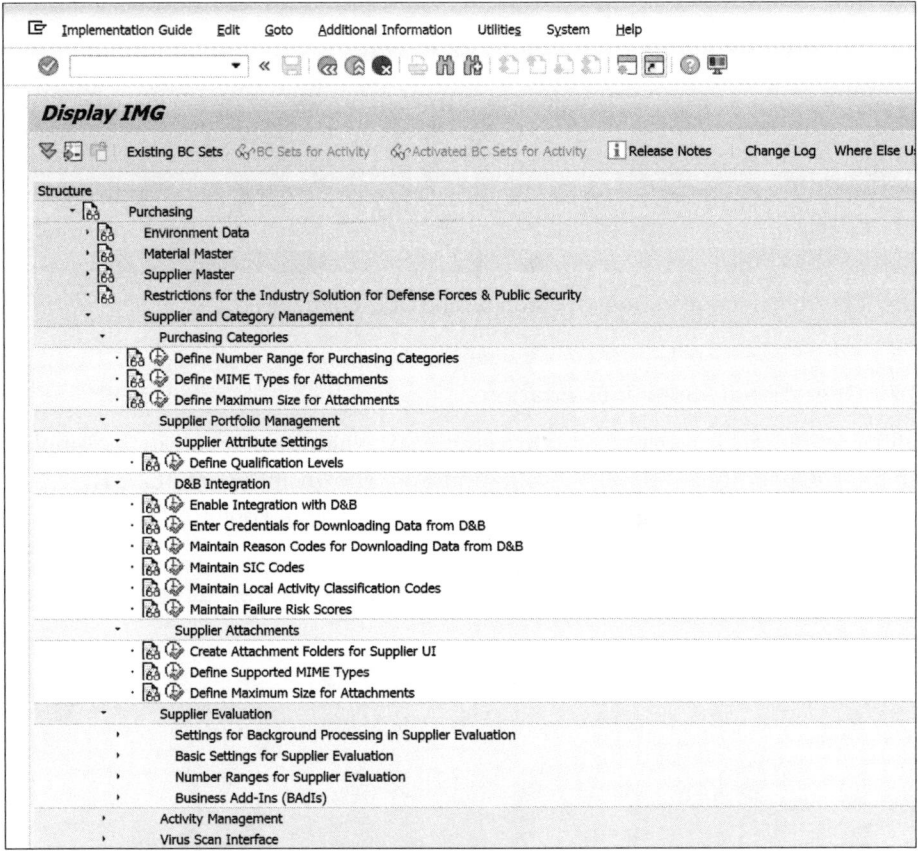

Figure 11.23 SPRO: Supplier and Category Management

Next, select **Define Number Ranges** as shown in Figure 11.24.

11.4 Configuration

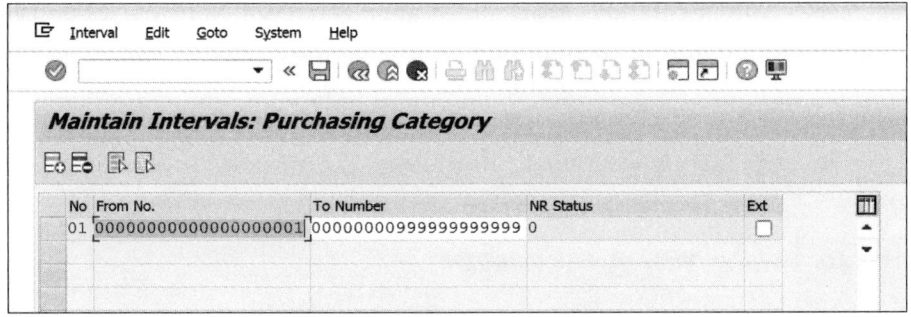

Figure 11.24 Define Number Ranges for Purchasing Categories

Once you've defined your number ranges, save and move to IMG menu path **Materials Management • Purchasing • Supplier and Category Management • Purchasing Categories • Define MIME Types for Attachments and Define Maximum Size for Attachments**. *MIME* here stands for Multipurpose Internet Mail Extensions, which allows you to further define which types of attachments are allowed, as well as their maximum size.

Next, proceed to **Materials Management • Purchasing • Supplier and Category Management • Supplier Portfolio Management • Supplier Attribute Settings • Define Qualification Levels**. Here, you can define qualification levels required by your organization by selecting **New Entries** and entering both a key and a description, as shown in Figure 11.25.

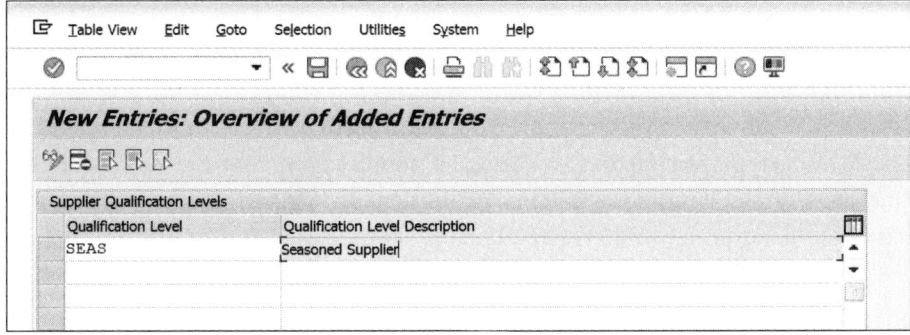

Figure 11.25 Supplier Qualification Levels

Next, if required, you can activate integration with Dunn & Bradstreet via **Materials Management • Purchasing • Supplier and Category Management • Supplier Portfolio**

429

11 Supplier Management

Management • D&B Integration • Enable Integration with D&B. Note that a Dunn & Bradstreet subscription is required prior to setting up this configuration. Select the switch for Dunn & Bradstreet integration, mark it **Active**, and save, as in Figure 11.26.

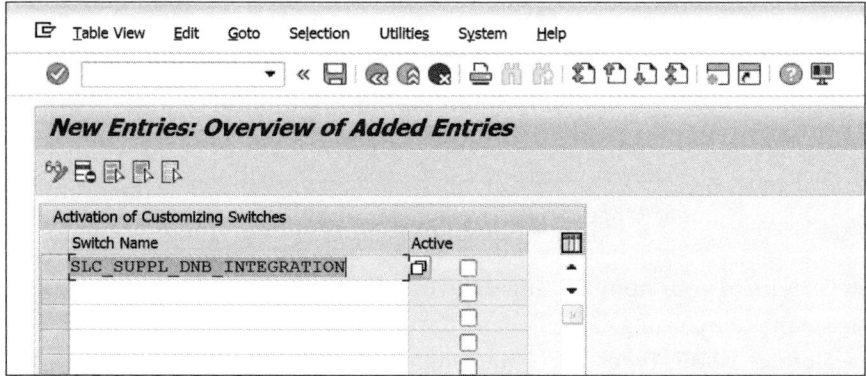

Figure 11.26 Dunn & Bradstreet Activation

In the remaining activation steps, you must maintain your credentials for logging in at Dunn & Bradstreet in **Materials Management • Purchasing • Supplier and Category Management • Supplier Portfolio Management • D&B Integration • Enter Credentials for Downloading Data from D&B**. If you have reason codes for downloading, or other settings for Failure Risk Scores and codes, you maintain them in the general section **Materials Management • Purchasing • Supplier and Category Management • Supplier Portfolio Management • D&B Integration** under the applicable configuration areas.

11.4.2 Supplier Evaluation Configuration

For supplier evaluation configuration, you must configure the number ranges in **Materials Management • Purchasing • Supplier and Category Management • Supplier Evaluation • Number Ranges for Supplier Evaluation** (see Figure 11.27). Any objects you plan to use will require a number range. If using, define number ranges for the following:

- Questions
- Sections
- Question and Section Groups
- Evaluation Questionnaire

- Supplier Evaluation Templates
- Supplier Evaluation Requests
- Evaluation Responses
- Evaluation Scorecards

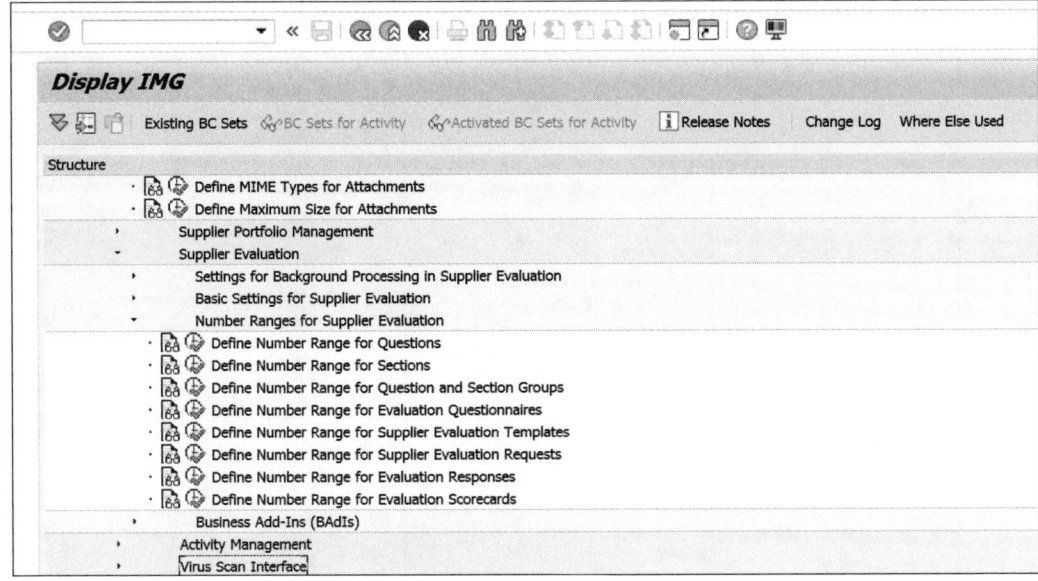

Figure 11.27 Define Number Ranges for Supplier Evaluation

Next, define a language for the question library for questionnaires via IMG menu path **Materials Management • Purchasing • Supplier and Category Management • Supplier Evaluation • Create Question Library for Supplier Evaluation**. You'll need the /SRMSMC/REPORT_EXEC_ADMIN role assigned to you to run this transaction. Select a language on the first screen, as shown in Figure 11.28.

Then, execute the transaction. Your question library has now been created. If you want to use another language other than the one you've defined here, you'll need to create a translation of the question. Once the library is activated, you can further define and assign MIME types and attachment sizes as for the previous area in **Materials Management • Purchasing • Supplier and Category Management • Supplier Evaluation • Maintain Settings for Mails and Other Texts in Evaluation** or **Define MIME Types for Attachments** or **Define Maximum Size for Attachments**.

11 Supplier Management

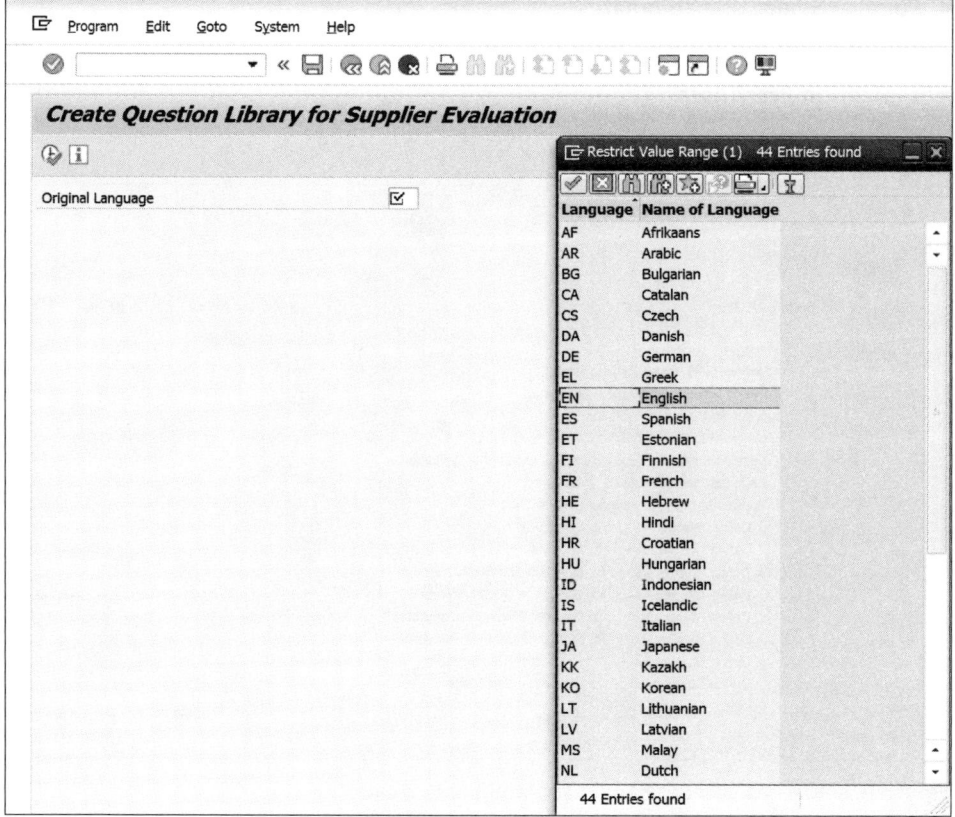

Figure 11.28 Define Language for Question

11.5 Integration with SAP Ariba

SAP Ariba Supplier Lifecycle and Performance is a newly released product; there isn't a version of SAP S/4HANA with a prebuilt SAP Ariba Supplier Lifecycle and Performance integration generally available yet. In a standard SAP Ariba Supplier Lifecycle and Performance integration with SAP S/4HANA, the main part to be integrated with the SAP ERP backend is the supplier master record. This exchange can leverage the existing MDG-S integration with SAP Ariba, which enables Master Data Governance for Supplier (MDG-S) to integrate directly and exchange supplier master data with SAP Ariba solutions. If your requirements are more extensive, you can build a custom integration leveraging the SAP Ariba Cloud Integration Gateway. Add-ons and documentation to support your integration requirements are available at *service.sap.com*.

11.6 Summary

A procurement operation run without any kind of reflection or analysis of its supply base is unable to make improvements over time, much less realize the true potential in SAP S/4HANA or its marketplace. Never before have supplier evaluation, classification, segmentation, and analysis been as deeply embedded and dynamic as in the SAP S/4HANA environment today. Organizations can segment and classify their suppliers, assign KPIs, and perform analysis while executing transactions simultaneously in a fluid manner, knowing that the data they're viewing is current and that the comparisons they're making between suppliers is underpinned by sound classification and segmentation of their major spend areas. In the next chapter, we'll dive deeper into general spend-analysis topics, which further compliment the robust supplier management capabilities in SAP S/4HANA Sourcing and Procurement.

Chapter 12
Reporting and Analytics

From a tech perspective, due to the immense advances and cost reductions in in-memory processing, as well as commensurate achievements and simplifications on the algorithmic side—that is, the software side—it's now more possible than ever before to view key procurement reports and conduct drilldown analysis in real time in an SAP S/4HANA environment. This means commensurate improvements in overall insight, reaction, and prediction times, as well as supplier/buyer satisfaction.

SAP S/4HANA represents a reunification of sorts of online transaction processing (OLTP) with online analytical processing (OLAP) for SAP ERP.

Procurement analytics and reporting are a necessity for any procurement operation. Procurement analysis and reporting are divided into two distinct areas in SAP S/4HANA Sourcing and Procurement: Spend Visibility and Real-Time Reporting and Monitoring (Figure 12.1). *Spend visibility* focuses on categories of spend and spending with groups of suppliers. In SAP S/4HANA, spend visibility comprises everything related to an organization's spend. *Reporting and monitoring* is more broad-based and can include general reports pertaining to procurement master data and transaction document status.

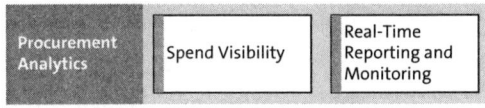

Figure 12.1 Procurement Analytics in SAP S/4HANA Sourcing and Procurement

This chapter will provide an overview of the approaches to reporting and analytics in SAP S/4HANA, as well as the complementary uses and connections available for traditional, business warehouse-based reporting, in which data is offloaded into a business warehouse, used to construct cubes, which then provides analysis drill down reports for the business user.

12 Reporting and Analytics

12.1 Spend Visibility

Like finance and controlling, a procurement department has a strong focus on spending. Unlike finance, the chief interests of which are cash flow and controlling costs, procurement seeks to understand what is being bought and whether more optimal approaches exist for categorizing and grouping this spend, as well as supporting it via agreements with suppliers. Spend visibility, also called *spend analysis*, provides the procurement team with reporting in this area, combining financial/transactional reporting in which payments are being made to suppliers with the upstream areas, meaning the requisitioning, sourcing, and contracting areas of the transaction. The difference between a classic approach to spend visibility and the approach in SAP S/4HANA is detailed in Figure 12.2.

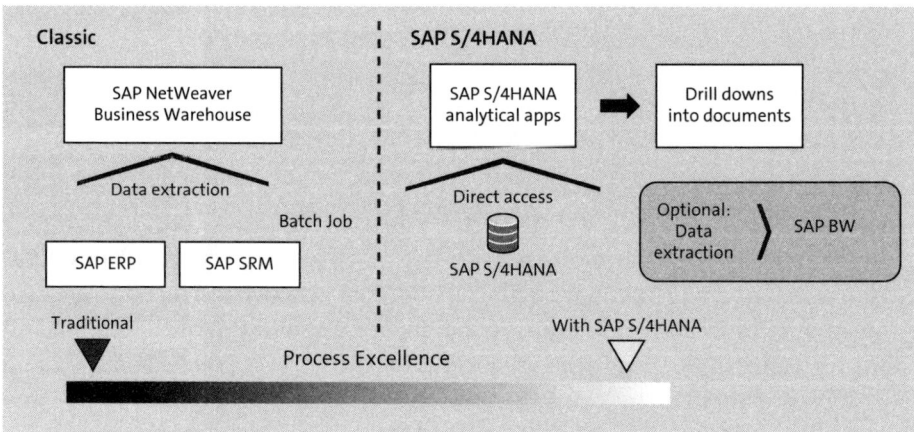

Figure 12.2 SAP S/4HANA Sourcing and Procurement Spend Visibility

In a classic approach for spend visibility, the SAP ERP system didn't conduct an extraction in real time, and there were no KPI options. Because the data had been extracted to another environment, drilling down into the minutia of a transaction or supporting financials wasn't always possible, either. For this, you had to return to the transaction system to further query data and/or rebuild your data cubes in your business warehouse to show the sought-after data. SAP S/4HANA still allows for extraction of data to a business warehouse if required, but you can also conduct KPI-based analysis in real time in the transacting system. This makes the view into your spending up-to-date and actionable in an immediate timeframe when required. With its Multidimensional Spend Report, SAP S/4HANA Cloud offers further extensions for spend reporting in later releases (1708 and above), as detailed in the next section.

12.1.1 Multidimensional Spend Reporting in SAP S/4HANA Cloud

The Multidimensional Purchasing Spend Report in SAP S/4HANA Cloud allows for purchasing spend to be analyzed dynamically by company code, region, plant, and other variables. The user can drag and drop dimensions, as well as change and adopt filters, dimensions and measures in rows, and columns. Users can flip between a table, bar, or split chart display.

12.1.2 Navigation and Procurement Overview Page

The same applies to monitoring and reporting in SAP S/4HANA Sourcing and Procurement. Buyers and executives can analyze and report on spend, contracts, and suppliers, as well as monitor business-critical situations in the Procurement overview page using *analytical cards* and worklists. *Analytical cards* are screen elements in an overview page. An overview page can show many charts and figures on one page, and the user can navigate to further applications by clicking the figures and/or charts contained in these cards, as shown in Figure 12.3. Here, the user selects a general app area and then drills into a card to further access an app.

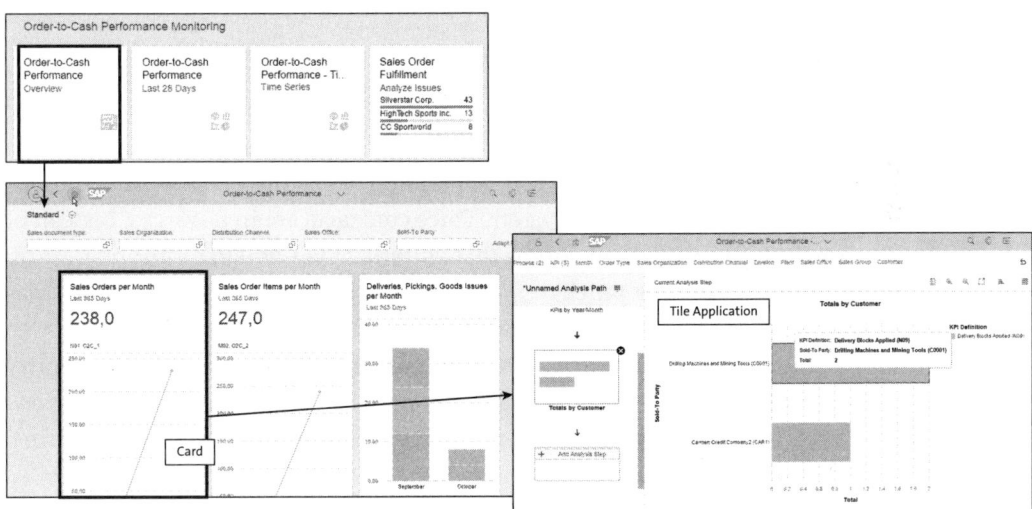

Figure 12.3 Navigating via Cards in SAP Fiori Elements

12   Reporting and Analytics

The Procurement overview page app provides a graphical dashboard display of key procurement and supplier management reports, as in Figure 12.4.

Figure 12.4 Procurement Overview Page

12.2   Contract Expiration

The first step in the evolution of contract reporting is to get the contracts out of the filing cabinets and into the SAP ERP system. Once contracts are in a system, instead of shuffling through paper files and hoping that you still have enough room and time on a contract to execute another purchase, you can begin to report on these contracts and identify ones that are expiring. Both cloud and on-premise editions of SAP S/4HANA Sourcing and Procurement shipped with this functionality early on, via the Quantity Contract Consumption SAP Fiori app. This app provides a comprehensive overview of all contracts in the system and all data related to them, such as validity timeframe, current released and target amounts, and material group.

Another app is the Contract Expiry app, which shows target value and consumption, providing a clear visual indicator of the amount left on a contract, as shown in Figure 12.5.

SAP S/4HANA has a mandate to raise process intelligence using its new, real-time reporting capabilities. From SAP S/4HANA version 1709 and SAP S/4HANA Cloud version 1705 onwards, the Quantity Contract Consumption app not only reports on existing expiration trajectories for contracts but also makes predictions using the predictive analytics algorithm in the system. This algorithm leverages historical consumption data to make predictions about when a contract will be completely consumed. The algorithm's predictive capability will be further enhanced in future releases to include situational and contextual awareness capabilities.

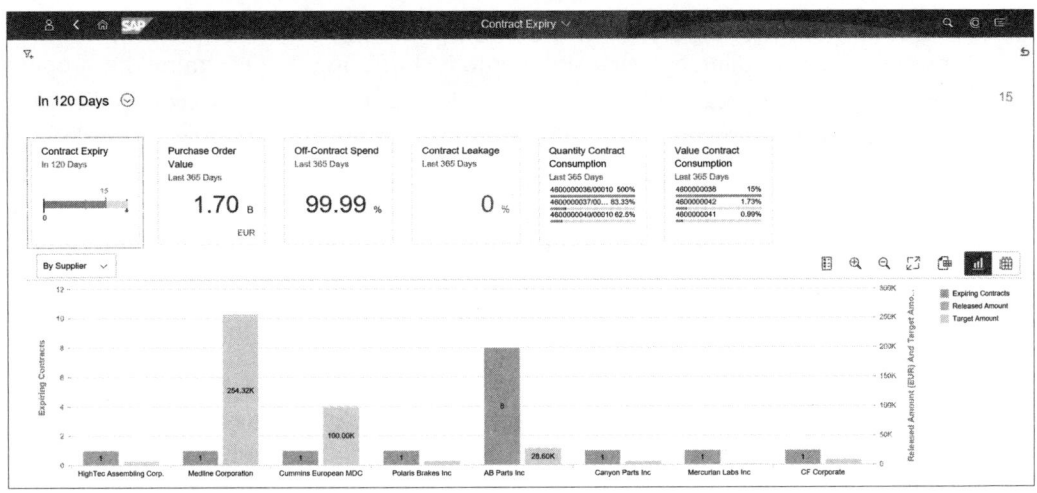

Figure 12.5 Contract Expiry App

12.3 Sourcing

The sourcing cockpit and functionality in SAP S/4HANA remains similar to that in previous versions of SAP ERP, and this is by design. For further innovation in sourcing topics, the go-to solution area is SAP Ariba. In SAP Ariba Sourcing, the collaboration and reporting capabilities are more robust than in SAP S/4HANA. Still, if you're evaluating sourcing from an existing supplier in SAP S/4HANA, you do have several supplier-performance reports at your disposal, such as the following SAP S/4HANA apps:

- Manage Sources of Supply
- Operational Supplier Evaluation Last 365 Days
- Overall Supplier Evaluation Last 365 Days
- Supplier Evaluation by Quantity Last 365 Days
- Supplier Evaluation by Price Last 365 Days

- Supplier Evaluation by Time Last 365 Days
- Supplier Evaluation by Questionnaire Last 365 Days

Because these analytics and reports are being generated in real time in the transaction system, they also can be brought to bear on the transactions taking place. For example, beginning in SAP S/4HANA Cloud version 1708, analytical information about the supplier is available at the transaction level. Rather than choosing a name and number for a supplier, by using simple product offerings to determine the supplier eligibility, this approach allows the user to look at the supplier's record holistically and not just at a supplier record. This allows a user to choose a supplier with eyes wide open, rather than grabbing the first eligible supplier off the list. A user now sees scores and other data that differentiates suppliers and can drive purchasing patterns of the organization towards the best-performing suppliers rather than ones that managed to appear at the top of the list based on their name or numerical code.

This new approach towards in-flight purchasing analytics can be summarized at functionality, value-proposition, and capabilities levels:

- **Functionality**
  When assigning a source of supply to an open purchase requisition, analytical information is embedded. The user can click the supplier record as in Figure 12.6.

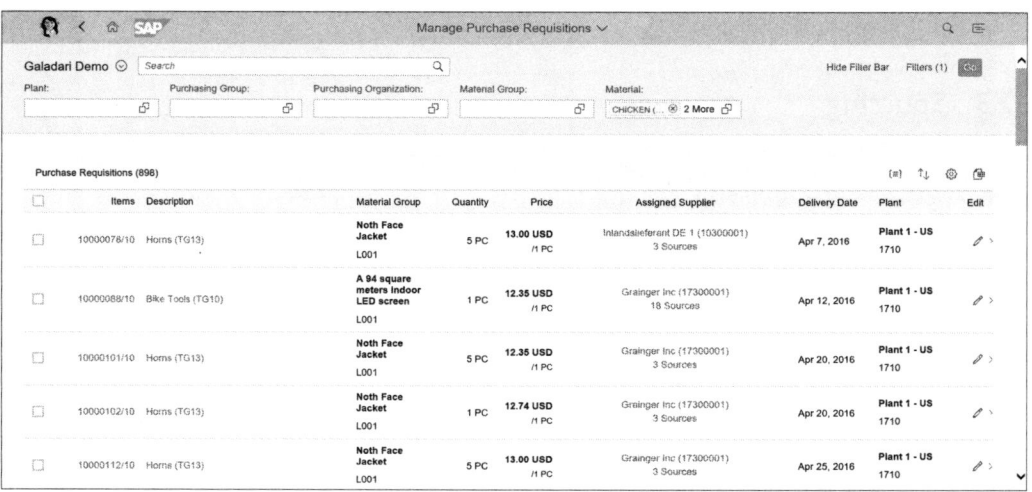

Figure 12.6 Source of Supply Drilldown

- **Value proposition**
  Provides the purchaser additional information (spend by supplier and supplier

evaluation score) about available sources of supply to support the decision, as shown in Figure 12.7.

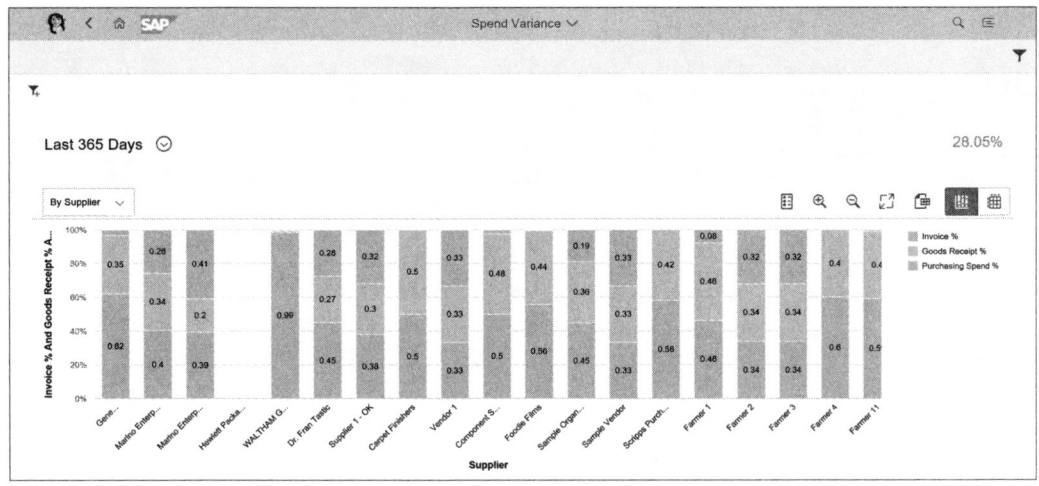

Figure 12.7 Spend by Supplier

- **Capabilities**
  For each valid source of supply, shows additional information via embedded analytics (price, evaluation score, and spend).

Both the SAP Ariba Sourcing and Sourcing Suite solutions offer additional sourcing and reporting capabilities. One of the key differences between the two versions is the support for direct materials sourcing in the Sourcing Suite version. The SAP Ariba Strategic Sourcing Suite version also offers integration with SAP Ariba Supplier Lifecycle and Performance Management.

12.4 Supplier Performance

Suppliers can also be evaluated in real time, providing instant insight into performance issues or improvements. From these reports, a user can then drill further into individual purchase orders and other documents, including surveys, to obtain a complete, real-time view. Figure 12.8 shows such a performance report for suppliers over time. Suppliers with steep drop-offs in recent performance need to be analyzed further for financial difficulties and supply chain relevance, and transactions correspondingly must be moved to more reliable performers.

12 Reporting and Analytics

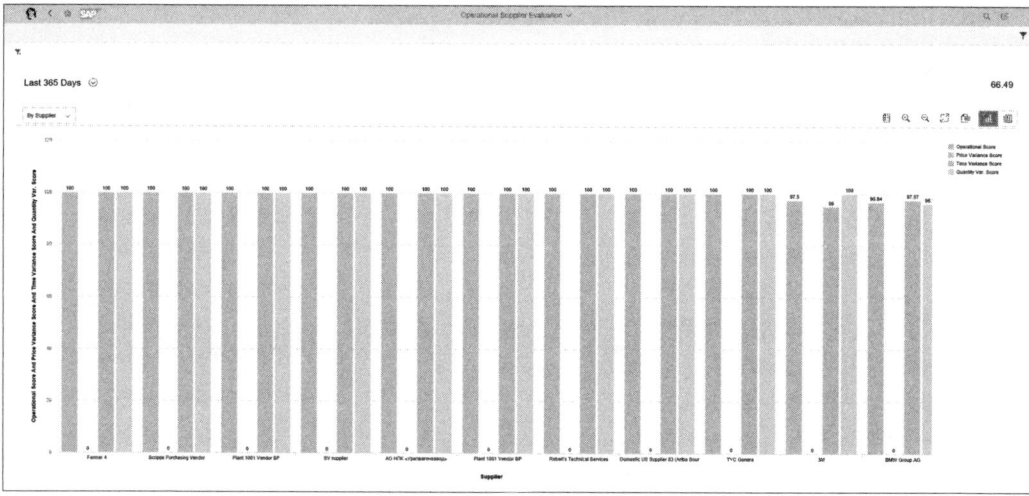

Figure 12.8 Supplier Valuation Scoring

Because these analytics capabilities are now available directly in the SAP ERP environment, they can be embedded at the document level for additional insight at the time of transaction. This is the subject of the following section.

12.4.1 Purchasing Documents Reports and Embedded Analytics

Monitoring purchasing documents in the SAP Business Suite in SAP ERP was done using SAP GUI transactions such as Transaction ME3L or ME4L and others. With SAP S/4HANA, these legacy reports are transformed and harmonized using the SAP Fiori UX, with additional charts and visual filters to support the user in analyzing specific business situations, such as overdue orders or next-scheduled items on a scheduling agreement. The user can navigate seamlessly from table to object pages or download a report to Excel.

This embedded analytics approach extends to other transactions and documents in SAP S/4HANA Sourcing and Procurement, such as contracts. In the Monitor Purchasing Contracts Items app, a user can navigate from line items in the contract to its release history and to an option to renew the contract. Without having to go into another app, the user can review the contract consumption and extend the validity or increase the value of the contract where required, as in Figure 12.9. In this app, a user also can see an overview of all of the contracts by spend type, select an individual contract to see how much remains of it, and then review consumption patterns over time to get an idea as to fluctuations in spending on this contract.

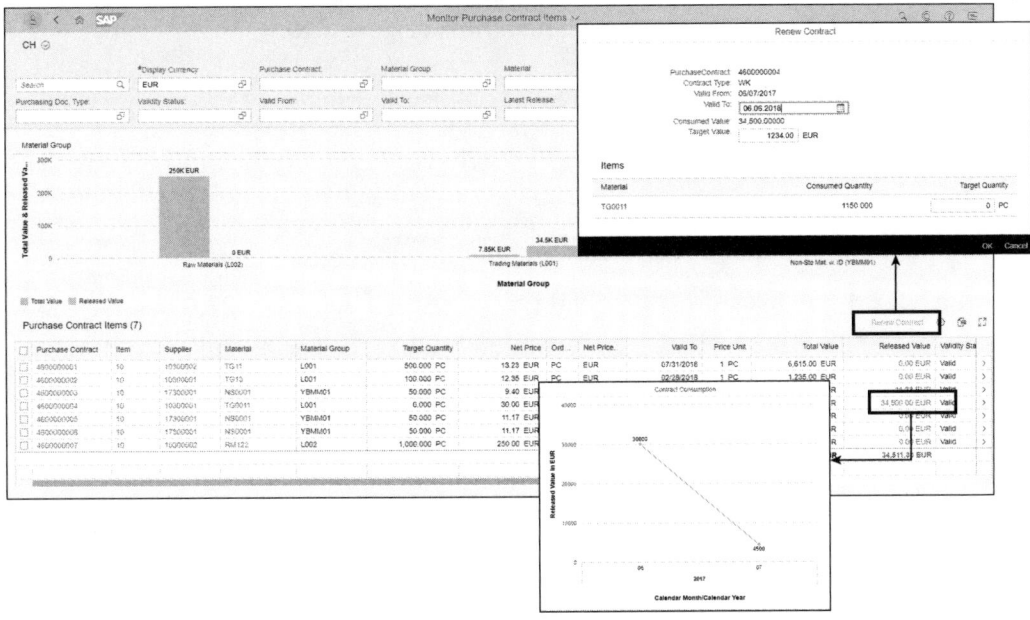

Figure 12.9 SAP S/4HANA 1708 Monitor Purchasing Contract Items App

12.4.2 Predictive Analytics

As mentioned earlier, contract reporting uses predictive analytics capabilities in recent releases of SAP S/4HANA. Predictive analytics is an exciting new area, combining traditional historical data and artificial intelligence-driven, algorithm-based analysis to drive further accuracy in forecasting.

In later releases of SAP S/4HANA Cloud (1705 onward) and SAP S/4HANA, Sourcing and Procurement reporting also boasts predictive capabilities on top of providing the historical reporting, with capabilities to predict the following:

- Purchase order spend based on open purchase requisitions
- Predictive analytics for contract consumption

The next section looks at further analytics and reporting apps available in SAP S/4HANA.

12.5 Accounts Payable Analytics and Reporting

The UI platform for analytics and reporting in SAP S/4HANA is app-centric. The core dashboard apps of a typical buyer are shown in Figure 12.10.

Value Contract Consumption	Quantity Contract Consumption	Contract Expiry	Off-Contract Spend	Contract Leakage	Unused Contracts	Purchasing Spend	Non-Managed Spend
4600002643 33.34% 4800002539 2% 4800002425 0%	4600000123/... 8528.57% 4600000338/... 2121.82% 4600000634/000...1400%	119	100 %	0.17 %	0	100 %	88.51 %
Spend Variance	Purchase Order Value	Invoice Price Variance	Purchase Order Average Delivery Weighted (In Days)	Overdue Purchase Order Items		Purchase Requisition Item Changes	Purchase Requisition Item Types
0.4 %	1.34 B EUR	169.34 ┃ 1000	-2.64	16 K	No. of Overdue I...16.44K Open Net Value 1.89B Overdue Days 105	27.02 K	330
Purchasing Group Activities		Purchase Requisition Average Approval Time		Purchase Requisition To Order Cycle Time		Purchase Requisition No Touch Rate	
13.66 K	Group 002 8.42K Group 001 3.33K Group 003 1.9K	0	Days Medium-Cost 0 Days High-Cost 0 Days Very High-Cost 0	30.25	Days Medium-Cost 6.45 Days High-Cost 1.25 Days Very High-Cost 9.13	14 %	High Touch % 86% Low Touch % 0% No Touch % 14%

Figure 12.10 SAP S/4HANA Sourcing and Procurement Dashboard

These apps show actionable values on their respective tiles, whether for contract consumption, leakage, volumes, PO values, price variance, or order cycles. The user can set KPIs, and the apps refresh their data automatically. These analytics apps also can be refreshed manually without going into the app itself by clicking the **Now** icon in the lower left-hand corner. Note that some measures appear in green and others in red. The red measures indicate that the KPI threshold set has been exceeded. A user thus is notified instantly in a simplified manner if something is going off target, without needing to enter the report itself.

SAP S/4HANA analytics and reporting apps extend the entire process flow for procure-to-pay. On the payment side, there are a comparable number of analytic options and reports, to provide accounts payable and invoice users with up-to-the-second insight into payables and cash flow position.

There is a variety of analytic apps for use by accounts payable roles in the SAP S/4HANA system. These apps include the following:

- Aging Analysis
- Overdue Payables

- Future Payables
- Cash Discount Forecast
- Cash Discount Utilization
- Days Payable Outstanding
- Invoice Processing Analysis
- Supplier Payment Analysis (Manual and Automatic Payments)
- Supplier Payment Analysis (Open Payments)

Let's take a closer look at each of these apps.

12.5.1 Aging Analysis

The Aging Analysis app is useful for viewing aging payables across the organization. This will allow you to identify negative trends in total payables, net due, and overdue amounts. You can then react to these negative trends and take appropriate actions to counter them.

The **Aging Analysis** tile displays the **Payable Amount** KPI (Figure 12.11), which is calculated as the sum of total open payables. Open payables are defined as the sum of past-due payables and future payables.

The Aging Analysis app allows you to do the following:

- Display the payables amount, including the overdue amount and the net due amount, by company, aging, business area, reconciliation accounts, currency, payment method, and supplier group.
- Use the company code, aging interval, business area, reconciliation account, and payment method filters to focus your aging payables analysis.

Figure 12.11 SAP S/4HANA Aging Analysis Tile

12.5.2 Overdue Payables

The Overdue Payables app is used to check overdue payable amounts to your suppliers by company code, supplier group, supplier, and reason for payment block. You can monitor the status of the overdue payments for critical suppliers. Use this app to take action on payables due to your key suppliers.

The **Overdue Payables** tile shows three metrics (see Figure 12.12):

- **Uncritical Overdue**
  The sum of all uncritically overdue payables amounts
- **Critical Overdue**
  The sum of all critically overdue payables amounts
- **Overdue Payables**
  The sum of uncritically overdue payables and critically overdue payables

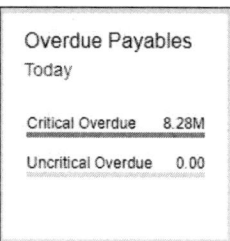

Figure 12.12 SAP S/4HANA Overdue Payables

In configuration, you can define the threshold for critically overdue in days for your company. Note that payables due on today's date are included in the calculation.

The Overdue Payables app, as shown in Figure 12.13, allows you to do the following:

- Display the overdue payable amount and the payable amount that isn't yet overdue.
- Distinguish between critically overdue amounts and uncritically overdue amounts.
- Analyze the payable amount by different views, including company code, supplier group, reason for payment block and supplier.
- Break the overdue payable amount into four intervals before today when you analyze the amount by supplier.

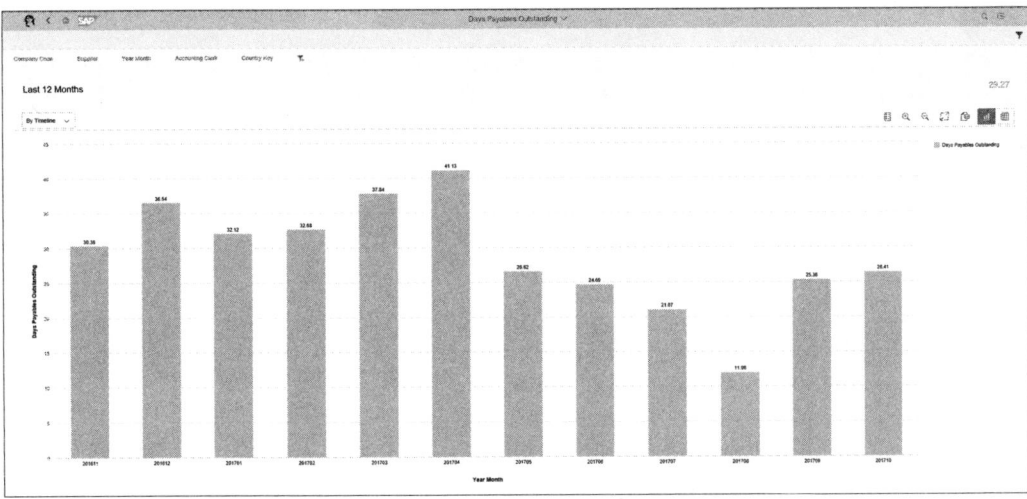

Figure 12.13 SAP S/4HANA Overdue Payables Report

12.5.3 Future Payables

The Future Payables app allows you to analyze your future payables in a variety of ways.

The **Future Payables** tile (see Figure 12.14) displays the **Future Payables** KPI, which is calculated as the total amount of all invoices due in the future.

Figure 12.14 SAP S/4HANA Future Payables Tile

You can analyze accounts payable for predefined due periods by drilling into the Future Payables app. For each due period, you can drill down further to the 10 suppliers with the largest amounts payable, as shown in Figure 12.15. These due periods are customizable.

12 Reporting and Analytics

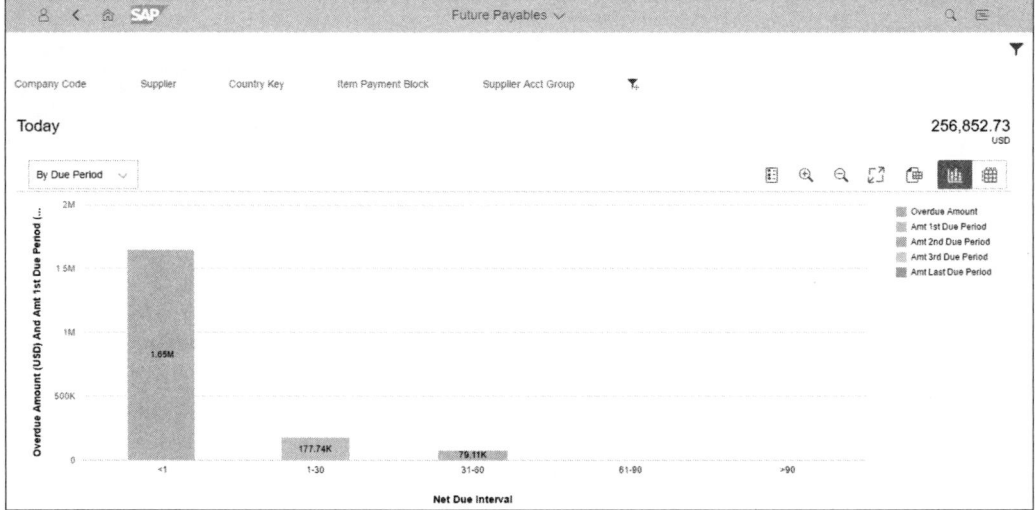

Figure 12.15 SAP S/4HANA Future Payables Report

Within this report, you can do the following:

- Analyze the top ten suppliers with the highest amounts payable and check the numbers of open items for these suppliers.
- Analyze future accounts payable by company code. For each company code, you can drill down further to the top ten suppliers with the largest amounts payable.
- Filter accounts payable based on payment blocking reasons. For example, you can choose a certain reason that a supplier is blocked and search for suppliers blocked for that reason. You can also navigate to the **Supplier** object page as well.

12.5.4 Cash Discount Forecast

The Cash Discount Forecast app lets you predict all available cash discounts in the short-term future period.

The **Cash Discount Forecast** tile (see Figure 12.16) displays the **Available Amount** metric, which is defined as the total amount of cash discounts available on open invoices.

12.5 Accounts Payable Analytics and Reporting

Figure 12.16 Cash Discount Forecast Tile

Drilling into the Cash Discount Forecast app (Figure 12.17), you can do the following:

- Display the cash discounts expiring in the future. Cash discounts are available on the key date, but will expire by the end of the period you define.
- Analyze the expiring cash discounts by company or by payment terms by displaying the expiring cash discounts, the available cash discounts on the key date, and the expired cash discounts before the key date. The available cash discounts on the key date refer to the cash discounts available from the key date to the future.
- Analyze expiring cash discounts by payment day by displaying the cash discounts that are expiring between that payment day and the next. You also can display the cash discounts for blocked within the set period. You then can take action to pay these invoices before the discounts expire.

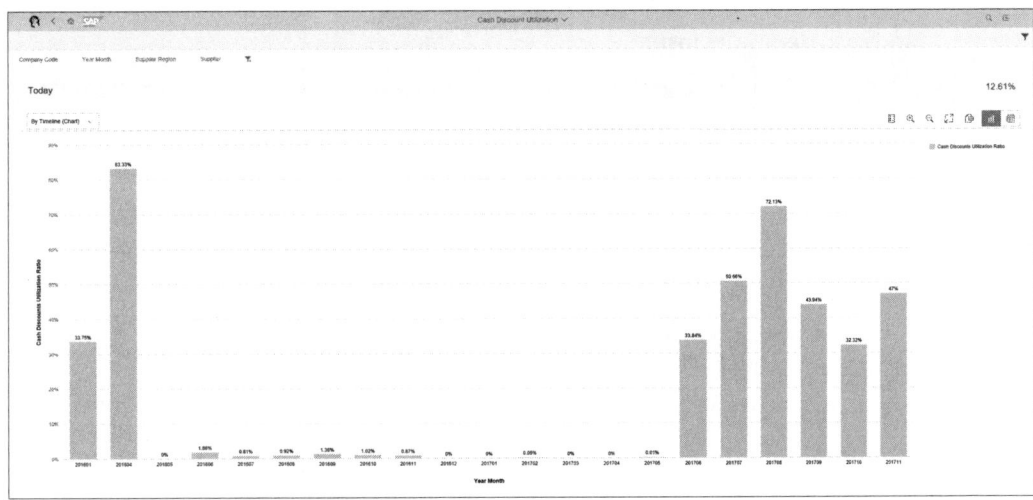

Figure 12.17 Cash Discount Forecast Report

12.5.5 Cash Discount Utilization

The Cash Discount Utilization app allows for monitoring of cash discount utilization in real time. You can find out which company codes or locations could make better use of the cash discounts available to them. You can also determine the reasons for cash discount loss so that it can be avoided in the future.

The **Cash Discount Utilization** tile, shown in Figure 12.18, displays the **Cash Discount Utilization Ratio**. This is defined as the sum of cash discounts taken divided by the sum of cash discounts offered over a defined time period in the past through today.

Figure 12.18 Cash Discount Utilization Tile

The app allows you to perform the following tasks:

- Display the utilization rate of cash discounts in a defined period in the past. This is defined as the cash discounts taken divided by the sum of the cash discounts taken and cash discounts lost.
- Compare the current versus the targeted utilization rate and measure compliance.
- Check whether the current utilization rate is acceptable, needs attention, or is critically low. This utilization-rate level is configurable in the SAP S/4HANA system.
- Analyze cash discount utilization by company, country, supplier group, payment terms, and cause of cash discount loss.
- Distinguish between discounts expired and discounts missed and display their corresponding amounts when you analyze cash discount utilization by cause of cash discount loss, as shown in Figure 12.19.
- Distinguish between cash discounts taken and cash discounts lost.

12.5 Accounts Payable Analytics and Reporting

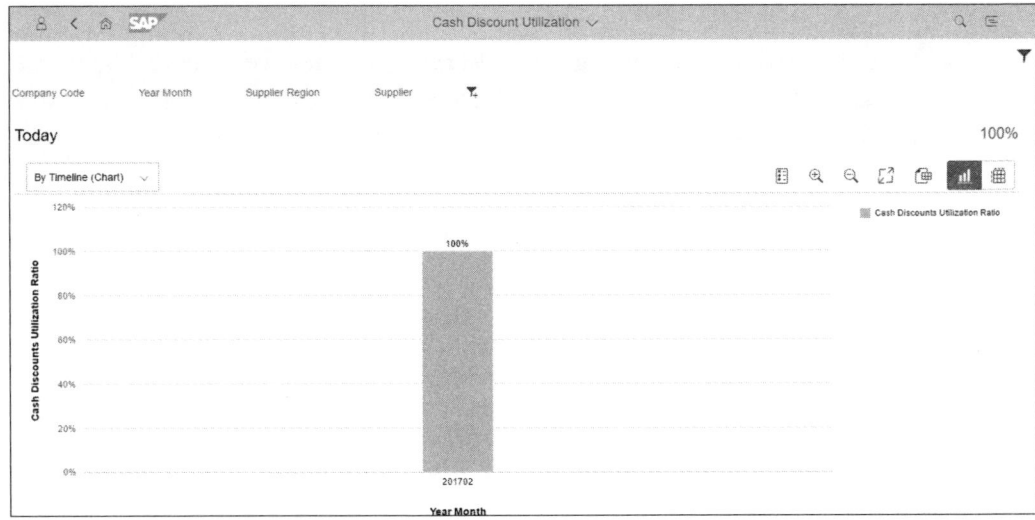

Figure 12.19 Cash Utilization Report

12.5.6 Days Payable Outstanding

The Days Payable Outstanding app gives you information to analyze and understand the key accounts payable performance indicator: days payable outstanding (DPO). DPO measures the number of payables a company has at the current moment. It lets you drill down to find suppliers with low or high days outstanding. You can view the data by company code, supplier, supplier's country, and timeframe, in either a chart or a table view.

The **Days Payable Outstanding** tile shown in Figure 12.20 shows a monthly breakdown of DPO for the last year.

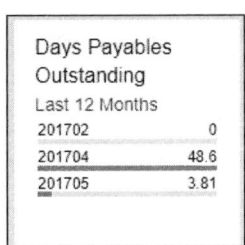

Figure 12.20 Days Payable Outstanding Tile

451

12 Reporting and Analytics

The Days Payables Outstanding app allows you to analyze DPO in a variety of ways:

- View days payable outstanding in the last rolling calendar year. For each month, as in Figure 12.21, you can drill down to the 10 suppliers with the highest/lowest days payable outstanding.
- View the top 10 DPOs by supplier.
- View DPO by company code. For each company code, you can drill down further to the top ten suppliers with the highest/lowest DPO value.
- Filter DPO by supplier.

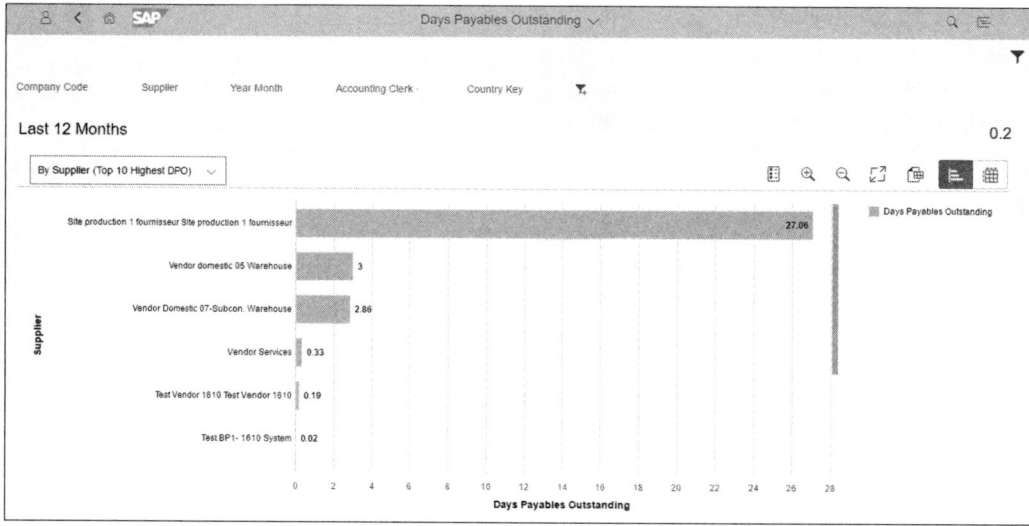

Figure 12.21 Days Payable Outstanding App

12.5.7 Invoice Processing Analysis

The Invoice Processing Analysis app lets you see information about the invoices processed in a period, such as the total number of posted invoices and posted line items.

The **Invoice Processing** analysis tile in Figure 12.22 displays the **Total Amount** metric, which is defined as the sum of the amounts of invoices posted in the designated period.

12.5 Accounts Payable Analytics and Reporting

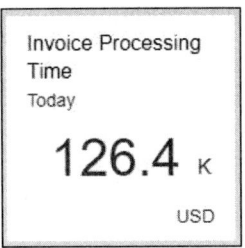

Figure 12.22 Invoice Processing Analysis Tile

The Invoice Processing Analysis app can be used to perform the following tasks:

- See the total amount of invoices and line items posted in a certain month, as shown in Figure 12.23.
- See the total amount of invoices and line items posted for a certain supplier or by a specified user.
- See the total amount of invoices and line items posted in each of the following four processing statuses:
  - **Free for Payment**
  - **Cleared**
  - **Blocked**
  - **Parked**

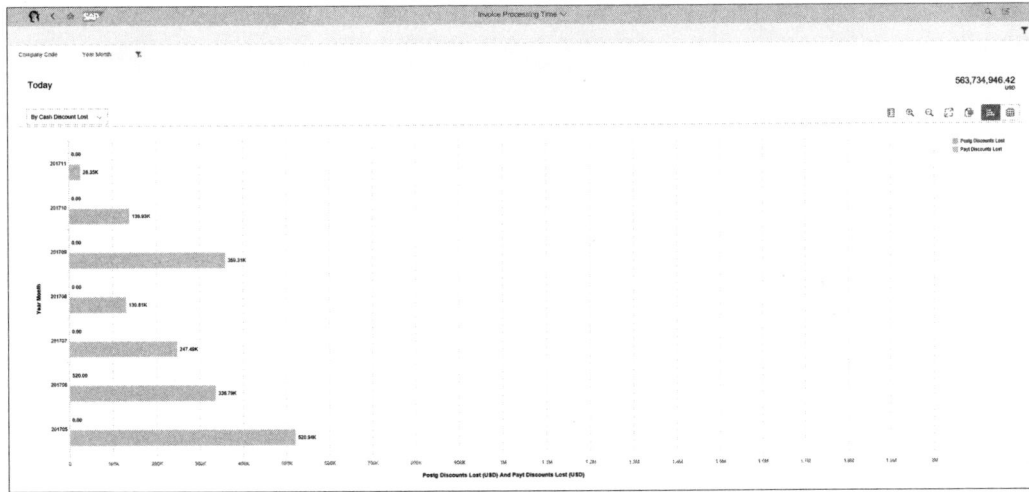

Figure 12.23 Invoice Processing Time

12.5.8 Supplier Payment Analysis (Manual and Automatic Payments)

The Supplier Payment Analysis (Manual and Automatic Payments) app is used to get insight into payments made in the last 365 days. Automatic payments are all payments posted directly by Transaction F110. Manual payments include all other payments made in the SAP S/4HANA system. The **Automatic and Manual Payments** tile (see Figure 12.24) shows the **Payments for the Last Year** metric, which is defined as the sum of the amount of payments that were made today through 365 days in the past.

Figure 12.24 Automatic and Manual Payments Tile

The Supplier Payment Analysis (Automatic and Manual Payments) app lets you perform the following tasks:

- Display aggregate data for all payment documents posted in the last year, as shown in Figure 12.25
- Display payment data by company code, supplier, user, or currency

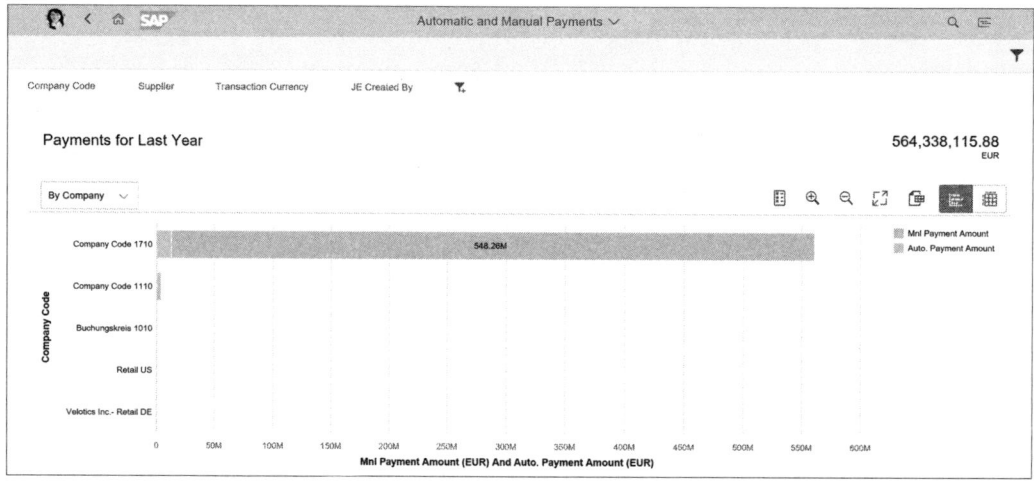

Figure 12.25 Automatic and Manual Payments Chart

12.5.9 Supplier Payment Analysis (Open Payments)

The Supplier Payment Analysis (Open Payments) app is used to get insight into open payments. You can look at open payments by company code, supplier, user, or currency, for example.

The **Supplier Payment Analysis** tile (see Figure 12.26) shows the **Open Payments** metric, which is defined as the sum of the amount of payments not cleared with invoices. Down payments are excluded from this analysis.

Figure 12.26 Supplier Payment Analysis Tile

This app can be used to perform the following tasks:

- Display data for all payment documents not reconciled with invoices
- Display payment data by company code, supplier, user, or currency, as shown in Figure 12.27

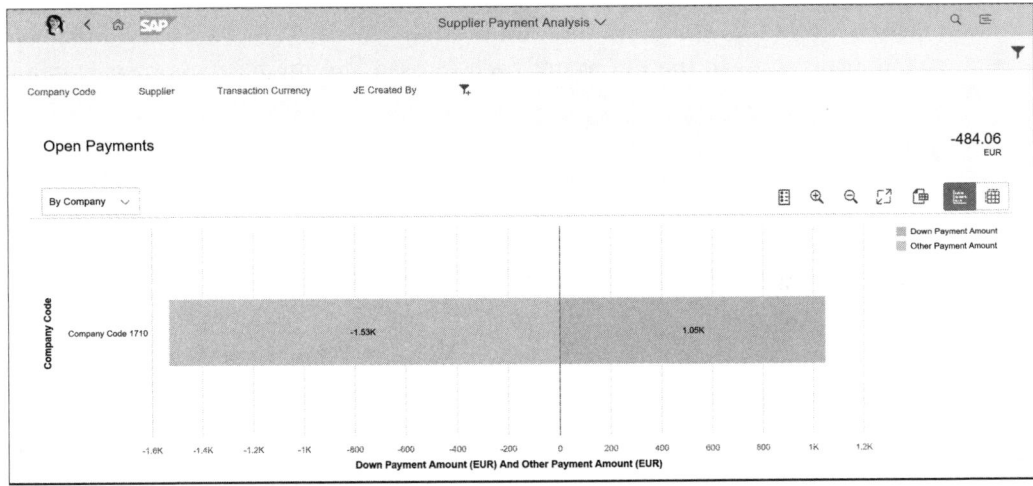

Figure 12.27 Supplier Payments Report

12   Reporting and Analytics

Accounts payable apps provide up-to-the-second information and analysis in a consumable format to optimize account payable's understanding of key metrics and cash position. As with procurement apps, SAP S/4HANA boasts a wide array of analytics apps and approaches for AP that weren't available, or in some cases even possible, in previous versions of SAP ERP. If a user requires an app that isn't available as a standard part of SAP S/4HANA, there's an option to build your own app or extend the existing standard ones. The next section looks at the extensibility of the analytics apps.

12.6 Configuration

Analytics apps can be assigned in a dashboard form for a user or a general role that then gets assigned to a user group. Once this role is assigned, you then have several options for the reporting app for display and further analysis. The **Legend** button in the app allows you to display or hide the legend. You can also zoom in and out and display the report full screen. This is especially useful when communicating reports during meetings, akin to putting a PowerPoint deck in display mode and removing the extraneous control icons to show the audience the essential report. You can also display graphs as tables and export to Excel using these buttons.

12.6.1 Creating a Key Performance Indicator

As discussed in Section 12.6, you can set KPIs to allow dashboard tiles to visually alert business users that their KPI thresholds have been crossed (indicated with red). Green displays mean the KPI hasn't been crossed and the business metric/area is operating as per budget/plan. To set a KPI, you must have the analytics specialist role assigned.

With this role, you now have multiple tiles available and corresponding options for working with KPIs.

Using this role, complete the following steps to set up a KPI:

1. **Create a KPI**
   Define the data source and measure
2. **Create an evaluation**
   Set evaluation criterion, prompt, values, and so on
3. **Create a tile**
   Choose the drilldown type and catalog to be saved

4. **Configure a drilldown**
   Set the dimensions/measures and visualization type

12.6.2 Configuring Real-Time Reporting/Queries

There are a multitude of procurement-centric analytics apps available in stock SAP S/4HANA. There are also nonstandard, custom reports you can build, as well as other analytics tools in the deep and wide analytics tools portfolio from SAP, which you can use for procurement reporting and analytics. There is an SAP Fiori-based set of apps called *Report Design Modeler apps* available in SAP S/4HANA Cloud from version 1702 onwards. These apps allow users of SAP S/4HANA Cloud to create and manage reports.

For SAP S/4HANA and SAP S/4HANA Cloud, there are two main types of users: key users, or IT users creating reports; and business users, who consume the reports. In some instances, business users also create the reports they're consuming, thereby playing both roles. Key users aren't quite technology users, but they aren't business users either. Key users build reports for business users with various tools and may span multiple departments and divisions of business users with their reports and analysis. To build reports, key users leverage the tools outlined in the following sections.

12.6.3 Exploring Virtual Data Model and Core Data Services in SAP S/4HANA

There are two SAP Fiori app browsers available for understanding and exploring the Virtual Data Model (VDM) and Core Data Services (CDS). The VDM is a structured representation of SAP S/4HANA database views. The VDM follows consistent modeling rules and provides direct access to SAP data via SQL and OData requests.

With an SAP HANA database, a paradigm for application development shifts from the app server directly to the database. To take advantage of this shift, SAP has introduced CDS, a data-modeling architecture that allows database models to be defined and consumed at the database level instead of the app-server level, taking advantage of SAP HANA's speed. CDS views aren't persistent, defined as the projection of other entities.

The Query Browser is part of a toolset aimed at business users, and the View Browser is part of the kit for key users.

Drilling into the Query Browser shows possible fields for query and details for running a selected analytical query with SAP Lumira, designer edition for multidimensional analysis.

Once on the overview screen, you can select which query you want to review.

On the detailed screen of the query, you can review the details of the selected analytic view, including its attributes and measures.

The View Browser shows input fields and output of CDS views and can display the data of the selected CDS views. SAP Lumira, designer edition is part of the View Browser app and supports analytic queries and multidimensional analysis.

The Custom CDS Views app allows you to take the following actions:

- Display a list of all predelivered data sources and existing custom CDS views.
- Preview details of available data sources and custom CDS views.
- Create a CDS view.

Similar to the CDS app, you can also create custom analytical queries in the Custom Analytical Queries app, shown in Figure 12.28. In this app, you can take the following actions:

- Create and manage analytical queries.
- Create calculated or restricted measures.
- Create additional parameters.
- Define which dimensions will be shown in rows and columns or as free dimensions.

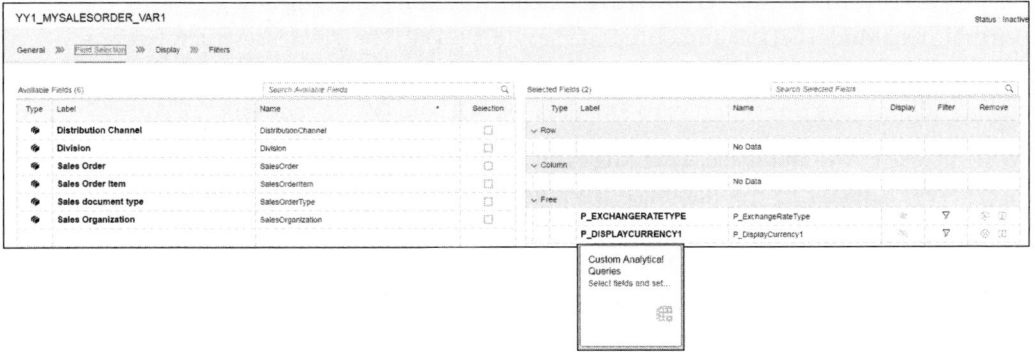

Figure 12.28 Custom Analytical Queries App

12.6.4 Integration of SAP S/4HANA with SAP Analytics Tools

There is also a portfolio of analytics solutions under the SAP BusinessObjects banner. Figure 12.29 outlines the various tools on offer by user.

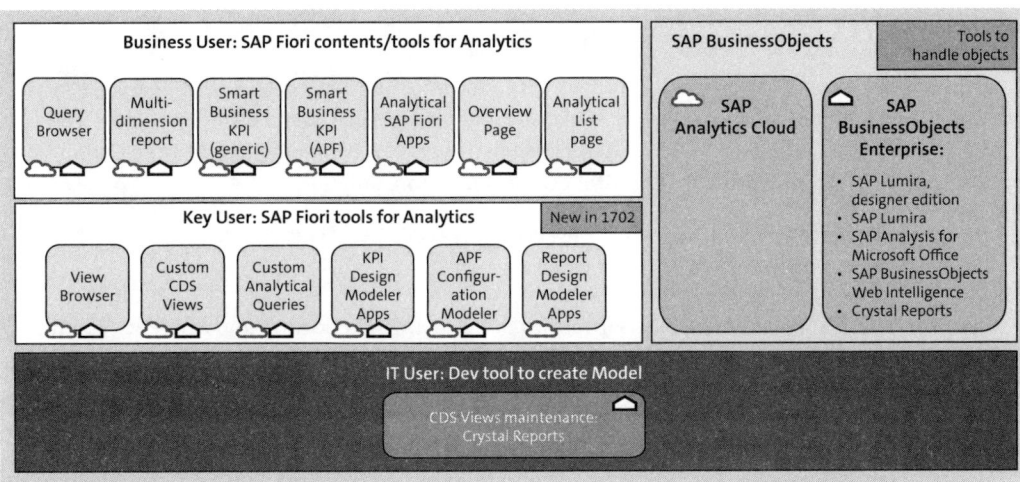

Figure 12.29 User Types for SAP BusinessObjects Tool Offerings

For further build out of reports, key user tools such as custom CDS views and View Browser are provided to go spelunking down at the database level for wisdom nuggets and views, as well as custom report creation. The resulting reports can then be consumed by the business user.

The business user can set KPIs directly and also has direct control over the Query Browser and apps. This way, a business user doesn't have to go through an intermediary for day-to-day analysis. In Table 12.1, the key user and business user tools are further explained. Analysis Office, for example, allows business users to directly analyze and report on data, whereas SAP Lumira, designer edition and SAP Lumira require a degree of expertise and specialization on the key user's part, who then creates reports for the general business users.

SAP Analytics Solution	Description/Application
SAP Lumira, designer edition	SAP Lumira, designer edition supports IT users creating SAP Lumira, designer edition applications to be consumed by business users.
SAP Lumira	Key users leverage SAP Lumira to create analytic *stories* used by business users.
SAP Analysis for Microsoft Office	Business users analyze CDS views with SAP Analysis for Microsoft Office.

Table 12.1 SAP BusinessObjects Tools for SAP S/4HANA Reporting and Analytics

459

SAP Analytics Solution	Description/Application
SAP BusinessObjects Web Intelligence	Key users and/or IT users leverage SAP BusinessObjects Web Intelligence to create reports using Query Panel and SAP BusinessObjects Web Intelligence document definition for business user consumption.
SAP Crystal Reports	IT users leverage SAP Crystal Reports to create reports for business users.

Table 12.1 SAP BusinessObjects Tools for SAP S/4HANA Reporting and Analytics (Cont.)

Multidimensional reporting tools such as the Floorplan Manager/Web Dynpro have the following characteristics in SAP S/4HANA:

- Dynamic analysis is possible—that is, slicing, dicing, and drilling down with many attributes.
- Analytical queries based on CDS views are used as a source.
- Web Dynpro objects are used in the backend system.
- No SAP Fiori app is available as a tool to create such reports directly.

The direction for these SAP Analytics reporting tools is to make them interoperable. For example, SAP Lumira and SAP BusinessObjects Explorer, both data-visualization tools, are being integrated, and you can export data from SAP Lumira, designer edition, a tool for building custom dashboards, into SAP Lumira. The SAP Analytics add-in for Microsoft Office, a Microsoft-focused tool for enterprise performance management, is converging with SAP analytics add-in for Microsoft Office, another analytics tool used in conjunction with Microsoft software.

> **Note**
>
> For the most recent interoperability updates for SAP Lumira and SAP Lumira, designer edition, visit *https://blogs.sap.com/2016/05/20/sap-lumira-and-design-studio-convergence/*.

12.7 Integration with Cloud Applications

Especially for hybrid environments, in which you're leveraging both SAP S/4HANA as the digital core and SAP Ariba and/or SAP Fieldglass to drive your procurement transformation, you'll need to look at analytics and at where data is stored and analyzed.

12.7.1 SAP Fieldglass

SAP S/4HANA natively integrates with SAP Fieldglass. This integration can be activated via guided configuration; middleware is not required. If you do require mediated connectivity for technical or policy reasons, you can leverage the SAP Cloud Platform to mediate the data transfers. Master data can be transferred, including purchasing organizations and plants, as well as transactional data such as supplier-initiated invoices. As such, you can integrate and incorporate the supplier-initiated invoices in SAP Fieldglass into overall spend reporting and analysis apps found in the Accounts Payable and Purchasing areas of SAP S/4HANA, outlined earlier in this chapter.

12.7.2 SAP Ariba

For SAP Ariba, you can integrate the spend management solutions bidirectionally, transferring data between SAP Ariba and SAP S/4HANA. The main mechanisms for this are as follows:

- Direct connectivity or mediated connectivity with SAP. Here, you implement SAP ABAP transports to send and receive SOAP-based data files directly to and from the SAP Ariba system. The mediated connectivity approach makes use of SAP Process Orchestration (SAP PO) to broker the transaction.
- Manual import and export of files from the spend management UI. This approach entails identifying what data you wish to export from SAP Ariba, locating the source using SAP Ariba resources and documentation, and exporting and importing the data manually into SAP S/4HANA's reporting tools and data structures.
- Automated file transfer using the SAP Ariba data transfer tool. You can automate the transfer of CSV files between spend management and external systems. The data transfer tool includes a command-line utility that facilitates CSV transfer in batch mode to SAP S/4HANA, as well as a *DB connector*, a command-line utility that connects the SAP Ariba data transfer tool with a JDBC-based ERP system.
- Real-time transfer using SOAP APIs. You can create web services to transfer data between systems using SOAP-based protocols.

When deciding where to conduct an analysis, it helps to consolidate the data from all applicable transactions and systems. In the case of SAP Ariba, if your buyers are conducting most of their business in SAP Ariba area, then it can make the most sense to extract SAP S/4HANA data and perform the comprehensive analysis in the cloud.

Conversely, if you're running the procurement operations mostly in SAP S/4HANA, with some SAP Ariba solutions involved and SAP Fieldglass for contingent labor, it may make the most sense to bring the cloud data into SAP S/4HANA, then analyze it comprehensively using the apps and extensibility on offer.

12.8 Summary

The apps-based approach of SAP S/4HANA Fiori, the topic of the next chapter, extends to analytics, as does the real-time, in-system processing of analytics and reporting in the transacting system. For Sourcing and Procurement, there are extensive reporting and analytics apps on offer from the initial stage of the process all the way through to accounts payable. In addition, users can extend their views and analysis via SAP BusinessObjects tools and integrated tools, as well as build customized reports. Integrated tools such as the *Report Design Modeler apps* in SAP S/4HANA Cloud, viewing browsers, and customization options create a further platform from which to drive real-time insight and, ultimately, better performance in SAP S/4HANA analytics and reporting in general and in SAP S/4HANA Sourcing and Procurement in particular. Next, we'll discuss the SAP Fiori UI approach in SAP S/4HANA.

Chapter 13
Customizing the SAP Fiori UI

This chapter focuses on the UI technology underpinning SAP S/4HANA and several future SAP solutions, as well: SAP Fiori. Based on user roles and business processes, SAP Fiori is a design language that underpins the UX in SAP S/4HANA.

One of the biggest challenges for SAP ERP has been UI and design. SAP Fiori focuses on users and design, simplifying and reimagining processes while embracing open standards and service orientation on the technology side. Perhaps equally important for SAP S/4HANA, SAP Fiori is built to run with in-memory and cloud applications. From a business user standpoint, SAP Fiori stands for simplification and reimagined processes, distilling transactions and processes into role-focused apps and easy-to-navigate screens. SAP Fiori is the go-to UI technology for SAP solutions.

13.1 The SAP Fiori User Interface

Many UI approaches of the past created an overwhelming cockpit of controls, buttons, and levers, confounding users looking to accomplish specific tasks in the system. SAP Fiori instead emphasizes role-based interaction, while still allowing for adaptability and flexibility to allow users to apply functionality beyond a single path or process. This emphasis on simplicity, rather than feature overload, carries over into the other core tenets of SAP Fiori:

- *Role-based*: designed for you, your needs, and how you work
- *Adaptive*: adapts to multiple use cases and devices
- *Coherent*: provides one fluid, intuitive experience
- *Simple*: includes only what's necessary
- *Delightful*: makes an emotional connection

For example, in SAP Fiori, you can click on a tile such as **Workflow Inbox** and enter the Approvals app (shown in Figure 13.1). Unlike previous workflow approval layouts, you only see the fundamentals: the request list and an expanded window showing the content of a selected request.

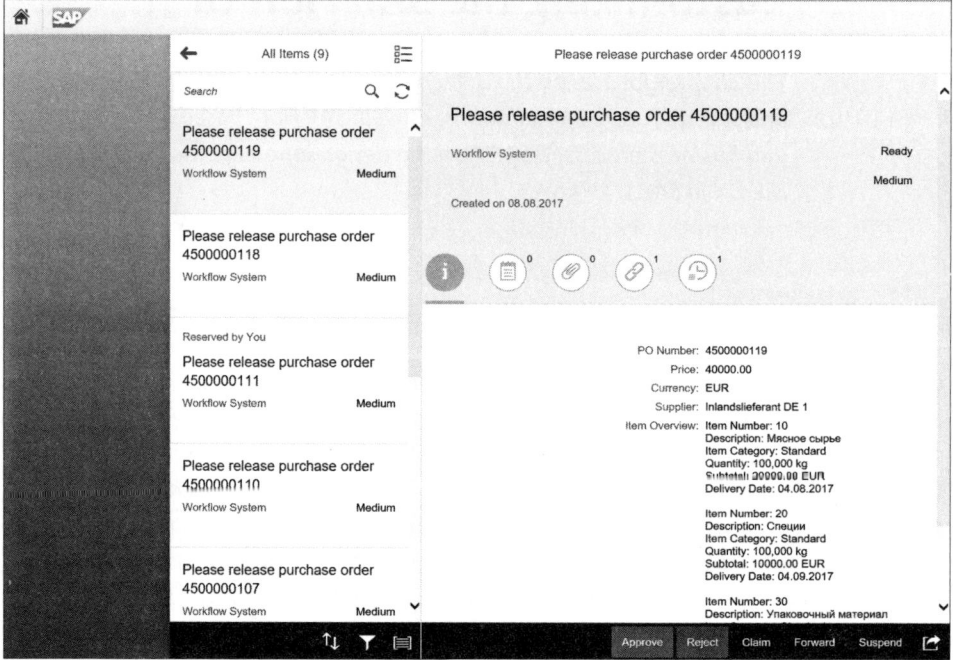

Figure 13.1 SAP Fiori Approvals App

Approvals is quite straightforward from a UI perspective and doesn't need a lot of bells and whistles. Either you approve something or you reject a request, perhaps communicating directly with the user during the process to further refine the order or understand a nuance. Beyond this, there need not be a slew of features. The app is in line with this thinking and with SAP Fiori's approach and principles overall.

13.1.1 SAP Fiori Launchpad

As of SAP S/4HANA 1610, SAP Fiori is the sole UI option. A user can update her profile and access her applications/notifications all via a single landing page called the *SAP Fiori launchpad*, as shown in Figure 13.2.

By clicking the shell header icons located at the top of the window, a user can navigate to his last activities in the system or to key notifications, as shown in Figure 13.3. The anchor bar at the top replaces the group menu options.

13.1 The SAP Fiori User Interface

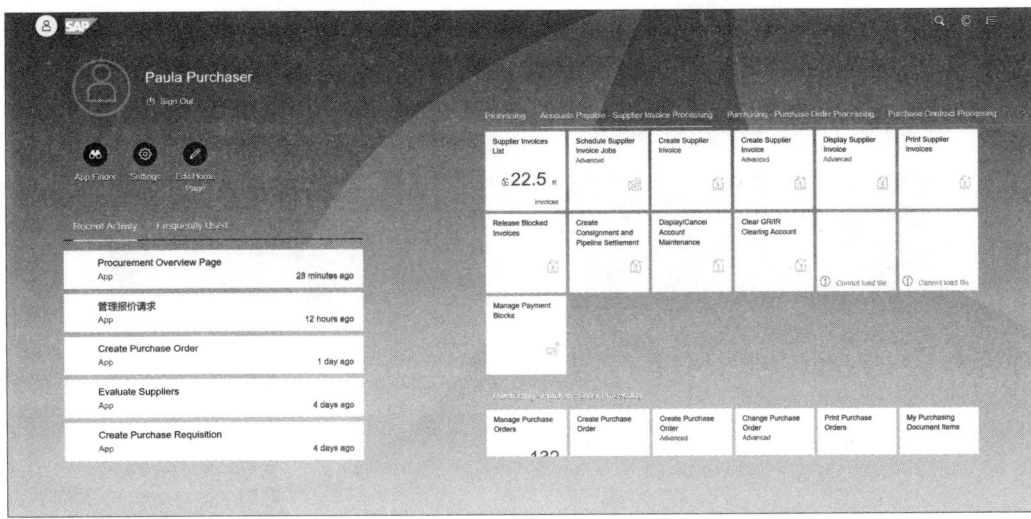

Figure 13.2 SAP Fiori Launchpad Overview

Figure 13.3 SAP Fiori Header Icons and Anchor Bar

Front and center are the apps, which can be made available as tiles or as links, as shown in Figure 13.4.

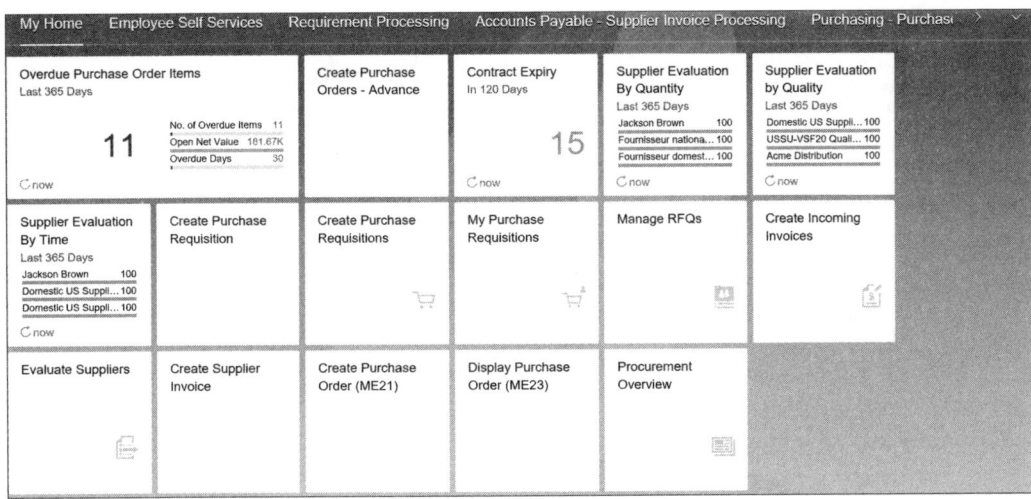

Figure 13.4 SAP Fiori Tiles

465

13   Customizing the SAP Fiori UI

Color-coding and dynamic charts in the tiles are used to update the user about important issues without having to drill into specific areas. A search option shown in Figure 13.5 allows you to search across and within apps, including individual business objects, to find immediate answers.

Figure 13.5 SAP Fiori Search Bar

If you need to drill into a business object or app, you can do so directly from the search results, as shown in Figure 13.6.

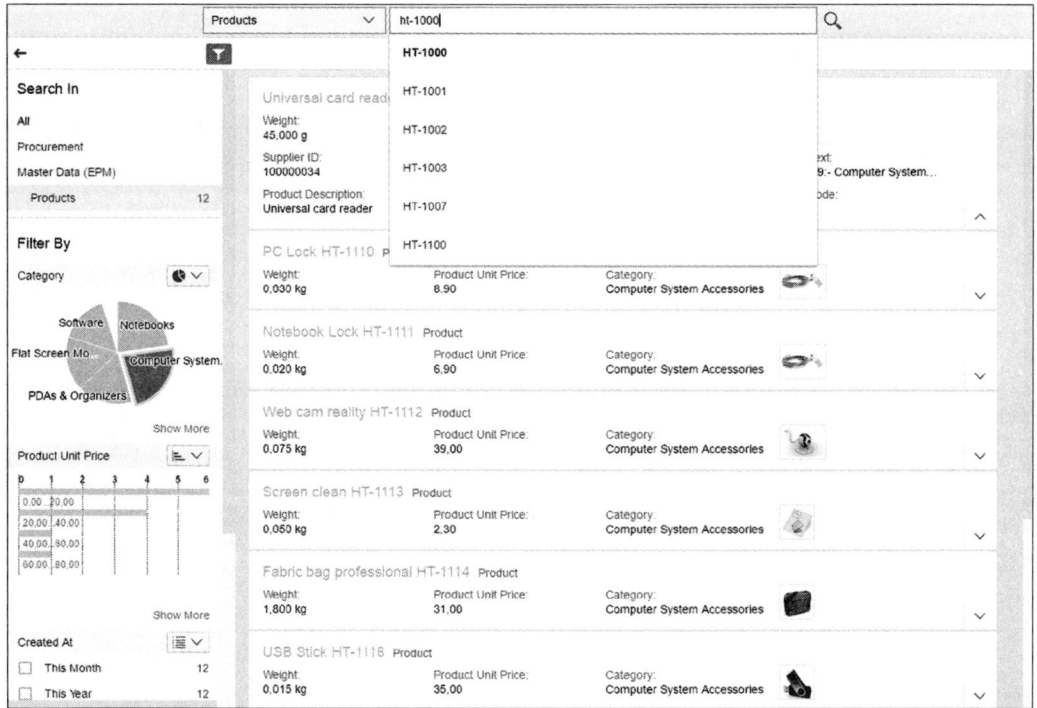

Figure 13.6 From SAP Fiori Launchpad Search Results to App or Business Object

You also can enter edit mode to personalize groups, tiles, and link menus, and launch into other applications in SAPUI5, Web Dynpro ABAP, SAP GUI for HTML, or URLs. You have to be on a device supporting these UIs for this launch to be successful, however.

The supported UI technologies include the following:

- Unified Rendering (Web Dynpro, ABAP/Java, HTML GUI, BSP, HTMLB)
- SAPUI5 (SAP Fiori, SAP Fiori launchpad)
- WebClient UIF (SAP CRM)
- SAP Portal Content Management by OpenText (Ajax Framework Page, SAP Fiori Framework Page)
- SAP NetWeaver Business Client (for desktop and HTML)

> **Note**
> Support is planned for SAPUI5 for Custom Libs and SAP GUI for Windows GUI.

SAP Fiori supports the following platforms:

- SAP NetWeaver AS for ABAP
- SAP Portal Content Management
- SAP Cloud Platform

These changes put all the core information and access at the user's fingertips while leaving some "whitespace" free for a featureless desktop rather than overloading the layout with distractions and nonessential functionality. In the SAP Fiori approach, no general newsfeeds or bulletin boards are found, just the key areas relevant to the user's role.

> **SAP Fiori 2.0 Design Concept**
> SAP Fiori 2.0 leverages a new Belize theme with light and dark flavors to further refine the SAP Fiori visual language, as well as a clean and consistent layout to convey content and clarity. SAP Fiori 2.0 addresses some of the shortcomings from 1.0, including standardizing screen elements, icons, and color, as well as unifying interaction and adopting application design.

13.1.2 SAP General User Interface

The SAP GUI has underpinned previous versions of SAP ERP, spanning back decades now. The screenshot in Figure 13.7 may look very familiar to long-time SAP users, even though it's a screenshot of an SAP S/4HANA SAP GUI screen. Little has changed here, and the transaction code bar still remains in the upper left-hand corner.

13 Customizing the SAP Fiori UI

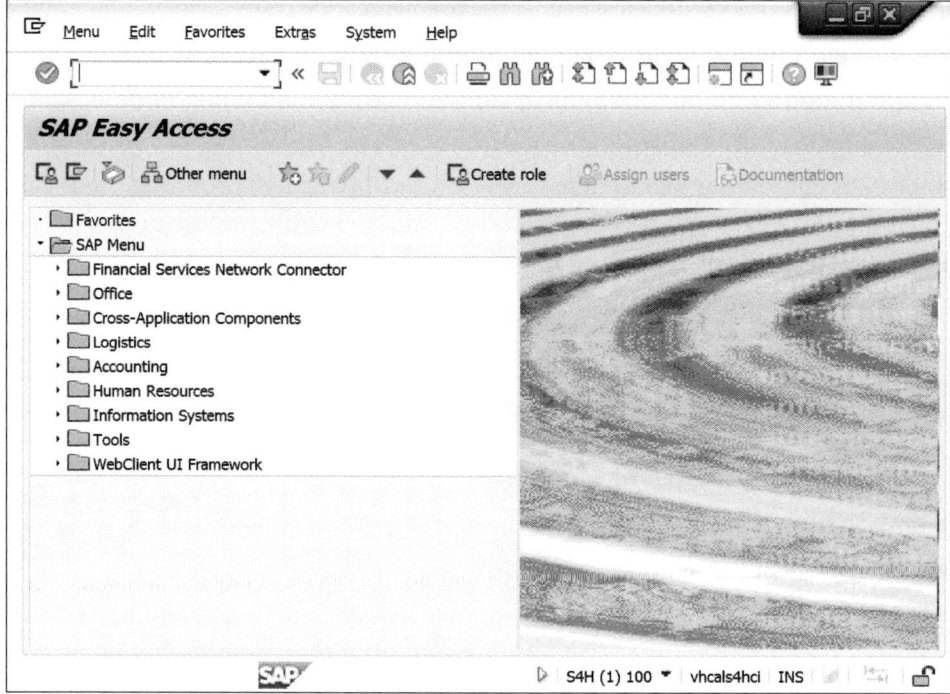

Figure 13.7 SAP GUI

In SAP S/4HANA, you can launch SAP GUI either out of HTML or Business Client approach. There are limitations and advantages to both options. Despite some limitations, SAP GUI HTML is the recommended approach for SAP GUI running the Belize theme. The SAP GUI limitations on the HTML side are as follows:

- Office integration is view-only.
- No Bar chart (GANTT), Netchart and SCM Planning Grid controls.
- No new ABAP Editor control (ABAP development needs SAP GUI for Windows).
- Limited support for client interaction (Upload/Download/Execute, etc.) especially in new browsers.
- Limited keyboard navigation.
- Lower performance compared to SAP GUI for Windows.

However, HTML does support Personas features. *Personas* is the personalization framework integrated into SAP GUI and multiple operating systems via its browser-based approach. A native Belize theme experience in SAP GUI will be available for SAP

GUI for Windows 7.5 and SAP Business Client 6.5. As far as using older themes in SAP Fiori, though possible, it isn't recommended, and not all the new features will be enabled using an older theme.

13.1.3 SAP Fiori Architecture

Before you begin implementation or configuration of SAP Fiori for SAP S/4HANA, it's important to understand the underlying SAP Fiori architecture for the different editions of SAP S/4HANA. There are differences between logging into SAP S/4HANA Cloud and SAP S/4HANA.

In SAP S/4HANA Cloud, users log in via the service's web dispatcher and, once authenticated, access the SAP Fiori UI. From there, the user can then can access the business-logic layer of SAP S/4HANA Cloud via SAP Fiori apps and the general UI.

In an on-premise version of SAP S/4HANA, the user logs into the SAP S/4HANA frontend server either via a browser to access the web dispatcher and system hosted internally or via an on-premise desktop/VPN, as per Figure 13.8. Cloud users go directly to SAP S/4HANA without a mediated connection as in the on-premise version.

For mobile devices, SAP Fiori provides the SAP Mobile Platform, which leverages the SAP Fiori frontend server, as per Figure 13.8.

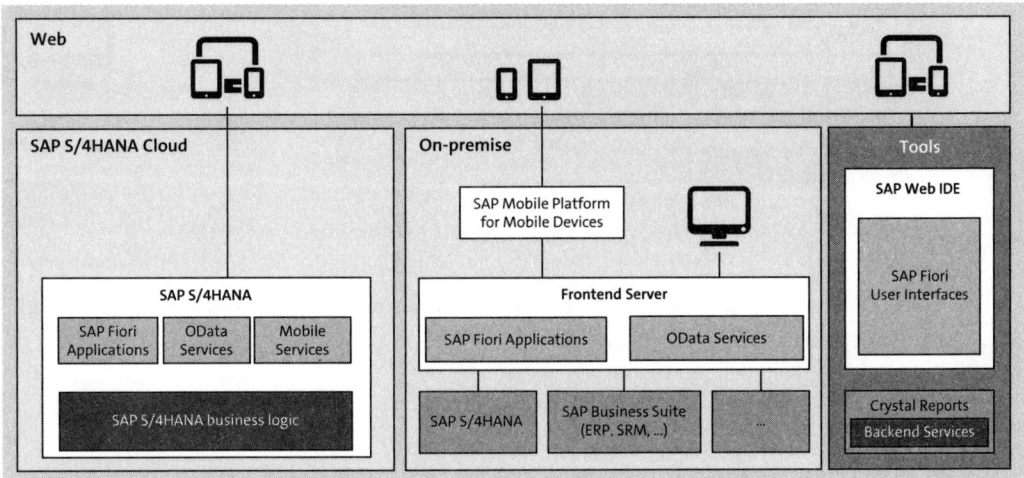

Figure 13.8 SAP Fiori Architecture Overview

From an architecture standpoint, the main difference between SAP S/4HANA Cloud and on-premise is the frontend server requirement. This is the SAP S/4HANA view with the changed access pattern to the SAP HANA database. From a sizing perspective, the approach stays the same, only load pattern changes. The desktop's path runs from the web dispatcher directly to the SAP S/4HANA SAP NetWeaver ABAP backend, whereas the mobile devices run through the web dispatcher to the SAP Frontend Server (FES), and then onwards to the SAP NetWeaver ABAP backend and SAP S/4HANA database.

As shown in Figure 13.9, the main technical components of SAP Fiori on SAP S/4HANA are the frontend server, including SAP Gateway, SAP NetWeaver/ABAP, including an SAP Gateway add-on, the SAP HANA database, SAP Web Dispatcher, and the SAP Mobile Platform.

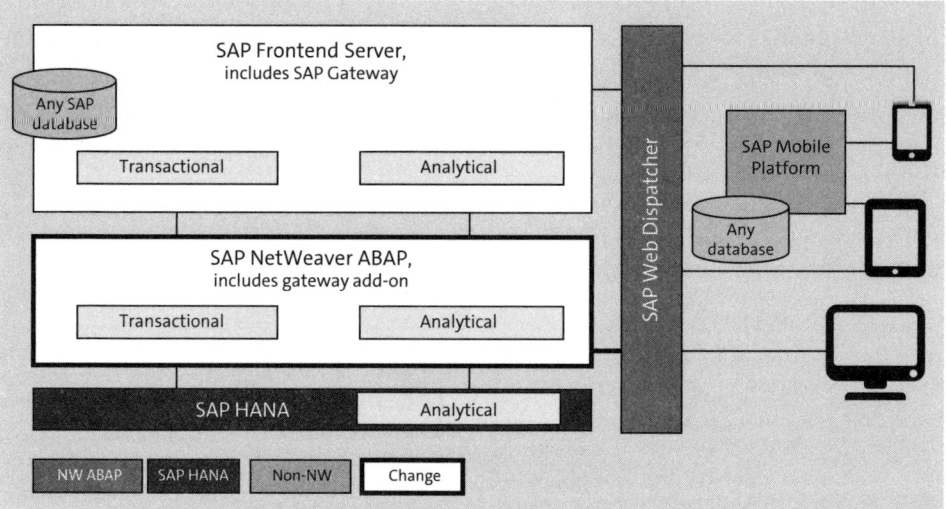

Figure 13.9 SAP Fiori on SAP S/4HANA: Architecture Simplified System View

From SAP S/4HANA, a user can access the SAP Fiori launchpad via a supported web browser and launch the following:

- SAP Fiori apps
- SAP GUI for HTML
- Web Dynpro apps

SAP Business Client

Another way to support SAP Fiori is via the SAP Business Client. The SAP Business Client approach replaces the web browser with a dedicated UI called the SAP Business Client. This approach provides more focused throughput on the transaction side, meaning faster speeds, and it's sometimes favored for desktop users performing specific transactions in the system for this reason. Future support is planned for a Windows SAP GUI in the SAP Business Client UI approach to SAP S/4HANA, as shown in Figure 13.10. The Windows SAP GUI in the SAP Business Client version will initially come in the classic SAP GUI design, with the SAP Fiori theme planned for future releases of this approach.

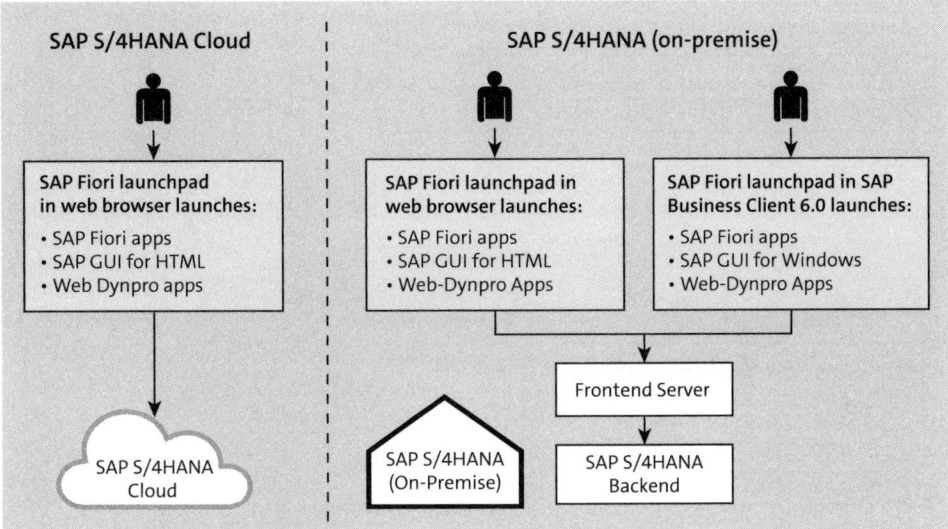

Figure 13.10 SAP Business Client UI Approach for SAP S/4HANA

Central Hub vs. Embedded: Deploying SAP Gateway

Further drilling into the general architecture of SAP Fiori for SAP S/4HANA, you can deploy the SAP Gateway either in a separate, central hub or in an embedded fashion, as in Figure 13.11 and Figure 13.12. Depending on your role in the project, you may or may not be tasked with deciding the approach here, as it's typically more of an IT decision. However, knowing the trade-offs, even at a functional level, is helpful for understanding how your SAP Fiori environment works.

13   Customizing the SAP Fiori UI

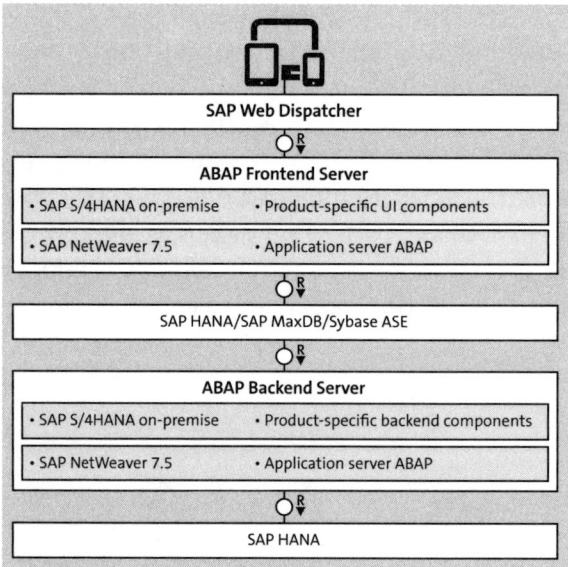

Figure 13.11 Fiori Landscape – Central Hub and Embedded Options for SAP Gateway (Part 1)

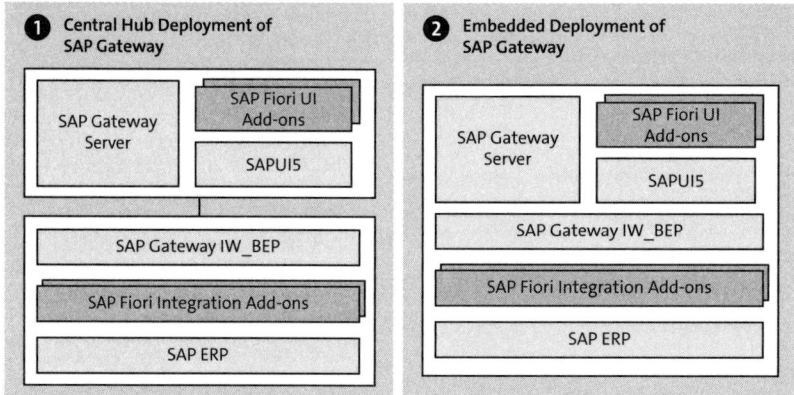

Figure 13.12 Fiori Landscape – Central Hub and Embedded Options for SAP Gateway (Part 2)

The central hub approach is more typical in productive environments than the embedded, though the embedded option is lightweight and allows for speedier setup of test environments. Key advantages of an embedded deployment are as follows:

- No additional SAP NetWeaver ABAP system needed; less TCO
- Less runtime overhead, as well as no remote-call

- Direct access to metadata and business data
- Later scale-out to central hub deployment possible

However, some of the concerns for an embedded approach are as follows:

- Innovation speed of SAP Fiori UI and backend must be synchronized
- Update strategy must reflect dependencies between software components
- SAP backend must fulfill minimum system requirements
- Possible scale-up of SAP backend (resizing)

Currently, the majority of customers are on a central hub deployment, which has its own advantages and considerations, as illustrated in Figure 13.13.

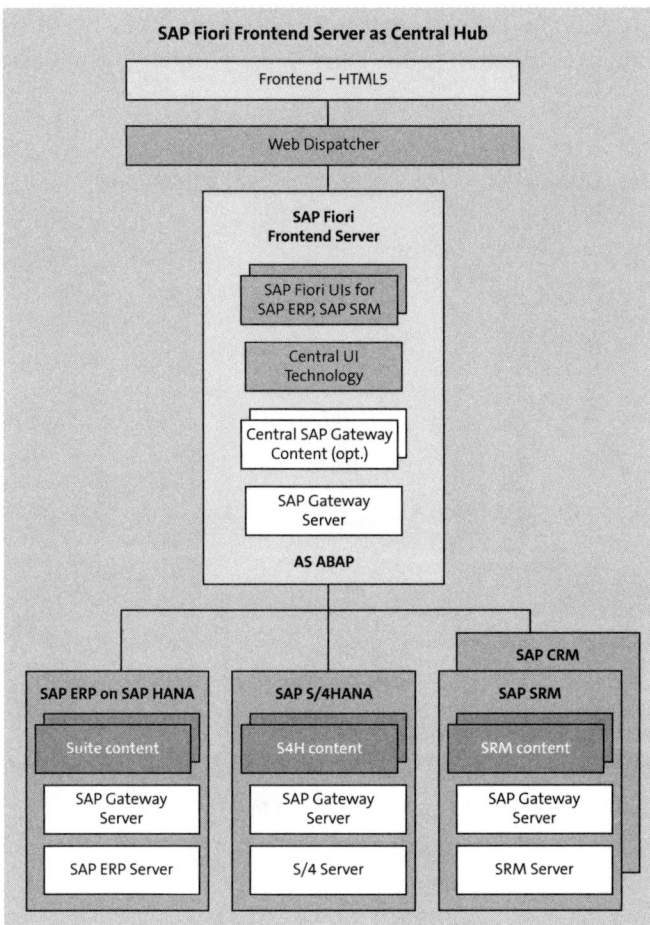

Figure 13.13 Central Hub Deployment for SAP Fiori Frontend Server

Regardless of the deployment approach for the SAP Fiori frontend server, SAP Fiori 2.0 is mandatory for all SAP Fiori apps on SAP S/4HANA version 1610 and beyond, and 1610 apps require an SAP database. Existing apps at this 1610 level and beyond currently run on the Belize theme. It's also possible to run older apps on SAP Fiori 2.0 in their respective classic themes. Not all functionality may be accessible for older apps without adjustments.

13.2 User-Driven UI Tuning Options

In SAP S/4HANA Sourcing and Procurement, as in other areas in SAP S/4HANA Enterprise Management, the first thing a user sees at login is the SAP Fiori launchpad, shown in Figure 13.14. The SAP Fiori launchpad displays tiles for apps, as well as other information, serving as the main entry point to SAP Fiori apps on mobile and desktop devices.

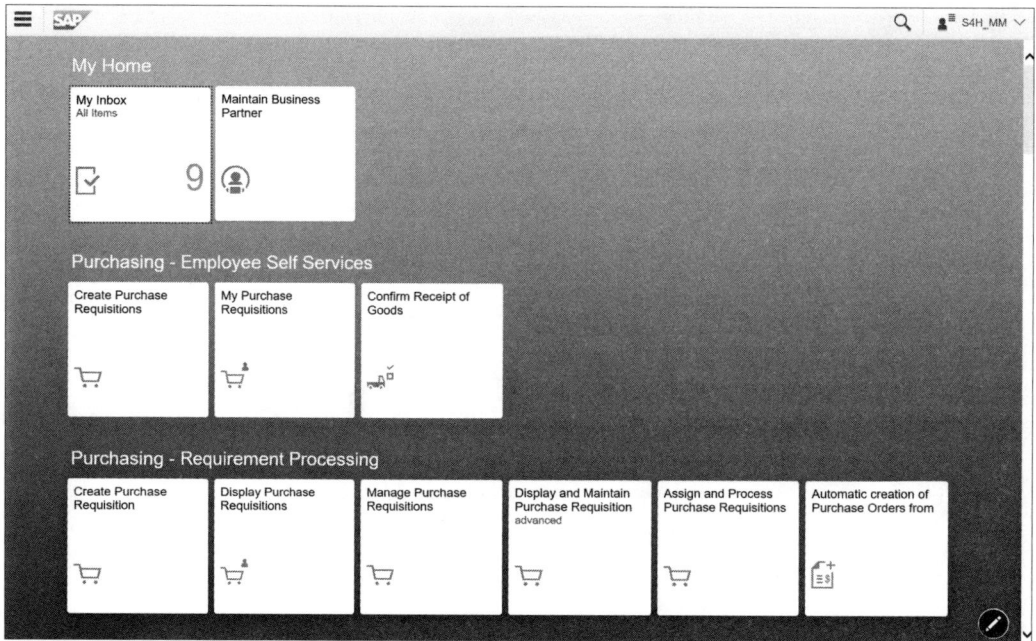

Figure 13.14 SAP Fiori Launchpad for SAP S/4HANA Sourcing and Procurement Users

13.2 User-Driven UI Tuning Options

A user can add, remove, and bundle tiles in the SAP Fiori launchpad and tailor the launchpad to serve as a starting point for all work in the system. The SAP Fiori launchpad automatically adjusts the screen and apps to the type of device being used.

13.2.1 SAP Fiori Edit Mode

You can arrange the dashboard and other apps by going into **Edit** mode, as shown in Figure 13.15. Here, you can move the app tiles and even delete tiles that aren't relevant to/desired for your dashboard. You can also add groups to group relevant apps together and allow for easier navigation.

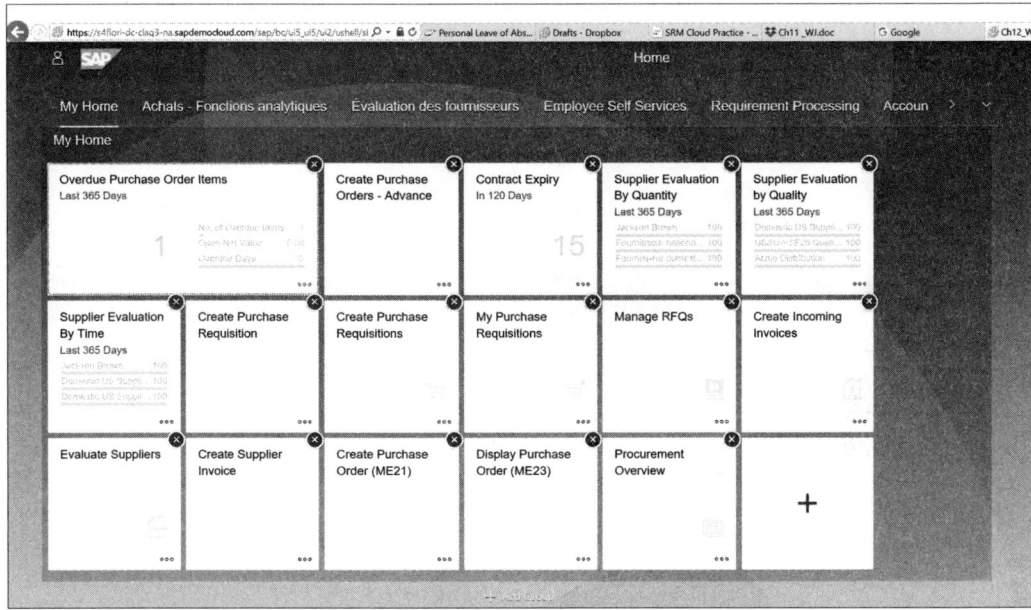

Figure 13.15 SAP Fiori Dashboard in Edit Mode

13.2.2 SAP Fiori User Settings

To tune and adjust the UI, you don't need to have configuration access. By going into the **Settings** area, as shown in Figure 13.16, you can tune several areas in SAP Fiori.

475

13 Customizing the SAP Fiori UI

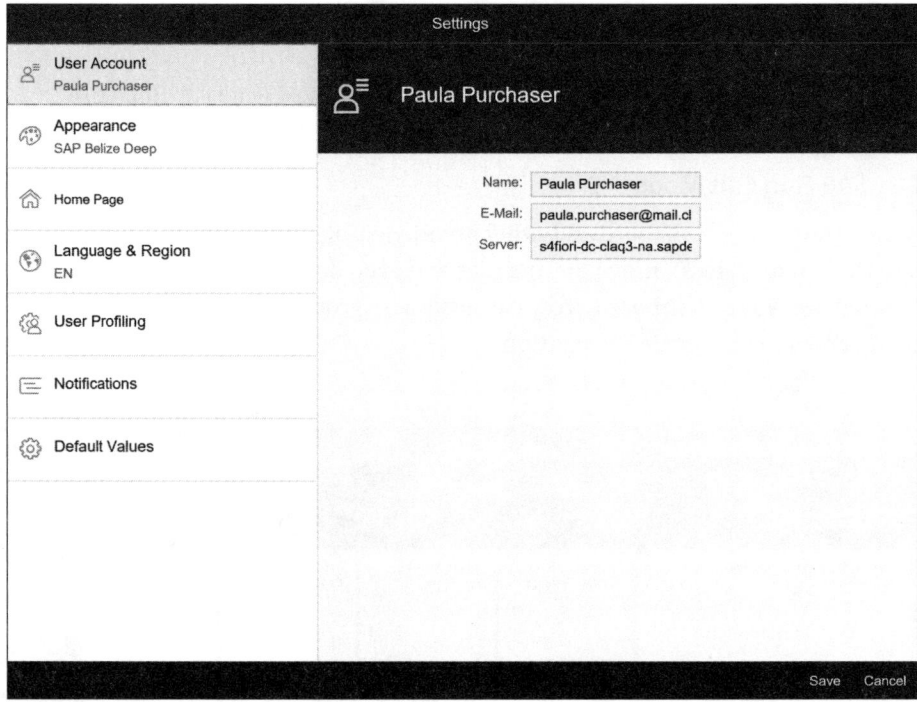

Figure 13.16 User Settings in SAP Fiori

The areas you can change include the following:

- **User Account**
  You can change the user account.

- **Appearance**
  The appearance of the screen can be changed from the standard Belize setting to a different **Theme**. You also can activate **Cozy Content Spacing** (Figure 13.17), which eliminates spacing between screen icons and buttons.

- **Home Page**
  Here, you have the option of showing all of the content or one group at a time.

- **Language & Region**
  Here, you can set the language, date, and time settings.

- **User Profiling**
  If this feature is turned on, SAP Fiori logs searches and other selections during usage to enable smart searching in the system. For example, if you search for the same thing often and select similar items from the search results, these items will

be displayed more prominently. An administrator can also turn this feature off, as shown in Figure 13.18.

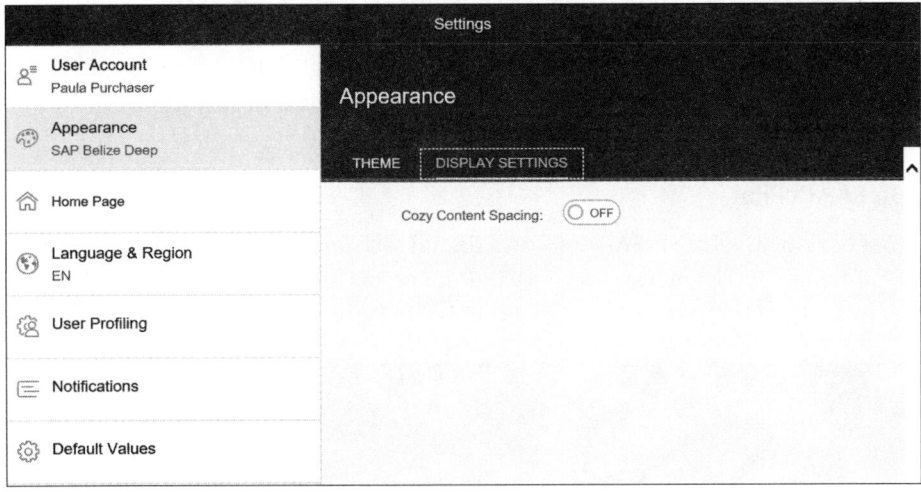

Figure 13.17 Cozy Content Settings

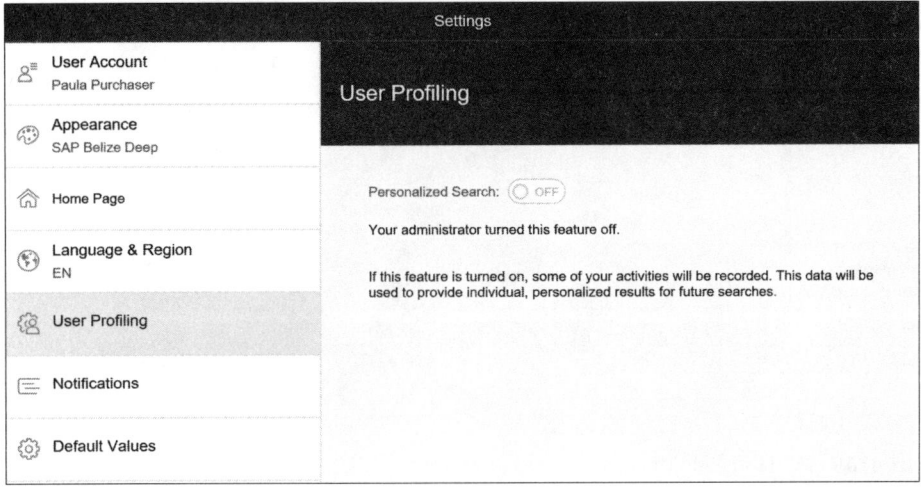

Figure 13.18 SAP Fiori Personalized Search

- **Notifications**

    If notifications are enabled in your apps, this is where you'll see app notifications. Otherwise, a message will appear that notifications aren't activated for your apps.

13　Customizing the SAP Fiori UI

- **Default Values**
  This is a very useful area, especially for users conducting routine transactions in the system. Here, you can set financial defaults for controlling, such as controlling area and cost center. You can also set accounting defaults, such as company code, business area, and/or G/L account. Finally, you can set defaults for supply chain management, such as bank information, supplier, plant, and customer.

13.2.3　SAP CoPilot

Another usability feature is SAP CoPilot, a digital assistant for enterprise, available as of SAP S/4HANA 1705. You can turn SAP CoPilot on via an icon in the upper left-hand corner of an SAP Fiori screen. The icon is circled in Figure 13.19.

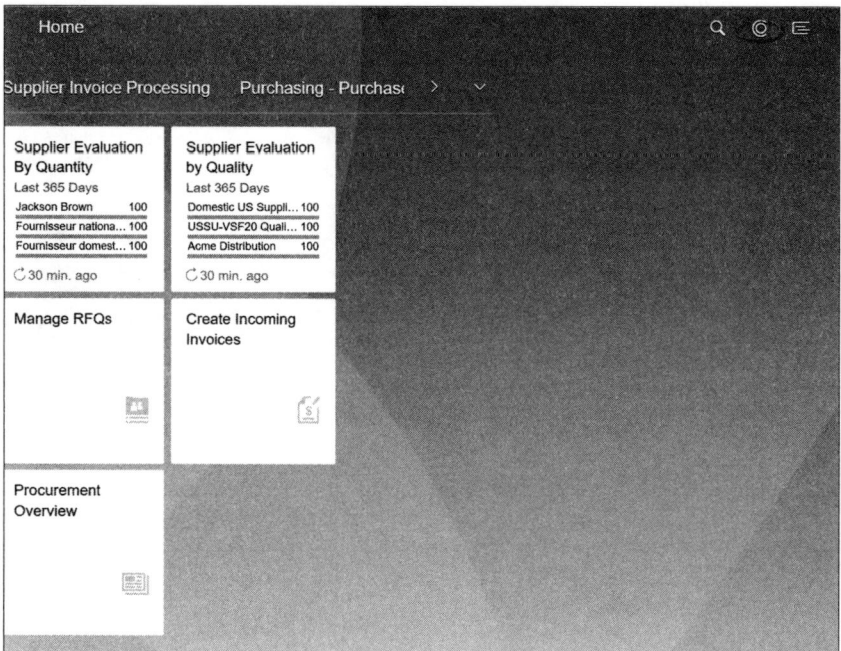

Figure 13.19　SAP Fiori CoPilot Icon

After turning on SAP CoPilot, a user can perform the following actions:

- Create notes when working with apps and have these notes linked to the apps.
- Create intelligent screenshots that allow you to navigate in the app to where the screenshot was taken. When sharing the apps, colleagues can follow the screenshot to the particular place in the app where the screenshot was taken, provided they

13.2 User-Driven UI Tuning Options

have access to the app. This allows for faster collaboration and issue resolution when using screenshots in support cases.

- SAP CoPilot recognizes business objects mentioned in chats, notes, or on the screen in general, allowing you to add business objects as such in screenshots, notes, and chats.
- The context extends to the chat feature in SAP S/4HANA, so there's no need to send emails and attach screenshots if you prefer chat. You can also save the chats, along with the attachments, for later use.
- Quick actions allow you to create business objects via QuickCreate UIs, which simplify the process by defaulting content from SAP CoPilot.

Classic transactions in SAP, even if they retain essentially the same fields, receive an overhaul in SAP Fiori in terms of appearance. These transactions are usually a couple of layers deeper into the process, rather than on the opening page. A key one for SAP S/4HANA Sourcing and Procurement is the well-known PO Transaction ME21N. This is now the "advanced" version for creating a PO in SAP S/4HANA (see Figure 13.20), in which, as discussed in Chapter 4, a user can create a framework order and other more involved types of purchase orders.

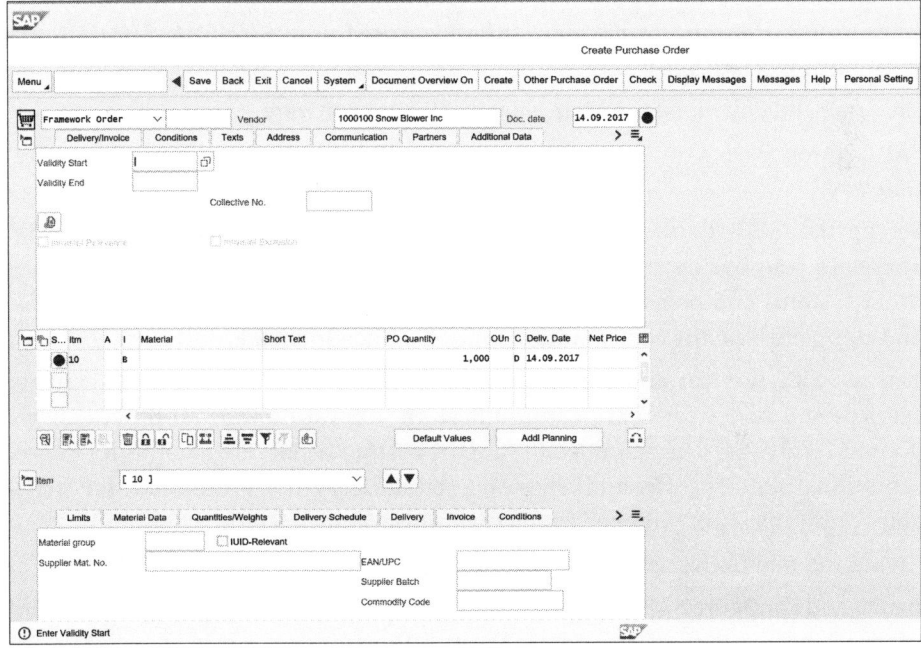

Figure 13.20 SAP Fiori: Create Purchase Order—Advanced

13 Customizing the SAP Fiori UI

In this transaction, the fields are mostly the same as in an SAP ERP environment, but the look and feel has been updated to align with SAP Fiori principles and approaches. This is the general approach taken by SAP for all classic transactions remaining in SAP Fiori and SAP S/4HANA.

13.3 SAP Fiori Configuration

This section provides a general overview of the installation of and required components for SAP Fiori. You should always check on *service.sap.com* prior to installing an SAP system to obtain the latest installation guides and notes.

13.3.1 Installing SAP Fiori

To install SAP Fiori, the technical SAP Basis team on your project will need to complete the following steps:

1. Install SAP NetWeaver 7.5x with the latest SPS. The supported databases are SAP HANA, SAP Adaptive Server Enterprise (ASE), or SAP MaxDB.
2. Follow the SAP S/4HANA SAP Fiori Foundation Configuration Guides found at *https://service.sap.com/public/rds* • **SAP Best Practice for SAP S/4HANA** • **S/4HANA** • **UX Best Practice for SAP S/4HANA**.
3. Generate and download the Maintenance Planner software.
4. SAP Gateway Basic Configuration; this refers to the baseline configuration of SAP Gateway.
5. Set up trusted RFCs/system aliases/SAP Fiori launchpad initial configuration. These are your basic set up steps for enabling the system to communicate with other systems and be configured. Configure your RFCs, define the system alias, and complete baseline configuration for SAP Fiori launchpad.
6. Activate SICF services and OData services. In Transaction SICF, you can activate services and nodes for HTTP communication. Activating OData services allows your RESTful APIs to be extended to support custom needs. *REST* stands for Representational State Transfer and relies on a stateless, client-server-based and cacheable communication protocol, which typically leverages HTTP.
7. Create and maintain standard SAP Fiori roles.
8. Install and configure SAP Web Dispatcher. SAP Web Dispatcher is required for on-premise installations of SAP S/4HANA and functions as a broker between the user's browser and the SAP S/4HANA system.

9. Activate Enterprise Search (fact sheet applications). SAP Fiori fact sheets provide overview information on a business object. By enabling search, you can identify related fact sheets while searching for an item, such as a material master.
10. Load search indexes. Indexes allow a search to run faster and more comprehensively.
11. Setup the SAP BW client on the SAP S/4HANA system for Embedded Analytics.
12. Activate SAP NetWeaver Business Client/WebGUI for HTML/Web Dynpro applications on the backend system.

13.3.2 Embedded and Central Hub Deployment for SAP Fiori

You then either configure a central hub or embedded deployment of SAP Fiori. The central hub and embedded options are the two main ways to set up the system, and each has advantages and concerns. In general, the central hub approach is used for larger production systems and systems required to handle large volumes of users, transactions, and queries. An embedded deployment approach is often used for development and functional testing systems, for which volume requirements are not as pronounced, and sometimes for more modest production systems supporting smaller organizations.

Central hub installation means you install the frontend and backend components on different systems. A central hub deployment requires more effort to set up, but allows you to separate your SAP Solution Manager installation from your SAP Fiori apps, making your apps available to business users without having to run SAP Solution Manager. This approach also allows you to consolidate your SAP Fiori apps into one launchpad, even when using multiple systems. You can perform the development either in the SAP Gateway system or directly in SAP Business Suite. Developing directly in SAP Business Suite allows you to reuse data easily because the data is in the system in which the development is taking place. Developing on SAP Gateway allows for a loosely coupled, noninvasive approach to development that can also fulfil security requirements because SAP Gateway can be placed in a separate area from the SAP S/4HANA system.

An embedded approach doesn't require an SAP Gateway system and therefore reduces setup and costs. Development is done directly in the SAP Business Suite system, allowing for similar advantages as found in the central hub option for developing on SAP Business Suite; that is, less intermediation between systems is required. Once you've installed the system with either the embedded or central hub option, you're ready to install SAP Fiori apps.

13.3.3 SAP Fiori Apps Reference Library

With SAP Fiori installed, go to *www.sap.com/fiori-apps-library* to discover, explore, and implement SAP Fiori apps. In the SAP Fiori apps reference library, you can search for apps, obtain recommendations based on your user profile and transaction code usage, analyze an app both on a functional and technical level, and, finally, implement the app in your system. In the library, you can search and filter for apps by business area, product type, and technical. Based on your backend transactions and installed software, the search functionality provides suitable app recommendations as well. You then can explore individual apps, reviewing app details and versions, and finally download the selected apps. Once downloaded, you further review the version, prerequisites, and dependencies. To implement the selected SAP Fiori apps, you integrate these apps with Maintenance Planner, SAP Solution Manager's cloud-based maintenance planner for planning all changes in your system landscape. Finally, you can export to task lists for automatic configuration.

Implementing Procurement-Specific SAP Fiori Apps

Let's now explore the process of implementing an app from the SAP Fiori apps reference library. For procurement-specific apps, you can search and filter for over 300 apps associated with the procurement processes in SAP S/4HANA, as shown in Figure 13.21.

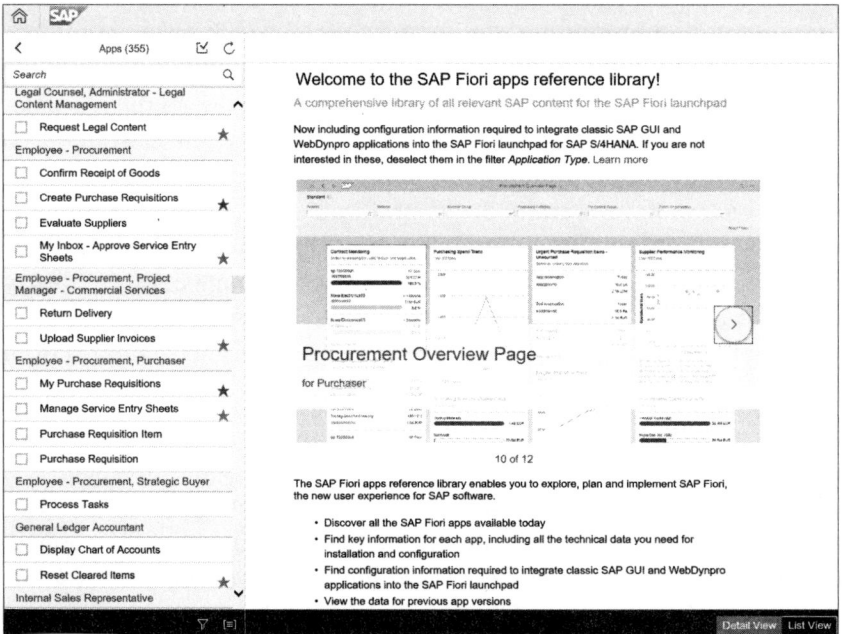

Figure 13.21 SAP Fiori Apps Reference Library: Procurement Apps

13.3 SAP Fiori Configuration

One popular app for procurement is the Create Purchase Requisitions app (see Figure 13.22). Let's walk through how to install or evaluate this app.

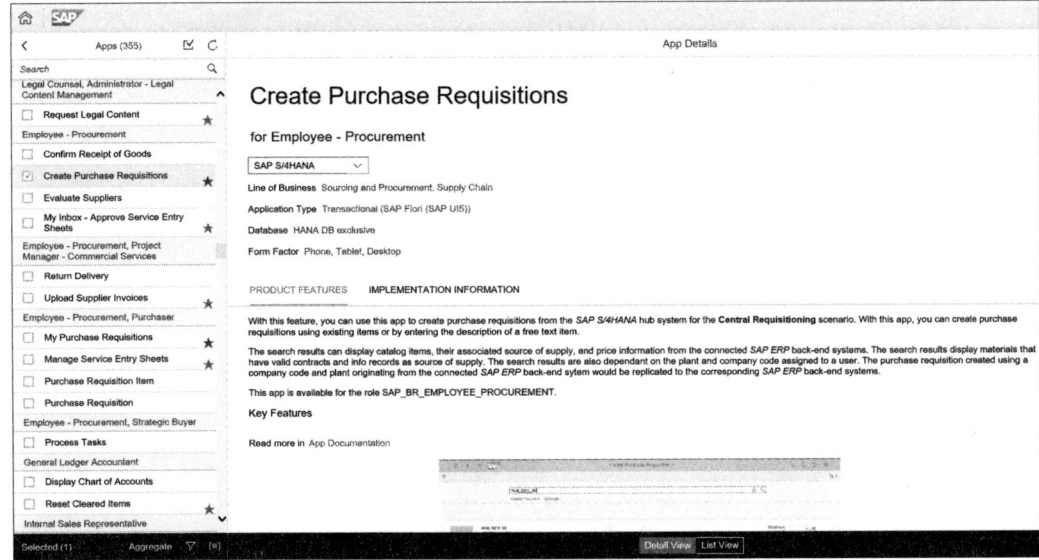

Figure 13.22 SAP Fiori Apps Reference Library: Create Purchase Requisition App

To begin, select whether the system for the installation is in the cloud (**SAP S/4HANA Cloud**) or on-premise (**SAP S/4HANA**), as shown in Figure 13.23.

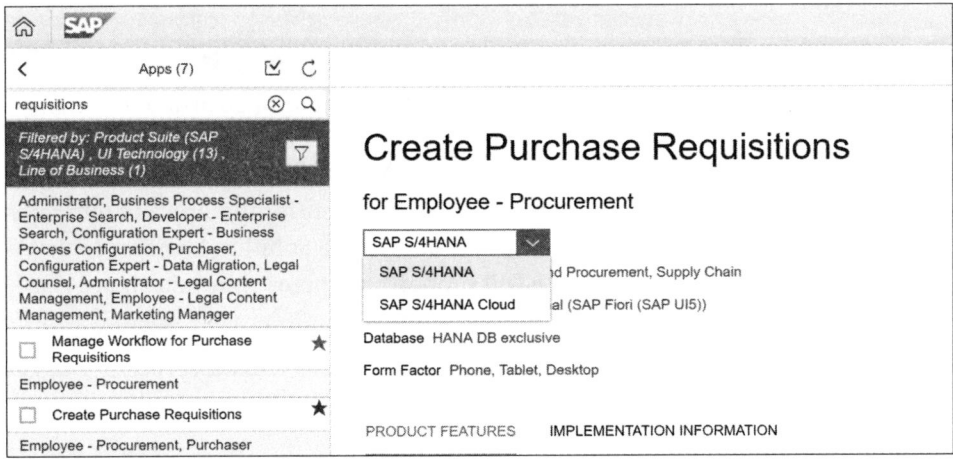

Figure 13.23 Create Purchase Requisitions App: Cloud or On-Premise

Once you've selected your system, you'll need to verify whether your system can support this app. Under **IMPLEMENTATION INFORMATION**, you can select your desired SAP S/4HANA version and access all of the implementation information available to install and use this app in your system, as shown in Figure 13.24.

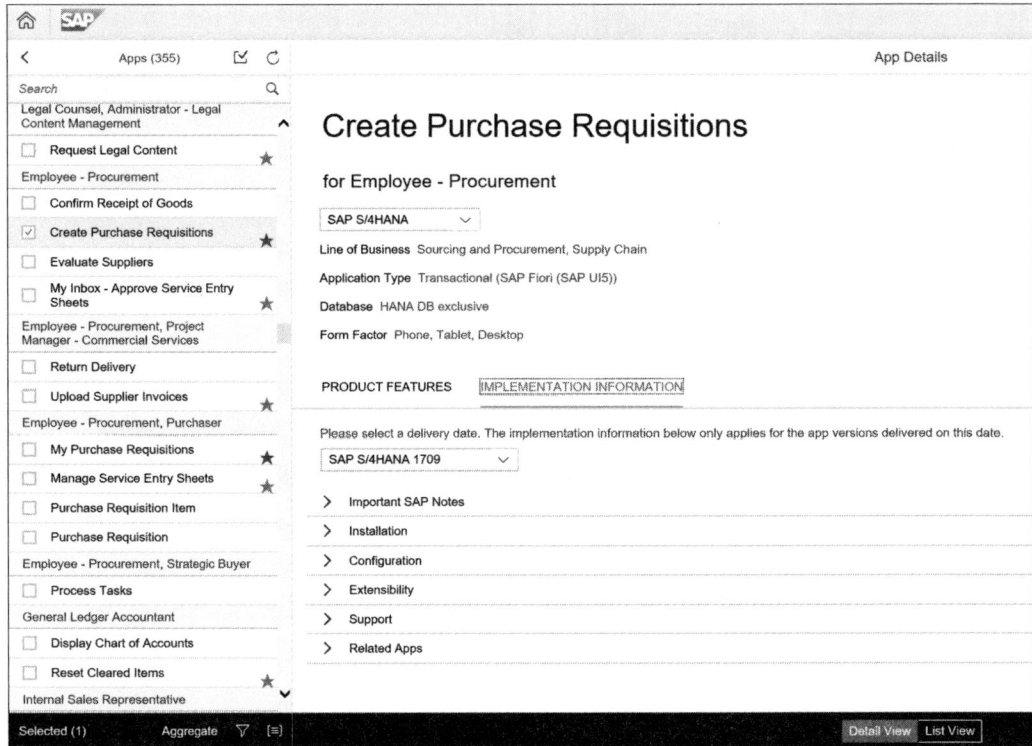

Figure 13.24 SAP Fiori Apps Reference Library: Create Requisition Implementation Information

The **Installation** section reviews the required components for this app and reiterates the guidance for the using Maintenance Planner via SAP Solution Manager to determine whether your system landscape will support the app, as shown in Figure 13.25.

In the **Configuration** section, each app may have different areas requiring configuration. For the Create Purchase Requisition app, ICF nodes, OData services, a target mapping, a business catalog, a group, a role, and search connectors all must be activated.

13.3 SAP Fiori Configuration

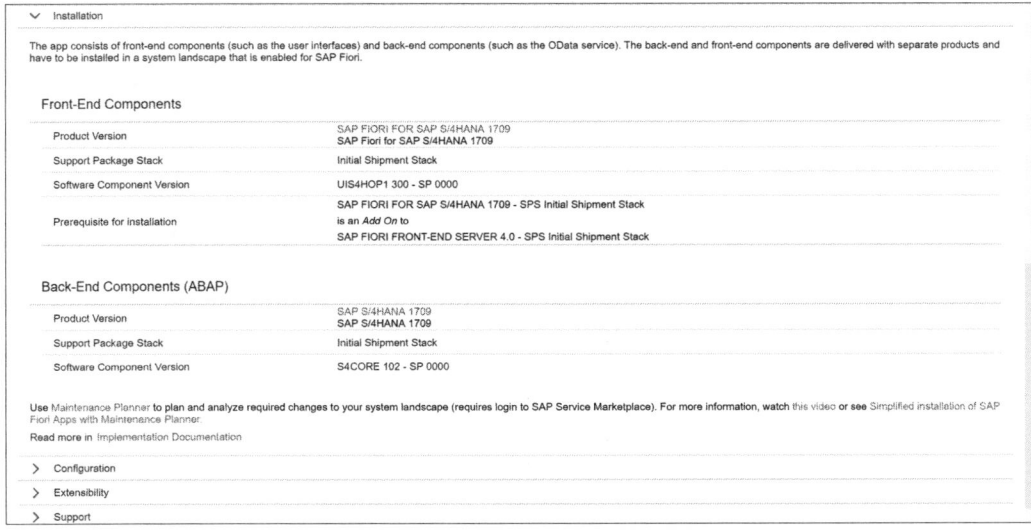

Figure 13.25 Installation Section for Create Purchase Requisition App

Upon completing the configuration, you can review the **Extensibility** section to identify areas of the app that are extensible, the **Support** section to determine areas to reference for support, and the **Related Apps** section to see groups of apps with similar functionality if required.

Unlike the SAP Fiori settings and the SAP CoPilot features, to which every user may have access, very few users will have authorization to install and/or configure additional apps in the system. The installation of apps is usually managed by a core system team in coordination with their technical resources and SAP Basis team. Each installation, depending on the app, may vary in its steps and areas of review. The SAP Fiori apps reference library also provides recommendation functionality to aid in identifying new relevant apps for your user community, as discussed in the following section.

Recommendations in SAP Fiori Apps Reference Library Search

You can obtain app recommendations based on your system usage, which allows for further apps to be proposed. The recommendations are driven in part by the transaction codes you currently use in the backend system, highlighting applicability as shown in Figure 13.26. Here, the search has yielded several relevant results, but from a system-readiness standpoint, only some of the required components for these recommended apps have been installed.

485

13 Customizing the SAP Fiori UI

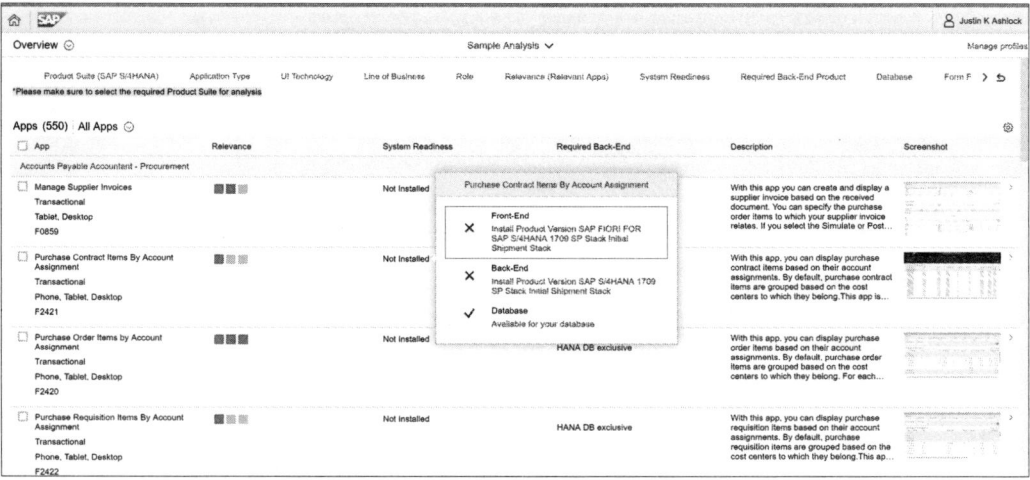

Figure 13.26 SAP Fiori App Recommendations Analysis

To get recommendations, you first select your profile. You can then upload profiles via CSV files to tune the search recommendations still further.

13.4 Summary

SAP Fiori is the de facto UI platform and technology for SAP solutions, and for SAP S/4HANA in particular. In this chapter, we explored the SAP Fiori UI, including the SAP Fiori launchpad, the SAP Fiori architecture, and SAP Fiori configuration. In the next chapter, we'll conclude with a summary of this book and of SAP S/4HANA Sourcing and Procurement.

Chapter 14
Conclusion

As reviewed in this book and in Figure 14.1, SAP S/4HANA covers a host of procurement processes both natively and in concert with SAP Cloud solutions.

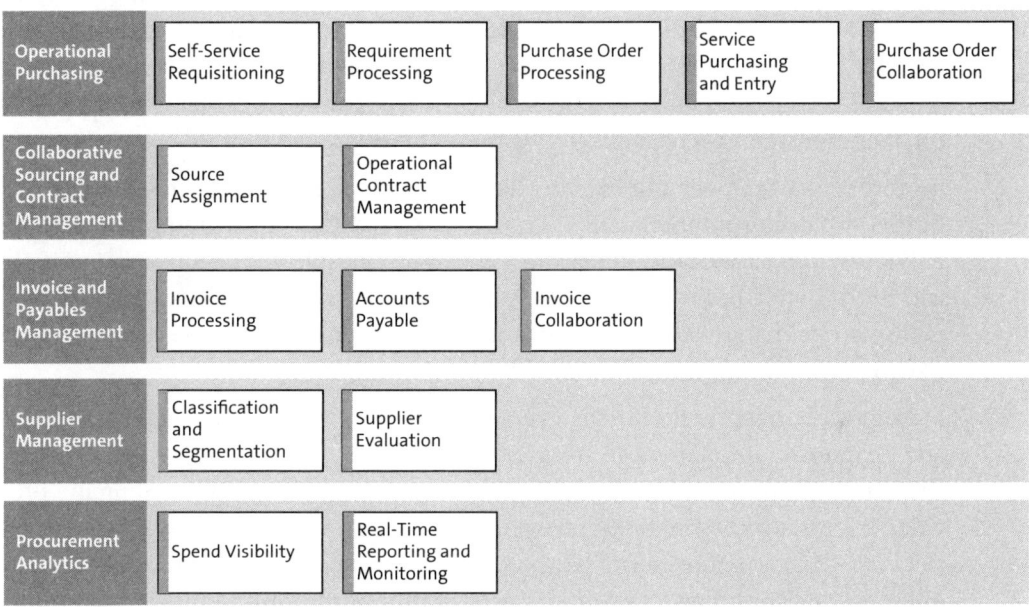

Figure 14.1 SAP S/4HANA Sourcing and Procurement Processes

Underpinning all of these areas is a layer of organizational and transactional master data, which is either defined during the project or at the inception of the original system. Many SAP S/4HANA implementations are greenfield or reimplementations today, requiring a strategy, design, and definition for master data; a refresher on this topic was provided in Chapter 3—we say a *refresher* because many of the concepts remained the same from previous versions of SAP. One major change for procurement topics in particular is the vendor master. The vendor and customer masters are consolidated in SAP S/4HANA into a unified business partner record. There are several steps prior to a system conversion that need to be performed to convert supplier data to this new model and format.

As covered in Chapter 5, operational purchasing in SAP S/4HANA is similar to the previous iterations of self-service procurement in SAP ERP, with a larger emphasis on content management in the form of extensibility with the SAP Ariba Catalog and SAP Ariba guided buying areas in the cloud, as well as native catalog indexing/management functionality. Operational purchasing in SAP S/4HANA also leverages the Ariba Network for purchase order and invoice collaboration.

A core procurement area that continues to be covered by ERP is direct procurement and automated processes driven by MRP. Chapter 6 outlined significant changes to MRP and other direct procurement areas in SAP S/4HANA, as well as key integration points via SAP Ariba Supply Chain Collaboration for Buyers and Ariba Network. Direct procurement documents and processes, from scheduling agreements to inventory collaboration, can now be managed via these solutions.

Inventory management, outlined in Chapter 7, remains a core area for SAP S/4HANA; further expansion of functionality is now available with the embedding of SAP EWM. Previously run as a sidecar application, it is now possible to run SAP EWM directly within the digital core of SAP S/4HANA and remove some of the redundant movement steps to manage goods. Resource-intense inventory management analytics are also much more accessible and timely in SAP S/4HANA.

Managing contracts and sourcing events in SAP S/4HANA was detailed in Chapter 8 and Chapter 9. Although these areas have remained largely similar to their counterparts in previous SAP ERP iterations, the integration with SAP Ariba Sourcing provides extensibility in the cloud and turnkey collaboration with suppliers on the Ariba Network. Contracts continue to be a core area for managing spend, and SAP S/4HANA offers more clause management and presignature tools for crafting optimal terms and language within an operational contract.

Accounts payable bookends the source-to-pay process covered in SAP S/4HANA and SAP Ariba, but it's a core area for savings realization and efficiency gains. Chapter 10 explained the recent developments in accounts payable for SAP S/4HANA and integration points with OpenText VIM and SAP Ariba Invoicing products.

Chapter 11 on supplier management showcased the power of SAP S/4HANA for analytics. Supplier reports can be driven by KPIs and real-time indicators to provide insight and performance readings in real-time. Dashboard and survey functionality allows for SAP ERP users to include subjective feedback in addition to the objective feedback they typically provide on a transaction level, creating a holistic view of supplier performance.

Purchasing analytics in general has greatly evolved in SAP S/4HANA, and Chapter 12 laid out the major changes and improvements to this area and analytics/reporting in general. The main areas include all of the new reports and apps on offer, capable of providing insight in real time as the transactions occur, as well as the continued extensibility and integration with further reporting tools from SAP BusinessObjects. For reporting areas continuing to require a business warehouse for data, SAP S/4HANA leverages a robust set of SAP BusinessObjects tools, such as SAP Crystal Reports, SAP Lumira, SAP Lumira, designer edition, and SAP Analysis for Microsoft Office. Future releases of SAP S/4HANA will continue down this path of convergence, offering deeper integration and cross-functionality with SAP BusinessObjects' toolsets.

The discussion of UI in SAP S/4HANA is driven by SAP Fiori. SAP Fiori represents a comprehensive platform and roadmap for SAP S/4HANA, with the goal of making system interaction intuitive on all devices, especially mobile, as well as providing app-based decision-making support and transaction simplification. Chapter 13 outlined the strategy for SAP Fiori, discussed purchasing apps, and covered the extensibility and customization options available today and planned for tomorrow. The final section of Chapter 14 looked to the future of procurement in SAP S/4HANA and procurement technology in general.

Future State of Procurement Solutions

SAP S/4HANA represents a significant step in reunifying transactions with analytics in one enterprise-grade environment. Corporate procurement processes have yet to take full advantage of the new level of speed and integration with SAP's various cloud solutions, such as SAP Ariba, SAP Fieldglass, and Concur. SAP S/4HANA introduces a further reunification in the procurement area, unifying customer and supplier in the form of a holistic business partner record. This is also being mirrored in SAP Ariba and other cloud solutions for procurement; customer and supplier contracts are maintained in the same area, and organizations play dual roles in the Ariba Network as both customer and supplier.

With real-time analytics in a transacting system comes the possibility of artificial intelligence-based learning and machine-to-machine transactions. Already, there are solutions that leverage these approaches, such as SAP Supply Base Optimization, which leverages predictive analytics libraries and linear programming to negotiate target prices and define award splits.

14 Conclusion

Further machine-based learning approaches for procurement, under the overall SAP Leonardo initiative, can be found on the invoice-processing side, in SAP's Cash Application. Here, labor-intensive invoice-matching processes are automated, using machine learning to match criteria from historical processing and thus automatically match and clear payments. It is safe to say, without hyperbole, that this area is still very much in its early years of growth and development. Another fast-growing area for procurement and automation is the Internet of Things (IoT). *IoT* and the *Industrial Internet of Things* (IIoT) refer to vast networks of devices connected to the Internet, from phones to machines to appliances. All of these connection points represent an opportunity to drive and automate procurement activities to support continued operations and avoid unexpected maintenance issues or failures. Already these connected devices communicate large amounts of information with SAP systems, from location to wear and tear. Machines on the shop floor and elsewhere can be set up to notify users of pending maintenance or parts needing replacement, and then order services and replacement parts.

Enormous amounts of structured and unstructured information is generated each day in the digital world, which is often referred to as *big data*. SAP S/4HANA already allows for predictive modeling and analysis. Having been architected from the beginning to manage large data sets in a more efficient, compressed manner allows SAP S/4HANA to incorporate and monitor external factors as well as internal ones and drive this insight into the transactions being conducted.

Consumer-level UX is a much-used term these days in procurement systems. As consumers experience simplified processes in purchasing in their everyday lives, they begin to expect similar experiences in their workplaces. Rather than a corporation dictating a process and experience, current and future procurement processes and systems will need to innovate continuously and upgrade often, just to keep pace with the relentless momentum in the consumer marketplace while maintaining seamless process integration with other areas of the business necessary for cash flow management, compliance, and production targets. With SAP Ariba, SAP Fieldglass, Concur, and SAP S/4HANA Sourcing and Procurement, SAP intends to remain the leader in this race.

The Author

Justin Ashlock spent over half of his 20-year-plus career in technology at SAP America, serving as the lead consultant for hundreds of global SAP customer projects and engagements supporting over $100 billion in procurement and logistics activities worldwide. Justin currently leads SAP's Supplier Relationship Management (SRM) Cloud practice for SAP North America, focusing on SAP S/4HANA Sourcing and Procurement, Materials Management, SAP Ariba upstream/downstream, integration solutions, SAP SRM, as well as SAP CLM/Sourcing. He holds a bachelor's degree from the University of California, Berkeley, and a master's degree in business administration from the University of Notre Dame.

Contributors

Robert (Bob) Gotschall is a platinum consultant in sourcing and procurement and in materials management and operations at SAP Americas. He has more than 19 years of full lifecycle SAP implementation experience, and 35 years of information systems design and implementation experience in total.

Chelliah Soundar has more than 10 years of experience in SAP customer projects in the areas of sourcing and procurement and materials management. Currently, Soundar is supporting SAP S/4HANA implementation projects globally as an SAP S/4HANA product expert in SAP's elite team, the regional implementation group.

Index

A

ABC Analysis for Cycle Counting app 265
Accounting data 114
Accounts payable 393
   analytics 444
   reporting 444
Accounts payable and invoicing 40
Activated appliance 57
Advanced shipping notifications 135
Aging Analysis app 445
Analytical cards 437
Analytics 435
Analyze PIR Quality app 183
Approve Bank Payments app 402
Ariba Catalog 37, 39
Ariba Network 36, 145, 165
Ariba Network for Purchase Order and
   Invoice 39
Assign and Process Purchase Requisition
   app 149
Attribute value mapping 121
Authorization check 309
Automated and direct procurement 171
   configuration 212
Automated procurement 172
Automated requirements processing 149
Automatic Creation of Purchase Orders from
   Requisition app 149
Automatic settlements 373

B

BAdI
   BD_MMPUR_REQ_APPR_PRV 163
   MM_PUR_CTLG_BDI_SRH 163
   MMPUR_CAT_CLL_ENRICH 163
   MMPUR_CAT_PROXY_INFO 163
   MMPUR_CATALOG_ENRICH_DATA 163
Bank information 113
Batch Information Cockpit app 276
Batch management 105, 230

Batch number 105
   assignment 105
Batch Overview app 276
Big data 490
Blanket agreement 293
Blanket purchase orders 199
Business area 81
Business partner 114
   creation 115
   SAP S/4HANA 116–117
Buyer-driven requirements processing 149
Buyer-side processes 412

C

Cash Discount Forecast app 448
Cash Discount Utilization app 450
Catalog via web service 162
Categories for Legal Content app 318
Change Inbound Delivery app 241
Change Physical Inventory Count app 260
Change Physical Inventory Document
   app 258
Chart of accounts 81
Check report
   1623677 122
   2216176 122
   2399368 122
   974504 122
   CVI_FS_CHECK_CUSTOMIZING 122
   PRECHECK_UPGRADATION_REPORT 122
Classification and Segmentation 413
Clear GR/IR Clearing Account app 384
Clear Outgoing Payments (Manual Clearing)
   app 395
Client 80
Cloud computing 47
Collaborative sourcing 29, 341
Collaborative Sourcing and Contract
   Management 293
Combined Scorecard app 427
Company 81
Company code 81
   creation 87

Confirmation and return delivery 140
Consignment orders 208
Consignment stock 206
Constant model 186
Consumable item 136
Consumer-level UX 490
Consumption-based planning 172
Contact person 121
Contract
   quantity contract 294
Contract and source determination 192
Contract consumption 299
Contract creation 294
Contract dashboard reporting 300
Contract expiration 438
Contract Expiry app 304, 438
Contract Leakage app 303
Contract management 29
   configuration 305
Contract workflow 309
Contracts
   apps 301
   contract release order 294
   item category 307
   release procedure 307
   texts 308
   value contract 294
Contracts management 293
Controlling area 81
Conversion phase 129
Core data services 457
Country-specific chart of accounts 82
Create Balance Confirmations app 406
Create Consignment and Pipeline Settlement
   app 386
Create Correspondence app 405–406
Create Dunning Notices app 406
Create Evaluated Receipt Settlement
   app 388
Create Inbound Delivery app 241
Create Material app 101
Create Outbound Deliveries app 245
Create Periodic Account Statements app ... 406
Create Physical Inventory Document
   app 257
Create Physical Inventory Documents—Regular
   Stock app 264

Create Purchase Order app 153
Create Purchase Order via Purchase Requisition
   app 149
Create Questionnaire app 426
Create Single Payment app 400
Create Standard Letters app 406
Create Supplier Invoice app 379
Create Supplier Invoice—Advanced app 381
Credit control area 81
Credit management 113
Credit memo 372
Cross-catalog search 157
Custom code 63
Customer
   object page 285
Customer attributes 121
Customer/vendor integration 111, 118
   BAdIs 126
   conversion steps 119
   mapping checks 129
   preparation phase 119
cXML 355

D

Date set 331
Date types 323
Days Payable Outstanding app 451
Define object links 336
Delete Correspondence Requests app 406
Direct procurement 31, 135
Display Inbound Delivery app 242
Display Material Documents List app 272
Display MRP Key Figures app 182
Display MRP Material Issues app 182
Display Physical Inventory Progress app ... 268
Display PI Document Items for Materials
   app 269
Display Stock in Transit app 252
Display Stock Overview app 277
Display Supplier Balances app 405
Display Supplier Invoice—Advanced app ... 390
Display Warehouse Stock app 278
Display/Cancel Account Maintenance app ... 386
Document content set 332
Document holding 376
Document parking 376

Index

Document stamps 328
Document status 335
Document types 333
   configuration 212
   definition 306
   LP 196
   LPA 196
Document types for purchase order 215
Document types for requisition 213
Document types for scheduling
   agreement 216
Dunn & Bradstreet 429

E

Electronic data interchange 133
Enter and Post PI Count w/o Document
   app 261
Enter Inventory Count app 259
Enter PI Count w/o Document app 260
Entity types 324
Expiry notification setting 300
External contact set 331
External contacts 325
External sourcing 339

F

FD02 117
FD03 117
FD05 117
FD06 117
Federal Supply Class 104
Final reports 127
FK01 117
FK02 117
FK03 117
FK05 117
FK06 117
Flexible workflow 359
Forecast collaboration 189
Forecast commit 191
Forecast dashboard 191
Forecast delivery schedule 310
Forecast planning 185, 217
Forecast review 190

Forecast-based planning 173
Forecasting 185
Full conversion 53
Future Payables app 447

G

Goods issues 244
   shipping integration 244
Goods Movement Analysis app 288
Goods Movement Reporting app 271
Goods movements 231
Goods receipt 143
   creation 141, 143
Goods receipt with reference to purchase order/
   production order 233
Goods receipt-based invoice verification ... 374
Goods receipts 232–233
Goods/service receipts 135
Group chart of accounts 82

H

Hybrid cloud 48

I

IDocs 112
Implementation 45
Importing catalog data 160
Importing images 160
Inbound Deliveries for Purchase Orders
   app 240
Inbound delivery object page 286
Indirect procurement 32, 172
Industrial Internet of Things (IIoT) 490
Infrastructure as a service (IaaS) 47
Initial stock entry for blocked stock 233
Initial stock entry for quality inspection
   stock 233
Initial stock entry for unrestricted use
   stock 233
Integrated object model 116
Integration platform as a service (IPaaS) 47
Internal contact set 331
Internal contacts 324

495

Internet of Things (IoT) 490
Inventory management 223–224
 analytics 288
 data model 225
 material master 226
 object pages 281
 reporting 270
Inventory overview pages 270
Inventory Turnover Analysis app 183, 289
Invoice and payables management 30, 369
Invoice collaboration 407
Invoice documents 375
Invoice entry
 using EDI 377
 via the Ariba Network 377
Invoice postings
 simulation 378
Invoice processing 370, 379
 reporting 389
 results 373
Invoice Processing Analysis app 452
Invoice reduction 377
Invoices 135
Item categories 307

J

JSON file 162

K

Key performance indicator 456

L

Landscape transformation 46
Legal content management 315
 customizing 322
Linked object set 331
Linked object types 326–327

M

Maintain MRP Controllers app 180–181
Maintenance planner 61
Manage Activities app 414, 419

Manage Automatic Payments app 397
Manage Change Requests app 181
Manage Context for Legal Content app 316
Manage External Requirements app 181
Manage Internal Requirements app 181
Manage Legal Transactions app 321
Manage Material Coverage app 181
Manage Outbound Deliveries app 247
Manage Payment Blocks app 396
Manage Payment Media app 401
Manage PIRs app 181
Manage POs app 181
Manage Production Orders or Process Orders
 app 181
Manage Purchase Categories app 418
Manage Purchase Contracts app 182
Manage Purchase Requisitions app 181
Manage Purchase Requisitions—Professional
 app 149
Manage Purchasing Category app 414
Manage Purchasing Info Records app 182
Manage Quota Arrangement app 195
Manage Scheduling Agreement app ... 196, 311
Manage Scorecards app 423
Manage Source Lists app 182
Manage Sources of Supply app 181, 439
Manage Stock app 181, 235
Manage Supplier Down Payment Requests
 app 399
Manage Supplier Line Items app 404
Manage Supplier Quotation app 182
Manage Workflows app 359
Manage Workflows for Scheduling Agreements
 app 196
MAP1 117
MAP3 117
Mass Change to Purchase Contract app 298
Mass Changes to Scheduling Agreements
 app 196
Master data 99
 definition 212
Material
 object page 283
Material document 282
Material Document app 183
Material Documents Overview app 237, 272

Index

Material group 100
   creation 104
Material Inventory Values—Balance Summary
   app 183, 279
Material Inventory Values—Line Items
   app 183, 280
Material master 100
   configuration 109
   creation 101
   field 110
   record 100
   updates 108
Material master record tabs 102
Material masters 175
Material Shortage Profile app 184
Materials requirements planning 173
MATNR field 110
Migrating SAP SRM shopping carts 146
MK01 117
MK02 117
MK03 117
MK05 117
MK06 117
MK12 117
MK18 117
MK19 117
MMPUR_CATALOG_ENRICH_DATA 163
Monitor Batches and Payments app 402
Monitor External Requirements app 180
Monitor Internal Requirements app 181
Monitor Material Coverage app 180, 184
Monitor Production Orders app 178
Monitor Production Orders or Process Orders
   app 181
Monitor Purchase Contract Items app .. 304
Monitor Tasks app 414, 419
Monitoring financial inventory values .. 279
Movement types 142, 233
   101 233
   201 244
   261 244
   301 248
   303 248
   305 248
   311 248
   313 248

Movement types (Cont.)
   333 244
   551 244
   561 233
   563 233
   601 244
   641 244
   643 244
MRP Cockpit Reuse Component app 181
MRP Live 175
Multidimensional spend reporting 437
Multipurpose internet mail extensions 429
Multitenant environment 68
Multitier purchase orders 201
My Inbound Delivery Monitor app 243
My inbox 350
My Inbox—Approve POs app 181
My Purchase Orders—Due for Delivery
   app 246
My Purchasing Document Items app ... 181

N

New implementation 46, 53
Number ranges 350

O

Object link descriptions 335
Object pages 391
Off-Contract Spend app 302
Online analytical processing (OLAP) 435
Online invoice entry 375
Online transaction processing (OLTP) 435
Operating chart of accounts 81
Operating concern 81
Operational procurement 32, 133
Operational purchasing 29
Operational Supplier Evaluation Last 365 Days
   app 439
Organizational structure 79
   example 83
   objects 83
Outbound delivery
   object page 287
Outline purchase agreements 293

497

Output Material Documents app 238
Overall Supplier Evaluation Last 365 Days
  app 439
Overdue Materials—Stock in Transit
  app 251
Overdue Payables app 446
Overview Inventory Management app 271
Overview Inventory Processing app 271
Ownership 230

P

Payables management 369
Physical count 256
Physical inventory 254, 256
  apps 257
  reporting 266
Physical Inventory Analysis app 268
Physical Inventory Document Overview
  app 267
Physical inventory documents 255
Picking Components for Process Orders
  app 178
Planned order 174
Planning 185
Plant
  creation 90
  definition 90
Plants 84
Platform as a service (PaaS) 47
PO processing 135
PO/invoice automation 167
Post Goods Movement app 238
Post Goods Receipt for Delivery app 239
Post Goods Receipt for Purchase Order
  app 234
Post Outgoing Payments app 394
Postprocessing orders 123
Postprocessing phase 130
PPO request 123
Predictive analytics 443
Preupgrade checks 129
Print Correspondence Requests app 406
Print Physical Inventory Documents app .. 263
Print Supplier Invoices app 383
Private cloud 47

Process Physical Inventory Count Results
  app 263
Process Tasks app 414, 420
Procurement 27, 35, 38, 136
Procurement analytics 30
Procurement Overview Page app 182
Procure-to-pay 29
Product type 108
Profile sets 330
Profiles 329, 332
Program
  LSMW 112
  *MM_PUR_CTLG_EXT_COM_CUR_*
  UPD 158
Public cloud 48
Purchase Contract app 182
Purchase Contract Item app 183
Purchase Contract Items by Account
  Assignment app 303
Purchase contracts 295
Purchase info record 218
Purchase order 133
Purchase Order app 182
Purchase order collaboration 135, 144
Purchase order number ranges 214
Purchase order processing 152
Purchase order-based invoice
  verification 373
Purchase orders 201
Purchase Requisition app 139, 183
Purchase Requisition Item app 182
Purchasing categories 414
Purchasing data 113
Purchasing groups creation 97
Purchasing Info Record app 182
Purchasing information record 193
Purchasing organizations 85
  creation 94

Q

Quality gates 77
Quality management 229
Quality management collaboration 209
Quantity Contract Consumption app 299
Quota arrangements 195, 218
Quote automation for procurement 342

Index

R

Real-time reporting 457
Release Blocked Invoices app 382
Release creation profile 314
Release Reminder Purchase Requisition
  app 149
Reminder set 332
Reorder point planning 172, 188
Report
  BBP_MIGRATE_SCEN 147
  BBP_SC_MIGRATE_TO_PR 147
  CVI_PRECHECK_UPGRADE 128
  FSBP_IND_SECTOR_MAPPING_
    CHECK 127
  MDS_LOAD_COCKPIT 128–129
  MMPUR_MIGR_EBAN 147
  NOTE_2324208_DDIC 112
  NOTE_2331298 112
  PPH_SETUP_MRPRECORDS 178
  PPH_SETUP_MRPRECORDS_SIMU ... 178
  PRECHECK_UPGRADATION_
    REPORT 127–128
  PRECHECK_UPGRADATION_REPORT ... 127
  RMMDVM10 178
  RMMDVM20 178
Reporting 435
Reporting and monitoring 435
Request for price 342
Request for quotation 341, 343–344
  configuration 350
  document types 351
Request Legal Content app 319
Request Physical Inventory Recount app ... 262
Requirement processing 135, 148
  navigation 151
Requisition creation 138
Requisition number range 212
Requisitioning 133
Requisitions 137
Requisition-to-pay 135
Return delivery 143
Revise Payment Proposals app 398

S

SAP Activate 45, 69, 71
  deploy phase 72
  discover phase 71
  explore phase 72
  prepare phase 72
  realize phase 72
  run phase 72
  workflows 74
SAP analytics add-in for Microsoft Office ... 460
SAP Appliance 58
SAP Ariba 31, 36, 165, 461
SAP Ariba Cloud Integration Gateway ... 367
SAP Ariba Discovery 410
SAP Ariba integration
  inventory management 290
SAP Ariba Procurement 36
SAP Ariba Sourcing 36
SAP Ariba Spend Management 461
SAP Ariba Strategic Sourcing Suite ... 441
SAP Ariba Supplier Lifecycle and
  Performance 410, 432
SAP Ariba Supplier Network Collaboration ... 171
SAP Ariba Supply Chain Collaboration for
  Buyers 38, 190, 220
SAP Basis 57
SAP Best Practices 57, 69–70
SAP Business Client 471
SAP Business Suite 43
SAP Business Suite in SAP ERP 442
SAP Business Suite powered by SAP
  HANA 225
SAP BusinessObjects Explorer 460
SAP Cloud 38
SAP CoPilot 478
SAP ERP
  materials requirements planning ... 175
SAP Extended Warehouse Management ... 82
SAP Fieldglass 164, 461
SAP Fiori 177
  architecture 469
  configuration 480
  installation 480
SAP Fiori 2.0 467

Index

SAP Fiori apps
  MRP 178
SAP Fiori Apps reference library 482
SAP Fiori launchpad 464, 474
SAP Fiori UI 463
SAP Fiori UX 442
SAP Gateway 480
SAP GUI 195
SAP GUI for HTML 466
SAP Hybris Marketing Cloud 46
SAP Integrated Business Planning 220
SAP MaxDB 480
SAP Model Companies 69
SAP Model Company 71
SAP NetWeaver Application Server 159
SAP NetWeaver AS ABAP 467
SAP NetWeaver Enterprise Search 159
SAP Note
  1164979 159
  1454441 122
  1623677 127
  1623809 122
  2309153 122
  2312529 112
  2324208 112
  2331298 112
  2340095 113
  2346269 112
  2376996 158
  2383051 119
  2405714 112
  974504 129
SAP S/4HANA 164, 225
  installation 57
  materials requirements planning 175
  workflows 147
SAP S/4HANA Cloud ... 43, 46, 66, 145, 165, 437, 440
SAP S/4HANA Cloud, private option 46
SAP S/4HANA Enterprise
  Management 21, 42, 45, 55, 79
SAP S/4HANA Sourcing and Procurement
  SAP Fiori apps 42
SAP S/4HANA Sourcing and Procurement roles
  Accounts payable accountant—R0005-12 42
  Employee procurement—R0056-12 41

SAP S/4HANA Sourcing and Procurement roles (Cont.)
  Manager procurement—R0091 42
  Operational purchaser—R0128 42
  Strategic buyer—R0153 42
SAP S/4HANA sourcing and procurement roles 41
SAP SRM deployment 146
SAP SuccessFactors 168
SAP SuccessFactors Employee Central 168
SAP Supplier Lifecycle and Performance 410
SAP Supplier Relationship
  Management 134, 339, 409
SAP Supply Base Optimization 209
SAPr Gateway 471
SAPUI5 466
Schedule MRP Runs app 181
Schedule Order Conversion Runs app 182
Schedule Purchasing Jobs app 182
Scheduling agreement 196, 309
  creation 311
  document types 312
  with release document 310
  without release document 310
Scheduling agreement number ranges 216
Scheduling agreement release
  collaboration 198
Scheduling agreements
  customizing 312
Search templates 160
Seasonal model 186
Seasonal trend model 186
Self-service procurement 137
  configuration 154
Self-service requisitioning 135, 137
Serial number 106
Serialization 105, 107, 231
SERV record 108
Service purchasing 164
Service purchasing and entry 135
Services procurement integration 165
Shopping cart creation 138
Shopping cart processes 145
Slow or Non-Moving Materials Analysis
  app 290
Software as a service (SaaS) 47
Source lists 218

Index

Source-to-pay 29, 172
Sourcing 439
Sourcing and procurement 27
Sourcing optimization 341
Sourcing process flow 340
Spend analysis 436
Spend visibility 435
Stock balances reporting 273
Stock identity 253
Stock management 227
   location 228
   material 228
   usability 228
Stock ownership 254
Stock transfers 248
   one-step 248
   reporting 251
   shipping integration 251
   two-step 248
Stock transport scheduling agreement 310
Stock type
   blocked 229
   customer returns 229
   quality inspection 229
   unrestricted use 229
Stock usability 253
Stock—Multiple Materials app 183, 275
Stock—Single Material app 183, 273
Storage locations 84
Strategic procurement 32, 34
Strategic sourcing 38, 339
Subcontracting 201
   in SAP S/4HANA 203
   order collaboration 205
Subsequent credit 372
Subsequent debit 372
Supplier
   object page 284
Supplier account management 403
Supplier accounting document object page 392
Supplier and category management configuration 428
Supplier app 183
Supplier collaboration 35
Supplier creation 111

Supplier evaluation 421
   configuration 430
Supplier Evaluation by Price app ... 425
Supplier Evaluation by Price Last 365 Days app 439
Supplier Evaluation by Quantity app 423
Supplier Evaluation by Quantity Last 365 Days app 439
Supplier Evaluation by Questionnaire app 425
Supplier Evaluation by Questionnaire Last 365 Days app 440
Supplier Evaluation by Time app ... 424
Supplier Evaluation by Time Last 365 Days app 440
Supplier Evaluation/Operational Supplier Evaluation app 427
Supplier invoice 372
Supplier invoice documents 371
Supplier invoice object page 392
Supplier invoice verification 373
Supplier Invoices List app 389
Supplier management 30, 409, 411
   with the Ariba Network 412
Supplier master 111, 113
Supplier Payment Analysis (Manual and Automatic Payments) app 454
Supplier Payment Analysis (Open Payments) app 455
Supplier payment processing 393
Supplier performance 441
Supplier quotation 347–348
Supplier Quotation app 359
Supplier quotations 346
Supplier Self-Service 339
Supplier self-services 145
Synchronization 128
System conversion 46, 52, 61

T

Table
   MATDOC 226
   MCHB 226
   MKOL 226
Target audience 21
Test phase 130

Index

Time-phased planning 173, 189
Transaction
   ANZE 194
   BMBC 276
   BNK_MONI 403
   BP 112
   CVI_FS_CHECK_CUST 127
   CVI_PRECHECK_UPGRADE 127
   ESH_COCKPIT 159
   F.18 406
   F.27 406
   F.61 406
   F.62 406
   F.63 406
   F.66 406
   F110 454
   F150 406
   F18P 406
   FD01 117
   FLETS 110
   MASS 112
   MB51 273
   MB52 278
   MB5T 253
   MB80 187
   MB90 238
   MD01 176
   MD01N 185
   MDAB 178
   MDRE 178
   ME11 194
   ME12 194
   ME13 194
   ME21N 479
   ME31K 295
   ME31L 312
   ME32L 312
   ME33L 312
   ME35L 312
   ME37 312
   ME39 312
   ME84 312
   ME9L 312
   MEQ1 195
   MEQ2 195
   MEQ3 195

Transaction (Cont.)
   MEQ4 195
   MEQ6 195
   MI01 257
   MI02 258
   MI04 259
   MI09 260
   MI10 262
   MI11 262
   MI20 263
   MI21 263
   MI22 269
   MI31 264
   MIBC 265
   MIDO 269
   MIR4 390
   MIRO 381
   MM01 .... 101, 108
   MM02 .... 101, 108
   MM03 .... 101, 108
   MMBE 277
   MMPUR_CAT_EXT 162
   MP30 186
   MR11 384
   MR11SHOW 386
   MR90 384
   MRBR 382
   MRKO 387
   MRRL 388
   OBY6 89
   OIS2 106–107
   OMSF 104
   OX01 96
   OX02 88
   OX08 95
   OX10 90
   OX15 87
   OX17 96
   OX18 91
   PA30 155
   PPOMA 155
   SFW5 122
   SW05 122
   VL06I 243
   VL10B 246
   VL31N 241

Index

Transaction (Cont.)
   VL32N 241
   VL33N 243
   VL34 240
   XD99 112
   XK99 112
Transfer postings 253
Transfer Stock—Cross-Plant app 250
Transfer Stock—In-Plant app 249
Translate Purchasing Categories
   app 414, 418
Trend model 186

U

UI tuning options 474
Umbrella agreements 293
United Nations Standard Product and Service
   Codes 104
Unused Contracts app 301

V

V+21 117
V+22 117
V+23 117
V-03 117
V-04 117
V-05 117
V-06 117
V-07 117
V-08 117
V-09 117
V-11 117

Valuated goods receipts 142
Value Contract Consumption app 299
VAP1 117
VAP2 117
VAP3 117
VD01 117
VD02 117
VD03 117
VD05 117
VD06 117
Virtual data model 457

W

Warehouse 84
   creation 93
Web Dynpro 419
Workflow inbox 148

X

XD01 117
XD02 117
XD03 117
XD05 117
XD06 117
XD07 117
XK01 117
XK02 117
XK03 117
XK05 117
XK06 117
XK07 117

Interested in reading more?

Please visit our website for all new book
and e-book releases from SAP PRESS.

www.sap-press.com